Lexington May — 48 —

My Dear Husband —

You will think indeed, that old age, has set its seal, upon my humble self, that in few or none of my letters, I can remember the day of the month, I must confess it as one of my peculiarities; I feel wearied & tired enough to know, that this is Saturday night, our babies are asleep, and as Aunt Maria B— is coming in for me tomorrow morning, I think the chances will be rather dull that I should answer your last letter tomorrow — I have just received a letter from Frances M, it related in an especial manner to the boy, I had desired her to send, she thinks with you(as good persons generally agree) that it would cost more than it would come — and it might be lost on the road, I rather expect she has examined the specified articles, and thinks as Levi says, they are hard bargains — But it takes so many changes to children, particularly in summer, that I thought it might save me a few stitches — I think I will write her a few lines this evening, directing her not to send them — She says Willie is just recovering from another spell of sickness, Many or none of them were well — Springfield

Mary Todd Lincoln

―――

HER LIFE AND LETTERS

Mary Todd Lincoln in January, 1862.

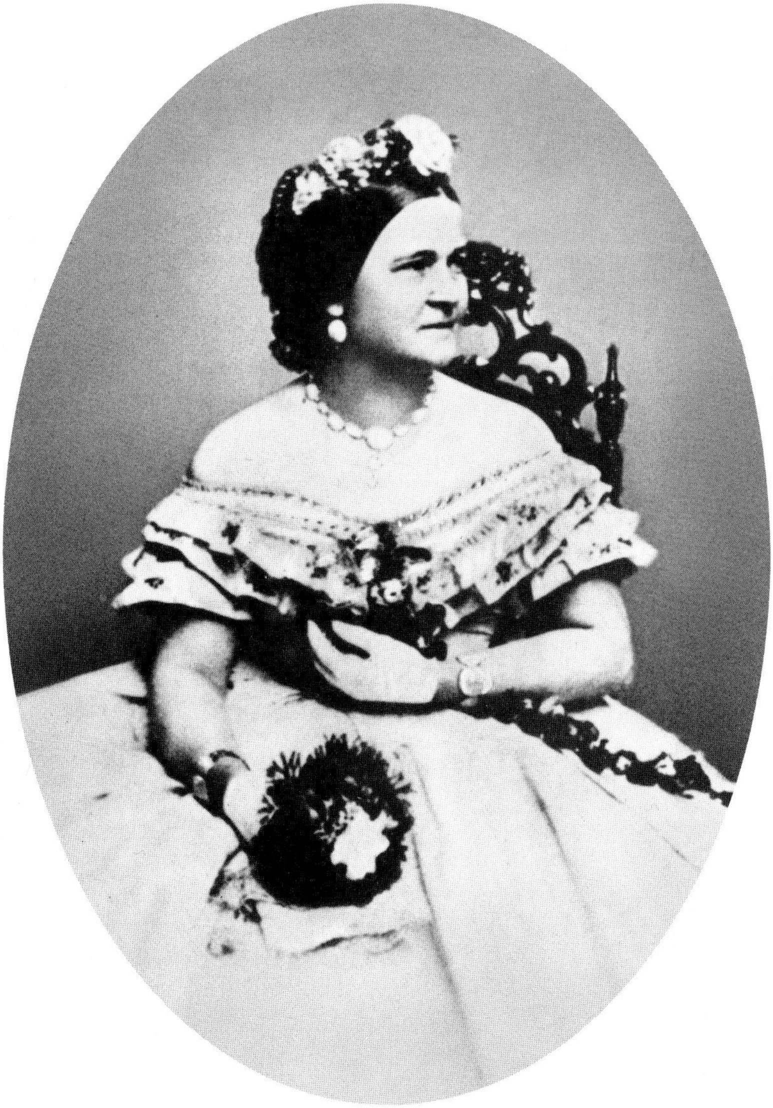

MARY TODD LINCOLN

Her Life and Letters

JUSTIN G. TURNER

LINDA LEVITT TURNER

With an Introduction by Fawn M. Brodie

Alfred A. Knopf   New York   1972

This is a Borzoi Book published by Alfred A. Knopf, Inc.
Copyright © 1972 by Justin G. Turner and Linda Levitt Turner
Published in the United States by Alfred A. Knopf, Inc., New York,
and simultaneously in Canada by Random House of Canada Limited, Toronto.
Distributed by Random House, Inc., New York.
Library of Congress Catalog Card Number: 69–10700
ISBN: 0–394–46643–8

———

Grateful acknowledgment is made to the following
for permission to reprint material:
Harcourt Brace Jovanovich: Nine letters
from MARY LINCOLN: WIFE AND WIDOW
by Carl Sandburg and Paul Angle (1932).
Harper & Row: Seventeen letters
from MARY, WIFE OF LINCOLN
by Katherine Helm (1928).

———

Manufactured in the United States of America
First Edition
Published September 27, 1972
Second Printing, November 1972

Acknowledgments

This book would not have been possible without the cooperation, assistance, and generosity of many people. We are indebted, first of all, to Robert Todd Lincoln Beckwith, younger of President and Mrs. Lincoln's two surviving descendants, for his approval and encouragement of the project; second, to Margaret A. Flint, former Assistant State Historian of Illinois, who gave us every consideration in our researches at the Illinois State Historical Library and who read the manuscript with vast care, as did the distinguished Lincoln scholar Paul M. Angle, whose wise suggestions made a great difference to its final form.

At various stages, from the inception of the work to its completion, we received considerable guidance from David C. Mearns, Roy P. Basler, and Oliver H. Orr, Jr., of the Library of Congress; Philip M. Hamer, Oliver W. Holmes, Albert H. Leisinger, Jr., and Diane Feller of the National Archives; James C. Ketchum, Curator of the White House and Betty C. Monkman of the Curator's Office; Norma Cuthbert, Herbert C. Schultz, and Jean F. Preston of the Henry E. Huntington Library; Robert Rosenthal, J. Richard Phillips, and Margaret McFadden of the University of Chicago Library; Margaret Scriven, Archie Motley, and Mrs. Howard Chudacoff of the Chicago Historical Society; Rodney G. Dennis III and Donna Packer of the Houghton Library, Harvard University; Harley Holden of the Harvard University Archives; R. Gerald McMurtry, Director of the Lincoln National Life Foundation; and Lloyd Ostendorf, the distinguished authority on Lincoln photographs.

Of great help in securing copies of Mary Lincoln's letters and in supplying us with information were: Barbara S. Hobson of Brown University; Dorothy W. Bridgwater of Yale; Alexander P. Clark of Princeton; William A. Pease of Franklin and Marshall College; Margaret Butterfield Andrews of the Rush Rhees Library, University of Rochester; James Hickey and Mildred Schulz of the Illinois State Historical Library; Rudy Clark of Lincoln Memorial University; Raymond Dooley, President of Lincoln College; David A. Randall and Elfrieda Lang of the Lilly Library, Indiana University; Edna L. Jacobsen of the New York State Library; Ben Weisinger of New York City Community College; Henry Cadwalader and John D. Kilbourne of the Historical Society of Pennsylvania; Sue Gillies of the New-York Historical Society; Mary K. Meyer of the Maryland Historical Society; and Josephine D. Allen of the National Park Service.

We are also grateful to the following people for their assistance in the long (and not always fruitful) process of locating Mrs. Lincoln's letters: Lawrence S. Thompson of the University of Kentucky; Howard Peckham of the University of Michigan; Lawrence W. Towner of the Newberry Library; Dorothy J. Smith of Allegheny College; Robert Vosper and James Mink of the University of California at Los Angeles; and, especially, Philippa Calnan of Parke-Bernet Sotheby's.

Particular thanks must be extended to those friends and scholars who gave us the benefit of their own research and showed continuing interest in the project: Ray Billington, Ralph G. Newman, Wayne C. Temple, Herman Blum, Carl Haverlin, Mort Lewis, Nathaniel Stein, and Irving Stone. It is our privilege to include in this category five distinguished individuals—William H. Townsend, Allan Nevins, Harry E. Pratt, Lloyd C. Dunlap, and Ruth Painter Randall—who are no longer alive to receive our thanks, but without whose help, interest, and advice this book would have been a great deal less than it is.

No small factor in the successful execution of an effort such as this was the good will of autograph dealers and collectors. Charles Hamilton, Ralph G. Newman, King V. Hostick, Paul C. Richards, and David Kirschenbaum were generous with advice and cooperated with us whenever it was possible for them to do so without endangering the interests of their clients. It is their graciousness and that of private collectors that have meant the most to us, for it cannot be denied that the monetary value of a manuscript diminishes, however slightly, with the publication of its text. Those collectors who were willing—and often eager—to share their treasures with the readers of this volume include Philip D. and Elsie O. Sang, Herman Blum, Dolly and Richard Maass, Katrina Kindel, Mrs. Stanley Holland Graves and her daughter Frances Sweeney, Elizabeth M. Benner, Gertrude Hollowbush, Edward Lustgarten, Catherine Newell, and John Reed.

In a number of cases we were privileged to reproduce letters published in scholarly journals, so carefully copied and annotated that we were saved the most difficult research chores. Among these were the letters published by Philip D. Sang under the title "Mary Todd Lincoln: A Tragic Portrait" in the *Journal of the Rutgers University Library;* by Charles V. Darrin, grandson of Mary Lincoln's friend Hannah Shearer, in the *Journal of the Illinois State Historical Society*, and by Francis Whiting Hatch, who produced "Mary Lincoln Writes to Noah Brooks" for the same publication.

For their patience and enthusiasm in seeing this long and complicated project through to its completion we are deeply indebted to Angus Cameron and Regina Ryan of Alfred A. Knopf, and to Ruth Ann Skippon, whose copyediting was accomplished with a discerning eye for content as well as style. Our thanks also go to Charles B. Bloch, Walter R. Schmidt, and Dr. Sarle H. Cohen for their efforts on behalf of the project.

We could not have done without the careful typing of Jean Beard and Helen O'Neill, whose standards of accuracy were as high as ours.

Special appreciation of course goes to members of our family. They not only bore with us through the years it took to finish our work, but actively contributed to its progress. Charles and Barbara Turner Sachs, who did much of the preliminary research and offered us continual advice and assistance out of their experience in the field of autographs; Rosalind Levitt, who read the book in the proof stage and contributed the perceptive suggestions of a writer and reviewer, and finally, Gertrude Turner, Paul S. Turner, and Rachael Levitt, who believed in the project and helped it along in a thousand ways— to all, our love and our thanks.

Contents

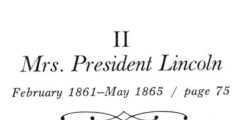

IV
A Land of Strangers
October 1868–August 1871 / page 487

* ✦ *

V
The Destroying Hand of Time
October 1871–July 1882 / page 593

* ✦ *

Illustrations

Introduction by Fawn M. Brodie

The publication in full of Mary Todd Lincoln's letters is both a memorable addition to Lincoln literature and an unexpectedly rewarding volume in its own right. It is superbly annotated by Lincoln scholar and collector Justin Turner and his daughter-in-law, Linda Levitt Turner. Their connecting narrative, deceptively low-keyed, leads the reader deftly from one group of letters to another, and one is inevitably captured by this compelling and doom-ridden story. Even those who know Carl Sandburg's brief biography with its accompanying letters and Ruth Painter Randall's scholarly but overprotective volume will be startled by the fresh material and cumulative impact of the Turner collection. Here, if ever, one sees that the whole letter is better than the fragment, and that six hundred letters, many of them written in moments of desperation, can become an austere verbal portrait more authentic than biography.

Although most of the correspondence between Lincoln and his wife is lost, the few surviving early letters and many portions of her letters to others serve as a corrective to the canard of Lincoln's law partner, William Herndon, who detested Mary Lincoln, that during the entire twenty-three years of his marriage "Lincoln knew no joy." Here we see tender domestic exchanges, with Mary, visiting her father's home in Lexington, Kentucky, writing to Lincoln in Washington in 1848:

> I wish instead of writing, *we* were together this evening. I feel very sad away from you. . . . I must bid you goodnight—Do not fear the children, have forgotten you, I was only jesting—Even E[ddy]'s eyes brighten at the mention of your name—

The editors give us Lincoln's reply with its oft-quoted barb, "Will you be a *good girl* in all things if I consent . . ."; but we see later that he could write gently, "Father expected to see you all sooner; but let it pass; stay as long as you please, and come when you please. Kiss and love the dear rascals."

Here too we have Mary Lincoln's description of an eleven-hundred-mile political tour with her husband in the summer of 1859; "Words cannot express what a merry time, we had, the gayest pleasure party, I have ever seen." To portrait painter Francis B. Carpenter she described Lincoln in his last cheerful days, when the war was virtually over, and he had become "almost boyish in his mirth & reminded me, of his original nature, what I had always remembered of him, in our own home . . ."

But along with the tenderness her rage is also evident. One reads again of that extraordinary episode at Grant's headquarters at City Point, shortly before Appomattox, when Mary Lincoln saw her husband riding horseback beside the attractive young wife of Major General Edward O. C. Ord and attacked "like a tigress" not only Mrs. Ord but also the President in front of a group of officers. We are told that she then shut herself up for three days in her cabin on the *River Queen*, later reporting that Lincoln on the third night dreamed that the White House was on fire; she went home "to see that all was well." What enriches the old painful story, with all its psychological subtleties, are her own telegrams and letters covering the episode. We learn that she took the dream so seriously she twice wired frantically to Washington. Still a mystery is how much of Lincoln's anxiety was real—for he pondered his own dreams —and how much was artful manipulation of his difficult wife.

Of far greater consequence than such tantalizing additions to what is already known about the marriage is the emerging evolutionary portrait of Mary Lincoln herself, painted by her own pen. Tormented throughout her later life by what she called "the vampyre press," and unsympathetically described by most Lincoln historians, who could not forgive her a single indiscretion that added to his burdens, she has generally been dismissed as an erratic and tactless shrew and a spendthrift, who further desecrated her husband's memory by degenerating into insanity, as though what she suffered could have been avoided by a simple act of will. However, although there are evidences of neurotic and obsessional behavior in scores of these letters, one never sees explicit psychosis. As the Turners point out, "she has, interestingly and ironically enough, refused to testify to her own madness." What surprises one is the evidence of her continuing struggle to save herself from the psychosis she feared, which finally did for a time engulf her in 1871, after the death by pleurisy of her youngest son, Tad.

In 1862 she wrote to the governor of New York begging clemency for a young woman convicted of killing her husband when she discovered he had a mistress. Mrs. Lincoln's moving phrase, "She must have acted under the influence of a mind, distrait," is surely out of her own heart. Again and again in her letters we see her making a decision—as she put it explicitly in a letter to Mary Jane Welles on December 29, 1865—"the better . . . for my reason."

There has never been a good clinical study of Mary Lincoln and the etiology of her illness. Dr. W. A. Evans' *Mrs. Abraham Lincoln: A Study of Her Personality and Her Influence on Lincoln* (1932) is disorganized and thin, and these letters will surely stimulate a new and more subtle book-length analysis. Mary was not yet seven when her mother died in childbirth, only to be replaced by a disliked stepmother. Nine additional children followed. It is not surprising that Mary described her childhood as "desolate," and referred to the boarding school to which she was sent as her only real home. With her mother's death she had suffered her first abandonment, and it ill-prepared her for the devastating losses that followed. In the letter that begins this collection, written to her dearest friend, Mercy Levering, Mary Todd at twenty-two wrote the following: ". . . to me it has ever appeared that those whose presence was the sunlight of my heart have departed." It would prove to be the theme of her whole benighted life.

Nevertheless we see great promise in the early letters, written by a high-spirited, intelligent young woman, unusually well educated, described by James Conkling as "the very creature of excitement." She delighted in the "unladylike" game of politics, and had the wit and wisdom to recognize genius in the ungainly lawyer her Edwards relatives looked upon as too far beneath her for marriage. Fond of dancing and cheerful parties, she wondered, "Why it is that married folks always become so serious?" Deeply scarred when Lincoln, for reasons that are still obscure, broke off their engagement, she wrote to Mercy Levering an anguished but nevertheless graceful and cadenced letter:

> . . . as I have not met *him* in the gay world for months, with the usual comfort of misery, imagine that others were as seldom gladdened by his presence as my humble self, yet I would that the case were different, that he would once more resume his Station in Society, that "Richard should be himself again," much much happiness would it afford me . . .

The couple was reunited after eighteen months, and Lincoln became, as she wrote later, "Always—lover, husband—father & *all all to me*, Truly my all . . ."

The Turners tell us that she liked being treated by Lincoln as a "child wife," though one suspects that to be told to "be a *good girl* in all things" would also rouse resentment. But by the restrictions of nineteenth-century society, Mary Lincoln in any case would have been permitted very little role besides that of docile wife and mother. A good brain may not have been expected automatically to atrophy, but with most women it did. Still, despite the occasional bursts of temper and malicious wit that alienated Billy Herndon, she might have conformed to the mold and lived out her whole life with her psyche intact. But little Eddie died of diphtheria in Springfield, and the beloved Willie died of malarial fever in the White House, causing her to give way to paroxysms of grief that no one of her friends could tolerate save Mrs. Gideon Welles, who had seen six of her own children die. With Willie's death, "neurasthenia" and migraine, the commonest of female ailments, became her internal prison within the larger prison of the female world. The religion which told her that his dying was punishment for her "worldliness" only served to compound her despair.

Still we see her pulling herself up out of the morass of depression—"had I not felt the spur of necessity urging me to cheer Mr. Lincoln, whose grief was as great as my own, I could never have smiled again." And in the still more nightmarish struggle after Lincoln's assassination, she fought against the demoralizing effects of her own guilt, for she had been partly to blame for the decision to attend the theater on that fatal Good Friday. To Francis Carpenter she wrote on November 15, 1865, "In the evening, his mind was fixed upon having some relaxation & bent on the theater. Yet I firmly believe, that if he had remained, at the White House on that night of darkness, when the fiends prevailed, he would have been horribly *cut to pieces*—Those fiends, had too long contemplated, this inhuman murder, to have allowed, him, to escape."

There had been, of course, evidence of neurotic behavior even before Willie's death and her husband's murder, and the newspaper editors of the time lacked the decency to cover it with silence. The role of First Lady permitted no indiscretions whatever, whether of finance, politics, protocol, or affection. There was no allowance for a separate identity outside the Dolly Madison stereotype, and the reporters watched Mary Lincoln for variations from it like circling turkey buzzards. Failing to report her numerous visits to army hospitals, they followed her instead on her wild shopping expeditions. They exaggerated her political meddling, distorted her innocent flirtations (surprisingly documented in these letters), and libelously insinuated that she was a Confederate spy.

No one, least of all her husband, whom she described as "a monomaniac on the subject of honesty," could possibly have understood why—with soldiers in want of blankets—she paid $2,000 for a single gown, and $1,000 for a cashmere shawl, or why she bought 84 pairs of gloves in a single month. She kept the cost of these and other extravagant purchases from Lincoln, turning frantically to wealthy men, whom she begged surreptitiously to pay her bills lest the President be informed.

Her obsessional hunger for elegant clothes was as enduring a theme in her letters as in her life. At ten she and a young friend had cut sticks and tried to fashion hoops to go under their skirts—in imitation of the style of adult clothes—only to be humiliated for it by Mary's stepmother. Sycophants in the White House quickly learned that to praise Mrs. Lincoln's lovely shoulders and fabulous dresses was a certain guarantee of her favor. Even her mourning veils had to be "the very finest, & blackest and lightest."

After Lincoln's death, a punishing and niggardly Congress, which could not forgive her shopping sprees, denied her a pension. Private efforts to relieve her want failed, this in the same year that Grant was given three houses and $100,000 for his services to the nation. Jay Cooke, who made millions from the war, could not be persuaded to cancel her loan of $2,000. Finally, in a gesture of rage and desperation, she offered her collection of beautiful dresses and jewelry for sale in New York City, but the Republican party and press, instead of being shamed, condemned and ridiculed her pathetic indiscretion.

To her mulatto friend Elizabeth Keckley, former seamstress in the White House, whose stories of slavery had helped to turn Mary into an "*extreme* Republican," she wrote a letter on October 6, 1867, describing an unexpected meeting with her old friend Charles Sumner in a railroad dining car. This is surely one of the saddest episodes in the annals of American presidential families:

> . . . my black veil was doubled over my face. . . . I immediately *felt* a pair of eyes was gazing at me. I looked him full in the face, and the glance was earnestly returned. I sipped my water, and said, "Mr. S[umner], is this indeed you?" His face was as pale as the table-cloth. . . . He said "How strange you should be on the train and I not know it!"
>
> As soon as I could escape from the table, I did so by saying, "I must secure a cup of tea for a lady friend with me who has a headache." I had scarcely returned to the car, when he entered it with a cup of tea borne by his own aristocratic hands. I was a good deal annoyed by seeing him, and he was so agitated that he spilled half of the cup over my *elegantly gloved* hands. *He* looked very sad. . . . I apologized for the absent lady who wished the cup, by saying "in my absence she had slipped out for it." His heart was in his eyes, notwithstanding my veiled face. I never saw his manner *so* gentle and sad. . . . When he left me, *woman-like* I tossed the cup of tea out of the window, and tucked my head down and shed *bitter tears.* . . .

Later, when she lapsed into severe psychosis, this woman for whom clothes were such an obsession wandered about a corridor in a Chicago hotel half-clad. Committed to a private sanitarium by the action of her only surviving son, Robert Lincoln, she repaid him with a furious letter of hate, demanding the return of the clothes and jewelry she had given as presents to his young wife. No one seems to have guessed that her clothes had long since become a symbol if not a substitute for her own person.

Mary Lincoln's letters, like her life, illuminate the appalling lack of either understanding or therapy for mental illness in her time. The press callously called her a lunatic (and as an obsessive newspaper reader she did not miss a single aspersion), although in her long struggle for equilibrium there were periods of relative stability, when she was merely lonely and frightened. She improved noticeably when Congress, at last, in 1870, thanks to the heroic efforts of Sally Orne and Charles Sumner, granted her a pension of $3,000 a year, confounding the venomous obstructionism of men like Senator Richard Yates of Illinois, who said publicly on the Senate floor that if Lincoln himself "could speak from the abode of heaven," he would oppose a pension for his wife. One of the happier sections in this volume is that which reproduces her warm letters to her grand-nephew, Edward Lewis Baker, Jr., who in the last years of her life became a much-loved substitute for Tad.

But in the end she slipped back into what she called "my terrible fate," undergoing *"daily crucifixion,"* ceaselessly wandering, searching for health in Canada and Europe, carrying thousands of dollars of securities about on her person, buying useless curtains, jewels, fabrics, and the inevitable gloves, haunted continually by a fear of destitution. She died at the age of sixty-four in her sister's home, where she had spent her last three months in seclusion, sleeping on one side of the bed only, reserving the other space for the President. At her funeral the Reverend James A. Reed likened the Lincolns to two pine trees with branches and roots intertwined. Though only one was struck by lightning, "they had virtually both been killed at the same time. With the one that lingered it was slow death from the same cause."

Editors' Note

In 1866, congratulating her friend Senator Charles Sumner on his forthcoming marriage, Mrs. Abraham Lincoln wrote felicitously, "Henceforth you will not stand *alone*, in your greatness." Sadly and ironically, no American statesman has seemed to stand so conspicuously alone in his greatness as Lincoln himself. In the ninety years since his widow's death, those of her countrymen who have thought of Mary Todd Lincoln at all have tended to regard her not only as somehow unworthy of her remarkable husband, but also as an embarrassment to his memory. The foundations for this national rejection were laid in part by William H. Herndon, Lincoln's law partner and biographer, who infected a generation of historians with his hatred of her. Only rather recently has the tide of opinion begun to turn. Mrs. Lincoln's biographers, most notably the late Ruth Painter Randall, recognized the injustice done her and endeavored to redress it. Mrs. Randall saw Mary Lincoln not as Herndon's "female wild cat of the age," but as a loving, well-meaning woman, whose undeniably erratic behavior was largely the result of mild mental illness, exacerbated by the tensions and shocks she experienced throughout the course of her life. In presenting her historian's brief, Mrs. Randall occasionally, and not unexpectedly, succumbed to a bias of her own— this one entirely sympathetic.

It is our belief that the most balanced view of Mary Lincoln— one that offers neither condemnation nor apology—can be obtained from reading her letters. More than six hundred of them survive, nearly all revealing and, in their cumulative effect, shattering. Like all letters, these have far greater value as evidence than the most candid diary or autobiography. Each one was written on a particular day under a specific impulse, with no thought that it would be judged in a larger context or, for that matter, read by anyone other than the person to whom it was addressed.

Because of their value to students of the Lincoln era (and, one hopes, to the general reader as well), and because they reflect so accurately the experiences and attitudes of a woman who was significant in her own right, we have chosen to include all the available letters in this collection, to present the documentary record as it stands.* Mary Lincoln lived for seventeen years after her husband's death, and most of her existing letters derive from this period. Certainly these years involved much that was sad and disagreeable: the loss of a beloved husband and the concomitant fall from status; the demeaning search for funds and the helplessness of a woman who was crippled as much by the attitudes of the age in which she lived as by her own weaknesses; the "Old Clothes Scandal"; Herndon's invention of the Ann Rutledge love story; the protracted battle with Congress for a pension; the death of Tad and a mental breakdown. Yet the letters from this period are as interesting, in a biographical sense, as those written in earlier years. They are longer, less self-conscious, less dignified. If anything revealed Mrs. Lincoln's anguish and the nature of her obsessions, it was her sixty-seven letters to Alexander Williamson from Chicago and her twenty-five letters to Sally Orne from Frankfurt. Amid the woeful rhetoric of these later letters there is much worth preserving: retrospective glimpses of the Lincoln marriage; allusions to old Washington intrigues; devastating character sketches of prominent personalities; descriptions of foreign scenes; and, always, unconscious self-revelation. To whom Mary Lincoln wrote, and how often, is frequently as significant as what she wrote. Even her ninety-two business letters to Jacob Bunn, arid though they are, prove a point by their consistency and sheer number: that for four years following her release from a sanitarium, Mrs. Lincoln's mind was remarkably lucid.

For all their unwitting self-revelation, Mary Lincoln's letters present problems for those who study them. They constitute, first of

---

* The only items in Mrs. Lincoln's handwriting that we have omitted are brief, formal invitations, which exist in profusion.

all, an almost totally one-sided record. She and, later, her son Robert destroyed the letters she received with such efficiency that less than fifty addressed to her are still in existence. This circumstance has made extensive annotation necessary, as have the number of proper names mentioned and events alluded to, the legion of separate correspondents, and the fact that Mary Lincoln was prone to complicated and less-than-straightforward ways of expressing herself.

Although parts of her letters have appeared in print, less than one third have been published in their entirety, and most of these are in books now long out of print or in historical journals of limited readership. Through the generosity of curators and private collectors, we were able to secure for this volume a great many documents whose existence was virtually unknown but to a small group of scholars. Time and again we found that these obscure letters, when placed in context, contained the answers to questions raised by other, more familiar ones—an experience affording the joys that come to any solver of intricate puzzles.

We were also fortunate, in most cases, to have had access to original manuscripts or to photostats of them. (A listing of sources and locations will be found at the back of the book.) Mary Lincoln's penmanship was exquisite and legible even in later years when her sight began to fail. Her style, on the other hand, was as complex and changeable as her nature: pithy and to the point one minute, the next, tortured and convoluted. She had the Victorian letter writer's proclivity for elaborate syntax and a personal addiction to commas and dashes; she could write an eight-page letter as a single paragraph. In transposing her letters into type, we have tried to retain as much of their unique flavor and appearance as possible, avoiding the use of *sic*, except when proper names are misspelled. Where Mrs. Lincoln, in her haste or confusion, left out part of a word, or an entire word or words, we have made the logical interpolations in brackets, but only when necessary to clarify meaning. The reader will soon grow accustomed, as we did, to her eccentricities of style, to her failure to remember to close quotes and parentheses, and to what now would be considered outmoded usage. Our only major alteration in the appearance of the letters was made for the purpose of saving space: Mrs. Lincoln would almost always head a letter with, for example, "Hon. David Davis" and then indent "My dear sir." We have deleted the formal address, identifying the recipient above the letter.

Telegrams are distinguished from letters but are treated for what they were: not the staccato outpourings of the modern teletype machine, but longhand documents, written out by the sender for transmittal over the wires or, on receipt, by a telegraph clerk. Mary Lincoln frequently wrote out her own messages on whatever scrap of paper came to hand. In cases where two copies of the same telegram exist—one as she wrote it out, the other as it was received— we have of course used the one in her handwriting.

She was generally scrupulous about dating her letters, although she did not always date them accurately. She once confessed to being unable to remember the day of the month, and often left off the year. On the basis of internal evidence, it was seldom difficult to place un-dated letters or those misdated either by Mrs. Lincoln or by some un-known collector or archivist. Other clues lay in the size and state of the handwriting and in the style of the notepaper used. (Mrs. Lin-coln would order personal stationery, usually initialed, on the aver-age of once every four months, run through it, and then order a new design.)

In cases where we did not see the original manuscript—it being either lost, destroyed, or otherwise inaccessible—we were obliged to use a version that had appeared in print. Although the style and lan-guage of these letters are unquestionably Mary Lincoln's, in many instances they were either transcribed carelessly, polished for smoother reading, or cut for reasons of discretion. (This *caveat* does not of course apply to every letter taken from a secondary source. We have been privileged to have been able to make use of documents meticulously copied and annotated, usually by their owners, in schol-arly journals. These sources are discussed in the Bibliography and Acknowledgments.)

The narrative passages interspersed among the letters were de-signed to supplement and analyze the documentary record rather than to stand alone as biography. Whatever judgments are expressed in the commentary are, unless otherwise noted, our own and are based primarily on our study of the letters, although we have made liberal use of other sources, which are listed in the Bibliography.

The collection is as definitive as it was possible to make it. However, two or three catalogued letters were unaccountably missing from the vaults of some redoubtable archives and a very few were withheld from us by owners whose motives can only be surmised. Some we may simply have overlooked. When inquiries to major European archives failed to yield results, we concentrated our search on American collections. Even now, a cache of Mary Lincoln's letters may be lying undiscovered in an attic or buried in a manuscript collection abroad, and there is every reason to believe that new ones will be constantly coming to light.

It is our hope that this volume will be regarded not merely as another addition to the enormous body of knowledge known as Lincolniana. To us, the chief interest of Mary Lincoln's letters lies in their self-portrait of a woman who had the intelligence, energy, and compassion to have been ranked among the outstanding first ladies of the land, an anomaly in her era, but who came to the White House at the most tragic hour in a nation's history and was destroyed by the experience.

J . G . T .

L . L . T .

April 1972

I

The Very Creature
of Excitement

December 1818
———
February 1861

On December 13, 1818, Eliza Parker Todd, wife of a prominent banker in Lexington, Kentucky, gave birth to her fourth child, a girl. Eliza and her husband Robert, who were cousins, already had two tiny daughters, Elizabeth and Frances, and a son named Levi. The baby was christened Mary Ann and welcomed into a happy family, into a life which was serene, ordered, and utterly secure.

The infant's distant ancestors on both sides had been Scottish Covenanters of hardy breed. Successive generations of forebears had migrated to America early in the eighteenth century, scattered to Pennsylvania and Virginia, and then followed the pioneer's path westward into frontier Kentucky. The family in its various branches —Todds, Porters, Parkers—boasted Revolutionary War heroes and Indian fighters, successful farmers and merchants, politicians and philanthropists. Wherever they settled they seemed to thrive. They married and intermarried, held on to their money, led useful lives, and considered themselves aristocrats.

By the time Mary was born the struggle against the wilderness was over for the Todds. There was little about them to recall it, beyond a strain of aggressiveness and practicality. Even those who grumbled that the family set too much store by money and property conceded that they attached equal importance to education, personal integrity, and public service. Todds had been among the founders of Lexington and of the university called Transylvania which gave the city much of its reputation as a cultural oasis in the raw western country. They had excellent taste in friends, and they themselves were good people to know.

Mary was the only one of Robert Todd's daughters to venture outside of a comfortable, patrician milieu, to show some daring in her choice of husband. In the teeth of family opposition, she married Abraham Lincoln, a penniless young lawyer born in the backwoods and largely self-taught, in whom she, almost alone at first, saw greatness. His dazzling success was therefore especially sweet to her, but flaws in her character, emotional instability, and a series of tragedies clouded her later life and brought the world down about her ears. A nation which erected a marble temple to her husband—as surely a house of worship as any cathedral in the capital—prefers not to think of her, but when it does, dismisses her as a shrew, a spendthrift, a madwoman. Why, despite spirited and scholarly defenses of her, do most Americans still harbor unpleasant feelings about Mrs. Lincoln? How much was she herself to blame for her unfortunate reputation, and how much of it was due to circumstance, inner demons, or the gossip of her enemies? Was her marriage a happy one?

There is perhaps no better means of reaching for the answers to these questions, of seeing all facets of Mary Lincoln's character, without bias pro or con, than by letting her speak for herself. In letters written over four decades, she has left behind a record of her life more trustworthy than autobiography, more revealing in its way than a diary. When this unwitting self-portrait is set in historical perspective and rounded out by the testimony of those who knew her or who have studied her, we begin to glimpse the truth about Abraham Lincoln's wife and in so doing add a new dimension to our understanding of Lincoln.

The earliest existing letter in Mary Todd's hand dates from July 1840, when she was twenty-one years old. To learn of her childhood and adolescence, those years now recognized as formative, we must rely on reminiscence and a somewhat sketchy record. It is known that three more children came after her: Ann, born in 1820; Robert, who died in babyhood; and George Rogers Clark, named for the great soldier-explorer. Eliza Todd died the day after this last, difficult birth; the year was 1825, and Mary was only six. Seventeen months later, Robert Todd remarried and went on to father nine more children (eight of whom lived) by his second wife, a Frankfort woman of good family named Elizabeth ("Betsy") Humphreys.

In a letter written in 1871, Mary Todd Lincoln described her childhood as "desolate"; difficult it certainly was. The loss of her mother must have had its effect on a little girl who was, from all accounts, sensitive and high-strung to begin with. Dr. W. A. Evans, in a clinical analysis of Mrs. Lincoln's personality [1] attributed many of her later problems to this traumatic circumstance. She was, he surmised, overly indulged at first, and later, in the chaos of a large family, denied proper training in such useful virtues as patience and self-control.

Our only intimate glimpse of Mary Todd as a child is in a tender memoir written by Elizabeth Humphreys Norris, a niece of Mary's stepmother.[2] In the late 1820's "Lizzie" Humphreys came from Frankfort to Lexington for her education, sharing Mary's room and many of her secrets. Seventy years later, mindful of her subject's reputation, she looked back in love and indignation to recall the child she knew as happy, high-spirited, affectionate, and somewhat precocious. Both girls attended a remarkable school founded by a former Episcopal bishop named John Ward. Dr. Ward was a pioneer in co-education and a "regular martinet," according to Mrs. Norris. Mary toed the line with the rest of his students, aided by a quick mind and a retentive memory. She was a religious child in an era when piety was considered particularly becoming in the young.

Yet somewhere along the way she acquired a few worldly tendencies which defied inhibition, among them a need for amusement and a passion for pretty clothes. Mary, remembered Mrs. Norris, always "wanted to be in fashion." Despising the demure little dresses then worn by young girls, she craved above all else a set of hoops. "But how to get it was the trouble—It would be a preposterous and unheard of request. . . . But come it must, at all hazards." [3] (This last observation is startlingly reminiscent of one made by Julia Taft Bayne of Mrs. Abraham Lincoln, thirty years

[1] W. A. Evans, M.D. *Mrs. Abraham Lincoln: A Study of Her Personality and Her Influence on Lincoln.* New York, 1932.
[2] The quotations which follow are taken from a three-part letter written by Mrs. Norris in 1895 to Mrs. Lincoln's half-sister Emilie Todd Helm, who was preparing a family history. The letter was formerly owned by Justin G. Turner.
[3] Mrs. Norris placed Mary's age at ten when the following incident took place.

later: "She wanted what she wanted when she wanted it and no substitute!") [4]

Mary Todd was ever resourceful. She and Lizzie pulled some willow branches from a neighbor's tree, raced home and stitched secretly into the night, determined to transform their prim, straight little skirts into something spectacular for Sunday school next day. The results were "grotesque," and when Betsy Todd saw them in the morning, she ordered the girls to change. Mary reacted first with a flood of tears, and then with a temper tantrum, the first and only one Lizzie ever saw her have and, according to her recollection, justified. "She felt we were badly treated—and expressed herself freely on the subject—I was angry too, and said quietly to myself as much as she had uttered, but I loved [Mrs. Todd] and had not the heart to make a loud denunciation."

Mary Todd tried to be as sedate and sweetly hypocritical as most other young females of her acquaintance, but occasional cracks in the ladylike veneer revealed a stubborn nature, a shrewd, independent mind, and a sharp tongue. Even loving Lizzie Norris had to admit that Mary, as an adolescent, "now and then indulged in sarcastic, witty remarks that cut. But," she insisted, "there was no malice in it. She was impulsive & made no attempt to conceal her feelings, indeed it would have been an impossibility had she desired to do so, for her face was an index to every passing emotion."

The face that so often betrayed Mary Todd was, as she entered womanhood, pretty and intelligent; yet the features were not definite enough to be called "striking," nor refined enough for classic beauty. She had a small, upturned nose, a broad forehead, wide-set blue eyes, and a rosy complexion framed by soft brown hair that glistened with bronze highlights. Her least attractive feature was a prominent chin, which caused her thin mouth to fall into tight, stern lines, and gave her, especially in later life as her face became full, a faintly hard-bitten expression. Yet even this judgment is based on portraits and photographs, stiffly posed. In life, we are told, the little mouth smiled a good deal, the eyes were merry and kind. She was somewhat sensitive about her lack of height; although she achieved a respectable five feet two inches, the contrast with her husband's lanky six feet four would later offend her

---

[4] Julia Taft Bayne. *Tad Lincoln and His Father.* Boston, 1931, p. 49.

vanity so much that she would never allow herself to be photographed with him. Yet she had a rounded figure, buxom and ideally suited to the fashions of the day, and exquisitely shaped arms and hands that moved in quick, graceful gestures when she spoke. She had learned early in life how to use her wiles to win her father's favor, and when things went well she was a delight. Only when she was unhappy or frustrated would her composure dissolve in tears or in uncontrollable rages that sent milder souls scurrying for cover.

In 1832, when Mary was thirteen, her sister Elizabeth, barely out of childhood herself, was married to Ninian Wirt Edwards, son of Ninian Edwards, who had been the third governor of the Illinois Territory, later U.S. senator, and first governor of the state. Since the bridegroom was still in his junior year at Transylvania University, the couple remained in Lexington until he graduated, at which point they moved to Illinois, first to Belleville, then to the bustling prairie town of Springfield, where they set up housekeeping in grand style.

Elizabeth had gone from one political milieu to another. In addition to mercantile interests and his presidency of the Lexington branch of the Bank of Kentucky, Robert Todd had held minor political office and wielded major political influence. He was close to Henry Clay and on cordial terms with nearly every other prominent Whig in Fayette County and beyond. With lavish hospitality, he and his wife entertained senators, governors, congressmen, party officials, and general visitors from all over the country and abroad, often allowing the older children to listen in on after-dinner conversations. This early exposure to political talk would have a lasting effect on Mary Todd; by the age of fourteen she was a fiery little Whig, who could not think of enough dreadful things to say about Andrew Jackson. Her particular hero was Clay, whom she once described as "the handsomest man in town," with the finest manners of anyone except her father. Her future husband may at the time have been worshipping Clay from afar, but Mary knew him well enough to extract an invitation to the White House for that inevitable day when the Mansion would be his home.[5]

[5] These and the following recollections of Mary Todd's girlhood in Lexington are derived from two major sources: Katherine Helm. *The True Story of Mary, Wife of Lincoln.* New York, 1928, and William Henry Townsend. *Lincoln and the Bluegrass.* Lexington, 1955.

"Putting Mr. Clay in the White House" was for years the chief preoccupation of the men who met with Robert Todd, but pursuit of this elusive dream eventually gave way to heated debate on the issue of slavery. So celebrated was the beauty, refinement, and cultural ambiance of Lexington that it had been dubbed "The Athens of America." But, like its ancient counterpart, it was also a slave-holding community, and Robert Todd, one of its leading citizens, was a slaveowner, though on a limited scale. When it occurred to Mary in childhood that the servants in her father's house were not free to depart, she quickly dismissed the matter. Why—and where —would they wish to go? They were tenderly looked after, treated with that loving condescension dignified by the expression "members of the family." Mary respected and confided in her own Mammy Sally (in family reminiscence, the archetypal southern mammy), who had cared for her from birth, petted and prodded her, and put her in fear of the "debil."

Inevitably her eyes were opened to the brutal aspects of the system, for Lexington had its share of auction blocks and slave jails, its public whippings and hangings. From her front window Mary could probably have seen those slow-moving lines of manacled black men, women, and children driven along Main Street to be sold South. She knew—and was pleased to know—that Mammy Sally distributed food to runaways headed for Canada. These early memories, reinforced by later experience, would go far toward making Mrs. Abraham Lincoln more ardent an abolitionist than her husband.

By the autumn of 1832 Robert Todd's elegant house on Main Street was crowded to the bursting point with children, relatives, servants, and visitors. Betsy Todd could only have been grateful to see Mary go off to board weekdays at a fashionable young ladies' academy on the Richmond Pike, founded by a pair of French émigrés, Madame Victorie Charlotte LeClere Mentelle and her husband Augustus. In four years at Mentelle's, Mary acquired not only a solid grounding in English literature and an excellent reading knowledge of French, but also the ability to carry on a conversation in a perfect Parisian accent. Mastery of the rules of etiquette and the steps of the polka, the schottische, the galop, and the waltz completed her education for society, which she proceeded to enter with a vengeance.

Although she could flutter a fan with the best of them, Mary Todd was "smart" and seldom troubled to pretend otherwise. Wide reading and a fascination with human nature and public affairs gave her something to say, and more often than not, she said it, tempering her frankness with wit and with the aptness of her observations. An eye for the ridiculous and an ear for speech patterns and dialects made her a devastating mimic; she also discovered that a little exaggeration made a good story better.

But even the cleverest girl could have no career in that day other than matrimony. By the time Mary Todd was finished at Mentelle's she was seventeen and eligible for this next step. Her older sister "Fanny" had already left for a long visit to the young Edwards family in Springfield where, under Elizabeth's shrewd matchmaking eye, she was keeping company with a physician and druggist named William S. Wallace, whom she would marry in May of 1839. Fanny taken care of, Elizabeth next invited Mary to Illinois.

In addition to her two older sisters, Mary had an uncle in Springfield, Dr. John Todd, and three cousins, all distinguished lawyer-politicians: John Todd Stuart, Stephen T. Logan, and John J. Hardin. Stuart had recently taken on as junior law partner a young state legislator named Abraham Lincoln, whom he had met when both had served in the Black Hawk War. It is doubtful that Mary met Lincoln on her first visit to Springfield in 1837. Although good things were already being said of him, he was still too much of an unknown quantity—and too uncertain of himself— to have penetrated that tight, aristocratic circle dominated by Ninian and Elizabeth Edwards.

For reasons that are somewhat obscure, Mary Todd returned to Lexington after only three months in Illinois. Back at home she immersed herself in advanced classes with her old mentor Dr. Ward (taking what her biographer, Ruth Painter Randall, termed "a sort of post-graduate course," unusual for a girl of her time and background).[6] It was probably Dr. Ward's academic program which held her in Lexington for two years thereafter;

[6] Ruth Painter Randall. *Mary Lincoln: Biography of a Marriage.* Boston, 1953, p. 28.

certainly her relations with her stepmother were far from placid. Betsy Todd was a good woman, but domestic responsibility and frequent childbearing left her neither the time nor the patience for dealing with a strong-willed eighteen-year-old. In all her conflicts with Betsy, Mary had one consistent champion: her Grandmother Parker, an outspoken, indomitable old lady who persisted in an antipathy to her dead daughter's successor and, living nearby, was able to provide shelter and succor whenever one of Eliza's children needed it. Mary needed it often.

In time she found herself drawn back to Springfield, where a sense of push and excitement more than compensated for the somewhat primitive conditions. As soon as the little city became capital of Illinois in 1839, it was flooded with politicians, lawyers, and young Easterners with a sense of adventure and large ambitions. Ninian and Elizabeth knew everyone who mattered. When Mary arrived to make her permanent home with them in October of 1839, she quickly re-established herself as a fixture of the young set which gathered evenings at the Edwardses' imposing hilltop home—that lively group which called itself "the Coterie" and was called by those it excluded "the Edwards clique." The shifting personnel of the Coterie included the town's prettiest, most marriageable girls and promising young men, several of whom—Stephen A. Douglas, Edward D. Baker, James Shields, Lyman Trumbull, and, a new recruit, Abraham Lincoln—would make their mark in history.

The girls in the Coterie had the best of it. There were plenty of exceptional men to go around, and femininity was appreciated. At the same time there was a freedom of exchange, an easy equality between male and female which emboldened a clever girl like Mary Todd to speak her mind on any subject without fear of being ignored or ridiculed.

She had read enough to make light literary pronouncements, and her experiences in her father's house had given her a zest for political and social gossip, conversational staples with the Coterie. She could milk the last drop of drama or humor from a story, and with one pithy retort could silence a fool or convulse a roomful of people. She was plumply pretty and bursting with healthy high spirits. James C. Conkling, a young lawyer and a charter member of the Coterie, wrote of her at the time: "She is the very creature of excitement you know, and never enjoys herself more than when in society and surrounded by a company of merry friends." [7] Ninian W. Edwards gave an even more telling description of her charms: "Mary could make a bishop forget his prayers." [8]

Shortly after her return to Springfield, Mary Todd was introduced to Abraham Lincoln at a ball. In the two years since her first visit, Lincoln had managed to carve a niche for himself in Springfield society by virtue of his association with Stuart and a growing respect among the townspeople for his intellect and integrity. By December of 1839 his name was sufficiently prominent to have been listed on the invitation to a cotillion, along with those of Douglas, Edwards, and other members of the Coterie; perhaps it was on this occasion that he and Mary met.

An amusing legend has grown up about the initial encounter between Mary Todd and Abraham Lincoln. Family tradition has it that the tall, gaunt lawyer bent over the belle of the ball and blurted out: "Miss Todd, I want to dance with you the worst way." Later, Mary commented drily to a cousin: "And he certainly did." [9] But Lincoln apparently made an impression on her consciousness as well as on her dancing slippers. He was in every respect—background, looks, manners, mentality—totally unlike any man she had ever met. She became almost immediately intrigued by him, and he by her.

There is no need here to recount the early struggles of Abraham Lincoln, or to list the forces that molded his mind and character. It is sufficient to say that, at thirty, he was already an extraordinary man, and sufficient to grant Mary Todd the sense to have seen it. Although his activities were attracting increasing attention, and he never lacked for masculine company, his private life in 1839 was essentially lonely and barren. Several years earlier he had given up on a desultory courtship of Mary Owens, a girl he had met in New Salem, who had all the qualifications for a good and loyal wife. But there had been something lacking in their relationship, something that went beyond Lincoln's gnawing conviction that he could not keep a wife in comfort. The missing "something" was

[7] James C. Conkling to Mercy Ann Levering, Springfield, September 21, 1840. MS. in the Illinois State Historical Library, Springfield.
[8] Quoted in Helm, p. 81.   [9] *Ibid.*, p. 74.

that special feeling compounded of powerful physical attraction and congeniality of mind. When Mary Todd, blithe and blooming, turned the full force of her charm upon him, laughed at his stories, talked earnestly with him of poetry and politics, and smiled up into his face, Abraham Lincoln was lost.

Before long he was abandoning those lazy, comfortable sessions of talk with his cronies at Speed's store to go and visit with the girl he called "Molly" at the Edwards mansion. His long body in its ill-fitting garments made a strange sight amid the dainty, elegant furnishings in Mrs. Edwards' parlor, where he would perch precariously on a horsehair sofa, mesmerized by Mary's animated chatter and practiced coquetry.

Although she seemed determined to make Lincoln fall in love with her, Mary Todd was not yet ready to commit herself to one man, despite the fact that she was approaching the dangerously advanced age of twenty-two. In the summer of 1840 she left Springfield and its major attraction to spend several months in Columbia, Missouri, as the guest of her uncle, Judge David Todd. The judge's daughter Ann was close to her age, and the two had fine times together, dressing up for parties and balls, taking long jaunts to neighboring cities with companies of friends, and exchanging confidences far into the night.

If Mary missed Lincoln in Columbia, she also missed a girl named Mercy Levering, who had come to Springfield from Baltimore to visit her married brother Lawrason at about the same time Mary had arrived to stay with Ninian and Elizabeth. The Edwards and Levering homes stood together on the rise now crowned by the Illinois Centennial Building, and throughout the winter of 1839–40 the two girls had been almost inseparable. Mary revealed to Mercy her growing interest in Abraham Lincoln and hung on all the details of Mercy's romance with James C. Conkling (the couple would marry in 1841). Shortly after Mary left for Missouri, Mercy temporarily retreated to Baltimore, but the friendship was maintained through the post. A letter to Mercy dated July 23, 1840, is the earliest existing one in Mary Todd's hand. (In it, she referred to a "lengthy document" she had sent soon after arriving in Columbia, but wrote, "as you did not mention having received it, I feared it had not reached you." The "lengthy document" is as lost to posterity as it was to Mercy.)

The July letter and the two which followed it enjoy another distinction: they are the only existing ones written by Mary Todd in the period before her marriage. That makes them precious documents which deserve consideration separately for the light they shed on this young woman's experiences and emotions at three critical junctures; taken together, they are remarkably revealing of her youthful personality, her intellectual bent, and her qualities as a correspondent.

She wrote in a small, clear, slanted script, filling each sheet to its edges, scarcely ever pausing for paragraphs. She usually finished off a long letter by cross-writing her closing words over the top of the first page, a thrifty habit she clung to all her life. To the florid epistolary conventions of the era were added her own stylistic quirks, which give her writings a characteristic look, even when set in type. She had a marked aversion to the period as a means of punctuation; her sentences flowed on and on, random thoughts rushing in upon one another in a simple stream-of-consciousness style. In place of periods, she made lavish and interchangeable use of dashes and commas, a predilection which became increasingly pronounced in later years. Her pages were inundated by a hail of commas; they shattered sentences into tiny fragments, occasionally severing subject from predicate, verb from object, adjective from noun, but remaining maddeningly absent in the customary places. She underlined firmly and frequently, with her peculiar emphasis. Her spelling was good, but far from perfect (certain words such as "pilgrimage" and "villainous" she stubbornly misspelled for forty years); when carried away by an idea, emotion, or grievance she could become hopelessly lost in her own syntax.

Nothing of her later prolific output can match these three early letters in depth of thought, in color, and charm. It is easy to see what attracted Abraham Lincoln to her. Behind the sentimental effusions, the protestations of eternal fidelity, lay a genuine capacity for warmth, sympathy, and joy. There were traces of melancholy, of vague, unfulfilled longings, as well as a certain tart humor and a philosophical approach to human frailties, including her own. Evidence of literary leanings can be found in her feeling for the apt quotation, in her gift for language, in descriptive phrases that verged on the poetic. But most noteworthy—and most charac-

teristic—were her unabashed interest in other people's lives and
her habit of alternating candid opinion with guarded remarks, the
latter sometimes prefaced or followed by the expression "between
ourselves." A social tidbit was to be kept "between ourselves";
so were the revelations of a young girl's delicate emotions; so, later,
would be acerbic comments on prominent political figures and,
still later, the wild imaginings of a troubled mind.

Historians have detected in the first letter to Mercy Levering
elaborate hints of Mary Todd's attachment to Abraham Lincoln,
although he is never mentioned by name. She had seen him some
weeks earlier when a political speech had taken him to Roche-
port, Missouri, and he had made a brief stopover in Columbia.
Since then she had received letters from Springfield, which she
claimed were "entirely *unlooked for*," but apparently welcome
nonetheless. Many young men, including one of distinguished
ancestry, showed an interest in her, but she assured Mercy that
her hand would never be given without her heart. For all her love
of excitement, she imagined hers was to be "a quiet lot"—a not unreasonable expectation were she to bind up her life with that of a
struggling young lawyer named Lincoln.

To Mercy Ann Levering

Columbia [Mo.] July 23d 1840

Many thanks Dearest Merce for your kind letter yet in spite
of the pleasure of hearing from you it brought many feelings of
sorrow and regret, to know that you were as near as St Louis, &
[I] was debarred the happiness of seeing one I love so well, a few
days before receiving yours, Elizabeth [Edwards] wrote to me &
spoke of the possibility of seeing you again as you did not quit
these western wilds until August & then you would accompany
your Brother home, in spite of the *agreeable visitation* I have already made, I had determined to forego all, once more to see you,
and shorten my visit here—You will readily credit me Dearest
when I tell you my time has been most delightfully spent, this por-

tion of the state is certainly most beautiful, and in my wanderings
I never encountered more kindness & hospitality, as my visit was
particularly to my relations & did not expect to remain for any
length of time, I was not anxious to mingle with the strange crowd,
and form new associations so soon to be severed, yet every lady
almost that called extended an invitation to us to spend an evening
with them, so I have necessarily seen more society than I had anticipated, on yesterday we returned from a most agreeable excursion to Boonville, situated immediately on the river and a charming
place, we remained a week, attended four parties, during the time,
once [sic] was *particularly* distinguished for its brillancy & *city
like* doings, the house was very commodious, four rooms & two
halls, thrown open for the reception of the guests, in two, dancing
was carried on with *untiring vigor*, kept up until 3 o'clock, however, Cousin [Ann] & myself were more genteel left rather earlier
Your risibles would have undergone a *considerable state of excitement*, were you to have seen the "poetry of motion" exercised in
the dance, had our grandfathers been present in the festive halls of
mirth, they would undoubtedly have recognised the familiar airs
of their youthful days, all the old Virginia reels that have been
handed down to us by *tradition*, were played, your Cousin Sep methinks would have enjoyed the danse, no insinuations meant, save
his extreme fondness for this fascinating amusement, and the rapid
manner they hurried through the figures, at the end of each cotillion. I felt exhausted after such *desperate exertions* to keep pace
with the music. Were Missouri my home, with the exception of
St Louis, Boonville would certainly in my estimation have the
preference a life on the river to me has always had a charm, so
much excitement, and this *you* have deemed necessary to my well-
being: every day experience impresses me more fully with the belief. I would such were not my nature, for mine I fancy is to be a
quiet lot, and happy indeed will I be, if it is, only cast near those,
I so *dearly love*, my feelings & hopes are all so sanguine that in
this dull world of reality tis best to dispel our delusive day dreams
so soon as possible Would it were in my power to follow your kind
advice, my ever dear Merce and turn my thoughts from earthly
vanities, to one higher than us all, every day proves the fallacy of
our enjoyments, & that we are living for pleasures that do not

recompense us for the pursuit—I wrote you a lengthy document, soon after reaching this place, as you did not mention having received it, I feared it had not reached you. The mail comes in to day, and I am on the wing of expectation, hoping to hear from my dear sister Fanny. Dr Wallace I hear has been sick, & Fanny I fear is unable to play the part of devoted nurse at *this time*, to both child & husband—Every week since I left Springfield, have had the felicity of receiving various numbers of their interesting papers, Old Soldiers, Journals & even the *Hickory Club*,[1] has crossed my vision. This latter, rather astonished your friend, *there* I had deemed myself forgotten—When I mention *some letters*, I have received since leaving S- you will be somewhat surprised, as I *must confess* they were entirely *unlooked for*. this is *between ourselves*, my dearest, but of this more anon;[2] every day I am convinced this is a stranger world we live in, the *past* as the future is to me a mystery, how much I wish you were near ever have I found yours a congenial heart, in your presence I have almost *thought aloud*, and the thought that paineth most is that such may never be again, yet, I trust that a happier day will dawn, near you, I would be most happy to sojourn in our earthly pilgrimmage, to me it has ever appeared that those whose presence was the sunlight of my heart have departed—separated far and wide, to meet when? In Boonville I met with two or three former schoolmates, endeared to me by ties of early memories, also several young gentlemen I [had known][3] well in Kentucky. I need not speak to you of the pleasures of such an agreeable meeting, Cousin Anne & myself did not *know* [quiet?] whilst there, this at all times, I have deemed a hard lesson, yet in this instance, the task was still severer, to have so many beaux "dancing attendance" on us at one time, and the little throng were hosts within themselves, our Sucker [Illinois] friends would have opened their orbs, at such strange doings, I there met with a young Cousin, by my Mother's side, who has but

[1] These were *The Old Soldier*, a Harrison campaign paper published in 1840, one of whose editors was Abraham Lincoln; the *Sangamo Journal*, Springfield's leading newspaper, staunchly Whig in outlook; and *The Old Hickory*, the Democratic campaign paper and voice of the Hickory Clubs. Perhaps the last was sent by one of Mary Todd's beaux, the Democrat Stephen A. Douglas, after she had "deemed [herself] forgotten" by him.
[2] This passage is considered to refer to Abraham Lincoln.
[3] Manuscript torn.

a few weeks since, wended his way westward, a young lawyer, and gives hopes of bright promise already the old lawyer's, have extended a *patronising* smile & I trust & feel that he may one day, ere long weave a bright chaplet of fame, for his youthful brow—Were you to see him, I almost fancy & hope that *others* in your eye would be forgotten,[4] no other Cousin save *him* would I deem worthy your acceptance—and he has that Dear Merce which I have heard you say would be *indispensable*, good morals & Religion and the most affectionate heart in the world, yet I much fear yours is a *gone case*, though far separated, do not deem your confidence misplaced, tell me all—every thing, you know the deep interest I feel for you, time can never banish your remembrance, how desolate I shall feel on returning to Springfield without you, your kind & cheering presence has beguiled many a lonely hour of its length. Mrs [Lawrason] L[evering] must feel lost, and little Anne too, has lost a play mate. Martha Jane [5] I am told seldom wanders on the hill,[6] still blest with her *little friend's* society, be it so "I care not though she be dearer," Merce she can now have an opportunity of making *dead sets* at the youngsters. I can answer for the security of your claims, tell me, were my suspicions unfounded? To change our subject to one of a *still warmer* nature, did you ever feel such oppressive weather as we have had of late, though you perhaps did not experience the intensity of the heat, at this time, no doubt, you are sailing o'er the waters blue, what an agreeable trip will be yours dearest, & I trust every happiness may attend you. I shall expect a lengthy account of your journeyings, crossed & recrossed. I feel exacting, yet bear with me, my great desire to hear from you is a sufficient palliation for my fault, so at least I deem it. Cousin & myself take the world easy, as usual, with me you know, allow but few of its cares, to mar *our Serenity*, we regularly take our afternoon *siestas*, and soon find our spirits wafted [to the] land of dreams—Then will I think of thee—Still [it does] not require so mighty of effort, to bring you [to] mind, for the brightest associations of the [past year] are connected with thee

Will Todd [7] has been here some part of the time, is now here,

---

[4] An oblique reference to James C. Conkling, Mercy's beau.
[5] Martha Jane Lowry, soon to be the bride of Sidney Abell.
[6] The rise on which the Edwards and Levering houses stood.
[7] William S. Todd, son of Mary's uncle, Dr. John Todd.

and sends his best respects, if not *love*, you will pardon the familiarity of the youth as in times past, he is agreeable surprised to find himself "not too young to enter society" here, that slight ever haunts him he is uncertain as to whether he will locate himself in Missouri, tis difficult at this time, to get any where into business, and perhaps he will yet again return homeward. There is a very lovely & interesting young lady, residing here whom rumor says will one day be a cousin of ours & *John Todd* [8] is the happy man, surprised at her taste, he is certainly very clever, yet he did not shew off to the same advantage whilst with us, as here he was a general beau—Cousin Ann, is betraying her womanly curiosity wonders what I am scribbling so much about—I soon close without having said half enough—Though I can fancy you pale and exausted—So in mercy will spare you—Ann says you cannot fail being pleased with Missouri, she is so much attached to her native state, that I fear nothing will ever draw her hence, not even *the leader in Israel*, though that will never be methinks—she hopes one day not far distant with some faithful swain, you may pitch your tent here, and then she will have the happiness of seeing you, & with this wish she sends much love—Uncle has just returned from Court, and insists upon our taking another jaunt as travelling is absolutely necessary to Cousin's health, I know not how this will be, ere long I must quit this land, your letter if you please direct to Springfield as I am confidant I shall be there ere you have time to receive & answer this, and do my dearest girl, write very soon, you know not the happiness one of your letters affords—If you conclude to settle in Missouri, *I will do so too*, [there] is *one* being here, who cannot brook the mention of my return, an agreeable lawyer & grandson of *Patrick Henry—what an honor!* Shall never survive it—I wish you could see him, the most perfect original I had ever met, my beaux have *always* been *hard bargains* at any rate, Uncle and others think, he surpasses his *noble ancestor* in *talents*, yet Merce I love him not, & my hand will never be given, where my heart is not—Cousin A has a most devoted hero who watches her every look, with a *lover's eye*, and I have long told her she was a coquette in a *quiet* way—and they are said to be the most danger-

[8] John B. S. Todd, oldest son of Dr. John Todd.

ous ever—Be as *unrese[r]ved* as you find me, I forget myself writing to you, pass my imperfections lightly by, and excuse so miserable a production from your most attached friend

Mary

⌒ ⌒ ◇ ⌒ ⌒

Mercy Levering was not to hear from Mary Todd for several months after Mary's return from Missouri. The letter which finally reached her in December 1840, though long and gossipy as usual, was unrevealing on the subject of Mary's involvement with Abraham Lincoln. Lincoln's name is mentioned twice, but most casually, considering that he and Mary Todd were either engaged or about to become so.

She was busy with parties, trips, politics, and home chores —or so she said. She was enjoying the companionship of Matilda Edwards, Ninian's attractive young cousin from Alton, and fending off the attentions of Edwin B. Webb, a lawyer who suffered from two visible disadvantages, his age and status as a widower with two children—and from a third, perhaps no less obvious: the fact that Mary Todd's heart belonged to Abraham Lincoln. There is little in the letter to indicate that Mary was going through the emotional crisis which would come to a head a few weeks later. Her mention of "the *crime* of *matrimony*" is perhaps the most significant allusion it contains. She, like her friend Mary Lamb, was "about perpetrating" such an offense and, although she was too proud to admit it, her sister and brother-in-law were not pleased.

To Mercy Ann Levering

Springfield Dec [15?] 1840—

Many, very many weary days have passed my ever dear Merce, since mine has been the pleasure of hearing from you, some weeks since I received your kind, soul cheering epistle & had I been *then* told such a length of time would have intervened ere I had availed myself of an oppurtunity of replying to it, I would not have given credence to the tale, yet such has been the case & I feel that I owe you many apologies & sincerely trust our future correspondence may be more punctual, my time has been much occupied of late, you will be surprised to learn, I have scarce a leisure moment to call my own, for several weeks this fall, a formidable supply of *sewing*, necessary to winter comfort, engaged our constant attention, now the scene is changed, Mr Edwards has a cousin from Alton spending the winter with us, a most interesting young lady, her fascinations, have drawn a concourse of beaux & company round us, occasionly, I *feel as Miss Whitney* [unidentified], we have too much of such useless commodities, you know it takes some time for habit to render us familiar with what we are not greatly accustomed to—Could you step in upon us some evenings in these "western wilds," you would be astonished at the change, *time* has wrought on the hill, I would my Dearest, you now were with us, be assured your name is most frequently mentioned in our circle, *words of mine* are not necessary to assure you of the loss I have sustained in your society, on my return from Missouri, my time passed most heavily, I feel quite made up, in my present companion, a congenial spirit I assure you. I know you would be pleased with Matilda Edwards, a lovelier girl I never saw. *Mr Speed's* [9] ever changing heart I suspect is about offering *its young* affections at her shrine, with some others, there is considerable acquisition in our society of *marriagable gentlemen*, unfortunately only "birds of passage." *Mr Webb*, a widower of modest merit, last winter, is our *principal lion*, dances attendance very frequently, we expect a very gay winter, evening before last my sister gave a most agreeable party, upwards of a hundred graced the festive scene. I trust the period is not very distant when your presence will be among us to cheer us & moreover, I trust *our homes* may be near, that as in times past, so may it *ever be*, that our hearts will acknowledge the same kindred ties, memory oftimes reverts to bygone days, & with the past your memory is intimately blended, well did you say "time has borne changes on its wing," Speed's *"grey suit"* has gone the

[9] Joshua Fry Speed, a Springfield storekeeper, at that time Abraham Lincoln's closest friend.

way of *all flesh*, an interesting suit of *Harrison blues* have replaced his *sober livery, Lincoln's, lincoln green* have gone to dust, Mr Webb sports a *mourning p[in]* by way of reminding us *damsels*, that we *"cannot come it,"* of the new recruits I need not mention, some few are gifted & all in our humble estimation interesting, *Mr C[onkling]* seems to have *given up* all, when deprived of his "own particular star," I have not met him, to have a chat since Martha Jane's marriage, I have often wished for the sake of his society & your *dear self* he would be more social. Harriet Campbell [1] appears to be enjoying all the sweets of married life, *Mrs Abell* [Martha Jane], came down two or three weeks since, have seen but very little of her, her *silver tones*, the other evening were not quite so captain like as was their wont in former times, why is it that married folks always become so serious? Miss Lamb, report says is to be married, next week, Mr *Beauman* [2] *I caught a glimpse of a few days, since, looked becomingly* happy at the prospect of the change, that is about to await him. I am pleased she is about perpetrating the *crime* of *matrimony*, like some of our friends in *this place. MJL* for instance, I think she will be much happier. I suppose like the rest of us *Whigs* though you seem rather to doubt my *faith* you have been rejoicing in the recent election of Gen [William Henry] Harrison, a cause that has excited such deep interest in the nation and one of such vital importance to our prosperity—This fall I became quite a *politician*, rather an unladylike profession, yet at such a *crisis*, whose heart could remain untouched while the energies of all were called in question?—You bid me pause, in your last, on the banks of *"Lionel"* [3] & there glean a needful lesson, by marking the changes, the destroying hand of time had written on all, a moments thought, would suffice to assure me that all *is not*, as it then was, the icy hand of winter has set its seal upon the waters, the winds of Heaven visit the spot but roughly, the same stars shine down, yet not with the same liquid, mellow light as in the olden time, some forms & memories that enhanced the place, have

[1] The former Harriet Huntingdon, whose wedding to James Campbell was attended by both Mary Todd and James C. Conkling.
[2] The transcribed Sangamon County marriage records at the Illinois State Historical Library record the wedding of Mary R. Lamb to Joseph G. Bouman as having taken place on December 21, 1840. On this information is based the tentative date for this letter, which was written during the preceding week.
[3] The girls' pet name for the "Town Branch," a stream that ran through Springfield.

passed by, many weary miles are you dear Merce removed from us, the star of hope, must be our guiding *star*, and we must revel in the happy anticipations of a reunion, may the day be not far distant—Once more, allow me my dear friend to wish you were with us, we have a pleasant jaunt in contemplation, to Jacksonville, next week there to spend a day or two, Mr Hardin & Browning [4] are our leaders the van brought up by Miss E[dwards] my humble self, Webb, Lincoln & two or three others whom you know not, we are watching the clouds most anxiously trusting it may snow, so we may have a sleigh ride—Will it not be pleasant?

Your Brother's family, are well, and all speak of you most frequently, & wonder when you expect to wander *westward*, we cannot do much longer without you, *your mate*, misses you too much from her nest, not to marvel at the delay, do trust a friend & be more communicative in your next, feeling as you must do the great interest I take in you, would deny me the consolation of being a sharer in your joys & sorrows, may the latter be never known to you—The State House is not quite completed, yet sufficiently so to allow the Legislature to meet within its walls. Springfield has improved astonishingly, has the addition of another *bell* to the Second Church, it rings so long & loud, that as in days past we cannot mistake the trysting hour—I trust you do not allow your sister to sing you any more such melancholy dirges I know *by sad experience that such dolorous ditties* only excite one's anxiety to see a beloved object, therefore tell her for the sympathetic feel[ings] I entertain towards you dearest, bid her cease the strain—The weather is miserably cold, & my stump of a pen keeps pace with the times, pass my imperfections lightly by, as usual, I throw myself on your amiable nature, knowing that my shortcomings will be forgiven—Fanny Wallace sends much love to you, her little urchin, is almost a young lady in size, Elizabeth has not been well of late, suffering with a cold, I still am the same ruddy *pineknot*, only not quite as great an exuberance of flesh, as it once was my lot to contend with, although quite a sufficiency—I must close, write very, very soon if you love me—ever your attached friend

Mary

[4] John J. Hardin, Mary Todd's cousin and a distinguished colleague of Abraham Lincoln in the Illinois legislature; Orville H. Browning, then an Illinois state senator.

At about the time Mary Todd wrote to Mercy Levering in December of 1840, she and Abraham Lincoln had reached an "understanding" and were talking openly of marriage. The next thing anyone knew the engagement was broken, presumably (and shockingly) at the gentleman's instigation. The falling-out occurred on New Year's Day of 1841, a date subsequently dubbed by Lincoln the "Fatal First" of January. Springfield gossiped then, and historians gossip today, for the causes of the break and the manner in which it came about were never made entirely clear. (One searches Mary Lincoln's letters in vain for facts; to rely upon her recollections of the period is to conclude the whole thing never happened.) Katherine Helm, in her biography of her aunt, contended that Lincoln, suddenly "panic-stricken" at the prospect of providing for this pampered creature, used her flirtation with Stephen Douglas as an excuse to end their relationship.[5] William H. Herndon, who knew Mary Todd Lincoln and disliked her, told yet another tale, this one most unlikely. In his *Life of Lincoln* he quoted Joshua Speed, the young storekeeper who was Lincoln's closest confidant in 1841, as saying that Lincoln simply decided he did not love Mary enough to marry her and was about to send her a letter to that effect when he was persuaded by Speed to tell her in person. Herndon maintained that Lincoln relented in the face of Mary's tears, and wedding plans went forward. On the appointed day—January 1, 1841 —with minister and guests assembled for the ceremony, the groom failed to appear.[6]

This ridiculous story, which portrayed Lincoln as a cad and a weakling, has since been demolished, most effectively by the late Ruth Randall in her meticulously documented study of the Lincoln marriage. Basing her views on subsequent events, on known fact and reliable reminiscence, Mrs. Randall put the lie to Herndon's statements and in so doing provided a key to the muddled

[5] Helm, pp. 87–8.
[6] William H. Herndon and Jesse W. Weik. *Herndon's Life of Lincoln.* Cleveland, 1930, pp. 168–70. (This edition, with an Introduction and notes by Paul M. Angle, was a reissue of the volume originally published in 1889.)

events of early 1841. She offered two factors as probably combining to precipitate the break-up and the eighteen-month estrangement that followed: Lincoln's extreme sensitivity, coupled with the adamant opposition of Mary Todd's family, particularly Ninian and Elizabeth Edwards. As her guardians, they had deemed it acceptable for her to see Lincoln along with other young men on the "safety in numbers" theory. When it gradually became apparent that her feelings were serious, they were at first bewildered, then mildly perturbed, and finally determined to make her see the unsuitability of such a match.

Their attitude was not lost on Abraham Lincoln. Several years earlier, he had written to Mary Owens of her dreary prospects as his wife: "I am afraid you would not be satisfied. There is a great deal of flourishing about in carriages here, which it would be your doom to see without sharing in it. You would have to be poor without the means of hiding your poverty." [7] The same feelings of inferiority that had haunted Lincoln with Miss Owens were intensified with Mary Todd. Determined to spare her misery, he asked to be released from his promise. Some said that, in accordance with custom, she wrote him a formal letter breaking off the engagement, but no such letter has ever been found.

The dignity with which Mary Todd bore this sad and embarrassing turn of events was remarked on by many, but nowhere is it more apparent than in the letter she wrote Mercy Levering in June of 1841; there is wistfulness there, but no vindictiveness. Her fond references to Lincoln indicate that she sympathized with his agony and bore him no ill will, although she certainly would have had he deserted her at the altar, as Herndon claimed. Her hope that "Richard should be himself again" alluded to the depression which had engulfed Lincoln after their parting on the "Fatal First." It was a deep, lugubrious melancholy which, for a week, actually made him physically ill. After the rupture Lincoln wrote to John Todd Stuart: "I am now the most miserable man living. If what I feel were equally distributed to the whole human family there would not be one cheerful face on the earth." [8] Ninian Edwards declared

[7] Abraham Lincoln to Mary Owens, May 7, 1837. MS. owned by Mrs. George H. Vineyard, St. Louis, Missouri.
[8] Abraham Lincoln to John Todd Stuart, January 23, 1841. MS. owned by the heirs of Stuart Brown.

later that Lincoln had gone "crazy as a Loon." [9] Others described him as "incoherent," "distraught," and, at the very least, "unsettled." Yet, except for the brief period when his health broke down, Lincoln managed to function. He was in almost daily attendance at the legislature, and as time wore on appeared more and more often among his friends—avoiding, of course, those places where he might meet Mary Todd.

To Mercy Ann Levering

Springfield June 1841

When I reflect my own dear Merce, that months of change have passed by since I last wrote you, and that your letters during that time have been far, very far more unfrequent than I could have desired, these circumstances would lead an *unknowing one* to imagine that time had wrought its changes upon us, and lessened the love which I feel has ever been ours towards each other, time and absence only serve to deepen the interest with which I have always regarded you & my greatest regret is that so many long & weary miles divide us—My late silence would doubtless lead you to imagine that you were only occasionally remembered, I have been much alone of late and my thoughts have oft been with thee, why I have not written oftener appears strange even to *me*, who should best know *myself*. that most difficult of all problems to solve, my evil genius Procrastination has whispered me to tarry til a more convenient season & spare you the infliction of a letter which daily experience convinces me would be "flat, stale & unprofitable," yet henceforth I trust it may not be thus with us, were you aware of the delight given by hearing from you, dearest Merce, surely you would more frequently cheer my sad spirit—the last two or three months have been of *interminable* length, after my gay companions of last winter departed, I was left much to the solitude of my own thoughts, and some *lingering regrets* over the past, which time can alone overshadow with its healing balm, thus has my *spring time* been passed, summer in all its beauty has again come,

---

[9] Quoted in Randall, p. 41.

the prairie land looks as beautiful as it did in the olden time, when
we strolled together & derived so much of happiness from each other's society—this is past & more than this I can scarcely realise that
a year of change has gone by since we parted, may it not be that
another has rolled on, and we still remain separated, the thought of
meeting solaces many a lonely hour—I have much much to tell you,
of all that is daily occuring around us, that I scarcely know where
the narrative should commence, at present a cousin of Mr Edward's
from Alton,[1] is on a visit to us, the June Court is in Session & many
distinguished strangers grace the gay capitol, we have an unusual
number of agreeable visitors, some pleasant acquaintances of last
winter, but in their midst the *winning widower* [Webb] *is not*,
rumor says he with some others will attend the Supreme Court next
month, in your last, you appeared impressed with the prevalent idea
that we were *dearer* to each other than friends, the idea was neither
new nor strange, dear Merce, the knowing world have coupled our
names together for months past, merely through the folly & belief
of *another* [Lincoln?], who strangely imagined we were attached
to each other, in your friendly & confiding ear allow me to whisper
that my *heart can never be his*, I have deeply *regretted that his constant visits, attentions* && should have given room for remarks,
which were to me unpleasant, there being a slight difference of
some eighteen or twenty summers in our years, would preclude the
possibility of congeneality of feeling, without which I should never
feel justifiable in resigning my happiness into the safe keeping of
another, even should that other be far too worthy for me, with his
two *sweet little objections*—We had such a continual round of company, gayety && last winter, that after their departure the monotony
of the place was almost unbearable, now that I have become habitu-
ated to quiet, I have resumed my frequent & social visits to Mrs
Levering, and if your ears do not oftimes burn, there can be no
truth in the old adage, all, all reminds me so much of your dear,
kind self, a few evenings since I was most forcibly reminded of you,
by seeing *Jacob Faithful* [Conkling], we spent the evening at Mrs
[James L.] Lamb's, and in one quiet, sequestered nook in the room
he was seated sad & lonely, no doubt his thoughts were busy with
you & the past, to me he has proved most *untrue* as I never see him,

[1] Probably Matilda Edwards.

e'en for your loved sake, he *comes not*. Mr Speed, our former most constant guest has been in Kentucky for some weeks past, will be here next month, on a visit *perhaps*, as he has some idea of deserting Illinois, his mother is anxious he should superintend her affairs, he takes a friend's privilege, of occasionally favouring me with a letter, in his last he spoke of his great desire of once more inhabiting this region & of his possibility of soon returning—*His* worthy friend [Lincoln], deems me unworthy of notice, as I have not met *him* in the gay world for months, with the usual comfort of misery, imagine that others were as seldom gladdened by his presence as my humble self, yet I would that the case were different, that he would once more resume his Station in Society, that "Richard should be himself again," much, much happiness would it afford me—My sister Fanny returned some weeks since from her visit east, her health & spirits much improved, regretted much that the hurry of business prevented the Dr visiting Baltimore, as she was very desirous of seeing you. Mrs *Beauman* [sic], Miss Lamb, that was is now on a visit to Mrs Mather [2] looks very well, says she is very happy, and much pleased with her new home—Mrs Abell, has been here, for a great while, owing to the warm weather, or something, sports loose wrappers, & looks quite *dignified*,—Our agreeable friend Mrs Anderson was in town a few days since spoke of having received a letter from you, and was about doing herself the pleasure of replying to it, I have never paid her a visit, since the time we went out together with William Anderson,[3] who is soon to be married to a lady in Louisville—strange perversity of taste—Think you not so? The interesting gentleman, whom Mrs Roberts gave you for a beau is now a resident of this place, Mr [Lyman] Trumbull, is Secretary of State, in lieu of *Judge Douglass*,[4] who has been rapidly promoted to office —Now that your fortune is made, I feel much disposed in your absence, to lay in my *claims*, as he is talented & agreeable & sometimes *countenances* me—I regret to see that my paper is so rapidly disap-

[2] Mrs. Thomas Mather, wife of the president of the State Bank in Springfield.

[3] Possibly William G. Anderson, a former Democratic legislator with whom Lincoln had quarreled in 1840. Their differences perhaps account for Mary Todd's subsequent comment on the "taste" of Anderson's fiancée.

[4] In 1841 Stephen A. Douglas (who was then spelling his name with a double "s") was appointed a judge of the Illinois State Supreme Court, in which capacity he would serve until his election in 1843 to the U.S. House of Representatives.

pearing, miserable scrawl as this has been, I feel much disposed to continue it—As with you, I always have so much to communicate, E[lizabeth] sends you much love & *desires you would hasten your movements westward as your* friends continue to remember you with the same unchanging affection—Miss Whitney whom I have not visited since you left & for some time before, called up to day & requested me to accompany her as far as Peoria, on her bridal tour as she is to be married in a few days to a widower of some *ten months* standing, residing in the northern part of the state—

Miss Rodney [5] is also to be an attendant, as you may imagine I declined the honour and being strangers, was somewhat surprised at the request—Your brother's family are all well, write very, very soon to your ever attached friend

Mary—

The period following the broken engagement was perhaps the lowest point in Abraham Lincoln's life. Joshua Speed chose that time to return to the family plantation near Louisville, and Lincoln, who had severed his connection with John Todd Stuart, attempted to adjust himself to a new partnership with Stephen T. Logan.

Speed's return to Kentucky occasioned an exchange of letters with Lincoln in which each man offered advice and solace to the other. Although the young lawyer was deeply absorbed in his own problems, he was happy to counsel Speed, who had courted dozens of girls and was bewildered by his strong feelings for one: Fanny Henning, a lovely creature whom Lincoln met on his visit to Speed in August of 1841. When Speed decided he had "reasoned" himself into his attachment to Fanny, Lincoln replied merrily, "Was it not, that you found yourself unable to *reason* yourself *out* of it? . . . Were not those heavenly *black eyes*, the whole basis of all your

[5] Anna Rodney, one of Mary Todd's close friends and a bridesmaid at the Lincoln wedding. She was the grandniece of Caesar Rodney of Delaware, a signer of the Declaration of Independence.

early *reasoning* on the subject?" [6] He clearly wrote from the heart.

Joshua Speed married Fanny Henning in February of 1842 and became, to everyone's surprise, a thoroughly doting husband. Lincoln found himself both pleased for his friend and uneasy over his own situation. He, too, could be happy, he wrote the bridegroom, were it not for the "never-absent idea, that there is *one* still unhappy who I have contributed to make so. That still kills my soul." [7]

Mary Todd was indeed unhappy parted from Lincoln, but she was too well-bred to let it show. For a year and a half after the broken engagement the two remained apart, thinking often of each other, but neither able to take the first step toward a reconciliation. If the Edwardses were relieved, others who also had the interests of the couple at heart felt that a dreadful mistake was being made. Among these was Lincoln's friend and physician, Dr. Anson G. Henry, who, it was said, took it upon himself to carry to Lincoln assurances of Mary Todd's continuing devotion. Another proponent of the match was Simeon Francis, editor of Springfield's Whig newspaper, the *Sangamo Journal*. During the summer of 1842 Francis and his wife determined to reunite the couple by arranging a surprise meeting at their home. Mary and Lincoln arrived separately, neither expecting to encounter the other, and were shyly delighted when Mrs. Francis urged, "Be friends." [8] They met secretly at the Francis home many times thereafter, and before long the plans for marriage that had been so abruptly cancelled in 1841 were revived, this time in utmost secrecy.

Those who knew Mary well might have guessed the truth, for she had never seemed happier. In September of 1842, she and her friend Julia Jayne jointly composed a rollicking story and verse poking fun at General James Shields, a young Democratic politician who was full of Irish blarney and outrageous vanity. The piece was good enough for publication in the *Sangamo Journal* as one of the "Rebecca Letters," a satirical series to which Lincoln had also contributed. "Jimmy" Shields was not amused. When he demanded

[6] Abraham Lincoln to Joshua Speed [January 3?, 1842]. MS. in the Illinois State Historical Library, Springfield.

[7] Abraham Lincoln to Joshua Speed, Springfield, March 27, 1842. MS. in the Illinois State Historical Library, Springfield.

[8] Quoted by Octavia Roberts in an article, "We All Knew Abr'ham." *Abraham Lincoln Quarterly*, March 1946, p. 27.

to know who was responsible for this affront to his dignity, Lincoln gallantly claimed authorship in order to protect Mary. To his astonishment and disgust, Shields challenged him to a duel, which fortunately got no farther than a confrontation. Neither Lincoln nor his lady could bring themselves to speak of the incident again.[9]

For several months Mary kept her own counsel, acknowledging very little to her friends and making especially certain that her sister and brother-in-law knew nothing of her plans. On the morning of November 4, 1842, the day the couple had chosen for their wedding, the news had to be broken to Mary's guardians at last. The demands of convention and family solidarity won out over the Edwardses' understandable consternation, and they insisted that if the ceremony had to take place it would take place in their home.

That evening Mary Todd and Abraham Lincoln stood before Dr. Charles Dresser, the Episcopal minister, and repeated their vows in the presence of only thirty relatives and friends. The words Lincoln had had engraved on Mary's wedding ring, "Love Is Eternal," were to prove appropriate—and prophetic. The marriage was a triumph of love over the odds, and that love would survive everything, including death.

There was no wedding trip for the Lincolns. The newly married pair drove through a blinding rainstorm to a hotel-boardinghouse called the Globe Tavern, where they were to live, paying four dollars a week for their room and meals, until after the birth of their first child on August 1, 1843.

Mary Lincoln, who presumably could have spent her confinement in her sister's commodious home, elected instead to have her child amid the stark surroundings of the Globe. Assuming that the choice had been hers, that decision to go it alone gives evidence of the streak of stubborn independence that was then such an important facet of her nature. If the Edwardses would still not accept Mr. Lincoln entirely, she would not seek their help even in this exigency. Her husband's presence was enough to sustain her

---

[9] Mrs. Lincoln *wrote* of it, however, after one of her late husband's biographers had the temerity to discuss it in a book. See letters to Josiah G. Holland (December 4, 1865); to Mary Jane Welles (December 6, 1865); and to Francis B. Carpenter (December 8, 1865).

through her ordeal. Fortunately the birth was easy and the baby strong. He was named Robert Todd after his maternal grandfather, who shortly thereafter journeyed to Springfield to get a look at his tiny namesake.

It soon became apparent that the Globe—noisy, crowded, and confining—was no place for an infant. And so the little family moved on, spending the winter of 1843–44 in a rented three-room frame cottage at 214 South Fourth Street. The following spring Lincoln paid Dr. Dresser $1,200 and turned over to him a small lot in exchange for his house on the corner of Eighth and Jackson Streets. He was now earning about $1,500 a year at his practice, but money was in short supply and young Mrs. Lincoln felt keenly the need to pinch pennies. She knew that much of Springfield (and perhaps Lexington as well) clucked over her reduced circumstances; although she accepted her lot cheerfully, she never forgot the pain of poverty. Her father helped a bit by advancing small sums of money, but some time passed before Abraham Lincoln was able to pay off "The National Debt," his rueful name for the obligations that had been hanging over his head since New Salem days.

"Why is it," Mary Todd had written Mercy Levering in 1840, "that married folks always become so serious?" She had her answer now. Before her marriage she had known nothing but ease and luxury; she had grown to womanhood surrounded by people to amuse her, servants to do her bidding. She could stitch neatly and entertain graciously, but this was the sum of her domestic preparation. Now she had to keep a house clean and warm, make and mend clothes for three, attend to the urgent demands of an infant, and feed a husband at strange and unpredictable hours. These responsibilities were so overwhelming in aggregate that one or the other often suffered until she was able to afford help. Lincoln, no stranger to physical labor, cooperated by chopping wood, building fires, grooming the horse and sometimes even tending the baby, but for six months out of the year he was traveling the judicial circuit, leaving his wife to handle all but the heaviest chores herself.

On March 10, 1846, a second son was born and named Edward Baker, after a friend and political ally of Lincoln. By this time the financial stringency had eased somewhat. More money

brought Mrs. Lincoln regular help; with it came freedom to social-
ize and shop, and nicer things to shop for. Her passion for lovely
things and her erratic attitude toward money matters may have begun to manifest themselves even while the marriage was still in its
difficult "period of adjustment." In making purchases for herself,
her family, or her home, she indulged her expensive tastes whenever possible; in most other areas she showed a talent for cutting
corners that embarrassed even her thrifty husband.

Both Lincolns had a great deal to learn about each other, and
a great deal to cope with. Mary seldom hesitated to speak her mind
when something or someone displeased her and, though her anger
passed quickly and led to deep remorse, she acquired a reputation
for sharpness. She was abnormally sensitive to slights, real or imagined. Although she feared no human being and looked into the
future with boundless, almost blind confidence, she was terrified
of small things. A thunderstorm could throw her into a panic and
bring on one of those miserable sick headaches that sent her to bed
for days at a time. Perhaps it was on such occasions, disagreeable
though they were, that she learned the uses of illness. Friends and
family have attested that Lincoln was not himself when his wife
was sick; often he dropped everything to care for her, his customary
abstracted expression giving way to a look of anguish that she must
have found reassuring in its way. (During her widowhood the only
compensation for her abominable health was the sympathy it
brought her and the way in which it kept her young son Tad by
her side, "his dark loving eyes—watching over me, remind[ing] me
so much of his dearly beloved father's.") [1] A deep-seated insecurity
caused her to demand constant proof of her husband's love. Lincoln
tried not to cross her unnecessarily and shielded her as best he
could from the harsher aspects of human existence.

Not all the couple's early strains could be laid at Mrs. Lincoln's door. Abraham Lincoln had entered into marriage cheerfully
unaware of the amenities so important to polite society. Though his
instincts were kindly and his dignity inborn, his dress and demeanor
were informal, and his language often indelicate. He could be
glum and uncommunicative when his wife wanted to talk; he was

---

[1] Mary Lincoln to Sally Orne, Frankfort a Maine December 29, 1869.

absent-minded yet coolly deliberate where she was literal, impulsive, and impatient. His habit of avoiding quarrels by withdrawing either physically or mentally at the first storm signals was exasperating to a woman who rather enjoyed a healthy set-to that cleared the air. Those long absences from home while on the judicial circuit were trying times for Mary Lincoln, especially when she was pregnant, but her husband obviously craved the change of scene and the broad legal experience the trips afforded him.

Mary Lincoln's longest-running grievance against her husband stemmed from his confidence in, and affection for, William H. Herndon, a bright but erratic young man whom he had taken on as junior law partner when he set up his own firm in 1844. "Billy" Herndon had gotten off to a poor start with Mrs. Lincoln. At a ball before her marriage he had told her, by way of clever compliment, that she danced with the ease of a serpent. She did not care for the comparison, said so, and from that moment on viewed Herndon with contempt. She felt, with some cause, that he was not a gentleman, that his loudly proclaimed opinions were shabby and ridiculous. She disapproved of his drinking habits and unorthodox religious views, and considered Lincoln's association with him demeaning.

Herndon was proud of his "dog-sagacity," his ability to "read" people virtually on a few moments' acquaintance. He assumed that his partner felt as uncomfortable married to a former member of the Coterie as he would have himself. His conviction that Mrs. Lincoln was haughty and mean only succeeded in making her so where he was concerned. She kept him at arm's length, never once inviting him to eat in her home and staying away from the office as much as possible. The fact that Lincoln divided hard-earned fees equally with Herndon could only have fueled her rage.

The result was a lifelong war of attrition between Mary Lincoln and her husband's law partner, each combatant busily working to discredit the other, with Lincoln (and, later, the memory of Lincoln) the prize over which they fought. With the publication of his *Life of Lincoln* in 1889, Herndon would seem to have won the battle. Written from his notes by a collaborator, Jesse W. Weik, the book provided a refreshingly candid, earthy view of the late President, but it did scant justice to his widow. Herndon consistently cast her in a disparaging light, blamed her for Lincoln's attacks of melancholy, and insisted that she had married to avenge Lincoln's first "desertion" of her, and that he had married out of a misplaced sense of honor. There was a confiding tone about Herndon's "revelations" which endowed them, in many instances, with an air of authenticity. Certain incidents, such as the aborted wedding ceremony, were made up out of whole cloth. But Herndon's cruelest offense against Mrs. Lincoln was his invention of the Ann Rutledge romance, of which we will learn more later.

"Many of [Mr. Lincoln's] ways," recalled Mary's half-sister Emilie, "such as going to his own front door and other mannerisms, Mrs. Lincoln did not like, and upon one occasion a member of her family said, 'Mary, if I had a husband with a mind such as yours has, I wouldn't care what he did.' " [2] No remark could have been calculated to please its hearer more. Most of Mrs. Lincoln's nagging at her husband resulted from her inordinate pride in, and ambition for, him. More certain every day that she had made the right decision in marrying him, she wanted others, particularly her family, to share her pride and applaud her choice. Emilie, who visited Springfield twice and saw the Lincolns constantly, claimed to have witnessed nothing but happiness in the little house on Eighth Street, and those of Mary's relatives who looked eagerly for signs of serious trouble there found only passing difficulties. Unlike many married couples of the day, these two had consciously chosen each other for reasons that made their life together continually rewarding: mutual respect, shared interests and—another factor that was clearly present although it is seldom emphasized—a physical passion that never diminished.

In time, and with some difficulty, the Todds were won over, although Ninian Edwards, a converted Democrat, had no use for his brother-in-law's politics. Most of the family was as pleased as Mary when in 1846 Abraham Lincoln was elected to Congress for a term to begin in 1847. He had worked toward this goal for some years, cultivating a wide acquaintance among the local Whig chieftains, campaigning steadily and mingling with the people of his district. Mrs. Lincoln, as ambitious for her husband as he was for himself, was elated at his emergence on the national scene. No

---

[2] Quoted in Randall, p. 89.

doubt she considered herself partly responsible for his increased polish and determination, and relished her position as the wife of a public personality. Soon she was going about gaily predicting that Abraham Lincoln would one day be President of the United States. Those who later cited the remark as an example of her arrogance seemed to have forgotten that she was right. Even had she not been, her prediction was scarcely out of place. From girlhood on, Mary Todd Lincoln had been on close terms with men who were widely spoken of as presidential possibilities. If the office had lain within their grasp, surely it was within Mr. Lincoln's as well, for she knew him to possess qualities of mind and leadership far surpassing those of any man she had met in her father's or sister's house, including Stephen Douglas and the great Henry Clay.

Congressman-elect Lincoln and his family set out for Washington in October of 1847, stopping en route to visit the Todds in Lexington. Mrs. Lincoln came to the reunion in quiet triumph, showing off her newly distinguished husband and two lively, sturdy little boys. The visit only lasted three weeks, for the Lincolns had a long journey and many responsibilities ahead of them. In Washington they rented rooms in Mrs. Ann Sprigg's boardinghouse on Capitol Hill; there they lived *en famille* for several months until Mrs. Lincoln decided to return to Lexington with the children. One suspects that her life in Washington was something of a disappointment: no one made the slightest fuss over the wife of a freshman congressman, and no boardinghouse could contain for long the likes of Bobby and Eddy Lincoln, who, with their father busier than ever before, were constantly at their mother's skirts. She would miss her husband acutely, but she could look forward to a long, leisurely visit with the relatives and friends she had left behind seven years before.

And so, while Abraham Lincoln worked to bar slavery in the District of Columbia, his wife sank blissfully back into a life in which slavery was the cornerstone of comfort. During this prolonged separation, the Lincolns exchanged a number of letters, few of which survive. The letter which follows is one of only three from Mary Lincoln to her husband that remain to us; it is the longest, and the only one dating from the period before the presidency.

Yet this single letter, together with three Lincoln wrote her from Washington, provide more eloquent testimony as to the nature of their relationship than all of Herndon's wishful theories.

"When you were here," Lincoln had written on April 16, 1848, "I thought you hindered me some in attending to business; but now, having nothing but business—no variety—it has grown exceedingly tasteless to me. . . . I hate to stay in this old room by myself." After touching briefly on his activities, he had teased her by writing: "All the house—or rather, all with whom you were on decided good terms—send their love to you. The others say nothing." He had then commented on several points she had made in an earlier letter and had finally asked solicitously, "You are entirely free from head-ache? That is good—good—considering it is the first spring you have been free from it since we were acquainted. I am afraid you will get so well, and fat, and young, as to be wanting to marry again. . . . Get weighed, and write me how much you weigh." [3]

On an evening in May, from her father's house in Lexington, Mary Lincoln sat down to write her husband a gay, gossipy letter which held a note of profound longing. One can almost picture her as she sat in an upstairs bedroom, windows open to the scents of a warm spring night, enveloped in comfort and the certainty of her husband's love.

To Abraham Lincoln

Lexington May—48—

My dear Husband—

You will think indeed, that *old age*, has set *its seal*, upon my humble self, that in few or none of my letters, I can remember the day of the month, I must confess it as one of my peculiarities; I feel wearied & tired enough to know, that this is *Saturday night*, our *babies* are asleep, and as Aunt Maria B[ullock] is coming in for me tomorrow morning, I think the chances will be rather dull that

---

[3] Abraham Lincoln to Mary Lincoln, April 16, 1848. MS. in the Illinois State Historical Library, Springfield.

I should answer your last letter tomorrow—I have just received a letter from Frances W[allace], it related in an *especial* manner to THE BOX I had desired her to send, she thinks with you (as good persons generally agree) that it would cost more than it would come to, and it might be lost on the road, I rather expect she has examined the specified articles, and thinks as *Levi* [4] says, they are *hard bargains*—But it takes so many changes to do children, particularly in summer, that I thought it might save me a few stitches—I think I will write her a few lines this evening, directing her not to send them—She says Willie is just recovering from another spell of sickness, Mary or none of them were well [5]—Springfield she reports as dull as usual. Uncle S[amuel Todd] was to leave there on yesterday for Ky—Our little Eddy, has recovered from his little spell of sickness—Dear boy, I must tell you a story about him—Boby in his wanderings to day, came across in a yard, a little kitten, *your hobby*, he says he asked a man for it, he brought it triumphantly to the house, so soon as Eddy, spied it—his *tenderness*, broke forth, he made them bring it *water*, fed it with bread himself, with his *own dear hands*, he was a delighted little creature over it, in the midst of his happiness Ma [6] came in, she you must know dislikes the whole cat race, I thought in a very unfeeling manner, she ordered the servant near, to throw it out, which, of *course*, was done, Ed-screaming & protesting loudly against the proceeding, *she* never appeared to mind his screams, which were long & loud, I assure you—Tis unusual for her *now a days*, to do any thing quite so striking, she is very obliging & accommodating, but if she thought any of us, were on her hands again, I believe she would be *worse* than ever—In the next moment she appeared in a good humor, I know she did not intend to offend me. By the way, she has just sent me up a glass of ice cream, for which this warm evening, I am duly grateful. The country is so delightful I am going to spend two or three weeks out there, it will doubtless benefit the children— Grandma [7] has received a letter from Uncle James Parker of Miss[ouri] saying he & his family would be up by the twenty fifth of June, would remain here some little time & go on to Philadelphia

[4] Levi Todd, Mrs. Lincoln's oldest brother.
[5] "Willie" was William S. Wallace, Mrs. Lincoln's brother-in-law; Mary was his daughter.
[6] "Betsy" Humphreys Todd, Mrs. Lincoln's stepmother.
[7] Elizabeth Porter Parker, Mrs. Lincoln's maternal grandmother.

to take their oldest daughter there to school, I believe it would be a good chance for me to pack up & accompany them—You know I am so fond of *sightseeing*, & I did not get to New York or Boston, or travel the lake route—But perhaps, dear husband, like the *irresistible Col Mc*,[8] cannot do without his wife next winter, and must needs take her with him again—I expect you would cry aloud against it—How much, I wish instead of writing, *we* were together this evening, I feel very sad away from you—Ma & myself rode out to Mr Bell's splendid place this afternoon, to return a call, the house and grounds are magnificent, Frances W. would *have died* over their rare exotics—It is growing late, these summer eves are short, I expect my long *scrawls*, for truly such they are, weary you greatly —if you come on, in July or August *I* will take you to the springs —*Patty Webb's*[9] school in S[helbyville] closes the first of July, I expect *Mr Webb*, will come on for her. I must go down about that time & carry on quite a flirtation, you know *we*, always had a *penchant* that way. ~~With love~~ I must bid you good night—Do not fear the children, have forgotten you, I was only jesting—Even E[ddy's] eyes brighten at the mention of your name—My love to all—

Truly yours
M L——

✦

The indulgent tone which marked Abraham Lincoln's April 16 letter to his wife is also present in two others that have been preserved. On June 12 he dealt with her desire to rejoin him in Washington: "Will you be a *good girl* in all things, if I consent? Then come along, and that as *soon* as possible. . . . I shall be impatient till I see you."[1] Nothing made Mary Lincoln feel more

---

[8] Colonel John A. McClernand, then Democratic congressman from Springfield, later a Union general.
[9] Daughter of Edwin B. Webb.
[1] Abraham Lincoln to Mary Lincoln, June 12, 1848. Photostat in the Illinois State Historical Library, Springfield.

cherished and secure than being addressed in such a patient, almost fatherly fashion; friends reported her as pleased rather than offended when Lincoln referred to her as "my child-wife." That patience and a firm hand were necessary is evident from still another letter, dated July 2, 1848, in which Lincoln mentioned an occurrence, the nature of which would in time become distressingly familiar. "Last wednesday, P. H. Hood & co, dunned me for a little bill of $5.38 cents and Walter Harper and Co, another for $8.50 cents, for goods which they say you bought. I hesitated to pay them, because my recollection is that you told me when you went away, there was nothing left unpaid." Surely it was not the inconsequential amounts involved which inspired this gentle reproof on Lincoln's part, but rather his wife's casual attitude toward debts. When money was available, he never begrudged her its use, especially when it contributed to her peace of mind. "By the way," he ended, "you do not intend to do without a girl, because the one you had has left you? Get another as soon as you can to take charge of the dear codgers. Father expected to see you all sooner; but let it pass; stay as long as you please, and come when you please. Kiss and love the dear rascals." [2]

Apart from his courageous stand against the Mexican War, Abraham Lincoln's single term in Congress was all promise and no fulfillment. It did, however, establish his position in local Whig councils and make him a conspicuous figure at the 1848 convention which nominated Zachary Taylor for President. Lincoln's ability as an orator was beginning to be recognized. He was asked to campaign for Taylor on a speaking tour of the New England states, for part of which Mrs. Lincoln joined him. At that time Whig aspirants to the congressional seat in Lincoln's district had a gentleman's agreement to rotate in office. When his two-year term expired, Lincoln was prepared to step aside for his wife's cousin and his former law partner, Stephen T. Logan. Logan ran on Lincoln's record—and lost.

As a reward for his efforts his party offered him the secretaryship of the Oregon Territory. Mrs. Lincoln's objections, reinforcing

[2] Abraham Lincoln to Mary Lincoln, Washington, July 2, 1848. Photostat in the Illinois State Historical Library, Springfield.

his own doubts, caused him to reject the offer out of hand. Her distaste for the prospect of raising her children in a wilderness, far from family, friends, and the little luxuries she prized, may have been selfish, but it at least succeeded in keeping Lincoln close to the center of political activity.

In July of 1849, Robert Todd died in a cholera epidemic which swept Lexington. When his son George challenged the probate of the will, Abraham Lincoln was chosen to protect the interests of his wife and her three sisters in Springfield. (Ann, the youngest, had by this time followed a well-worn path to matrimony; her husband, Clark Moulton Smith, was one of Springfield's most successful merchants.) In October Lincoln journeyed to Lexington for the litigation involving the estate, taking his wife and two sons along. A few months after their return to Springfield, word arrived of a second death in the family. Grandmother Parker, Mary Lincoln's faithful friend of old, had passed away. The news reached the couple at a bad moment: their four-year-old son Eddy was desperately ill, apparently with diphtheria.

Together the Lincolns nursed their boy for fifty-two days and nights, until he was beyond reach of their help. When he died on the morning of February 1, 1850, the young mother collapsed in grief and shock. She seemed unable to stop weeping; only her husband could persuade her to take an occasional bite of food.

After Eddy's death, mostly to comfort Mary, Abraham Lincoln began attending the First Presbyterian Church in Springfield. Until then he had known no formal religion beyond the fundamentalist prayer-meetings of his backwoods boyhood; there is reason to believe he had had a thoughtful young man's usual complement of doubts. Although he would never be as frequent a churchgoer as his wife, nor officially join the congregation, he rented a family pew which he and Mrs. Lincoln would occupy for the next decade—she having abandoned the Episcopal church she had attended for years with her sister Elizabeth. Lincoln came to have vast regard for the pastor, Dr. James Smith, who had conducted Eddy's funeral service and whose wisdom and kindness had been responsible for Mary Lincoln's return to the faith of her ancestors. Dr. Smith was the author of *The Christian's Defense*, a book designed to challenge the skeptic, and Lincoln, who had an aggressive skeptic in his own law office, had read the work with interest. From 1850 on Dr. Smith was a welcome caller at the house on Eighth Street, engaging Abraham Lincoln in probing philosophical discussions and providing Mary Lincoln with the strength to look ahead.

It was no easy task. Lincoln at least could bury his grief in activity and draw on that well of resignation which enabled him to give tragedy its place in the scheme of things. The man who was by nature melancholy, solitary, and self-doubting would from then on gain in assurance and magnetism. His wife, on the other hand, had suffered a setback. The humor and control that had sustained her in the past became increasingly submerged in fearfulness, self-indulgence, and in sudden outbursts of rage, often directed at her husband or a servant and occasionally overheard by the neighbors. Lincoln, who knew something of black moods himself, could only cope and commiserate, feeling that she was powerless to help herself and knowing, with it all, that she loved and needed him more than ever.

Within a month after Eddy's death, Mary Lincoln was pregnant again. Her third son was born on December 17, 1850, and named William Wallace after Frances' husband. "Willie" was a charming, beautiful little boy whose sunny presence did much to ease the pain in his parents' hearts. A fourth and last son was born on April 4, 1853. Called Thomas after his paternal grandfather, he was immediately nicknamed "Tad" by Lincoln, who decided that the baby's large head and tiny, squirming body resembled nothing so much as a tadpole. "Tad" he remained for the rest of his life.

Mary and Abraham Lincoln loved children and understood them. Perhaps because both had had unhappy childhoods, they cosseted and indulged their three boys to such an extent that the most permissive modern parent might have had reason to find fault. Lincoln let them run wild in his office, where they climbed the furniture, scattered papers, and made Billy Herndon want to pitch them out the window. Mrs. Lincoln unashamedly paraded their accomplishments before visitors, gave them elaborate birthday parties, and often joined in their games, throwing dignity to the winds. It must have saddened her a bit not to have had a daughter to dress up, instruct, and confide in; a sympathetic daughter might have made a considerable difference in her later life. For, despite her emotional highs and lows, Mary Lincoln was a consistently good mother and a generous one. Many of her letters, including the one which follows, show her to have been as concerned about her sons' appearance and well-being as she was about her own and her husband's.

To Elizabeth Dale Black [3]

Springfield Sep 17 1853

My dear Mrs Black

Mrs Remann [4] sent me word to day, that your husband was here, & would leave in the morning for St Louis. May I trouble you to undertake the purchase of a white fur hat, for a boy of 6 months, I presume ere this, the fall styles have been received, I should like white trimmings & white feather, if you find any to your taste, of the prettiest quality. Would you be kind enough also, to have me a drawn satin bonnet made of this brown, lined with white, I have some small brown feathers for the outside, also inside trimming, which I suppose is not necessary to send down, please have it made to *your* taste, if fine black lace, will be used this fall, perhaps *that* would be pretty with it, for the outside. I can put the feathers & flowers inside my self. I send you a string for the size of the hat,—if I am not too troublesome, may I have them about the first of October? I should think a pretty hat, would cost about four dollars, but if more, I do not object, as it will *last all* my boys.

We would be much pleased to see you in Springfield, it appears a long time since you left. Will you excuse this hasty scrawl & believe me yours truly

Mary Lincoln

[3] Wife of William Black, a Springfield storekeeper who had recently moved his business to St. Louis.
[4] Mary Black (Mrs. Henry) Remann, widowed sister-in-law of Mrs. Black and one of Mrs. Lincoln's closest friends.

In the early 1850's Abraham Lincoln was practicing law with considerable success. He never abandoned his political ambitions, but pursued them half-heartedly, confining his oratory to campaign speeches for others. Then in May of 1854 came an event which galvanized him into renewed activity: the passage of Senator Stephen A. Douglas' Kansas-Nebraska Bill. Though accompanied by repeal of the Missouri Compromise, the Douglas solution in itself nullified both that achievement and Clay's Compromise of 1850 by permitting each state entering the Union in future to decide, on the basis of "popular sovereignty," whether it would be slave or free. Lincoln now found himself propelled into returning to the state legislature, but his campaign speeches indicated that he had bigger things in mind. Not only did he criticize the Douglas law; he began voicing his own revulsion for the "peculiar institution" itself. Election to the legislature, when it came, was clearly not enough. Wishing to combat the new legislation in the body in which it had originated, Lincoln resigned his seat to run for the United States Senate.

In February of 1855 the Illinois legislature met to elect a second senator. Lincoln, who had engaged in what he called an "agony" of maneuvering, was almost certain of victory against a field of opponents, two of whom had a curious link with each other and with his and his wife's past. Lyman Trumbull had been a member of the Coterie and was now the husband of Mary Lincoln's long-time friend Julia Jayne, co-author of the "Rebecca Letter" that had nearly provoked a duel. James Shields, the incumbent senator and another former Coterie member, was the very man the two girls had ridiculed.

At the end of the first ballot, Lincoln led the pack with forty-five votes of the fifty-one needed to elect. Shields was close behind with forty-one and Trumbull a poor third, with only five. After nine ballots it became clear that the Shields candidacy was only a front for that of Governor Joel Matteson, a Democrat known to favor the Douglas bill. Lincoln, disliking Matteson's methods as well as his opinions, threw his own considerable strength to Trumbull, who at least was anti-Nebraska, enabling Trumbull to win. Mrs. Lincoln did not appreciate her husband's magnanimity. She had been desperately anxious for his election and saw no reason why, with triumph close enough to taste, it had not been Trumbull who had made the generous gesture and thrown his support to Lincoln. Thereafter a chill fell over her relations with the Trumbulls; the ice would thicken with the events of subsequent years.

After the election Lincoln turned again to his law practice, appearing in courts throughout the state and handling cases of increasing importance. His lucid, logical mind, his reasoned approach to legal situations, the human way in which he could present an argument, brought clients great and small to his door, and respectable fees into the family coffers. Mrs. Lincoln also drew consolation from her husband's repeated assurances that his retirement from active politics was only temporary. The Whig party was dying, disintegrating under the force of the slavery question, and a new party which called itself "Republican" was beginning to attract to its ranks those who opposed the extension of slavery into the territories. This being Lincoln's major concern, he had no alternative but to "unwhig" himself and join the Republicans. Mary Lincoln was torn between loyalty to her husband and a nostalgia for the old Whig associations. Douglas' bill had opened a wound of dissension and violence, and the air was thick with a sense of onrushing calamity.

In the election of 1856 John C. Frémont, the first Republican presidential candidate, was defeated by James Buchanan, a Democrat from Pennsylvania. Shortly afterward, Mrs. Lincoln wrote her half-sister Emilie, now the wife of Ben Hardin Helm of Kentucky, a letter which provides a foretaste of the difficulties she would face in dealing with her family in the South. Somewhat skittishly she defended Lincoln's politics, assuring Emilie, quite truthfully, that though a Republican he was not an abolitionist. Yet, considering the Lincolns' intellectual rapport, the meshing of their opinions and ambitions, her mention of her personal preference for Fillmore, the "Know-Nothing" candidate whom Lincoln had fought to defeat, strikes a jarring note. Perhaps her reference to her heart being "Southern in feeling" and the rather parochial notions which followed were carefully calculated to placate Emilie and the rest; perhaps they revealed a genuine ambivalence, in which she was not alone at the time. Clearly, her views on this occasion were not her husband's; had he chanced to read this letter, he might have been puzzled and shaken by its content.

Both Lincolns had a special fondness for "Little Sister" Emilie, a pretty, perceptive girl eighteen years younger than Mary Lincoln. The three existing letters Mrs. Lincoln wrote her are loving, candid, and larded with choice items of gossip. The letters to Emilie span nearly a year—a good year for Mary Lincoln. They show her to have been leading a busy and exciting life, filled with trips and parties, including a "handsome" entertainment the Lincolns themselves gave in February of 1857, followed by a summer's journey to the East which took them as far as New York and Canada. If she was awed by the grandeur of Niagara, Mrs. Lincoln was intoxicated by New York City; from that time on she found it difficult to resist its delights.

No longer was she a young girl hearing enviously of the achievements of other womens' husbands; no longer was she the wife of a poor young lawyer, scraping for the smallest luxuries. She was basking in the reflected light of her husband's rising star, entertaining and being entertained by some of the wealthiest and most influential people in Illinois. Her home, newly enlarged, was modestly but elegantly furnished, and her clothes—always her clothes—were of the richest materials and the most modish, extravagant cut. In 1856 and 1857, Mary Todd Lincoln began to come into her own as helpmeet and hostess.

To Emilie Todd Helm

Springfield Nov 23rd 1856

With much pleasure, my dear Emilie, I acknowledge, the receipt of one of your ever acceptable letters, & notwithstanding many weeks have passed since writing you, I have frequently *intended* doing so, & you have been oftentimes in my thoughts.

Mr E[dwards] expressed great pleasure at meeting you last summer, you know you have a very warm place in his heart. You have been such a wanderer around with your good husband, and a letter might have failed reaching you, I must try & devise some excuses—for my past silence, forgetfulness you know it could not be—

Besides, there is a *great deal* in getting out of the habit of letter writing, once I was very fond of it, nothing pleases me now better than receiving a letter from an absent friend, so remember dear E- when you desire to be particularly acceptable, sit thee down & write one of your agreable missives & do not wait for a return of each, from a staid matron, & moreover the mother of three noisy boys—

Your Husband, I believe, like some of the rest of ours, has a great taste for politics [5] & has taken much interest, in the late contest, which has resulted very much as I expected, not hoped—

Altho' Mr L- is, or was a *Fremont* man, you must not include him with so many of those, who belong to *that party*, an *Abolitionist*. In principle he is far from it—All he desires is, that slavery, shall not be extended, let it remain, where it is—My weak woman's heart was too Southern in feeling, to sympathise with any but Fillmore,[6] I have always been a great admirer of his, he made so good a President & is so just a man & feels the *necessity* of keeping foreigners, within bounds. If some of you Kentuckians, had to deal with the "wild Irish," as we housekeepers are sometimes called upon to do, the south would certainly elect Mr Fillmore next time—The democrats in our state have been defeated in their Governor, so there is a crumb of comfort, for each & all—What day is so dark, that there is no ray of sunshine to penetrate the gloom? Speaking of politics, Gov's && reminds me of your questions, relative to Lydia M.[7] the hour of her patient lover's deliverance is at hand, they are to be married, privately I expect, some of us who had a hand-

[5] Ben Hardin Helm, although a West Point graduate, was pursuing a legal and political career. He served in the Kentucky General Assembly and as Commonwealth Attorney for his district. His father had been a two-term governor of Kentucky.

[6] Milliard Fillmore, President of the United States, 1850–3. A somewhat recalcitrant Whig, he was in 1856 nominated for President by the American Party, successor to the Know-Nothings, on a pro-slavery, anti-immigration platform.

[7] Lydia Matteson, daughter of retiring Democratic Governor Joel Aldrich Matteson, would marry John L. McGinnis, Jr. later that month.

some dress for the season, thought, it would be in *good taste* for Mrs Matteson, in consideration of their being about to leave their present habitation, to give a general reception. Lydia, has always been so retiring, that she would be very averse, to so public a display. This fall in visiting Mrs M[atteson] I met with a sister of Mr McGinnis, a very pretty well bred genteel lady from Joliet— she spoke of being well acquainted with Margaret K- [8] in Kty—

Frances W- returned from her visit to Pennsylvania, two or three days since, where she has been spending the fall. Mr Edward's family are well. Mr B & Julia [9] are still with them. Miss [Louisa] Iles was married some three weeks since, I expect you do not remember her, which gave rise to some two or three parties. Mr [Robert] Scott is frequently here, rather playing the devoted to Julia Ridgeley [sic], I suspect, whether any thing serious I do not know. I expect the family would not be very averse to him. Charley R[idgely] was on a visit to him, in Lex- this fall—*He*, it is said, is to be married this winter to Jennie Barrett—a lovely girl, you remember her—I am very sorry to hear that our Mother, is so frequently indisposed. I hope she has recovered from her lameness— Tell her when you see her that our old acquaintance O. B. Ficklin [1] took tea with us—an evening or two since, made particular enquiries about her—still as rough & uncultivated as ever altho some years since married an accomplished Georgia belle, with the *advantages* of some winter's in Washington—Ma & myself when together, spoke of our minister Dr Smith, who finding his salary of some $1600 inadequate, has resigned the church. Uncle & some *few* others are desirous of getting Dr [John H.] Brown, your former pastor in Lex- within the last year, both his wife & himself, have been a great deal here, he has purchased lands, and appears rather identified with the country. I must acknowledge, I have not admired him very much, his wife appears pleasant but neither I think would suit the people. Dr Smith is talented & beloved, & says he would

[8] Mrs. Lincoln's half-sister, Margaret Todd Kellogg, wife of Charles Kellogg of Cincinnati.

[9] Mr. and Mrs. Edward Lewis Baker. Julia Baker was the daughter of Mr. and Mrs. Ninian W. Edwards; her husband was editor of the *Illinois State Journal*, formerly the *Sangamo Journal*. (He should not be confused with Edward D. Baker, after whom the Lincolns' second son was named.)

[1] Orlando Bell Ficklin, Illinois state legislator and lawyer who served as co-counsel with Lincoln on behalf of the Illinois Central Railroad.

stay if they would increase his salary, yet notwithstanding the wealthy in the church, as usual, there are many very close. But I am speaking of things that will not interest you in the least—If you do not bring *yourself* & Husband to see us very soon we will think you are not as proud of *Him*, as rumor says you should be—Do write soon, in return for this long & I fear dull letter from yours truly

Mary Lincoln

To Emilie Todd Helm

Springfield, February 16   57

Think not, dear Emilie, altho' weeks have passed, since your welcome letter was received, that you have been forgotten or that I have not *daily proposed*, writing you, yet something has always occurred to oppose my good intentions—This winter has certainly passed most rapidly, spring if we can call the month of *March* such, is nearly here. The first part of the winter was unusually quiet, owing to so much sickness among children with scarlet fever, in several families some two & three children were swept away— Within the last 3 weeks, there has been a party, almost every night & some two or three grand fetes, are coming off this week—I may perhaps surprise you, when I mention that I am recovering from the slight fatigue of a very large & I really believe a very handsome & agreable entertainment,[2] at least our friends flatter us by saying so—About 500 hundred were invited, yet owing to an *unlucky* rain, 300 only favored us by their presence,[3] and the same evening in Jacksonville Col [William B.] Warren, gave a bridal party to his son, who married Miss [Cordelia] Birchall of this place, which occasion, robbed us of some of our friends. You will think, we have

[2] An invitation to this party, in Mrs. Lincoln's hand, is owned by the Illinois State Historical Library. It is addressed to Mrs. Henry Remann and reads: "Mr and Mrs Lincoln will be pleased to see you on Thursday evening Feb 5th at 8 o'clock."

[3] How Mrs. Lincoln managed to squeeze three hundred people (much less the expected five hundred) into the downstairs rooms of a modest house in midwinter, and with women wearing crinolines and hoops, is—to use Lincoln's words on another occasion—"a matter of profound wonder."

enlarged *our borders*, since you were here [4]—Three evenings since Gov Bissell [5] gave a very large party. I thought of you frequently that evening, when I saw so many of your acquaintances, beautifully dressed & dancing away very happily. And as enquiries were made about you, during the evening, by both beaux & belles, you could not fail to be remembered—I wish you would write me more frequently, and tell me all about yourself. You have so much leisure & such a literary Husband, that you will become a regular bleu— Your old laugh, will soften the *solemnlity* of such a character and the Emilie, of former times, will shew herself—Miss Dunlap, is spending the winter with her sister Mrs Mc[Clernand] looking very pretty, but the beaux do not appear so numerous as the winter you passed here—Within the last two or three weeks, I have often wished that *Dedee* [6] was here, yet the first part of the winter, was so quiet, that I feared she would not have enjoyed herself, I hope another winter, both Kitty [7] & herself will come out & we will endeavour to make it as pleasant as possible for them—

Dr and Mrs Brown—also Mr Dwight Brown & lady, are residing here. The former has charge of the 1st [Presbyterian] Church—Whether the arrangement, will suit all round, remains to be proved—I must hasten to conclude, as I am interrupted by company. Write soon, hoping to be remembered to your Husband & I remain yours truly

Mary Lincoln.

To Emilie Todd Helm

Springfield Sept 20th [1857]

My Dear Emilie.

So long a time has passed since your last letter was received that I scarcely know how to ask you to excuse my silence. Forget-

---

[4] Some historians maintain that this statement alludes to additions made to the Lincolns' home during 1856; it is equally possible that Mrs. Lincoln was referring to the widening of their social circle.

[5] William H. Bissell, formerly a free-soil Democrat, elected Governor of Illinois in 1856 on the Republican ticket.

[6] Elodie Todd, Mrs. Lincoln's half-sister.

[7] Katherine Todd, youngest of Mrs. Lincoln's half-sisters.

fulness, it has not, or could ever be, for I have oftentimes resolved & *resolved* to write. I only pray you, return "good for evil" and let me hear from you, more frequently. Mr Lincoln, frequently meets Mr Wintersmith [8] in Chicago, and he has so frequently thrown out gentle *insinuations*, in regard to yourself & your *expectations*, that I expect dear Em, ere this, they are fully realised & that now, you are a *happy, laughing, loving Mama.*[9] Do write me, all the news. I feel anxious to hear from you. This summer has strangely & rapidly passed away—some portion of it, was spent most pleasantly in travelling east,[1] we visited Niagara, Canada, New York & other points of interest, when I saw the large steamers at the New York landing, ready for their European voyage, I felt in my heart, inclined to sigh, that poverty was my portion, how I long to go to Europe. I often laugh & tell Mr L- that I am determined my next Husband *shall be rich.*

You can scarcely imagine a place, improving more rapidly than ours, almost *palaces* of homes, have been reared since you were here, hundreds of houses have been going up this season and some of them, very elegant. Gov Matteson's house is just being completed the whole place has cost him he says $100,000 but he is now, worth a million—

I saw Elizabeth, this afternoon. Julia & Mr Baker are in Peoria, at the fair, from thence go to St Louis. At the county fair, here last week, Julia's last quilt (which makes her third one) a very handsome silk one, took the premium, she trusts for the like fate at Peoria & St Louis—she has nothing but her dear Husband & silk quilts, to occupy her time. How different the daily routine of some of our lives are—It is getting very late, dear Emilie, and I must close, my little billet—Shall I apologise for this scrawl? I know, I ought to be ashamed of it—When you read this, like a good sister, sit down & write me a good long letter, all about yourself—

[8] Robert L. Wintersmith, a merchant and politician of Elizabethtown, Kentucky, would serve in 1860 as his state's sole Lincoln elector.

[9] On September 2, 1857, Emilie Helm gave birth to a daughter, Katherine, who became a distinguished portraitist and biographer of her aunt, Mrs. Lincoln.

[1] A pleasure trip probably taken on the proceeds of Lincoln's legal services to the Illinois Central Railroad.

Mr L- is not at home, this makes the fourth week he has been in Chicago.[2] Remember me to your Husband.

Yours affectionately
Mary L——

To Mary Brayman [3]

Saturday afternoon [c1857] [4]

My dear Mrs Brayman

If your health will admit of venturing out, in such damp weather, we would be much pleased to have you, Mr B- & the young ladies come round, this eve about seven & pass a social evening also any friend you may have with you.

Yours truly
Mary Lincoln.

In 1855 Abraham Lincoln had "got it into his head" to try to be a U.S. senator and narrowly failed in the attempt. Three years later opportunity again presented itself as Senator Stephen A. Douglas, a leader of the Northern Democrats, came up for re-election. On June 16, 1858, Lincoln was nominated by the state Republican convention to contest Douglas' seat. " 'A house divided against itself cannot stand,' " he quoted in his acceptance speech, nor could

[2] Lincoln left for Chicago on September 1, 1857, and returned a week after this letter was written.
[3] Wife of Mason Brayman, a Springfield lawyer with whom Lincoln was associated in his work for the Illinois Central Railroad. Brayman later became a Union general.
[4] The approximate date of this letter is based on the particularly small, precise script characteristic of Mrs. Lincoln's letters in the 1850's.

"this government . . . endure . . . half *slave* and half *free*." [5]
Determined to force the "Little Giant" into the open on the slavery
question, Lincoln challenged him to that series of debates which
was to constitute one of the most memorable chapters in American
political history.

The debates were especially thrilling to Mary Lincoln: the
significance given them, the carnival atmosphere surrounding them,
the impressiveness of her husband's bearing and rhetoric. Although
she only attended one, the final confrontation at Alton on October
12, she followed the newspapers avidly, radiating a confidence that
infected even her cautious husband. Once, in a railway depot
during the campaign, Lincoln companionably told the journalist
Henry Villard: "Mary insists . . . that I'm going to be a Senator
and President of the United States, too." [6]

Caught up in the excitement of it all, believing Lincoln's
entire future to be at stake, Mrs. Lincoln never wavered in her
loyalty to the Republican cause, now merely an extension of her
loyalty to its spokesman. Years before she had compared her husband favorably to her old beau "Steve" Douglas, saying, "Mr. Lincoln may not be as handsome a figure, but the people are perhaps
not aware that his heart is as large as his arms are long." [7] On
another occasion, "her head thrown back and her eyes shining with
pride," she declared, "Mr. Douglas is a very little, little giant by
the side of my tall Kentuckian, and intellectually my husband
towers above Douglas just as he does physically." [8] So much for the
man her Springfield relations had wanted her to marry!

Douglas at first appeared to have the upper hand. A dynamic
and convincing orator, he also had the reputation of a man of action.
In his stocky, handsome person he bore all the prestige of a U.S.
senator responsible for one of the most significant pieces of legislation ever introduced in Congress. Some of the aura surrounding
Douglas faded, however, in the face of his opponent's inexorable
logic, moral fervor, spare and elegant language, and skillful de-

[5] Abraham Lincoln. "A House Divided": Speech at Springfield, Illinois, June
16, 1858.
[6] Henry Villard. *Lincoln on the Eve of '61: A Journalist's Story.* Edited by
Harold G. and Oswald Garrison Villard. New York, 1941, p. 6.
[7] Quoted in Herndon, p. 238.
[8] Quoted in Helm, p. 140.

bating technique; time and again Douglas found himself backed
into a forensic corner before he realized what had happened.

The debates were to destroy Douglas's presidential hopes, but
he retained his Senate seat. When the vote of gerrymandered electoral districts negated Lincoln's popular majority, the defeated candidate assured friends—and a disappointed wife—that all was not
lost. He was now a figure of national prominence, a leader of his
party, his name only slightly less lustrous than that of Seward or
Chase. In the year and a half following the election Lincoln traveled
frequently and extensively, often taking his wife with him, leaving
her behind when he thought a trip would be brief and busy. In
February of 1859, he went to Chicago only to be summoned home
by a wifely note to a family friend, O. M. Hatch.

To Ozias M. Hatch [9]

[February 28, 1859] [1]
Monday morning

Mr Hatch.

If you are going up to Chicago to day, & should meet Mr L-
there, will you say to him, that our *dear little Taddie*, is quite sick.
The Dr thinks it may prove a *slight* attack of *lung* fever. I am
feeling troubled & it would be a comfort to have him, *at home*. He
passed a bad night, I do not like his symptoms, and will be glad, if
he hurries home.

Truly your friend
M. L.

[9] Secretary of State of Illinois 1857–65, and a close friend and associate of
Lincoln.
[1] Date based on records of Lincoln's travels. Lincoln was in Chicago on legal
business at this time.

In 1859 Mary Lincoln began a correspondence with a friend and former neighbor, Mrs. John Henry Shearer. Hannah Shearer was the sister of a local Baptist clergyman, Noyes W. Miner, also a close friend of the Lincolns. She had moved to Springfield from Brooklyn, New York, with her two young sons after the death of her husband, Edward Rathbun, and in 1858 had married Shearer, a physician. For nearly a year the couple lived directly across Eighth Street from the Lincolns, until a tubercular condition obliged the doctor to move with his family to the mountain town of Wellsboro, Pennsylvania.

The letters Mary Lincoln wrote Hannah Shearer in 1859 and 1860 give vivid glimpses of her activities during the busy period when Lincoln was turning the senatorial defeat into the larger victory. These were days in which she seemed to have her feet planted firmly in Springfield and her eyes on distant horizons. Her letters were filled with the stuff of small-town life: news of social events, of marriages, births and deaths, of feuds and friendships among neighbors. (She was never without a few personal grudges of her own, and her skill at insinuation and gentle backbiting was never more apparent than in these letters.) From such narrow concerns she swung easily, gaily, into discussion of travels with her husband. For Abraham Lincoln these trips involved legal and political affairs of high moment; for his wife, who thrived on good times and excitement, they were pure pleasure.

To Hannah Shearer

[INCOMPLETE]   [*Springfield, April 24, 1859*]

I suppose she took the occasion of saying this to you, when she was informed of our alienation, a *noble hearted woman*. In another world she may discover, when too late, what the fate of the liar & hypocrite is! [2] I have always heard so much from the connections & those who were thrown in contact with *that woman*, always to avoid her. As before said, Mrs D [3] mentioned this, carelessly, and allow me to assure you, that I would as soon have her to say this, as anything else, her name & *tongue* is well established. My seamstresses bear such different testimony to my *honesty* & justice, that it is a matter of unimportance & therefore, we will forever drop the subject.

Even if I had recognized her as an acquaintance, whether the person she was scandalising, had ever been or still was a friend, she would not have dared ventured such an assertion in my presence.

This is Easter Sunday, & Julia Baker's renowned "baby" is to be christened this afternoon. If I felt well, I would try & attend church out of compliment, perhaps I may. Mr Dubois' family and Mr Hatch, took tea, with us a few evenings since, & then & there, be sure you were remembered. Mr & Mrs D[ubois] Mr H[atch] Mr L & myself are expecting to leave here in a little more than two weeks, for Council Bluffs. [4]

. . . Kansas about the 18th of May. I hope nothing will prevent our journey. In case we go, I hope you will write so soon as you receive this. I want to hear from you before we start. There is a good deal of scarlet fever around us. Tell Ed, John Kent died a week ago with it. Mrs Pascal Enoss [sic] is dead & buried. Mrs Matteson called here on yesterday, regretted that you had left, said she had always intended calling to see you, when she became settled . . . such a coarse picture, [5] the other looks so much better. Mr Ayers went on a week ago, for Mrs W & Delia. [6] I wish they would take the next house which is still untenanted. My heart aches when

[2] The first page of this letter was lost; it is not known to whom Mrs. Lincoln was referring. (Ellipses throughout indicate missing portions.)

[3] Probably the wife of Jesse K. Dubois, a close friend of the Lincolns, elected State Auditor in 1856.

[4] The purpose of this trip was to enable Lincoln to look over Iowa land which the owner, Norman B. Judd (see p. 64), wished to convey to him as security on a debt. The trip was not taken until August, and Mrs. Lincoln apparently remained in Springfield.

[5] A daguerreotype of himself that Lincoln presented to Dr. Shearer in 1859.

[6] E. J. Ayres was a Springfield drygoods merchant; "Mrs W," Mrs. Solomon Wheelock, his mother-in-law; "Delia," Ardelia Wheelock Ayers, his wife.

I think of you, away from us, dear one. The first ride I take, I am going to stop to see your sister.[7] Not one of them deplores your absence more than I do, I believe I may say, as *much*.

With kind regards to the Dr & the boys, I remain ever your attached friend

Mary Lincoln

To Hannah Shearer

Springfield June [26, 1859]

My Dear Mrs Shearer:

I can scarcely realise that three or four weeks have passed since your last welcome letter was received, each day has found me proposing to write, and yet my promises to myself, always unfulfilled. I trust with either of us, it may never again occur—for it is a great trial for me not to hear from you. Owing to some business, Mr L- found he had to attend to in Chicago, our trip to Council Bluffs, has been for the present deferred, however I accompanied Mr L- to Chicago, and passed a few days very pleasantly. For the last two weeks, we have had a continual round of *strawberry* parties, this last week I have spent five evenings out—and you may suppose, that this day of rest, I am happy to enjoy. You need not suppose with our *pleasures*, you are forgotten. I shall *never cease* to long for your dear presence, a cloud always hangs over me, when I think of you. This last week, we gave a strawberry company of about seventy, and I need not assure you, that your absence was sadly remembered. *Miss* [Cornelia] *Curran*, Mr [Jackson] Grimshaw's bride was present. After raspberry time, we will resume, doubtless our usual quiet. About the last of June Mr L contemplates his visit to Council Bluffs, and I presume, I will accompany him. And during the month of July, I hope to pay a visit to Chicago. You know I enjoy, city life. Mr & Mrs Dubois are well. Mr Hatch told me last evening, he was going to visit his native New Hampshire hills, this summer, he is still as pleasant as ever. Mrs Trumbull made her first

[7] Mrs. Chauncey G. Parrish, who lived just outside of Springfield.

appearance, last evening, looking as stately & *ungainly* as ever. Altho' she has been in the city 10 days, this has been about the first notice that has been taken of her. Tis unfortunate, to be so unpopular. The Wheelocks, have moved, as they expected. I suppose you were *startled* at Delia, being so smart. In whom can we trust? I have tried to gain courage, to make a call on Mrs P- [8] "over the way." As yet, I have not had the *courage*. If I could cease to *dwell* upon your memory, I should be far happier. Mrs Mc[Clernand] spent two months in Ky, not much improved, I fear, she still has a bad cough. What would I not give, for a few hours conversation, with you this evening. I hope you may never feel as lonely as I sometimes do, surrounded by much that renders life desirable. I hope you will not become so interested in your new home, as to lose your interest in us. Altho' as you are likely to remain there at present, I trust much pleasure & happiness, will be yours. I have been afraid of our horse, or I should have been out to see your sister, before this, for any one connected with you, will always interest me. I am not satisfied with your letters. They are too short. Do write more lengthy epistles, tell me everything about yourselves. With kind remembranses to the Dr & boys, I must close. I hope *very very* soon to hear from you. Mr Lincoln sends his love.

Yours affectionately
Mary Lincoln

I dare not look over, this, it is written so hastily.

To Hannah Shearer

Springfield August 28th [1859]

My dear Mrs Shearer,

Notwithstanding some *two months*, have passed, since I wrote you last, and no answer has been returned to my missive, yet in-

[8] A probable reference to the wife of a local Baptist minister, George W. Pendleton. Mrs. Shearer's brother was also a Baptist clergyman, and perhaps there was a rivalry between the two men. Such a situation would explain Mrs. Lincoln's comments on the Pendletons.

clination prompts me to send you a few lines. I am feeling quite lonely, as *Bob*, left for College, in *Boston*,[9] a few days since, and it almost appears, as if light & mirth, had departed with him. I will not see him for ten months, without I may next spring, go on to see him. I believe when I wrote you, I anticipated a quiet summer at home. Within a week, after we started unexpectedly on an excursion,[1] travelled *eleven hundred* miles, with a party of eighteen. Many of the party, were your acquaintances, Mr & Mrs Dubois, Mr & Mrs Tom Campbell,[2] Mr Hatch *of course*, and some few others,[3] I believe you knew. *Words* cannot express what a merry time, we had, the gayest pleasure party, I have ever seen. Mr Lincoln says I may go up to the White Mountains, Niagara & take New York & Philadelphia, in our route. Will go on, in time to bring *Bob* home next summer, if *one dare* anticipate, so far in advance.

Your Sister Mrs Parrish, has moved to town, and I am going this very evening to see her, they are some six or seven blocks from here. I do not wonder, they left the farm, it was so dreary. Do write, when you receive this and give an account of yourselves. About this time, you will be starting for New York, I hope you will have a pleasant time—

If I had not devoted so long a time, in writing to R[obert] this afternoon, and as I am called away or I should write you a long letter. What a world, we would have to talk about, were we to meet. I shall never cease to miss you. Mr & Mrs Pendleton *speak* of removing from Springfield. I presume the Dr will not wonder. If I had leisure or opportunity, I would like to tell you of some few handsome parties, that have been given this summer, at Mr Ridgely's in his

[9] In 1920 Robert Lincoln wrote Mrs. Shearer's son, William Lincoln Shearer: "The letter in which my mother spoke of me . . . was written at the time I went east to pass the entrance examinations of Harvard College. In this I failed, and so passed a very valuable year to myself at Phillips Exeter Academy in New Hampshire. This enabled me to pass the Harvard examinations in 1860 without difficulty." Quoted in the article " 'Your Truly Attached Friend, Mary Lincoln,' " by Charles V. Darrin. *Journal of the Illinois State Historical Society*, Spring 1951, p. 15.

[1] A trip designed to assess the property of the Illinois Central Railroad in connection with litigation.

[2] Mrs. Campbell was the former Ann E. Todd of Columbia, Missouri, Mrs. Lincoln's first cousin. (See letter of July 23, 1840.)

[3] The others included Mr. and Mrs. Stephen T. Logan, John Moore, and William Butler, probably with their wives.

new house, and some other places. I hope you will not lose all interest in us. For I *can never* cease to love you.

Write soon, to your attached friend

Mary Lincoln

To Hannah Shearer

Springfield Oct 2d. [1859]

My Dear Mrs Shearer.

By some strange coincidence, I believe each of our last letters were dated on the same day. Therefore if we were inclined to be ceremonious, we would scarcely know, how to set about it.

Since I last wrote you, I have again been wandering. Mr L & myself visited Columbus & some beautiful portions of Ohio, & made a charming visit to Cincinnati. I am again at home and Mr L- is in Wisconsin.[4] I miss Bob, so much, that I do not feel settled down, as much as I used to & find myself going on trips quite frequently. I have invited Miss Cochran [unidentified] and she is spending some weeks with me, so I have a good opportunity of leaving home. Mary, the same girl, I had last winter, is still with me, a very faithful servant, has become as submissive as possible.

Betty Stuart & Chris Brown [5] are to be married the 20th of this month, will have quite a wedding & some parties are expected, which will be a pleasant change for us. Did you make your visit to New York. Write & tell me all about yourselves.

Mr Miner's [6] family & Mr and Mrs P[arrish] I understand went down to the St Louis fair. Mr P[endleton] is about moving away. Col McClernand is nominated by his party, for Congress & as the district is democratic, will doubtless be elected. Sarah's health is still very delicate *still her cough*, he speaks of sending her to Alabama this winter.

[4] The trips to Ohio and Wisconsin were political speaking tours.
[5] Elizabeth Stuart, daughter of Mrs. Lincoln's cousin, John Todd Stuart, and Christopher C. Brown, a lawyer.
[6] The Reverend Noyes W. Miner, Mrs. Shearer's brother.

One of the seven wonders has taken place. Mrs Dubois has a daughter, born two or three days since. Until the last hour *no one* suspected her, as she looked smaller, than she ever had done. Sometimes I thought her countenance had changed, but that was all. She is doing well & much pleased.

Mr Hatch, made one of his social, agreable calls last evening —enquired very particularly for you—no sign of his marrying.[7] We are having beautiful weather, and I hope it will continue. How dearly I should love to see you. Next summer you must meet me in New York. Bob & myself expect to be somewhat of travellers. We are going up to spend a week at the White Mountains. Won't you join me? This is the third letter, I have written within the last two hours, so you will excuse the style, &&. With respects to the Dr & love to the boys, I remain your attached friend

Mary Lincoln

To Ozias M. Hatch

Monday afternoon Oct 3d [1859][8]

Mr Hatch

By way of impressing upon your mind, that friends must not be *entirely* forgotten, I would be pleased to have you wander up our way, to see us this evening, altho' I have not the inducements of meeting company to offer you, or Mr Lincoln to welcome you, yet if you are disengaged, I should like to see you.

Respectfully
Mary Lincoln

[7] Ozias M. Hatch would marry Julia R. Enos in December of 1860.
[8] On this date Lincoln was in Chicago completing the speaking tour mentioned in the preceding letter.

To Hannah Shearer

Springfield Jany 1st [1860]

My dear Friend,

For some time past, I have intended writing you, but each day has brought its own separate calls, causing a delay, which has been unintentional. I have only a few moments, now at my disposal, it is quite late in the evening & tomorrow I must rise early, as it is *receiving* day. How I wish you were with us. The weather is *intensely* cold, and our winter, has been rather quiet. Gov & Mrs Matteson, give a large entertainment on Wednesday evening, Mr L- *gives me* permission to go, but declines, the honor himself. I should like to go, but *may probably* pass the evening at home. Since I last wrote you, I have passed a week very pleasantly in St Louis. You know I have four *own* cousins, who keep house in the city, & live very pleasantly. Yet my time by especial invitation was passed at my cousin Judge [John C.] Richardson's. They live in a very handsome house, four stories, plenty of room & some Kentucky *darkies*, to wait on them.

Whilst there, Julia Dean Hayne [9] had a benefit, our Springfield *Ned* Taylor [1] (who is passing the winter in St Louis) came up and we all went together. Ten years ago, about the time of her debut, I saw her in Washington, she has failed greatly since then. Perhaps you are aware, that Mrs McClernand accompanied her Husband this winter. I never saw persons *so elated* in my life. Poor woman, she cannot feel comfortable away from home, with her poor health. I saw your sister Mrs P[arrish] a few days since, she is so good a woman I love her very much. I need not assure you, that I am writing under, unpleasant circumstances. Such a pen, may you never handle *such another*, boys *disposed* to be noisy. Speaking of *boys*, Willie's [ninth] birthday [2] came off on the 21st of Dec. and as

[9] A celebrated New York actress, known professionally by her maiden name, Julia Dean.
[1] Possibly Edward J. Taylor, formerly associated with Charles R. Hurst in a drygoods business in Springfield.
[2] An invitation to this party, in Mrs. Lincoln's hand, is in the Illinois State Historical Library. It was addressed to "Little Isaac Diller," son of a local pharmacist.

I had long promised him a *celebration*, it duly came off. Some 50 or 60 boys & girls attended the gala, you may believe I have come to the conclusion, that they are nonsensical affairs. However, I wish your boys, had been in their midst. Do, like a dear friend, begin the New Year well, & answer this scrawl, so soon as you receive it. Knowing, I will not have an hour, at my disposal for some days I *venture* to send it. With kind regards to the Dr & the boys, I remain your attached friend,

Mary Lincoln

Let *the flames* receive this, so soon as read.

In October of 1859 an Illinois housewife named Mary Lincoln had, with all the casualness of a wealthy, worldly woman, asked Hannah Shearer to join her in New York or the White Mountains the following summer. The trip was never taken. Mrs. Lincoln's mind and time that summer were occupied with far more important matters. In February of 1860 her husband had traveled to New York himself to deliver his celebrated speech before the Cooper Union. Widely reprinted, the address set forth his views on the heightening national crisis and made him a significant contender for the Republican presidential nomination. His New York commitment was followed by a tour of the New England states, including a stop and a speech at Phillips Exeter Academy in New Hampshire, where young Robert was preparing for Harvard. The years of speechmaking, maneuvering, and unremitting toil in the political fields were at last seeing their reward. On May 18, 1860, at the climax of the Republican convention in Chicago, Abraham Lincoln won his party's nomination over the claims of the most influential Republican of the day, Senator William H. Seward of New York.

His chances for election were improved by the fact of divided opposition: Stephen A. Douglas was running for the Northern Democrats and John Breckinridge for the Southern Democrats; a third faction, the Constitutional Union Party, was represented by John Bell. Because Lincoln's position on the issues was well known, and the potentially explosive political situation made caution the order of the day, he remained in Springfield from the time of his nomination to the day of the election, November 6.

He was hardly alone, and hardly idle. The leaders of his party who traveled about the country speaking in his behalf found time to make pilgrimages to his door, putting Mary Lincoln to her first great test as hostess and diplomat. The candidate went to his headquarters in the State Capitol nearly every day, reading and answering mountains of mail, conducting delicate, long-distance negotiations with supporters all over the country. Artists flocked to Springfield to paint his portrait or carve his features, journalists came from distant parts to see and talk with him and send their papers firsthand reports of this strange-looking, compelling man on whose strength and wisdom might well depend the fate of the republic. All the stir was heady tonic for Mary Lincoln. Important men who had once been only names appeared at her door, lounged in her parlor, sat at her table. She listened to snatches of talk and seldom hesitated to venture her opinions to her husband and to others. She still devoted herself to her sons and to her duties at home, she could still be shattered by family tragedies, but her husband's fate in the coming contest absorbed her almost completely. A few letters which have been preserved provide a cross-section of her concerns during 1860, one of the happiest years of her life.

To Mark Delahay [3]

Springfield May 25th 60

Dear Sir:

One of my boys, appears to claim prior possession of the smallest flag,[4] is inconsolable for its absence, as I believe it is too small to

---

[3] Lawyer and publisher of the *Kansas Territorial Register*, a prominent anti-slavery organ. Delahay had helped to organize the Kansas Republican party and was a strong Lincoln supporter. He was distantly related to Lincoln's stepmother.

[4] On his way home from the Chicago convention, Delahay had stopped in Springfield with two convention flags and inadvertently carried both away with him.

do you any service, and as he is so urgent to have it again—and as I am sure, the largest one, will be quite sufficient, I will ask you to send it to us, the first opportunity you may have, especially as he claims it, and I feel it is as necessary to keep one's word with a child, as with a grown person—Hoping you reached home safely, I remain yours respectfully

Mary Lincoln

To Adeline Judd [5]

Springfield June 13th [1860]

My dear Mrs Judd,

Your very acceptable letter was received some days since & under *other* circumstances, than those by which we are, at present surrounded, my silence would be inexcusable. Mrs C. M. Smith,[6] whom you perhaps remember, lost a son of ten years of age, on yesterday, has been sick some weeks with *typhoid* fever. I trust never to witness *such suffering ever* again. He is to be buried this afternoon. The family are almost inconsolable, & for the last week, I have spent the greater portion of my time, with them.

Nothing would give me more pleasure, than to join you in your excursion to Minnesota, I am quite *unnerved* just now, and we have so much company, that I could scarcely leave home, if it was in September or later, perhaps I might do so, it has always been one of the *many* anticipations of "my future" to visit *Minnehaha*—Our oldest boy, has been absent, almost *a year*, a *long year*, & at times I feel *wild* to see him, if I went any where, within the next few weeks, I should wish to visit him. If any thing, should prevent your trip, at the present time, and you would ever conclude to take the same excursion, I would be very happy to accompany you, if I could gain courage, feeling much depressed, from recent occurrences, I know

---

[5] Wife of Norman B. Judd, general counsel for the Rock Island Railroad and Republican state committee chairman. Judd headed the Illinois delegation to the Republican convention of 1860, and placed Lincoln's name in nomination for the presidency.

[6] Mrs. Lincoln's youngest sister, Ann.

well, that nothing would benefit me more, than such an *excursion*. Hoping, you will accompany your Husband, in some of his visits to Springfield, I remain yours very truly,

Mary Lincoln

I am too well aware of your goodness, not to feel assured, that you will excuse *this note*. Mr L- joins me in kind regards to your Sister & Mr Judd.

M.

To John Meredith Read [7]

Springfield Aug 25th [1860]

Dear Sir:

Mr Brown [8] of your city has taken a miniature likeness of my Husband, which I think is perfect. I see no fault or defect whatever. Allow me to express the great pleasure it afforded us, of seeing so excellent a representation of yourself.

I have the honor of being yours respectfully

Mary Lincoln

To Hannah Shearer

Springfield Oct 20th [1860]

My Dear Mrs Shearer:

Your last kind letter was received a week or two since & if every moment of my time was not occupied, should have answered

[7] A Philadelphia jurist and politician who was a prominent supporter of Lincoln's presidential candidacy.

[8] J. Henry Brown, a Philadelphia artist, had come to Springfield with a commission from Read to paint a miniature of Lincoln on ivory that would show the candidate to be considerably nicer looking than political caricaturists depicted him. Two days later, Lincoln himself wrote Read that the likeness was "without fault."

it sooner. You used to be worried, that I took politics so cooly you would not do so, were you to see me now. Whenever I *have time*, to think, my mind is sufficiently exercised for my comfort. Fortunately, the time is rapidly drawing to a close, a little more than two weeks, will decide the contest. I scarcely know, how I would bear up, under defeat. I trust that we will not have the trial. Penn. & Indiana have made us fair promises for Nov.[9] & I trust other doubtless [doubtful] states will follow in their footsteps. You must think of us on election day, our friends will feel quite as anxious for us, as we do for ourselves. I called round to see Mrs Miner a few days since, she was looking very well & enjoyed her trip east exceedingly. You must allow me to thank you for the beautiful collar, you sent me, although I did not require any assurance of the kind to convince me of your kind recollections. I suppose Mrs M- gave you a history of passing events in S- since you left. I believe I have always known less than any one else of what is transpiring in our midst. This summer, we have had immense crowds of strangers visiting us, and have had no time to be occupied, with home affairs. How much I wish I could see you & have some of our long talks together. If Mr L- *is elected*, I hope that time will come, I trust that we may all meet at *Phillipi*. There was a Douglas meeting here a few days since, over which their chief presided. Mrs McClernand, gave them a reception at which they expected *hundreds*, but they only numbered thirty. This rather looks as if his greatness had passed away. Our boys often wish they could see Ed & Miner.[1] I have never ceased to miss you all. I know that I should not send you such a scrawl, but were you to see my pen, you would wonder that I could write as well. Write soon. With kind remembrances to all, I remain your affectionate friend,

Mary Lincoln

[9] In the local elections of October 9, 1860, Pennsylvania and Indiana had shown overwhelmingly Republican sentiment.
[1] Mrs. Shearer's two sons, Edward Rathbun, Jr. and James Miner Rathbun.

To Dyer Burgess [2]

————

Springfield, Oct 29th [1860]

Dear Sir:

Your letter of the 24th was received a day or two since, to which I reply. Mr Lincoln has never been a Mason or belonged to any secret order, since he has been a man, he has had no time to devote to any thing out of the line of his business, even if he had been so disposed. Hoping that some day, you may make each other's acquaintance, and that health & happiness will always be yours, I remain very respectfully

Mrs A. Lincoln

To Samuel Byram Halliday [3]

————

Springfield Dec 31 1860

Dear Sir:

Allow me to return my acknowledgments, for the handsome books, you sent me, which were received on yesterday. The volume Mr Lincoln brought home with him last spring,[4] I read with much interest, also some of my friends. My Husband retains a lively recollection, of his visit to the Inst[it]ution,[5] whilst in New York, also

[2] Reverend Burgess of Constitution, Ohio, was a member of an anti-Mason faction in the Republican party. He had expressed his desire to support Lincoln but would not do so until he could be convinced that Lincoln had never belonged to a secret society.

[3] A New York clergyman who had made his mark in the field of work programs for the poor. He eventually became assistant pastor of Henry Ward Beecher's Plymouth Church.

[4] *The Lost and Found; or Life Among the Poor*, a collection of short stories of children abandoned or mistreated by their parents.

[5] The Five Points House of Industry, a school and training center for needy children, one of whose founders was Dr. Halliday.

of your polite attention to him. I shall always prize, the works you sent me, and wish you much success, in so benevolent a cause.

I remain very resp

Mrs A. Lincoln.

"I scarcely know, how I would bear up, under defeat," Mary Lincoln had written Hannah Shearer shortly before the election of 1860. Fortunately she was never put to the test. On November 6 she remained at home, edgy but hopeful, while her husband went to his office, then to the courthouse to cast his ballot, and, that night, to a gathering at the telegraph office to get the returns. When a Republican victory was forecast by the capture of New York, close to ten thousand people across the street set up a mighty cheer and called for a speech from the soon-to-be President-elect. For once Lincoln did not give himself up to the multitudes. Turning to Lyman Trumbull, he said: "I guess I'll go down and tell Mary about it," and started for home.[6]

One can well imagine her exultation on learning the news. Twenty years earlier she had fallen in love with a struggling young lawyer of uncommon strength, decency, and intellect. She had invested her whole soul in him, had dreamed great dreams for him, and now they had come true. Notwithstanding the hardships of their early married life, despite tensions, frustrations, and the tragedy of a child's death, her years with Lincoln had been good ones. At times he had been far from an ideal husband; his interests and ambitions had taken him away from the hearth more frequently than she would have liked, and his mind was often roaming in far countries she could not reach. But with the absences and absent-mindedness had come compensations. Lincoln was appreciative of her virtues and tolerant of her faults; he pampered her like a child yet heeded her wishes and respected her judgments more than many a Victorian husband. Above all she had the satisfaction of knowing

[6] Quoted in Randall, p. 186.

that she had seen earlier than most what he might attain and had helped him to attain it.

Mrs. Abraham Lincoln traveled to New York early in January 1861 to outfit herself for the eventful days ahead. She was determined to show Washington and the world that she was no small-town frump come out of the West with trunks full of dowdy clothes. She wanted a wardrobe equal to any grand occasion she might be called upon to attend. Not even the illustrations in *Godey's Lady's Book* had prepared her for the glittering array of fabrics, jewels, furs, and head-dresses available to women of means. Fussed over by merchants who knew a victim when they saw one, she embarked on what proved to be only the first of a series of giddy shopping sprees. She took full advantage of the credit lavishly extended the wife of the President-elect and kept her debts from her husband, who from that time forward would be far too preoccupied to notice what she was up to.

The New York trip marked a turning point in other respects as well. For the first time Mary Lincoln was lionized by people of such power, wealth, and sophistication as she had never encountered before. They sought her out and appeared to hang on her every word. The attention went to her head. Soon she was expounding on matters of great delicacy, giving forth opinions based on hearsay or fragmentary knowledge. One reporter claimed to have heard her say that her husband had finally decided to name William Seward Secretary of State due to "pressures" upon him, the implication being that he would not have done so otherwise. Whether she said precisely that or not, she did make many outspoken references to matters of personality and policy, without regard for the consequences.

Such behavior may have been, by the standards of the day, "unwomanly," and by any measure unwise, but it should not have been unexpected. From an early age, Mary Todd Lincoln had been conditioned to politics and to expressing herself spontaneously on the subject. She had spoken up to Henry Clay as a girl, and had been led by a doting father to believe that her childish opinions had worth. Her years as a center of attention in the Coterie had done little to cramp her style; then had come marriage to Abraham Lincoln. Through all the vicissitudes of his career, Lincoln had to an extraordinary degree confided to her his plans, his positions, his opinions of others. He seldom took her advice unless it coincided with his private judgments, but listened to her with a kindly interest which encouraged her to keep talking. Lacking Lincoln's breadth of vision, his magnanimity and subtlety, she came to view politics through the glass of her own volatile nature. To her it was at once an intricate game of maneuver and manipulation and a great drama based on themes of punishment and reward. She had always been susceptible to gossip and fascinated by the interplay of personalities among her acquaintance. She was in many respects a shrewd judge of character and of human motivation, especially in its negative aspects. Although a want of discretion had made her enemies in Springfield, they were social enemies, harmless enough. She was a long time learning that it was one thing to disparage the motives of a neighbor, quite another to impugn publicly the integrity of a Cabinet member.

Though much of the growing criticism of her was the result of envy or of attempts by Lincoln's foes to discredit him through his wife, some of it was justified. Proof that Mary Lincoln occasionally went in over her head lies in a letter to be found among the papers of David Davis, a Bloomington judge who was one of Lincoln's closest friends and his campaign manager in 1860. Knowing Davis to be influential in the matter of Cabinet choices, she wrote him from New York, warning him against efforts then being made to promote Norman B. Judd for a Cabinet post. The letter, marked *Confidential*, was somewhat malicious; it was also unnecessary: Davis, for political reasons, was determined to keep Judd out of the Cabinet. It is the only letter of its kind she is known to have written before her husband assumed the presidency, but others in similar vein would follow it. Never would she fail to justify her interference with high-sounding references to the welfare of the nation.

By the time she returned to Springfield, other, more vicious stories were circulating about her, most of them unfounded. A visitor purported to give an "eyewitness" account of a hysterical scene between Mrs. Lincoln and her husband over an appointment she apparently wished him to make and to which he objected. She was also accused of accepting bribes in exchange for using her influence with the President-elect in the realm of appointments. That both Lincolns—particularly Mrs. Lincoln—accepted gifts from well-wishers is known fact, but that Lincoln (whom his wife once described as "almost a monomaniac on the subject of honesty"[7]) would allow himself to be used by the donors, or fail to be aware that he was being used, is highly unlikely.

To David Davis

New York Jany 17th [1861]

Confidential

Dear Sir:

Doubtless you will be surprised, to receive a note from me, when I explain the cause, of my writing, I believe your honest, noble heart, will sympathise with me, otherwise I am assured, you will not mention it. Perhaps you will think it is no affair of *mine*, yet I see it, almost daily mentioned in the Herald, that *Judd*[8] & some *few* Northern friends, are *urging* the *former's* claims to a cabinet appointment. *Judd* would cause trouble & dissatisfaction, & if Wall Street testifies correctly, his business transactions, have not always borne inspection. I heard the report, discussed at the table this morning, by persons who did not know, who was near, a party of gentlemen, evidently strong Republicans, they were laughing at the idea of *Judd*, being any way, connected with the Cabinet in *these times*, when honesty in high places is so important. Mr Lincoln's great attachment for you, is my present reason for writing. I know, a word from you, will have much effect, for the good of the country, and Mr Lincoln's future reputation, I believe you will speak to him on this subject & urge him not to give him so responsible a place. It is strange, how little delicacy those Chicago men have. I know, I can

[7] Mary Lincoln to Abram Wakeman, Soldiers' Home, September 23, [1864].
[8] Norman B. Judd was one of many Lincoln supporters in line for Cabinet posts, but consideration of his name brought great opposition from former Whigs in the Republican party. Lincoln ultimately appointed Judd minister to Berlin and later he became a member of Congress.

rely on what I have written to you, to be kept private. If you consider me intrusive, please excuse me, our country, just now, is above all.

Very Respectfully,
Mary Lincoln

There was much to be done before the Lincolns' departure for Washington. The house on Eighth Street, with all its memories, had to be vacated for a tenant, some household articles sold, others stored, still others packed for use in the White House. A huge reception had to be held for everyone in Springfield who mattered to the Lincolns. Mrs. Lincoln handled many of these chores herself, for her husband was intensely preoccupied. He was attempting to form a new government at a time when the Union was disintegrating and the future lay bleak under gathering clouds of war. For months there had been threats on his life, ghastly effigies sent through the mail, dark hints that he would never live to be inaugurated. Because of the dangers all about, it was with some difficulty that Mary Lincoln persuaded her husband to allow her to accompany him on the long train journey to Washington; perhaps they had a real set-to on the subject, for she did not leave Springfield with him but joined him the following day in Indianapolis with Willie and Tad.

On the rain-swept morning of February 11, 1861, the Lincolns stood on the threshold of a new life. The former prairie lawyer was about to take leave of Springfield to assume the highest office in the land. His wife was among the crowd of relatives, friends and townspeople come to bid him farewell. Young Robert stood stiffly at his father's side on the train platform as, in a voice trembling with emotion, Lincoln addressed the throng. "Here I have lived a quarter of a century," he said, "and have passed from a young to an old man. Here my children have been born, and one is buried. I now leave, not knowing when, or whether, ever I may return." [9]

[9] *Farewell Address at Springfield Illinois*, February 11, 1861. ["A" Version.]

As the cars rolled eastward out of the Springfield depot, Mary Lincoln turned away, no doubt reflecting that this was the proudest moment of her life. But there was sadness as well. She was preparing to leave behind close friends and those who were of her blood—people who understood, sympathized, who would remember her tragedies, and, in the end, forgive her shortcomings. Now the eyes of the nation would be upon her. Few people would understand and still fewer would be ready to forgive.

Mrs. President
Lincoln

February 1861
———
May 1865

No President's wife in history had a more turbulent career in the White House than Mary Todd Lincoln. None took up her duties under more difficult circumstances; none was so consistently criticized, none so vulnerable to criticism. In a sense Mrs. Lincoln was doomed before she set foot in Washington. Her efforts to make a good impression, to serve her husband well, were hampered from the start by an impulsive, nervous temperament, a loose tongue, and a mind filled with quirks and delusions. Moreover, conditions in Washington in February of 1861 were volatile enough to have tried the nerves of a woman far more stable than she. The capital was a troubled city, girdled by hostile territory and dominated by an entrenched aristocracy: men who were jealous of their power and women who had for decades held undisputed social sway. As the Union broke apart, the atmosphere grew thick with hatred, rumor, and divided loyalties. Some of the capital's most prominent citizens were Tidewater gentry whose contempt for westerners was exceeded only by their loathing for Yankees and Republicans. Others were ardent supporters of the Union, quick to suspect the Kentucky-bred Mrs. Lincoln of secessionist sympathies.

Once the Confederacy had been formed and had elected its leaders, a reconciliation between North and South seemed the vainest of hopes. Every day brought closer the threat of a war in which brother would be set against brother. As a minority President, Lincoln trod on uncertain ground; he was hated in the South and suspect among extremist elements within his own party. He too was judged by Washington society on surface appearances and judged harshly. They called him "the backwoods President" and dismissed him as a boor and a buffoon. He appeared to be more uncouth than Andrew Jackson, who at least had had the decency to be a Democrat.

Even before the Lincolns arrived in the capital there were indications of trouble ahead. Their twelve-day journey East was in most respects a triumphal tour, yet crowds were often overzealous in their efforts to see and touch the President-elect and occasionally endangered his safety in their exuberant good will. The continual call for speeches and public appearances put Lincoln under an appalling strain. He had to clarify the issues for his countrymen and prepare them for the trials ahead without jeopardizing any eleventh-hour accommodation with the Confederacy. He had to hold passions in check by appearing calm and confident, by stressing the common aspirations of "one people," while concealing as best he could his own growing sense of despair.

That eastward progress which had begun as a public love-feast ended on a note of terror and ignominy. When the train entered Pennsylvania, the famous private detective Allan Pinkerton informed Lincoln that a band of Confederate "plug-uglies" was planning to sabotage bridges and rail connections outside of Baltimore in order to halt the presidential train and seize its most illustrious passenger. Not until Pinkerton's intelligence was corroborated by others did Lincoln reluctantly agree to separate himself from his family and entourage and travel through Baltimore by night on an unmarked train with Pinkerton and an old friend, Ward Hill Lamon, as his only companions and bodyguards.[1]

Lincoln insisted that his wife be among the few informed of the plan in advance; he feared she might become "very much excited" by his unexplained absence. It was the gesture of a thoughtful husband, but a gesture made in vain. When Mrs. Lincoln was told of the ruse and the reasons for it, she was plunged into panic and nearly gave the plan away by her visible agitation. She was not free of anxiety until she was notified of her husband's pre-dawn arrival in the capital and until her own train had passed safely through restless crowds in Baltimore. The experience was a searing one

[1] Lincoln's nocturnal adventure and his wife's reaction to it are discussed in *Lincoln and the Baltimore Plot*. Edited by Norma B. Cuthbert. San Marino, 1949.

for a high-strung woman, and it would leave its mark, planting in her consciousness a seed of dread that would grow and grow until, four years later, it blossomed into hideous reality.

The Lincoln family was reunited on the afternoon of February 23 at Willard's Hotel in Washington, where they would stay until the inauguration on March 4. Here Mrs. Lincoln got her first taste of the strains and suspicions that would cloud her happiness in the White House and place her on the defensive for the rest of her life. Few of the ladies of Washington condescended to call on her at Willard's, and their slights stung her deeply. Born into a distinguished family, she was horrified to realize that she was being dismissed as a parvenue; longing to be a great lady, she was given scant opportunity to display the best that was in her. It was difficult to decide which hurt the most, the subtle ostracism of the social leaders of the city, or the outright abuse of letter writers and certain segments of the press.

Some of the most influential newspapers in the land had already published malicious allusions to Mrs. Lincoln's southern antecedents, her lack of discretion, her unseemly interest in her husband's appointments. Ordinarily responsible journalists spiced their political commentary with arch references to her appearance, manners, and conversation (although some found themselves pleasantly surprised at her poise). Lincoln was disturbed by abuse of himself but bore it with equanimity, putting it down as the price of holding office at a time when feelings ran high. He had a government to form and worries enough without dwelling on the ravings of those who wished him ill. His wife had no such preoccupation and no ready means of defending herself against unjust accusations. She had to find a way of proving that she was a well-bred, intelligent, and sophisticated woman, loyal to her husband and her country, and more than qualified for the demanding role that history had thrust upon her. She must also make it clear that she knew something of political infighting herself: no one was going to take advantage of her or her husband if she could help it!

Inauguration day came and went in a blaze of somber glory. Many of Mrs. Lincoln's Springfield relatives had journeyed East in honor of the occasion, only to shudder at the gloom which pervaded everything: the troops that guarded the route to the Capitol, the extreme tension in the air, the slurs and sneers overheard from all sides. "We are not enemies but friends," Lincoln declared as he stood in the thin winter sunlight beneath the half-finished Capitol dome. His appeal to "the better angels of our nature" no doubt touched his wife as deeply as it did others. No one could have wished more ardently than she that some miracle would occur so that all would indeed be well.

After the ceremonies the Lincolns entered the White House for the first time to rest and dress for the inaugural ball, the only even remotely gala occasion of that dismal day. In the evening, wearing a magnificent blue gown with a blue feather in her hair, Mrs. Lincoln entered the ballroom on the arm of Senator Stephen A. Douglas, an old friend whose presence at her side served as a sentimental link between the pleasant past and the proud new life on which she was embarked.

As Abraham Lincoln turned his mind and energies to the agonies of a divided nation, his wife set about the task of making a national monument and public meeting place into a livable home for her family. By the end of March all her relatives had returned to their homes, with the exception of her cousin and close friend Elizabeth Todd Grimsley, who had consented to stay on to help her through the first taxing weeks in the White House. As soon as she had the leisure to resume her correspondence, she was nudging William Seward and Ward Hill Lamon about appointments, flattering Simon Cameron, the new Secretary of War, and urging her friend Hannah Shearer to visit her soon in her splendid new home.

To William H. Seward [2]

Washington March 22d [1861]

Dear Sir

Our friend Col [George S.] Mygatt, a resident of Cleaveland comes to us very highly recommended, as a gentleman, and an earnest Republican. He was an applicant for the collectorship of the port of C[leveland] that place was given by Gov Chase [3] to another although he had been one of *his* earnest supporters. He desires the consulship of Honolulu & brings the highest testimonials from prominent men of Ohio. It would be very gratifying, if his request would be granted. Trusting you will pardon, the liberty I have taken, I remain very respectfully,

Mrs A. Lincoln

To Hannah Shearer

Washington March [28, 1861]

My dear Mrs Shearer.

I scarcely thought when we parted at Harrisburg,[4] that so long a time would pass, before I would send you a letter, yet I feel assured, if you were aware how much *every moment* is occupied, you would excuse me. We suppose, that the crowd will be gradually leaving the city, and henceforth, we may hope, for more leisure, *that blessed* assurance, frequently quiets my nerves. Last week, both of the children, had the measles slightly, altho' the papers represented them as quite ill.

[2] Former governor and senator from New York and Lincoln's major rival for the Republican nomination, now Secretary of State.
[3] Salmon P. Chase, former governor of Ohio and Lincoln's first Secretary of the Treasury. Mrs. Lincoln bore Chase a strong dislike and took this opportunity for a gentle criticism of him to Seward, whom she also distrusted.
[4] Dr. and Mrs. Shearer had traveled on the presidential train with the Lincolns from Philadelphia to Harrisburg.

We have given our last *general* levee until next winter, our cabinet dinner comes off this evening, a party of 28 will dine with us. Our friends have all left, except Mrs Grimsley [5] & Mr and Mrs Kellogg [6] of Cincinnati. The latter leave for home, tomorrow. Mrs G will remain a week or two longer.[7] This is certainly a very charming spot & I have formed many delightful acquaintances. Every evening our *blue room*, is filled with the elite of the land, last eve, we had about 40 to call in, to see us *ladies*, from Vice P. Breckinridge [8] down.

I want you to spend the month of May, with us. W at that time, is perfectly charming. We can pass, many pleasant hours, together, the drives around here are fine, and our carriage we find *very luxurious*. Remember that I shall certainly expect you. As will be most agreeable to us, we will not have any other friends with us. Be sure & bring your boys, with you, the pleasure grounds here, are exquisite. I shall claim the month. I am beginning to feel so perfectly at home, and enjoy every thing so much. The conservatory attached to this house is so delightful. We have so many choice bouquets. My sister Mrs Edwards writes that she cannot settle down at home, since she has been here. We *may perhaps*, at the close of *four* years, be glad to relinquish our claims.

One day this week, we went down to Mt Vernon. A visit we can again pay, when you are with us. Like a dear friend, do not wait for a regular return of letters, remember how little time, is at my disposal. Remember me to your Husband & boys, and believe me ever your attached friend

Mary Lincoln

[5] Elizabeth Todd Grimsley was the daughter of Dr. John Todd and wife of Harrison Grimsley of Springfield.

[6] Charles H. and Margaret Todd Kellogg were Mrs. Lincoln's brother-in-law and half-sister.

[7] Mrs. Grimsley stayed longer. She discussed her visit in her article "Six Months in the White House." *Journal of the Illinois State Historical Society*, October 1926–January 1927.

[8] John C. Breckinridge, senator from Kentucky and vice-president of the United States 1857–61, was distantly related to Mrs. Lincoln's stepmother. Nominated for the presidency in 1860 by proslavery Democrats, he would soon depart Washington to serve the Confederacy.

To Simon Cameron [9]

March 29th [1861]

Dear General—

I understand that you *forgive me*, for all *past offences*, yet I am not Christian enough, to feel the same towards *you* as you pass me so "lightly by" when you visit the White House—

Very truly yrs
M. Lincoln

To Ward Hill Lamon [1]

Thursday April [11, 1861]

Mr Lamon:

I trust you will *redeem your promise* in reference to Woods [sic].[2] If you *exert* your influence with Mr L I am sure *you* will succeed. Some one must have prejudi[ci]ng Mr L against W-. I believe him to be a clever man & would make an efficient Commissioner.[3]

Respectfully
Mrs A. Lincoln

[9] A former Pennsylvania senator whom Lincoln named as his first Secretary of War under considerable pressure. Cameron served in that capacity until scandals and inefficiency in his department forced his removal in January 1862. He was then appointed minister to Russia, which post he held for a year before returning to his home state.

[1] A close Illinois friend of Lincoln's, appointed U.S. Marshal for the District of Columbia, April 12, 1861.

[2] William S. Wood, who had arranged the Lincolns' train trip to Washington, was at this time being considered for the post of Commissioner of Public Buildings. He served for some months, but was not confirmed by the Senate.

[3] Lamon's reply to this letter was dated April 11, 1861, and read in part: "Mrs. L: I never was false to a promise or a friend or knowingly did a dishonorable act. *I will visit Mr. Lincoln on the subject at once.* I regret that anyone has prejudiced Mr. L. against Mr. Wood. . . ." MS. in the Henry E. Huntington Library, San Marino, California.

If one were to judge by her letters, written from Washington and in later years, Mary Todd Lincoln felt no particular reverence for the past history or symbolic significance of the White House. Rarely did she measure her conduct or her husband's by that of the Mansion's previous tenants. There is no mention in her correspondence of Martha Washington, Abigail Adams, Dolly Madison, or Eliza Monroe. To her, the President's house seemed a suitably splendid domicile for the most successful politician in the land. In the past his name may have been Jefferson or Jackson, Pierce or Polk; in 1861, mercifully, it was Lincoln.

Yet, for all its magnificence of scale, its standing army of servants, the White House had little then to commend it as a showplace, or even as a comfortable dwelling. On their first full day in residence, Mary Lincoln and Elizabeth Grimsley explored the building from cellars to attic, in mounting distress at the way in which it had been allowed to deteriorate. For decades hordes of visitors and office seekers had tramped the stairs, loitered in the corridors, spat on the carpets and floors, and invaded the privacy of presidential families. The impressive state rooms had been reasonably well maintained, but the family quarters on the second floor were in shocking disrepair and cluttered with shabby, broken furniture which Mrs. Lincoln later described as "abominable," not fit for "the humblest cabin." [4] Some pieces looked as if they had been "brought in by the first President," wrote "Cousin Lizzie" with fine historical abandon. [5] Out they went.

A major overhaul was clearly in order—a fact that even Congress acknowledged by voting what was then the munificent sum of twenty thousand dollars expressly for the purpose of refurnishing and renovating the Executive Mansion. Mary Lincoln was overjoyed at news of the appropriation. She saw in it an opportunity not only to create a comfortable home for her family, but to show the

[4] Mary Lincoln to Alexander Williamson, Chicago, January 26, [1866].
[5] Elizabeth Todd Grimsley. "Six Months in the White House," p. 47.

snobbish ladies of Washington that she had civilized taste and a knowledge of the very latest styles in furniture and decor. Before she finished her work the White House would be the most sumptuous and fashionable home in the nation, a brilliant setting for lavish entertainments.

She might have chosen a better time to indulge this ambition. As the nation drew closer to war, living in Washington was like sitting on a powder keg. On April 12 Fort Sumter was fired upon. With his government barely a functioning entity, with appointments still to be made and policy formulated, Abraham Lincoln was called upon to shoulder the wartime burdens that would weigh him down until the day of his death.

At the news of Fort Sumter Mary Lincoln became as concerned as the rest of Washington that the federal enclave would be invaded by Confederate troops. As southern loyalists began to depart the city, the remaining population, including the Lincolns, waited anxiously for further military protection. At last the Sixth Massachusetts Regiment managed to fight off a Baltimore mob and get through to Washington, where it was shortly reinforced by the Seventh New York Regiment. The capital was now as safe—and as cheerful—as any armed camp. The pall of gloomy anticipation that hung over the city that spring was reflected in a homesick letter the President's wife wrote a Springfield friend.

To Mrs. Samuel H. Melvin [6]

Washington, April 27, 1861—

My Dear Mrs Melvin:

Cap Todd,[7] leaves to day for S & I take the liberty of enclosing some photographs of the boys, also, a little bonnet cap, for my sweet

[6] The wife of a dealer in drugs and medical supplies and a close friend of Mrs. Lincoln in Springfield. Mr. Melvin was chairman of the Pew Committee of the First Presbyterian Church.

[7] Captain Lockwood Todd, brother of Elizabeth Grimsley.

little namesake. Thousands of soldiers are guarding us, and if there is safety in numbers, we have every reason, to feel secure. We can only hope for peace!

Our boys, remember your dear little sons, with much affection. I trust the day *may come* when they will be reunited. I had intended requesting Mr Melvin to have given me a promise, that on our return to S- we would be able to secure *our particular pew*, to which I was very much attached, and which we occupied some ten years, may I hope that he will be able to do so.

With kind regards to your family & all friends, I remain ever sincerely

Mary Lincoln

To Ward Hill Lamon

[New York] May 12, 1861

Dear Sir:

I feel that an apology is due you for having sent you a dispatch about the appointment of [George H.?] Plant or [Job] Angus. We heard it mentioned positively, on yesterday that Plant would receive it [8] and as the commission was brought very near the lady of the house [9] I am sure you will think I am right in taking so great an interest. The men who are applying for the situation are very unsuitable, deficient in intelligence, manners, and it may be, morals. May I ask the favor of you, to speak to Mr L. on the subject. I know he has confidence in your judgment.

Very respectfully,
Mrs A. Lincoln

[8] Either the Commissionership of Public Buildings or some lesser post in the same department.
[9] A reference to the fact that the Commissioner of Public Buildings worked closely with the President's wife on White House matters.

To Caleb B. Smith [1]

[*May 31, 1861*]

Hon Mr Smith

We boarded some months, with Mrs Sprigg,[2] & found her a most estimable lady & would esteem it a personal favor, if her request, could be granted.

Mrs A. Lincoln

Throughout the grim spring of 1861 Mary Lincoln soothed her nerves by spending time with her children and making excursions about the city and near countryside. But the easiest way to forget her fears was to concentrate on the task of redoing the White House and spending the twenty thousand dollars placed at her disposal. She had always sought security in possessions and found shopping an excellent morale-booster, but she had begun to lose her sense of proportion on the subject. She dismissed the fact that the government now had to defray the huge expense of arming, clothing, and feeding tens of thousands of men; what was hers was hers, she reasoned, and the President's family could not under any circumstances be expected to live like transients in a rundown hotel.

In mid-May she traveled to Philadelphia, Boston, and New York with Elizabeth Grimsley and others. In New York the two women attended services at Henry Ward Beecher's Plymouth Church and the theater at Laura Keene's. When she was not holding court at the Metropolitan Hotel, Mrs. Lincoln was shopping at A. T. Stewart, Lord & Taylor, Arnold & Constable, and other noted

---

[1] Secretary of the Interior, 1861–3.
[2] Mrs. Ann G. Sprigg, who kept the boarding house on First Street where Lincoln had lived as a Congressman. Mrs. Lincoln's note was appended to a similar one from the President himself. Mrs. Sprigg's request is not known.

drygoods stores. She purchased a carriage at Brewster's for $900. She visited Haughwout & Company, dealers in glassware and china, where she ordered, among other things, a Haviland dinner service in "solferino and gold," emblazoned with the arms of the United States. So attractive was it that she purchased a second set with her own initials in place of the national seal. It cost eleven hundred dollars and, though it has been assumed that Lincoln himself paid the bill, comptroller's records recently discovered in the National Archives show otherwise. Even before her return, an article appeared in the Philadelphia *Sunday Dispatch*, written by the paper's New York correspondent. The reporter had apparently followed Mrs. Lincoln from store to store and talked with the clerks. His description of her purchases, served up to the public seasoned with sarcasm, read in part:

> "Mrs. President Lincoln," as the ladies call her, was shopping to a considerable extent in this city in the early part of the week. She has evidently no comprehension that Jeff. Davis will make good his threat to occupy the White House in July for she is expending thousands and thousands of dollars for articles of luxurious taste in the household way that it would be very preposterous for her to use out in her rural home in Illinois. The silver plate from Houghwout [sic], and the china services from the same . . . will admirably suit the mulberry-colored livery of her footmen . . . and possibly may help very nicely to get rid of the apparently exhaustless $25,000 a year salary of Mr. Lincoln. So may the elegant black point lace shawls she bought at Stewart's for $650 each, and the real camel's hair cashmere at $1,000. . . . Let me do Mrs. Lincoln the justice to say that she was dreadfully importuned to enter into extravagances of various kinds; but I heard her, myself, observe at Stewart's that she could not afford it, and was "determined to be very economical." One thousand dollars for a shawl was quite as high as her sense of economy would permit her to go in these excessive hard times! [3]

During her first year in the White House Mary Lincoln bought bell-pulls, brocades, and books; she acquired handsome draperies,

[3] This article appeared on May 30, 1861, in the Columbus, Ohio, newspaper, *The Crisis*, edited by Samuel Medary, who reprinted it from the Philadelphia *Sunday Dispatch*. It was published in *Lincoln Lore*, No. 1492 (June 1962).

ornately carved furniture, custom-made carpets and wallcoverings. Back and forth to New York and Philadelphia she went, in an orgy of spending, paying top prices for everything. On the heels of her purchases came expenditures for cleaning, repair, and modernization of the Executive Mansion. Windows were washed, floors polished, rooms painted. Potomac water soon flowed through taps, furnaces supplanted fires, candles gave way to gaslight in every room. Inevitably the day dawned when she discovered, in something close to panic, that the $20,000 appropriation had been exceeded by $6,700, most of it owed a Philadelphia wallpaper firm.

She hastily dispatched Major Benjamin Brown French, appointed Commissioner of Public Buildings in December 1861, to plead her case with the President, since she herself could not bear to face him. In a letter to his sister-in-law, French recalled Mrs. Lincoln's desperate plea that he tell her husband "that it is common to overrun appropriations—tell him how *much* it costs to refurnish he does not know much about it, he says he will pay it out of his own pocket (tears) you know, Major, he cannot afford that . . . . you must get me out of this difficulty, it is the last . . . *but* do not let him know you have seen me."

Mary Lincoln had just cause to shrink from her husband's wrath, which the Commissioner recalled as terrible indeed. Lincoln refused to authorize an additional appropriation to meet the deficiency, telling French, "It can never have my approval—I'll pay it out of my pocket first—it would stink in the nostrils of the American people to have it said that the President of the United States had approved a bill overrunning an appropriation of $20,000 for *flub dubs*, for this damned old house, when the soldiers cannot have blankets." The man who was born in a dirt-floored cabin was honestly bewildered. "The house was furnished well enough," he said, "better than any one we ever lived in. . . ." [4] Congress eventually settled the question by burying the additional appropriation in the next year's budget, and the issue was, for the moment, resolved. But in the end it was the very people Mary Lincoln desired to impress who were the loudest in criticizing her extravagance.

[4] Benjamin Brown French to Pamela French, December 24, 1861. MS. in the Library of Congress.

To Mary Brayman

June 17th [1861]
Executive Mansion

My Dear Mrs Brayman:

Your note, was received a day or two since. I submitted it to Mr Lincoln, with accompanying letters, from what he has said, I presume, the appointment will be made.[5] I trust your health is good this season, I hope if you visit the East, this summer you will take Washington, en route. Mrs Baillache [sic][6] & boy, are they well? Mrs B- looked delicate, when I last saw her. In N. York, I procured an excellent dressing maid & seamstress, the girl Ellen, whom I brought from S- is not expert with her needle, or does not understand arranging or dressing a lady. Yet she is the most reliable, truthful, kind hearted girl about children, I have ever known. As I have procured a girl, who will be more *necessary* to me at present, and as she [Ellen] will return home soon, I would recommend her to Mrs Baillache, as nurse—She is so kind I dislike to part with her, now as my boys, have grown too large, to require a nurse. We brought a man, with us, who takes care of them, most of the time. I was grieved to hear of Mrs McClernand's death—Her friends & orphan children, will never cease to miss her. With kind regards to all, I remain ever your friend

Mary Lincoln

[5] Probably the appointment of Mrs. Brayman's son-in-law, William H. Bailhache, as a quartermaster in Springfield. Bailhache, partner of Edward Lewis Baker as proprietor and editor of the *Illinois State Journal*, would in 1863 be accused of gaining financially as a result of his quartermaster's position. Mrs. Lincoln's brother-in-law, Ninian W. Edwards, appointed to the commissary, was accused and dismissed along with Bailhache.
[6] Ada (Mrs. William H.) Bailhache, the Braymans' daughter.

To John Fry [7]

Executive Mansion
June 20, 1861

My Dear Sir:

It gives me great pleasure to be the medium of transmission of these weapons,[8] to be used in the defense of national sovereignty upon the soil of Kentucky.

Though some years have passed since I left my native State, I have never ceased to contemplate her progress in happiness and prosperity with sentiments of fond and filial pride. In every effort of industrial energy, in every enterprise of honor and valor my heart has been with her. And I rejoice in the consciousness that, at this time, when the institutions to whose fostering care we owe all we have of happiness and glory are rudely assailed by ungrateful and paricidal hands, the State of Kentucky, ever true and loyal, furnishes to the insulted flag of the Union a guard of her best and bravest sons. On every field the prowess of the Kentuckians has been manifested. In the holy cause of national defense they must be invincible.

Please accept, sir, these weapons as a token of the love I shall never cease to cherish for my mother State, of the pride with which I have always regarded the exploits of her sons, and the confidence which I feel in the ultimate loyalty of her people, who, while never forgetting the homage which their beloved State may justly claim, still remember the higher and grander allegiance due to our common country.[9]

Yours, very sincerely,
Mary Lincoln

[7] A colonel from Boyle County, Kentucky.
[8] Three days earlier, Lincoln had written Secretary of War Cameron, asking that he furnish a pair of navy revolvers and a sabre so that "Mrs L. can send them with her compliments. Mr Fry is an acquaintance of hers and a good and brave man." MS. in the Illinois State Historical Library, Springfield.
[9] The editors have been unable to locate the original of this letter, but the smoothness of its style indicates that it was either written out for Mrs. Lincoln's signature or edited for publication.

No matter how determinedly Mary Lincoln busied herself with her children, her social responsibilities, and the adornment of her home and person, the tragic fact of war began to press in on her. Ironically enough, the first major casualty of the conflict was one which touched her and her family directly. On May 24, 1861, before a single massive engagement had taken place, Colonel Elmer E. Ellsworth, the gallant young commander of the Fire Zouaves, was killed in the act of hauling down a Confederate flag flying over a tavern in Alexandria. Ellsworth had read law for a short time in Lincoln's Springfield office and had ridden the train to Washington as military escort. There he had become so much a part of the family he had caught the measles from Willie and Tad. The body of the young hero was brought to the East Room to lie in state. A military funeral followed, after which the bloodstained flag that had wrapped itself around Ellsworth's feet as he fell was presented to Mrs. Lincoln. She immediately had it put out of sight.

On July 11 she pleaded with Hannah Shearer to come to Washington, or at least to join her in a trip to the fashionable seaside resort of Long Branch, New Jersey. She was especially anxious that her friend, who was expecting a child, have a long, relaxing visit in Washington; her own desperate hunger for companionship can be read into every line of her letters. Mrs. Shearer was never able to come to the White House. Ten days after Mrs. Lincoln's letter was written, the first Battle of Bull Run resulted in a demoralizing defeat for the Union Army. The North was shocked into an awareness of its vulnerability. The sound of cannon was heard in the streets of Washington, and the sight of ambulances bringing in the wounded in steady streams carried with it the dread that the city was in imminent danger of invasion.

"I have passed through so much excitement," wrote Mary Lincoln to Mrs. Shearer on August 1, "that a change, is absolutely necessary." Although she longed to escape from the fear and frustration which stifled the capital as oppressively as the swampy summer heat, she could not leave until after the visit of Prince Jerome

Napoleon of France. At that time, when the chance of foreign intervention on the side of the Confederacy was a clear threat, Jerome's visit was of particular importance: he was a cousin of the Emperor of France.

Here was a moment of high drama for Mary Lincoln, who always thrilled at the presence of royalty, even of the Bonaparte variety. On the night of the official dinner she entered the State Dining Room on the arm of the Prince and practiced her French on him most of the evening. The grand occasion was not without its unhappy consequences, however, for there was considerable carping about the amount of money a wartime government had spent amusing Jerome. Even in her widowhood Mrs. Lincoln would not be allowed to forget it.

On August 13 she finally departed Washington, with Willie, Tad, Mrs. Grimsley (who would soon go home to Springfield), and her husband's secretary John George Nicolay in her entourage. Mrs. Shearer and her sons joined the party in Philadelphia and went on with them to New York, where an enterprising reporter picked up their trail and followed them to Long Branch, sending back gushing accounts of Mrs. Lincoln's dress, baggage, accommodations, and social activities. Each public occasion was minutely described, from her inspection of a life-saving station with former New Jersey governor William A. Newell to her attendance at a "grand hop" in her honor that evening. Afterwards she returned to New York for more shopping, and Robert came down from Cambridge to join her. From there the group traveled to upstate New York for a courtesy call on the Sewards in Auburn and stops at Saratoga and Niagara, returning to Washington during the first week of September.

To Hannah Shearer

July 11th 61.
Executive Mansion

My Dear Friend,

After your long silence, I regret to receive a letter stating that you cannot make "the promised visit." I am now sitting down, to explain to you, why you *must* keep your word, & what a *quiet*, comfortable time, you will have, by so doing. In the first place, there is no place in the country, so safe & well guarded as Washington. No matter what your state or feelings are, you will have a pleasant time. We expect to go out to the "Soldier's Home" [1] a very beautiful place 2½ miles, from this, in about three weeks. We will ride into the city every day, & can be as secluded, as we please.

I have a proposal to make to you, we expect to visit Long Branch," to remain a week or ten days, about the last of the present month. We have invitations from three different hotels, with suites of rooms, offered us in each, if you are not well, sea bathing, will be beneficial to you. We have railroad passes, and the trip will cost nothing, which is a good deal to us all these times. How I want you to lay all difficulties aside, join us at Philadelphia. We will let you know the exact time, and make a visit to L.B. We go on to New York, and pass a day, going & returning.

Mrs Grimsley, is still with me, & will accompany us to Long B., but will leave us at New York, for home. From Long Branch, you must return with me to W. & pass a month or two. You will certainly gratify me in this. Bring your boys with you, it will be more pleasant all around. I am going to take my boys, with me, with a servant man, who will take charge, of your children also. Remember I claim you for two months. Do not disappoint me. You shall be kept perfectly quiet. Mrs Grimsley you will love very much. She is very anxious, to have you join us. It will give you strength, for a year to come. We go to the sea shore, to be perfectly quiet. We are invited, to bring any friend with us, we desire, and there is no one I am so anxious to see, as your dear self. If you are not well, my word for it, you can always keep yourself, as quiet as you wish.

I feel that I must have you with me. I wish, I could hand you over the magnificent bouquet, just sent me, the magnolia is superb. We have the most beautiful flowers & grounds imaginable, and company & excitement enough, to turn a wiser head than my own. But when Congress adjourns, and we go out to our retreat, we

[1] Each summer the Lincolns made their residence at the Anderson Cottage on the grounds of the Retired Soldiers' Home at what is now Upshur Street and Rock Creek Road, N.W.

will be quiet enough. There are so many lovely drives around W. and we have only *three* carriages, at our command.

I want you to write, directly you receive this. If you love me, give me a favorable answer. I have set my heart on having you with me,

With kind regards to the Dr & boys I remain ever

Your attached friend,
Mary Lincoln

P.S. I have had quite a variety of letter paper & note, with your initials embossed on it, but have as yet, met with no opportunity of sending it.

To The Cambridge (Mass.) Telegraph Office

[TELEGRAM] [2]   *July* [18?] *1861*

Mrs Lincoln is very much alarmed, has her trunks packed to leave.[3] Did you receive message for Robert T. Lincoln of this morning. Why no answer—

To Hannah Shearer

August 1st [1861]
Executive Mansion

My Dear Friend.

For some days past, I have tried to get a moments leisure to answer your letter, you can scarcely imagine how I am pressed for time.

[2] Not in Mrs. Lincoln's handwriting.
[3] This telegram, which bears no day of the month, might have been Mrs. Lincoln's initial frightened reaction to the defeat at Bull Run; more likely, she was reacting to Robert's July 17 wire to his father saying he had the mumps.

This day week, the 8th of Aug. we leave here, for New York. I want you to meet us at the Philadelphia depot that day. You must not fail me. I have passed through so much excitement, that a change is absolutely necessary. The Prince & suite are expected in Washington & on Saturday, we dine them at *8 o'clock* P. M. Very different *from home*. We only have to give our orders for the dinner, and *dress* in proper season. I will take no refusal from you. We remain a day or two in New York, in passing through. I think it probable I may take my boys. If I do not, and you desire it, you could leave your boys in Brooklyn, until our return from the branch. We would be pleased to have them with us, and I am determined to bring you all home with me. The boys would enjoy it here. Answer immediately.

Ever your attached friend

Mary Lincoln

From her first exposure to her sister Elizabeth's lively Coterie in Springfield, Mary Lincoln had relished all forms of social activity. Even before she became mistress of the White House she was well known as an accomplished hostess. Now, in addition to her regular Saturday receptions, her evening levees, and official dinners, she would frequently entertain at small private gatherings in the Executive Mansion or at the Soldiers' Home, the presidential summer retreat northwest of the city. Sometimes her guests were politicians or generals with whom Lincoln wished to speak informally; more often they were good, old friends who could be counted on to make the President laugh and reminisce. But when the cares of office kept him at his desk far into the night, Mrs. Lincoln was left to her own devices socially. In time she managed to assemble in her Blue Room a salon of sorts, into which drifted such noted personages as Senators Charles Sumner and Ira Harris; Assistant Navy Secretary Fox and former Governor Newell of New Jersey called often with their wives, and the poet-journalist N. P. Willis was often present to lend the gatherings a literary tone.

But at the core of her new coterie were gentlemen of quite a different stamp, some of whose past histories would have horrified her Springfield friends and perhaps herself as well not a year before. Ladies of good family and those in the public eye customarily avoided persons who had about them the faintest breath of notoriety, who were too much of the world. Though Mary Lincoln was quick to impugn the "morals" of those whom she did not like, she ignored the fact that many of her new companions were somewhat deficient in that area. If a man, once granted entrée to the White House, flattered and made much of her, brought her gifts, amused her with anecdotes and choice morsels of gossip, she accepted him without question in her circle. In common with many another sheltered Victorian female, she had an insatiable curiosity about the fashionable world. This, together with her need for amusement and an earthy streak in her nature, drew her to quick-witted, irreverent people, and to the informed malice that was their stock in trade.

There is a similar ring to descriptions of some of the men who were her favorites. One of these was a charming international adventurer named Henry Wikoff, who, after insinuating himself into her confidence, sent a stream of "inside" reports to the New York *Herald*, which had hired him for the purpose. In a day when the methods of the press were frequently unethical, "Chevalier" Wikoff, as he styled himself, excelled at his assignment. In December of 1861 parts of Lincoln's forthcoming annual message to Congress were published prematurely in his paper; only after his arrest did he confess to having obtained secret information. After his release he was forbidden the White House on Lincoln's order, but not before Mrs. Lincoln had innocently suffered implication in the affair. Later she would laugh about Wikoff, for he was fun while he lasted. The nature of his appeal was delineated by the publisher-politician John W. Forney, who knew him well: "Ranging through all society, he can talk of love, law, literature and war . . . can gossip of courts and cabinets, of the *boudoir* and the *salon*, of commerce and the Church . . . of Dickens and Thackeray . . . of Lincoln and Stanton, of Buchanan and Pierce, of the North and the

South, of the opera and the theatre, of General Sickles and Tam-
many Hall. . . ." [4]

Dan Sickles, Wikoff's close friend and another of Mrs. Lincoln's "courtiers," had as a congressman been the central figure
in a scandal that had rocked Washington society during Buchanan's
administration. Sickles' young wife Teresa, bored and unhappy
due to his frequent absences and flagrant womanizing, had taken
a lover, Philip Barton Key. When Sickles learned of the affair he
shot Key dead in ambush; he was acquitted of murder, it was said,
only because of his influence with the President. Even after he became a general, Sickles remained a flamboyant, faintly disreputable
figure who was, nonetheless, according to a biographer, "a diverting companion, a man of easy charm and ready conversation that
rippled with theatrical allusion and humorous anecdote." [5]

Another frequent White House caller was Oliver S. Halsted,
Jr. A number of Mrs. Lincoln's letters to him came to light in the
mid-1950's; before that, a note in her hand to a "Mr Halstead"
was assumed to have been written to the journalist Murat Halstead;
the new letters change the picture entirely. "Pet" Halsted was
the black sheep of a prominent New Jersey family, a graduate of
Princeton. During his youth he had acquired a fondness for questionable company and a skill at persuasion that would in wartime
make him an effective lobbyist for munitions manufacturers. "No
public character was so well known in Washington as he," wrote
a correspondent for the New York *Tribune*. "His was a swagger
that was more than magnificent. He went everywhere, knew every-
body, and cut a large figure in social as well as political life. There
was nothing he did not know—nothing he could not do. There were
no bounds to his ambition. . . ." More to the point, in Mrs. Lincoln's case, was the fact that Halsted was "lavish in his expendi-
ture and as generous as a prince, when he had money." [6]

Mrs. Lincoln delighted in the company of her new friends,
basked in their attention, and praised them to her husband. Later
she would learn to her grief that such persons were notoriously
unreliable, "summer friends" who were happy to amuse the Presi-

---

[4] John W. Forney. *Anecdotes of Public Men*. New York, 1877, p. 367.
[5] W. A. Swanberg. *Sickles the Incredible*. New York, 1956, p. 242.
[6] Quoted in Robert V. Bruce. *Lincoln and the Tools of War*. Indianapolis and
New York, 1956, p. 231.

dent's lady, happy to exchange favors with her, but were of scant consolation to a lonely widow, shorn of influence and desperate for money.

One of Mary Lincoln's most serious areas of difficulty, both in her Washington years and later on, sprang from an essentially egalitarian impulse. She developed the habit of confiding in servants, entrusting them with her secrets, sending them on confidential errands, exacting personal favors which put her under obligation to people whose loyalty could not always be tested. Mary Ann Cuthbert, housekeeper at the Executive Mansion, Thomas Stackpole, an engineer on the staff, and Edward McManus, chief doorkeeper, were among those who served the President's wife in a private as well as an official capacity, and as a result acquired a hold over her. Even her dressmaker and trusted friend Elizabeth Keckley would, from motives more misguided than malicious, betray her in the end.

Her ordinarily shrewd grasp of human nature seemed to fall away in the face of flattery, leaving her vulnerable to anyone who combined a facile tongue with a knowledge of her weakness. One such individual was John Watt, who had been head groundskeeper at the White House for some years before the Lincolns arrived and had already been accused of everything from padding expense accounts to forging payrolls. Watt immediately took Mrs. Lincoln's measure, finding that her poise and authoritative air masked a profound insecurity. She talked a good deal of money, but the only thing she seemed to know about it was how to spend it. Watt succeeded so well in winning her confidence that in time she was revealing her financial difficulties to him. She was probably most interested to learn that there was a way of juggling accounts so that funds paid out for one purpose could be charged to another and no one the wiser. Soon she was accepting Watt's judgments of White House personnel and using her influence to have his enemies dismissed. These machinations were not lost on Lincoln's two secretaries, Hay and Nicolay, and John Hay in particular turned against Mary Lincoln because of them. (Hay's private name for President Lincoln was "the Tycoon"; for Mrs. Lincoln, "the Hellcat.")

However misguided her loyalty to Watt, Mary Lincoln went

to extravagant (and dangerous) lengths to protect him from his own indiscretions. Somehow her defense of him became inextricably bound up with her hatred for a gentleman named William S. Wood. Wood, a friend and protégé of William Seward, had been delegated to arrange the Lincolns' train journey from Springfield to Washington and had accompanied them on the trip. At Mrs. Lincoln's urging he had been named to the post of Commissioner of Public Buildings, pending confirmation by the Senate.[7] Her interest in the appointment was natural, for whoever held the post would come into regular contact with her in matters dealing with the furnishing and renovation of the White House, and she cherished grandiose plans in that direction. In his capacity as Commissioner, Wood had escorted her on her May shopping expedition to New York. The fact that the Commissioner had to approve all purchases for the White House legitimized Wood's presence, but that did not stop tongues from wagging over his travels with Mrs. Lincoln.

Perhaps some of this gossip reached her and threw her into a panic; perhaps Wood's failure to be confirmed (on grounds of a conflict of interest) and his association with Seward, whom she detested, caused her to turn against him; he might have taken liberties with her confidence. Whatever the reason, by September of 1861 her loathing for the man knew no bounds. When Wood set out on a campaign to expose John Watt, she wrote a series of letters in defense of her employee; in nearly every one she lit into Wood in terms that were nothing short of slanderous.

Watt, like Wikoff, was out of the White House by February of 1862; it was he who had given the "Chevalier" the advance wording of Lincoln's speech. There were later tales of Watt's attempting to blackmail the President by demanding twenty thousand dollars for three letters written by Mrs. Lincoln; he was supposedly bought off cheaply with the threat of imprisonment. Charges that Watt was a secret secessionist, so vigorously denied by Mary Lincoln, may have been true; it is more likely that he was simply a scoundrel with his eye on the main chance.

Lincoln's enemies, of all persuasions, decided early that his wife was his Achilles heel. They played up every rumor concerning her for all it was worth, including one that she herself was a Rebel

[7] Mary Lincoln to Ward Hill Lamon, April [11, 1861].

sympathizer—perhaps a Rebel *spy*—the most vicious and far-fetched accusation of all. Much of the talk spread among people who had never even met her, and the stories were magnified as they descended from second to third hand. Mary Lincoln had faults in plenty, some of a serious and disturbing nature, but her loyalty to her husband and to the Union were the strongest forces in her life. Nonetheless both the Democratic and abolitionist press attacked her and made fun of her. Extravagance soon became "stealing," indiscretion became "treason," and innocent friendships with other men became something too shocking to mention. William O. Stoddard, who acted as her personal secretary and smoothed her path in many ways, described Washington society as "a jury empaneled to convict on every count of every indictment which any slanderous tongue may bring against her." He could not understand it. "As you look at her and talk with her, the fact that she has so many enemies strikes you as one of the moral curiosities of this venomous time, for she has never in any way harmed one of the men and women who are so recklessly assailing her." [8]

If Mary Lincoln ever "harmed" anyone, it was for no other end than to protect herself, her husband, her country, or those to whom, on whatever basis, she had reason to be loyal. Unhappily, she could give criticism more easily than she could take it; as she wrote James Gordon Bennett, her nature was "very sensitive." Whether the criticism came from family, friend, or foe, that same sharp sensitivity often caused her to retaliate with a flood of innuendo or invective that at its worst could match anything directed at her.

To Caleb B. Smith

Sept. 8th [1861]
Executive Mansion

Dear Sir:

You will kindly excuse me for troubling you, but I much regret that Mr Wood still pursues the attack, and tries to bring the

[8] William O. Stoddard. *Inside the White House in War Times.* New York, 1890, p. 52.

charge of dishonesty upon Mr Watts [sic] who in all his accounts with us, has been rigidly exact. Circumstances have proved, that Mr Wood, is the last man, who should bring a charge against any one, very especially against one, who has been tried & always proven exact in his dealings. From remarks made by eyewitnesses, in reference to Wood, he is either deranged or drinking. Many testify, that he is acting very strangely, & as he is *now known*, not to be the right man,[9] he is trying to place, a just man on a level with himself. Major French,[1] who has long known Mr Watts, will bear testimony to his good name—I heard much of Wood, in N. York—and all agree that he is not a good man—He is bitterly disappointed, that we read him aright & that he is displaced—and is *capable* of saying any thing against those who tried to befriend him—when he was so undeserving.

I remain very sincerely your friend
Mary Lincoln

[*To Oliver S. Halsted, Jr.?*] [2]

[*September 9, 1861*] [3]

I fancy the "blue room," will look dreary this evening, so if you and the Gov.[4] are disengaged, wander up & see us—I want to become accustomed to *vast solitude* by degrees. The paper is ready for your notice—Bring the Gov with you

Truly your friend
Mary Lincoln

[9] A reference to Wood's rejection by the Senate.

[1] Benjamin Brown French of New Hampshire, who would succeed Wood as Commissioner of Public Buildings, had held the post during the Pierce administration.

[2] On the basis of subsequent correspondence, there is reason to believe that this note was sent to Oliver S. Halsted, Jr. The reference to the "paper" indicates that the call was not purely social.

[3] This letter was given its tentative date by Clyde C. Walton, former Illinois State Historian.

[4] "The Gov" in this case might have been William A. Newell, former governor of New Jersey, who frequently accompanied Halsted on his visits to the White House.

To Simon Cameron

Sept. 12, 1861
Executive Mansion

Dear Sir:

Will you allow me to thank you, for your kindness, in making the appointment in Major Watts [sic] case,[5] instead of infantry he preferred cavalry, and in order to be attached to the [White] house. This is an especial request & if you would make it out in writing this morning, the kindness will always be remembered. I have heard some strange things as coming from *Woods* [sic]. Will you allow Mr Watts—to explain to you. We understand he [Wood] has been making some false charges against Mr W, his reputation has become so well established, we feel particularly grateful, he will no longer mortify us. May I rely on you, in settling Major Watt's business this morning & oblige yours very respectfully,

Mary Lincoln

To John F. Potter [6]

Sept 13th [1861]
Executive Mansion

Mr Potter:

I am very much surprised to hear that a letter has been received in the Commissioner's office—charging Major Watts as a Secessionist. I know him to be a Union man, & have many oppor-

[5] In August of 1861, John Watt was awarded a lieutenant's commission which was later revoked following charges of disloyalty. In 1863, he re-enlisted as a private. Nearly thirty years later Watt would write Cameron, asking for a recommendation. "You know very well," he declared, "what difficulties I had to contend with in regard to Mrs. Lincoln. . . . I paid about $700.00 for Mrs. Lincoln on one trip to Cambridge, Mass." Excerpts published in catalogue of Howard S. Mott, Sheffield, Mass., no date. Item 191.
[6] Representative from Wisconsin and chairman of a House committee investigating disloyalty in the government departments.

tunities of hearing of & judging him. The day after the battle of Manassas, I never saw a more troubled man. The charge originates in a tool of Woods [sic], who is now proved to be a very bad man, to my own knowledge, who does not know, what *truth* means, all hands, acknowledge Woods to be a most unprincipled man, so much so, that the President, to save his family from disgrace— When the Senate *would not* confirm him, [re]nominated him until the 1st of Sep. with a promise from him, he would resign. Knowing Mr Watts, found out much about *him*, when he was in office— he supposes Watts, was one of the means of his removal—and employs men, to bring false charges against him—This man, who has brought charges against Watts—brought a piano to this house, and *is* closely allied to Woods—which does not say much for him —The charge is false, many can prove to the contrary—There is no better Union man, that [than] Watts, & no one who has a greater contempt for Jeff Davis—

Yours sincerely
Mary Lincoln

To Elizabeth Todd Grimsley

Sept. 29th '61
Executive Mansion

My dear Lizzie:

I have been intending writing you for some days. I have been quite sick with *chills* for some days, this is *my day of rest*, so I am sitting up—I am beginning to feel very weak. If they cannot be broken in a few days, Mr Lincoln wants me to go North, & remain until cold weather—Where so much is demanded of me— I cannot afford to be delicate, if a different climate will restore my health—If at the close of this week, I am still sick, I expect I will go up to Boston, take quarters at the *Revere House* for two or three weeks—& return here in November. I trust however, I may not be under the necessity, yet I am feeling *very far* from well—September and early in Oct—are always considered unhealthy months here

—my racked frame certainly bears evidence to the fact. Have just received a note from Willis [7]—with all his weaknesses—he is kind hearted. Gov Newell & Halstead [sic] are frequently here *as who is not?* I presume you are aware, your brother is elected to Congress.[8] I received a letter from *Elizabeth* E[dwards] the other day—very kind and aff yet very *characteristic*—said if *rents* and means permitted, she would like to make us a visit I believe for a season— I am weary of *intrigue*, when she is by herself she can be very agreeable, especially when her mind is not dwelling on the merits of fair daughters & a talented son in law, such personages always *speak for themselves.* I often regret E. P. E. little *weaknesses*, after all, since the *election* she is the only one of my sisters who has appeared to be pleased with our advancement—you know this to be so—Notwithstanding Dr W- has received his portion, in life, from the Administration,[9] yet Frances always remains *quiet.* E. in her letter said—Frances often spoke of *Mr L's* kindness—in giving him his place. She little knows, what a hard battle, *I* had for it—and how near, he came getting *nothing.* Poor *unfortunate* Ann, inasmuch as she possesses such a miserable disposition & so false a tongue—How far dear Lizzie, are we removed, from such a person. Even if Smith, succeeds in being a rich man, what advantage will it be to him, who has gained it in *some cases* most unjustly, and with such a woman, whom no one respects, whose tongue for so many years, has been considered "no slander"—and as a child & young girl, could not be outdone in falsehood—"Truly the Leopard cannot change his spots" —*She* is so seldom in my thoughts I have so much more, that is attractive, both in *bodily* presence, & my mind's eye, to interest me. I grieve for those, who have to come in contact with her malice, yet even *that*, is so well understood, the object of *her wrath*, generally rises, with good people, in proportion to her *vindictiveness.* What *will you name*, the *hill* on which *I* must be placed. *Her*, putting it on *that* ground with Mrs Brown, was only to hide her envious feeling toward you. Tell Ann for me, to quote her own expression, *She*

[7] Nathaniel P. Willis, poet and editor of the popular magazine *Home Journal* (which later became *Town & Country*) was one of the most consistent of Mrs. Lincoln's "courtiers."

[8] John B. S. Todd, a brigadier general in command of Missouri troops, took a leave of absence from the army to stand for election as delegate to Congress from the Dakota Territory.

[9] Mrs. Lincoln's brother-in-law, William S. Wallace, who had suffered financial difficulties, was appointed by Lincoln a local paymaster of volunteers.

is becoming still further removed from "Queen Victoria's Court"—How foolish between us to be discussing, such a person. Yet really it is amusing, in how many forms, human nature can appear before us—*Nicolay* told me, that Caleb Smith, said to him, a few days since that he had just received a letter from Kellogg—of Cin- that he did not know why he had *not* received his appointment as *Consul*—Is not the idea preposterous? Did I tell you that *"Hollis"* [unidentified] has been here, came to see me frequently, and always enquired with much interest, after you—The "Cap" [unidentified] also dined here, a few days since, still as refined and elegant as ever —I have so much to tell you, I do not know, what first to write about. *Wykoff* [sic], the "Chevalier," enlightened me about Baker's & Julia's proceedings in New York in Feb- Looked a little quizzical, about her not remaining in W- as she had expected a long stay and much gayety—Did you say, she only numbered 5 *months*—I thought she had *gently insinuated* when she was here—Hill Lamon, I believe is now in *Ill.* mustering recruits—I know you will be sorry to hear, that our colored Mantuamaker, Elizabeth,[1] lost her only son & child in the battle of Lex Mo- She is heart broken. She is a very remarkable woman herself—The weather is so beautiful, why is it, that we cannot feel well. The air feels very much like the *early days*—when I used to have chills in Ill- those days have passed & I know I have no cause to grieve over my lot—If the country, was only peaceful, all would be well. If I thought, sending your Father, a pass, would bring him here, I would do so with pleasure. Give my best love to them both. Mrs Don[n] Piatt,[2] calls here in an hour's time. I must mount my white Cachemere & receive her—We now occupy the stately guest room—She spoke last winter of the miserably furnished rooms. I think she will be astonished at the change—I am not well enough to go down—Write very soon—very often to—

> your attached cousin—
>
> Mary Lincoln

William[3] has given me $3.00 to hand you—I will have it in bill shape, to send you in a few days, when I write next—Strange he called upon you.

---

[1] Elizabeth Keckley. Her unique relationship with Mrs. Lincoln is discussed on pp. 112–13.

[2] Wife of a prominent Ohio journalist and lawyer-politician. The Piatts had accompanied the Lincolns to Washington on the presidential train.

[3] Probably William Slade, Lincoln's Negro valet.

To Thomas A. Scott [4]

Executive Mansion
Oct 3d 61

Col Scott:

A friend of mine, has written me from Kentucky, that he himself has, from 500 to 1000 of the finest young Ky horses, he is a good Union man & wishes to dispose of them to the Government, at Gov- prices. If you could favor me with the authority to Major [J. W.] Belger, Quarter Master [of U.S. Volunteers] at Baltimore, to buy the horses at government prices, subject to Government inspection, I would be much obliged to you. Being a native of Kentucky, it would be a great pride to me, to know that this selection had been made. I ask this as an especial favor. Lieut Watts, is going to Baltimore this evening, and it would give me great pleasure, if he could hand the order to Major Belger—In the battle for the Union, it would gratify me, to see the horses used, from my native state. Hoping I will receive a favorable answer, I remain

yours very sincerely
Mary Lincoln.

To Montgomery Meigs [5]

Oct 4th 61
Executive Mansion

Gen Meigs:

I wrote Col Scott,[6] not knowing that you had the contract about horses. I made an especial request, & the *only one*, I *have* ever *made* of you, to be kind enough to authorize Major Belger, to purchase

---

[4] Vice-president of the Pennsylvania Railroad, appointed Assistant Secretary of War by Cameron in 1861.

[5] Shortly before this letter was written, Brigadier General Meigs had been appointed U.S. Quartermaster General.

[6] See preceding letter.

500 or 1000 young Ky horses, belonging to an especial friend of mine in Ky- a strong Union man. It would be a particular pleasure to me to have, as Kentucky is my native state—some horses from there on the battle field—May I hope, as this is the only request, I have asked of you, or ever again that you will grant it?

Very Respectfully

Mrs A. Lincoln

Please answer immediately.

To Hannah Shearer

Oct 6th 61

Executive Mansion

My Dear Mrs Shearer:

I had scarcely supposed, that so long a time would elapse, ere I should have written you, but indisposition has prevented me. For the last ten days, I have been sick with chills, am now beginning, to feel better—I am pleased to hear that you reached home in safety, I felt quite anxious to hear from you. The weather has again become quite warm, & so dusty, there is no comfort in riding—We will welcome cool weather, *dust*, I presume we will never be freed from, until *mud*, takes its place—We are as far removed, as ever on this eastern shore, it appears, *from war*—If we could accomplish our purpose without, resorting to arms & bloodshed, how comfortable, it would be—But that is impossible. Mr Lincoln, has gone out to day, to pay a visit to Gen Banks [7]—Our friends Gov Newell, Halstead, && are generally about here—The diplomatic corps, have returned to the city, quite a number of strangers are daily coming in & our "blue room," in the evenings, is quite alive with the "beau-monde"—Gen McClellan [8] has just sent me in, a box of grapes from

[7] Major General Nathaniel P. Banks, a former congressman and governor of Massachusetts, at this time had command of the Department of Annapolis. He was conferring with Lincoln at the encampment of the 19th New York Regiment near Rockville, Maryland.

[8] Major General George Brinton McClellan, commander of the Army of the Potomac.

Cin- They are delicious. I wish you were here, to share them with me—I often receive delightful fruit from New Jersey. Do write me, & tell me how you are coming on—You have so much more leisure, than I have, why do you not write? I want to hear, all about yourself—When *any thing* happens, make the Dr write—I send you a few scraps of my dresses, I send you a sample of an evening silk, *lights* up beautifully—to be flounced—I will enjoy it, because it is a variety, *not figured*—Lizzie Grimsley, I frequently hear from —she is well & recovered her trunk some time since—*Hay* [9] has just returned from Ill—When you receive this,—I want you to sit down & write me a long letter—With regards to the Dr & boys, I remain your attached friend

Mary Lincoln

To Carlos E. Farnham [1]

Executive Mansion
October 15th, 1861

My dear Sir:

I owe you an apology, for allowing your kind note to remain so long unanswered. Unavoidable circumstances alone prevented a reply. My own name is "Mary," it would of course greatly gratify me to have one of your little girls called by that name, I think either "Ella" or "Alice," very pretty names. With many wishes, for your welfare & that of your family, I remain

Very respectfully
Mary Lincoln

[9] John Hay, assistant private secretary to the President. Hay, who later collaborated with John G. Nicolay on a celebrated biography of Lincoln, entered the diplomatic service in 1865. As Secretary of State under McKinley and Roosevelt, he was responsible for formidable achievements in foreign policy, including the "Open Door Policy" in China and the negotiations which led to the construction of the Panama Canal.

[1] The father of twin girls, born on the day of Lincoln's first inaugural. His brother, Frederick Farnham of Tunbridge, Vermont, had written Mrs. Lincoln, almost in fun, asking her for permission to name one of his nieces after herself, which prompted the above letter, rather long after the fact.

To W. Hindhaugh & Company [2]

[*October, 1861*]

Gentlemen:

There is no misunderstanding, in the matter, Mr Wood, without any order or unsolicited, had Mr L. measured, for a suit of clothes.[3] Of course, it was not supposed, they were a present from *you*, but Wood mentioned, that they were to be presented to the President—and nothing more was thought of it, until your bill was presented—Mr Wood, was requested to select the summer suit.

I remain very respectfully
Mary Lincoln.

To James Gordon Bennett [4]

Oct 25th 61
Executive Mansion.

Dear Sir:

It is with feelings of more than ordinary gratitude, that I venture to address you, a note, expressive of my thanks for the kind support and consideration, extended towards the Administration,[5] by you, at a time when your powerful influence would be sensibly felt. In the hour of peace, the kind words of a friend are always acceptable, how much more so, when a "man's foes, are those of their own household," when treason and rebellion, threaten

[2] A firm of New York tailors whose business was located in the Fifth Avenue Hotel.

[3] There appears to have been some controversy surrounding the purchase of these garments. On October 16, Mrs. Lincoln wrote Hindhaugh's, "It is now brought to our recollection, that whilst passing through New York last February, that Mr Wood had the President measured for a suit of clothes, unordered and uncalled for as he was well supplied with clothing." (Excerpt published in Parke-Bernet Catalogue, Foster Sale, December 3, 1957. Item 149.) The above letter probably followed.

[4] Influential publisher of the New York *Herald*.

[5] Bennett was hardly a constant administration supporter, but perhaps Mrs. Lincoln believed a little flattery could make him so.

our beloved land, our freedom & rights are invaded and every sacred right, is trampled upon! Clouds and darkness surround us, yet Heaven is just, and the day of triumph will *surely* come, when justice & truth will be vindicated. Our wrongs will be made right, and we will once more, taste the blessings of freedom, of which the degraded rebels, would deprive us.

My own nature is very sensitive; have always tried to secure the best wishes of all, with whom through life, I have been associated; need I repeat to you, my thanks, in my own individual case, when I meet, in the columns of your paper, a kind reply, to some uncalled for attack, upon one so *little desirous* of newspaper notoriety, as my inoffensive self.[6] I trust it may be my good fortune, at some not very distant day, to welcome both Mrs Bennett & yourself to Washington; the President would be equally as much pleased to meet you. With an apology, for so long, trespassing upon your time, I remain, dear Mr Bennett, yours very respectfully

Mary Lincoln

To Caleb B. Smith

Executive Mansion
[*October* 26, *1861*][7]

Dear Sir:

Mr Watts came to me this morning, and asked me if I would address you a note. He says, he will ever be deeply grateful to you,

[6] On October 21, 1861, the *Herald* had published an editorial condemning the Northern press for its attacks on Mrs. Lincoln. As a case in point they reprinted a paragraph from the Springfield (Mass.) *Republican*, which read in part: "Her friends compare Mrs. Lincoln to Queen Elizabeth in her statesmanlike tastes and capabilities. She is by no means a simple, domestic woman. . . . She has ere this made and unmade the political fortunes of men. . . . Nothing escapes her eye. She manages the affairs of the White House (I do not mean State affairs) with ability, and will see to it that the 'old man' does not return to Springfield penniless." The *Herald* replied by praising Mrs. Lincoln's "intelligence, capacity and amiability" and by contrasting her reticence and dignity with the aggressiveness of certain "strong-minded" women of abolitionist connections. The President's wife, declared the *Herald*, was a woman of "remarkable ability and goodness of heart . . . a highly gifted lady." It is no wonder she was pleased.
[7] Date of receipt, as noted on letter.

if you would *to day*, attend to some business, which he says he has spoken to you about. He expresses great friendship & gratitude to you, and if you will *kindly* release him from his present trouble, he promises and I *know will keep his word*, that you will not be embarrassed by him again & will be too happy to serve you henceforth in any way. Very sincerely your friend

Mary Lincoln

If money for White House furnishings came out of the federal till, money for Mrs. Lincoln's clothes did not—and thereby hung a tragic tale. Now that she was the focus of so much attention, she determined to pay whatever price in time and money was required to appear at her best at all times, to live up to her own image of how a President's wife should look. The day after she moved into the White House an acquaintance sent over a mulatto dressmaker and former slave named Elizabeth Keckley, who had once been in the service of no less a personage than Mrs. Jefferson Davis. "I cannot afford to be extravagant," Mrs. Lincoln firmly informed "Lizzie" Keckley at the outset. "We are just from the West, and are poor." [8]

Whenever she suffered pangs of conscience about having spent large sums of money she did not have, the President's wife indulged in petty haggling over price, invariably with those who were in no position to make demands. Perhaps the humiliations of her early married days in Springfield had fostered this growing obsession about poverty; it could have resulted from guilt and a subconscious acknowledgment that there was something wrong about her compulsion to buy, something not quite normal.

Mrs. Keckley understood her client's ambivalence, for she was a woman of rare intuition. She also had the kind of positive personality to which Mrs. Lincoln always responded. As the Presi-

---

[8] Elizabeth Keckley. *Behind the Scenes, or, Thirty Years a Slave and Four Years in the White House.* New York, 1868, p. 85.

dent's wife grew to depend on her "mantuamaker" for advice and support, Mrs. Keckley became her closest female confidante. She was an unobtrusive witness to much that occurred in the family quarters of the White House, and the memoirs she left of her service there provide invaluable source material for historians of the Lincoln marriage.

Mary Lincoln's interest in clothes as well as her penny-pinching proclivities are also evident in the letters she wrote her favorite milliner in New York, "Madame" Ruth Harris. The most elaborate headdress, made to precise specifications, must be ready in no time and must not cost more than $5.00. The letters to Madame Harris crop up all through Mrs. Lincoln's years in Washington. They provide fascinating insight into her skill as a designer, her meticulous attention to changing styles, her awareness of her own best features, and her sureness of taste.

She had a particular penchant for elaborately trimmed, long-trained gowns, cut low enough to show to advantage her rounded shoulders, bosom, and arms. She was incorrigibly vain, and nothing pleased her more than to be complimented on her appearance—especially by her husband, to whom she would often present herself, dressed for a splendid occasion, in hopes of an approving comment. On one such evening Lincoln's eyes traveled with a mixture of appreciation and chagrin from his wife's striking décolletage to her trailing satin skirt. "Whew!" he exclaimed, "Our cat has a long tail tonight," adding, in that gently teasing manner he invariably adopted when dealing with his wife's lesser foibles, "Mother, it is my opinion, if some of that tail were nearer the head, it would be in better style." [9]

She ignored the remark, for she felt he knew nothing of "style." Neither did those who called her overdressed, underdressed, too girlishly dressed. A correspondent for *Frank Leslie's Illustrated Newspaper*, in describing a gala White House reception, bestowed upon Mrs. Lincoln the sort of gushing praise she adored receiving, all the more as it came so seldom:

> She was attired in a lustrous white satin robe, with a train a
> yard in length, trimmed with one deep flounce of the richest black
> Chantilly lace. . . . The dress was, of course, décolleté and with

[9] Keckley, p. 101.

short sleeves, displaying the exquisitely moulded shoulders and arms of our fair "Republican Queen". . . . Her headdress was a coronet wreath of black and white crêpe myrtle, which was in perfect keeping with her regal style of beauty. Let us here add, *en passant*, that Mrs. Lincoln possesses that rare beauty which has rendered the Empress of the French so celebrated as a handsome woman.[1]

The eye of the beholder made all the difference, and none was more jaundiced than that of James W. Nesmith, a crusty senator from Oregon who returned from the same reception and sputtered in a letter to his wife, "The weak minded Mrs. Lincoln had *her bosom* on exhibition, and a flower-pot on her head, while there was a train of silk, or satin draging on the floor behind her. . . . I could not help regretting that she had degenerated from the industrious and unpretending woman that she *was* in the days when she used to cook old Abes dinner and milk the cows with her own hands."[2]

A more balanced and personal view came from the President himself. Once, at a reception, he stood watching his wife at a distance, as she moved from group to group, her manner almost regal in its blend of dignity, poise, and the simple warmth designed to put people at their ease in formal situations. Turning to a woman at his side, the President said with unmistakable pleasure, "My wife is as handsome as when she was a girl, and I, a poor nobody then, fell in love with her; and what is more, I have never fallen out."[3]

[1] Quoted in Carl Sandburg and Paul Angle. *Mary Lincoln: Wife and Widow.* New York, 1932, p. 97.
[2] James W. Nesmith to his wife, Washington, February 5, 1862. MS. in the Oregon Historical Society, Portland. Quoted by permission.
[3] "A Kindly Word for Abraham Lincoln's Widow," signed C.E.L. *The Christian Register*, September 7, 1872. Quoted in Randall, pp. 219–20.

To Ruth Harris [4]

Washington
Nov. 21st 61

My dear Mad[ame] Harris.

I want you to make up a purple *silk* velvet headdress of the *exact shade* of the flowers in this dress, similar to the crimson velvet one, you made me, real silk velvet strings, behind—trimmed exquisitely with heartease before & behind, of the same shade—I want it very beautiful, exercise your taste, to the utmost. Please let me have it by Wednesday. I presume by this time, your bill is paid— be very moderate with this purple headdress—you must not ask me over $5.00 for it—I want it the exact shade of this purple & real —a little green & gilt would not hurt it—I want a lovely affair—the velvet gracefully twisted

I hope to receive the headdress in three days, at furthest.

Truly your friend
Mary Lincoln

To Ruth Harris

[*November 22, 1861*]

Mad Harris.

I wrote you on yesterday—I will also get you to make me a *real* black velvet headdress twisted as you did the crimson, the true real velvet bow & strings behind of your richest velvet—also a bow on the top—A bow also on the purple with a loop—in case I take off the flowers—Remember a bow & loup in front on each—To be made

[4] Mrs. Lincoln's principal milliner in New York. "Madame Harris," as she styled herself, was listed in New York City directories as "widow." She ran her establishment together with her son, first in a shop on Broadway, then in new quarters on Brevoort Place.

in your handsomest style—In front & behind a handsome bunch of black berries—with those peculiar leaves—your richest berries —without they are of the best & most stylish, I do not want them —Remember under the flowers of each—in front & back—bows & loups—Please send them by Wednesday or Thursday Express—

Truly

Mrs Lincoln—

All of the richest velvet—

To "Mr Anthony" [5]

—————

Washington, [November, 1861]

Dear Sir—

At Mr Brady's gallery here, in the city, they tell me, they sent on some of my photographs. On yesterday the principal persons, at the establishment told me they would send you a dispatch to have them destroyed. You will certainly oblige me, by doing so—The only one at all passable, is the one, standing, with the large figured dress—back almost turned—showing only side face—You will readily remark, which is the one—This you might retain—On Monday —I will sit for another, which we will send you, if you destroy the others.[6] Please answer—

Very respcty—

Mary Lincoln

[5] Either Edward or Henry T. Anthony, successors and agents in New York of Mathew Brady, the photographer.

[6] Contrary to Mrs. Lincoln's wishes, four poses taken at this sitting were preserved. The original print of the one she preferred (and the most flattering) is in the National Archives. It is reproduced in the section of illustrations following page 164.

To William A. Newell

Nov 27 [*1861*]

My dear Sir:

   We have concluded to go down the river on Friday [7] and I hope you will be able to come on and accompany us. If you can make it convenient we will be happy to have you dine with us Thursday eve.[8] at half past five o'clock. Quite a pleasant little party will accompany us down the river. With kind regards to Mrs Newell, I remain

Truly your friend
Mary Lincoln

To Thomas W. Sweeney [9]

[TELEGRAM]   *Dec 15* [*1861*]

Col Sweeney [sic]
1226 Chestnut Street
Philadelphia
W- [1] will be at Continental Hotel this evening Pray see him

Mrs Lincoln

[7] The trip was never taken.
[8] Thursday, November 28, 1861, was Thanksgiving Day. Also invited for dinner that evening were General Nathaniel Banks, Colonel John Cochrane, and Lincoln's old friends, Mr. and Mrs. Joshua Speed.
[9] Assessor of Internal Revenue at Philadelphia and another of Mrs. Lincoln's particular friends and confidants.
[1] "W-" could have been anyone, but it was probably John Watt.

To George Sykes [2]

Executive Mansion
Dec 15th [1861]

Gen Sykes

Peter Vermin [?], who has been for years, in the employ of this house, has always been found to be, very honest, temperate & a very worthy man—You will find him very upright in his dealings & never drinks—Any kindness extended to him, will always be appreciated, by those with whom, he has lived & we are assured you will find him, the right kind of man.

Respectfully,
Mrs A. Lincoln

To Robert T. Lincoln

[TELEGRAM]
Through War Department   Jany 7th 1862

Robert T. Lincoln
Cambridge Mass-

Have you received the passes, sent to you a week since—From Boston to Washington? Return answer, through War Department answer immediately

Mrs A. Lincoln

By order of President through War Department

[2] Brigadier General Sykes was at this time in command of the Regular Infantry Brigade in Washington.

To Joanna Newell

Jany 15th [1862]
Executive Mansion

My dear Mrs Newell,

It will afford us, much pleasure, if the Gov. yourself, the Major,[3] & the young ladies, will join us, in an informal dinner, to day, at 5 o'clock. This letter,[4] I send to the Gov. was received this morning, I hope, it will give satisfaction.

I remain very truly,
Mary Lincoln

[*To Benjamin Brown French?*]

Executive Mansion
Washington
[*February 1, 1862*]

This draft is entirely incorrect. The President or myself are not indebted to this person, and he draws without any authority whatever. In future any such draft, from this source, please pay no attention to, as we have no business transactions, ever with this person.

Very respectfully,
Mrs Lincoln

No matter what the crisis facing her at a given moment, Mary Lincoln never lost sight of the staggering burdens borne by her hus-

---

[3] John Newell, brother of the former governor, appointed an army paymaster.
[4] Not preserved.

band. She tried to make the family quarters at the White House a pleasant haven in which Lincoln could forget his cares for brief periods. If she concealed her own problems from him, particularly her growing indebtedness, it was as much out of a desire to spare him undue anxiety as to protect herself. Although she worried constantly about his health and safety and about the progress of the war, she tried not to betray her apprehension in his presence. She encouraged him to eat well, to go for drives in the sunshine, and to spend as much time as possible with his two younger sons, knowing how he adored them and how a brief glimpse of one or the other could sustain him for an entire day.

Eleven-year-old Willie, who had many of his father's characteristics, was closest to Mrs. Lincoln, but both boys were indulged by their parents and given free run of the White House and its grounds. Of the two, it was Tad—quick, nervous, and temperamental like his mother, and an incurable prankster besides—who took endless advantage of his prerogatives as the President's pet. Tad invaded the attic where the White House bell system was located, setting off an insistent pealing that sent people scurrying from office to office until the culprit was revealed. He once made significant inroads into a supply of strawberries being prepared for a state dinner and another day trained a toy cannon on a Cabinet meeting. On one memorable occasion he stood at the foot of the grand staircase collecting from each caller a five-cent "entrance fee," which he solemnly announced was for the benefit of the Sanitary Fund.

Willie went along with most of Tad's schemes and war games, but he was softer by nature, more studious, more reasonable and totally lacking in that sharp acquisitive sense in which the younger boy so closely resembled his mother. He often sought sanctuary from Tad's hyperactivity in his mother's room, spending hours there with books, pencils, and writing tablets. He shared her love of reading, especially poetry, and was gifted with a wisdom and spirituality that were almost uncanny in one so young. In time Mary Lincoln came to depend upon Willie as he depended on her and proudly prophesied that he would be the comfort of her declining years.

———

Life was pleasant for the Lincolns during the Christmas season of 1861—as pleasant as possible under the circumstances. The alterations in the White House were all but complete. Robert, tall, handsome, and surprisingly mature, was home from Harvard for the holidays. With her family around her, Mary Lincoln was experiencing the first real contentment she had known in months.

But it was not her fate to enjoy even a relatively happy state for long. Clouds of war, suspicion, and hatred had already muted the joys of her first year in the White House; high-strung nerves and chronic ill health were destroying her resiliency, and worry over her husband's well-being was eroding her peace of mind. Now this woman, who loved her family so fiercely, was about to receive a blow that would further alter her outlook and turn the trappings of her new life to tinsel.

Early in February 1862 Willie came down with a slight chill from which it was presumed he would recover. But the fever (probably malarial in origin) raged out of control, and there was nothing the doctors could do to help him. On the night the boy's illness became acute, a White House reception was scheduled to take place, a huge, spectacular private party with which Mrs. Lincoln had taken vast pains. Since it was too late for the affair to be cancelled, the distraught parents were forced to preside over the gaiety while longing to be with their sick child. Mrs. Lincoln left the reception a number of times to sit by Willie's bed, only to return to her duties with leaden steps. Modern drugs might have cured Willie in a week; at that time all physicians and parents could do was watch helplessly as his life ebbed away. He died on February 20, at five in the afternoon.

Both the President and his wife were inconsolable. Whatever stability Mary Lincoln had possessed at the time of Eddy's death had long since fallen away under the pressures of her new existence, and she was more alone, frightened, and despairing than ever before. For three months following the funeral, she lay lost in the most abject misery, wild grief alternating with periods of paralyzing depression. She was unable to function, or to write to her family or friends. To be reminded of her son was agony.

Lincoln in his own sorrow searched desperately for some means of salvaging his wife's sanity, but there were limits to what he could do. His days were filled with concerns of vital importance, with decisions that affected the lives of millions. The most he could do was arrange for a nurse to look after her and to supervise Tad's slow recovery from the same illness that had taken the life of his brother. But it soon became apparent that only someone close to Mrs. Lincoln, someone of her own blood and part of her past, could provide the special comfort she so badly needed. It was Robert Lincoln who finally prevailed upon his aunt Elizabeth to move into the White House until his mother gained control of herself, an unenviable assignment but one which Mrs. Edwards did not hesitate to take on. The experience was worse than she had expected. Deeply depressed by her sister's state of mind, Elizabeth stood the strain for two months and then departed the White House at an "urgent summons" from home.

Mary Lincoln was in the throes of what today would be considered a mild nervous breakdown. On one especially bad day, Lincoln took her gently by the arm and led her to a window, pointing out in the distance a building in which mental patients were confined. Elizabeth Keckley, who witnessed the incident, heard the President say quietly, "Mother, do you see that large white building on the hill yonder? Try and control your grief or it will drive you mad, and we may have to send you there." [5] Only Lincoln's need of her enabled Mary to regain a semblance of equilibrium. Some years later she told her half-sister Emilie, "If I had not felt the spur of necessity urging me to cheer Mr. Lincoln, whose grief was as great as my own, I could never have smiled again." [6]

This second shared tragedy had a profound effect on the religious views of both the President and his wife. Lincoln, the onetime skeptic, felt increasingly the need to believe in something in order to deal with his burdens. He could often be found in quiet moments reading the Bible, and appeared the stronger for having done so. Mary Lincoln, the erstwhile traditionalist, seemed shaken to her very soul. Like most "good women" of her day, she was a devoted churchgoer; many of her most intimate friends were ministers, and her saddest letters abounded in appeals to heaven. But

[5] Keckley, pp. 104–5.
[6] Helm, p. 226.

close analysis of her writings and remarks reveals that, after Willie's death, her private beliefs evolved into a curious creed, blending formal Christian teachings on the immortality of the soul with strong infusions of spiritualism, then at the zenith of its popularity.

Wanting desperately to believe that "a very slight veil separates us, from the 'loved & lost' . . . that though unseen by us, they are very near," [7] she began to seek out mediums who, it was said, could call the dead from their graves to speak to those who mourned them. Expectant, emotionally overwrought, gullible as usual, she became involved with a succession of outlandish characters, whose seances she attended faithfully in hopes of communicating with Willie. On several occasions Lincoln went along out of curiosity and a desire to watch over his wife. But when she fell prey to an obvious charlatan who called himself Lord Colchester, it was the President's trusted friend Noah Brooks who came to the rescue. Brooks joined one of Colchester's seances in seeming good faith and at the crucial moment rose and walked in the direction of sounds supposedly coming from the beyond. He found the medium with a bell, banjo, and drum and received a blow on the head for his pains. Brooks later confronted Colchester with the wound and ordered him out of town. [8]

In years to come, after spiritualists had been discredited, Mary Lincoln was embarrassed to admit having dealt with them, but there can be no doubt that she was taken in at first. Whether she was "sitting" with Colchester, Mrs. Cranston Laurie of Georgetown, or the famous Nettie Colburn Maynard, she continually sought proof that Willie was somewhere near at hand. Late in 1863, when Emilie Helm was staying at the White House, Mrs. Lincoln entered her room one night and said, with a strange glint in her eyes, that, were it not for the fact that Willie came often to comfort her, she would still be "drowned in tears." To Emilie's horror she continued, "He comes to me every night, and stands at the foot of my bed, with the same sweet, adorable smile he has always had; he does not always come alone; little Eddie is sometimes

---

[7] Mary Lincoln to Charles Sumner, near Chicago, July 4, 1865.

[8] Brooks described the incident in one of his newspaper dispatches, which were rewritten as *Washington in Lincoln's Time*. Edited and with an Introduction by Herbert Mitgang. New York, 1958, pp. 66–8.

with him." Emilie could only shudder and wonder what was happening to her sister's mind.[9]

This was just one area in which Mary Lincoln was losing her grip on reality; there would be others as time went on. Few of her friends and family had any idea of how to handle her moods—the age of psychiatry was yet to come. All they could do was share Mrs. Keckley's belief that she was a "peculiarly constituted woman,"[1] cheerful and reasonable one minute, the next irrational and impossible to deal with. With his sensitive intelligence and his special understanding of his wife, Lincoln must have sensed that disturbing forces were at work within her mind and personality, and he often had cause to despair at her behavior. But he was unfailingly patient, using all the gentle firmness and fatherly tolerance he possessed to soothe her and set her back on the path of reason.

Several months passed before Mrs. Lincoln could lift her pen and write to her friends again. When she did, it was upon the black-bordered stationery of mourning, and the major theme was sadness. To Julia Sprigg, a close friend of Springfield days, she wrote longingly of Willie and posed the question she would ask herself repeatedly in years to come: "Can life be endured?"

To Clement Heerdt & Company [2]

[TELEGRAM]   [*February, 1862*][3]

Clement Heerdt & Co
93 Water Street
New York City

The wine is required by Wednesday, of this week. Please forward it, immediately by Adams Express.

Mrs Lincoln—

---

[9] Helm, pp. 226–7. Curiously, there are no references to such other-worldly visitations in Mrs. Lincoln's letters. As will be noted later, it is almost impossible to read extreme psychosis into any document in her hand.

[1] Keckley, p. 182.

[2] New York wine merchants.

[3] This telegram was probably dispatched in connection with the levee held on February 5, over which the Lincolns presided as their son Willie lay ill.

To Francis L. Vinton [4]

Executive Mansion
Sunday morn—April 13 [1862]

Mrs Lincoln returns Rev Dr Vinton's, interesting sermons, with her sincere thanks for his kind consideration.

She asks his acceptance of a bouquet, and hopes the acquaintance so agreably commenced, may be renewed ere long.

To Ruth Harris

Executive Mansion, [*May 17, 1862*] [5]

Madame Harris

I will get you to send me, for a lady now visiting me— [6] a *very fine* black straw—trimmed stylishly with colors—I want it got up with great haste & make the price as reasonable as possible—Please send on so soon as possible—I want it very pretty, I am in need of a mourning bonnet—which must be exceedingly plain & genteel. I want one made of crape with folds, bonnet of blk crape—that is trimmed with it. I want the crape to be the *finest jet black* English crape—white & black face trimmings—Could you obtain any black & white crape flowers? small delicate ones—I want it got up, with great taste & gentility—I should like you to select 2 sets—collars & undersleeves—blk & white crape mixed—want them very plain & genteel—I hope you will give great satisfaction with the bonnets— The black one must be exceedingly, plain rich, very best material

---

[4] Assistant rector of New York's Trinity Church, and one of a number of clergymen who offered spiritual consolation to the Lincolns after the death of their son Willie on February 20, 1862. Lincoln had been much impressed with Dr. Vinton's comforting conclusions on the subject of death and had requested a collection of his sermons for perusal.

[5] An envelope exists addressed by Mrs. Lincoln to "Madame Harris & Son" and is postmarked on this date.

[6] The bonnet may have been a gift for Mrs. Rebecca Pomroy, a nurse who cared for Mrs. Lincoln after Elizabeth Edwards left for Springfield.

& genteel—I want a *very very* fine black straw for myself—trimmed
with folds of *jet fine* blk crape—White & blk face trimmings five
white & blk crape flowers—besides the blk & white ruche—I also
want it very fine & plain—Please send me the one or two bills, you
had against me in the winter—I have them here also,

> with regards to your Mother—
> I remain, truly yours,
> Mary Lincoln

blk crape bonnet to be made as light as possible

To Mrs. Phineas D. Gurley [7]

_____

May 19, '62

My Dear Mrs Gurley.

Our consul at Smyrna, sent me a few boxes of figs. I take the
liberty of sending you a taste of raisins & figs, a little different from
those, we get here. Hoping your daughter's health is improving, I
remain truly,

> Mary Lincoln

To Ruth Harris

_____

Executive Mansion
[*May, 1862*]

My Dear Madame.

Your bonnets were received on yesterday. The black with colors—I liked very much. Also the blk crape—I wished a much finer
blk straw bonnet for mourning—without the gloss. Could you not
get such a one? I want you to send me a bow of blk crape, for the

---

[7] Wife of the pastor of the New York Avenue Presbyterian Church, attended by
the Lincolns.

top of the blk straw bonnet, *exactly* like the one, on top the blk crape bonnet—of the *same crape* two bows on each side of the loup —bound—like the other—I wrote you about the veils—did you receive the letter—I want you to select me the *very finest*, & blackest & lightest long crape veil & bordered as they bring them—Please get me the finest that can be obtained—want a short *very very* fine blk crape veil, round corners & folds around—want one of very fine blk silk net—with folds around for summer—round at corners & short—The *long veil* I, should like to have by Friday—want it very fine—blk & light—please send *this* immediately.

I liked the undersleeves & collars—Please have me *two more*, white & blk collars mixed, with cuffs to match—no undersleeves— I want the genteelest & tastiest you can find or have made—I liked the style of the blk & white reversed—Do not forget the bow, for the bonnet—And the long veil, I want immediately.

I have your money ready for you—

Very truly yours
Mrs Lincoln

To Julia Ann Sprigg [8]

May 29th [1862]
Executive Mansion

My Dear Mrs Sprigg:

Your very welcome letter was received two weeks since, and my sadness & ill health have alone prevented my replying to it—We have met with so overwhelming an affliction in the death of our beloved Willie a being too precious for earth, that I am so completely unnerved, that I can scarcely command myself to write. What would I give to see you & talk to you, in our crushing bereavement, if any one's presence could afford comfort—it would be yours. You were always a good friend & dearly have I loved you. All that human skill could do, was done for our sainted boy, I fully

[8] John C. and Julia Ann Sprigg had lived a block south of the Lincolns in Springfield.

believe the severe illness, he passed through, now, almost two years since,[9] was but a warning to us, that one so pure, was not to remain long here and at the same time, he was *lent* us a little longer—to try us & wean us from a world, whose chains were fastening around us & when the blow came, it found us so unprepared to meet it. Our home is very beautiful, the grounds around us are enchanting, the world still smiles & pays homage, yet the charm is dispelled— everything appears a mockery, the idolised one, is not with us, he has fulfilled his mission and we are left desolate. When I think over his short but happy childhood, how much comfort, he always was to me, and how fearfully, I always found my hopes concentrating on so good a boy as he was—when I can bring myself to realize that he has indeed passed away, my question to myself is, "can life be endured?" Dear little Taddie who was so devoted to his darling Brother, although as deeply afflicted as ourselves, bears up and teaches us a lesson, in enduring the stroke, to which we *must submit*. Robert will be home from Cambridge in about 6 weeks and will spend his vacation with us. He has grown & improved more than any one you ever saw. Will we ever meet, & talk together as *we have* done. *Time* time how many sad changes it brings. The 1st of July, we go out to the "Soldiers' Home," a very charming place 2½ miles from the city, several hundred feet, above, our present situation, to pass the summer. I dread that it will be a greater resort than here, *if possible*, when we are in sorrow, quiet is very necessary to us. Mr [Jesse K.] Dubois, I suppose has reached home, ere this. I see by the papers that Mr [William S.] *Burch* is married—We have some pieces of furniture, still remaining at his house, may I ask a favor of you—It is this—If Mr [George N.] Black can have room for them, can they be moved, to any place above his store, where he may have room for them. The sofa, at Mr Burch's was new, a few months before we left. May I also ask you, to speak to Mr Black, and see if the 8 boxes we left with him, are all there. I fear we have been troublesome friends—I send you a list of the articles sent me by Mr B. If you feel the least delicacy about this— I will not wish you to do it. Whenever you have leisure, I hope you will write me. With love to all, I remain ever your attached friend

Mary Lincoln

[9] A siege of scarlet fever.

To John E. Wool [1]

Dear Sir:

Allow me to return you, my most sincere thanks, for your kindness in recommending my friend, Mr Stackpole [2] and any further service you can render him, will be duly appreciated by the President & myself. We are very anxious to have our friend have the place as Sutler, to the School of Instruction, to oblige him and any thing, you can do to forward it—will be pleasantly remembered.

> With kindest regards I remain,
> Very respectfully,
> Mrs Lincoln
> A. Lincoln [3]

As Mr Stackpole is visiting Baltimore, I take the liberty, of sending you a bouquet.

To Benjamin Brown French

July 26th [1862]

Dear Sir:

Happening to be in N.Y. & having a day of leisure—in accordance with your letter, which mentioned there was an appropriation of $250—I selected some books for the library—$75.00 worth were selected in W[ashington] and the remaining $150.00—in

---

[1] Formerly in command of the Department of Virginia, Major General Wool had just been given command of the Middle Department, based at Fort McHenry.
[2] Thomas Stackpole, guard and engineer at the White House.
[3] This is one of the rare documents bearing the signatures of both President and Mrs. Lincoln. Lincoln also sent a separate recommendation of his own.

N.Y.[4]—There is a very poor set of Waverly—also Shakespeare in the house library, so I replaced each with a fine new edition—I presume, with your usual kindness, you are willing to leave such things to my judgment. No one has the interest of the place, more at heart than myself. I cannot express how disappointed I felt not [to see] Mr Tuck [5] & yourself, when you called out. Hoping you will visit us again, I remain sincerely your friend

Mrs Lincoln

To Mrs. Charles Eames [6]

July 26th [1862] [7]
Soldiers' Home

My Dear Mrs Eames,

I have just placed the carte-de-visite,[8] of your sweet little girl, in my Album for which allow me to thank you, also for the agreable note, you left for me. *At the time*, I was making a short & unexpected visit to the North,[9] undertaken with much reluctance, yet found to be more pleasant, than I could have hoped, with spirits so depressed—In the loss of our idolised boy, we naturally have suffered such intense grief, that a removal from the scene of our misery was found very necessary. Yet, in this sweet spot, that his bright nature, would have so well loved, *he is not with us*, and the anguish of the thought, oftentimes, for days overcomes me.

[4] Bills for these books are reproduced in Harry Pratt. *The Personal Finances of Abraham Lincoln.* Springfield, 1943, p. 180–1. They are from Richstein's in Washington ($75.15) and Crowen's in New York ($113.00). Perhaps more books were ordered, for Lincoln in a note dated August 26, 1862, directed French to pay $175.00 to Crowen and enclosed a personal check for $124.25 covering those books he wished to retain for his private library.

[5] Amos Tuck, former U.S. representative from New Hampshire, and a personal friend of both the President and his wife.

[6] Wife of a prominent government lawyer and a social leader of Washington.

[7] Misdated "1864" in a hand not Mrs. Lincoln's.

[8] The exchange of "cartes-de-visite," bearing a photograph of the sender on one side and an autograph message on the other, was a popular custom of the day.

[9] Mrs. Lincoln had been in New York from July 10 to 17 and then had gone on to Boston.

How often, I feel rebellious, and almost believe that our Heavenly Father, has forsaken us, in removing, so lovely a child from us! Yet I know, a great sin, is committed when we feel thus.

We are truly delighted, with this retreat, the drives & walks around here are delightful, & each day, brings its visitors. Then too, our boy Robert, is with us, whom you may remember. We consider it a "pleasant time" for us, when his vacations, roll around, he is very companionable, and I shall dread when he has to return to Cambridge. I presume, you will not return to W. before cool weather, *thus far*, we have found the country very delightful.

It will be so late in the season, ere, we return to the city, that I yet hope to welcome you *here*. Hoping you may pass the summer pleasantly, I remain

ever sincerely,
Mary Lincoln

To Jeremiah T. Boyle [1]

[TELEGRAM]   [*August 21, 1862*]

I presume you have received a dispatch from Mrs Preston.[2] If you can consistently, will you not grant her request?

Mary Lincoln

----

[1] A Union brigadier general who was serving at this time as military governor of Kentucky.

[2] Margaret Wickcliffe Preston, wife of General William Preston of the Confederate army and an intimate girlhood friend of Mrs. Lincoln, probably wished to pass through the Union lines in order to see her husband. This telegram, poorly written out in pencil, was sent with one from Lincoln to Mrs. Preston, which read in part: "Your despatch to Mrs. L. received yesterday. She is not well. Owing to her early and strong friendship for you, I would gladly oblige you, but I cannot absolutely do it. If Gen. Boyle and Hon. James Guthrie . . . see fit to give you the passes, this is my authority to them for doing so." MS. in the Brown University Library, Providence, R.I.

To Ozias M. Hatch

Saturday morning,
[September 28, 1862] [3]

A tempting bowl of raspberries, sent by a kind sister, induced me to extend invitations to two or three friends to take tea with us this evening. Hoping you will not fail to remember us by your presence, I remain,

Your friend,
Mary Lincoln

To Ozias M. Hatch

Soldiers' Home Sabbath Morning
[September 29, 1862]

Dear Sir:

Mrs Brayman & a Lady friend from N.Y—expect to take a drive with me—perhaps to the *lunatic* asylum, which commands a splend[id] view of Washington & (where Gen Hooker is now stopping.[4] We are going about 2½ or 3 o'clock & if you are at leisure, will be pleased to have you accompany us—The carriage can be sent for you at the hour designated or you can meet us at the Executive Mansion.

Your friend
Mary Lincoln

[3] Ozias Hatch was in Washington in late September and early October 1862. On October 1, he left with Lincoln on a five-day battlefield tour.

[4] Major General Joseph Hooker had been wounded in the foot at the battle of Antietam on September 17, 1862. Due to overcrowding in Washington hospitals, he was recuperating in quarters made available to him in the asylum for the insane, and there received many distinguished callers including, apparently, the President's wife.

To John E. Wool

Executive Mansion
Wash Sep 30, 1862

Dear Sir:

Capt T. Stackpole is quite desirous of a "Sutler's" place, & we knowing him, to be so honest & faithful, would be much pleased to have him receive the favor at your hands.

Very rept
Mrs Lincoln

To Daniel E. Sickles [5]

[Soldiers' Home]
Sept. 31st. [1862] [6]

My Dear Sir

Allow me to assure you, of the gratification it gave the P to see you last evening. In our daily circles, your name is frequently & deservedly mentioned, as being among the most prominent & energetic of our brave Union defenders. I should like to have had a social chat with you, about Virginia affairs & if you remain a day or two in the city, hope to have the pleasure of seeing you again. We always have so many evening callers, that our conversations, necessarily are general. When we are within hearing, as we on this elevation have been, for the last two or three days, of the roaring cannon, we can but pause & think. Yet, as to Washington, yielding to the Rebels, a just Heaven would prevent that! If you

[5] Sickles, formerly Democratic representative from New York, was a colorful and controversial figure who had become a personal favorite of the Lincolns. By the time this letter was written, he had succeeded in raising a brigade of troops from his home state and had become a general.

[6] The date is obviously in error; study of perpetual calendars indicates Mrs. Lincoln was often careless in dating letters.

are in W. on Monday, and, if you have leisure & of course, are so disposed, can you not drive out about 11 o'clock, in the morning Mr L. has so much to excite his mind, with fears for the Army, that I am quite considerate in expressing my doubts & *fears* to him concerning passing events. If more convenient to you, I could see you tomorrow morning, at the same hour, designated, yet would prefer Monday.

Your friend,

M. L.

A line directed to care of "Edward McManus,[7] especial messenger" will receive attention.

On New Year's Day of 1863 the Lincolns' old Illinois friend Senator Orville H. Browning chanced upon the President's wife driving out in her carriage and was invited to ride with her. Of their conversation he wrote in his diary: "Mrs. Lincoln told me she had been the night before, with Old Isaac Newton [8] out to Georgetown, to see a Mrs. Laury [sic], a spiritualist and she had made wonderful revelations to her about her little son Willy who died last winter, and also about things on earth. Among other things she revealed that the Cabinet were all enemies of the President, working for themselves, and that they would have to be dismissed." [9]

If ever there were a case of Mary Lincoln being told what she wanted to hear, Mrs. Laurie's "revelation" about the Cabinet was that. The President's wife was suspicious of several of his major

---

[7] "Old Edward" McManus had been doorkeeper and messenger at the White House since the administration of Andrew Jackson.

[8] Browning may have been wrong in stating Mrs. Lincoln's companion to have been Commissioner of Agriculture Isaac Newton. Jesse Newton, an official of the Interior Department, was known to have been an ardent spiritualist and a friend of the President's wife. She might have spoken to Browning of a "Mr. Newton," leading the Senator to make his erroneous assumption. See Jay Monaghan. "Was Abraham Lincoln Really a Spiritualist?" *Journal of the Illinois State Historical Society*, June 1941.

[9] Quoted in Sandburg and Angle, p. 203.

appointees. Fiercely loyal to her husband, accustomed to defending him automatically since the day Elizabeth Edwards first looked down her nose, she honestly believed that she operated in his best interests when she assailed these gentlemen in conversation and correspondence. Washington politics had for her an air of Byzantine intrigue, with Lincoln the unwary victim of powerful predators who were endlessly conniving to ruin and replace him. She was perfectly correct, of course, even though, as she managed to concede occasionally, her interference made her appear to be "strong-minded"—the last thing a lady wished to be. She never admitted, even to herself, that Lincoln may have been a more sensitive judge of character than she—and a better politician. Instinct led her to immediate, passionate likes and dislikes, but the same mind that saw so quickly the unpleasant truth about a situation or personality leapt just as swiftly to wrong conclusions. Lincoln moved coolly and cautiously in assessing others, bringing many considerations to bear on his final judgments. It seems clear, moreover, that he had begun withholding these judgments from his wife, lest she compromise him with an idle remark. And so she saw him as a "saint," naive, trusting, determined to see the best in the worst of people. He deserved to be warned against those who, in her opinion, were taking advantage of him or plotting against him. Her stream of advice on the subject was so relentless that Lincoln once said in exasperation that if he continued to listen to her he would soon be without a Cabinet.

She knew that Secretary of State William Seward had been bitterly disappointed to have been passed over for the Republican nomination in 1860, and that he intended to wield as much influence as he could in his subordinate role. Despite the fact that the President preferred her to stay out of such matters ("My husband always enjoined upon me to be quiet," she would confess years later),[1] Mrs. Lincoln could not contain her antagonism. When Seward had all but insisted that he hold the first official reception of the new administration, the mistress of the White House had turned on him and snapped, "It is said that you are the power behind the throne. I'll show you that Mr. L. is President yet." [2]

---

[1] Mary Lincoln to Alexander Williamson, Chicago, December 14, [1866].
[2] Quoted in Randall, p. 239.

Still another highly placed official whose motives she distrusted was Salmon P. Chase, Secretary of the Treasury. Her repeated warnings to her husband of the Ohioan's ambitions were superfluous to say the least. Others were cautioning him as well, the President had eyes and ears, and Chase himself allowed his name to be mentioned as an alternative to Lincoln in 1864. Her dislike of Chase was mild, however, in comparison to her hostility toward his lovely and spirited daughter Kate, who in 1863 became the wife of Senator William Sprague of Rhode Island. As her father's hostess and confidante, Kate was one of the most talked-about women in the capital, second only to Mrs. Lincoln. She shared her father's desire to live in the White House and considered that she would have made a much more fitting ornament there than its rightful resident. Her ambitions were no secret, and the President's wife despised her for them.

All her life Mary Lincoln aroused great extremes of feeling among women in general. Those for whom she had a real affinity adored her and received in return almost smothering affection; those with whom she was forced to compete found her a formidable adversary. Aside from Mrs. Keckley, who was in a category all her own, her closest friends in Washington were the settled wives of congressmen, generals and administration officials, near her own age and with similar backgrounds and interests. She had much in common with Mrs. Gideon Welles, wife of the Secretary of the Navy, especially after Willie's death: Mary Jane Welles had lost six children. She also formed lasting attachments to two other women she saw from time to time in Washington, and who proved to be friends in need: Mrs. James H. Orne of Philadelphia, whose wealthy husband was a heavy contributor to the Republican party and to the war effort, and Mrs. James W. White, wife of an immigrant Irishman who had risen to become a justice of the New York City Superior Court.

The staid matrons with whom Mrs. Lincoln surrounded herself in Washington stood in sharp contrast to the sort of men who had rushed to fill the vacuum left when the old society chose to spurn the President's wife. These women were good, reliable, and no competition whatever. Mary Lincoln had little use for those females, unknown to her personally, who clustered about her husband at White House functions. Although she herself could be coy and flirtatious, she resented it mightily when Lincoln showed even passing interest in a woman who was young, intelligent, or attractive. She could never accept the fact that most of the attention bestowed on the President by the ladies was as innocent as her own girlish coquetry, and, more often than not, was followed by requests for favors. When he was not with his family, Lincoln was happiest talking politics and exchanging anecdotes with other men. Yet he was refreshingly direct in his dealings with women, treating them gently but refusing to regard them as children or imbeciles. This was a rare quality in that day; women welcomed it and responded to it.

Late in October 1862 Mary Lincoln went north for her second trip away from Washington since Willie's death. (She had made a brief excursion to New York and Boston the previous July.) This time Tad traveled with her, and Elizabeth Keckley joined them for a few days in New York. She was gone for nearly a month, and three letters written on that trip indicate that she was beginning to come alive again after her terrible spring. Two of these letters are to Abraham Lincoln. They are rare personal documents which somehow found their way into the welter of official correspondence now housed in the Library of Congress. In the first, Mrs. Lincoln recounted some of her activities in New York and then proceeded to offer unabashed—and once again superfluous—advice on military matters; the second bespoke her passionate concern for the welfare of former slaves, homeless and helpless in the large cities of the North. A third letter from New York, addressed to Governor Edwin D. Morgan, gives evidence that her intercession in public matters was not always negative: her appeal on behalf of Mary Real was as heartfelt and right-minded as her later attempts to find government jobs for deserving individuals, many of them Negroes.

To James Gordon Bennett

Oct 4th 1862
Soldiers' Home

My Dear Sir:

Your kind note, sent by Mr Delille, has been received and justly appreciated. I hope to have the pleasure of seeing the gentleman, this morning, as I believe, he speaks of leaving in the afternoon. It is so exceedingly dusty, it is quite an undertaking to visit W- even from this short distance, however, as he has been the bearer of a note from *you*, I scarcely feel like having him leave, without seeing him. From *all parties*, the cry, for a "change of Cabinet" comes. I hold a letter, just received from Gov Sprague, in my hand, who is quite as earnest, as you have been on the subject. Doubtless if my good, patient Husband, were here, instead of being with the Army of the Potomac, both of these missives, would be placed before him, accompanied by my womanly suggestions, proceeding from a heart so deeply interested, for our distracted country. I have a great terror of *strong* minded Ladies, yet if a word fitly spoken and in due season, can be urged, in a time like this, we should not withhold it. As you suggest the C was formed, in a more peaceful time, yet some two or three men who compose it, would have *distracted* it—Our country requires no ambitious fanatics, to guide the Helm, and were it not, that their Counsels, have very little control over the P- when his mind, is made up, as to what is right, there might be cause for fear. With many apologies for so long a note, I remain, my dear Mr Bennett

Very Respectfully yours
Mrs Lincoln.

To "Mrs Lester" [3]

Executive Mansion
[No date]

Mrs Lester—

I would be very much pleased to see you at the house this evening. Mr Lincoln will be with us.

Very truly
Mary Lincoln—

To Abraham Lincoln

[New York]
Nov 2d [1862]

My Dear Husband—

I have waited in vain to hear from you, yet as you are not *given* to letter writing, will be charitable enough to impute your silence, to the right cause. Strangers come up from W- & tell me you are well—which satisfies me very much—Your name is on every lip and many prayers and good wishes are hourly sent up, for your welfare—and McClellan & his slowness are as vehemently discussed. Allowing this beautiful weather, to pass away, is disheartening the North— [4]

Dear little Taddie is well and enjoying himself very much— Gen and Mrs Anderson [5] & myself called on yesterday to see Gen

[3] Unidentified.
[4] At the time this letter was written, General George B. McClellan and his Army of the Potomac were encamped in northern Virginia. The battle of Antietam in September of 1862 had been an important but costly Union victory, but McClellan's continued failure to land a decisive blow or to pursue the enemy after a successful engagement led to his removal from command in mid-November.
[5] Major General Robert Anderson, defender of Fort Sumter.

Scott [6]—He looks well, although complaining of Rheumatism. A day or two since, I had one of my severe attacks, if it had not been for Lizzie Keckley, I do not know what I should have *done*—Some of *these periods*, will launch me away—All the distinguished in the land, have tried how polite & attentive, they could be to me, since I came up here—Many say, they would almost worship you, if you would put a fighting General, in the place of McClellan. This would be splendid weather, for an engagement. I have had two suits of clothes made for Taddie which will come to 26 dollars—Have to get some fur outside wrappings for the coachman's carriage trappings. Lizze [sic] Keckley, wants me to loan her thirty dollars—so I will have to ask for a check, of $100- which will soon be made use of, for these articles—I must send you, Taddie's tooth—I want to leave here for Boston, on Thursday & if you will send the check by Tuesday, will be much obliged—

One line, to say that we are occasionally remembered will be gratefully received by yours very truly

M. L.

I enclose you a note from Mr Stewart,[7] he appears very solicitous about his young friend. Mr S. is so strong a Union man—& asks so few favors—if it came in your way, perhaps it would not be amiss to oblige—

To Abraham Lincoln

[*New York, November 3, 1862*]

My dear Husband—

I wrote you on yesterday, yet omitted a very important item. Elizabeth Keckley, who is with me and is working for the Contra-

---

[6] General Winfield Scott, aging hero of the Mexican War, had served briefly as General-in-Chief of the Union army and was now living in retirement at West Point.

[7] Alexander T. Stewart, owner of New York's most glittering drygoods emporium, specializing in imported articles. Mrs. Lincoln, one of his best customers, probably already owed him a great deal of money. Stewart's note, addressed to the President but conveniently left open for Mrs. Lincoln's perusal, dealt with an army promotion.

band Association, at Wash [8] is authorized by the *White* part of the concern by a written document—to collect any thing for them—*here* that, she can—She has been very unsuccessful—She says the immense number of Contrabands in W- are suffering intensely, many without bed covering & having to use any bits of carpeting to cover themselves—Many dying of want—Out of the $1000 fund deposited with you by Gen [Michael?] Corcoran, I have given her the privilege of investing $200 her[e] in bed covering. She is the most deeply grateful being, I ever saw, & this sum, I am sure, you will not object to being used in this way—The cause of humanity requires it—and there will be $800 left of the fund—I am sure, this will meet your approbation—The soldiers are well supplied with comfort. Please send check for $200 out of the fund—she will bring you on the bill

With much love
Yours &

Please write by return mail
[On envelope] Please answer by return mail & send c——

To Edwin D. Morgan [9]

Metropolitan Hotel
New York, Nov. 13th [1862]

My Dear Sir:

Allow me to express my extreme regret at being unable to see yourself & Mrs Morgan, when you did me the honor of calling some days since. I have been frequently urged since my arrival here, to make an appeal to you, in behalf of the unfortunate woman, Mary

---

[8] The "Contraband Relief Association" had been organized in the summer of 1862 on a suggestion by Mrs. Keckley herself before the congregation of her "colored church," or so she claimed in her memoirs. Composed of both Negroes and whites, its membership worked to raise money to alleviate the sufferings of former slaves adrift and destitute in northern cities. Keckley, pp. 113–14.

[9] A political protégé of Thurlow Weed, Morgan had been governor of New York since 1858. He was leaving office to command the Department of New York as a Major General.

Real,[1] convicted of man slaughter, and now in Sing Sing. The case, with all its details, must be quite familiar to you, the painful particulars, therefore, will be unnecessary to discuss—

I think, *her*, entitled to your clemency—She must have acted under the influence of a mind, distrait, besides there is but little evidence, that she contemplated or committed the deed, she is punished for. Pray, let me know, if my signature, to a petition for mercy, with other names of respectability, will induce you to remit her sentence? I am confident, the District Attorney, will readily recommend her pardon—An early answer, will oblige me, & I shall feel grateful if you think proper to signalize your retirement from office, by an act of grace, which I cannot but feel, is well deserved.

Very Respectfully,
Mrs A. Lincoln.

To Gustav E. Gumpert [2]

[TELEGRAM]
[*New York*], *November 26, 1862*

Augustus Gumpert [sic]
Barnum's Hotel
Baltimore

Please bring Tad home immediately [3] he can come on Tom Cross's [4] car.

Mrs Lincoln

---

[1] A 25-year-old woman who shot her husband dead on learning he had a mistress. Her six-day trial, exhaustively covered by *The New York Times* in mid-October 1862, aroused great public sympathy for a "wronged woman." The verdict was manslaughter in the third degree (with mitigating circumstances); Mrs. Real was sentenced to two years and six months of hard labor at the state prison at Sing Sing. There is no record that Governor Morgan responded to Mrs. Lincoln's appeal for clemency.

[2] "Gus" Gumpert was a well-to-do Philadelphia tobacco dealer, with whom Mrs. Lincoln did business and of whom Tad was fond.

[3] Both of Tad's parents were out of Washington on this date, and the excursion to Baltimore was probably designed as a distraction.

[4] A White House messenger who often had special charge of Tad.

To "Mrs Goddard" [5]

Executive Mansion
Dec 6th 62

My dear Mrs Goddard:

Your kind note was received. Mr Lincoln says, Gov Seward will forward your package, with the greatest pleasure. Hoping to have the pleasure of seeing you, ere you leave the city, I remain very sincerely your friend

Mary Lincoln

To William A. Newell

Washington, Dec. 16, [1862]

My dear Sir:

Your kind note was received a day or two since, for which allow me to thank you. Also for the delightful cider you so generously sent. Mr L. enjoys it very much. Your friends inquire about you as you visit Wash- so much less frequently than in former times. It is doubtless a subject of congratulation to you that you can sometimes dispense with so tedious a journey and that your business detains you more at home. I trust however, during the winter you will bring Mrs Newell to the city. So many changes have taken place since we last met. From this time until spring each day will be almost a gloomy anniversary. My precious little Willie is as much mourned over & far more missed (now that we realize he has gone) than when so fearful a stroke as to be called upon to resign Him came. Your kindness can never be effaced. With regards to Mrs Newell, I remain sincerely your friend

Mary Lincoln

[5] Possibly Mrs. John H. Goddard, whose husband Lincoln appointed as Justice of the Peace for the County of Washington in 1864.

To Charles Sumner [6]

Executive Mansion
Dec 30th 1862

Mrs Lincoln presents her compliments to the Hon Mr Sumner, & begs leave to ask him, if he is acquainted with the address, of the venerable Mr Josiah Quincy,[7] as Mrs L. is about sending an excellent photograph of the President to him, and is anxious that it shall reach him, by the 1st of Jan—

The first public reception at the White House after Willie's death was held on New Year's Day of 1863, two weeks after the defeat at Fredericksburg. It was a gloomy occasion, especially for Mary Lincoln, who commented dolefully to Benjamin French, standing beside her in the receiving line, "Oh Mr French, how much we have passed through since last we stood here." [8] The strain eventually became too great, and the President's wife left the reception long before it was over. Memories of Willie were never far below the surface; the approaching anniversary of his death promised to be particularly painful. But as she grew more resigned to her loss the wild, uncontrollable grief diminished.

Having passed through what she termed "the fiery furnace of affliction," [9] she was developing something of a conscience and a heightened concern for others. Beginning in late 1862 and continuing through the remainder of her years in Washington, she wrote innumerable letters of recommendation and intercession on

[6] Senator from Massachusetts from 1851 until his death in 1874. Mrs. Lincoln was one of his most devoted admirers. Their friendship is discussed on pp. 185–6.
[7] Distinguished former congressman from Massachusetts and president of Harvard College.
[8] Quoted in Randall, p. 320.
[9] Mary Lincoln to Hannah Shearer, November 20, 1864.

behalf of friends—and strangers. If she urged a diplomatic post for John Jay of New York, a comfortable Customs House berth for Joseph Hertford of Illinois, she also acted as a one-woman employment bureau for deserving persons who wanted work as clerks, night watchmen, lamplighters. Many of these were former slaves.

The thousands of wounded languishing in military hospitals throughout Washington benefitted from her loving, almost maternal sympathy. She carried them flowers from the White House conservatory, had delicacies sent from the White House kitchens, and distributed among them some of the gifts sent her family. She made her hospital calls alone or with a friend such as Mary Jane Welles; the visits were frequently unannounced and were rarely reported in the press, with the result that few were aware of this tender and courageous side of Mrs. Lincoln's character. The tours must have been dreadful ordeals for a woman who, with all her tragedies, had led a sheltered life. But the same nerves that quivered at the dropping of a book, the slamming of a door, somehow remained steady amid the ghastly sights, sounds, and smells of the overcrowded wards. The same woman who begrudged a few extra pennies to a milliner, who was hounded by debt, made innumerable personal gifts to and solicitations for the hospitals.

But the most significant area of change had come in Mary Lincoln's attitude toward those she would refer to as "all the oppressed colored race." [1] In 1856 she had apologized for Lincoln's affiliation with the Republican party, assuring Emilie Helm that he was not of that pestiferous breed, an abolitionist. She had even hinted that having a few submissive Negroes about the house might be preferable to coping with "wild Irish" help. [2] By 1863, the noted antislavery journalist Jane Grey Swisshelm had come to recognize that the President's wife, whom she had at first distrusted on the basis of hearsay, was in fact "more radically opposed to slavery" than her husband and had "urged him to Emancipation, as a matter of right, long before he saw it as a matter of necessity." [3]

Mary Lincoln's conversion to abolitionism resulted from many

---

[1] Mary Lincoln to Charles Sumner, April 5, [1864].
[2] Mary Lincoln to Emilie Todd Helm, Springfield, November, 1856.
[3] Jane Grey Swisshelm in a letter to the editor of the Chicago *Tribune*, July 20, 1882, five days after Mrs. Lincoln's death.

factors, not the least of which were the President's own progressively stronger feelings on the subject and her own kindness and sense of justice. Talk with Mrs. Keckley had revived girlhood memories of the brutalities of the slave system; Lizzie had had experiences which rivaled in horror and despair anything in abolitionist literature. But perhaps the most potent influence on Mrs. Lincoln's political thought was her extravagant admiration for Senator Charles Sumner of Massachusetts, the leading antislavery spokesman in Congress; we shall learn more of their friendship later.

To Edwin M. Stanton [4]

Feb 11th 1863

Dear Sir:

Allow me, to intercede with you, and respectfully ask for the retention of Mr Frank Jones, as a Cadet, in the Military Academy at West Point. He is a young man, of more than ordinary promise of Quaker origin, & his Father is exceedingly anxious, as well as his son, to have a trial of six months longer.

Mr F. Jones, labored under peculiar disadvantages, during the past six months, in having a roommate, who did not desire his advancement & consequently every obstacle was thrown in his way, that could be devised, to impede his progress in his studies. This was an appointment, the President, was much pleased to make and may I not rely on your great kindness of heart, in, giving him another trial? You will gratify many persons by so doing and oblige yours very gratefully

Mrs Lincoln.

[4] Secretary of War, 1862–7.

To Montgomery Meigs

[*Undated*]

Will Gen Meigs, please render justice to this man, who has not received pay for his boat—

Mrs Lincoln

To Mary Jane Welles [5]

Feb 21st 63
Executive mansion

My dear Mrs Welles:

Allow me to thank you for your sympathising & kindly re-membrance, of *yesterday*,[6] when I felt so broken hearted. Only those, who have passed through such bereavements, can realise, how the heart bleeds at the return, of these anniversaries,—I have never been able, to express to you, how I grieved over your troubles,[7] our precious lambs, if we could only realise, how far happier they *now* are than when on earth! Heaven help the sorrowing, and how full the land is, of such! Any morning, you may have leisure, I should like to see you. I would enjoy, a little conversation with you—

Ever sincerely—
Mary Lincoln

[5] Wife of Gideon Welles, Secretary of the Navy, 1861–9.
[6] The first anniversary of Willie Lincoln's death.
[7] Hubert Welles, young son of the Secretary and his wife, had died the preceding November. He was the sixth child the couple had lost.

To Mrs. Charles Heard [8]

March 4, 63
Executive Mansion.

My Dear Mrs Heard:

I will be gratified if you will visit me about 8½ o'clock, this eve, sans ceremonie also Mr H- & Mrs [Abner] Doubleday.[9] I am not expecting company, only perhaps, your friend Mrs Lamon, may look in upon us.

Very truly,
Mary Lincoln

If you attend the party at Mr Chase's this eve—we will excuse you, at a suitable *hour*.

To Peter H. Watson [1]

March 10 [1863]

Hon Mr Watson,

Having been acquainted, with the family of Mrs Redwood,[2] in earlier years, and as she is very solicitous, to procure writing from your Department, for one of her Daughters—Will you not confer a favor upon me, by granting her request? By so doing, you will greatly oblige   yours Res—

Mrs Lincoln.

---

[8] Wife of a New York drygoods merchant.
[9] Wife of the Union general who is perhaps best known as the developer of modern baseball.
[1] A former legal colleague of Lincoln, now Assistant Secretary of War.
[2] On June 27, 1861, the President had appointed William H. Redwood, Jr. cadet "at large" at West Point. It can be assumed that this was his mother, and that she was asking permission for her daughter to visit the Academy.

To George Harrington [3]

Executive Mansion
[March 20, 1863]

Dear Sir:

I am under many obligations to you, for your frequent kindnesses to me, and will only request you to add another name, in the place of *Ellen Shehan*,[4] & will promise, not to trouble you again. The woman, who is most estimable, is named Elizabeth Keckley, although colored, is very industrious, & has just had an interview with Gov Chase, who says he will see you & I am sure, it rests with you. She is very unobtrusive, and will perform her duties, faithfully. I do not believe, I am making a vain request of you—and I will not again trouble you—

Please insert her name in place of the other, I presume you will not, object, to her not entering upon her duties, until the middle of April. You see Mr Harrington, I am calcu[la]ting on your kindly agreeing to my proposal

Very Respectfully,
Mrs Lincoln.

To Thomas W. Sweney

Executive Mansion
[April, 1863] [5]

Col Sweeney [sic]:

About *1 o'clock* to day, Taddie & myself are going in the carriage about a mile & half out to carry some flowers && to the

---

[3] Assistant Secretary of the Treasury, 1861–5.

[4] In an earlier letter to Harrington, Mrs. Lincoln had expressed what were apparently second thoughts about Miss Shehan, whom she had recommended for a job in the note-cutting room of the Treasury Department. "The girl, Ellen," she had written, "is not worthy the place, has made use of some expressions which I cannot countenance in one I have recommended to so eligible a station." (Excerpt published in Carnegie Book Shop Catalogue No. 274. Item 296.) Action was swift. Miss Shehan had been appointed to the position on March 17; on March 19, one day after Mrs. Lincoln's letter was written, she was dismissed. The above communication followed.

[5] The approximate date of this letter is based on the style of notepaper on which

sick soldiers, if you are disengaged, will you go with us. Taddie, as usual is appropriating you, for a ride on horseback this afternoon to the Navy Yard. It is *sometimes*, unfortunate, to be a favorite, with so exacting a young *man*.

Your friend
Mrs Lincoln

To George Harrington

April 22d [*1863*]

Mr Harrington will confer a great favor on Mrs Lincoln if he will give places to Miss Coburn & her friend,[6] in the Treasury Clipping De[partment].

To Gustav E. Gumpert

[TELEGRAM]

[*Undated*]

Mr Gumpert
1226 Chestnut Street
Philadelphia, Penn.[7]

Send the name immediately of the young man who desires a clerkship. The place is given to him. Name only required. I write you today—Please attend to the contents.

Mrs Lincoln

Send name to day—by telegraph—

---

it was written. Mrs. Lincoln ordered stationery on an average of once every four months, used it up, and then invariably reordered a new design. This habit has facilitated, in many instances, the placement of undated letters.

[6] It is possible that "Miss Coburn" was Nettie Colburn (Maynard), a spiritualist whose seances Mrs. Lincoln attended after Willie's death. Jay Monaghan, in his article "Was Abraham Lincoln Really a Spiritualist?" states that Mrs. Lincoln obtained a position for Miss Colburn in the Interior Department in 1862, in order to keep her in Washington. Perhaps this was a later effort to get her a job. The "friend" may have been Parthenia Hannum, Miss Colburn's companion and associate.

[7] The address was that of Thomas W. Sweney.

To Mary Jane Welles

May 17th [1863]

My dear Mrs Welles—

The pretty neck scarf, I will willingly accept, if you will retain the one I send you—I trust your health is benefitted by your visit North—With kindest regards, I remain, very truly yours

Mary Lincoln

To Thomas Stackpole

[TELEGRAM] [8]
Through War Department June 1st 63

Cap Thomas Stackpole
Astor House—
New York City—
Your letter will reach you this p.m. at 6 o'clock—

Mrs L

[8] This telegram was written out by Mrs. Lincoln on the back of a scrap torn off from the corner of a most curious document in an unknown hand. On the reverse side of the sheet can be discerned the words: ". . . me how where they cannot amalgimate . . . royal Blood Collar of our . . . . this state of Confusion without . . . am sure you have no good Spirit . . . . all order and Love to us all in . . . . and in the Spirit Land . . . . for you to Look to god and . . . in this great time of trial . . . . so long been shared . . . Dis Honor be minded . . . and me too . . . Washington . . . Country. . . ."

To George B. Butler

[TELEGRAM]
Through War Department   June 5th 1863

Mr George B. Butler
Care of A. T. Stewart
5th Avenue, New York City

I have just received word from Sec Stanton, that an order was made to-day relieving Lt Butler [9] from duty—

Mrs Lincoln

To John Meredith Read [1]

June 16th [1863]
Continental Hotel [2]

Mrs Lincoln presents her kindest regards to Judge Reid [sic] & regrets she was unable from indisposition to receive himself & Lady & trusts, when they visit Washington, she will have that pleasure.

---

[9] Mr. Butler's son, George, Jr., had lost an arm in combat. Later Butler wrote Mrs. Lincoln that his handicapped son was pursuing a successful career as a painter. She must have been gratified to have been able to do a favor for anyone associated with A. T. Stewart.

[1] Identified on p. 65.

[2] Mrs. Lincoln and Tad had been staying at the Continental Hotel in Philadelphia since June 8. She sent several telegrams to the President on this visit; only his replies have been preserved. On this date he wired her: "It is a matter of choice with yourself whether you come home. There is no reason why you should not, that did not exist when you went away. As bearing on the question of your coming home, I do not think the raid into Pennsylvania amounts to anything at all." MS. in the Illinois State Historical Library, Springfield.

To Antonio Bagioli [3]

[TELEGRAM]
Through War Department   1 July 1863

Mr Bajioli [sic]
No 43 West 32nd Street
New York City

A letter directed to you, was sent a few days since, enclosing an important paper for Mr Eugene Little [unidentified] of your city. Please send me a telegram, stating whether it was received by the young man, direct to Edward McManus—Executive Mansion—send through War Department

On July 2, 1863, while driving from the White House to the Soldiers' Home, the President's wife was in a carriage accident, one of several she would suffer in Washington. Sustaining a serious injury to her head, she was incapacitated for three weeks under the care of a nurse; at one point the wound became infected and had to be opened. Worse, Lincoln was hardly in a position to hover at her bedside. As she lay sick and dazed, a tremendous three-day battle was being fought near the little town of Gettysburg, Pennsylvania. The repulsion of this northernmost offensive of Lee's army—and the simultaneous capture of Vicksburg on the Mississippi—proved the turning point of the war, but no one knew it at the time, and Lincoln agonized over the fact that the Confederate forces were allowed to retreat without pursuit.

As soon as she was able to travel, Mrs. Lincoln left Washington which was sweltering through one of the worst heat spells on

[3] Signor Bagioli, a noted musician and teacher, was the father of General Daniel E. Sickles' estranged wife Teresa. Mrs. Lincoln's business with him is unknown.

record, for an extensive trip north. She took Tad with her, and Robert joined them for a long sojourn in the White Mountains, sandwiched between the inevitable stops in New York. During this two-month separation and another later in the year, the Lincolns exchanged dozens of telegrams and letters—certainly many more than have been preserved—inquiring after each other's health and well-being and keeping each other posted on events. None of Mrs. Lincoln's letters for the period remains, but there is a record of her having asked a newspaper correspondent who followed her up Mount Washington, for a piece of paper on which to write a note to the President. She took ten minutes to add a postscript and then said to the correspondent with a smile, "I am sorry to trouble you, but you know a woman's letter is incomplete without a postscript." [4]

Back in New York at the end of September, she seemed disturbed over rumors of an epidemic in Washington; Lincoln wired her to come home, assuring her it was safe and indicating that he missed her and Tad acutely. But before she could arrange her return trip, a long telegram from the President caught up with her at the Fifth Avenue Hotel. In the midst of his terse summary of the Union defeat at Chickamauga, there was a single sentence of tragic import: "Of the [Confederate] killed, one Major Genl. and five brigadiers, including your brother-in-law Helm." [5] Since the telegram had been dispatched through War Department channels, it would have been most inappropriate for the President to have expressed sorrow over the death of an enemy officer, but private reminiscence records him as unbearably grieved.

Ben Helm's fate and its effect on the Lincolns was sadly representative of the heartbreak suffered by divided families everywhere and of the national tragedy itself. Early in 1861, Helm, a West Point graduate, had visited Washington where the President had offered him the coveted post of U.S. Army paymaster, with the rank of major. Lincoln had used every possible argument to persuade Helm to accept, even pleading that Mrs. Lincoln needed Emilie in Washington. Obviously torn, the young man had con-

---

[4] From an article by a correspondent of the Boston *Journal*, "Mrs. Lincoln at Mount Washington," reprinted in the Cincinnati *Gazette*, August 14, 1863. Quoted in Randall, p. 326.

[5] Abraham Lincoln to Mary Lincoln, Washington, D.C., September 24, 1863. MS. in the Illinois State Historical Library, Springfield.

sidered the offer carefully but in the end had returned home to become an officer in the Confederate Army.

His death at Chickamauga was not the first loss to afflict the Lexington branch of the Todd family, which was almost entirely southern in its sympathies. All but one of Mary Lincoln's young half-brothers and sisters were, like their mother, staunch Confederates, as was her full brother George. Their allegiance was used to great effect against her although she had neither seen nor heard from most of them in years. Her half-brother Sam was killed at Shiloh in April of 1862; another, Alexander, at Baton Rouge the following August. David would die later from wounds received at Vicksburg. The deaths of Sam and Alexander had come hard on the heels of Willie's passing and had affected Mary Lincoln deeply, especially that of "Little Aleck," but she could hardly make a display of her grief. Even in private she indicated that something of a shell had formed over her heart. A friend visiting her early in 1862 had been astonished to hear her say that she hoped all of her brothers fighting for the Confederacy would be either captured or killed. When the friend protested, she said, grimly and truthfully, "They would kill my husband if they could, and destroy our Government—the dearest of all things to us." [6]

But "Little Sister" Emilie was, and always had been, an exception. She was dear to both Lincolns, who regarded her as the daughter they had never had, and on this occasion her grief was theirs. In December of 1863, shortly after Mary Lincoln returned from her New York trip, the young widow was at the White House with her older daughter Katherine and pregnant with a third child. Emilie had not intended coming to Washington. She had been in Atlanta where her husband was buried and was starting North for Kentucky when she was stopped at Fortress Monroe, Virginia, and prevented from crossing into Union-held territory unless she took the Oath of Allegiance, something her fine conscience would not permit her to do. The officer who detained her finally communicated word of the impasse to the President, who wired back without hesitation, "Send her to me." [7]

[6] Rev. N. W. Miner, "Mrs. Abraham Lincoln, A Vindication." MS. in the Illinois State Historical Library, Springfield.

[7] This telegram and excerpts from Emilie Helm's diaries describing her White House visit, are quoted in Helm, pp. 219–33.

The reunion that followed was weighted with sorrow and restraint. Great care was taken at first to steer conversation out of the deep, dark waters of politics, war, the deaths of Ben and Willie. But in a quiet moment Lincoln broke down and said to Emilie, "You know, Little Sister, I tried to have Ben come with me. I hope you do not feel any bitterness or that I am in any way to blame for all this sorrow." Emilie later wrote of the incident, "I answered it was 'the fortune of war' and that while my husband loved him and had been deeply grateful to him for his generous offer, he had to follow his conscience. . . . Mr. Lincoln put his arms around me and we both wept."

There were other wrenching moments during Emilie's stay. Once, when Emilie came upon her sister reading a newspaper, Mrs. Lincoln looked up and said with a rush, "Kiss me Emilie, and tell me you love me! I seem to be the scapegoat for both North and South!" It was soon apparent to Emilie that the source of her sister's unhappiness lay much deeper than the wounds inflicted by her critics. After the unsettling episode when Mary announced that Willie and Eddy had stood by her bed, Emilie wrote in her diary, "It *is* unnatural and abnormal, it frightens me. It is not like sister Mary to be so nervous and wrought up. She is on a terrible strain and her smiles seem forced."

When Lincoln begged Emilie to stay on at the White House (despite adverse public comment on her presence), he gave as his reason the fact that his wife's nerves had "gone to pieces." Emilie had to concur, telling the President, "She seems very nervous and excitable and once or twice when I have come into the room suddenly the frightened look in her eyes has appalled me. I believe that if anything should happen to you or Robert or Tad it would kill her." But no amount of urging could persuade Emilie to make her home in Washington, even for a little while, and she left before the first of the year for Kentucky and her mother.

To Edward McManus

[TELEGRAM] [8] *New York, July 28, 1863*

Edward McMannus [sic]
Executive Mansion

Did Robert leave this morning for New York, I hope the President is well answer this immediately [9]

Mrs A Lincoln

To Edward McManus

[TELEGRAM] *New York*
September 21, 1863

Edward McManus
Executive Mansion

Go to Col. McCullum [sic] [1] and ask him to send the green car on to Philadelphia for me and make arrangements for a special car from New York to Philadelphia. Send me a reply immediately.

Mrs. Lincoln

To Abraham Lincoln

[TELEGRAM] *New York*
September 22, 1863

A. Lincoln:

Your telegram received. [2] Did you not receive my reply I have telegraphed Col McCullum to have the car ready at the earliest

---

[8] Not in Mrs. Lincoln's handwriting.
[9] Lincoln himself answered, writing his message at the bottom of the sheet on which the incoming telegram was recorded: "Bob went to Fort-Monroe & only got back to-day—[He] Will start to you at 11 AM to-morrow. All well A. Lincoln." MS. in the Brown University Library, Providence, R.I.
[1] Daniel C. McCallum, Director of Military Railroads.
[2] Lincoln had wired earlier that day: "Did you receive my dispatch of yesterday? Mrs. Cuthbert [see p. 171] did not correctly understand me I directed her to tell

possible moment. Have a very bad cold and am anxious to return home as you may suppose. Taddie is well.

Mrs. Lincoln

To Abraham Lincoln

[TELEGRAM] [3]   *War Dept.*
                                                  Nov 18th 63 [4]

Hon A. Lincoln
Gettysburg, Pa.

The Dr has just left. We hope dear Taddie is slightly better [5] will send you a telegram in the morning.

Mrs Lincoln

To "Mrs Blair" [6]

Nov 20 [1863]

My Dear Mrs Blair

Some tickets, have been sent us, for the concert this evening, pardon my sending you, three or four. Your children, perhaps may be interested in attending. The weather, is certainly *not* very inviting—

Very truly
Mrs A. Lincoln [7]

---

you to use your own pleasure whether to stay or come; and I did not say it is sickly and that you should on no account come. So far as I see or know, it was never healthier and I really wish to see you. Answer this on receipt. A. Lincoln." MS. in the Illinois State Historical Library, Springfield.

[3] Not in Mrs. Lincoln's handwriting.

[4] On the following day Lincoln delivered his historic address at the dedication of the soldiers' cemetery in Gettysburg.

[5] Tad was at this time ill with a severe case of scarlatina.

[6] Probably the wife of Montgomery Blair, Postmaster General, 1861–4.

[7] This note was written out on a visiting card engraved with Mrs. Lincoln's name as above.

To John W. Garrett [8]

[TELEGRAM] [9]   *[New York]*
                                 December 1, 1863

To Mr Garrett   Balt & O R R
Camden Station
Be kind enough to have a special car at New York for me on Tuesday morning at Seven oclock I wish to return on that day to Washn

                                        Mrs Lincoln.

To Abraham Lincoln

[TELEGRAM]   *New York*
                                 December 4, 1863

Abraham Lincoln
President United States.

Reached here last evening. Very tired and severe headache. Hope to hear you are doing well.[1] Expect a telegraph to-day.[2]

                                        Mrs. Lincoln

To Abraham Lincoln

[TELEGRAM]   *December 6, 1863*

A. Lincoln

  Do let me know immediately how Taddie and yourself are.[3] I will be home by Tuesday without fail; sooner if needed.

                                        Mrs. Lincoln

[8] President of the Baltimore & Ohio Railroad.
[9] Not in Mrs. Lincoln's handwriting.
[1] Lincoln was convalescing from a mild case of smallpox.
[2] Lincoln replied on December 5: "All doing well." MS. in the Illinois State Historical Library, Springfield.
[3] Lincoln replied to this message on December 6: "All doing well." MS. in the Illinois State Historical Library, Springfield.

To Edward McManus

[TELEGRAM]   *New York*
                             December 6, 1863

Edward McManus
Executive Mansion

Let me know immediately exactly how Mr. Lincoln and Taddie are.[4]

Mrs. Lincoln

To Abraham Lincoln

[TELEGRAM]   *New York*
                             December 7, 1863

A. Lincoln

Will leave here positively at 8 a.m. Tuesday morning. Have carriage waiting at depot in Washington at 6 p.m. Did Tad receive his book.[5] Please answer.[6]

Mrs. Lincoln

[4] Lincoln replied on December 7: "All doing well. Tad confidently expects you to-night. When will you come?" MS. in the Illinois State Historical Library, Springfield.

[5] Mrs. Katrina Kindel of Grand Rapids, Michigan, is the owner of a card bearing the legend "Taddie Lincoln from his loving Mother Dec. 4th 63." The card was probably in the gift book sent from New York.

[6] Lincoln replied an hour after his wife's telegram was received: "Tad has received his book. The carriage shall be ready at 6. pm tomorrow." MS. in the Illinois State Historical Library, Springfield.

Eighteen sixty-four loomed large at the White House. In November Lincoln would have to go before the electorate and ask for confidence in his leadership at a time when that leadership was extremely uncertain. Although thousands of volunteers had begun pouring into the Union ranks after the victories at Gettysburg and Vicksburg, and foreign intervention on the side of the Confederacy was no longer a possibility, the end of the war was nowhere in sight, and Lincoln's political opponents were ready to take advantage of the fact.

On March 10 a long search was ended: the President named Ulysses S. Grant commander of all the Union armies. Grant had been responsible for the fall of Vicksburg and for other badly needed victories in the West. He was a scruffy, taciturn soldier with no pretensions other than the certainty that he could win the war. Mrs. Lincoln had her opinion of Grant, which she voiced in her usual vehement terms to her husband. If McClellan had been a "humbug," Grant was a "butcher." When the President argued that Grant had been successful in the field, she answered, "Yes, he generally manages to claim a victory, but such a victory! He loses two men to the enemy's one. He has no management, no regard for life. . . . I could fight an army as well myself." To this Lincoln could only reply lightly, "Well, mother, supposing that we give you command of the army. No doubt you would do much better than any general that has been tried." [7]

The President's house was the scene of considerable social activity throughout 1864; its chatelaine planned to leave no stone unturned to insure her husband's re-election. The undersides of some of those stones revealed a few unappetizing specimens, but Mary Lincoln forged ahead, determined to cultivate anyone who could conceivably be of use politically. She gave receptions, dinners, and intimate "at homes," did favors when she could, and made judicious offerings of flowers and small gifts.

The ratio of gifts received to gifts given nonetheless continued high. Mary Lincoln had a child's passion for presents, accepting all, from the humblest to the most impressive, with impartial delight. Grapes sent from Ohio, apple cider from New Jersey, figs from the

[7] Keckley, pp. 132–4.

Consul at Smyrna, were sampled and passed around. Pieces of crude furniture fashioned by rural craftsmen were valued as tokens of love and loyalty. But there was so much more! Mrs. Lincoln's treasures—and they *were* hers, not the nation's, she insisted—included an elaborate tablecover imported from Constantinople, yards of lace and China silk, fabrics embroidered in France, books, jewelry, and such novelties as Wheeler & Wilson's de luxe model sewing machine, silver plated and inlaid with pearl and enamel. A gold and enamel brooch, set with forty-seven rose diamonds, and cuff pins set with twenty-seven diamonds each were presented Mrs. Lincoln by "her friend William Mortimer." Donors were noted and remembered.

This lavish hoard was augmented by the gifts Mary Lincoln gave herself: bonnets, gowns, slippers, and shawls; diamond earknobs, tiny gilt clocks, sets of china, silver, and crystal. She gloated happily over her possessions, thrilled at their newness, used some of them once or twice and others not at all. The mere sight of a diamond brooch from Tiffany or Galt, glittering in its box, was enough to give her profound pleasure—until a month later her eye was caught by still another, prettier piece, and the first was forgotten.[8]

Her susceptibilities were no secret. Shopkeepers welcomed her visits to their establishments, set out their finest goods for her inspection, and extended her almost unlimited credit. By the spring of 1864 her appetite for luxury goods became a matter of public concern. In May the New York *Herald* described her most recent visit to that city as a "business trip" and left no doubt as to the nature of her "business." "From the early hours . . . until late in the evening," reported the paper, "Mrs. Lincoln ransacked the treasures of the Broadway dry goods stores. The evenings were spent in company of a few private friends."[9] Some years later, the journalist Mary Clemmer Ames, no friend of Mrs. Lincoln, wrote of the popular indignation felt toward her at the time: "While her sister women scraped lint, sewed bandages, and put on nurses' caps, and gave their all to country and to death, the wife of the President of the United States spent her time in rolling to and fro between Washington and New York, intent on extravagant purchases for herself and

[8] A partial listing of Mrs. Lincoln's jewelry collection can be found in her letter to Alexander Williamson, January 3, 1866.

[9] New York *Herald*, May 2, 1864.

the White House. Mrs. Lincoln seemed to have nothing to do but 'shop,' and the reports of her lavish bargains, in the newspapers, were vulgar and sensational in the extreme." [1]

Mary Lincoln was far from being the callous creature described by her detractors. In one part of her consciousness—the healthy part—she was deeply affected by the costs and casualties of the war. But there were areas in which she could not think clearly, in which she was increasingly weak and deluded: money was foremost among them.

No matter how many economies she introduced into her household, no matter how much she or her friends managed to scrape together to hold her creditors at bay, she was always short of funds and haunted by debt, for the simple reason that she could not stop buying. The cheerful, rich atmosphere of the shops, the mental effort of choosing between two cashmere shawls (and then taking them both) were charms to banish dark thoughts of battlefield slaughter and Washington intrigue, forebodings of illness and sudden death. She had worked out an elaborate rationale for her purchases, convincing herself that wearing clothes of rich, imported materials was nothing less than a patriotic obligation, because of the revenue such stuffs brought into the treasury. She also felt an obligation to be well-dressed at all times, so as not to do injustice to her position and invite critical comment. Finally, she was certain that, should any serious financial difficulty overtake her, her possessions could be sold for a considerable sum. As the election approached, she confessed to Mrs. Keckley that she owed over $27,000 to the New York stores, particularly to A. T. Stewart. (One white point lace shawl, later valued at $2,000,[2] provides an indication of how the totals must have run up.) Lincoln was given to comment that his wife was more anxious than he over the outcome of the election, never guessing the true reason for her concern. "If he is re-elected," Mrs. Lincoln confided to her dressmaker, "I can keep him in ignonorance of my affairs; but if he is defeated, then the bills will be sent in, and he will know all." [3]

---

[1] Mary Clemmer (Ames). *Ten Years in Washington or Inside Life and Scenes in Our National Capital as a Woman Sees Them.* Hartford, 1882, p. 237.
[2] From a listing in the New York *Semi-Weekly Tribune*, October 8, 1867.
[3] Keckley, p. 150.

Never one to minimize her troubles—or her importance—Mary Lincoln began to imagine herself as being responsible for her husband's defeat, just when her financial deliverance depended on victory. She told Mrs. Keckley that if her husband's enemies discovered the extent of her indebtedness they would use the information against him so effectively as to cast doubt on his own integrity. He would be thrown out of office. Unable to take the long view, well aware of the President's own concern over his re-election, Mrs. Lincoln was, in Mrs. Keckley's words, "almost crazy with anxiety and fear." [4]

Panic eventually gave way to a plan: those Republican politicians who had grown affluent on presidential patronage must recognize an obligation to rescue Mrs. Lincoln from a predicament which, if publicized, could imperil the party's chances in November. Defeat would not only deprive the Union of its victory and of Lincoln's services, but would cost these gentlemen their own comfortable positions. They must pay her debts.

Beginning early in 1864, Mary Lincoln set out on her own campaign to woo the vulnerable: Cabinet officials, local satraps, "fat cats," and holders of government contracts—to call in the political debts owed her husband and in some cases, she did not hesitate to imply, herself. In personal confrontations tears flowed from a well of genuine distress. "That lady," Commissioner of Agriculture Isaac Newton told John Hay, "has set here on this here sofy & shed tears by the pint a begging me to pay her debts which was unbeknownst to the President." [5] When weeping failed to bring results —as in Newton's case—she employed her considerable skill at cajolery. Rufus F. Andrews, Marshall O. Roberts, Abram Wakeman, "Pet" Halsted, Simeon Draper and others of their ilk were treated to the company and confidences of the President's lady. All were gently reminded of past favors and no doubt assured of continued consideration. There is evidence to indicate that these efforts bore fruit in the way of loans, direct payments, or some form of intercession with creditors. Assistance came in the end not so much from gratitude or greed, but from fear: fear of Mrs. Lincoln's influence,

[4] *Ibid.*, p. 151.
[5] Quoted in *Lincoln and the Civil War in the Diaries and Letters of John Hay.* Edited by Tyler Dennett. New York, 1939, p. 274.

The Lincoln home at the corner of Eighth and Jackson Streets in Springfield in the summer of 1860. Lincoln is standing in the front yard, with Willie beside him; Tad is astride the fence

Mary Lincoln with Willie and Tad in Springfield, soon after Lincoln's election to the Presidency in 1860

OVERLEAF

The earliest known photographs of the Lincolns, taken in Springfield in 1846, the year Lincoln was elected to Congress

Mary Lincoln in two formal poses taken in 1861 and early 1862 by Mathew Brady

LEFT
*President Lincoln
and his youngest son, Tad,
on February 9, 1864*

ABOVE LEFT
*Tad Lincoln in Frankfurt
at the age of seventeen*

ABOVE RIGHT
*Elizabeth Todd Edwards in 1859,
holding her grandson, Edward
Lewis Baker, Jr., the "Dear Lewis"
of Mrs. Lincoln's later years*

RIGHT
*Robert Lincoln
at the time of his marriage*

*"Little Sister" Emilie Todd Helm and her husband,
General Ben Hardin Helm, in his Confederate uniform*

LEFT
*Mary Lincoln as she looked during her first year
in the White House, photographed by Brady*

Three of Mrs. Lincoln's closest confidants in Washington:
Charles Sumner (above); Elizabeth Keckley and Abram Wakeman (opposite)

Simon Cameron and William H. Herndon

OPPOSITE
David Davis, Eliza Slataper and Mary Jane Welles

Mrs. Lincoln's wardrobe being examined at the time of the
"Old Clothes Scandal" in 1867. The drawing is from Harper's Weekly

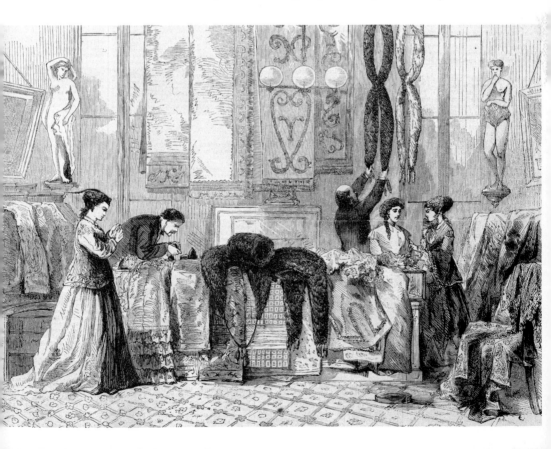

Pages from two of Mary Lincoln's letters; the one at top, left, written to Emilie Helm in 1857, the one at bottom, left, written to Noyes W. Miner in 1882

Mary Lincoln during her early widowhood

*The last known photograph of Mary Todd Lincoln,
said to have been taken during the late 1870's by a
spiritualist. A ghostly figure of the late
President has been superimposed on the photograph*

fear of defeat in November, fear that she knew too much of lower-echelon corruption.

A glimpse into some of these maneuverings can be found in two groups of letters discovered relatively recently. The first were those written to "Pet" Halsted; the second, those addressed to Abram Wakeman, a shrewd, genial New York politico who had served as congressman in the fifties, then as Postmaster of New York City. In September of 1864 Lincoln appointed Wakeman Surveyor of the Port of New York as a sop to the powerful Seward-Weed machine. It was, next to the Customs House, the most sought-after patronage post within the gift of the administration.

It is not known precisely at what point in 1864 Mrs. Lincoln's acquaintance with Wakeman blossomed into a confidential relation-ship, but he was in and out of Washington as she was in and out of New York, and their paths must have crossed frequently. She would insist years later that she had been instrumental in securing him what she called the "lucrative" post of Surveyor.[6] Considering the political exigencies of the hour, her claim cannot be taken seriously, but she at least must have added her voice to those urging the ap-pointment. And why not? With his direct wire to Seward, Thurlow Weed and James Gordon Bennett, with his intimate knowledge of New York politics, Wakeman was a mine of information and a valuable friend.

It is interesting to contrast the letters Mrs. Lincoln wrote to Wakeman in 1864 and 1865 with those she was writing Charles Sumner during the same period. The two sets of documents reflect sharply the two sides of her personality. With the Massachusetts senator she took pains to be gracious and dignified, even in asking favors, to write well and to display the best side of herself: her com-passion for the oppressed, her love of music and literature. The let-ters to Wakeman are for the most part careless in construction and somewhat belligerent in tone. They are excellent examples of Mary Lincoln's talent for combining candor with caution and of her tend-ency to endow the mildest machinations with an air of vast and mys-terious import. Domestic difficulties at the White House take on the air of Borgian plots; individuals are identified only by initials. Some statements are so guarded as to be nearly incomprehensible. She

[6] Mary Lincoln to Messrs. Brady and Keyes, September 14, [1867].

continually urged Wakeman to destroy her letters and hold his tongue—admonitions that would crop up frequently in future correspondence as her troubles multiplied. She would have been horrified to learn how rarely such requests were heeded.

To Catherine Sumwalt [7]

[TELEGRAM] *Washington*
Monday January 4th [1864]

Mrs C. C. Sumwalt
No 66 S Sharp St
Baltimore Maryland

Meet, a lady, who has some work for you at Baltimore Depot at 8 o'clock this p.m. on green car.

Mrs L.

To Julian Dartois [8]

[TELEGRAM]
Through War Department   Monday Jany 11th [1864]

J. Dartois—
Broadway New York

My narrow width white fringe, has not yet reached me—I need it very much—

Mrs Lincoln

[7] The 1864 Baltimore city directory lists Mrs. Sumwalt as a dressmaker.
[8] An importer and manufacturer of "ladies' new trimmings."

To Benjamin F. Butler [9]

Executive Mansion
Washington, Jany 15th, 1864

My dear Sir:

Capt Stackpole a most worthy man & an especial friend of the President is anxious to have his vessel, to go into the Oyster trade, he is anxious, for a permit from you, to that effect. Any kindness shown him, will be gratefully appreciated by the President and Mrs Lincoln— [1]

Very R. Mrs Lincoln

To Daniel E. Sickles [2]

Washington
Feb 6th 64

Major. Gen Sickles
Brevoort House

I am pleased to announce to you my entire innocence as to flowers & music—A sensation, doubtless emanating from the host & the proprietor of the Conservatory—W[ood] [3] by placing a card on

[9] Another former politician who raised a regiment and became a major general. He had been recently appointed commander of the Department of Virginia and North Carolina (later the Army of the James).

[1] This recommendation was followed by one from the President.

[2] Sickles, who had lost a leg at Gettysburg, was for the moment inactive and living in New York.

[3] Fernando Wood, who, as Democratic mayor of New York, in 1861 had made the interesting suggestion that New York City secede from the Union and become a "free city." In January 1864 Wood, now a congressman, gave a large reception. Among the flowers was a bouquet from Mrs. Lincoln prominently displayed with her card. The card, which has been preserved, read "Compliments of Mrs. A. Lincoln, Executive Mansion, Jany 25th." Apparently more cards were written to give the impression that she had supplied all the flowers for the occasion; it was also said that she had sent the Marine Band. Mrs. Wood had in fact asked that she do so; she had refused, but for courtesy's sake had sent the bouquet. (See *The New York Times*, January 28 and February 4, 1864.)

each vase of flowers, for political effect—With the exception of two political public receptions, they [the Woods] have not entered the [White] house—all of my, friends, who know my detestation of disloyal persons will discredit the rumor—You know me too well to believe it—

Tell your friend—Mrs R-, V- has now called—

Mrs Lincoln—

To E. N. Drury

[RECEIPT] [4]

White House, Washington, D. C.
February 18th 1864

Received of Lieut. E. N. Drury, a package addressed, "Little Master Lincoln," "care of Mrs Lincoln".—from Mr Ellsworth,[5] Vergennes, Vt.

Mary Lincoln

To Daniel E. Sickles

Saturday Feb 20th [1864]

My Dear Sir.

Having ascertained Mr Foster's [6] number, which is 450-6th St. immediately by—Gov Chase's residence—I take the liberty of informing you. A visit to him, may afford you, an hour's pleasant past time—We have never had so distinguished & brilliant a mati-

[4] Not in Mrs. Lincoln's handwriting, but signed by her.
[5] Ephraim D. Ellsworth, father of the late hero and friend of the Lincolns, Elmer E. Ellsworth (see p. 92). After Colonel Ellsworth's death, Lincoln had undertaken to ensure his father financial security by appointing him to several posts, the last of which was at the Champlain Arsenal at Vergennes.
[6] The Washington city directory for 1864 lists no "Mr Foster" at the above address. His identity is therefore in doubt, but he may have been Thomas Gales Foster, eminent spiritualist speaker, who also held a position in the War Department. Sickles is known to have participated in at least one of the seances to which Mrs. Lincoln became addicted after Willie's death.

nee, as that of *to day*, you must have been indisposed or I am sure
you would have favored us, with your presence— The President, is
a little better to day,[7] was able to visit the "blue room;" to night, I
will try & persuade him, to take some medicine & rest a little on the
morrow—Do not fail us tomorrow eve to dinner, at 6½ o'clock.

Sincerely yr friend
M. L.

To Larz Anderson [8]

[TELEGRAM] *Feb 21st* [1864]

Mr Larz Anderson
Cincinnati—

I assure you that it is a great disappointment, not having the young
gentlemen,[9] with us at this time—Can they not, still come on?

Mrs Lincoln

To Clement Heerdt & Company

[TELEGRAM]
Through War Department   *Feb 25th 64*

Clement Heerdt & Co
93 Water Street
New York—

Please send immediately 1 basket champagne, the "Widow Cliquot"
brand, the other basket of any choice quality you consider desirable.

Mrs Lincoln—

---

[7] The nature of Lincoln's illness is not known. That chronicle of minutiae, *Lincoln Day by Day* (Washington, 1960), makes no mention of his having been indisposed and, indeed, indicates that on the preceding day he engaged in normal activity and spent the evening at the theater.

[8] Brother of Major Robert Anderson, and father of Robert's friend and classmate, Frederick P. Anderson.

[9] Probably Fred and friends.

To Clement Heerdt & Company

[TELEGRAM]   *Feb 26–64*

Clement, Heerdt & Co
93 Water Street
New York—

A telegram was sent you in reference to a basket of champagne—
Please send a basket of the kind requested also another one, of the
choicest quality, you have in store

Mrs Lincoln—

To "Mr Sanford" [1]

*Executive Mansion
March 4th [1864]*

Mrs Lincoln presents her compliments & sincere regrets to Mr Sanford, that owing to a slight indisposition, she was unable to see him,
last evening. If disengaged, to day at 3½ o'clock, she will be pleased
to have him join them in a drive at that hour. If agreeable to him,
then carriage, will wait upon him at that hour. Very truly,

Mary Lincoln

---

[1] "Mr Sanford" could have been Mr—later General—E. S. Sanford, vice-president
of the Adams Express Company and president of the American Telegraph Company, who was appointed head of the military telegraph. Another possibility is
James T. Sanford, one of a group of New York merchants who contributed heavily
to the Republican party.

To Mary Ann Cuthbert [2]

[TELEGRAM]
Through War Department   [*March 6, 1864*]

Mrs Cuthbert
Metropolitan Hotel
New York

There is a letter for you at your Hotel here—will be one tomorrow morning also—Write & telegraph

Mrs Lincoln

To Mary Ann Cuthbert

[TELEGRAM]   *Friday morning*
Through War Department   *March 7, 1864*

Mrs Cuthbert
Metropolitan Hotel

Do not leave New York, until tomorrow, Saturday evening.

Mrs Lincoln

To Mary Ann Cuthbert

[TELEGRAM]
Through War Department   [*March 9, 1864*]

Mrs Cuthbert—
Metropolitan Hotel
New York

Meet Thomas Cross Monday morning, 9 or 10 o'clock—No 1226 Chestnut Street Philadelphia. Let Charles [3] come on home

Mrs Lincoln

[2] Seamstress and later chief housekeeper at the White House. Like many other White House employees, Mrs. Cuthbert often ran errands for Mrs. Lincoln. Subsequent correspondence reveals a confidential relationship between the two women, especially in the area of Mrs. Lincoln's debts.
[3] Probably Charles Forbes, a White House staff member, who, like Tom Cross, often watched over Tad.

To Mary Ann Cuthbert

[TELEGRAM]   [*March 10, 1864*]

Mrs Cuthbert
Care of Mr Warren Leland,
Metropolitan Hotel, New York City
Come back—

                                                    Mrs Lincoln

Request for a Pass

                                                    March 11th [*1864*]

Please give Washington Sanford [sic] [4] a pass, to go over the Long
Bridge, to "Camp Distribution." [5]

                                                    Mrs Lincoln

To Charles Sumner

                                            Executive Mansion
                                            Tuesday morning
                                            March 28, 1864

My dear sir:

    Words, are scarcely an atonement, for the inadvertent manner,
in which I addressed you on yesterday, therefore, I pray you, accept
this little peace offering, for your table, a few fresh flowers, brought
up, by the gardener. I am aware, that you, do not usually frequent
large crowds, or attend receptions, they are certainly, *somewhat* of
an annoyance, but a necessity, which of course, in this house cannot

[4] George Washington Sandford, listed in Interior Department records as a "laborer" at the White House.
[5] "Camp Distribution" in Virginia, also known as "Camp Misery," was a gathering place for the army's derelicts.

be dispensed with. Yet, in reference, to your expected attendance, my words were mere badinage.

We have no good news, from that brave youth, Col Dahlgren,[6] fears are now entertained that he is certainly killed. Trusting that your kind nature, will excuse me, I remain respectfully

Mrs Lincoln

To Emmanuel Uhlfelder [7]

[TELEGRAM]
Through War Department   *April 1, 1864*

E. Uhlfelder
Broadway
New York

Two weeks ago, I sent you a check for your bill. Please return the bill receipted.

Mrs Lincoln

To Edwin A. Brooks [8]

[TELEGRAM]   [*April 1, 1864*][9]

Edwin A. Brooks
Opposite Metropolitan Hotel
New York

Two weeks ago, I sent you a check for your bill. Please return the bill—receipted.

Mrs Lincoln

[6] Colonel Ulric Dahlgren, son of Admiral John A. Dahlgren, former Chief of Ordnance for the navy and inventor of several innovative weapons. Young Dahlgren, though he had lost a leg, was widely known for his commando exploits. On March 7, 1864, he was killed in an unsuccessful attack on a position near Richmond; his mutilated body was captured by the Confederates and displayed as an object lesson.

[7] A dealer in "fancy goods."

[8] An importer and manufacturer of boots and shoes.

[9] This telegram was written out by Mrs. Lincoln on the same sheet as the preceding one.

To Charles Sumner

Tuesday
April 5th [1864]

My Dear Sir:

I take the liberty of introducing to your disguished notice, these two colored persons, who come to us very highly recommended, from some of our most loyal families of Phil- The man calls himself "Mr Hamilton & the woman Mrs Johnson [1] Both appear to be very genteel & intelligent persons, the latter has devoted all her time & labor for the last three years to our suffering & wounded soldiers. They promised some of our prominent Phil- friends they would call to see you, whom all the oppressed colored race, have so much cause, to honor && the liberty I am sure I am taking you will excuse.

Our friend, whom we all *so* loved & esteemed, has so suddenly & unexpectedly passed away—Mr Lovejoy! [2] An all wise power, directs these dispensations, yet it appears to our weak & oftentimes erring judgments. "*He* should have died *hereafter*."

With great respect,
Mary Lincoln

[*To A. T. Stewart*] [3]

Washington
April 16th [1864]

Private

Your letter has been received, and I write to thank you, for your patience and soliciting as an especial favor to me, (having

---

[1] Francis B. Carpenter, in his book *Six Months at the White House* (New York, 1866), p. 199, described Caroline Johnson as "an estimable colored woman . . . an active nurse . . . who had once been a slave." Hamilton was a minister.

[2] Owen Lovejoy, the noted abolitionist congressman from Illinois.

[3] There is no salutation on this letter and, though the envelope in which it was sent has been preserved, the name and address of the recipient have been torn off. It was probably written to A. T. Stewart who, at one point, threatened to sue Mrs. Lincoln for money owed him.

been a punctual customer & always hoping to be so, a delay of the Settlement of my account with you, until the 1st of June—when I promise, that without fail, *then*, the whole account shall be settled. I deeply regret, that I am so unusually situated & trust hereafter, to settle as I purchase. I desire to order, a black India Camel's Hair shawl, yet in sufficient time, will see you, to give directions.

With many apologies, for thus writing to you & hoping as the 1st of June, is so nearly approaching, and anticipating a favorable answer, I remain very Resp—

Mrs Lincoln

To Warren Leland [4]

[TELEGRAM]
Through War Department [*April* 27, *1864*]

Mr Warren Leland
Metropolitan Hotel New York

We [5] leave Wash- on the 7 o'clock this evening train, will reach New York, on the 4 or 5 oclock train tomorrow morning. Please have carriage waiting

Mrs L-

To Abraham Lincoln

[TELEGRAM]
New York City
April 28, 1864

Hon A. Lincoln
President United States

We reached here in safety. Hope you are well. Please send me by mail to-day a check for $50 directed to me, care Mr Warren Leland, Metropolitan Hotel, Tad says are the goats well? [6]

Mrs Lincoln

[4] Manager of the Metropolitan Hotel.
[5] Mrs. Lincoln and Tad.
[6] Lincoln replied on the same day, "The draft will go to you. Tell Tad the goats and father are very well—especially the goats." MS. in the National Archives.

To Abram Wakeman

May 3rd [1864]

Mrs and Miss Haight of N. Y.[7] accompany Mrs Lincoln in a drive to the Soldier's Home, this morning at 12 o'clock & Mrs L. would be pleased to have Mr Wakeman accompany them.

To Mary Jane Welles

Executive Mansion
May 27th 64

My Dear Mrs Welles:

I was quite unable during several hours yesterday to leave my bed, owing to an intensely severe headache & although it has left me, yet I am feeling so weak this morning that I fear, that I shall be prevented from visiting the Hospitals today. I cannot venture to promise about *tomorrow*, yet, will say Monday morning, if you are disengaged at 11 o'clock. I believe, you are likewise, a sufferer, from these bilious attacks & know how much inclined to *nausea* they leave you—During the day, I will endeavour to have the gardener, pick the few first strawberries & send them to you for Gen [John C.?] Robinson, they are not very ripe and very scarce, yet the taste is pleasant for an invalid. With high regard, I remain

Mary Lincoln

[7] Possibly the wife and daughter of Representative Edward Haight of New York.

To Phineas D. Gurley

July 15th [1864]
Executive Mansion

Dear Sir:

You will doubtless be pleased to hear, that the lady from Va, who made an application for employment for her husband, has been successful. He was employed as *lamp lighter* and she is represented, as being very grateful. It would have been very sad indeed, if they had been left, uncared for, when they proved themselves, so loyal. Be kind enough to accept this bouquet, with the best wishes of yours Respectfully,

Mary Lincoln

To George D. Ramsay [8]

Wednesday Morning
July 20 [1864]

My Dear Sir:

An intense headache, caused by driving out, in the heat of the day, deprived me of the pleasure of seeing yourself & niece, when you called. I *begin*, to consider myself quite unfortunate, as regards yourself, for it is such a pleasure, *especially*, at such a charming place as *this* [the Soldiers' Home], to receive one's friends. I trust Mrs Ramsey [sic] Miss R & yourself, will favor me by frequently driving out, these delightful evenings. Cuthbert mentioned to me on yesterday, that one of your children, was sick, I shall be pleased to learn, of its recovery. Trusting you will remember us, in our *country* retirement, & with kindest regards to your family, I remain ever sincerely your friend

Mary Lincoln

[8] Brigadier General Ramsay was at this time Chief of Ordnance for the U.S. Artillery.

To Robert T. Lincoln

[TELEGRAM]   *Executive Mansion*
Through War Department   July 29th [1864]

Mr Robert T. Lincoln
Union Hotel
Saratoga New York—

It is very warm & dusty here. If agreeable to you, remain a week or
ten days longer—on Monday will send you what is necessary.[9]

Mrs Lincoln

To Mercy Levering Conkling [1]

Soldiers' Home
Saturday morning
July 29th [1864]

My dear Mrs Conkling:

Mr Lincoln informed me last evening, that you had accompanied Mr Conkling to Washington. As we are contemplating going down to Fortress Monroe to day,[2] about 3 or 4 o'clock, it will
afford us great pleasure, to have you join us. We propose returning
on Monday morning & in *this* excessively warm weather, we may
perhaps be able to find an *occasional* cool breeze, on the river.

Anticipating the pleasure of seeing you, I remain sincerely
your friend

Mary Lincoln

[9] It is safe to assume that what was "necessary" to Robert was money.
[1] Mrs. Lincoln's girlhood friend. See letters of July 23, 1840; December 1840;
June 1841.
[2] The trip, designed to enable Lincoln to discuss the combining of several departments under the command of General George G. Meade, was postponed until
Monday, the 31st. On the same date, Mrs. Lincoln wrote General Ramsay a
three-page note (full text unavailable) saying, in part, "Mr L- & myself with
two or three friends contemplate leaving for Fortress Monroe to day about
three or four o'clock. It will afford us great pleasure to have you join our party
as we return Monday morning. . . . The President has already several gentlemen friends to accompany him. . . ." Published in Parke-Bernet Catalogue,
Madlener Sale, January 29, 1958. Item 207.

To George A. Hearn [3]

[TELEGRAM]   *Executive Mansion*
Through War Department   Aug 1 1864

To George A. Hearn
Broadway
New York

Will you send your check to day.[4]

Mrs Lincoln

To "Mrs Agen" [5]

Campbell Hospital
Washington, D.C.
Aug 10th 1864

My dear Mrs Agen—

I am sitting by the side of your soldier boy. He has been quite sick, but is getting well. He tells me to say to you that he is all right. With respect for the mother of the young soldier.

Mrs Abraham Lincoln

---

[3] A New York drygoods merchant, founder of Hearn's Department Store.
[4] (Will send your check today?)
[5] This is the only known letter written by Mrs. Lincoln for a soldier she visited in the hospital. James Agen had been stricken with fever in the army near Richmond. According to his later recollections, he was visited twice by a woman who first brought him flowers and, on a second visit, wrote his mother for him. He did not know who the woman was until his mother showed him the above letter when he returned home. It was published in the Chicago *Times Herald* in June 1897 along with Mr. Agen's story.

To Abram Wakeman

Soldiers' Home
September 23 [1864]

My Dear Mr Wakeman

I am just recovering from a little tedious indisposition and pour passer le temps and perhaps to interrupt you in your numerous engagements, I am now writing. You doubtless rejoiced with us over Sheridan's last victory; [6] these successes, will be beneficial in the rapidly approaching Election. I fear you had not a very encouraging report to make of your conversation with Mr L as regards Mr B[ennett] and General S[ickles]. A little notice of them would strengthen us very much I think. The P feels very kindly he assured me, towards General S and appreciates a kind expression of Mr B's very much; altogether, it is strange. I see that the miserable "World" is criticizing very much, a sermon preached by your pastor, Dr Thomson [sic],[7] last Sabbath. Of course, it would be far too loyal for their rebellious minds. Also in yesterday's paper they continue their villanous aspersions. Poor Mr L who is almost a monomaniac on the subject of honesty, they positively assert that to a near relative of his, a lady, he gave an order for a contract.[8] In the first place, he has neither brother nor sister, aunt or uncle, and only a few third cousins, no nearer ones; that clears him entirely as to any connection. Those whom he would have cared to see prospering, did not really require his assistance. At any rate on no terms would either male or female receive, his signature to enable them to profit by our Government. The P.'s own salary is not over $10,000 in gold, taxes $900.[9] With such an establishment to keep up, you may imagine

6 On September 22, General Philip Sheridan had routed a superior force under Jubal Early in the battle of Fisher's Hill, Virginia. The victory all but wiped out Confederate resistance in the Shenandoah Valley.

7 The Reverend J. P. Thompson, New York Congregationalist minister. His sermons at the Broadway Tabernacle were widely reprinted in northern papers and praised for their erudition, eloquence and loyalty to the Union cause.

8 The *World* article on September 22, 1864, was one of a series of pre-election editorials questioning the integrity of "Honest Abe." It accused him of encouraging irregularities in the St. Louis Quartermaster's Department. Mrs. Lincoln's summary of its major point was accurate, and her anger justified.

9 Lincoln's nominal salary was $25,000 a year, taken in greenbacks. The actual tax he paid in 1864 was $1,183 (refunded to his family, with other amounts,

we have not enriched ourselves. In truth, I have had to endeavor to be as economical as possible; more so than I have ever been before in my life. It would have been a great delight to me to have had the means to entertain, generally as should be done at the Executive Mansion, it would have been my pride and pleasure, so when the World dares to insinuate aught against us, the public should take them in hand. With the exception of what I have said to you as regards our friend, Mr. W.[1] It is the first thought or conversation I have ever had on the subject of contract. In his case and because he has exerted a friendly influence without any reward, you, I am sure, will make your word good in his case. He is truly a disinterested friend. I have not received the letter. I presume you have handed it to him. I will be pleased to receive a line from you when you have any news. I hope some day to have the pleasure of knowing Mrs Wakeman.

Truly your Friend
Mary Lincoln

To Abram Wakeman

Oct 23rd [1864]

My dear Mr Wakeman—

I have been much amused in looking over the *Sunday Mercury* to see that some kind Merchant, has been so generous towards us![2] When will their vile fabrications cease: Not until they find Mr L reelected. This is the reason, that makes their falsehoods so desperate! Please say *not a word*, to *anyone* not even W[eed] about the 5th Avenue business.[3] I write in *great* haste—

Your friend
M. L.

---

years after his death as a result of a ruling that the presidential salary was not subject to taxation). The greater portion of Lincoln's salary was invested in government securities.

[1] "Mr W" was Thurlow Weed, newspaper publisher and a Republican "boss" of New York, one of whose protégés Wakeman was.

[2] The editors have been unable to locate this issue of the *Mercury*, but the reference was probably to reports that Mrs. Lincoln had been forgiven a debt.

[3] Possibly an incident or meeting that took place at the Fifth Avenue Hotel.

To Elizabeth Keckley

[TELEGRAM]
Through War Department   [*November 2, 1864*] [4]

Mrs Elizabeth Keckley
153 West 47th Street
New York

On Tuesday, at noon, I sent you a letter, with check enclosed, for full amount, for both articles—leave the goods with Mrs Martin [unidentified].

Mrs Lincoln

To Gideon B. Welles

Executive Mansion
Washington, Nov 2d, 1864

Hon Sec Welles—

James Eager, desires a situation, as Watchman or messenger. He is a very worthy man & any business given him, will be faithfully attended to & thankfully received.

Very respectfully
Mrs Lincoln—

To Edwin M. Stanton

November 9th [1864]

Sec of War

H. Kelly is allowed a furlough of two days, to Baltimore & return—As *he* is a faithful attendant at the W. H. Door—and if the Sec of Way [sic] will give a transportation ticket, it will oblige

Mrs L

---

[4] The date is stamped on the face of the telegram.

Election day of 1864 was bleak and rainy in Washington. As the President slogged across to the War Department telegraph office to receive the returns, his wife paced her room in a fever of anxiety until news of victory arrived. A four-year reprieve had been granted her. Breathing easier, she could tell Mrs. Keckley, "Now that we have won the position, I almost wish it were otherwise. Poor Mr. Lincoln is looking so broken-hearted, so completely worn out, I fear he will not get through the next four years." [5] Lincoln's deteriorating health was not the only thing she had been almost too frantic to notice for months. In the last year of their life together, there appears to have been a lack of communication and considerable tension between the President and his wife.

Much of the strain was the inevitable result of Lincoln's wartime presidency; it arose despite intensified mutual devotion and a fierce dependency on Mrs. Lincoln's part. Friends noted that the President only seemed truly happy and relaxed in the presence of his wife or Tad. To Mary Lincoln, her husband represented all that was strong and good; he was her "lover—husband—father—*all*"; [6] because of him, she was a person of consequence. She thought she knew him absolutely, but she did not; no one did. More and more the Lincolns were shutting off from each other significant areas of their lives. Concealment of her debts and political dabblings had become second nature to Mary Lincoln, and she lived in terror that her husband would discover these involvements. He had long since ceased to confide in her, partly out of sheer preoccupation, partly out of a desire to spare her unnecessary stress, but mostly because she could not always be trusted with a secret. In that last year she considered herself fortunate if, at the end of the day, Lincoln stopped by her room, drugged with weariness, for a brief chat before bed. Although he continued to inform her of military developments, his news usually came after the fact and was available a day or so later

[5] Keckley, p. 157.
[6] Mary Lincoln to Sally Orne [Frankfurt, December 12, 1869].

in the public prints. Irritated by her persistent questions and importunities, he made abrupt, inadequate replies, with the result that she fed on rumor, building a mountain of conjecture on a shred of evidence, and then working herself into a state.

After the election she became agitated by gossip that General Nathaniel Banks was being considered for a Cabinet post, probably Secretary of War—he, "a speculator and associate of secession with General Butler!" [7] There was only the dimmest possibility of Banks' receiving such an appointment, and a single query to the President allayed her fears. But before she went to her husband she had already dashed off frantic notes to Charles Sumner and "Pet" Halsted on the subject.

In the past her loyalty and sense of propriety would never permit her to discuss with others her differences with Mr. Lincoln or to utter in public a disrespectful remark to him or about him. Richard Oglesby, soon to be Governor of Illinois, reported her as having attended in 1864 a presidential speech which was apparently not a particularly noble effort. According to Oglesby (and to others within earshot), Mrs. Lincoln dismissed the talk as "the worst speech I ever listened to in my life," adding, "I wanted the earth to sink and let me through." [8] A letter to Abram Wakeman, written in January 1865, constituted a further breach in family solidarity. Mary Lincoln confessed to having had a "scene" with her husband over the dismissal of a servant. Such scenes were "novelties" with them, she insisted (neglecting to add that Lincoln rarely bothered to argue). A more significant "novelty" was the fact that she felt "strangely disposed" to discuss the matter with a third person. Never again would she "provoke discussions, lest *forbidden subjects* . . . be introduced." [9] Too many "*forbidden subjects*" do not make for candid communication between husband and wife. But if Mr. Lincoln would not talk to her of substantive matters, there were

---

[7] Mary Lincoln to Charles Sumner [Washington, November 20, 1864]. The appointment of Banks was being actively promoted by Mrs. Lincoln's good friend General Daniel Sickles. It is not known whether she was aware of the fact, but it was one of many instances in which her close friendships and violent enmities came into seeming conflict; another was the Abram Wakeman—Thurlow Weed alliance; still another, the warm association of Charles Sumner and Salmon P. Chase.

[8] Quoted in Sandburg and Angle, p. 111; reported in the Washington *Star*, February 23, 1864.

[9] Mary Lincoln to Abram Wakeman [Washington], January 30, [1865].

many who would, and she turned increasingly to others for enlightenment and companionship. One of these was Wakeman, another, Senator Charles Sumner of Massachusetts.

Of all the distinguished gentlemen who called at the White House, Sumner was Mrs. Lincoln's overwhelming favorite. Her admiration for him bordered on awe. Brilliant and elegant, aloof to the point of arrogance, Sumner was the very model of the aristocrat as public servant. He was a genuine intellectual, a renowned orator and a power in the Senate. But his major reputation lay in his commitment to the freedom and advancement of the American Negro, and to what was in his judgment a concomitant goal: the total subjugation of the South in payment for its crime against the Union and humanity. All of these qualities and attitudes made him one of the most compelling, controversial figures in the history of American public life, and a source of intense fascination to his contemporaries, including Mrs. Abraham Lincoln, who thought him "in many respects . . . *a peculiar* man."[1]

The Senator in his early fifties was still austerely handsome and still a bachelor, the latter condition intriguing in itself. The fact that he allowed Mary Lincoln to enter his limited circle of confidants enhanced her image of herself as a cultivated woman. It was gratifying to her that Sumner so readily laid aside his momentous concerns to join her at the opera; flattering that he came so often to relax in her drawing room, where he entertained her with anecdotes of his acquaintances in government and diplomacy, read her letters from foreign statesmen, or engaged her in earnest discussion of the works of Whittier, Longfellow, Emerson and the other New England savants who were his personal friends. The essence of Sumner's appeal was revealed in a letter Mrs. Lincoln wrote her friend Sally Orne years later: "*I* was pleased," she recalled, "knowing he visited no other lady—His time was so immersed in his business—and that cold & haughty looking man to the world—would insist upon my telling him all the news & we would have such frequent and delightful conversations & often late in the evening—my darling husband would join us & they would laugh together like *two* school boys."[2]

[1] Mary Lincoln to Alexander Williamson, Chicago, August 19, [1866].
[2] Mary Lincoln to Sally Orne, Frankfurt [November 12, 1869].

That picture of the "cold & haughty looking" Mr. Sumner convulsed in boyish mirth is so ludicrous as to be almost inconceivable. Moreover, it would seem that as 1864 wore into 1865, he and Lincoln had less and less to laugh about. It was inevitable that some observers would see Sumner's attentions to the President's wife as carefully calculated; they said he was using a social friendship, fostered by her, to convert the President to his own views on emancipation and reconstruction. Others claimed the opposite: that Lincoln had, in effect, "assigned" Sumner to Mary for his own purposes— one of which was simply to keep him coming to the White House. The endless subtleties of this three-cornered relationship make for fascinating conjecture; all that can be said with certainty is that Lincoln and Sumner got on so well in her presence that Mrs. Lincoln was unaware of the slightest divergence in their views. Possibly sensing that the President was no longer educating his wife, Sumner became her mentor, her Melbourne—perhaps for no other purpose than the sheer challenge of it. Building on a base of abolitionist sentiments which had grown in her over the years under a variety of influences, including his own, he proceeded to make of her a thoroughgoing radical. "I never failed to urge my husband to be an *extreme* Republican," she would write later, and it is clear that the seeds of that urgency were planted and watered by Sumner.[3]

Yet the Senator was not so naïve as to have overestimated Mrs. Lincoln's influence on her husband in a matter of such importance as the future course of the republic. Had Lincoln lived to put into effect a conciliatory policy, Mrs. Lincoln might have been in for an awkward time; in the months before the assassination the ties of courtesy and camaraderie that bound the two men together were already showing signs of strain.[4] Yet whatever they were worth politically, Sumner's frequent visits in the presidential parlor were in themselves enjoyable occasions, and his pleasure in Mary Lincoln genuine. She was a gracious hostess, a spirited conversationalist— delightfully indiscreet—and, above all, an adoring disciple. No more convincing proof of Sumner's regard can be found than in his loyalty to her in her widowhood, at a time when such loyalty could no longer have yielded him the slightest advantage.

[3] Mary Lincoln to Elizabeth Keckley, Chicago, October 29, [1867].
[4] Mary Lincoln to Charles Sumner, Executive Mansion, April 11, 1865, *note*.

To Mercy Levering Conkling

Nov 19th [1864]

My dear Mrs Conkling

Whilst we were sojourning, in the Green Mountains last summer, your kind letter, was sent me from Washington & knowing my feelings of friendship, I am sure you will attribute my silence to any motive, save indifference. We are surrounded, at all times, by a great deal of company, we have *now*, been so long living among the Eastern people, that we number many of them, among our dearest friends, yet notwithstanding the ties, thus formed, in the midst of this fearful strife, the friends of the "long ago," are ever most pleasantly & affectionately remembered. And *these* are times, to make us very capable of judging of both, friends & foes, if we had not, had the discernment, to have had realized the consciousness, before— With me, "quickly comes such knowledge—yet we can afford to smile & be cheerful, over the triumph our party has won & I am not unconscious, I assure you & am deeply grateful for the renewed honor done, my noble & good Husband, who notwithstanding the great distinction conferred upon him, will ever remain true to *his friends*, & disinterested, in all that concerns himself. It has been gratifying, from all quarters, to receive so many kind & congratulatory letters, so fraught, with good feeling, & the White House, has been quite a *Mecca* of late—I consider myself fortunate, if at eleven o'clock, I once more find myself, in my pleasant room & very especially, if my tired & weary Husband, is *there*, resting in the lounge to receive me—to chat over the occurrences of the day—I received a letter from Lizzie Grimsley on yesterday. *She*, is a noble, good woman & has been purified, through much trial. I am pleased to learn that Uncle & Aunt,[5] still retain a reasonable share of health— She has been a very loving daughter. She writes me about poor, silly, Julia Baker! How unfortunate a Mother, must consider herself, to *so rear*, a child—Naturally weak, how much better, to have brought her up a good, domestic woman—One of the wives, of our

---

[5] Dr. and Mrs. John Todd of Springfield.

most distinguished Major Generals, who is spending the winter at Willard's, a person who is disinclined to think evil of any one—& one of my most intimate friends, said to me, a few days ago, "Are all the stories, relative to *a Mrs Baker*, who stopped two weeks, at the W. H. correct?" I, quietly remarked, what were the stories, you heard, she said, "one of our most distinguished officials in Washington told me & vouched for its truth—that Mrs B- so conducted herself, that she would have disgraced the City, got up in the morning, at daylight, rode out, with a *gentleman*, in a close[d] carriage, leaving her Husband in bed, miserable silly man!—After respectable visitors at 11 o'clock at night, had, bid good evening—Mrs B's voice, was heard at two o'clock—with gentlemen, in the library, on the same floor, with the President's apartments, the latter, disclaiming against such proceedings"—This was all true,—I could but admit, the fact, & could but agree with her, when she said, that "*such a woman*, would be frowned, down at an Hotel"—Lizzie, tells me, *she* is this Winter "*outshoddying*, shoddy"—in diamonds—how absurd! Robert writes me, he is hoping to have a visit from Clinton—[6] this winter—do not fail, my dear friend to send him & remember your promise. I shall be most happy, to welcome you at the *Inauguration*. If you can think over any plants, you *have not* & desire; let me know—

With kind regards I remain

M. L.—

To Hannah Shearer

Nov. 20th 1864

My *very dear* Friend.

Since we were so heavily visited by affliction, almost three years since, the loss of our darling, idolized Willie, with the sensitiveness of a heavy sorrow, I have shrank, from all communication, with those, who would most forcibly recall, my sorrows to my mind.

[6] Clinton L. Conkling, son of Mr. and Mrs. James C. Conkling, a student at Yale and a close friend of Robert.

Now, in this, the hour of *your* deep grief,[7] with all my *own wounds* bleeding afresh, I find myself, writing to you, to express, my deepest sympathy, *well knowing* how unavailing, *words*, are, when we are broken hearted.

The fairest, are most frequently taken, from a world of trial, for some wise purpose, which we cannot understand. I am glad, that you still have two dear children, left to comfort you. And a Husband so perfectly devoted to you. And *yours*, is so loving a nature, that it is absolutely necessary, for you, to have some one, to lean upon, & look up to. It is a most fortunate circumstance, that you married, when you did.[8] When, I tell you, I am writing to *Lizzie Grimsley*, for the *first time* to day since our heavy loss, you will appreciate & understand, that you are not *alone*, as regards my silence. I am very deeply attached to you both, yet since I last saw you, I have sometimes feared, that the *deep waters*, through which we have passed would overwhelm me.

Willie, darling Boy! was always the idolized child, of the household. So gentle, so meek, for a more Heavenly Home. We were having *so much bliss*. Doubtless ere this, our Angel boys, are reunited for they loved each other, so much on Earth. *The World*, has lost so much, of its charm. My position, requires my presence, where my heart is *so far* from being. I know, *you are* better prepared than I was, to pass through the fiery furnace of affliction. I had become, so wrapped up in the world, so devoted to our own political advancement that I thought of little else besides. Our Heavenly Father sees fit, oftentimes to visit us, at such times for our worldliness, how small & insignificant all worldly honors are, when we are *thus* so severely tried. Please remember to your family & accept so much love for yourself, from your truly attached friend

Mary Lincoln

[7] Shortly before this letter was written, Mrs. Shearer had lost her oldest son, Edward Rathbun, Jr.

[8] A reference to Mrs. Shearer's second marriage.

To Oliver S. Halsted, Jr.

Washington
Nov 22d [1864]

Private
My good friend.

We have wondered what *has* become of you since the election
—I have had your money,[9] ready for you, for six weeks—It will be
handed you, when you come on—Gen Banks is here, working for
dear life, for the *Cabinet* [1]

Do come on & use your influence immediately—*He* is indefatigable, and *may* be appointed immediately—Heaven forbid! Can
you not come on, when you receive this, there should be no delay in
this matter—

In great haste

your friend
Mary Lincoln

See Judge White of New York [2]—

[9] Halsted had probably paid some bills for Mrs. Lincoln and was being reim-
bursed.

[1] Major General Nathaniel Banks had been defeated in the Red River Campaign
of May 1864, but was still in command of the Army of the Gulf. A discussion of
Mrs. Lincoln's attitudes on the subject of his possible appointment can be found
on p. 184.

[2] James W. White was from 1861–4 a justice of the New York City Superior
Court. An Irish immigrant, he had founded in 1840 the *New York Freeman's
Journal*, a Catholic newspaper which in 1861 was banned from the mails in
New York by court order for "encouraging the rebels . . . [and] expressing sym-
pathy and agreement with them." By that time, however, the owner and editor
was James A. McMaster. Rhoda White, the Judge's wife, later became one of
Mrs. Lincoln's closest friends.

To Edward Grosjean [3]

————

[TELEGRAM]   [*No date*]

Mr Grosjean
(Chestnut Street
Phil—

    The letter, in which the check was enclosed was by mistake directed to

Crosjean, instead of Grosjean,
        Please enquire at P. O—Philadelphia

Mrs Lincoln

To Charles Sumner

————

Executive Mansion
[*November 20, 1864*]

My dear Sir:

    Our best Republican friends, those who have been the most ardent supporters of the Administration, through the *last* trying conflict,[4] are very much exercised over the attempts which Gen Banks himself is making & urging most *strenuously*, for *imaginary* services, also the leading Conservatives who would like to use Banks are urging him, for the Cabinet. Our *true* friends write me frequently & deplore such a prospect, I am sure *such* an appointment will not meet with your approbation, will you not exercise your great influence, with the friends who have a *right*, to demand some thing at the hands of a Government they have rescued, from tyranny? I feel assured *now*, whilst this subject, is agitated, your voice & your pen, will not be silent. Gen Banks, is considered a *weak failure*,

---

[3] An embroidery designer.
[4] The campaign of 1864, in which George B. McClellan, former commander of the Army of the Potomac, was the Democratic candidate for President.

overrated, and a speculator & associate of secession with Gen Butler,[5] all parties have learned to respect, a strong and resolute man. I
believe, Gen Banks, would *bow*, as submissively to *Gen McClellan*
if he were in power, as to Mr L- himself. Perhaps, you will consider
it unbecoming in *me* to write to you thus, the whole country is anxious about this, and it is very natural, that discriminations, should
be made, between true loyal men & those, whom the country consider, *time servers*—The services, of such, are certainly, not required, at a momentous time, like this! I can scarcely believe that
these views will not meet with your own ideas on the subject,[6] if I
have erred please excuse me.

Gen Banks has been in W- for ten days past, unremitting in his
attention to the President. I fear the appointment or the promise of
it *might* be made, ere Congress meets, *you* can do much, in this case,
any communication on the subject, will be considered private.

Your friend

Mary Lincoln

To Oliver S. Halsted, Jr.

Nov. 24th [1864]

Mr Halstead [sic]—

I write you in great haste, to say, that after *all* the excitement,
Gen Banks, is to be returned to his command, at New Orleans,[7] and
the *Great Nation*, will be *comforted* with the idea, that he *is* not to
be in the Cabinet. With kind regards to Mrs H- I remain your friend

Mrs Lincoln—

[5] Mrs. Lincoln's statement that Benjamin Butler was an "associate of secession"
stemmed from his support in 1860 of the southern wing of the Democratic Party.
Since then, however, his treatment of civilians under his jurisdiction at New
Orleans had been so harsh that he was removed from command of the military
government there in December 1862 and replaced by Banks. Banks was also a
Democrat.
[6] They did.
[7] Although Lincoln ordered Banks to return to his command at New Orleans
he remained in Washington four months longer.

To Charles Sumner

Executive Mansion
Nov 24th [1864]

Hon. Mr Sumner

I do not regret, than [that] an opportunity offers, for an apology, for having written you so candid & as it *now* appears, so unnecessary a letter, as I did, a few days since. I regretted writing you, immediately after the note was sent, the great excitement the rumor created was the cause of my doing so & knowing that a word from you, to your Republican friends might prevent the appointment— Seward & Weed were said to be urging it very earnestly, Mr L- now says, neither of these gentlemen have ever mentioned the subject to him, he has had no idea of it himself, & that Gen Banks, is to return to his command in New Orleans immediately. This will be pleasant tidings to many—who made pilgrimmages to this city, in *pious* indignation!—The recollection is truly amusing. And now trusting that I have made the "amende honorable," for my *sympathetic interest* in Gen Banks, and with apologies for having trespassed upon your valuable time, I remain

Respectfully &&
Mary Lincoln

To Edwin M. Stanton

December 8th [1864]

Sir

The applicant Robert E. Parker is a strong Union man, and if you can grant his petition,[8] which I send enclosed, you will bestow a personal favor upon me.[9]

Mrs. Lincoln

[8] See letter to James A. Hardie, December 16, 1864.
[9] Not in Mrs. Lincoln's handwriting.

To Ruth Harris

Dec 11th [1864]

My Dear Madame,

Your last note has been received—I sent the velvet—which you will doubtless receive to day—I did not wish *any lace* on the outside —therefore the bonnet must cost but $25.00 which is more than I had expected to pay for a bonnet—furnishing the velvet myself— the feather must be long & beautiful—lace trimmings *very* rich & full; the outside you can arrange to your taste—

You can certainly procure black velvet ribbon—of the shade of the velvet of the bonnet—for strings—a finger length wide— very rich. I saw some in N.Y. when there—I do not think the edge *inserted* on the ribbon would look well. Qu'en pensez-vous? It is a bonnet for *grand occasions* & I want it to be particularly stylish & rich. Very especially, blk velvet is so *expens[ive]*, do not fail to turn in the sides of the front, more than an inch of course, it will some day, have to undergo, a new foundation—I am sure, you will not fail me in this. Another favor, I have to request. Can you have my bonnet, sent me Express, on Monday next, leaving N.Y. on that day, and will you, send down to Tiffany & Co- for a blk velvet headdress, which he had as a measure, & enclose with the bonnet. Some of the narrow blk velvet ribbon, which you sent as a sample, with white edge, would look well, on one side of the front trim-ming. My strings must be one yard long each—*Do* have my bonnet got up in exquisite taste.

Very sincerely your friend
Mary Lincoln

To Ruth Harris

[TELEGRAM]   [*15 Dec 1864*]

Madame Harris
7 Brevoort Place 10 St
New York

I sent your letter & contents last Thursday—write if you have received it.

Mrs Lincoln

To James A. Hardie [1]

*Executive Mansion
Dec 16th 1864*

Dear Sir:

The applicant for post sutlership, Mr R. E. Parker, Jr. has been in the service of his country three years, in the 26th Penn Vols and is honorably discharged. I wish you would give him the post sutlership of the New Convalescent Camp at Fairfax Seminary, or Fort Delaware, or any other post, by doing this you will oblige—truly

Mrs Lincoln.

[To George Harrington?]

December 20, 1864

The President has sent his recommendations [Dec. 15, 1864] to Mr Fessenden,[2] concerning the appointment of [Gustav] Gumfert [sic]

[1] Formerly Assistant Adjutant General of the Army of the Potomac, at this time serving in the office of the Secretary of War.
[2] William Pitt Fessenden, Secretary of the Treasury, June 1864–March 1865.

as special [treasury] agent. Mr Gumfert says they are filed. If you would assist Mr G. in obtaining such a position, you would confer an especial favor upon me. I would be very much obliged to you, as I have desired Mr Gumfert to obtain such a place.

To Ruth Harris

Washington. Dec 28th [1864]

Madame Harris—

I can neither wear, or settle with you, for my bonnet without different inside flowers—As to inside flowers of black & white, I saw some beautifully fine ones, in two or three different establishments, in N.Y.—By going out, for them, you can procure them— I need to wear my blk velvet bonnet on Wednesday next. Do send me the flowers—By a little search you can procure them—I cannot retain or wear the bonnet, as it is—I am certainly taught a lesson, by your acting thus

I remain &
Mrs Lincoln

The public reception at the White House on New Year's Day of 1865 was a hopeful occasion, for the sweet scent of victory was at last in the air. General William T. Sherman, who had begun his march from Atlanta to the sea the preceding November, had presented the city of Savannah to the President as a Christmas gift. The devastation his troops had wrought in the rich heartland of Georgia was vast—and some said needlessly thorough—but it had broken the back of Southern resistance. Sheridan had finally succeeded in routing Jubal Early's forces in October, thus ending the four-month-long Shenandoah Campaign. All that remained was for Grant to wear down what was left of Lee's army, capture Richmond, and end the war. Grant had every possible advantage over Lee, but the Confederates continued to resist, and the fighting dragged on week after weary week.

With each day that passed the chances grew stronger that Robert Lincoln, then in his first year at the Harvard Law School, would see some war service, a possibility that filled his mother with dread. She had lost two sons before they were old enough to know what war was about; now she stood to lose a third, in the prime of his young manhood. For years Robert had begged his parents to allow him to leave college and enlist, and Lincoln knew that the President's son must not be considered a shirker. But Mary had become so overwrought at the idea of her oldest living son being exposed to danger that her husband had tactfully refrained from discussing the matter with her.

In January 1865 the President hit upon a compromise. He wrote to General Grant, requesting rather embarrassedly that his son be given a place in the general's "Military family," with a nominal officer's rank; he himself would pay Robert's keep. The young man was made a captain on Grant's staff and stationed for the most part well behind the lines, but his mother—her pride warring with her fears—was sure that he was in the thick of things.

That same month there was something of a flurry resulting from Mrs. Lincoln's abrupt dismissal of "Old Edward" McManus, who had served as doorkeeper at the White House since Jackson's day. Edward was described by John George Nicolay as a "short, thin, humorous Irishman, to be trusted equally with state secrets, or with the diplomatic management of the President's unpredictable young son Tad." [3] Apparently Edward could not be trusted with Mrs. Lincoln's secrets, which were many. Though the precise reasons for his removal remain a mystery, it is clear that he must have crossed her seriously or betrayed her confidence in some way. The doorkeeper left Washington in a vindictive mood, turned up in New York, and seemingly went to Thurlow Weed with vicious stories about his former employer—stories which of course got back to her. She dilated on the whole unpleasant business in a series of letters to Abram Wakeman written in the early months of 1865.

[3] Helen Nicolay. *Lincoln's Secretary, A Biography of John G. Nicolay.* New York, 1949, p. 121.

The letter describing her "scene" with Lincoln was the first of these. After she gave up fulminating on the transgressions of her former servant, she began writing harshly of Weed to a man who, interestingly enough, owed his political fortunes to Weed's sponsorship. We shall never know how Wakeman responded to her remarks or whether he encouraged them, for she took care to destroy his letters—along with nearly every one that was ever written to her.

To John A. Dillon [4]

[TELEGRAM]   [*Jan 5 1865*]

John O Dillon [sic]
No 161 Olive Street
St Louis Missouri

Robert will not be home, until Friday evening—I think it is probable he will go—I regret he is now absent—

Mrs Lincoln

To James K. Kerr [5]

[TELEGRAM]   [*January 9, 1865*] [6]

James K. Kerr
China Hall
Chestnut St. Philadelphia

We must have the China tomorrow—Send what you have   Our dinner comes off Monday, & on Saturday, the articles must be ready for use here—

Mrs Lincoln

[4] The St. Louis city directory for 1865 lists John A. Dillon as a "law student," boarding at the above address. Like most of Robert's friends, Dillon came of a wealthy, socially "correct" background. In 1872 he would found the St. Louis *Evening Post* which soon after merged with Joseph Pulitzer's *Dispatch*.
[5] A dealer in china and glassware.
[6] A stamped date can be dimly discerned on the face of the message.

To James K. Kerr

[TELEGRAM] [7]   [*Jan 10, 1865*]
11.43 *AM*

Mr Kerr
China House
Philadelphia
What is the meaning, that we do not have the China.

Mrs Lincoln

Answer immediately

To Simeon Draper [8]

[EXCERPT]   *January 26, 1865*

I am very desirous of placing under your auspices, in some sphere of usefulness to the government, either in the Custom House at New York or Savannah, a gentleman who is a personal friend of the President and our family from our own state "Illinois." Mr Jos Hertford [9] at present a clerk of the second class in the office of Second Auditor of the Treasury, is a good accountant and penman and capable of filling a more important position, than the one he now occupys.

Very truly yours,
Mrs A. Lincoln

Please oblige in this.

[7] This telegram was written out in a large, uneven handwriting by Mrs. Lincoln on a sheet torn from a pocket ledger and headed "Cash Account January."
[8] A prominent New York merchant and politician of the Seward-Weed faction, appointed in September 1864 to succeed Hiram Barney as Collector of Customs at New York.
[9] An ex-Chicagoan, Joseph Hertford had held a War Department clerkship and then moved on to the Treasury Department, first in Internal Revenue, then apparently in the above position. In 1863 Lincoln had tried unsuccessfully to have Hertford made a Treasury agent.

To Abram Wakeman

Executive Mansion
Jany 30th [1865]

My Dear Sir:

It will afford us much pleasure, to have you dine with us, *most informally* tomorrow evening at six o'clock. I name, an earlier hour, than usual, as the President, proposed to *me himself*, to attend the theatre to see [Edwin] Forrest in "Sparticus" [sic], Mr Forney,[1] whom you perhaps know, may accompany us. I have taken your advice, for I well know, how deeply grieved, the P feels over any coolness of mine. We have had quite a little laugh together, most fortunately for both my Husband and myself, who [would] have broken our hearts, had it been otherwise, notwithstanding our opposite natures, our lives have been eminently peaceful—The *serpents*[2] that have crossed our pathways, will be remembered by both of us, with *horror*, in after years. The communication made you this morning, will I am sure, always be sacredly guarded by you—As *scenes* are novelties with us, I felt strangely disposed to tell you. Thank Heaven, the storm has cleared away & I shall ever, *even in jest*, take especial pains not to provoke discussions, lest *forbidden subjects*, might be introduced—Excuse so long a note—I shall expect to see you, tomorrow at eleven o'clock,

Your Sincere friend
Mary Lincoln—

[1] John W. Forney, owner-publisher of the Washington *Chronicle*, considered the organ of the Lincoln administration. Forney also published the Philadelphia *Press* and served as clerk of the Senate from 1861–8.
[2] Subsequent correspondence indicates that the "serpent" was Edward McManus, elderly doorkeeper at the White House, whom Mrs. Lincoln abruptly dismissed in January 1865, for reasons that are obscure.

To Winfield Scott Hancock[3]

Executive Mansion
February 12th 65—

My Dear Sir:

My estimable friend Mrs Hughes [unidentified], understanding from me, that if possible, you would grant her request, relative to her son, entrusts me, with a note to you. She supplicates, in a very ardent & *motherly* style, for the promotion of her son, who is considered very promising; any favor granted in the case, will be truly appreciated, by yours very respectfully

Mary Lincoln

To Abram Wakeman

[*February 18, 1865*]

Dear Mr Wakeman,

If you have leisure today, at two P.M. I am assured you will be gratified if you make a call at our morning reception, the Senate, in both ladies && will be largely represented—Since I have certainly ascertained that E[dward McManus] has been up North—I am more shocked than ever, that any one can be so *low*, as to place confidence in a discarded menial's assertions, the game of espionage, has been going on, to a greater extent than we have imagined —if the "Heavens fall," E shall never be restored—Nicol[ay]. himself says, that E's mind is positively deranged, I have suspected it for some time. It will gratify Mr L if you pay your respects to him to day. I believe, if possible I shall love and venerate my blessed Husband more than ever—as E- inhabits a *three* story brick house

---

[3] A major general, at this time commanding the 1st Corps of Veterans. Mrs. Lincoln was acquainted with the family of the General's wife and had often singled out the couple socially.

& has it filled with lodgers no doubt, "Monsieur Thomson [uniden-
tified], will *quarter* there—and have many exciting chats—"How
have the mighty fallen" Please burn this note & if I should not see
you again, do not fail to see, *this* person, tomorrow & report of
course—I remain very respectfully—

Mary Lincoln

Private

To Abram Wakeman

Feb 20th [1865]

My Dear Sir

I have a moment of leisure this morning & will write you a
few lines. A note, this morning from the same disagreeable source
—takes particular occasion *not* to mention E[dward]'s visit to N.Y.
says two or three *distinguished* individuals of *his acquaintance* coming from W[ashington] had mentioned flying rumors—How false,
all this is! I could tell him, what a more noble & distinguished person, than he could venture to number among his friends, said to
me within the last 24 hours—that E had ventured into his room,
and began his complaints, that this Mr G- had informed against
him & caused his removal. This friend indeed, as might have been
expected from a source, that would scorn close communion with
menials, told E that he might leave his presence. If any information was given Mr W[eed] it emanated from E himself and those
whom he had entertained with his vile falsehoods. Coupling a
lady's name, with one with whom, I have never conversed & not
placed on even the footing, of one of our doormen, is indeed a
farce! The intellect that a kind & Heavenly Father, gave him, he
has thrown away, in a very strange manner. I have a funny story
to tell you of Mrs Trumbull. Excuse my great haste & say nothing about receiving a letter—from *me*, to Mr W.

Truly your friend,
—Mrs L

To Ruth Harris

[TELEGRAM]   *Feby 21st 65*

Madame Harris—
No 7- Brevoort Place,
New York—

If you please, send immediately, the things I wrote for—I am in great need of them.

Mrs Lincoln—

To Ruth Harris

Feb 24th [1865]

My dear Madame Harris

I feel that I owe you an apology, for my long delay, in settling my account with you. I enclose you a draft for $94.00- please give me credit on the bill & oblige

Yours very truly
Mrs Lincoln

Please return bill immediately

To Robert T. Lincoln

[TELEGRAM]   *Feb. 28, 1865*

Capt. Robert T. Lincoln
on Gen Grant's Staff
Gen Grant's Head Quarters

A message from your Father, will be sent you tomorrow, I have been ill or would have written All well now

Mrs Lincoln

To Abram Wakeman

[*March 12, 1865*] [4]

My dear Sir:

Nothing but the unusual excitement we have just passed through [5] & from which, we have not entirely recovered, would excuse me, in not having thanked you, for your *recent kindness* towards me—I write hurriedly to day & will not attempt to discuss so unnecessary a subject & one which certainly does not occupy mine, for a moment, yet when you chance to visit W[ashington] it will be quite amusing, to hear you account, some of the ludicrous scenes, you may have passed through, and which I am sure, gave you some trouble—Some other time, will answer, to talk over all this—Please say nothing about having received a line from me. If possible, I am sure you will always say a kind word to Mr & Mrs B[ennett] whose favor, it would be most *impolitic* to ignore—Weed may try to sour them—all this is between ourselves—

Very truly your friend
Mary Lincoln

To Charles Sumner

Executive Mansion
Sunday, March 19 [1865]

My dear Sir:

Whilst appointments are being made & vacancies filled, I trust you will not deem me intrusive by suggesting your *quiet* perseverance & that of your influential friends in urging the claim of Mr J. Jay, [6] who is so worthy of being recognized by the Govern-

[4] Date taken from a postmark on the envelope.
[5] Lincoln's inauguration, victories by Sherman and Grant.
[6] John Jay of New York, grandson of the Chief Justice and an outspoken abolitionist, had been proposed as minister to Spain in 1862, but did not receive the appointment. In 1869 he would be appointed minister to Austria.

ment. I am sure the President, feels most *kindly* towards him & listens patiently, when I speak to him, on the subject. I really believe you will have very little trouble, in succeeding, in obtaining some position of eminence for him. Our good friend, Baron Gerolt,[7] called to see me, on yesterday & proposes bringing the new Austrian Minister [Wydenbruck], to pay his respects this evening. Hoping the charming music, in "Faust," compensated, you for the two or three hours, passed away from your studies, which in Mr Lincoln's case I never regret, I remain, very truly,

Mary Lincoln

To Abram Wakeman

March 20th [1865]

My Dear Sir:

I find in my drawer, a rather pleasant photograph of my little Taddie, yet not so good a one, of Mr L- I take the liberty of enclosing it to you; it may interest your children—The papers appear to think it is one of Mr L's "last jokes," the offer made to Mr B.[8] lest *he* [Bennett] might consider, that it was intended as a *jest*, please, do not fail to express my regrets to him—*you* will understand—*even* give W[eed] to understand—that I regret, that Mr B- did not accept. We are having charming weather & I am most happy to say, that my blessed Husband's health, has much improved. We went to the Opera on Saturday eve; Mr Sumner accompanied us—we had a very gay little time. Mr S when he throws off his heavy manner, as he often does, can make himself very *very* agreable. Last evening, he again joined our little coterie, & tomorrow eve,—we all go again to hear "Robin Adair," sung in "La Dame Blanche by Habelmann.[9] This is always the pleasant time to me in W. spring-

---

[7] Baron Friedrich von Gerolt, minister from Prussia.

[8] On February 20, 1865, Lincoln had offered James Gordon Bennett the post of minister to France, which Bennett declined.

[9] Theodore Habelmann, one of the celebrated tenors of his day, was a member of Grau's opera troupe, whose performances were frequently attended by the Lincolns. *La Dame Blanche* was the last opera either of them saw.

time, some few of the most pleasant Senators families remain until June, & all ceremony, with each other is laid aside. Mr L- most probably, goes down to the front [1] (entre nous) this week & wishes me to accompany him—I gladly seize on any change, that will benefit him.

I write, as usual, in great haste

Very truly, your friend

M. L.

Two weeks after Lincoln's second inaugural, General Grant invited the President to visit his headquarters at City Point, Virginia, on the James. Mrs. Lincoln insisted on going too. She would bring Tad, see Robert, and enjoy a holiday of sorts, with all the family together. That the expedition turned out to be something less was no one's fault. Both the President and his wife were living under great emotional and physical strain; it was a weary pair that boarded the government steam yacht *River Queen* for the overnight trip to City Point.

Trouble developed almost immediately. On the 25th of March, Mrs. Lincoln found herself riding in a field ambulance with Mrs. Grant and Adam Badeau, a member of the General's staff. Badeau later recalled saying that he believed heavy fighting was ahead, since all officers' wives were being ordered to the rear, with a single exception: the young wife of General Charles Griffin, who had been granted a presidential dispensation to remain at the front. To Mary Lincoln this news had a shocking implication. In order to exact such a favor, Mrs. Griffin must have seen the President alone. Furiously she said to Badeau, "Do you know that I never allow the President to see any woman alone?" Badeau attempted to make light of the matter, but the damage was done. Mrs. Lincoln ordered the ambulance halted and jumped out, announcing her determination to discuss the subject with the President. The

[1] The proposed trip was to Grant's rear headquarters at City Point, Virginia.

first person she encountered was General George G. Meade, to whom she immediately put the question on her mind. Meade had the tact to reply that it was the Secretary of War, not the President, who had granted Mrs. Griffin permission to remain with her husband. Mary Lincoln was temporarily mollified, but her sense of injury persisted.

A review of the troops was scheduled for the following day. The President set out for it on horseback together with Major General Edward O. C. Ord, commander of the Army of the James. The President's wife followed with Mrs. Grant in a slow ambulance over corduroy roads, worrying every inch of the way that she would be late for the review. At one point the vehicle jounced so sharply that the occupants' heads struck the top, aggravating Mrs. Lincoln's unpleasant mood.

By the time she arrived, the review was already in progress. On learning that Mrs. Ord, a handsome woman and a skilled equestrienne, had ridden alongside the Commander-in-Chief on the way to the parade grounds, she was blinded with rage, certain that the troops had mistaken the General's wife for herself. As Mrs. Ord came forward to greet her, the accumulated tensions of two days— indeed, of four years—caused Mrs. Lincoln to lose all sense of discretion, of time and place. She gave Mrs. Ord a severe tongue-lashing, using language so abusive that the startled woman burst into tears. The rest of those present could only hang back in horrified silence, avoiding the eyes of the President.

Badeau later wrote of that day: "Mrs. Lincoln repeatedly attacked her husband in the presence of officers because of Mrs. Griffin and Mrs. Ord. He bore it as Christ might have done, with an expression of pain and sadness that cut one to the heart, but with supreme calmness and dignity. He called her 'Mother,' with his old-time plainness; he pleaded with eyes and tones, and endeavored to explain or palliate the offenses of others, till she turned on him like a tigress; and then he walked away, hiding that noble, ugly face that we might not catch the full expression of its misery." [2]

For the next three days, as Lincoln spoke with his generals of the conduct of the now inevitable surrender, Mrs. Lincoln re-

---

[2] This quotation and the preceding account are taken from Adam Badeau. *Grant in Peace.* Hartford, 1887, pp. 356–65.

mained "indisposed" in her cabin aboard the *River Queen*. Suddenly it was announced that she would return to Washington: the President had dreamt that the White House had caught fire in his absence, and his wife was being sent to see that all was well. She arrived in Washington on April 2, wired reassurances to Lincoln, and requested news. Lincoln sent her the news, and it was so exciting that from then on no further mention was made of the events of the preceding week. Richmond had at last been captured!

Anxious to be in at the kill, Mrs. Lincoln began assembling a party of friends to return with her to City Point and go on to Richmond with the President: Senator Sumner and his special guest, the Marquis de Chambrun, Secretary of the Interior and Mrs. James Harlan and their daughter Mary (a particular friend of Robert); Elizabeth Keckley, whose former home had been in nearby Petersburg, had asked to be included in the group. They arrived at Fortress Monroe on the fifth of April, whereupon some confusion resulted. Despite his wife's hints that he should await her arrival before going on to tour the captured cities, Lincoln had proceeded on his own. When she received word that Secretary of State Seward had been seriously injured in a carriage accident, she sent a series of anxious telegrams to ensure that the President's party would not return to Washington without her. Although Lincoln was close to exhaustion, and despite grave danger to his safety, he stayed on in order to escort his wife's party through Richmond and Petersburg.

No sooner had the *River Queen* re-docked at Washington than the Lincolns were overcome with a sense of deep disquiet. Returning to the White House in the state carriage with her husband, Sumner, and the Marquis, Mary Lincoln looked about her and said suddenly, "That city is filled with our enemies." Lincoln turned on her, visibly annoyed, and replied, "Enemies! we must never speak of that."[3] The vehemence of his retort could not have been lost on Sumner.

The feeling of foreboding was forgotten the next day, when word reached Washington that Robert E. Lee had surrendered his forces to Ulysses S. Grant at Appomattox Courthouse in Virginia.

[3] Charles A. Pineton (Marquis de Chambrun). "Personal Recollections of Mr. Lincoln." *Scribner's Magazine*, January, 1893, p. 35.

That evening the capital was illuminated in honor of the surrender. Crowds filled the streets and clustered about the White House, wild with joy. Elizabeth Keckley described the "grand and imposing scene" when the President "with pale face and his soul flashing through his eyes," stepped to a window to speak. A light was brought so that he could be seen, and the dressmaker thought fleetingly how easy it would be for someone in the vast, dark throng below to assassinate the Chief Executive and slip away undetected. When she mentioned this the next day to Mrs. Lincoln, she was told, "Yes, yes, Mr. Lincoln's life is always exposed. Ah, no one knows what it is to live in constant dread of some fearful tragedy. The President has been warned so often, that I tremble for him on every public occasion. I have a presentiment that he will meet with a sudden and violent end." [4]

To Charles Sumner

Executive Mansion
March 23 [1865]

My Dear Sir:

The President & myself are about leaving for "City Point" and I cannot but devoutly hope, that change of air & rest may have a beneficial effect on my good Husband's health. On our return, about Wednesday, we trust you will be inclined to accompany us to the Italian Opera, "Ernani," is set aside for that evening. Perhaps, we will have a large private box, some one or two other agreeable friends, will join us. From the "State Department" on yesterday, Mr Lincoln received Louis Napoleon's recent work, the Life of "Julius Caesar," It has been sent in pamphlet form & has to be sent to be bound, when it is returned to us, if you will allow me, to take the liberty of sending it to you, to read, you will doubtless be interested in it. In the coming summer, when we will be left to our solitude, I shall peruse it myself, for I have so sadly neglected, the little French, I fancied so familiar to me.

[4] Keckley, p. 178.

Judge Harris [5] called last evening, to say, farewell. He has been so kind a friend that I am quite as attached to him as if he were a relative.—

Very truly—

Mary Lincoln

Please excuse this very hasty note.

To Mary Ann Cuthbert

[TELEGRAM]   *Fortress Monroe*
Through War Department   March 24th 1865

Mrs Cuthbert Executive Mansion
Answer immediately

Send a telegram, directed to City Point, so soon as you receive this & say, if all is right at the house [6]—Every thing is left in your charge —be careful—

Mrs Lincoln

To Alphonso Dunn [7]

[TELEGRAM]   *12.45 PM, March 25, 1865*
By Telegraph from City Point, Va.

To Mr Dunn
Door Keeper
Ex. Mansion

Ask Cuthbert why my telegram of yesterday has not been answered. Reply immediately.

Mrs Lincoln

---

[5] Ira Harris, formerly New York State Supreme Court Justice, elected senator in 1861 with the support of the Seward-Weed machine.
[6] Mrs. Lincoln later declared that her husband had dreamt the preceding night that the White House had burned down. The tone of her telegram indicates the anxiety both she and Lincoln were experiencing, despite the impending victory.
[7] A former police officer, newly appointed White House guard and doorkeeper.

To Abraham Lincoln

[TELEGRAM]   *Executive Mansion*
                             Washington
                             April 2nd [1865]

A Lincoln
City Point
Arrived here safely this morning, found all well—Miss, Taddie &
yourself very much—perhaps, may return with a little party on
Wednesday—Give me all the news [8]

                             Mary Lincoln

Certification

                             Executive Mansion
                             Washington, April 3d. 1865

This is to certify that John F. Parker,[9] a member of the Metropolitan Police has been detailed for duty at the Executive Mansion by
order of

                             Mrs Lincoln [1]

---

[8] That evening Lincoln wired his wife: "At 4:30 p.m. to-day General Grant telegraphs that he has Petersburg completely enveloped from river below to river
above. . . . He suggests that I shall go out and see him in the morning, which
I think I will do. Tad and I are both well, and will be glad to see you and your
party here at the time you name." Published in *The War of the Rebellion: A
Compilation of the Official Records of the Union and Confederate Armies*. Series
I, Volume XLVI, Book III, pp. 447–8.
[9] John F. Parker was the only guard on duty at the President's box at Ford's
Theater on the night of April 14, 1865.
[1] This order and the one which follows were written out for Mrs. Lincoln's signature, which was hastily scrawled.

Certification

Executive Mansion
Washington, April 3d. 1865

This is to certify that Joseph Sheldon a member of the Metropolitan Police has been detailed for duty at the Executive Mansion by order of

Mrs Lincoln

To Charles Sumner

Monday morning
April 3d [1865]

Senator Sumner,

The Sec of War, has just left & says that Richmond was evacuated last night & is ours! This is almost too much happiness, to be realized! I can say no more—except that *Grant* is pursuing the enemy.

Very truly your friend
Mary Lincoln

To Abram Wakeman

Executive Mansion
April 4th [1865]

My Dear Mr Wakeman—

Your very kind note was received, but alas! too late to remedy the evil—I returned home on Sunday morning & left Mr L with a promise that I would return on Wednesday, tomorrow, with a choice little party of friends. The company had already been formed & of course I cannot retract. Pray, for me, lest any evil spirits, come near me—I trust in some way, *he* [Weed] may have left C[ity] P[oint] ere we arrive—It was the queerest coincidence last evening.

Baron Gerolt, Sumner and myself, were chatting away, when the Baron, brought up some reminiscences of a voyage across the Atlantic, when the "Chevalier" [Wikoff] was his room mate & how the latter person endeavoured to learn his the President's opinion of *his* "*book*" [2] The Baron told it in such a ludicrous way, that S- looking at me, we both laughed immoderately—we had a gay time over it —Returning to my room, I found your letter—I wish, I had time to tell you, of all we have passed through recently at the front, and how happy I am feeling, over our glorious victories. I wish you would join us at City Point—We will have a most charming party —I have much to say to you, I am expecting quite a number of friends, this evening—the buildings & city are to be illuminated. Lights will glare from windows from whence rebellious hearts, have been wont to gaze—from—Such is life! I wish you would drop me a line at City Point or perhaps you had better not, as I might not get it—We are expecting to visit R[ichmond] ere we return. Will you dine with us, in Jeff Davis', deserted banqueting hall? Mr Sumner accompanies our party—he is coming up this evening, with some friends from Boston—I write this in great haste—Remaining truly your friend

Mary Lincoln

I receive telegrams from my Husband every two or three hours. He has improved in health VERY GREATLY—And after 3 days of exposure to rebel shots my darling Boy [Tad] is well and happy.

To Abraham Lincoln

[TELEGRAM] *4 April 1865*

A. Lincoln
City Point

Glorious news! Please say to Captain Bradford [of the *River Queen*] that a party of seven persons, leave here tomorrow & will reach City Point, on Thursday morning for breakfast—

Mrs Lincoln

[2] Wikoff was, among other things, the author of a sensational memoir, *My Courtship and its Consequences*, dealing with his adventures in romance and diplomacy in Europe. It was a best seller of its time.

To Abraham Lincoln

[TELEGRAM]   *Fortress Monroe*
                    April 6 [1865]
                    4 o'clock Thursday morning

A. Lincoln

If Mr Seward, is not too dangerously injured [3] cannot you remain at City Point until we reach there at twelve noon to day. We have several friends on board & would prefer seeing you & returning on your boat, we are not comfortable here [4]—

Mary Lincoln

To Edwin M. Stanton

[TELEGRAM] [5]   [*Fortress Monroe*]
                        6 a.m. April 6, 1865

Hon Sec of War

I presume of course the president will leave immediately for Washington   If Mr Seward is not too severely injured—cannot the President, remain until we arrive at City Point, we would prefer returning on that boat, as this is not so comfortable   I am sure, if it can be consistently done you will oblige [6]

Mrs Lincoln

[3] On April 5 Secretary of State William Seward was thrown from his carriage in Washington and suffered a broken jaw and arm. The neck brace he wore after the accident saved him from death when he was attacked on the night of Lincoln's assassination.

[4] On another boat, *The Monohassett.*

[5] Two copies of this telegram exist: the above, as Mrs. Lincoln wrote it out, and another, as it was received.

[6] On April 6 Stanton wired Mrs. Lincoln at Fortress Monroe: "Mr Seward although severely injured is not in danger. I telegraphed the Prest. last night that you were on the road and also that the Surgeon Genl. saw no reason for alarm. There can be no objection to the President remaining at City Point until your arrival there and I have so telegraphed him." Mrs. Lincoln wrote in pencil on the face of this telegram, presumably to her husband; "We will be ready to leave tomorrow eve 6 o'clock do wait return with us. M. L." MS. in Lib. of Cong.

To Abraham Lincoln

Fortress Monroe
Apl 6 [1865]
9 a.m.

A. Lincoln—

If you are compelled to return before we see you, which I shall much regret, cannot you return on some other vessel, we are most uncomfortable on this & would like your boat—I know you would agree with me & we will be with you in six hours + at City Point.

Mary Lincoln

To Charles Sumner

[April 6, 1865]

Mr Stanton, I think would be better satisfied to know, that this news, had been received—If it is ascertained that Mr S[eward] is not *fatally* injured, I know that Mr Lincoln would prefer remaining to meet us [7]—And it does not appear to me, to be a necessity for our returning [to Washington]

M. L.—

Mr L Will, of course, use his own discretion about remaining at C-Pt.

---

[7] Alone in her cabin at an early hour, Mrs. Lincoln dashed off this note to Sumner. He replied: "The more I think of it, the more I feel that we must wait for the President." MS. owned by Victor Jacobs, Dayton, Ohio.

To Charles Sumner

Monday noon
[April 10, 1865]
Executive Mansion

Senator Sumner:

In honor of this great & glorious day *perhaps*, the gardener has sent up to my rooms, an unusual supply of flowers & I have concluded to exercise my *rejoicing* spirit, of the "Consummation so devoutly, to be wished," by having a bouquet left on the tables of yourself & the Marquis.[8] Mr L- told me the news, last night at ten o'clock, that Lee & his Army were in our hands & it would have been my delight, to have been able to send the communication to all of our recent travelling companions, well knowing how much sweeter your dreams would have been. If possible, this is a happier day, than last Monday,[9] the crowds around the house have been immense, in the midst of the bands playing, they break forth into singing. If the close of that terrible war, has left some of our hearthstones, *very, very* desolate, God, has been as ever kind & merciful, in the midst of our heavy afflictions as nations, & as individuals.

As always, truly your friend,
Mary Lincoln

To Charles Sumner

11th April '65
Tuesday morning
Executive Mansion

My Dear Mr Sumner:

Presuming, it would be agreeable for the Marquis, in visiting our Country, to witness *every* novelty that presents itself at this

[8] Charles Adolphe Pineton, Marquis de Chambrun, grandson of Lafayette, was on a visit to the United States.
[9] The day Richmond was captured.

eventful time, I have invited him to call informally this evening, about 8½ o'clock, as doubtless, a vast assemblage, will be gathered in front of *this* building, with music & anticipations of a little speech from the President. It would be very pleasant, both for the Marquis & ourselves, if you would accompany him.[1] I have had the *moral courage*, to write him a note in French. Tomorrow, I begin with a very excellent French teacher to perfect myself in that language—I am happy to say, that Mr Lincoln is feeling much better to day, Friday's pilgrimmage through the hospitals, although a labor of love, to him, fatigued him very much.

Very   truly,

Mary   Lincoln

P.S. I am very anxious to have a good view, for once of the illumination, the effect will be grand, I am sure, and in consequence of having the safest coachman in the Country, propose that the Marquis & yourself, accompanied by some other lady of course, besides myself, drive around quietly, for about half an hour this eve. It does not appear to me, that this *womanly* curiosity will be undignified or indiscreet, qu'en pensez vous?

M. L.

On April 12, 1865, Abraham Lincoln paused in his labors to pen an affectionate note to his wife. Although the letter no longer exists, it is known that Mary Lincoln kept it with her for years, reading and rereading it for comfort. It was, she wrote a friend, "playfully

---

[1] Sumner did not accept this invitation. In his book *Charles Sumner & the Rights of Man* (New York, 1971), p. 215, David Donald has written: "Anticipating that Lincoln would make some new pronouncement upon the subject of reconstruction, he [Sumner] had no intention of . . . allowing his presence to be used . . . to give symbolic approval. 'I . . . was unwilling,' he explained to Chase, 'to put myself in the position of opposing him at his own balcony or assenting by silence.' "

& tenderly worded, notifying, the hour, of the day, he would ride with me." [2]

Months later, when she could bring herself to recall that day —Friday, the fourteenth of April—she described her husband's mood as supremely cheerful. The couple drove out alone as far as the Navy Yard in raw, gusty weather, talking of past and future. "We must be more cheerful," Mrs. Lincoln remembered her husband as saying. "Between the war & the loss of our darling Willie—we have both, been very miserable." [3] In the years which stretched peacefully ahead they would travel together, out to the West as far as California, then perhaps to Europe. They might even make a special pilgrimage to Jerusalem, which Lincoln had often said was a city he longed to see.

That evening they were going to the theater, an event they would have anticipated with pleasure had they been a bit less weary. The availability of theatrical and musical entertainment had been one of the few wholly delightful aspects of their life in Washington. The President had enjoyed seeing his favorite Shakespearean plays performed by the troupes of Booth, Forrest, and Hackett; he could also find relaxation in such third-rate offerings as the one they would see that night, "Our American Cousin," a British potboiler in the repertoire of Laura Keene's company. Mrs. Lincoln loved the theater too but had a special predilection for the opera. She rarely missed a performance of the German and Italian troupes when they came to Grover's Theatre. Sometimes she persuaded her husband to join her, but mostly she had enjoyed the music in the cultured company of Charles Sumner. The Lincolns were the first presidential couple to make a habit of theater-going and to invite artists to the White House not only to entertain but as honored guests. Mrs. Lincoln in particular loved the excitement of stage performances and seemed fascinated by actors and singers as by all flamboyant personalities. There is no better measure of the impact of the events of April 14, 1865, upon her than the fact that, after that night, she never was known to set foot in a theater or concert hall.

[2] Mary Lincoln to Mary Jane Welles, near Chicago, July 11, 1865.
[3] Mary Lincoln to Francis Bicknell Carpenter, Chicago, November 15, 1865.

To James Gordon Bennett [4]

[EXCERPT]   [*April 13, 1865*]

We are rejoicing beyond expression, over our great and glorious victories and appreciate most gratefully your devotion to our cause and great influence exerted in crushing, this terrible rebellion.

To Charles Sumner

Thursday
the 13th [*April 1865*]
Executive Mansion

Senator Sumner:

The volume of "Julius Caesar" has been brought to the house, you will doubtless have much pleasure in reading it—Gen Grant, will be here this evening, & if you are disengaged, we will be pleased, to have you visit us. The Marquis, would, very probably be interested in seeing him—And I am going to have the Genl drive round & see the illumination. In great haste, very truly,

Mary Lincoln

To Ulysses S. Grant

Executive Mansion
[*April 13, 1865*]

General Grant—

Mr Lincoln is indisposed with quite a severe headache, yet would be very much pleased to see you at the house, this evening about 8 o'clock & *I* want you to drive around with us to see the illumination!

Very truly
Mary Lincoln—

---

[4] The catalogue offering this letter for sale states that it was accompanied by a "likeness" of John Randolph, a gift from Mrs. Lincoln.

To Abram Wakeman

April 13 [1865]

My dear Mr Wakeman

Having a few moments of leisure I have concluded to write you something about our visit to City Point. I can scarcely express what a charming time we have had, and *not* encounterng Mr W[eed] was the *most agreeable* feature of the excursion. I *am told* he has just left W for N.Y. I wish very much you had been with us, even our stately dignified Mr Sumner acknowledged himself transformed, into a lad of sixteen. We had a gay time I assure you, & Richmond we visited as a matter of course, & "the banquet halls" of Jeff Davis looked sad and deserted. Each & every place will be repeopled with our own glorious & loyal people & the traitors meet the doom which a just Heaven ever awards the transgressor. Please do not acknowledge to Mr W that you wrote me, he with a party was en route to City Point, there is no necessity that *he* should know, I had heard any thing about it. When you have leisure write me all the news and believe me always your friend.

Mary Lincoln

To Schuyler Colfax [5]

13 April 1865 [6]

It appears to have been arranged, (without Mr Lincoln's knowledge, that you were to accompany us, to the theatre this evening) that Gen Grant & staff, were to occupy the box usually assigned to us, therefore I shall have to waive, all ceremony & request you to accompany us some other evening soon. . . .

[5] Congressman from Indiana 1855–69; Speaker of the House 1863–69.
[6] It has been generally assumed that the performance to which Mrs. Lincoln had invited Speaker Colfax and General Grant was the fateful one at Ford's Theatre, yet the date on the above letter (and the presumed date on the one which follows) is April 13, and Mrs. Lincoln wrote "this evening." There is no

To Schuyler Colfax

[*April 13, 1865*]

Since sending you my note, I have found that Gen Grant's staff will not be seated with him, therefore, with much pleasure, I will send the carriage at 7 o'clock. . . .

———❖———

The only guard on duty at the presidential box at Ford's Theatre on April 14 was John F. Parker of the Metropolitan Police Force. Less than two weeks earlier, before rejoining her husband at City Point, Mrs. Lincoln had signed an order detailing Parker for White House guard duty. She was perhaps too elated then by the war news to consider whether an investigation had been made into Parker's qualifications, which were dubious to say the least. It was one of those small lapses destined to have fatal consequences.

Parker stationed himself at the back door of the loge as the Lincolns entered with their two last-minute guests, Major Henry R. Rathbone and his stepsister, Clara Harris, daughter of the Lincolns' close friend Senator Ira Harris of New York. The President sat down in a special rocker upholstered in red damask, and Mrs. Lincoln had her chair pulled close beside his. The play had been running only a short time when John Parker grew restless and abandoned his post; he never noticed a tiny hole that had been bored into the door of the loge earlier in the day by someone who had wanted a close view of the evening's occupants.

Despite its banality, "Our American Cousin" was entertaining enough, and the Lincolns were enjoying themselves hugely. The feeling of closeness that they had rediscovered on their ride that

———

way of accounting for this discrepancy except Mrs. Lincoln's habit of misdating letters. Neither Grant nor Colfax accepted the invitation: Colfax was about to leave for a trip West, and Mrs. Grant, it has been said, did not, after City Point, choose to spend an evening with Mrs. Lincoln.

afternoon still enveloped them in its happy glow. At one point during the third act, Mary Lincoln turned to her husband, slipped her hand in his, and leaned into his lap. "What will Miss Harris think of my hanging on to you so [?]" she whispered. Lincoln replied softly, "She wont think any thing about it." [7]

The next moment there was a sudden sharp sound, followed by a wild flurry of movement. Mrs. Lincoln, sitting so close to the President, must have realized before anyone else that something had happened to him. Her terrified screams were the first to rouse the audience; her arms, the first to reach out convulsively to keep her husband's body from slumping to the floor. Some accounts say she lost consciousness after that; others describe her wheeling frantically about the box like a caged animal. Whatever her actions, she was clearly in a state of shock and unmindful of the tumult that raged about her after the assassin had jumped to the stage. It was Laura Keene—not Mrs. Lincoln—who asked and received permission to cradle the President's head in her lap as the doctor probed his wound.

When the decision was made to move Lincoln to a house across the street, his wife could only follow dumbly, weeping and wringing her hands. Once admitted to the room where the President lay, she fell to her knees beside the bed, oblivious of staring eyes, sobbing, calling him by intimate names, crooning words of endearment, begging him to speak to her. When no conscious sound came from the form on the bed, she asked that Tad be sent for in hopes that Lincoln would at least respond to the son he had loved so dearly. Robert came, but not Tad.

After some time Mrs. Lincoln left the President's room and returned to the front parlor. As the night wore on, most of the leaders of the government came in and out of the house, among them her special friend Senator Charles Sumner, but she spoke to no one and acknowledged no one. Between spasms of weeping and stumbling trips to the President's bedside, she sat on the front room settee, dazed with shock. When her befuddled brain at last assimilated the fact that there was no hope, the hysterical crying began in earnest.

[7] Quoted by Dr. Anson G. Henry in a letter to his wife, Washington, April 19, 1865. Photostat in the Illinois State Historical Library, Springfield.

At six o'clock in the morning, as a steady rain started falling, the President's labored breathing began to slow. It ceased altogether at seven twenty-two. Robert Lincoln, transformed in an instant from weeping child to head of the family, quietly led his mother out of the room, out of the house, into the rain, and back to the empty Mansion she had left so happily a dozen hours earlier. "Oh, My God," she cried with an agonized backward glance, "and have I given my husband to die." [8]

The President was dead. It was essential that his widow be taken care of immediately at the White House for she could no longer stand upright. Elizabeth Keckley was sent for and arrived early in the morning to find Mrs. Lincoln tossing restlessly on a bed. The seamstress stood by, listening to her moans, her cries that her life was over, her pleas that death take her away. The sounds were dreadful: "the wails of a broken heart, the unearthly shrieks, the wild tempestuous outbursts of grief from the soul." Brought in to comfort his mother, Tad could only beg, "Don't cry so, Mamma! don't cry, or you will make me cry, too!" [9]

Mary Lincoln never knew at what point the President's body was returned to the White House, but she could hear the rain beating against the windows, the hammering of nails into the platform that would hold the coffin, the voices and footsteps of a thousand people, and the mournful tolling of church bells. As far as is known, she never saw the East Room draped in black, with crepe hanging over the mirrors and paintings, swathing the columns and chandeliers. Lincoln's remains lay in that room for a full day; there, on the nineteenth, a funeral service was held, with Robert the only immediate family member in attendance. At two o'clock the procession left the White House for the Capitol. The casket was placed in the center of the great Rotunda, and remained there for another day as crowds came to pay their final respects to the President. Mrs. Lincoln did not make an appearance.

At last, on the evening of the twentieth, Abraham Lincoln

[8] Quoted in a letter from James Tanner to Henry F. Walch, Washington, April 17, 1865. Published in "James Tanner's Account of Lincoln's Death" by Howard H. Peckham. *Abraham Lincoln Quarterly*, December 1942, p. 179.

[9] Keckley, pp. 191–2.

and his son Willie began their slow journey home to Springfield. Mrs. Lincoln was left behind in a house filled with phantoms. Secluded in her room, hours of wild grief alternating with periods of total prostration, she was completely unaware of what was going on in the rest of the Mansion. In the absence of an experienced doorkeeper, all sorts of people freely entered the White House, carrying off silver and china, ornaments, and even heavy furniture. Curtains and cushions were slashed and pieces of velvet carpet taken away as souvenirs. Her beautiful home—the nation's house—was a shambles and she could not have cared less.

Only a few people were admitted to her room, and only a few would have wanted to be there. She saw her sons, Mrs. Keckley, friends such as Mary Jane Welles, Elizabeth Lee, and Sally Orne. But the person who seemed to provide her with the most comfort was Dr. Anson G. Henry, an old friend from Springfield, now on leave from his post as Surveyor-General of the Washington Territory. Dr. Henry sat with the widow for hours at a time and assured her repeatedly that in death her husband was closer to her than in life. This was a concept she had accepted long ago, at the time of Willie's passing; it was reassuring to know that her beliefs were shared by so excellent a man as Dr. Henry.[1]

For the next month the only tasks that Mary Lincoln could face were those involved in carrying out the wishes of her late husband. She made decisions about his burial—controversial decisions that brought on a war of attrition lasting for months; she wrote letters of recommendation for persons the President had planned to help; she proceeded with the painful task of distributing mementoes among Lincoln's closest friends and supporters, but especially among those who had served him faithfully in a menial capacity: doorkeepers, guards, waiters, valets. She gave away almost all of his clothing and effects. Out of a seemingly endless supply of canes, she reserved one, a "simple relic," for Senator Sumner in memory of the President's "great regard." [2]

The rest of her belongings were packed in crates to be sent

[1] From letters written by Anson G. Henry to his wife, Washington, April 19 and May 8, 1865. MSS. in the Illinois State Historical Library, Springfield.
[2] Mary Lincoln to Charles Sumner, Executive Mansion, May 9, 1865.

on to Chicago, where she had decided to make her home. Chicago was close enough to Springfield to enable her to visit Lincoln's grave with relative ease, but far enough away to keep the town's associations from preying on her mind. There were over sixty crates in all, containing the accumulated possessions of a lifetime, including nearly every article of clothing she owned and every gift presented her as the President's wife. Many years later Mary Clemmer Ames would write: "The size and number of these boxes, with the fact of the pillaged aspect of the White House, led to the accusation, which so roused public feeling against her, that she was robbing the National House, and carrying the national property with her into retirement. This accusation . . . was probably unjust. Her personal effects, in all likeliness, amounted to as much as that of nearly all other Presidents' wives together, and the vandals who roamed at large through the length and breadth of the White House, were quite sufficient to account for all its missing treasures." [3]

From all over the world, Mary Lincoln received messages of condolence. In time she would attempt to answer many of them personally, for writing provided an outlet for her emotions, and even in her misery her sense of duty and politesse remained. One letter she cherished came from Queen Victoria, a woman whom she resembled in many ways. After the death of Prince Albert, Victoria had hidden away at Windsor and indulged her grief to the point where she was widely criticized. "No one can better appreciate than I can," wrote Her Majesty, "who am myself utterly *broken hearted* by the loss of my own beloved husband, who was the *light* of my life, my stay—*my all*—what your suffering must be." [4] Mrs. Lincoln's reply was so graceful and dignified that, had no names been affixed to the letters, it would have been difficult to determine which had been written by a queen and which by an American woman from Lexington, Kentucky.

Out of respect for Mrs. Lincoln's bereavement, the new President allowed her to remain in the White House for more than a month until she could pull herself together. During that period he did not

[3] Ames, p. 241.
[4] H. M. Queen Victoria to Mary Lincoln, Osborne, April 29, 1865. Copy in the Library of Congress.

call on her once, nor did he convey his condolences in writing. Although a note would certainly have been in order, Andrew Johnson could scarcely have been blamed for avoiding contact with her in her distraught state; he might also have known of her intense dislike of him (she had called him a "demagogue" months before).[5] What he did not know was that she believed the wild rumors linking him with Booth and his fellow conspirators.

To Andrew Johnson

Executive Mansion
April 29, 1865

My Dear Sir:

The bearer Mr Alexr. Williamson was for more than four years, connected with our family, in the capacity of tutor to my late son Willie and latterly to Tad. He enjoyed the complete confidence and had the best wishes of my late husband, so much so that about the middle of March when he had made up his mind to make certain prominent appointments in connection with the "Bureau of Refugees, Freedmen and Abandoned Lands," he in a conversation with Mr W. in the library, told him that he would "not forget him." I am most desirous that the promise should be fulfilled.[6]

Mr W- has all along been a devoted friend of our family and an unconditional friend of the Union, and as such I leave him and his case with perfect confidence in your hands.

I am
My dear Sir
Yours very Truly
Mary Lincoln

[5] Quoted in Keckley, p. 132.
[6] Williamson did not receive the appointment but remained in his position as clerk in the Second Auditor's office of the Treasury Department, to which he had been appointed in 1863. Mrs. Lincoln's mention of "four years'" service was an exaggeration which she probably thought would be helpful to Williamson.

To Andrew Johnson

Executive Mansion
Washington D.C. May 3d, 1865

President Johnson: —

I have the honor to respectfully submit the following recommendation,[7] which I sincerely hope will receive your favorable consideration.

The bearer of this is Mr Albert F. Pike. He is an applicant for a Cadet appointment to West Point. He is well qualified both by education and physique—having devoted himself with untiring energy to this end for the past three years—lately passing a creditable examination before a Board of Examiners.

He is thoroughly in earnest, the Mil'ty profession being his aim and ambition.

Mr Lincoln was intending, had decided in fact, to give him this appointment. And if any word or entreaty of mine at this time, can expedite this matter, I heartily trust it will avail in this young man's behalf—for I am deeply, not to say personally, intersted [sic] in his success.

An early notice with favorable action, will be regarded as a personal kindness by

Your obliged friend—
Mary Lincoln—

To Charles Sumner

Executive Mansion
Tuesday Morning
May 9th 1865

My Dear Mr Sumner:

Your unwavering kindness to my idolized Husband, and the great regard, *he* entertained for you, prompts me to offer for your

---

[7] This letter was written out for Mrs. Lincoln's signature by Oakes Ames, member of Congress from Massachusetts. On January 17, 1865, he himself had written Lincoln on behalf of Pike, who was a resident of his state.

acceptance this simple relic, which being connected with his blessed memory, I am sure you will prize. I am endeavouring to regain my strength sufficiently to be enabled to leave here in a few days. I go hence, broken hearted, with every hope almost in life—crushed. Notwithstanding my utter desolation, through life, the memory of the cherished friends of my Husband & myself, will always be most gratefully remembered.

With kindest regards, I remain always, yours very truly

Mary Lincoln

To Charles Sumner

11 May, 65

Mr Sumner

I deeply regret that I cannot see you this evening if you are not leaving, on the morning train, I will be pleased to receive a call from you at 12 o'clock tomorrow

Your friend

M. L.

To Charles Sumner

Executive Mansion
Sunday May 14th '65

Pardon the great liberty, I am taking in offering for your acceptance this likeness of Mr Bright [8] as having belonged to my beloved Husband & which he prized, in its rough state, as representing so noble & so good a friend of our cause, in this unholy rebellion. The news of the capture of Davis,[9] almost overpowers me!—In my

[8] John Bright, the great English reformer and statesman, an ardent admirer of Lincoln and supporter of the Union. The portrait of Bright had been mounted above the mantel in Lincoln's White House office.
[9] Jefferson Davis was captured on May 10, 1865, at Irwinsville, Georgia. Although he was held for two years at Fortress Monroe, he was never tried and was finally released on bail.

crushing sorrow, I have found myself almost doubting the goodness of the Almighty!

With sincere friendship [&] regard, I remain, your truly afflicted friend,

Mary Lincoln

Pray excuse, the haste in which this note was written

M. L.

To Andrew Johnson

[May, 1865]

His Excellency Andrew Johnson, President

You will confer a personal favor upon me by retaining as principal doorkeeper, Thomas F. Pendel. He has been a sober, faithful, and obliging servant.

Yours respectfully,
Mary Lincoln.

To "Mrs Off and Mrs Baker" [1]

Executive Mansion
May 16th [1865]

Mrs Off & Mrs Baker.

A note has been handed me this morning, written by our amiable friend Mrs Orne [2] & delivered I believe by yourselves. Bowed down as I am with my great sorrow, I cannot sufficiently

[1] A pair of volunteer nurses who came to the White House to present Mrs. Lincoln with a Bible, originally intended for the President. Too distraught to receive them, she wrote them this note of thanks several days later.
[2] Sally (Mrs. James H.) Orne was the wife of a wealthy Philadelphian who had performed many wartime services for Lincoln. She was one of Mrs. Lincoln's most loyal friends.

compose myself, to write you such a note, as at any *other* time, I should do—I am very sure my Beloved Husband, would have been most grateful for the gift of a Bible—a book so very dear to *him*, and which it was his delight to read; in his name & for his sake, I will accept & treasure the offering.

With the most grateful regard, I remain your

deeply afflicted friend
Mary Lincoln.

To Alphonso Dunn

May 20, 1865

The suit of clothes used by Mr [Matthew] Wilson[3] will be delivered to Mr Dunn, when he no longer requires them.

Mrs Lincoln

To H. M. Queen Victoria

Washington
May 21st, 1865

Madam:

I have received the letter,[4] which Your Majesty has had the kindness to write, & am deeply grateful for its expressions of tender

---

[3] A painter then working on a portrait of Lincoln. Lithographs based on this portrait were widely circulated after Lincoln's death.

[4] The letter from the British Queen was dated "Osborne, April 29. 1865" and read as follows:

> Dear Madam, Though a stranger to you I cannot remain silent when so terrible a calamity has fallen upon you & your country, & must personally express my *deep* & *heartfelt* sympathy with you under the shocking circumstances of your present dreadful misfortune.
>
> No-one can better appreciate than I can who am myself *utterly broken hearted* by the loss of my own beloved Husband, who was the *light* of my Life— my stay—*my all*,—what your sufferings must be; and I earnestly pray that you

sympathy, coming as they do, from a heart which from its own sorrow, can appreciate the *intense grief* I now endure. Accept, Madam, the assurance of my heartfelt thanks & believe me in the deepest sorrow, Your Majesty's sincere and grateful friend.

Mary Lincoln

On the twenty-third of May, Mrs. Abraham Lincoln, clad in black from head to foot, slowly descended the White House steps to be driven to the depot for her journey to Chicago. Few people came to bid her farewell, even fewer than had welcomed her to Washington four years earlier. To Mrs. Keckley, "it was so unlike the day when the body of the President was borne from the hall in grand and solemn state. Then thousands gathered to bow the head in reverence as the plumed hearse drove down the line. . . . Now the wife of the President was leaving the White House and there was scarcely a friend to tell her good-by. . . . The silence was almost painful." [5]

---

may be supported by Him to whom Alone the sorely stricken can look for comfort in this hour of heavy affliction.

With the renewed expression of true sympathy, I remain, dear Madam

Your sincere friend Victoria

It was intended both as a warm personal condolence and a diplomatic gesture. The Queen's ministers expected that the letter would be widely published to favorable comment, but Mrs. Lincoln unconsciously defeated the maneuver by keeping it to herself.

[5] Keckley, p. 208.

III

A World
of Anguish

May 1865

October 1868

At six o'clock on the evening of May 23, 1865, a somber party of travelers boarded a private railway car at the Washington depot. Mrs. Abraham Lincoln, accompanied by her two sons, her trusted friends Anson Henry and Elizabeth Keckley, and by Thomas Cross and William Crook of the White House guard, was leaving the capital to make her home in Chicago, a prospect she faced without the slightest interest. Crook recalled the fifty-four hour journey as a harrowing experience. When the President's widow was not weeping, he wrote, she "was in a daze; it seemed almost a stupor. She hardly spoke. No one could get near enough to her grief to comfort her." [1]

Before Crook and Dr. Henry returned to Washington, they saw the three Lincolns installed in an apartment at the Tremont House, then in its last days as Chicago's largest and most popular hotel. But a single week there was all the family finances could withstand, and Robert was sent off in search of less pretentious lodgings. He finally chose as temporary summer quarters a newly built hotel in the resort community of Hyde Park, seven miles south of town on the lake shore. His mother at first seemed satisfied with the arrangement and even managed some enthusiasm as she described the hotel, sight unseen, in an otherwise dolorous letter to her friend "Pet" Halsted.

---

[1] *Through Five Administrations: Reminiscences of Colonel William H. Crook: Bodyguard to President Lincoln.* Compiled and edited by Margarita Spalding Gerry. New York, 1910, pp. 71–2.

To Oliver S. Halsted, Jr.

Tremont House
Chicago
May 29th [1865]

My Dear Sir:

We arrived here some days since & I quite regretted that I did not see you again, before leaving W. as I had a good deal to say to you. May I trouble you with a message to our friend Mr Roberts [2] & say to him, that as soon as our boxes *can be reached*, at the Warehouse, I will send him the promised cane—At the same time, I trust you will accept a slight memento, I am sure, any little relic, of my Beloved Husband, will be valued by you—Life & the future looked to me, wretchedly desolate when we left W- realizing as *I now do*, that I am alone, my all, my Husband gone from me, the agony is insupportable. If I was not aware, that my precious Boys, depended upon me, for their happiness, I would pray our Heavenly Father, to remove me from a world, where I have been so bitter a sufferer. To rejoin my Husband, who loved me so devotedly & whom I idolized, would be bliss indeed. I am scarcely able to sit up & fear it will be some time, ere I can summon strength of mind or body either, to receive my friends. And some charming friends, we have here, persons who live delightfully & honored my darling Husband, always. My health is so miserable, that we may go out on the Michigan Lake Shore for the summer, Robert went out on yesterday to a place called "Hyde Park, a beautiful new Hotel, rooms exquisitely clean & even luxuriously fitted up, seven miles from the city—Cars passing every hour of the day—R. will come in each morning & return in the evening. It was on Michigan Avenue, that my indulgent Husband—proposed three months since, to purchase a handsome home, *this June*, so that instead of going North—we

[2] Marshall O. Roberts, a New York shipping magnate and prominent contributor to Republican campaigns. Roberts owned the *Star of the West* which in January 1861 had been hired to provision Fort Sumter. His subsequent activities in chartering and selling vessels to the U.S. Government during the war made him one of the most successful profiteers of the era.

might come here at our pleasure—Alas! every thing is greatly changed since then, & we must content ourselves, for the present, with my heavy *cross*—We cannot make any definite arrangements, until our business affairs are adjusted.[3] My blessed Husband, was so noble & generous, that he thought very little of future wants. Yet I would not recall one dollar, that he ever bestowed upon suffering humanity—For it was his heart's delight to do good & love all mankind—Remember me most kindly to Mrs H- and believe me, your true friend

Mary Lincoln.

— ✦ —

With his father's death it became impossible for Robert Lincoln to continue at the Harvard Law School, and he felt the deprivation keenly. He would now commute daily from Hyde Park into Chicago to read law in the Lake Street offices of Scammon, McCagg and Fuller, beginning what would be a lifelong pursuit of identity and success. The company of young people such as he had known in Cambridge and Washington (among them, Mary Harlan, the girl he loved) was lost to him for the duration. There were no more gay little excursions, no more parties, dances, and talk sessions, none of that exhilarating sense of participation he had known during his brief war service. Each evening he would return wearily to the Hyde Park apartment, where two people depended on him for strength he could not always summon.

Within a short time, Mary Lincoln stopped referring to her new residence as a "hotel"; it became that most demeaning of habitations, a "boarding house." The three rooms the family occupied proved to be small and inadequately furnished, a jarring comedown from the grandeur of the White House. Robert told Mrs. Keckley shortly before her return to Washington that he would "put up" with The Hyde Park for his mother's sake, but that he would "al-

---

[3] An oblique reference to unpaid debts.

most as soon be dead as be compelled to remain three months in this dreary house." [4]

If his reduced circumstances depressed Robert, his mother's mental and physical condition could only have deepened his gloom. Mrs. Lincoln was carrying the rituals and restrictions of a Victorian widowhood to alarming extremes. Her husband's death had brought into permanent dominance all that was unappealing—even abnormal—in her nature. The sophisticated, flirtatious woman who had delighted in clever talk, high fashion, the theater, and the opera, had vanished overnight. In her place sat an aging creature, garbed in funereal black, drowning in waves of anxiety and self-pity. From the moment of her arrival in Chicago, she immured herself in her rooms, rarely venturing on the streets (where she felt she would be conspicuous in her mourning), refusing to receive most callers and calling on no one herself. One reason she gave for her seclusion was her precarious health: the attacks of chills and migraine came more frequently than ever; incessant weeping caused her temples to pound and her eyes to burn and swell until she could scarcely see. But her chief purpose in hiding was to avoid conversation with those who had known her in happier days. Most of her Chicago acquaintances, basking in the postwar prosperity, had handsome, well-staffed homes, of the sort she too might have had had the President lived out his second term and retired to Chicago, as she claimed he had planned to do. After her brief taste of glory, she was once again what she had been in her early married days in Springfield: the least well off of anyone she knew. She had had a husband then and dreams for the future; now she had nothing, *was* nothing.

She complained bitterly of loneliness and a lack of true friends, but quite clearly preferred solitude to seeing pity in the eyes of strangers, or to witnessing the thinly disguised satisfaction of those she was certain had always disliked and envied her, including some members of her own family. Instead of erasing the differences between her and her sisters, Mary Lincoln's accession to the White House had created new tensions. None of the three had come to her after the assassination; none would visit her in Chicago. There is no trace of correspondence between Mrs. Lincoln and her sisters

[4] Keckley, p. 212.

during her early widowhood, nor did she mention them when writing to others. No record exists of her having asked for, or been offered, financial assistance from her cousins or brothers-in-law, at a time when she was desperately seeking the aid of strangers.

Living as a virtual recluse, she had, as she wrote Charles Sumner, "ample time to muse," [5] a condition nearly always disastrous for the recently bereaved. There was no one available, on a day-to-day basis, to flatter and fuss over her, to make light of her troubles or jump to her commands. She was alone with her burdens and without benefit of consistent, sensible advice.

She lived in letters to her eastern friends and to former associates of her husband, pouring her grief, bitterness, and humiliation onto the black-bordered pages, many of them stained with tears. Her correspondence filled the endless, empty hours during the day when she had nowhere to go, and at night when she could not sleep. It served as a catharsis for her troubled spirit, as her sole means of conducting her business and of making her wishes known. In the end letters became her chief contact with that "outside world," the inhabitants of which were cheerfully going on with their lives while hers was all but over.

In a letter to the editor of the New York *Evening Journal* in 1867, Elizabeth Keckley attempted to describe Mrs. Lincoln as she was in 1865 and for several years thereafter. "The most of her time," she wrote, "she devotes to instructive reading within the walls of her boudoir. Laying her book aside spasmodically, she places her hand upon her forehead, as if ruminating upon something momentous. Then her hand wanders amid her heavy tresses, while she ponders for a few seconds—then, by a sudden start, she approaches her writing stand, seizes a pen, and indites a few hasty lines to some trusty friend, upon the troubles that weigh so heavily upon her. Speedily it is sent to the post office; but, hardly has the mail departed from the city before she regrets her hasty letter, and would give much to recall it. But, too late, it is gone. . . ." [6]

Several themes recurred in the hundreds of letters she wrote in the first three years of her widowhood. The most consistent of these was her grief, her loneliness, her longing to leave a world

[5] Mary Lincoln to Charles Sumner, near Chicago, July 4, 1865.
[6] Keckley, pp. 311–12.

which had seen fit to punish her so. She was convinced that no human being had ever been visited by such adversity as she. The words "misery," "desolation," "agony," "affliction," surfaced again and again on a flood of woe that never abated.

A second major theme in her correspondence was her desire that all should honor the memory of the man to whom she now frequently referred as "my sainted husband." Throughout Mr. Lincoln's lifetime, she had taken it upon herself to protect him from his enemies and had been openly hostile toward those she believed were operating at his expense. If anything, she felt the charge more keenly after his death. By whatever means lay within her power, she would see to it that no one cast aspersions on his name, that he was remembered only for his nobler qualities, that all untruths circulating about him would be instantly refuted, and that any desire he had ever expressed would, if possible, be fulfilled. One such desire involved the site of his final resting place.

During the course of their visit to Virginia shortly before the President's death, the Lincolns had gone off alone for a drive through the countryside. They had stopped to wander through a secluded graveyard, lying peaceful and green in the spring sunshine. Strolling among the weathered stones, Lincoln had turned to his wife and said, as she remembered it, "Mary, you are younger than I. You will survive me. When I am gone, lay my remains in some quiet place like this." [7] That intensely private moment was to have far-reaching public consequences. Immediately after the assassination, a group of prominent Illinois citizens, calling themselves the National Lincoln Monument Association, contracted for six acres of land in the center of Springfield and, without consulting the President's widow, made preparations for the construction of a vault on the spot. No sooner had she learned of the Association's plans than she recalled the scene in the Virginia graveyard. She sent word from Washington that her husband was to be buried in suburban Oak Ridge Cemetery, and that provision must be made for herself and her sons in the same tomb—a matter of vast importance to her. When the Monument Association balked at her demand, a protracted controversy began, with Mary Lincoln standing almost

[7] Quoted in Isaac N. Arnold. *The Life of Abraham Lincoln*. Chicago, 1885, p. 435.

alone against a phalanx of eminent gentlemen, many of them old
and trusted friends.

She won out on her choice of Oak Ridge as the burial place,
but the group persisted in plans to erect Springfield's monument
to Lincoln not over his tomb, but on the original downtown site,
where it could be seen from any point in the city and would even
be visible from the railroad tracks. Mrs. Lincoln would have no
backtracking on the bargain. The tomb and monument would be
together and they would be at Oak Ridge. Throughout the first half
of June 1865, she fought the Monument Association with every
weapon at her command, emerging triumphant but with a number
of enemies who had once been friends.

To Richard J. Oglesby [8]

Hyde Park
June 5th 1865

Dear Sir:

I learn from the Newspapers & other sources, that your association have it in contemplation to erect a Monument to my
Husband's memory, on the Mather Block,[9] in the City of Springfield, instead of over his remains, in Oak Ridge Cemetery.

I feel that it is due to candor and fairness that I should notify
your Monument association, that unless I receive within the next
ten days, an Official assurance that the Monument will be erected
over the Tomb in Oak Ridge Cemetery, in accordance with my oft
expressed wishes, I shall yield my consent, to the request of the
National Monument association in Washington & that of numerous
other friends in the Eastern States & have the sacred remains de-

---

[8] A former general in the Union army, Oglesby had been elected governor of Illinois in 1864. He was chairman of the National Lincoln Monument Association.
[9] A large plot of elevated land near the center of Springfield, owned by the well-
to-do Mather family. The Illinois State Capitol now stands where the Lincoln
tomb and monument were to have been.

posited, in the vault, prepared for Washington, under the Dome of the National Capitol, at as early a period as practicable.

I remain, your deeply afflicted friend

Mary Lincoln.

To Harriet Howe Wilson [1]

Near Chicago
June 8th 65

My Dear Mrs Wilson.

Your very kind and truly sympathizing letter, was received a few days since, pray, receive the grateful thanks of my deeply afflicted heart, for the words of affection & comfort it contained. My precious Boys and myself, are left very desolate & brokenhearted, the deep waters of affliction have almost overwhelmed us and we find it very difficult, to bow in submission, to our Heavenly Father's will, the light of our life, has been taken away. I shall always feel most grateful, to your Noble Husband, for his unwavering friendship & faithful support of the President, which was highly appreciated, I assure you, by *his* grateful heart. I had truly hoped in the coming four years, we had anticipated residing in Washington, that Circumstances would have drawn you & myself together, and I should have been privileged to number you, with my cherished friends. Our Heavenly Father, has so disposed events, has removed my idolized Husband from me, my Boys, are deprived of their counsellor & protector, my all, & the one so devoted always to me, is removed from our sight forever! The knowledge, that my sons, depend upon me, for their comfort & happiness, alone, prevents me from pleading, with our gracious Saviour, to remove me, from a World in which we have been called upon, to suffer *so much.* In our griefs, we are said to be selfish, I hope you will excuse, my sending you, so lengthy a letter—We found, Chicago, at this Season

---

[1] Wife of Henry Wilson, the Massachusetts senator who was among the leaders of the radical Republicans in Congress and who would serve as Vice-President under Ulysses Grant.

of the year, very warm & dusty, and our rooms, at the [Tremont] Hotel, very noisy & confined. We considered outselves quite fortunate, in finding, a new, large & exceedingly neat Hotel just opened, seven miles out on the Lake Shore—trains passing to & fro every hour of the day & only consuming half an hour, in reaching the City—My son Robert, has entered a law office, to read & study for the summer, going into C- in the morning & returning in the evening. We occupy three very pleasant rooms & how gladly we would welcome, our Eastern friends, to see us, those who have known & loved my darling Husband, are very dear to us—

Please present, my kindest regards to your Husband & with love to yourself, I remain always, truly yours

Mary Lincoln

Request for Agreement [2]

[June, 1865]

It must be expressly understood and agreed upon, that *no one*, save the bodies of the President, his wife, sons & son's families, shall ever be placed, in the vault, that is to be built—Only on these terms, shall the sacred remains of Mr Lincoln, be placed there

Mrs A. Lincoln

To Richard J. Oglesby

Near Chicago
June 10th, 1865

Dear Sir:

I perceive by the paper of to day, that notwithstanding, the note, I recently addressed you, yourself & Mr Hatch are en route to

---

[2] This request in Mrs. Lincoln's handwriting was directed to the Lincoln National Monument Association at the time of the "battle of the gravesite."

Chicago, to *consult*, with me, on the subject. My determination is unalterable, and if you will allow me again to add, that without I receive the 15th of this month a formal & written agreement that *the* Monument shall be placed over the remains of my Beloved Husband, in *Oak Ridge* Cemetery, with the *written* promise that no other bodies, save the President, his Wife, his Sons & Sons families, shall ever be deposited within the enclosure; in the event of my *not* receiving a *written* declaration to that effect, I shall rigidly comply with my resolution. If I had anticipated, so much trouble, in having my wishes carried out, I should have readily yielded to the ~~wishes~~ request of the *many* & had *his* precious remains, in the *first instance* placed in the vault of the National Capitol—A tomb prepared for Washington the Father of his Country & a fit resting place for the immortal Savior & Martyr for Freedom—Lest you do not accede to my wishes, it is best that I should be apprised of your intended action, so that changes, *if come, they must*, shall be made ~~before the heat of summer~~ immediately.

Very Respectfully,
Mary Lincoln

To Richard J. Oglesby

Near Chicago
June 11th [1865]

Gov Oglesbey [sic]—

From to day's Chicago paper, I have clipped another interesting *editorial*,[3] such articles injure those *from whom* they emanate, far

---

[3] The editorial, headed "Mrs. Lincoln and the Springfield Monument Association," has been preserved with this letter. It read in part: "The National Monument Association held a meeting yesterday, and Gen. Oglesby said he had received a letter from Mrs. Lincoln who notified the association, that unless the monument were erected over the President's remains at Oak Ridge and a deed given to her and her descendants, of the lot on which it was to be placed, she would accept a proposition for the removal of the remains to Washington! This letter . . . caused a great sensation at the meeting, and some of the members, including one or two prominent citizens, talked of resigning their trust. It is evident that a majority, if not all, gentlemen forming the association, will feel compelled to reject Mrs. Lincoln's proposition. . . ."

more than myself. My wish to have the Monument, placed over my Husband's remains, will meet the approval of the whole civilized world, & if not carried out, and a favorable answer, given me by the 15th of this month, I will certainly do as I have said. It is very painful to me, to be treated in this manner, by some of those I considered my friends, such conduct, will not add, very much, to the honor of our state.

I enclose you a scrap, sent from *Springfield*, to the paper to-day doubtless emanating, from the fertile pen [of] *E. L. Baker—* [4]

Very resp-

Mrs Lincoln

For three years after President Lincoln's death financial embarrassment formed a grim accompaniment to his widow's grief and in time came to occupy her thoughts to the point of obsession. Mary Lincoln had feared poverty even when she was riding high; now that she was without a husband's earning capacity, and, worse, owed thousands of dollars to merchants and bankers in the East, that fear had become a mania. Poverty and privacy being nearly always mutually exclusive, she felt most bitterly her inability to afford a home of her own in a place of her choosing—and that place was *not* Springfield with all its memories of happier days. It was appalling to her that the family of Abraham Lincoln, who had given his life for his country, should be left to languish in boardinghouses, while "roving generals" (most notably the wildly popular U. S. Grant) had "elegant mansions, showered upon them." [5] The ingratitude and inhumanity of the Congress, the Republican party, the American people themselves, in condoning such a state of affairs, was another persistent motif in her correspondence.

She felt, with considerable justification, that those congres-

---

[4] Mrs. Lincoln's nephew-in-law Edward Lewis Baker, editor of the *Illinois State Journal*.

[5] Mary Lincoln to Alexander Williamson, Chicago, August 17, [1865].

sional leaders who eulogized Lincoln with such fervor could prove their regard in a tangible, humane way: they could vote his widow a sum of money which would permit her to live with a dignity befitting her former station. She wished nothing less than one hundred thousand dollars, the amount representing salary for the full term to which Lincoln had been elected. With these funds she could buy, furnish, and maintain a home, where she could nurse her grief in peace and comfort. She would not regard the money as charity, but as compensation for Lincoln's extraordinary service and sacrifice.

There were few who saw things her way. Even those who had truly revered Lincoln were reluctant to aid his widow, for a variety of reasons. First, no precedent existed for the payment of salary for an uncompleted term. A second obstacle to assistance seemed to be widespread knowledge of the size of Lincoln's estate. Much to Mrs. Lincoln's chagrin, the newspapers reliably reported it at $75,000 in cash and government bonds. Real estate holdings, consisting of the house in Springfield and some Iowa land, brought the total close to $85,000. Since the President had left no will, his estate was divided, according to law, equally among his widow and sons and placed under the administration of his old friend, Justice David Davis. The principal, all eventually invested in government securities, was substantial, but the income was only $1,500 to $1,800 a year for each, the amount fluctuating with interest rates and increasing slightly with the appreciation of the capital. Tad's portion would be left in trust until his twenty-first birthday.[6] "A clerk's salary"[7] was the term Mrs. Lincoln used to describe her income. She maintained, quite truthfully, that it did not go far in those inflationary times, and that, without access to the principal, she could never buy a home. No one seemed to understand this, and many persisted in believing that she was, as usual, living beyond her means.

In the end, respect for the martyred President was not transferable to his widow. Too many powerful persons knew her too well, by reputation if not personally. The men who had been Lincoln's enemies were now hers, and she had had a few run-ins of her

[6] The above figures, and a general discussion of Lincoln's estate can be found in Pratt. *The Personal Finances of Abraham Lincoln*, pp. 131–41.
[7] Mary Lincoln to David Davis, Chicago, 24th February [1867].

own. Her extravagance in Washington, the debts she had amassed, had been matters of common gossip, and a great many of those whose help she would now seek had been approached for assistance in earlier years. Then at least they had had selfish reasons for coming to her rescue; now that she could do them neither good nor harm, she could starve for all they cared.

There was little chance of her going hungry, but there was a distinct possibility that she would be "published" on her debts. Dread of this humiliating prospect lent a special urgency to her search for aid. In the beginning not even Robert was aware of the money his mother still owed in the East; she cherished his good opinion and, what is more, feared he would insist on her debts being paid out of the estate, leaving her next to nothing. Various persons have estimated the amount she owed in 1865 as being anywhere from $6,000 to $70,000; [8] the actual total was probably closer to $20,000, which was bad enough. It is likely that she herself had no clear idea of what she would be held accountable for. Study of her correspondence not only fails to yield a definitive figure; it provides some evidence that she was given close to $10,000 by a group of private contributors before she even began her major efforts to raise money. Whatever obligations remained, it must be said to her credit that she determined to obliterate them, in her own time and in her own way. To this end, she worried, schemed, and begged for nearly three years, reaching desperately for help wherever she could find it.

Nowhere can the nature of her efforts be seen more clearly than in sixty-four letters she wrote between 1865 and 1868 to a gentle Scotsman named Alexander Williamson who had been a tutor in the White House until Willie's death in 1862. Because he was fond of Williamson and impressed with his ability, the President had arranged a clerkship for him in the Treasury Department at the termination of his White House service. In April 1865 Mrs. Lincoln recommended Williamson warmly, if unsuccessfully, to Andrew Johnson for a new position in the Freedman's Bureau.[9] At some point prior to her departure for Chicago, she must have talked at length with her former employee, reinforcing her memory

---

[8] The first figure is hypothesized by Willard King in his book *Lincoln's Manager, David Davis*. Cambridge, 1960, p. 235; the second is from Keckley, p. 204.
[9] Mary Lincoln to Andrew Johnson, April 26, 1865.

of him as kind, intelligent, reliable, and needy—altogether the ideal person to handle a delicate assignment she had in mind, something she knew would ultimately benefit them both.

The assignment grew out of her most pressing problem: the need to settle her debts with dignity and dispatch. A solution seemed to lie with an agent in the East, someone who, for a price, would be willing to follow orders, run errands, and absorb the abuse that would have been directed at her had she undertaken to act in her own behalf.

What Williamson agreed to do must have been distasteful to a man of his sensibilities. It was certainly beyond his capacities. He was to lobby in Congress for the full four years' salary. He was charged with convincing creditors to reduce or withdraw certain of their claims, and with the occasional sale of articles for which their owner no longer had any use. Finally, he was required to present himself before a great many formidable gentlemen for the purpose of soliciting contributions for Mrs. Lincoln's relief, all the while pretending to be acting on his own initiative. The mission called for tact, perseverence, patience, and a good bit of gall. In Mrs. Lincoln's absence, Williamson was left to weave his own course among her complicated relationships in Washington, New York, and Philadelphia, and to discover, often by a humiliating process of trial and error, precisely what could (or could not) be revealed to whom. Although the risks were many, her assurances that compensation would be forthcoming in the event of success— assurances sincerely given—were too tempting to withstand.

Mary Lincoln's letters to Alexander Williamson have a quality all their own. The first one stands alone in its warmth and lack of references to money. But in coming months, as the full dimensions of her predicament became apparent, all attempts at graciousness were abandoned. Whenever a fresh grievance or strategy occurred to her, she dashed off a note to her harried representative. The letters were filled with garbled instructions and admonitions delivered in the manner of a stern schoolmistress, with criticisms— often warranted—of Williamson's methods, with frantic inquiries after his progress. Many of them were scrawled in pencil, some are nearly illegible, others barely coherent.

Her communications with such worthies as David Davis,

Charles Sumner, Elihu Washburne, and her several female friends may have been steeped in self-pity, but they showed some restraint and contained numerous professions of gratitude and respect. Not so with Williamson. By learning the worst of her secrets, the poor man unwittingly forfeited any claim he ever had to such deferential treatment and in time assumed the status of a servant. An occasional pang of conscience would prompt Mrs. Lincoln to commend his efforts wearily and grudgingly, and she even used her waning influence to help him keep his Treasury job in the face of wholesale dismissals. But for the most part, as with a servant, she seemed to care very little about his opinion of her, as long as he did as he was told.

The result was a curious, uneasy relationship, defined by distance and by the tacit hold each had over the other: Mrs. Lincoln, the power of the open purse; Williamson, the knowledge that she was to a considerable extent at his mercy. Neither was guaranteed the other's good faith. When Williamson wrote that he had made a contact as instructed, Mrs. Lincoln, lacking proof to the contrary, had to believe him. When she insisted that she had not received a single contribution, and thus could not send him his pitiful commission, he was forced to take her at her word. In working through Williamson, a comparative stranger (and an impecunious one at that), she was playing a dangerous game. In the hands of someone with less integrity, her letters could have provided fuel for blackmail. As it was, Williamson only occasionally used the relationship to advance his own interests. And if, as one must assume, his primary desire was to earn a quick dollar, he clearly got the short end of a poor bargain. For two years he worked for Mrs. Lincoln, nights and weekends, hinting often for some tangible sign of appreciation that never materialized. His frequent blunderings were a source of embarrassment to her, but she had no alternative other than to keep him going to the end of his usefulness.

Although she occasionally sent him expense money, there is no record that either profited materially as a result of their strange, symbiotic relationship. The inevitable frustration showed in every line of Mrs. Lincoln's letters, which are as fascinating to study as they are distressing to read. The psychologically oriented might regard them as the products of a neurotic personality, obsessive,

compulsive, occasionally hysterical and paranoid. Others might
view them as a reflection of qualities more reprehensible than abnormal: greed, coarseness, impatience, lack of candor, and love of
command. But a sympathetic observer might see their author as
an honest person at heart, willing to acknowledge her obligations,
charging at obstacles with prodigious energy and lonely gallantry.
So complex was Mary Lincoln's nature that something can be said
for all three viewpoints.

To Alexander Williamson

Hyde Park Hotel
June 15th 1865

My dear Sir:

Taddie has just received the name of the "Bucktail," [1] & bids
me write & thank you truly, for *all* your kindness to him. He says
two or three lessons a day & is at length seized with the desire to be
able to *read* & *write*—which with his *natural* brightness, will be *half*
the battle with him. I hope he will be able to write by fall so that he
may be able to write you a letter inviting you *out here*, to see him.
For all your great kindness, to my darling boys, may Heaven
forever bless you! I am sure my Angel boy, in Heaven, loves you as
dearly as ever, *He* was too pure for Earth & God recalled his own.
How deeply we have been made to drink of the bitter cup of affliction, is known to all, if it were not for my two remaining sons, I
would pray the Father, to take me *too* hence—Taddie has a lovely
nature & I have not the least trouble in managing him, he is all love
& gentleness. Robert, in our day of sorrow and adversity, manifests
himself as he really is, a youth of great nobleness—I was very much
surprised in yesterday's evening Chicago Journal, to see this article
I enclose, purporting to come from Stackpole.[2] My Beloved Hus-

---

[1] The "Bucktail" Regiment was the nickname given the Thirteenth Pennsylvania
Reserves, some of whom had been assigned to guard the President's family. A
mutual fondness had developed between Tad and many of the young soldiers.
[2] Identified on p. 129.

band's great tenderness & gentleness of character, is well established & in his great love for his children, it is well known, that I bore an equal part. His love for me, was in the same proportion, yet, when I read a story which gives S- as the author, saying I threatened to *whip* Taddie, for cutting up, *copper-toed* shoes, such articles, as my boys never wore—I am surprised. It is a new story—that in my life I have ever whipped a child—In the first place *they*, never required it, a gentle, loving word, was all sufficient with them—and if *I* have erred, it has been, in being too indulgent. I trust if S- has ever got up such a story—even in jest, he will discontinue it—I have relied on him, as a friend [3]—Do not, I pray you, let him have the piece, but return it to me, It would please Hanscom, the R- man [4]—to have such a piece, it may have been copied from his paper. As to *Copperheadism*,[5] I really believe, it would have been a happier day for *us* now, & my idolized husband would *now* have been living, if those, en masse holding office, would have abhorred & sternly treated these Copperheads as I *would* have done.

To Alexander Williamson

June 26th [1865]

Private—show no one this letter
My dear Sir:

I have just received your last note—Please hand the enclosed one to Mrs Cuthbert—I gave her some six papers [6] to keep for me until I called upon her for them—As it can be proved that she has them & it will not avail her to keep them—as I have the names of them—and they can be got from her, as they are my lawful property & I demand them—She must give them to you. What does she

---

[3] A significant statement, as subsequent correspondence reveals.
[4] Simon P. Hanscom, editor of the Washington *National Republican*.
[5] "Copperhead" was the epithet applied to northern Democrats who had opposed the government's war policy and had favored a negotiated peace. After the war it was enlarged to include those who opposed the reconstruction policies of the radicals in Congress.
[6] Probably either bills or some other evidence of Mrs. Lincoln's indebtedness.

mean, by having you write & ask what she must do with them & not send them—Speak kindly to her & say to her, on your authority—that she can be forced to give them up—Robert bids me thank you, about enquiring about the paper, yet prefers a thinner & finer paper, than perhaps Phillips [sic] & S [7] have. I will write you again about it. I write in great haste—remaining truly

your friend
M. L.

Please show *no one* the printed article I sent you & return it to me —R- says, he has not a line with him of his Beloved Father's writing —When he has access, to the papers, he will send you some.

⌣ ⌒⌒ ◇ ⌒⌒ ⌣

If Alexander Williamson served as Mary Lincoln's "secret agent," Justice David Davis was a legitimate, prestigious source of help. A lawyer and judge from Bloomington, Illinois, of acumen as impressive as his girth, Davis had known Abraham Lincoln well since their early days together on the circuit. In time he had become the most prominent member of that inner circle of counselors who had promoted Lincoln's political ambitions, engineered his nomination for President, managed his campaign, and helped him form his Cabinet. In 1862 Davis' loyalty had been rewarded by a seat on the U.S. Supreme Court, from which Olympian perch he had continued to give occasional advice on policy and patronage.

On the day following the assassination an urgent telegram reached Davis in Chicago. It was from Robert Lincoln, and it read: "Please come at once to Washington & take charge of my father's affairs." [8] "The Judge's" devotion to Lincoln, as well as his vast experience in business and the law, made him the family's natural choice for administrator of the President's estate, and this he became officially on June 16, 1865.

[7] Philps & Solomon, Washington stationers.
[8] Robert Lincoln to David Davis, Washington, April 15, 1865. MS. in the Illinois State Historical Library, Springfield.

Davis fulfilled his trust conscientiously for as long as his services were required; under his husbandry the estate increased in value from $85,000 to $110,000 when it was settled late in 1867. Robert was not only appreciative of "the Judge's" sagacity, but grateful for his kindness as well, even going so far as to call him "a second father." [9] Had Robert been the only one to be served, Davis might have welcomed his responsibilities. It was Robert's mother who caused him trouble. As guardian of the purse strings, he was thrown into uncomfortably close contact with her at a time and in an area in which her reactions tended to be emotional and erratic. She sent him scores of carefully worded missives, instructing him to take this or that step in her behalf, reiterating her need of money, repeating endlessly the details of her sufferings, and pleading with him to use his influence to secure an appropriation for her. In her current mood of anger and suspicion, she was not satisfied with Davis' replies. Try as she would, she could not make him understand the feelings which prevented her from moving back to the house the family owned in Springfield, rather than begging funds for a new home in Chicago. The physical comforts of the house on Eighth Street, she insisted, would hardly compensate for the mental anguish of returning there. She also detected in Davis what she believed to be a rich man's complacency. The man had not only amassed a large private fortune, but was secure in a lifetime appointment which he owed to Abraham Lincoln. Mrs. Lincoln assumed (incorrectly) that he had not the slightest understanding of what it meant to count pennies, to be without a home, to worry over the future. Although her letters to Davis were strewn with flowery compliments, she disparaged both his character and motives when writing to others, calling him on one occasion "*intensely* selfish" and declaring that he would actually prefer to see her suffer. She referred to him sarcastically as "our *warm hearted* friend" and dissected his every statement for signs of indifference, even enmity.[1]

Perhaps to some degree Davis did fail to appreciate her need for cosseting, her fear and loathing of poverty, and her persistent

[9] Robert Lincoln to Thomas Dent, September 12, 1919. Copy in the Illinois State Historical Library, Springfield.
[1] Mary Lincoln to Anson G. Henry, Hyde Park Place, July 17, 1865; Mary Lincoln to Simon Cameron, Chicago, April 6, [1866].

sense of injury. He wanted to help, but was simply too busy to give her the constant attention she craved, too honorable to pander to her anxieties with empty promises, and too dignified to beg in her behalf. If he did extend himself at all in an effort to secure her the four years' salary, he had as little success as anyone else. Her chief grievance against David Davis was his insistence that, by exercising prudence, she could manage to live on her income. He could not be faulted on this, for, in the beginning at least, he knew nothing of her debts—and she was not inclined to enlighten him on the subject, for fear he, like Robert, would feel obliged to pay them out of the estate. When bits of her secret, like the peaks of a vast iceberg, floated into view, Davis grew more determined than ever not to let her do anything foolish.

To David Davis

Hyde Park Place
June 27th 65

My Dear Sir:

From the articles, that are *now* appearing, in the papers *daily*, about our being left with $75,000- you can appreciate the motive, I had, in not desiring, *any* amount at all being given or indeed any thing, being said about it. Robert, explains, that the reason, the definite sum, was given, or any mention made, that it was owing, to its having to be drawn from Mr Harrington,[2] previous, to his leaving for Europe. Of course, *no less* than the true amount, should be given, yet when it comes, to be explained, as I am sure, it will be, in your letters, in reply, to those that are written you, on the subject, that one third, as it belongs to a son under age, cannot be invested in a *house*, for us to live in—and the ⅔ thirds—Robert's & my own portion, is all that is left us—Of course, we will be unable to secure a home, with this suitable, to our Station & as to keeping it up, it would be impossible—Coming from you, any explanation, would be well received and have much weight. The sum of $75,000

[2] Identified on p. 149.

sounds very formidable, at first, to those, who do not understand the *particulars*—And again, there *are many* & some not hundreds of miles away,[3] who cannot appreciate Station & with their own pockets, well filled, would like to see us, live very humbly—I hope, if it not very inconvenient, you will oblige us, by writing to those "anxious enquirers,"—I assure you, I am growing very weary of *boarding*, it is very unbecoming, when it is remembered, *from whence*, we have just come. In great haste

Very respectfully
Mary Lincoln

I send you a slip from Greeley's paper— [4] Very true & appropriate.

To Charles Sumner

Near Chicago
July 4th, 1865

From the *far* off shores of Lake Michigan, be pleased My Dear Mr Sumner, to accept my most grateful thanks, for the truthful and eloquent Eulogy on my lamented Husband [5] which in your kind thoughtfulness, you have sent me. In this quiet retreat, where I have ample time to muse upon my griefs & fully realise the extent of my *utter* desolation, the words of a friend so cherished as *you* were, by the great and *good* man, who has been called away, your words as testimonials in *his* praise are very welcomely received. Within the past week, the first paragraph of the address, has been commented upon in *so* complimentary a manner by the press; [6] that I have felt quite solicitous, to read the whole. And I find myself, as

[3] An oblique reference to the "Springfield clique" who had opposed Mrs. Lincoln on the monument and who she now believed to be operating against her interests.
[4] The New York *Tribune*. The clipping has not been preserved.
[5] Delivered before the Municipal Authorities of Boston on July 1, 1865.
[6] The memorable first paragraph began: "In the universe of God there are no accidents. From the fall of a sparrow to the fall of an empire or the sweep of a planet, all is according to Divine Providence, whose laws are everlasting. No accident gave to this country the patriot we now honor. No accident snatched this patriot so suddenly and so cruelly from his sublime duties. . . ." Sumner went on to a review of Lincoln's life, and ended by linking the late President to his own convictions regarding the Negro and the South.

I had anticipated, well repaid. It almost appears to me, that I am on the Sea Shore, land cannot be discerned across the Lake, some seventy-five miles in breadth. My friends thought, I would be more quiet here during the summer months than in the City. My great grief has left my nerves in a very weak state. I have not been able to summon sufficient courage, to receive but *very* few, of my friends, who, with all the world, *surely*, sympathize in my unutterable distress of mind. Little did I think, on that pleasant Sabbath Morning on the boat, [the *River Queen*] when my beloved Husband, so feelingly repeated, some of those heartbreaking lines of Longfellow, on "Resignation," how little did *his* deep loving nature suppose, that *those there*, so *near* & *dear* to *Him* would soon, be called upon to drink of *that bitter* cup & pass through *such* a Baptism of Sorrow! In other days of sadness & bereavement when he sadly repeated those lines to me, our griefs were *one* & therefore more easily assuaged. My belief, is so assured, that *Death*, is only a blessed transition, to the "pure in heart," that a very slight veil separates us, from the "loved & lost" and to me, there is comfort, in the thought, that though unseen by us, they are very near. When I last saw you, surrounded by darkness & despair it appeared to me that *Time* could do no more, yet *even* then, many events of great interest have transpired. When I seated myself, it was merely to return you my thanks for your kind remembrances; my apologies are due you for having thus trespassed upon your time.

I remain sincerely your friend
Mary Lincoln.

To Mary Jane Welles [7]

Near Chicago
July 11' 65

My Dear Mrs Welles

Your very kind letter, was received a few days since & you can well imagine, how much pleasure, it afforded me, to hear from

---

[7] Identified on p. 147.

you. I often thought of you, as you were travelling Southward; although the journey, was made at a *sad, sad* time, you will, I trust eventually, find your health, benefitted by it—Perhaps you have seen Lizzie Keckley, and she has informed you, *how*, we were situated for the summer. The house, has become crowded, with some of the very best Chicago people, each family keeping their carriages && I have, as you may suppose indulged in my privilege, of being very quiet & retired. Each morning, when it is pleasant, I walk in the beautiful park, adjoining the place—I, quite dread, when we shall have, to return, to the city—although persons, drive out every day, to see me, I receive but *very few;* I am *too miserable*, to pass through, *such* an ordeal, as yet. Day by day I miss, my beloved husband more & more, how I am, to pass through life, without *him* who loved us so dearly, it is impossible for me to say. This morning, I have been looking over & arranging a large package of *his* dear, loving letters to me, many of them written to me, in the "long ago," and quite yellow with age, others, more recent & *one* written from his office, *only* the *Wednesday* before, a few lines, playfully & tenderly worded, notifying, the hour, of the day, *he* would drive with me! Time, my dear Mrs Welles, has at *length* taught & convinced me, that the loved & idolized being, comes no more, and I must patiently await, the hour, when "God's love," shall place me, by *his* side again—where there are no more partings & *no more* tears shed"—For I have almost become blind, with weeping, and can scarcely, see sufficiently to trace these lines—How often my mind, dwells on your great kindness, to me, in my agonizing bereavement! Words, would fail to express my deep gratitude to you, for your great goodness to me, in my solitude. I often wish I could see you again. My boxes are still in a public warehouse in Chicago, where until we can get into a house & obtain possession of them, they will be inaccessible. I intend sending Mr Welles, one of the best canes, and it is quite embarrassing that I have so long delayed doing so. *You* will understand this.

With kind regards, to your family, I remain your truly attached friend,

Mary Lincoln.

To Elizabeth Blair Lee[8]

My Dear Mrs Lee:

The remembrance, of your great kindness to me, in my great sorrow, so overcomes me, with gratitude, that I would be doing my feelings injustice, if I did not express them to you. I suppose, Lizzie,[9] as she promised me, she would, called on you & informed you, how, we were situated, for the *summer*—Never, in my life, have I had the least idea, of the meaning of the word, *Desolation!* Although many persons, drive out to see me, yet, I am so *very, very* miserable, I have not had, the courage, to receive, but few. I have heard of Mrs Trumbull, calling, on some in the house, she met, my little Taddie, & did not enquire about me. As a matter, of course, I should not have seen *her*, without I was seeing every one; cold, unsympathizing persons, are unpleasant enough, when we are happy, but when we *are* otherwise, their presence is *terrible*. As they dined, with us last winter, in W- one, would suppose, the *world* had taught her, the civilities of life, to speak kindly, to the boy & ask, after the health of his Mother. Even, little Taddie, remarked, the breach of *politeness*. My darling husband & myself fully understood their selfish natures & were discussing them, at City Point. All this is *entre nous*. I am realizing, day by day, hour by hour, how insupportable life is, without, the presence of the *One*, who loved me & my sons so dearly & in return, was idolized. Tell me, how *can*, I live, without my Husband, any longer? This is my first awakening thought, each morning & as I watch the waves of the turbulent lake, under our windows, I sometimes feel I should like to go, under them. I receive letters, every day, from the many

---

[8] Wife of Rear Admiral Samuel P. Lee, daughter of Francis P. Blair and sister of Montgomery Blair, Lincoln's first Postmaster General. Mrs. Lee was one of the few persons who came to the White House to comfort Mrs. Lincoln after the assassination.

[9] Elizabeth Keckley had done sewing for Mrs. Lee, among others, before coming to the White House.

friends, who in my deep bereavement, appear to me, dearer than ever, yet I hesitate, in many cases, replying to them, for the sadness, of my letters, would only infect their kind spirits. The memory of your gentle kindness, is ever present, with me! Remember me most truly, to your brother, Judge Blair, your dear father & mother & all friends. If I did not see Gov & Mrs Dennison [1] before I left W- it was not because I did not esteem them, most highly—Do write me, when you receive this & believe me ever, your attached friend

Mary Lincoln

Taddie, wishes to know, how the *nannies*,[2] are getting on. That dear little boy, of yours, I expect enjoys their gambols!

To Anson G. Henry [3]

Hyde Park Place
July 17th 1865

My Dear Dr:

I had hoped, to have sent this letter, by to day's Steamer, but have been so seriously indisposed, this week, that this is the first day of it, I have been sitting up. *General* [John B. S.] Todd, called to see us, ten days since, said he had had a conversation with Sec Harlan,[4] the day before leaving, that was the Monday, day after you sailed. H- expressed *great regret*, that you had *so, suddenly*

[1] William Dennison, former governor of Ohio, succeeded Montgomery Blair as Postmaster General in 1864, holding office until 1866.
[2] Tad's pet nanny goats had been ordered sent to the Lee family when the Lincolns left the White House.
[3] Dr. Henry's long friendship with the Lincolns is discussed on pp. 29 and 224. In February 1865, Lincoln had reluctantly rejected Dr. Henry's request for appointment as Commissioner of Indian Affairs, on the grounds of his obligations to William P. Dole, who then held the office. "[Noah] Brooks says I am bound to have the place if Dole goes out," wrote Dr. Henry to his wife on March 3, 1865 (letter published in Harry E. Pratt. *Concerning Mr. Lincoln*, Springfield, 1944, pp. 116–20), which statement explains many of Mrs. Lincoln's remarks in this letter.
[4] James Harlan, former senator from Iowa and father of Robert Lincoln's secret fiancée, served as Secretary of the Interior from 1865–6, at which point his opposition to Johnson caused him to resign from the Cabinet in order to return to the Senate.

left, said *he had* intended, doing something for you. Robert, immediately wrote to him and insisted, that it was not too late & that
he, considered it due, his Father's memory, that *you* should be
provided for, in W- Altho' it has been over ~~two~~ a ~~weeks~~, since this
was written; not a word, have we heard from *him*. I see, by the
papers, this week, that *some* man, from Iowa, has been put in
Dole's place, and that *Holloway*,[5] has resigned—*Much*, doubtless
to old [Isaac] Newton's delight—*another*, *this last* is, of the selfish
ones—Mr Harlan, has acted in the most contemptible way! It has
become so much so with every one, that when I write to Wash- on
any subject or business, I receive no reply, it is so, with Robert also.
No *such sorrow*, was ever visited upon a people or family, as when
we were bereaved of my darling husband, every day, causes me to
feel still more crushed & broken hearted. If it was not for dear little
Taddie, I would pray to die, I am so miserable. I still remain
closeted in my rooms, take an occasional walk, in the park & as
usual see no one—What have I, in my misery, to do, with the outside world? I must not fail to thank you, for your most interesting
letter from New York, it is well for us, that you passed a day or two
there, & saw those, you did. Mr Bentley [6] wrote me from Detroit,
one day this week, said he would probably, be in Chicago, next week
—He appears, to be a very kind hearted man. *Judge* Davis, has been
holding court in Chicago, called out, & said *very complacently*, I
am glad, to see you are so well situated out *here* & remarked, that
there was not the *least indication*, that C[hicago] or *any other place*,
would *bestow* a house & we would have to *content* ourselves, with
boarding. I replied, "I board *no longer*, than next spring in *Ill*, *after*
that, if we have still to be *vagrants*, I prefer being so, in any *state*,
rather than where, *every man*, in the State, owes, my Husband, a
deep debt of gratitude." He said, will you take Robt with you too?
I replied, most certainly, he goes, where I do"—There is no doubt
he, Judge D, enters *entirely* into the feelings of the S[pringfield]
clique, I mentioned, that I had understood, that *Smith* [7] had been
making himself, as silly & *malicious* as ever, by endeavouring to
turn my best friends in N.Y. against me. He said, "not at all, he

[5] David P. Holloway, Commissioner of Patents.
[6] Norman S. Bentley, a wealthy New York merchant.
[7] Probably C. M. Smith, Mrs. Lincoln's brother-in-law.

could not believe it"—I told him very emphatically, *"it was so,"* I did not mention any names to him. With all our overwhelming sorrows, what enemies, we *do* have to contend with!—I can assure them here, that it is from no feeling of gratitude or love, for *them*, that I have returned *here*,—Judge D- is intensely selfish, and would rather, I really believe, prefer to see us, as we are, without a home, or the prospect of one, rather than have us comfortable—it is endurance vile—I assure you—and no prospect of a remedy—I ~~really~~ believe in my heart, that you are really, the only disinterested, sincere friend, left us. I trust for all your kindness, I will be enabled to repay some of it. It was very painful to us, I assure you, to find that you had to return home.[8] I had fondly hoped, that you, would have been settled in W[ashington] and we would have received frequent visits from you & Mrs Henry, whom I remember with much affection. Alas, alas, our families, are both situated alike, nothing but disappointments before us—and if myself & sons, are specimens, of American justice, God help, other people. I have written to Sen [George H.] Williams [of Oregon], and have as yet, had no reply. I have requested him, to inform me, of the first safe means, of sending some articles to you—our *poor boxes*, I fear, are long destined, to remain in the warehouse! I thought it best, not to send, for the present, those claims to Mr Brooks.[9] Some months later, perhaps, it would be better. Anything, *we do* is seized on—an especial way, of "being cared for, by the American people"—Robert, is so worried, that I am sick so much, that he has purchased a neat covered buggy, in which he can drive his horse, otherwise, he says he would sell the horse—As it was his Father's *last* gift, I would not consent to this, although I expect we will hear remarks, about our purchasing a buggy—I do hope, dear Doctor, you will write to us very frequently, what would I not give, to have one of our old chats together again. R- often remarks the same—I cannot express,

[8] Dr. Henry never reached home. Two weeks after this letter was written, the steamer *Brother Jonathan*, on which he was a passenger, sank off the coast of California, and the doctor was drowned.

[9] Mining certificates purchased by Mrs. Lincoln (see letter to Noah Brooks, May 11, 1866). Noah Brooks, journalist and intimate friend of Lincoln, was slated to have succeeded John Hay as the President's personal secretary, a post for which Mrs. Lincoln and Dr. Henry had lobbied furiously in Brooks' behalf. Appointed by President Johnson Naval Officer for the Port of San Francisco, Brooks had sailed for the West Coast with Dr. Henry but had left the ship at Panama.

how lonely & desolate we are.—And you have been almost, our only friend in our deep, deep affliction. Please present much love to Mrs Henry, who must indeed be rejoiced to see you. I will write you again in a few days, after seeing Bentley, *if he calls*—Do write, at least once a week. Robt & Tad send much love.

> Your truly attached friend
> Mary Lincoln

To James K. Kerr [1]

Chicago July 26th [1865]

Private—
My dear Sir:

When we left W. you promised on the 1st of July, you would send the China [ordered in the White House], since then, you have advised me, that a little further delay, was necessary, yet as almost, a month, has passed, since I last heard from you—I presume, certainly, by *this time*, it is now quite ready. Please write, as it will be a great disappointment to me, if you do not soon forward it, to me.

With kind regards to Mrs Kerr, I remain truly

> your friend
> Mrs L

To Anson G. Henry

Hyde Park Place
July 26th 65

My Dear Dr:

Although, I wrote you, a few days since, by the Overland Route, yet remembering that a steamer sails, next Saturday, I have concluded, to send you, a few lines—I did not receive your letter

---

[1] Identified on p. 198.

from Panama and I have written to Senator Williams & he has not replied. I have nothing new, just now to tell you, *this place*, has become a complete Babal & I grieve, that *necessity*, requires us, to live, in this way—Bentley, from the Detroit [Commercial] Convention came over to C- as usual, he was "hoping on, hoping ever"—there is a very *dim* prospect of success I think—I see, that one of the Editors of the Springfield *Mass*, R[epublican] paper, accompanies Mr Colfax, and is now, with him, in California—This Mr [Samuel] Bowles, will *throw* cold *water*, I fear on any of your or the [N.Y.] Tribune's efforts [to raise money]—in Cal- Taddie is not at home, the scarlet fever, is in the house & a lady who boards here, the daughter of Dr [Levi] Boone, a niece of Mrs Judge [Jesse B.] Thomas, who formerly lived in S. now in C- proposed for fear of the disease, taking Taddie, up to her Mother's, in the country—I am so miserable, it is painful to part with him, even for a day, yet it is best, he should be away—Taddie, has made many warm friends, in the house. I live, as secluded, as ever—as a matter of course—I long for a home, where I can bury myself & my sorrows. Sec Harlan wrote R. a letter, full of all manner of excuses about *not* appointing you—*he* is intensely selfish & I trust, I shall never see any of them again—I am sure, as *we* are not now in power, *they* do not desire it. Gov Oglesbey [sic] is in Chicago, and it appeared in two of the leading Journals, of the City, yesterday—purporting to be copied, from "Boston Transcript, that Mrs Lincoln, had already from the estate $100,000 and the *paper* was authorized to state—no more contributions would be received.[2] It, of course, emanated from Springfield, [Mass.?] and *those* people know, we have no home!—If you hear of any person, going to California or W[ashington] T[erritory] please advise me. I wish to send you what I have promised. I again reiterate, that when *you* left, our only true friend departed. Do write very often & give my best love to Mrs Henry. The world looks darker to me than ever & my heart aches, for my bereaved sons—[page torn]

Poor Robert, has borne his sorrows, manfully, yet with a

[2] Probably toward the "dollar fund" originated by Greeley through his New York *Tribune* for Mrs. Lincoln's benefit. About this time the Springfield (Mass.) *Republican* had published an article stating, "The scheme for a popular subscription to raise $100,000 for Mrs. Lincoln has been abandoned. It has been ascertained that the late President left an ample fortune. . . ." Quoted in King, p. 234.

broken heart. I wish to goodness, yourself & family, could have remained on this side—but, as it was *our* earnest wish, they, *at W-*
saw fit to disappoint us.

Your attached friend
Mary Lincoln

Mrs Trumbull has not yet honored me with a call, should she ever
deign, she would not be received—She is indeed "a whited Sepul-
chre."

To Alexander Williamson

Chicago,[3] *Aug 17th* [1865]

My dear Sir:

Your letter, was received on yesterday. We were quite surprised to learn of your speedy return to the U.S. [from Scotland]. I
trust, you found your Mother, in good health. Taddie is well &
sends you a photograph of himself, just taken. He is growing very
fast & I am sorry to say, he does not apply himself to his studies,
with as much interest as he should. We intend that he shall attend
school, regularly after the 1st of Sep. Your idea about the carriage,
is, very correct. I did not wish a notice of it, to appear in the W[ash-
ington] C[hronicle] but in Forney's Phil paper. There are too many
secessionists in W. to care, for any thing, belonging to us. As you
may suppose, no family ever felt their bereavement, more than we
do. My heart is indeed broken, and without my beloved husband, I
do not wish to live. Life, is indeed a heavy burden, & I do not care
how soon, I am called hence.

I wish you to see Cuthbert & tell her, I thought according to
her promise, she would have settled my business ere this. We have
to board, as our means will not enable us to purchase a home—each
of us, have only $500 a year— [4] hence, where everything is so ex-

---

[3] By this time Mrs. Lincoln had moved back into town, taking rooms at the
Clifton House, a popular, substantial, and genteel "hotel."
[4] The actual figure was $1,500 to $1,800. Since the original letter is unavailable
there is no way of ascertaining whether those who transcribed it for publication
inadvertently omitted a digit. If not, one can only assume that Mrs. Lincoln chose
to minimize her income to Williamson, for obvious reasons.

pensive, we can only board, in the plainest manner, on it. I explain to you, exactly & truly, how we are circumstanced, a greater portion of our means, is unavailable, consisting, in a house in S. & some wild lands in Iowa—notwithstanding my great & good husband's life was sacrificed for his country, we are left, to struggle, in a manner, entirely new to us—and a noble people would pronounce our manner of life, *undeserved*. Roving Generals have elegant mansions, showered upon them,[5] and the American people—leave the family of the Martyred President, to struggle as best they may! Strange justice this—I hope, the day may yet come, when I can repay *your* kindness to us—At present, seeking lodging, from one place to another, is insupportable, and added to my afflicting sorrow, renders life very desolate. My poor sad boys, are the only remaining ties, to a world rendered so miserable by my great loss. You need not show *Cuthbert* the *letter* or papers—please return them to me—talk to her. R & Taddie wish to be remembered.

Your friend
M. L.

Amid all the torments of her early widowhood, Mary Lincoln never lost her appetite for political gossip. Once, it had been her husband's welfare that had prompted her concern with public offices and public attitudes; now that her future comfort depended in large measure on the same factors, her interest in the minutiae of politics intensified. Not two months after Lincoln's death, she would dry her tears long enough to make brisk, perceptive comments about doings in official Washington: who was "in" or "out" at a particular moment, who had been awarded this or that minor government post, who was for or against President Johnson, for or against Mary Lincoln.

She still held emphatic opinions on prominent personalities. It disturbed her to see how "*pertinaciously*" William Seward clung to

[5] A sarcastic reference to the custom of honoring war heroes by giving them homes, paid for either by the government or by public or private subscription. U. S. Grant alone was presented with homes in Galena, Illinois, and Philadelphia; a third in Washington, D.C., was financed by a group of wealthy New Yorkers.

the office of Secretary of State, annoyed her that Ulysses Grant seemed to have his eye on the White House ("He makes a good general, but I should think, a very poor President.") [6] She rarely lost an opportunity to poke at old adversaries: Trumbull, Judd, Newton, even Andrew Johnson. Her respect and affection for Charles Sumner kept her in total sympathy with the radical element in Congress. She remained firm in her conviction that President Johnson's reconstruction policies bore no relation to what would have been Lincoln's; with his "wicked" and "contemptible" acts, the new President was ruining the country and undoing all that her husband had died for.

Some of her information on Washington affairs came from private sources, but because she seldom saved a letter, there is no way to determine who was telling her what. Much of what she learned and repeated derived from the public prints. Far from the center of events, cut off from ordinary social exchange, she was after 1865 a more compulsive newspaper reader than she had been in Washington. She subscribed to—or saw each day—the Chicago *Tribune*, *Times*, and *Evening Journal*. The *Illinois State Journal* kept her apprised of the activities of her friends and foes in Springfield, and the New York papers, the *Times*, *Tribune*, *Herald*, even the hated *World*, brought her into occasional touch with that glittering metropolis she had once loved so well.

The names of the great press chiefs of the day were as familiar to her as those of political figures, perhaps because most of them were not only active in politics but more influential than many an officeholder. She wrote of Horace Greeley, who, unlike James Gordon Bennett, was proving himself an ally; of Henry J. Raymond of *The New York Times;* of Lincoln's friend John W. Forney, who published and edited the Washington *Chronicle* and Philadelphia *Press*. She was displeased with Simon Hanscom of the Washington *National Republican* for, not unnaturally, "writing up" the Johnson family; with Samuel Bowles of the Springfield (Massachusetts) *Republican* for his attempts to thwart Greeley's plans to raise money for her; with her own nephew-in-law Edward Lewis Baker, editor of the *Illinois State Journal*, who had emerged as spokesman for the "Springfield clique."

[6] Mary Lincoln to Elizabeth Blair Lee, Chicago, August 25, 1865.

It is not difficult to envision the short, black-clad figure, seated in a chair with a huge newspaper before her, eyes darting swiftly over the columns of microscopic print, sharp chin jerking as her glance moved from one page to the next. Despite swollen eyes and an aching head, she could pick out the name "Lincoln" in a flash: no mention of the late President or of herself escaped her notice. She devoured editorials, articles, letters, social notes, dispatches copied from out-of-town papers, lists of arrivals at the large Chicago hotels. Often she went for her scissors to clip an item of interest for one of her correspondents. She sent Governor Oglesby of Illinois an editorial from the Chicago paper he read every day, in order to prove a point; mailed David Davis an item from the New York *Tribune*, "very true & appropriate"; forwarded her friend "Betty" Lee a scrap of newsprint to let her know that "all was made right, about the monument." [7]

At first she was both fascinated by and faintly suspicious of the press in general. Later, and with just cause, suspicion curdled into loathing. In 1867 war was officially declared between Mary Lincoln and "the vampyre press," [8] yet even then, and for years afterward, each remained interested in the other.

To Elizabeth Blair Lee

Chicago Aug 25th 1865

My dear Mrs Lee—

Your very kind letter was received several weeks since & I have delayed replying to it, until your probable return from Cape May. Doubtless, you have been much benefitted, by the sea air & the *newspapers* announce that *other distinguished* individuals, have followed your example. Notwithstanding *every* thing, how *pertinaciously* Seward, hangs on, to his Office—The thought of the Presi-

[7] Mary Lincoln to David Davis, Hyde Park Place, June 27, [18]65; Mary Lincoln to Elizabeth Blair Lee, Chicago, August 25, 1865.
[8] Mary Lincoln to Sally Orne, Frankfurt a Maine [sic], February 11, 1870.

dency, is nearer *his* heart *now*, than it has ever been—Gen Grant too, to judge from his *extensive* wanderings over the country, his mind, is evidently, *gradually* realizing, what he may *become* in the future—I think, *he* had better let "*Well*," alone. He makes a good general, but I should think, a very poor President—All this is entre nous—You must enjoy the quiet, of your charming country home— You have an unbroken little band, & hence every thing, to contribute to your happiness—How dearly I loved the "Soldier's Home & I little supposed, one year since, that I should be so *far removed* from it, broken hearted, and praying for death, to remove me, from a life, so full of agony—Each morning, on awakening, from my troubled slumbers, the utter impossibility of living another day, so wretched, appears to me, as an impossibility. Without, my beloved, my idolized husband, life, is only a *very heavy* burden & the thought, that I should soon be removed, would be supreme happiness to me—

I can scarcely express to you, how surprised I was, when you wrote me, that you did not have the poor little nannies, that my darling husband, loved so well!! Almost & indeed the last order, I gave at the White H- was, that on the morrow, they should be carried out, to your place—*Under* the *circumstances*, the servants knowing, that we would not be satisfied, without, they were placed with you—it was almost criminal, the neglect—What could have become of them, without doubt, was well known, to the crew, but *that act*, was only, in keeping, with many other such transactions. Bidding Adieu, to *that house*, would *never* have troubled me, if in my departure, I had carried with me, the loved ones, who entered the house, with me—Alas, alas, my burden of sorrow, is too heavy, for me to bear, *why*, have we been so terribly afflicted, I know your kind, sympathizing heart, would be saddened, if you could daily see, my poor boys & myself, so crushed, with our heavy bereavement. What would I not give to see your face once more, I learned to love you, very dearly, when you ministered so gently, to me, when I lay so crushed, in the first weeks, of my sorrow. *Time*, does not soften it, nor can I ever be reconciled to my loss, until the grave closes over the remembrance, and I am again reunited to *him*—the worshipped one—I enclose your dear little boy, a photograph of Taddie. Robert, considers them, shocking. Also—to show you, that all was made right, about the monument—this paper—Please present my love to all—and *do—do*, write me very soon—give me all the news—

> Your attached friend
> Mary Lincoln

To Alexander Williamson

Aug 30th [1865]

My Dear Mr Williamson

I find myself again troubling you. Please hand these letters to Cuthbert & Stackpole—They require immediate attention from them—Have a talk with them and have C- send me the papers, I requested her to do. I do not know, what she means—I write, in great haste—Your friend

> M. L.

To Sally Orne [9]

Chicago
Aug 31st [1865]

My dear Mrs Orne

Bowed down & heart broken, in my terrible bereavement, my thoughts, this last sad summer have often turned to you & I have remembered with most grateful emotions, your tender sympathy, in the first days of my overwhelming anguish. Time, does not reconcile me, to the loss, of the most devoted & loving husband, a sadly afflicted woman, ever possessed, how dearly, I long, my kind friend, to lay my aching head & sorrowing heart, by the side, of this dearly loved one. When the summons, comes for my departure, I will gladly welcome it—for *"there*, the weary, are at rest."

[9] Identified on p. 229.

As you may well suppose, I have led a life, of most rigid seclusion, since I left Washington—Chicago, is a very pleasant city & we have many charming acquaintances here, the few, whom I have been sufficiently composed to receive, have as a matter of course, deeply sympathized with me, in my great sorrow. I trust, some day, my dear Mrs Orne, I shall have the pleasure of seeing you here, you would be well repaid by a visit to the West. We are very differently situated, from what we would desire or from what should be expected, from our former station—We are deprived of the Comfort, *of a home*, where my poor sadly afflicted sons & myself, could *quietly* indulge our griefs—If my darling husband had lived out, his four years, he promised me, we should pass our remaining years, in a home, we both should have enjoyed. We are left, with only $1500- a year, each, to live upon, the interest on our money, and as a matter of course, must board, plainly and as genteel as possible, on this sum. I mention this, by way of excusing a subject, I will mention to you. A friend of my husband's & myself, presented me last February, a *very* elegant lace dress, very fine & beautiful—lace flounce about ~~an eighth~~ 6 inches, in width, for the bottom of the skirt— same pattern as dress—a double lace shawl, very fine, exactly similar pattern, with the request, that I would wear it, on the night of the Inauguration—for two hours, that evening, I did so, over a white silk dress, next morning, most carefully, the *gathers* were drawn from the skirt—and it was folded *tenderly* away—the flounce, was not used. I wore the article, reluctantly, as it was too elaborate for my style & too expensive, for my means—My desire is, to dispose of these articles, it cost, in New York, to import them $3,500—of course—if I can get $2,500—for them, it will be a great consideration to me. If you know, of any one, who would desire, such a dress, will you not gratify me, my dear friend, by informing me.[1] You may well be assured, only *dire* necessity, which I have never before, known, anything, about—would cause me to write so freely to you. The lace dress && is exquisitely fine, and was considered, a bargain at the $3,500. I have also—the most magnificent white moire an-

---

[1] Mrs. Orne was apparently of little help in this matter. Two years later, Mrs. Lincoln attempted to sell this "white point lace dess, unmade" along with other garments. It was listed in the New York Semi-Weekly *Tribune* of October 8, 1867, at a value of $4,000.

tique, that Mr Stewart says, he ever had imported—it was purchased last winter & never made up—$11 a yard—a yard wide. Some 16 yards in the dress I would sell at $125—I am so anxious to have my boys, in a quiet home of our own—& without I make some exertions of the kind, disposing of my articles, now unnecessary, I fear, I cannot succeed. If any of your friends would desire such articles, please advise me—they are rich & beautiful—Taddie was very grateful for your magic toys.

Your attached friend
Mary Lincoln

To Eliza Henry

Chicago Aug 31st 1865

My very dear Mrs Henry:

Bowed down & broken hearted and feeling so deeply for you, in your agonizing bereavement,[2] I feel justified in approaching you, at this time when, we all feel alike crushed. We have both been called upon to resign to our Heavenly Father, two of the best men & the most devoted husbands, that two unhappy women ever possessed. The terrible news, that our beloved friend, who so sympathized, with *us* in our irreparable loss, *is gone*, has been received by us, only a day or two since, my sons & myself have been overcome, by the startling & heart rending intelligence—

We consider that we have lost, our best & dearest friend, it had been my most ardent wish, that Dr Henry, should have received an appointment, in Washington, it would have been a great comfort to us, in our own overwhelming sorrow, to have had you both near us. In this great trial, it is difficult, to be taught resignation, the only comfort, that remains to us, is the blessed consolation, that our beloved ones, are rejoicing in their Heavenly home, free from all earthly trials & in the holy presence of God & his Angels, are singing the praises of the Redeemer. I long, to lay my own weary head,

[2] The drowning of Dr. Henry on July 30, 1865.

down to rest, by the side of my darling husband—I pray God, to grant me sufficient grace, to await *his* time, for I long, to be at rest. Without my idolized husband, I do not wish to remain on earth—Mr Wm S. Henry,[3] called a day or two since. I was confined to my bed & did not see him, Robert saw him & he left, your telegram. Robert, immediately wrote on to Washington, urging & pleading for the appointment, of your son in law. We pray & trust, the appeal, will be granted. You have no one, my dear friend, who could possibly feel for you, as I do, your grief is mine, in it, I am living over my own disconsolate state & the gratitude, we feel, for the dear Doctors recent, sympathy, for us, in all things together with the great love, we all bore him—makes your troubles, my own. How much, I wish, you lived nearer to us. We could then weep, together—over our dreary lot. The world, without my beloved husband & our best friend—is a sad & lonely place enough—Our poor, little family, would be a gloomy picture, for any one to see who has a heart to feel—It was a great trial, to me, when Dr Henry, left here in June, that I was unable to have access, to some boxes, stored in a warehouse, where was deposited a cane of my Husband's, a large family Bible & some others things, designed for presentation, to the Dr so soon, as I can get to them, I shall avail myself, of the first opportunity, of sending them to you. I can offer you in conclusion, of this very sad letter, my dear Mrs Henry, very little consolation, for I am so weary and heavy laden myself, over every thing, concerning us both—I trust you will write to me, for you are very dear to me, now & ever—With regards to your family, I remain always your attached friend

Mary Lincoln

To Alexander Williamson

Chicago Sept 9th 65

My dear Sir:

Your letter was received on yesterday. As to the carriage, had you not better ascertain, at what shop, in N.Y. you can deposit it,

[3] Son of Dr. Anson Henry.

before you *carry* it there?—Surely, there are, persons of means, *there* or in Phil- who would purchase it, if for no other reason, than it having been the property of my lamented husband. I received the newspaper, containing the sad intelligence of Dr Henry's death. The story it contains, that we were married at his house, is entirely unfounded. I believe both, his wife & himself were present, at our marriage. Taddie is going to a school [4] & for once in his life, he is really interested in his studies—After all, few children learn well, without some one, sharing their lessons—If his darling, precious brother Willie had lived, *he* Tad, would have been much further advanced.

I do not wonder that you shrink from the White House! All the sorrows, of my life, occurred there & that *Whited Sepulcure* [Johnson?] broke my heart.

I presented you the shawl, dressing gown & slippers, as a private gift, out of respect for your kind interest in our family & your great goodness to my little boys—You certainly did not desire me to write an article, for *you*, to put in the papers, saying that I had presented, these little relics to you. They were given you quietly & in the belief, that no parade, would be made over them, only your grateful appreciation of them, as having been worn, by the best man, the world ever saw.

I write in haste, remaining always

Your friend
M. L.

Taddie, sends his love.

To David Davis

Chicago
September 12th [1865]

My dear Sir:

A lady friend, whom I respect very much, visited me, on yesterday & remarked, that a gentleman told her, that *you* had told a

---

[4] Tad attended the Elizabeth Street School for the year 1865–6.

friend of his, that our means were very ample, & no assistance, was required to enable us, to live *very* comfortably—I replied to her, that there *must* be, some mistake, that it was impossible, you could have said this, or overrated an income, which enabled us to board, in the plainest manner *only*. I further added, what I *know*, to be correct, that the greater portion of those in Ill, who had received the highest favors, from my noble & generous husband, were, very evidently, the most indifferent, about our having a home, or the wherewithal to keep it up. Yet I assured, the lady, that I could not realize, that you, whom my husband so much respted & loved & knew exactly the small & limited state of our finances, could have made such an assertion. I told her, that when the time, came for action, when Congress met, & persons came to you for information, I felt assured, you would insist upon a liberal allowance, which the position, we had *held*, would justify, and that we should be enabled to live, in a manner not disgraceful, to the American Nation. She replied, "that *roving* Generals, had *homes*, thrust upon them, and it was shameful, that the President's family, had to live so humbly"—All this came from a dear friend—who felt—all she said. Whilst we are passing our days, at *boarding houses*, if my head, was not bowed down, with a sorrow deeper far, that [than] ever fell, to the lot, of a bereaved & heart broken woman; with my natural pride, I should feel greatly humiliated—hoping & being assured that better days, in *this* respect, may ere long, come to us—for the present, I accept, our most uncomfortable state. My beloved husband, assured me the latter part of March last, at City Point, that he had determined, not to spend a cent of his next four years salary, & that we would endeavour (which we could have easily done) [to] live on the interest of what he had accumulated—Alas, alas, all & every thing, is changed with us, yet through, your word & influence, from *this time forth*, very much depends, your word, with friends *now* & Congress, will assuredly have great weight. I only mention this to you, knowing that a misinterpretation, had been put, upon your words. Through Mr [Hiram W.] Beckwith's conversations with a friend, *I am told* that Sen Trumbull insists upon it, that we have quite a *large* fortune & the idea is ridiculous, that any thing, should be done for us. Coming from such a sordid, selfish creature, without *a soul*, almost, yet indebted to my great and good husband, for *all*, his Senatorial distinction; from *him*, this is not unexpected—Although I believe, he would be hissed, in the Senate, next winter, if he raise *his* voice, in such a strain. A package, has come to the P.O. office from Manchester, Eng. expressage, $14.88 cts. presuming, it is memorials [word unreadable] && we have concluded, to have it sent, to *dead* letter office. If it should prove, a sum sent us, from the "Mother Country," for a "*homestead*", for the *friendless*, it would be a *great mistake*. Mrs Wm H. Brown,[5] called last evening & appeared to be dissolved in tears—that so *great* & *distinguished* a *man*, as *Judd*, should be recalled from his Mission [as minister to Prussia]. I expect, he has occasionally within the last four years, caused *Motley*,[6] & a few other appreciative & learned persons, abroad, to blush for American *provincialism*. As Mr Trumbull also, came so largely into her ideas, of greatness, I thought, if I could not *endorse* her *amiable* views, silence would be the wisest course. They must have a high standard for society *here*—entre nous. If you have not written to Harper & Mitchell & May & Co [7]—please do not—I will attend to it, immediately, myself—With many apologies, for troubling you, with so lengthy a letter, I remain

Very respectfully,
Mary Lincoln

To James K. Kerr

Chicago Oct 12th [*1865*]

My dear Sir—

Your note is received, & I presume, the articles you sent will arrive to day. I shall always prize, the set, showing your goodness, in

---

[5] The wife of a Chicago banker and lawyer who had been associated with Lincoln.

[6] John Lothrop Motley, a learned, urbane historian and diplomat, served as minister to Austria, 1861–7.

[7] In his private notebook Davis recorded the receipt on August 2 and 10, 1865, of two statements from Harper & Mitchell and May & Co., respectively, for $817.14 and $628.01. Both were sent to Mrs. Lincoln for payment. The May & Co. bill covering, among other items, eighty-four pairs of gloves and receipted on March 5, 1866, is in the Illinois State Historical Library.

keeping your word, as I paid so heavily for the glass ware, when I could illy afford it, I assure you, in receiving the China, *that* is very much lightened—Are the coffee cups, the *small after* dinners ones, they should be so—It would take *so little more* to render it a *complete* set, of which, I wrote you, last week, Did you receive the letter? I cannot be satisfied, without I have, of the same kind, two dozen large size coffee cups & saucers—two dozen tea cups—2 sugar bowls—2 slop bowls some *small* meat dishes—or have you those, with the dinner set? the small plates you doubtless have with the dinner set—Have you water pitchers, with the dinner set? I should think so—Now, write me about these additional cups && it will never do *not*, to have *the set* complete. What should I do, for my breakfast & tea? This would not be like *you*, so true a friend, not to have it all right & complete—As to the note, which you desire me, to write to the Johnson family, regarding the remaining portion of the set—I would like you, to write me a copy & word it, as you think best —send it to me, I will copy & sign it & return it to you—Major *French*, I expect, will be satisfied, with *that* family, with *no* knowledge, of such things as are requisite, to set a table right, they will not make many demands—*this is between ourselves*—from him. But what you have prepared for the house Major F & Congress must settle with you. After that Mrs Sprague [8] must be your hope for purchases, in the future—do not forget, my remaining business I pray you. Show this letter, my expression about business or W. H.—to no one. Some day, I hope Mrs K & yourself, will visit C- your friend

M [L]

To Mary Jane Welles

My dear Mrs Welles

I have only been awaiting, your return to Washington, to reply, to your last, very kind note. I trust you find your health bene-

---

[8] Kate Chase (see pp. 136) was married on November 12, 1863, to the wealthy Senator William Sprague of Rhode Island. Lincoln had made a brief appearance at the wedding but Mrs. Lincoln, who disliked the bride intensely, was not with him.

fitted, by your summer travels, at any time, I am aware, you have to be, very careful with yourself. Your Son's, very tempting offer to Robert, to accompany him, to Havana, was declined with much regret; the temptation offered by *such a trip* was great & I almost marvelled that R- could withstand it. In consideration, of our recent afflictions, pressing so heavily upon us, Robert, thinks it is best, for the present, to be quiet, and attend to his studies, some future time, if your son, makes a similar request, I am very sure, it will be accepted. Robert, is very much attached to Edgar, and it would be a great pleasure for him, to have him visit him, in Chicago, some time. *At present*, we are situated very differently, from what, we could desire. We are boarding & as every thing is so enormously high here, quite as much so, as in W- our means, only allow us, to board genteely, and with this, I suppose, we must, *just now*, be content. My friends, all, live so handsomely here & if my beloved husband, had lived, when the time came for us to reside here, he meant to have a handsome home. He told me, last March, that he did not intend, using a dollar of his next four years salary, and as our outfit, in every particular, did not require replenishing, we could live very well, on the interest of the money he had. Alas, all is changed, and we find, we have to bow to our terrible fate, in *every respect*. The subject, just mentioned, however, troubles me, the least of my griefs. With my darling husband, *any* lot, would have been cheerfully borne. It has been, a great mortification to me, not to have been able to have fulfilled my promise ere this & sent your good husband his cane & yourself some worthy momento of the friend, you both loved so well & whom, *he*, respected so highly—I have not seen my boxes since I came to Chicago. They are stored away, in a warehouse, two miles distant & R- says, I cannot approach them, until we get into a house of our own—my blk crape mourning hat, sent from N.Y. I have not seen since May. All there together & this is the first summer, in twelve years, I have dispensed, with a carriage. You may imagine, that the bonnet I travelled here in, fully sufficed for the few walks, I have taken. I am too miserable my dear Mrs W- to care for *outward show* I only wonder, that I have my reason—Mr Dana—Ass. Sec of War [9]—resides here, has purchased a handsome

[9] After his government service, Charles A. Dana, formerly on the staff of Greeley's *Tribune*, edited the Chicago *Republican*, strongly anti-Johnson in editorial outlook, from July 20, 1865, to May 23, 1866. He ultimately became editor of the New York *Sun*.

residence, costing $28,000- & doubtless, designs making this, his future home. He is editing a popular paper—

I hope, my kind friend, you will write often to me, the remembrance of your past kindnesses so completely fills me, with gratitude, that I can never, cease to love & respect you. With kindest regards, to the Sec, I remain always truly—

Mary Lincoln

To Alexander Williamson

[EXCERPT]　　　　　　　　*Chicago*
　　　　　　　　　　　　　October 20 65

Your telegram is received. It may be just as well to let the carriage be sold at auction. Your cards [1] are just right, not too many—4 full packs. The Express bill says $5.00; the money I will enclose to you & send by Mr Isaac Arnold.[2]

To Francis Bicknell Carpenter [3]

Chicago Oct 26th 1865—

My Dear Sir:

In the midst of my overwhelming distress, the kind promise, you several times made me, in regard to my beloved husband's portrait, returns to my remembrance. Will you not, send us, one quite

---

[1] Probably printed visiting cards.

[2] An old friend of Lincoln's, whose distinguished career as a U.S. representative had just ended. He would serve until 1866 as auditor of the treasury for the Post Office Department.

[3] Carpenter, a popular portraitist, had just completed his painting of Lincoln's first reading of the Emancipation Proclamation before his cabinet. The painting now hangs in the old Supreme Court Chamber of the Capitol.

as accurate, as in the "Emancipation Proclamation? [4] *More*, we could not ask or expect. As one, whom my lamented husband, so highly respected—we will always hope, to see you, should you visit Chicago—I have always felt, great pride, in the success of your great painting, bowed down, with such intense sorrow, *think*, of what inestimable value, a portrait from your unerring skill would be prized by myself, and my Boys—Please present my regards to Mrs Carpenter—and be assured, of my sincere esteem.

Mary Lincoln—

To Oliver S. Halsted, Jr.

Chicago—Nov. 11th [1865]

Private

My dear Sir:

Your last letter is received. Mr B[entley] from what I infer from his letters, is waiting—"for the action of Congress"—Does he mean, to withdraw, what he has, if C- gives us an app[ropria]t[ion] —Urge him, to settle the fur business [5]—He writes, *he* & *Greeley* are going to W the first of the session—*Perhaps* he will take *Godfrey* [6] with him—I very much fear, those men will injure, our cause as to the four years, salary. They are certainly acting very mysteriously. Please write whenever you hear from them & I am sure, you will be

---

[4] Mrs. Lincoln received the portrait in December of 1866 (see letter to Carpenter, December 25, 1866), but it apparently did not remain in the family's possession. Rufus Rockwell Wilson, in his book *Lincoln in Portraiture* (New York, 1935, p. 310), noted that an unsigned portrait of Lincoln, owned at that time by the late William Townsend, "closely resembles . . . Carpenter's original Emancipation Proclamation portrait," and could well be the one referred to above.

[5] Isaac Newton told John Hay some years later, "There was one big bill for furs. . . . she got it paid at last by some of her friends—I don't know who for certain—not Sim Draper for he promised to pay it . . . but after Lincoln's death he wouldn't do it." (Quoted in Dennett. *Lincoln and the Civil War In the Diaries and Letters of John Hay*, p. 274.)

[6] Possibly either John A. or George Godfrey, partners in the firm of Godfrey & Holyoke, New York merchants.

a good friend to us in W- I hope you will be there, the 1st of the Session—In great haste,

I remain your friend
Mrs A. L.

To Alexander Williamson

[INCOMPLETE?]   *Chicago—Nov 11th* [1865]

My dear Sir:

Severe indisposition, has prevented an earlier reply to your last letter—I enclose you, a note from Stackpole, hold *on* to this & see, that he makes his word good—within the next few days—I, also enclose you all my bills, the one at Shuster's—and H[udson-] Taylor's —I have never heard a word from—since I left Wash. Enquire of Stackpole, if they have been settled. I owe no small bill, of any kind —to any one—Save $5.00—at Frank Taylors—in W- for a book. The book matter, at H. T.s can easily be covered, with library books —as there is a yearly app[ropriation] of about $300- to purchase books—for [the White] house, and for 3 years—the app has been untouched. If, by the 1st of Dec- you return me all these bills, *receipted*—I will send you $50- for an overcoat for yourself & some handsome things, for your wife & daughter. Please follow Stack. up, & have all, immediately attended to—the more *quiet*—the better. As to passes to N.Y. I have no business, at all, there—one little matter only—in the hands of a business man [Norman Bentley]—once free, from these harrassing accounts, the sun, will never *go down*, with my owing, a cent—Every thing is so changed with us, with no good, generous husband, to sustain me, as a matter of course, I must be, very circumspect—Yet, on your own business, if you ever desire to go to N.Y. If possible, from the Sec of W[ar] I will procure you, passes, on *my own* account. Mr French, was indebted, to *my* earnest persuasion—for getting his *present* position from the P- the latter had been told much against him—and of his former connection with the house in Pearce's [sic] time—Of course; there are always *those* to denounce in W- Mr L- liked Mr F very much himself, so did I, and I trust, he will remember, this is the last favor, a sadly bereaved woman & his friend, is requesting, of him. This must all be settled before C[ongress] meets—very quietly & not a word said —tell not, even your wife—Your proposition is very kind, yet notwithstanding, the thousands of letters, I have received of condolence, placing them before the public—would only seem like thrusting ourselves forward—another plan is in your power & with your great intelligence, with good management, you can do me great service. *It is this—*

To Leeds & Miner [7]

Chicago, Nov. 11th, 1865

Gentlemen—

Your letter, relative to the carriage, has been received. Considering it was so much out of repair, I think it sold very well. Can you inform me, who was the purchaser? As to Mr Williamson—for the last four years, he was tutor to my little boys, my husband & myself always regarded him as an upright, intelligent man. When leaving Washington, last May I directed the servant woman, to present him in my name and in consideration, for the high reverence, he Mr W always entertained for the President) a shawl, & dressing gown. In doing so I felt he would cherish & always retain, these relics of so great & good a man. My astonishment, was very great I assure you, when you mentioned that these articles were for sale. Mr W. certainly did not reflect, when he proposed such a thing. I wish you would write to him & remonstrate upon so strange a proceeding. Hoping, again to hear from you, on the subject, I remain very respectfully,

Mrs A. Lincoln

I am feeling very anxious, after again looking over your letter, about Mr Williamson's *proposed sale*, of these little relics—it sounds very

[7] New York commission brokers. See letter to Williamson, September 9, 1865.

badly *to me*, who in my deep affliction, am naturally very sensitive. If possible, *it must be prevented.*

M. L.

The following letter was written to the artist Francis Bicknell Carpenter, who came to know the Lincolns well during the six months he spent in the White House working on his celebrated painting of Lincoln's first reading of the Emancipation Proclamation before his Cabinet. In late 1865 Carpenter was planning a second project, a composite portrait of the Lincoln family as it existed in 1861, and had asked Mrs. Lincoln for photographs of herself and her sons. She replied to his request in a long, discursive letter, full of private references and ending with what seems to be her sole written recollection of Lincoln's last hours of life, and of her own feelings regarding the assassination.

For days after Lincoln's murder, his widow would recount the events of April 14 in excruciating detail to anyone who would listen. "She would go over these painful details until she would be convulsed with sorrow," recalled Lincoln's old friend Isaac N. Arnold. "When entreated not to speak on such a painful subject . . . she would apparently try to turn her thoughts elsewhere, but directly and unconsciously she would return to these incidents." [8] By the time she left Washington, Mary Lincoln had evidently drawn a veil over that day and its hideous climax. If the *fact* of her loss crept into nearly every communication, the manner in which that loss had come about was too appalling to discuss. On only two known occasions—in this poignant letter to Carpenter and in a rather startling one written to her friend Sally Orne on March 15, 1866—did she commit to paper her private beliefs about her husband's assassination.

[8] Arnold, p. 440.

To Francis Bicknell Carpenter

Chicago Nov 15th [1865]

My Dear Sir:

Your last letter, has been received—It would be utterly impossible for me, in my present nervous state, to sit for a photograph—although, I should like to oblige you, very much. There is an excellent painted likeness of me, at Brady's in N.Y. taken in *1861*—have you, ever seen it? I am sure you will like it & I believe, it was taken, in a black velvet.[9] I enclose you one of my precious, sainted Willie. You have doubtless heard, how *very* handsome a boy, he was considered—with a pure, gentle nature, always unearthly & in intellect *far, far* beyond his years—When I reflect, as I am always doing, upon the overwhelming loss, of that, *most* idolized boy, and the crushing blow, that deprived me, of my *all in all*, in this life, I wonder that I retain my reason & live. There are hours of each day, that my mind, cannot be brought to realize, that *He*, who is considered, so great and good, a God, has *thus* seen fit to afflict us! How difficult it is to be reconciled to such a bereavement, how much sooner, each one, of our stricken family, if the choice had been left to us, would have preferred "passing away," ourselves.

It strikes me strangely, how such a rumor, should be circulated —that Robert is in Europe.[1] The thought of leaving home, I am sure, has never *once*, entered his mind. He is diligently applying himself, to his law studies—a most devoted Son & brother. Every thing is *so fabulously* high *here*, that his third of the estate, an income of $1800 apiece—with taxes deducted—It requires the most

---

[9] A highly flattering standing pose which was actually a painted-over photograph. An original print is owned by Lloyd Ostendorf of Dayton, Ohio.

[1] In September, the Chicago *Tribune* had reprinted a report from the Cincinnati *Commercial*'s Paris correspondent, who claimed to have seen Robert Lincoln in that city. The *Tribune* in correcting the error declared: "Captain Robert Lincoln was at his usual place in this city last evening, in the enjoyment of good health, and was not aware of his being in Paris. The *Commercial*'s correspondent says all the papers commend the *condescension* of Captain Lincoln in studying law and preparing to work for a living." (Reprinted in the New York *World*, Weekly Edition, September 25, 1865.)

rigid economy, with Robert & the rest of us to clothe ourselves, plainly & weekly settle our board-bills. Is not this, a sad change for us! As a matter of course living, every where, *now* in the U.S. is high—Yet I cannot express to you, how painful to me, it is, to have *no* quiet home, where I can freely indulge my sorrows—*this*, *is* yet another of the crosses, appointed unto me. With my beloved husband, I should have had, a heart, for any fate, if "need be." Dear little Taddie! was named, for my husband's father, Thomas Lincoln —no *T*—for a middle name—was *nicknamed, Taddie*, by his loving Father. Taddie—is learning to be as diligent in his studies, as he used to be *at play* in the W. H. he appears to be rapidly making up, for the great amount of time, he lost in W- As you are aware, *he* was always a *marked character.* Two or three weeks since, a lady in an adjoining room, gave him, a copy of Mr Raymond's life of the President,[2] for me to read & return to her. After reading it, I remarked to Robert, in Taddie's presence, that it was *the most* correct history, of his Father, that has been written—Taddie immediately spoke up & said, "Mother, I am going to save, all the little money, you give me and get one of them." R. told him, he need not, as he would buy, a copy. I press the poor little fellow closer, *if possible*, to my heart, in memory of the sainted Father, who loved *him*, *so very dearly*, as well as the rest of us—How I wish you could have seen my dear husband, the last three weeks of his life! Having a realizing sense, that the un-natural rebellion, was near its close, & being most of the time, *away* from W, where he had endured such conflicts of mind, within the last four years, feeling *so encouraged*, he freely gave vent to his cheerfulness. Down the Potomac, he was almost boyish, in his mirth & reminded me, of his original nature, what I had always remem-bered of him, in our own home—free from care, surrounded by those he loved so well & *by whom*, he was so idolized. *The Friday*, I never saw him so sumpremely cheerful—his manner was even playful. At three o'clock, in the afternoon, he drove out with me in the open car-riage, in starting, I asked him, if any one, should accompany us, he immediately replied—"No—I prefer to ride by ourselves to day." During the drive he was so gay, that I said to him, laughingly, "Dear Husband, you almost startle me by your great cheerfulness,"

[2] Henry J. Raymond, editor of *The New York Times*, had published his book, *The Life and Public Services of Abraham Lincoln*, in 1865.

he replied, "and well I may feel so, Mary, I consider *this day*, the war, has come to a close—and then added, "We must *both*, be more cheerful in the future—between the war & the loss of our darling Willie—we have both, been very miserable." Every word, then uttered, is deeply engraven, on my poor broken heart. In the evening, his mind, was fixed upon having some relaxation & bent on the theater. Yet I firmly believe, that if he had remained, at the W. H. on that night of darkness, when the fiends prevailed, he would have been horribly *cut to pieces*—Those fiends, had too long contemplated, this inhuman murder, to have allowed, *him*, to escape. Robert informs me, that the best likeness of himself, is at Goldin's, in Washington, taken last spring. We have none, unframed. The attitude in the one, you sent me, of myself, is very good, my hands are always *made* in *them*, very large and I look too stern. The drapery of the dress, was *not* sufficiently flowing—and my hair, should not be so low down, on the forehead & so much dressed. I am sending you a long & most hastily written letter, which I pray you excuse. My sons desire to be remembered to you. Whilst I remain

Very Sincerely
Mary Lincoln

To Alexander Williamson

Chicago Nov 19th [*1865*]

My dear Sir:

Your letter is received. I pray, do not go neard *Seward* about my business—keep him out of my affairs. Do be quiet & cautious— about mentioning, this business to any one, save parties concerned— See Stackpole & have him settle it—I was not aware before, that the *latter*, was an *ex*-gardener. Find Stackpole, & have him, quietly, help you out, about it. Do not approach [Isaac] Newton or [Simeon] Draper, about my affairs. Should you see Rufus F. Andrews [3]—of

---

[3] Appointed by Lincoln Surveyor of the Port of New York in April 1861, but replaced by Abram Wakeman in September of 1864 in an attempt to accommodate the powerful Seward-Weed machine.

N.Y. at Willards—you could consult with him & he will aid you—he is a true friend—to no others—I beg you mention it—*This*, is a very critical time—When you speak to Sen's & mem[bers] mention *no* indebtedness *in any* quarter. Mr Newton, I am not indebted to—in any way—he *may* have some papers & I think he has, about a little N.Y. business—with which he has, no connection—Write & be very cautious—about my business—

Do not go—near Seward—if Stanton fails & H[arlan]—See Andrews—

be prudent

Talk to the Members, of the *shame*, it is, *we are*, *without* a home—

Your friend

M L

To Alexander Williamson

Chicago—Nov 26th [*1865*]

Mr Williamson

I again enclose you a line, *urging* you, not to take *any* assurance for granted, without having it *down*, in *black & white* follow Mr Speed [4] up—insist upon a written promise—Harlan's letter, is *very indefinite*. Do not write *notes*, to them, but go & insist & get the written promise. The first thing, I fear, that I will hear of is, that some of the *party* [of creditors], go to Judge D- on Wednesday next—Prevent this—by seeing the creditors & seeing the party—*who will* settle it imm—Do not allow it to be laid over until Con- makes us a little appropriation & our *all*, taken from us, in this way—I firmly believe, this is what Stack[pole] Stan[ton] && are waiting for—Follow up, this new lead—Have it settled through H[arlan] Speed && the day you receive this—see Colfax—Forney & some others—urge *our* claims in Con—so soon, as it meets—C[ol-fax] can have great influence—tell them we are miserably situated, without a home && which *they* all know—This is a *grateful Repub-lic*, to allow me, with all my heavy sorrows—to suffer thus!

In haste

[4] James Speed, brother of Lincoln's old friend Joshua Speed, served as U.S. Attorney General from 1864 to 1866.

To Alexander Williamson

Chicago—Nov 28th [1865]

My dear Sir—

I trust you will be very careful, *not*, to rely, *even*, on the *promises*, of Harlan & Atty Genl [Speed]—but get the *imm* payment made, or a written promise from them, which you can show—the creditors—*The 1st* of December *is Friday &* without those people, are paid, they will rush to Judge D- From what, Sec H[arlan] writes —it will only require a little energy, for you, to make every thing right, by *1st* of Dec. Never take a *verbal* promise in business matters. Will you go to Lizzie K. & see *why, she,* does not send my package, you say nothing about it, in your letters—and I am positively suffering for the articles she has. *Do* try & have them sent by Adams Ex—*free* of *cost,* when they arrive here—our means, are very much reduced—and it requires, the greatest economy, for me, to get along *at all,* where every thing, is so enormously high—Plead for our four years salary—for if only the first year is given—we are *consigned,* to a *boarding house,* all our days—Heaven, help, us *then! Mr French,* at Hudson-T[aylor] promised me, the "Mutual Friend" & Armadale [5] when they were published—free of charge—bound, as the set of Dickens *he* will understand—If they are not bound in the same way, get them, as they are—send them by Ex- *free also,* Money is more than scarce with us—See about *bill* business & Mr Speed— without a moment's delay. Be very cautious when you converse with members & Sen's—do not speak of *my private business* matters, to any *one*—Very truly—

Since I wrote the above, your last letter, has been received—*By all means*—see Genl Cameron,[6] he is, an excellent friend of mine. Do not let Stackpole escape you—as to letters of condolence && I have been solicited for them so much, that I would give offence to *many,*

[5] *Armadale* was a novel by Wilkie Collins, whose works many people (including Mrs. Lincoln) occasionally attributed to Charles Dickens. *Armadale* was published early in 1866.
[6] After Simon Cameron's service as minister to Russia, he returned to his native Pennsylvania in 1863 where he ran unsuccessfully for the U.S. Senate. He was at this time contemplating a second senate campaign.

if I allowed *them*, to be used—Allusions—*could* be made, to the thousands, that had been received by me [half page missing] Of course very delicately—It must not appear, that *I* am aware, of any thing, going on—As to Stackpole & Stanton, that is merely a *come off*, of Stanton—which *you* must guard against. Very little time left & much work to be done—Cameron, will aid, about the Congress business && [page torn]

Get *Genl Cameron* interested about *the four* years appropriation & have it urged to come up before Congress before the 7th of Dec when Congress first meets, before other appropriations are urged—

To Elihu B. Washburne [7]

Chicago
Nov 29, 1865

My dear Sir—

It has not been my intention of writing to you, on the subject, that involves my future comfort, notwithstanding my knowledge, of your great personal affection, for my beloved & most deeply lamented husband & your kind friendship, for me—All these assurances tempt me, to intrude myself *now* upon your remembrance, and I feel assured, that our cause in your hands—will be triumphant.

Broken down, as I am, with the greatest sorrow, that ever befell, a poor heartbroken woman—I am aware, I will not plead with *you*, in vain, to urge, the appropriation of the four years salary for us—in the first few days, of the session, before, other interests, are brought forward—The central portion, of the State, we have been *quietly* informed, are against our having a home & the means to keep it up—Simply, I presume, because, my son & myself, did not allow *them*, in the first shock, of our overwhelming bereavement, to manage, our affairs, as they pleased. This you will perfectly understand—Our ideas, of persons, were never very dis-

---

[7] U.S. Representative from Galena, Illinois, and a close personal friend of both Abraham Lincoln and Ulysses S. Grant.

similar—Baker—the unprincipled man of the Springfield J- has sent the co Editor—[David] Phillips on to Wash- is now there— Gov *Oglesbey* [sic], leaves this morning. With your great energy & noble heart, all their malice—can readily, be circumvented—If the appropriation, is brought forward, after the election of S[enate] it will succeed. Situated as we are, with only the means, to board, in the *humblest* manner, with no home, where I can bury myself, with my sorrows—with the weight of my other great grief—it is difficult to live and endure—so great a burden—

I trust you will pardon, my expressing myself so freely to you —I know in whom I trust, or I should not *thus* venture—I have been so wild in my despair, over the loss, of my idolized husband, that the dearest friends, I have been unable to see, yet, in the future, I hope, it may be more strengthening to bear the heavy accumulation of sorrow, I am called upon to endure—When you pass through Chicago, always call & see me—

I remain, very truly & sincerely
Mary Lincoln

To Derby & Miller [8]

Chicago—Nov 29th—65

Gentlemen.

By yesterday's Express, a volume, of the memoirs of my deeply lamented husband, was received. When I wrote to Mr Carpenter, I mentioned the circumstance, of Taddie's, desire to possess a copy, more as an anecdote than any thing else, *never* presuming, it would be communicated to any one. However, for your great kindness, please accept my most sincere & grateful thanks—remaining very truly.

Mary Lincoln

[8] New York publishers of Henry J. Raymond's biography of Lincoln, discussed in Mrs. Lincoln's letter to Carpenter of November 15, [1865].

To Alexander Williamson

Chicago—Dec 1st [*1865*]

Mr Williamson

I enclose you a letter, from a man, who presented my husband, with a very elegant hat, a year since [9]—Two hours, before I left the White House last May, I wrote a line, to Dr [Phineas D.] Gurley— presenting him, the hat, as a precious relic of my husband, knowing Dr G- would value it—on *his* account. I have never since heard, from Dr G- on the subject, yet attached no importance to *that*. Here comes this letter from the hatter—Of course in the hurry of departure, I could not remember, what particular servant, was intrusted with the order—It must h[ave] been given to Cuthbert—to give to some of the men to carry over—Could *she*, have presumed—to *give* it, to Burke.[1] Between ourselves I should not be surprised—at any thing—I want you to find Burke—and see if "Warburton."—name— is in the hat—and make him tell—who gave it to him. *She*, would not have dared, say *falsely* that I sent it to him. I took such particular pains, with my note to Dr Gurley, accompanying the hat—If Burke has'nt it—please see Dr G & ask him—if he ever received it— I am anxious, to hear about it—

Do have those bills settled, without an hours delay—you know it is to your interest—to relieve yourself of the money your wife used —For I have had to borrow some to make settlements—and I know you will feel interested, in seeing my affairs, settled up. Please talk to Thad Stevens, of Penn-[2] & urge our claims from *Con*[gress] Never say you hear from me. If Dr G- has the hat—of course—let

[9] According to Elizabeth Keckley, this was the last hat worn by Lincoln before his death.

[1] Edward Burke was a steward at the White House. It has been suggested by several historians that he and Edward McManus were the same person. (See letters to Wakeman, January 30 and February 18 [1865].). Close study of the letters of President and Mrs. Lincoln, as well as of Interior Department records, would seem to indicate that Burke and McManus were two separate individuals. Mrs. Lincoln apparently cared for neither.

[2] Representative Thaddeus Stevens, leader of the radical Republicans in the House.

him retain it—and if Cuthbert—*dared*, give Burke the hat—give her a solemn talk—

Your friend
M. L.

Return this letter to me, of "*Warburton*," and let no soul, see it.

❖

In writing of her husband, Mary Lincoln fell into the most exalted usage; Lincoln's image in her memory was taking on superhuman proportions. She was not alone in her reverence. The deification of the sixteenth President had begun at the instant of his passing. Contemporaries who had known Lincoln as shrewd and skeptical, with a genius for self-advancement, associates who were familiar with his ironic turn of mind and earthy turn of phrase, were now comparing his life to the Second Coming. Mrs. Lincoln was in the vanguard of the idolators and custodian of the shrine. She sprinkled her letters with such words as "sainted," "immortal," "martyr," "savior," and "worshipped." Inasmuch as this remarkable man had chosen to share his life with her, she felt herself entitled to a special respect, and whenever this respect was not forthcoming was filled with righteous rage. Only she had truly understood her husband, she insisted, as only he had truly understood her. There had been no secrets between them, and therefore no one but she could claim to be an authority on the character of Abraham Lincoln.

By late 1865 a formidable body of literature had accumulated on the subject of the late President—books, articles, pamphlets, pouring from the pens of authors eager to profit from an insatiable public appetite. Mary Lincoln read all she could of it, keeping a sharp eye out for anything which might present Lincoln in a false or unflattering light. Although she would later have reason to dislike Henry J. Raymond, the editor of *The New York Times* who became a congressman, she was highly pleased with his early biography of Lincoln. Appearing almost simultaneously with Raymond's work was *The Life of Abraham Lincoln*, a weighty effort on the part of

Josiah G. Holland, managing editor of the Springfield (Massachusetts) *Republican* and a historian of some repute. Holland sent Mrs.
Lincoln a copy of his book; in writing to thank him for it, she could
not resist adding a few qualifications to her general praise. She was
particularly perturbed by Holland's account of the duel Lincoln had
nearly fought with General James Shields over her "Rebecca verses"
in 1842. As soon as the encounter was behind them, both Mary
Todd and her champion had pushed it from their minds, as one will
suppress any memory that is painful or embarrassing. But there was
one person who had not forgotten it, who seldom forgot any morsel
of gossip about the Lincolns: Mary's *bête noire*, William Herndon.
The incident of the duel as recounted by Holland had come directly
from Herndon, along with other, more valuable information about
Lincoln's life in Springfield. If Mrs. Lincoln suspected the source,
she did not say so, but the thought of the public's feasting on that
foolish bit of ancient history agitated her more and more as time
went by. If the proprieties had permitted her to publish her version
in the newspapers, she might well have been tempted to do so.
Instead she confined herself to writing long, elaborate explanations
of the incident to Frank Carpenter and Mary Jane Welles.

To Josiah G. Holland

Chicago Dec 4th 1865

Private—
My Dear Sir:

The Biography of my deeply lamented husband, which you
have so kindly sent me, has been received and read, with very great
interest. After a careful perusal of the work, I find the statements,
in *most* instances, so very correct, that I feel quite surprised, as to
the extent of your *minute* information. From the description of my
husbands, early struggles, which he has, so frequently described to
me, to the foolish and uncalled for *rencontre*, with Gen Shields,[3]

[3] For the story of Shields' abortive duel with Lincoln, see pp. 29–30. Mrs. Lincoln's version is presented in the letters to Mary Jane Welles and Francis B.
Carpenter of December 6 and 8, 1865.

all are truthfully, portrayed. This *last* event, occurred, about six months, before our marriage,[4] when, Mr Lincoln, thought, he had some right, to assume to be *my* champion, even on frivolous occasions. The poor Genl, in our little gay circle, was oftentimes, the subject of mirth & even song—and we were *then* surrounded, by several of those, who have since, been appreciated, by the *world*. The Genl was very impulsive & on the occasion referred to, had placed himself before us, in so ridiculous a light, that the love of the ludicrous, had been excited, within me & I presume, I gave vent to it, in some *very* silly lines. After the reconciliation, between the *contending* parties, Mr L & myself mutually agreed, never to refer to it & except in an occasional light manner, between us, it was never mentioned. I am surprised, at *so* distant a day, you should have ever heard of the circumstance.

It is exceedingly painful to me, *now*, suffering under such an overwhelming bereavement, to recall *that* happy time. My beloved husband, had so entirely devoted himself to me, for two years before my marriage, that I doubtless trespassed, many times & oft, upon his great tenderness & amiability of character. There never existed a more loving & devoted husband & such a Father, has seldom been bestowed on children. Crushed and bowed to the earth, with our *great great* sorrow, for the sake of my poor afflicted boys, I have to strive, to live on, and comfort them, as well, as I can. You are aware, that with all the President's, deep feeling, he was *not*, a demonstrative man, when he felt most deeply, he expressed, the least. There are some very good persons, who are inclined to magnify conversations & incidents, connected with their slight acquaintance, with this great & good man, For instance, the purported conversations, between the President & the Hospital nurse, it was not *his* nature, to commit his griefs and religious feelings so fully to words & that with an entire stranger. Even, between ourselves, when our deep & touching sorrows, were *one* & the same, his expressions were few—Also the lengthy account, of the lady, who *very* wisely, persisted, in claiming a hospital, for her State. My hus-

---

[4] The verses appeared in the *Sangamo Journal* on September 16, 1842; thus the episode of the duel occurred six weeks, not months, before the Lincolns were married. A possible reason why Mrs. Lincoln misdated the episode is given on pp. 532-3.

band, never had the time, to discuss these matters, so lengthily with any person or persons—too many of them came daily, in review before him—And again, I cannot understand, how strangely his temper, could be at so complete a variance, from what it always was, in the home circle. There, he was always, so gentle & kind. Before closing this long letter, which I fear will weary you, ere you get through it—allow me again to assure you, of the great satisfaction the perusal of your Memoirs, have given me. I remain very truly & gratefully,

Mary Lincoln.

To Mary Jane Welles

Chicago Dec 6th 1865

My dear Mrs Welles.

Although weeks, have intervened, since your last kind letter was received, I need scarcely assure you, how greatly it pleases me, to hear from you & how fresh the remembrance of all your affectionate & Christian sympathy is, upon my poor, desolate heart. We were very much pleased to hear of the safe arrival of your son, in Washington, it is quite a trial to me, when I reflect, on the pleasure, *such a trip*, would have afforded my poor sad boy, Robert. He was conscientious, in what he considered his duty, to remain at home, for the present. Your son, sent him, a souvenir of his visit to Havanna, in some *cigarettes*, almost sufficiently tempting to induce "strong minded women," to resort to them, in a case of emergency. *Tomorrow*, is *Thanksgiving Day!* [5] How strangely the name, comes back upon my distracted memory, bringing with it, the beloved presence of my idolized husband, and our cheerful little family circle. If I could close my eyes & not awaken until the day has passed, *if possible*, I would be *less* miserable. *These anniversaries*, are so terrible, to the deeply bereaved! Time only makes me realize more

[5] After Lincoln proclaimed an annual day of thanksgiving in 1863, a celebration was customarily held on the last Thursday of November, but precedent was broken in 1865, as it would be occasionally in future years.

deeply, our great loss and the only consolation left me, is the *certainty*, that each day, brings me nearer, my "loved & lost." I have been reading over, Mr Johnson's Message [to Congress],⁶ and it appears to *me*, (or it may be, the tenacity, which very naturally clings to me, in regard to my husband,) that Mr Johnson dwelt very *lightly*, on *his*, great loss—I am sure, I cannot be mistaken in this—I have never heard, of any depth of expression, as coming from him, in regard to the late President. Have you? But I will not dwell upon this—it is too painful, to discuss—I thank you, very sincerely, for your kind wishes, in regard to our comfort in the future —if my husband's memory, and his invaluable service to his Country, does not justify Congress, in settling something upon *his* family, that will enable us, to live comfortably, in time to come, then of course, we, as the party interested, have nothing more to say. I greatly mistake, the American people, if we will be left *thus*, in our desolation. I have been trying to interest myself of late, in the different Biographies, of my Husband that have been sent me, from time to time. The last one, from the pen of Dr Holland, I have been looking over, this week. Some of his accounts are very minute & *one*, especially that he publishes, would have *pained* my husband, very much, if at *this* distant day, he had ever supposed, it would have appeared in print. In our little cotérie in Springfield in the days of my girlhood, we had a society of gentlemen, who have since, been distinguished, in a greater or less degree, in the political world. My great and glorious husband comes *first*, "a world above them all." Douglas, Trumbull, Baker, Hardin, Shields, such choice spirits, were the habitués, of our drawing room. Gen Shields, a kind hearted, impulsive Irishman, was always creating a sensation & mirth, by his drolleries. On one occasion, he amused me exceedingly, so much so, that I committed his *follies*, to rhyme, and very silly verses they were, only, they were said to abound in sarcasm causing them to be very offensive to the Genl. A gentleman friend, carried them off and persevered in not returning to them [sic], when one day, I saw them, strangely enough, in the daily paper. Genl Shields, called upon the Editor [Simeon B. Francis], and demanded the author. The Editor, requested *a day*, to reflect upon it—The

⁶ President Johnson's first message to Congress, read in the Senate on December 5, 1865.

latter called upon Mr Lincoln, to whom he knew I was engaged & explained to him, that he was certain, that I was the Author—Mr L. then replied, say to Shields, that "I am responsible." Mr L- thought no more of it, when about two weeks afterwards, whilst he was 150 miles away from S[pringfield] attending court, Shields, followed him up & demanded satisfaction. The party, with their seconds, repaired to "Bloody Island," opposite St Louis armed with swords, but doubtless, to the delight of each one, were reconciled. The occasion, was so silly, that my husband, was always so ashamed of it, that months before our marriage, we mutually agreed—never to speak, of it, ourselves—and it gradually passed out of the memories of all—This occurred, six months, before we were married & so far as our mutual relations, to each, other were—it would have been the same, eighteen months previous—We were engaged & greatly attached to each other—two years before we were married.[7] It was always, music in my ears, both before & after our marriage, when my husband, told me, that I was the only one, he had ever thought of, or cared for. It will solace me to the grave & when I again rest by *his* side, I will be comforted. [I] send you a long letter, yet I am sure, as you knew & appreciate—my darling husband—the occurrences of *his* earlier life, will—be uninteresting to you—a busy winter is before you, yet I feel assured, that you will remember me, by writing frequently to me. With regards, to all friends, I remain always truly & Affectionate

Mary Lincoln

To Alexander Williamson

Chicago—Dec 7th [1865]

My dear Sir:

I have not yet heard a word—from the articles Lizzie K. has —if they are not sent—have Lizzie, keep them until the 20th of Dec.

---

[7] It is interesting to note that Mrs. Lincoln here chose to ignore the broken engagement and the strained period of about 18 months that followed until the romance was resumed in the summer of 1842.

find Mr Wentworth—member of Con from—Ill-[8] and as he is coming to Chicago—then—if you request him, he will bring, the package—At the same time from Mr F[rench] at H[udson] T[aylor]—
you can get "Armadale & Mutual Friend" & send them along—
Do—have Stackpole—have the bills—cut down—without an hour's
delay—and have them, settled, *not to come back to me*, I would like
you, to be relieved, as well, as myself of your indebtedness—Be
perfectly candid with me—and if you do not see your way clear,
let me know—Stackpole *can*, accomplish, *all*, for you, if he chooses
—My Ill friends, the Members, will I hope & believe, help me out
—with Con- but I must be relieved of those bills—as we propose
—Call at Willard's & the hotels—but W's particularly & enquire
if on the registers—is a man named—Norman S. Bentley—name—
New York City. If you meet with his name, please telegraph me,
immediately I will explain, to you, hereafter—You appear to send
telegrams marked "D[eliver by] H[and]" you are more fortunate,
in that respect, than I am, I, hope you are eating a very comfortable
Thanksgiving dinner, to day, it is, a very *sad* day to me—your
friend &

To Francis Bicknell Carpenter

Chicago, Dec. 8th 1865

My Dear Sir:

The saddest of *all my very sad* days, has passed, *Thanksgiving*
day, and by way, of diverting my mind & memory, from the recollection of *yesterday*, I have concluded, to reply, to your very kind

---

[8] "Long John" Wentworth had been the first Republican mayor of Chicago,
serving from 1857–63. Now a member of Congress, he would introduce the House
bill for the payment of four years' salary to Mrs. Lincoln. The New York *World*,
on January 6, 1866, claimed that Wentworth was the only man to vote for the bill.
"There was a large lobby . . . from New York," continued the paper, "urging
this very appropriation and that the lobbyists were not wholly disinterested is
instanced in Long John's question to one of the patriots who said that the country
fairly owed this magnificent donation to the bereaved beneficiary. Wentworth
. . . asked him 'How much is your bill?' 'About seven thousand dollars,' said the
man. 'I thought so,' replied Long John."

note, so recently received. Only those, who have suffered & lost, what made life, so well worth, living for, can fully understand the return of anniversaries, that recall the past so vividly to the mind & make the day of general praise & rejoicing so painful, to the sufferer. But I will not complain, or return to my sorrows. I must endeavour to make the best, of the life, that is left me, for the sake of my sons, who have had so much, to try them. I thought, you would be satisfied, with the likenesses, of my darling little boys, "Willie & Taddie, taken in 1861—they will answer very well, for the picture, you propose painting. Even, in *that* likeness, of Willie, justice, is not done him, he was a very beautiful boy, with a most *spiritual* expression of face. He was a most peculiarly religious child, with great amiability & cheerfulness of character—It is impossible, for *time*, to alleviate, the anguish, of *such irreparable losses*—only the grace of God, can calm our grief & still the tempest. I wish you could have known, that dear boy, for *child*, he scarcely seemed to me. So unlike little Taddie, yet so devoted to him—Their love for each other, was charming to behold. Taddie, was quite worried, about the expression, he was said, to have made use of, on *that* Sabbath Morning,[9] he says "His Father was always so happy, when he was alone, with his Mother & himself, that he scarcely, believes, he said it." In his great grief, it is impossible for him to remember, all his utterances—I have been reading Dr Holland's Memoirs, of my husband—and was quite surprised, at the mention of a circumstance, in the "long ago," the publication of which, would have annoyed the President, very much. You may have heard, of the little coterie, we had in Springfield, years since, who have, all since in a greater or less degree, distinguished themselves, in the political world. Genl Hardin, Baker, Douglas, Trumbull—Shields and my great & glorious husband, always a "World, above them all," these men constituted, our society. Shields was always, a subject of mirth, his impulsiveness & drolleries were ir-

---

[9] Carpenter had quoted Tad in one of a series of articles he had written for the New York *Independent* following the assassination. His book, *Six Months at the White House*, expanding upon these articles, was published in 1866. The quotation referred to by Mrs. Lincoln was probably Tad's statement, made on the Sunday following his father's death: "I am glad he has gone [to heaven], for he never was happy after he came here. This was not a good place for him!" (Quoted in Carpenter, p. 293).

resistible. On one occasion, he made himself, so conspicuous, that I committed his follies, to rhyme & some person, looking over the silly verses—carried them off & had them published in the daily paper of the place. The sarcastic allusions irritated Shields & he demanded the author, of the Editor, the latter, requesting a few days, for reflection, repaired to Mr Lincoln, who having heard of it, through me, immediately told the Editor, that "he would be responsible." A few days after this, Mr L- almost forgetting the circumstance, went off some two hundred miles to court, and to make a foolish story, very short, was followed by Shields, demanding satisfaction. Mr L- accepted, scarcely knowing what he was doing, they repaired to St Louis, to "Bloody Island," with their "long swords," the choice of weapons, being left to Mr L- the challenged party. Genl Hardin, my cousin, stepped in their midst & effected a reconciliation. No doubt, much to *their* satisfaction. This affair, always annoyed my husband's peaceful nerves—and as it occurred six months, before we were married, he said, he felt, he could do, no less, than be my champion. However, if the same cause, had transpired a year & half before, it would doubtless have been the same result, as our mutual relations were *then*, the same. Last February, an officer of our army, presented himself, in the drawing room, of the W. H. on one, of those fortunate & especial occasions, when the President, was able to respond to my urgent invitation, to accompany me, to the drawing room, if "only for an hour."— *Private*—This Genl in the course of conversation, said, playfully, to my husband "Mr President, is it true, as I have heard that you, once went out, to fight a duel & all for the sake, of the lady by your side." Mr Lincoln, with a flushed face, replied, "I do not deny it, but if you desire my friendship, you will never mention it again—" Immediately, after the occurrence, months, before we were married, *we*, mutually agreed, on no occasion to allude to it & gradually it ceased to be mentioned. In the long lapse of years—I marvel that Dr H- should have heard, of this very unnecessary episode, in my lamented husband's life. All this is between ourselves—I must say, I was greatly surprised, to see a simple letter of mine, written, when my heart was bursting, with its great sorrow, in print. I will forgive you—in the hope, it may never occur again. If we are ever sufficiently well situated, to invite our friends to see us, I hope you will visit us, accompanied by Mrs C. and I can tell you, many things, of my dearly beloved husband, that I have not sufficient time or calmness to commit to paper. Taddie is greatly mortified, that you have exposed, his little waywardness—but he is a dear amiable loving boy, after all, and I presume, will forgive. Your friend,

Mary Lincoln.

To Elihu B. Washburne

Chicago—Dec 9th 65

My dear Sir:

Your kind & encouraging note, is received—My sole dependence, is in, your urgent *persistence* in the 4 years salary—with only the 25,000- added to my already, very small income, I could not *rent* the smallest house & furnish it, in C- Will you not bring it up & pass the bill on Monday or Tuesday next—if it is pushed forward & insisted upon, the *first days*, of your meeting—we will beyond the least possibility, of doubt, be successful—If otherwise—a fate, will await us, which *should* be, truly mortifying, to every American, who had any respect, for my dear husband. It would be a source of pride to me, if we are indebted to our future comfort & well being, to our Ill- friends—To yourself & Mr Wentworth—as the leaders— with urging it—*immediately* after the meeting of Con- on Monday or Tuesday—we will have success—I am anxious, to know what is to be our fate, in the matter—it will be, I am sure, *as you* say—Every one of our friends, feel, that you have a right, to direct it & carry it through—please do so, at an early hour—I fear *Gov O.* will work against us—I mistrust that *S-* set of people & with very good cause. I hope, certainly by this time next week, it will all be settled favorably—Praying you will excuse, my troubling you, so much, on a subject, that is of such vital importance to us I remain very truly—

M. L-

Please do not let Mr Wentworth or any one be content, with the first years salary—as Judge D- will tell you—our house, would have henceforth—to be a boarding house—every thing, is so fabulously high here & even if prices—come down—I could not rent, the plainest house & furnish it, with *only*, the additional year's salary—this you can readily imagine—and believe me—if *this* appropriation bill, follows, immediately after the resolutions && it will pass, unanimously—We should, in justice, to my husband's services, have $50,000- for a home & furniture & the hundred thousand to keep it up—the interest of it, would not be much more than $6,000- a year —Our estate is all unsettled—and every thing I have, may have to go, towards settling it—Please see all the members & Sen- & acquaint them, with these facts—If it comes off, next week, any sum you name, will be given us & I shall be so grateful for a home. With the $25,000- we can never have one, I assure you—

You will see yourself that imm- upon introducing it, into the house, it will become a law—*Before*, some outsiders, we could name, can work, *much* against us—I rely on you all, from this state, with your urgent persistence—it can be effected—

Again, I remain—Sincerely
M. L-

To Elizabeth Blair Lee

Chicago Dec 11th 1865

My dear Mrs Lee:

Your letters, are always *so* welcomely received, that although they come, at such distant intervals, yet so soon as I read them, my first thought, is to reply immediately—Although, it has been several weeks, since I last heard from you, the remembrance of your tender care and sympathy, is ever with me. You wrote me such a pleasant account, of your husband being with you & your great happiness in consequence, that I have earnestly hoped, he would be able to remain during the winter, in Washington. I suppose, you are quietly established, in your Winter home, in the city, with your health, I trust entirely restored. If your husband, is with you, I would risk, *your*, not giving much thought, to your physical condition and consider yourself, to be feeling very well. When I speak of others, and the comforting presence of those they love, surrounding them; notwithstanding the ardor & depth, of my own nature; with regard to myself, I feel and know & *now*, solemnly realize, that my overwhelming sorrow, removes me, from the world, in which henceforth, I have no share & what is more terrible to me, always is the thought—that the one, on whom I leaned for support & loving tenderness is so sadly & cruelly removed—and my poor boys, only remain—who rest their hopes on *Me*—God's ways are inscrutable! In happier days, I could never have believed, I could have lived an hour, without my idolized husband. Yet I, wretchedly, live on, the comforting thought, that our Maker, in *this*, will be gracious, by allowing me, soon to rejoin him—Where no more tears, shall be shed is a solace to me. As dear little Taddie, often says, "three of us on earth, & *three* in Heaven." I feel that *he* is only beckoning, to us, to be also "ready"—The comfort of my early life, always, before my marriage & ever afterwards, that my husband, always told me & his actions all proved, that he had never thought or cared for any one but myself—or I might have added had never noticed any other lady—This memory, is some solace, to me in my misery, & yet it reminds me, very sorrowfully, of all the devotion, I have lost—Still believing, as I do, that in their blessed home, they love us, *still more* transcendent[al]ly & are waiting to welcome us there, should be some consolation to us, in the midst of our deepest afflictions. Forgive, the sad strain, in which I write you. I am sure, *your* sympathizing heart *will*. I hope your Father, has recovered entirely, from his late accident, of which Mrs Welles, wrote me some weeks since—if it had been *very* serious, undoubtedly, we should have heard of it.—How, my beloved husband, revered & loved *him*. Will *the day*, never return, when I shall again see you, when I can pour out, my heart to you & in return, I can listen & enjoy your conversation, so full of cheerfulness and kind feeling for all. My own life, has been so chequered, naturally so gay & hopeful—my *prominent desires*, all granted me—My noble husband, who was my "light & life," and my highest—ambition gratified— and *that* was, the great weakness of my life. My husband—became distinguished above all. And yet, owing to *that fact*, I firmly believe he lost his life & I am bowed to the earth with Sorrow. Such is life! & we must submit, to the decrees of fate! Your busy season, will soon begin & my dear friend, you must occasionally remember me, in the midst of those, who love you no better than I do. I hope you will write to me often & tell me, about all my friends—whom in the midst of my trials, are remembered most kindly. With love to Miss Betty—your father & mother—not forgetting your husband— I remain, always affectionately

yours
Mary Lincoln

December of 1865 proved to be a month of particular misery and disappointment for Mary Lincoln. Creditors were pressing her on every hand, and no stratagem she or Williamson devised could still their demands. She was beginning to suspect the sincerity and zeal of several of those "summer friends" on whom she had counted so heavily, among them "Pet" Halsted, Rufus Andrews, and Norman Bentley. Davis seemed cold and unsympathetic; Williamson was proving tactless and ineffectual. Toward the end of the month, after Tad had recovered from a severe illness, she and Robert traveled to Springfield in order to be present in the city when Lincoln's body was taken from the receiving vault at Oak Ridge and placed in a temporary tomb, awaiting construction of the monument. She could not bring herself to witness the removal, but her visit was grim enough without the experience. It was the first time she had set foot in Springfield since the day she had left it, in high elation, nearly five years before. Memories rode on the winter wind, and her initial glimpse of the gravesite where one day she too would lie left her sick and shaken.

Then the Christmas season was upon her, the unhappiest Christmas she could remember. Just before she left for Springfield, she had received long-awaited tidings from the East, and they were anything but glad. In a move which seemed almost diabolically designed to rob her Christmas of any shred of hope or comfort, Congress had voted on December 21, 1865, to grant her one year's salary of $25,000, no more than had been given previous presidential widows. After the requisite deductions had been made, she came away with only $22,000, far less than she felt she needed or deserved. There no longer seemed any chance that she would receive the remaining three years' salary or any other form of government assistance. The leaders of a "*grateful* nation" clearly considered they had met their obligations to Mrs. Abraham Lincoln and hoped they had heard the last of her.

To David Davis

Chicago—Dec 13th [*1865*]

My dear Sir:

Your note, is just received. Although, I am suffering, to day, with one, of my severe headaches, by way of relieving your mind, I hasten to reply. Mr Williamson, in attending to some little business of mine, has acted very singularly—I shall write him & set it all straight. Any indebtedness, I have is easily settled—So—I hope you will give yourself no uneasiness—on the subject. I shall write to those gentlemen & apologise, for the indiscretion, of this person —which arose more from the head than heart—you will certainly, not again, be troubled *or*, those persons—Therefore, we will dismiss, the subject. Next week, we go down, to Springfield, on our most melancholy duty—which will only, be opening, my bleeding wounds, afresh—Cousin John Stuart,[1] is proving himself, a most excellent friend, I shall feel, forever grateful to him—Excuse my hasty note, for I am really not able, to sit up—

Very truly yours—
Mary Lincoln

[1] John Todd Stuart, a moving spirit of the Lincoln Monument Association, had consistently upheld Mrs. Lincoln's wishes before that body.

To Alexander Williamson

Dec 13th [1865]

Private

My dear Sir:

Judge D- has just written to me—enclosing *your* note (copied) to Mr Speed—sent by Harlan—with a note to Judge D—*asking* Judge D- *how*, I could be relieved and appealing to *him*—This is the explanation, of *his* sending for Stackpole—go to Stackpole & tell him, *not*, to go near Judge *D-* if the latter, send for *you*, *on no terms* go near *him*—Sec H was very innocent, by applying to *Judge D- This*, is the reward, of my persuading my husband—to put H in the Cabinet—You see *now*, there is no help—from these generous gentlemen—We must be *more* discreet, in the future—*Never* intimate to Speed H[arlan] or Sec S[tanton] that any letters were written to Judge- D- from *them*—only see, them each once more & say that Mrs L- intends—settling her own business—Let them *all* alone—afterwards for fear, you might have some difficulty, in your own affairs. We can discuss—them—when you come out—I am a little fearful Stanton, may be cross & refuse you a pass—in my next, I will write, the request—In the mean time, it would be better to see Stanton—be very polite & say quietly that Mrs L- is *now* settling her own business—do so with the other *two*—It is just as well, to let *well*, alone. It was a great pity, you wrote *letters* to these people, who are *not* gentlemen. Between ourselves—all this—Now, what remains for you, to do is this—make Stackpole—go—with you & have all the bills reduced. They *all*, could be brought, down to $3500—if Stackpole set to work, about it—say—to them Judge D- has nothing to do, with my affairs—*Otherwise, they* will be settled. It will be better—*not*, to write to Bentley see—if he is [in] Wash— if not, on your way out—stop in N.Y. to see him. If Andrews should come to Wash- have a private conversation with him—making both Bentley & himself, promise, to be quiet. Write me, how much, you *had* erased from Shuster's bill—When you get them cut down— send me the list—as I sent you—very much reduced—The Lamb bill you remember, I told you was wrong—[by] over two hundred at least—too much on the card. Have them, all reduced, as much as possible—Do keep, *perfectly quiet*, about my affairs. W- is such a *gossiping* place & every one—is ready to fly to *Judge* D—with my business—The latter is so close, that I prefer to keep my business to myself.

Pray—say nothing to Stanton Harlan or Speed—about—the two latter writing to Judge D- It will only irratate them & do no good—say—I have settled my own business and *then, after that— do not* go—*near them.*

Do remember, my advice, in all this—you will see it is, for the best.

To Alexander Williamson

Chicago—Dec 15th [*1865*]

My dear Sir:

I want you, to take my advice & *do not* go near—Judge Davis—Harlan Stanton or Speed—no matter how often & how much they send for you—Advise Stackpole also—*never,* to go near them. All, they desire is to be *inquisitive* and they are *not* friends & will *never* assist us—Therefore, let this, be an end, to *them*— When you see Bentley in Wash- telegraph me—On Monday— gather *all* your bills together—have Stackpole go—with you & have them lessened—greatly—get them all together. Do not write to Bentley—better *see* him. By Tuesday morning, you will receive a note to Stanton requesting a pass for yourself & Mr French [2] to come to Chicago—Stanton, is so irritable—I am, in some dread—lest he refuse. I do not know, how he can do so—I am beginning to have *very* little hope, for ourselves—in Con—they will try & cut us down, without doubt to—the *first years salary.* I am sure enemies are at work. Do pray, attend to these bills—I shall send a note to S[tanton] for a pass to Chicago—if he will *not grant* this, he certainly will give you one to N.Y. You can then *see* Bentley—I will give you his business place Also B. B. Sherman—banker Wall Street—*do not*

---

[2] E. F. French, friend and fellow clerk of Williamson in the Treasury Department.

write to them. With Judge Davis—I smoothed it over—saying your zeal, in my cause was great—but that the *Sec's* would *never* be troubled *again* and advised him, it was *my* business & he must dismiss *it*, from his thoughts—*Do* not *go* near Judge D- or the Sec's —*They*, are not friends—but for your *future*, in W- do not mention, the passing *of the* letter to Judge D- Treat it, with *silent contempt*. Get *those* bills together—have them cut down, without fail on Monday—so that you will be ready to start to Chicago—via New York —to see Bentley any hour—On next Wednesday evening, I go to Springfield—but will return on Friday the 22d—See to those bills —if you cannot *persuade*—Bentley to *undertake* them, with what *he has*, really belonging to *me*—then bring them to *me*—very greatly reduced—You have—*not* an hour to lose

Do not forget to get "Armadale & the Mutual Friend"—from French—at H[udson] T[aylor's]—bring them with you—F—promised them, as going, with the set I bought—I *must have*, this Christmas, *all* my articles from Lizzie Keckley—

To Elihu B. Washburne

Chicago—Dec 15 [1865]

My dear Sir:

I see by the papers, that your Committee, in reference, to our affairs, meets next Monday—May I urge you, in view, of the necessities of your case *insist* upon the *four years salary* & have the tax removed from it—The $10,000- off—the 4 years salary, would be a great deal to us, who have a home to obtain, furniture & [need] the interest to live on—It will be small enough & I shall have to exercise much economy with *that*—If a *grateful* American people—only give us the $25,000- our portion, is a boarding house forever—a *fitting* place, for the wife & sons, of the man—who served his country so well & lost his life in consequence—Those false friends—who urge —the Harrison *precedent* [3]—*he*—Pres- for *one month*, will perhaps

[3] The families of William Henry Harrison and Zachary Taylor, the first two Presidents to die in office, received no assistance or compensation from the government beyond full salary for the year in which the President died.

place it on the ground, that it would be an improper example—Perhaps, never in history, will such a case, again occur as ours—therefore there is *no* parallel—to our case. Every day, as you see, *is* strengthening the opposition, will you not relieve ~~me~~ my mind, atleast, of this small portion of its burden—by settling it in both houses of Congress—before next Wednesday morning—*after that*, believe me, most truly, there will be, no chance, for us—In the excitement of dispersing, before the holidays—It would undoubtedly pass & prevent *further* opposition to us—which *it is well known*, is going on, *from those*, who should be *our* friends. I will rely on yourself & Mr Wentworth, to have this carried before Christmas, also the tax removed—which will be, a great consideration. I see that an app- bill—was passed for W. H. of $50,000- Why cannot *ours*, be then urged, before others come up—to kill ours off—Please see to this—dear Mr Washburne

I remain very truly
Mary Lincoln

To Alexander Williamson

Chicago—Dec 16th [1865]

My dear Sir

Your last letter is received. I regret to learn, of the death of your Mother, it must be a gratifying thought to you, that you visited her, last summer, in Scotland—I enclose you a line to Mr Stanton. If he gives you a pass, I suppose you will be in Chicago, in about a week—we will all be pleased to see you. Little Tad—is suffering with a most terrible cold, I was up, with him, almost all last night, as he came very near, having the croup—Without he greatly improves—I will be unable to go down to Springfield this week—He is too unwell to leave or to take him—I see Mr Stanton, has gone up North, so I will address my note, to Genl Hardee [4] [sic] which I suppose, will be *just* the same—There was no neces-

---

[4] Major General James A. Hardie, military aide to Stanton in the War Department.

sity, that Speed, should have *those* bills—without he first, *promised* to pay. I *must have them.* Please go, to him, the day, you receive this & get them away, from him, or else *Judge D*, will soon have them. If you are coming to C- come by the way of New York—see Bentley—whose business place, is on *Beaver* St—somewhere—the number escapes me—B. B. Sherman banker Wall St will tell you —get every bill together—*The Galt* [5] *items*, only, give him, go to him & see if he *will* relieve me—*If not*, bring them, with you to C- and if you do not come, enclose them to me. It is rather singular— that the list on the card, should not be over $6,000—and you write me—*between* $6- & 7,000- this is a mistake—On that list, on the card—the Lamb list—was one hundred & 50—at least—*over*, the amount, of his own bill sent me & ($52- were erased from *that* bill). I do not understand—the bill increasing, rather than *diminishing*, in this way—nor I cannot have it—and since then too, the Shuster bill, has been cut down, so it cannot be, much over $5,000 even without, the bills, having been *lessened*—which Stackpole & your- self, can easily have done. There is little time, *now*, left for play— Urge Mr Bentley to settle them—if not, I must have every one of them—I am getting very tired, of having nothing accomplished— Only the added trouble, of every thing, going to *Judge D.* and I cannot have them, either returned to me—*greater*, instead of less— With urgent entreaty, Mr B- will settle them—*do*, be quiet, about your business—Telegraph me, each day, what you propose doing —I am very well posted, about my bills—& *even*, with what *has* been erased, my bills, as I sent them to you, cannot be much over $5,000—and you could have them lessened & if you try. I *must* have, my work from Lizzie—*this* Christmas. If you do *not* come out, see if Mr Wentworth, will be coming—If so—if it is not too large he will bring it—I hope you will be able to come.

do not go near *Judge D*—nor let Stackpole.

---

[5] **M. W. Galt,** a Washington jeweler. The firm of Galt & Company is still in business in the nation's capital.

To James A. Hardie

Chicago. Dec 16th 1865

My dear Sir:

Understanding that Secretary Stanton, is absent, from Washington, permit me to address you. Mr E. B. French [sic] & Mr Williamson are anxious to visit Chicago, during Christmas & would be very grateful and it would be very agreeable to us, if you would kindly allow them each a pass—Via New York in coming out to Chicago—& in returning, the shorter route. Mr Williamson, was Taddie's teacher & they, both are anxious, to see each other again —Trusting, you will grant them, the favor, of a pass I remain, very sincerely & truly

Mrs A. Lincoln

To Noah Brooks

Chicago. Dec 18, 1865

My dear Sir:

Several weeks have elapsed since your last letter, was received —and I thank you kindly, for your friendship, & sympathy for us, in our overwhelming bereavement. How inscrutable are the ways of Providence! *So soon*, after our terrible calamity, poor Dr H[enry] who so freely sorrowed with us, should be so unexpectedly called to rejoin, his great & good friend, who had just "passed before." Such is life & the shorter the race, the happier, for some of *us*.

I hope some person, will be appointed in the place of "Frank Hen[r]y," [6] a loyal man, who will be required to share, the small profits, of the office with his [Dr. Henry's] poor, afflicted widow. For, without doubt, she requires, such assistance.

[6] Francis Henry, a relative of the late doctor, was a clerk in the office of the Surveyor General of the Washington Territory and was assisting Mrs. Henry financially.

I received, the sum of, $400, in gold—from the gentleman, you mentioned, which I acknowledged in writing. Have you ever heard, any thing about it? You spoke, of sending, the other amount, of over $2,000 in gold—in November—as it has not yet arrived, I presume there has been some detention. I scarcely think Congress, will give us more than the *first year's* salary. Genl Grant, has been recently presented, with his third magnificent mansion, within the last eighteen months, the last one, one of the Dougla[s]'s houses.[7] All this, is strange inconsistency. My little Taddie, is very much indisposed, with a bad cold—and I write you, in great haste. My husband, was so earnest a friend of yours, that we will always remember you, with the kindest feelings & will always, be pleased to hear from you.

Your friend truly
Mary Lincoln

To Sally Orne

Chicago Dec 24th 65

My dear Mrs Orne.

I am sitting up, for the first time, in three days, whilst the girl, is arranging my room, so I have concluded, whilst I am left to myself, to write you a line. You will not wonder, at my illness, when I mention, that last week, I visited, the resting place of my beloved husband. On the evening train returning, I had a very severe chill, doubtless caused by, the intensely cold weather and my great excitement of mind. Never, did I so greatly wish, to be placed, by his dear side—as when I visited that spot. The temporary vault, is just completed, containing apartments—for my darling husband, myself & four sons—*Two* of the latter are now resting there, side by side—By my husband's side—is a niche, for my coffin—as a matter of course, I was not present, at the removal, but passed the

---

[7] Mrs. Lincoln was in error. The house had formerly belonged to John C. Breckinridge.

morning, of the same day, there, accompanied, by my dear son Robert & Cousin John T. Stuart. The latter has faithfully, carried out all my wishes, in regard to this sacred resting place—where all my thoughts centre—I pour my sad tale, into your sympathizing ear, knowing, how well, your affectionate heart, can appreciate, the deep & overwhelming sorrow of mine. Dear little Taddie, often says, "dear Mother, three of us here, *three*, in Heaven"—How true alas, it is, my own breaking heart, can testify—Think, of the sorrowful memories, this Christmas brings me! I dare not, pause to think—I was apprised of the result, of the Congressional action, in my case, before I went, to Springfield—but not, until my return here, prostrated with sickness—have I thought it over & fully realized, that no more home, in future, is to be mine where I can bury myself & my sorrow—and have this continually aching head, relieved by *quiet*—The latter, I can *now* no more expect, although, it has been so earnestly desired. The *first years salary*, given us— *nominally* $25,000—is in fact, only $20,000—one month's salary, having been drawn by my husband—and the tax of $2500- will bring it very near, the sum I state [8]—With this sum, I could not, at this time, purchase a house here—and my income of $1800 besides —would neither furnish it, of course or keep, it up—I must so soon, as I sufficiently recover, I will send you, some hair—do you know only a bunch, as large as one of our finger's, was saved me—You shall have, as much as I can possibly spare you—I wish it was more —I am truly miserable—do write me & believe me ever truly

Mary Lincoln

[8] On December 21, 1865, Congress voted to pay Mrs. Lincoln one year's presidential salary of $25,000. The net figure after deductions (see p. 324) was $22,025.34, placed in seven percent federal bonds of 1865, payable in thirty years ("seven-thirties"). The figure cited by Mrs. Lincoln as "tax" would ordinarily have been withheld in accordance with temporary measures enacted during the war. However, because the payment was considered a donation, technicalities prohibited the government from withholding tax on it. The tax was collected subsequently, but in 1872, as a result of an Attorney General's opinion that any diminution of presidential salary was unconstitutional, the money was refunded the estate along with amounts previously withheld from President Lincoln's salary. A detailed discussion of this matter can be found in Pratt. *The Personal Finances of Abraham Lincoln*, pp. 125–7

To Benjamin B. Sherman [9]

Chicago, Ill.
December 26, 1865

My dear Sir:

Although my son wrote you a letter on yesterday, I have concluded to write and thank you, most gratefully, for your kind interest in our deeply afflicted family. We have, indeed, lost our all; the idolized husband and father is no more with us, and, if possible, our adverse fate and the great injustice of a people who owed so much to my beloved husband does not contribute toward lessening our heavy trials. Sir Morton Pelo [sic] [1] gave a farewell dinner to his friends in New York in return for their polite attentions to him. We are homeless, and in return for the sacrifices my great and noble husband made, both in his life and in his death, the paltry first year's salary is offered us; under the circumstances, such injustice has been done us as calls the blush to any true, loyal heart. The sum is in reality only $20,000, as the first month's salary was paid my husband, and I presume the tax on it will be deducted from it. The interest of it will be about $1,500. I am humiliated when I think that we are destined to be forever homeless. I can write no more. I remain, very respectfully,

Mary Lincoln

P. S.—I omitted to say, my dear Mr Sherman, mentioning to you what has been told me several times lately; persons apparently reliable saying that to their knowledge $10,000 in money toward the

[9] A New York grocery merchant and banker, mentioned in Mrs. Lincoln's letter to Williamson of December 16, 1865. Sherman was treasurer of a dollar fund for Mrs. Lincoln's assistance. It is possible that the $9,000 mentioned in her note to Francis Spinner of December 30, 1865, represented the proceeds of this fund.
[1] Sir Morton Peto was a British financier who had visited the United States during the war years and translated his support for the Union into investments in northern railroads. *The New York Times* of October 31, 1865, devoted the first five columns of its front page to an account of Sir Morton's lavish farewell dinner at Delmonico's, including menu, guest list (a remarkable assembly of the country's notables, headed by Generals Grant and Sherman), and several of the speeches in honor of the host.

dollar fund had been raised in Boston. I mention this so that you might write to Boston to ascertain the truth of this report. Knowing my anxiety to have a home where we could at least have some privacy and your good feeling for us in our distress will, I am sure, induce you to write about this to B[oston]. Excuse my troubling you in this matter &. I agree with R[oberts?], it is best not to advertise; if there is anything at such an hour as this, it will be forthcoming.

M. L.

To Alexander Williamson

Chicago—Dec 26th [1865]

My dear Sir:

About a week since, I received a telegram, in which you said, you would write the *next* day. Not a line since the telegram has been received—I supposed you would be on here, at Christmas—I requested you to bring or send, *all* my bills, you have—*this*, is not certainly acting as a friend—Will you go, PRIVATELY & kindly to Mr Galt—and ask him, if there *is*, any thing on my bill, he would allow me to return. *He* has always treated me, as a gentleman—I would willingly return—the gold ear rings & breast pin—with grecian pattern—The two gilt clocks—many little things—if *he* says *so*—if you choose, show him this note—I would not inconvenience, Mr Galt, for he has been very patient—but, in my great trouble— he will not be unmindful—It is most singular—Lizzie K. does not send, the articles she has of mine—plenty of opportunities occur— Without any delay, fail not, to send, me the bills & when Con- gives me the money, which of course will be very soon, I will settle—Say this to Mr G- & *all* parties. Judge D- has nothing, to do, in the matter—Your silence, is very remarkable, at this time.

Your friend Sincerely—
Mrs A. L.

To Mary Jane Welles

My dear Mrs Welles—

Your last very kind sympathizing letter is received: How well assured, I am, from your past appreciation, of our overwhelming griefs, that you were pained, with the recent decision of Congress —which leaves us, forever without a home—In reality, we are only given $20,000, one month's salary, had been paid, my darling husband, and the tax of $2500— will be deducted, from the remainder. The $20,000- will not be sufficient here, to procure us a home— besides we would require, to have it furnished, and means to keep it up—What a *future* before us—The wife & sons, of the Martyr President, *compelled* to be inmates of boarding houses, all their lives. I am bowed with humiliation at the thought—how much *such* a thought, would have pained my beloved husband, who, last March, expressedly told me, that he did not intend using a cent, of his next four years salary, as we had every thing handsome we required—he intended living on what he had and reserved, his means, for a handsome home. One block from the warehouse, where our goods are stored—was burnt to the ground, a week since—and we are in daily fear, that what little, we have, may share the same fate. The precious relics, belonging to my husband, are a continual source of anxiety to me—Yet I *had anticipated* we would soon, have *had*, a place, to put them—but alas! my hopes, like every thing else, that is pleasant, has vanished—each morning as I awaken from my troubled sleep, I wonder—if it can be true—that after my noble husband's services to his Country & dying in its cause—all this great sacrifice, is ignored. We, without *him*, our all, are forever to dwell, as we *now* are doing, Living Monuments of a Nation's ingratitude! Without a home to she[l]ter us, we, of course, are bound, to no particular spot, to keep together the few of us, who are left, was, one, of my cherished wishes—A visit to Springfield & the Cemetery—where my beloved one's rest, last week—convinced me, that the further removed, I am, the better, it will be, for *my reason*, from *that* spot. I am now sitting, up, the first day since my return,

I am almost too miserable to live—Three days of each week, almost, I am incapable of any exertion, on account of my severe headaches —Our physician says, I must go, out more, in the open air—As I have become known here, and my deep mourning, is very conspicuous, as the interest, of the $20,000 is only $1500- All I can do with it is to procure a carriage—and *this* interest will keep it up. Besides—the sum, *so generously* bestowed upon us, by a *grateful* nation, we each, have $1800- to live upon. In what way, could I convert *that* sum—into a house—This is certainly, not an age of miracles. I consider that so far, as our poor afflicted family is concerned, the close of the year 1865—with the *indignity*, to say the least, thrust upon us by this *great nation*, is very well worthy, of the dark deeds, that have been committed—Sir Morton Peto—in return for the *polite civilities* of his American friends gave them a dinner in N.Y. costing $25,000. The councils of our Nation—deny, the family of the man, who lost his life in their cause—a home. I was pained to learn that Senator [Edwin] Morgan, quoted the "Harrison-precedent," he a president, for a month—his family with an elegant place, on the Ohio—my husband—gave up, everything connected with himself—gave his all—to his Country—I bow my head in deep sorrow that, broken hearted, as I am, we are thus left, without shelter, to return to—in our grief.

Please burn this, for I have written in the bitterness of my sad heart.

My dear Mrs Welles [2]—I fear, we are as much indebted, if *not more*, to those, who *in* my dear husbands, life, professed, the greatest affection for him—and received the highest favors at this hands, those who *now* are occupying enviable stations, and are ungrateful to the *giver*. Trumbull—who *twice*, has owed his present position, to my husbands popularity [3]—and a few others—have had a hand *in this*—knowing me, as you do, *you* with your kind tender heart can understand, how, I feel, when I reflect, that cut off, as we so unjustly & cruelly, have been, from the means to procure a home— it has truly overcome me. The new vault, was completed in S- con-

[2] This portion of the letter was affixed overleaf of the preceding lines in the bound volume of the Welles papers in the Library of Congress. Since it bears no date, it is assumed that it was a postscript to the letter of December 29.

[3] See pp. 43–4 for a discussion of Lincoln's generosity in throwing his votes to Trumbull in the senatorial election of 1856. The second instance referred to was Lincoln's position at the head of the ticket in the election of 1860.

taining places—for my husband, myself & 4 sons—2 sons & my husband, are now far beyond the reach of care, in their glorious home. When my good cousin—Mr John Stuart, pointed to the vacant niche by my beloved husband's side, which he said, was reserved for me—bowed down—with such anguish—as I trust no other unhappy being has ever before been called upon to suffer— I felt & prayed—that my own appointed time, would not be far distant. I am troubling you with a long tiresome letter—whatever our sorrowful fate, in the future, may be you shall never again, hear complaints from me—I feel that we have beeen, very unkindly treated—the last words, almost that Judge Davis said to me last fall was—if Con- only gives you, the *first years* salary—you will be unable, in the future, to have a home—Those, who, got off, on the Harrison & Taylor precedent, were well aware—in what state, *such a decision* would leave us. With much love & gratitude—I remain truly yours—

So soon as I am able, I will send, your husband & yourself what I have promised—Without a home every thing will be scattered—and what is not *cherished* by us—we will have to part with —as a necessity—

To Alexander Williamson

Chicago—Dec 29th [1865]

My dear Sir:

Your note of 26th Dec. is just received. There is *now* no necessity of going to New York   I never heard of a "French Society," to aid me & *Mr Bentley*, was in Wash several days—last week— Send me the bills—and attend to *the Galt matter*—I am sorry—I made a mistake about the passes. For all your kindness, to us *always* I excuse you, from the [word blotted out] and will return you the note. "A fellow feeling makes us wondrous kind" I am poor myself & can sympathize with you, in that respect. R[obert] is waiting for this letter—

Your friend
M. L.

To Francis E. Spinner [4]

Clifton House, Chicago
Dec 30, 1865

My Dear Sir:

Mr Wentworth called last evening and proposed writing you to day relative to the $25,000 in seven-thirties, the remaining $9,000 [5] in money. I trust, notwithstanding the arduous duties of your office, your health remains good. I am very gratefully yours,

Mary Lincoln.

To Sally Orne

Chicago, Dec 30th 65

My dear Mrs Orne:

Your truly kind & sympathizing letter was received, a day or two since—The reflection is painful to me, that writing, as I did, from the impulses of my saddened heart, realizing, as I frequently have, the great kindness of your nature, perhaps I should have been more careful in the expression, of my feelings—yet "from the heart, the mouth speaketh. Left, as we are, without the *possibility* of a home—*the thought* had preyed, upon a mind, overwhelmed, with its great sorrow, and my health, much impaired, by the terrible vicissitudes, I have passed through, the past year. However, you will allow me to close this trying subject, by saying, that the decision, by our National Representatives—that the family of the Martyred President, shall be homeless wanderers forever—is well worthy of the scenes enacted, *during the year*—We, as an afflicted family, *well knew*, we had lost our *all*—the *nation*, has sealed the decree, by their vote, that there, is to be, no privacy, for us, in the

---

4 Treasurer of the United States, 1861–75.
5 This amount was probably the proceeds of B. B. Sherman's "dollar fund," the "given sum" mentioned in Mrs. Lincoln's letter to Williamson of March 25 [1866]. Spinner seems to have acted as banker for Mrs. Lincoln and her benefactors.

future, our grief & we, ourselves—can have, no retirement. Mr Wentworth, called to see me, last evening, he is a plain, out spoken man, yet, he has great kind feeling, for us, in our trials. *He*, never received a favor, at the hands of my noble & good husband, yet he deeply deplores, the great injustice, we have met with, at the hands, of a nation, who should *at least*, have desired to see us, comfortable. At the same time, he says, it would be utterly useless, to expect, a redress of our grievances, at the hands of Congress. Many, who would be willing to have us, enjoy a competency, are afraid to vote for it, for fear of their constituents—all these reasons, would continue *against us*—and if the subject was again agitated in Congress —we would meet with *the same sad fate*—They would shield themselves, under the plea, of "the *Harrison* precedent, a man, who was President, only a month—and who had a beautiful homestead, on the Ohio. From the moment, my husband, entered upon the duties, of his Office, his *own* business matters, were entirely ignored—yet, the widows & fatherless, of our patriotic soldiers, [were] seldom left [by] him, uncared for—and *his* means were known, to be limited —for *he*, had never thought, of himself. Yet, last March, down the river, he promised me, not to use, any of the next four years salary but, would reserve it, for a home & surroundings, worthy of the Nation & the position, he had occupied. Gen Grant whose services to his *country*, were certainly *not*, *superior*, to my husband's, within the last eighteen months, has had three elegant mansions, presented him, a salary of $13,000- a year, he enjoys. On New Year's day, he is to be presented with $100,000- raised in New York —an elegant library, in Boston—and the *prospect*, of *his*, being made [full] *General* with his salary increased to $25,000 a year! Life is certainly, *couleur de rose* to *him*—if it is, all *darkness* & *gloom* to the unhappy family, of the fallen chief. *Perhaps, Mr Fessenden,*[6] who took particular pains, to speak, against our appropriation, and who had enjoyed, the *honor* of a place, in the Cabinet will deliver, a feeling eulogy, on the *12th of Feb!* I trust, my dear Mrs Orne your health, is entirely recovered & you have enjoyed a "Merry Christmas"—How dearly, I should love, to see you, once more, and have a long talk, with you, you never appeared to me, as a stranger

[6] William Pitt Fessenden, successor to Chase as Secretary of the Treasury, had recently been returned to his former Senate seat from Maine.

—and your cheerfulness, impressed my darling husband, *so agreeably*.

　　With regards, to your family, I remain truly—

Mary Lincoln

To Alexander Williamson

———

Dec 31st [*1865*]

Mr Williamson

　　I write you a line, in haste [to] [7] say that Mr Wentworth, called last [even]ing—Lizzie—might just as well, have [sent the] skirt, she has—I want you to go [the hour] you receive this & tell her, I do not [want any c]ollars undersleeves—*without* she [herself has] made them—If she has made them [let her keep] them, until she sends the skirt, [by] private conveyance. What did you mean, by writing, in your last note "S. says he has $1500—in hand— Write me, who, you mean, by S. and the meaning, of the expression ["in hand"] I Write, in haste, for I am [very] much, indisposed.

Your friend

M. L.

To Francis E. Spinner

———

Chicago Jan 1, 1866

Dear Sir:

　　Thinking it was likely that you would attend to Mr Wentworth's request so soon as practicable, I wrote you in what form to send the money, as this last was my only reason for writing. I will trust to your friendship for not saying you have received a line from me on the subject. With assurances of high esteem, I remain, yours truly,

Mary Lincoln.

———

[7] A corner of the original letter is torn off.

To Alexander Williamson

Chicago—Jany 3d 66

My dear Sir:

Your note is received. Mr Galt is very kind to allow me, to return the articles—I will enumerate & the prices, on the bill. As a matter of course—they were never taken out of their cases— never worn—scarcely looked at & never shown to any one—so, if he will let me return them, at the price—I gave him, for them, I shall be much obliged & he will be acting, as he has always— towards me—as a true gentleman—As they have never been out, of their cases—I am sure—he will let me return them for the price he asked—

1	Ball breast pin & ear nobs	$25.00
1	gold card case—	100.00
1	Pear[l] & diamond ring—	440.00
1	pair band bracelets—	60.00
1	shawl pin ball & chain—	25.00
2	gilt clocks—$50—	100.00
1	set Onyx—Breast pin & earings—	60.00
1	pair white Onyx—& Diamond sleeve buttons	30.00
1	diamond & pearl bracelet—	550.00
1	d[itt]o do do —	550.00
1½	do[zen] Silver gilt coffee spoons	
	$40—per dozen—	60.00
1	pair Enameled sleeve buttons—	40.00
1	pair Enamelled Bracelets	50.00
2	shawl pins $3 each	6.00
~~1~~	~~Opal & diamond ring each $30.~~	
1½	dozen—nut picks & spoons—	56.00

In consideration of the great scarcity of means, if Mr Galt— will allow me to return these articles—at the price, they were pur- chased—it would confer, the greatest favor upon me—please, carry him, this paper, and see—if he will do so & write immediately, so that I may return, these articles, by Express & he can erase them

—from the bill—if he is *merciful* enough, to do so—return me—
this paper—With his approval—immediately & oblige your friend

Mrs A. L.

~~2 sets Ice cream sp.~~

Send me Hudson Taylor's bill—by return mail

To Sally Orne

Chicago Jan 4th 66

My Dear Mrs Orne:

I write you, a hurried line, this morning, enclosing, a very
few hairs, from my beloved husband's head. I regret, I have so
few to spare you, as I have only a bunch, as large as one of our
fingers. I was told before I left Washington, that quite a quantity
was cut off, to be reserved for me, was placed in the wardrobe, in
the guest room, at the W. H. As some officers were present at the
time, it was presumed, it was taken, from where it was placed. Your
appreciative heart will prize, even the few hairs, I send you. May
Heaven bless you, for *thus*, having reverenced my great and good
husband. I enclose you a scrap from this morning's paper.[8] The
country, is certainly "growing smaller by degrees, & beautifully
less." I almost wish, that the *necessities* of the case, did not require
me, to retain the small portion, so *ungraciously* bestowed upon me.
I have passed the last two mornings, my dear friend, at a warehouse a mile distant among the few goods we have, trying to as-
sort them & see what disposition, I can make of them. *For,* boarding
in such narrow quarters & so curtailed for means, I must dispose
of every thing, not necessary, to be retained. As I was leaving off
black, last March, I find myself, with several dress patterns on
hand. If I am not asking too great a favor, should I send them on
to you, to be placed in a store for disposal—would I be imposing,
too much, on your great goodness. The price of living here is fabulous, board is quite as high, as in Wash. and our last resort—a plain
yet genteel boarding, does not exempt, us, from charges, that I

[8] Not preserved.

shall have to exert myself, in the future, to meet. I will write no more to day, for I became so thoroughly chilled on yesterday that my limbs—ache with pain and I am sure, the terrible trials we are passing through—will only pain your gentle heart, by the recapitulation—

With much love, I remain always truly,
Mary Lincoln

To David Davis

Chicago Jany 5th 1866

My dear Sir:

Robert, informs me, that he has written to you, for $800—Be kind enough, to send the rest of the interest, which is due, in Wash —and please draw & send me, the interest now due—in S[pringfield] So that we may divide it—among us three, for our wants—We can place, any of the interest, we do not immediately need, in the Chicago—bank to draw when required. This month, I shall begin— and keep a faithful record, of all money, paid for dear little Taddie, from this time onwards—so that no mistake or trouble, may arise. I remain very respectfully,

Mary Lincoln

To Sally Orne

Chicago, Jany 10th [1866]

My Dear Mrs Orne—

You will think that *sickness*—as well as great sorrow, is my appointed lot—as this is the first hour, I have been up, since I last wrote you. *Congress*, yesterday voted $77,000. for the expenses— of the *current year*, at the W. H!—*We*, have not the means, to furnish the humblest cottage, if we had it—I see, that the *New York* Union league—through Gov [sic] Morgan request, the rest of the four years salary for us—It has been referred to the Committee of Means—*where* it will rest, without some of our friends—come to my aid. Will you favor me, by writing when you receive this, to *all* your Phil. Members—also to Mr *Stephens* [sic] of Penn. What have we done, that such cruel injustice & even cruelty, should be, thus exercised, towards us—Please request the Phil members to urge, upon Mr Stephens—the necessities of the case, that we are without a home—& are living most uncomfortably. Congress—appropriate $77,000 for W. H and the family, of the man, who sacrificed his life for his country—barely able to meet expenses, in a boarding house—A generous Nation, will certainly not permit this—The Committee *of Means*—meet the beginning of next week, to report, may I urge you, to write a line—so soon, as you receive this—I am not able, to write any more—I remain truly & aff

Mary Lincoln

To David Davis

Chicago Jany 11th 1866

Judge Davis

I enclose you an exact copy of Genl Spinner's—letter [9]—re-

[9] The letter was copied out in Mrs. Lincoln's hand. It read:
"My dear Madam—After I wrote you, the Comptroller came to the conclusion that the amount of Salary, that had accrued to Mr Lincoln, in the month of April, including the day of his death, and the tax on the whole amount paid or now to be paid, from that day back to the 3d of March last, must also be deducted from the $25,000—The tax part will be retained here, and the small draft, will be sent to the Hon Mr Davis—Administrator of the Estate—The matter then stands thus—

Paid to Judge Davis heretofore	$1981.67cts
To be paid to him now—	847.83
Income tax on the above—	145.16
Draft enclosed to you—	$22025.34
	$25000.00

Your tax as income on your receipt has not been with-held here, because it is not considered as a salary but as a donation, and will therefore be collected from you, by your Collector of Internal Revenue. If I can be of service to you please command me. Very respectfully yours F. E. Spinner Tr. U.S." The $847.83 was the balance of salary due the President at the time of his death and, as such, went into the estate rather than to Mrs. Lincoln.

ceived to day. Be pleased to write me, on what authority, he can deduct the half month of April—from the pay—Also—why $847.83 is paid to *you*—now—It is a pitiful offering at best & most ungraciously bestowed, yet there is no reason—why, *by degrees*, they wish to extract most of it from the original sum. Please explain this letter & oblige

Mrs L.

To Francis E. Spinner

Chicago Jan 11, 1866

Dear Sir:

Since you were so kind as to offer to correct the money coming to me in seven-thirties, I enclose you the draft endorsed to your order for that purpose. I will leave it to your discretion as to which of the issues to take at the present market price. The draft will purchase $22,000 listed bonds and leave some margin. Please send me a draft for the surplus. With kind thanks for your service I remain, very truly

Mary Lincoln.

To Sally Orne

Chicago—Jany 13th [*1866*]

My Dear Mrs Orne—

Your kind letter is received & I cannot express to you, how grateful I am, that you accede to my request, I will early, in the week send the articles—I regret to learn of the indisposition, of your little girl, I trust she will improve. Do you visit Wash- this winter?

I understand the "New York World," is visiting its spleen & spite, against the Government, by attacking poor *me!* [1] Broken down, as I am, with my agonizing sorrow, it might at least have spared me *this* cruelty. But coming from *such* a *source*, it is not to be regarded. Any article of furniture, I ever saw, at the W. H— in all humility be it spoken, I would not have given it houseroom— Only an appropriation for furniture & repairs, of $25,000—was ever made in my husband's administration—and I never had the power, to order a chair or the least article of furniture. As to the contents of my poor boxes—the editor of that noble article—would be welcome to all, of their contents—save my clothing—if he was a loyal man. The contents are very generally, composed of wax work— Country quilts—made by old women, who bowed the knee in reverence to the good & great man. Old rude chairs—made by veteran hands—These things coming from such patriotic persons—were more precious than gold to my darling husband—Our surroundings, if closely searched, would certainly bear no evidence—of acquisitions, not our own—to place myself & sons, in even an humble home, I design to part with every superfluous article—and will trouble you, little as I possibly can—in carrying, out my design. I write in haste—I shall never forget your great kindness & forbearance to me, in my great great sorrow—

ever your affectionate friend
Mary Lincoln

Genl Spinner—sent me, two days ago, a check for $22,025—deducting 6 weeks [salary] & interest [tax]—and writing that *I* must pay the income tax, on it—reducing it to *$20,000-* which will only enable us, to board, a little more comfortably. In consequence, you will agree, with me, that I must arouse myself—for a little action.

---

[1] On January 6, 1866, the *World* had covered the New Year's reception at the White House, writing: "No one could look about the house without being almost shocked at the downright shabbiness of the rooms and furniture. To be sure, more than one hundred thousand dollars have been 'appropriated' for furnishing and fixing the Executive Mansion within four years. But exactly *ninety* boxes were furnished by a certain official for packing up curtains, carpets, vases, pictures, and 'knickknacks' of all sorts that were carried away not many months ago. The thirty thousand dollars appropriated two weeks ago . . . will scarcely pay the outstanding local bills of the former occupants . . ."

To Alexander Williamson

Chicago—Jany 17 [1866]

Private

My dear Sir:

Certainly, it must be a joke of the season, that I should desire on [to] transport, from the W H any rubish in the way of furniture, I ever saw *there*—If it was *regal*—in its grandeur, I should be conscientiously indisposed to purloin, what did not belong to me—Such effrontery is amusing, yet no one ever left there, without encountering such a villanous charge—even my great sorrow—did not spare poor *me*. The *same charge*—I have heard time & again, against Buck—& Miss Lane [2]—in every case—none of us, would have given —such miserable broken furniture houseroom. As I never had the liberty, of ordering a chair—so, I cannot plead guilty, to handling any of the pitiful $25,000 only give[n], for our four years—Do caution Mrs Williamson—not to mention any business matters—it was unnecessary for you to mention, to any one about them—pray, say no more to any one—I *have little* or *no faith* in *Bentley*—he can talk very well, *that* is all. I hope he will settle the Wash accounts— and *keep* still—you remember, I have Shuster's accounts—a little over $400 by next mail—please send the list as you have it—of all—I want Hudson T- item bill—send me the list, adding Shuster's & oblige truly—

M L

Do not breathe my affairs, to no one

[2] President James Buchanan and his niece and hostess, Harriet Lane, had preceded the Lincolns as White House occupants.

To Oliver S. Halsted, Jr.

Chicago Jany 17 [1866]
evening

My dear Sir:

I write you a line in great haste, to say, that I have just received a telegram from Mr Godfrey—saying Mr Bentley, *refused* to settle the business—What *do* they mean, by keeping the money. I hope they will spare us any *newspaper* notices—half the country, believe *these men*, have secured us a fortune & I positively *believe &* *know*, they have done us more harm than good. If I had done—as I will do in the morning, *two* months since, I believe we would *now* have a home—B[entley] and S[tackpole?]—all prattled about the *fur* business in Wash until it injured the cause. Do not let *Bentley* or S. into any of your plans—as I trust you have some—but it is *now* or *never* with us—That old Comm French at Wash—I believe—to pocket $77,000—started the *box* business story & deprived us of a home. There is no *greater scamp*, in the country, than *that* man. I hope you are securing something for us—in N.Y I fear the Union league—can get nothing out of those ungrateful people in W—Do advise me of *what* success, you have—Please go to Godfrey—*Saturday* morning & say—that Thursday morning (tomorrow)—his draft wil be sent—which I wish him to acknowledge imm—truly

M L

To Alexander Williamson

Chicago—Jany 19th [1866]

My dear Sir:

I rise from a bed of sickness, to reply to your letter—Please go to Hudson T. the *hour* you receive this letter—Tell them on the 9th day of Feb- *my* word for it, their bill, shall be settled *Prevent* Hudson T- or [his assistant] Mr French, going to, those *time servers—Judge D- Harlan* or *Speed—they* are too *contemptible* to speak of—*Ease* Hudson-T- until *9th* of Feb positively—Write to *Andrews—*about it *he* will help you out, with *them all—Bentley* you *see, promises well.* Go to Hudson T- without fail, when you read *this* Tell *them*—the promise will be *kept*—watch for Andrews—at Wash—*he* will have *this* money raised for you—Write to him & *urge* him—I have never had the items of Hudson T's bill *Mr* French, *is* a gentleman and will give it to you—Ease Hudson T *until* 9th Feb. *Andrews* will help us—

Please see to all this—immediately & oblige—

To Oliver S. Halsted, Jr.

Chicago Jany 21st [1866]

My dear Mr Halsted—

Your letter, was written on Friday, Jany 12th and on Thursday Jany 18th I sent the check [3]—for the money—The time—the *ten* days, will extend to Monday 22d—but from a letter, received this morning, which I enclose you, I fear—he Godfrey will be disposed to deceive me—Yesterday or this morning—at farthest, he *must* have received the check—In my great distress, do not allow this *cruel* imposition to be practised upon me—It would break me up entirely & it would be an unlawful act—Go—the moment, you receive this to Godfrey—and have it all right—send me the receipt —If he is disposed to *play false*, do not allow it—you can manage it. You know, my narrow means & will not allow me to be wrongly treated in this—Go, the hour you receive this to Godfrey & telegraph me. In great haste & trouble

truly & gratefully
M L

Please, do not mention, all this, to any one.

[3] This statement, together with the frantic tone of the entire letter, would seem to indicate that Mrs. Lincoln did make an effort to pay her debts herself.

To Alexander Williamson

Chicago Jany 26th [1866]

My dear Sir:

Your last note was received on yesterday. I had seen the "Herald" article before, when I was in the W. H.—I felt it was a degradation to have to submit to such abominable furniture && if it had been my own, even occupying, the humblest cabin, would not have given it room—that villanous & criminal falsehood—was gotten up, by the *party*—who wished to have *all* the spoils to themselves,[4]—and in consequence was rewarded, in *truly American* style, by *quite* a $100,000- to fit up the *W. H. We*, will see, how, much of it will be used for *that purpose—His Yankee* pockets, are capacious, perhaps his love for gain, will be discovered ere long. I am receiving letters, *now*, constantly, on *this* subject, and it *is* being traced, to the smooth faced, Com[missioner]—all, those barbarous stories, of W. H. depredations. The New York World," did not *lose*, I imagine, by its correspondence. *He* was kicked out of *that place* in Pierce's time—and if Johnson, knows what he is about, he will not have *him* long remain, where he is—Every one, understanding, the miserable state of W. H. furniture && knowing, from whence, those villanous falsehood's emanated, & better still, *appreciating* me & knowing, that I desire *only*, what is my own—this week, I have received letters, from most of my distinguished friends, of course *not* alluding, to such low stuff, as French & his surroundings are. *He* is very obsequious, to the *new* powers—and a *blunderer, I* always found him at receptions—*He*, has secured $75,000—which should have been mine—and deprived me of a home, yet *such* a *villain*, does not always prosper—In consequence of his *recent* success—he can afford—to place himself, pompously, in Newspapers! Eh bien! "let him laugh who wins"—*This* communication is confidential—but keep your *eyes* open, to the *house* & proceedings generally. All, you write me, is as safe, as if never written. *Old Newton*, is another old scamp. And both, have worked,

---

[4] A reference to Benjamin Brown French, Commissioner of Public Buildings.

against me. Be quiet, about all *this*, & you can soon judge for yourself. How heartless & hollow, I have found, all those who were so much indebted to us! If I had not this great overwhelming sorrow upon me, and knowing what I now do, I should have no desire, to return to a world so entirely selfish, and who would prefer to attack an innocent & helpless woman, in her deep affliction, than a strong man, who could soon, *quiet* the assailant. Dear little Taddie, goes to school, & does not miss an hour—He is already, very much beloved in C. his teacher speaks of him in the highest & most affectionate term[s]. *One* of the Bucktails, resides here, and T. takes great comfort, in visiting him. He is married & keeps house.

Watch for Mr Andrews at the Hotels, and write him at 47 Wall St. N.Y. I wish all my business settled, early in Feb.—no matter how poor I am left. *Quiet*, the *Wash* creditors until then— *After that*, never a cent will I owe. Andrews—is influential, & quietly can see me through all—I see that *Hanscom*—another of the low & sycophantic *time servers*, is writing the Johnsons *Patterson's* [5] && up! What a world this is! Write me longer and more especially —show my letters to no one & be quiet about contents, I pray you.

Yr friend

M L

To Alexander Williamson

Chicago—Jany 27th [*1866*]

My dear Sir:

Your note, is just received. *The day*, you receive *this* letter, please go around, to *each*, *person*, whom I am owing, and say, that positively, on the *11th* day, of February, I will pay each their demands—Mention, *this date*, to *Shuster H. Taylor* & *all*—Does Andrews reply to your letters? You telegraph *free*, why not send *him*—a telegram, *when* you receive this, 47 Wall St—never mention *my* name, in it—The exact sum, of the indebtedness is $6,189.40

---

[5] Martha Patterson was Andrew Johnson's daughter and hostess. Her husband, David Patterson, was at this time running, successfully, for a seat in the U.S. Senate.

cts [6]—let Andrews know this. Send *me often* a telegram & as you communicate free, in this way—send to Andrews—B[entley] can do nothing, I fear—Do not let A- *escape* you, at the Hotel—he could help me, through this business, if he choose—*He*, wrote two months ago & made many fair professions—Tell *him*, I will be *published*, if I do not settle this sum, by *11th* of Feb. Which is true—Telegraph me, when you receive this—I pray you, say nothing, of this business, to any one—Once free from *these incumbrances*—I shall always remain so—Tell—Mr French, at Hudson T's—I think he might keep his word & send me the remaining volumes *free*, of Dickens, as he promised—*If* they are not, bound exactly like the others— it does not matter so much—that is, if he *keeps his* word—and throws them in. You see, I have *very few days* to go upon—so please, be untiring with A's—telegraph often, both of us—& write

Your friend
M.L.

Go round, with[out] delay, to *each one*, of the party—The *11th* without fail—

To Alexander Williamson

Chicago Feb 2nd [1866]

My dear Sir:

Last Feb. Stackpole seeing me pressed about some money matters—borrowed me $2,000 from Fahnstock [sic] [7]—privately—

[6] This amount, owed to a group of Washington merchants, was considerably less than the total amount of Mrs. Lincoln's indebtedness at the time of her husband's death. A $2,000 loan from Jay Cooke's bank was still outstanding (see letter to Williamson, February 2, 1866); the jewelry bill at Galt had not yet been settled; many other, lesser obligations had been paid or settled (the mysterious "fur business") by the time this letter was written, and others would be so within the next year. Because of Mrs. Lincoln's confusion and frequent lack of candor in money matters, it is impossible to determine the precise amount of her indebtedness from those of her letters which exist.

[7] Harris C. Fahnestock headed the Washington branch of Jay Cooke's bank (with Cooke's brother Henry), playing an important role in financing the Union war effort. By the time he went to New York in March of 1866 to head Cooke's New York operations, he had already made his reputation as one of the most astute financiers in the country.

as through me he gained many favors, from my good husband. On hearing my express anxiety, about the inability to pay Mr Fahnstock—of his own will—he wrote me—this agreement which I send you. Before I left I said to Stackpole, "Remember the loan from Fahnstock—*He* said do not feel uneasy about that, it will never come back to you. Last summer—Judge Davis, spoke of Stackpole's name, being on my husbands—account book, for almost $400—borrowed 3 years & ½ since—the interest of course *now* would bring it [to] $500, now—I said to Judge D- "Never mind, that now." waiting to see, what S- would do—I write *all this* to you, *most sacredly* & *confidentially*—Breathe not a word—save to S. Please go & see him, within the hour, after receiving, this note & papers —Never allow him, to approach—*within a yard*—of this written promise of his—do not let him lay a finger on it—if he is so unforgetful of his written word—I am not—He certainly will keep his word & pay it—if he does not, he must assist & give written pledges to Fahnstock—as he is owing us—at least $500—now—Stackpole will not be so ungenerous—pressed down, as I am, on all sides—If you can telegraph *free*, do so, the moment—you see S- do write also—I am sure—having this paper, in my possession S's natural good heart, will prompt him to do right. If he settles it, as his *written* promise binds him, to do—I will release him, from the money, due the estate—Tell him this—Please hand this *separate* line to Fahnstock—and say nothing to the *latter*, about *the* S- business—until you see & converse, with S——and until I *write* you, to do so—Let these two papers—pass into no one's hands—for an instant, retain them—*very* safely, until you hear from me *again*—S- gained many favors through me & made much & must like an honest man, keep his word.

Mention this subject to no one but telegraph & write—see S- without delay—no time, is to be lost—

Say nothing to Fahnstock if you please of *this* or any *one else* —save S——do not part, with *these* papers—for your life.

To Alexander Williamson

Chicago. Feb 5th 66

My dear Sir:

Your last note was received. Mr Bentley & Mr Halsted, write me, they will be in Washington on *10th* next Saturday. B. writes, he has engaged rooms for *that* date. Please, do not wait to be notified by them—but call for yourself, at Willard's. Do not labor, under the impression, for an instant—that B- or any one else, is settling, they are only acting, as agents—by means of borrowing & with great difficulty, I will be enabled to raise the $6,000- which settles my indebtedness, in Wash- or any where else [8]—*Thank Heaven!* although raising the means—to make these settlements will leave me in very moderate & quite reduced circumstances—I shall forever remain free from the thraldom of debt, after this—*if I am numbered with the poverty stricken. This*, is a grateful return for the services, my noble husband, rendered his country *His family*, left in *genteel poverty—As to Mr Andrews*—three weeks ago—he wrote me a flattering letter, as to what would be done for me, since then, no answer, can I get from any of my letters—does he reply to yours?—you say nothing, about him, in your letters—*If you hear* from him or *see* him, I should think, you would write. When, you see, Andrews, tell *him*, I had expected his assistance, in my business —and tell him; that I had to borrow the money, to pay Wash claims —and if through any quarter, he can assist me in redeeming it, I shall be glad. Explain to Bentley & Halsted—the Stackpole matter, & let them see F[ahnestock] also—much, was done for S- in my husband's administration & he realized much money, from my own good nature to S- as well as my husband's—S- *must*, have *forgotten* —the promissory note or he would not have allowed F. to send it to me—I will enclose all the bills—tomorrow—the outside envelope directed to you—Please hand to B or H- on Saturday next—the bills. The money, I will send to Genl Spinner—Bentley can draw it from him—I trust Galt will allow me, to return some articles & cut down

---

[8] See letter to Williamson of January 27, [1866], *note*.

bill—I shall have to part, with much that I have of personal effects—
to redeem, this money borrowed—Please, be quiet, about my affairs
& do not allow the cred- to think, any one but myself settles these
bills—for it will be untrue—*See* the *cred* after the payment is over
& make it straight, as regards, *that*—Have B- and H- see Stackpole
—I wish you would write more lengthily about matters

yr friends [sic]

Write almost every day when B- & H- are in Wash—

To Alexander Williamson

Chicago—Feb. 9th [1866] [9]

My dear Sir:

I very much fear, from a note received on yesterday from Mr
B[entley]—that he may not go to Wash watch for him & H[alsted]
either of them, can settle the claim—You surprise me, by *still*
dwelling upon it, that either of these parties—will add a cent to it.
Mr Andrews—has made me such fair promises, that all I desired
was, that he would assist me, in redeeming the loan from the bank
—He does not *now* reply, to my letters—*he*, is like all the rest of the
world, a friend in sunshine. If neither B or H- are in Wash—next
Monday—you must telegraph me (free) if they are not there—
please go round to the parties & tell them the money is in W- and
you are waiting to hear from me—in your disappointment at the
non appearance of *the two persons*—I trust however—we will not
have to submit—to such a trouble. On Monday, show Fahnstock—
S[tackpole's] written promissory note—Do have *that*—all made
right for me—for I am utterly reduced in consequence of payments
&& Tell Mr Bentley—if you see him—that [A. T.] Stewart never
wrote or loaned me a cent—*Be sure & do this*—also say to Andrews
& Bentley—that I had to borrow from bank in what I have settled—
Say also to B—— that I did not mean Mr Halsted—*at all*, when I

[9] On February 10, 1866, the day after this letter was written, Congress voted
Mrs. Lincoln the traditional franking—free mailing—privilege of ex-Presidents
and presidential widows.

spoke of "summer friends"——telegraph me Monday—Tuesday & write me particulars.

Yr friend
M L

read & seal S's note before delivering it.

To Alexander Williamson

Feb 17th 66

My dear Sir:

I am greatly indisposed, but will sit up, long enough to write, you a few lines. I have not yet received a line from Bentley,[1] he has not sent me either—a receipted bill yet. *He* is a very *strange* man. You say, you gave the promissory note, to B- I greatly fear, *he never* showed it, to Fahnstock. *The note* will certainly exempt me from the payment—Consult with F- and do not let—Stackpole succeed over us—*He*, S, is owing the estate, *now*, $500—and must settle it immediately or be sued—If *he*, S, settles with F-, without further trouble, *he* will be excused from the debt. *Tell S- this.* I sent $5,500 —to Spinner—wanting *seven hundred*, of sufficient, for entire payment, I now greatly regret, I did not send a check—to each party— instead of placing it in *B's* hands—it *may* be, *weeks*, before the bills are returned to me receipted or I shall know, to what parties—the *seven hundred*, is due—Bentley, is really "fuss & feathers"—and appears *never* to complete any thing. I have exhausted myself & means, in these payments,—and I cannot express to you—how reduced I am in means—I could not rent, the smallest cottage—and in the future know not, how I shall possibly get along—*Old* French has "feathered his nest," at my expense—$83,500—besides $30,000 more. If *ten thousand*, goes into the *W. H.* it is more than I believe. *He*, is a *smooth* faced, *avaricious* villain and he got up his story of losses—for his own peculiar benefit—*You* can aid me *now* & help

---

[1] Williamson had telegraphed to Mrs. Lincoln on February 15, 1866: "Received your telegram. Mr. Bentley started for New York yesterday evening. He worked hard to square your Affairs but without any success. He wrote you fully yesterday evening." MS. owned by King V. Hostick, Springfield, Illinois.

yourself a little, at same time. Keep sacredly secret about it, but *work—from this hour*. See & converse with *Hooper, Ally* [sic] of *Mass—Morgan* of *Sen*, Stewart & Nye of Sen—*Lane* of *Kansas Sprague* [2] & others—get up a little article headed, to secure a home for Mrs L- go—to these men & *others*—& have them subscribe to it —every thousand contributed, you shall [get] $35—of each thousand —represent to them—in what a *homeless* state you are informed, by reliable parties—who are well informed as to the manner, we are compelled to live—Carry your paper & they will sign it. Do not go near Wentworth—Washburn [sic]—Raymond [3]—[Henry] Wilson or Fessenden—you can think of suitable persons—never breathe you hear from *me* or that I write to you—that would ruin all. You can say, out of my own means—I have settled the estate, & am left, really impoverished—Say, Chicago residents tell you this—that we are compelled to board—in the plainest manner. By getting up a *heading* and presenting it to suitable parties & urging them to sign it,—you will advance my cause & your own, at same time. There will be "no fail," if you try it—Consider this communication, as sacred as possible, breathe it not even to your wife. Bentley—has always done us more harm than good, if it had not been for that silly "dollar Con" [4] *we* would now have a handsome home. See 3 or 4 parties each day & place *the writing* before them to sign their names. You will see how successful you will be—Telegraph each day—Have the F[ahnestock] business settled to S[tackpole's] account—Never say to any person, with whom you converse, that you hear from me—Represent to *them all*, the disgrace it is—we are compelled to live as we are doing—work upon their feelings & have them sign—their names.

Private—Your reward will be sure. Take *no one* into *your* confidence—*any name* you get, *telegraph* [5]—In the event of *success*—

[2] The men listed by Mrs. Lincoln were as follows: Representatives Samuel Hooper and John B. Alley of Massachusetts; Senators Edwin Morgan of New York, Andrew Stewart of Pennsylvania, James W. Nye of Nevada, James H. Lane of Kansas, and William Sprague of Rhode Island, all Republicans.

[3] Henry J. Raymond, editor of *The New York Times*, elected to Congress from New York in 1865.

[4] A reference to the "dollar fund" for Mrs. Lincoln's assistance organized by Bentley, B. B. Sherman, and other substantial citizens in New York.

[5] Williamson telegraphed on this date: "Received telegram. Seen Fahnstock [sic], but says he will have nothing to do with Stackpole's note. Is in no hurry

you, yourself—will be much benefitted. I write in haste, for I am positively quite ill—Yr friend

To Alexander Williamson

Chicago Feb 20th [1866]

My dear Sir:

I have seated myself to day, to write you a letter of an entirely confidential character, which if you follow my wishes in—to the *very letter*, will result in successful benefit to *you* as well as myself. Never allow a word, that this letter contains, during *your life* to escape *you*. I believe I can rely on you. If something does not come to me *now*, for a *home*, I shall *forever*, be without one, a wanderer on the face of the earth. "Nothing venture, *nothing* have."—My proposition is this—and on each $1,000—raised from the parties I wish you to address—I will give you $50 I *never* fail in a promise —and I want to see *your* condition bettered as well as my own and *God* knows, we both require it, even to live comfortably. I want you, the hour you receive this note, to write to Hon Larz Anderson of Cincinnati [6] & Hon Sam Galloway of Ohio [7]—men of great wealth & nobleness of character and very intimate friends of my husband, who if *they* thought, *his* family required aid, would freely bestow it. It is my last resort, but I sincerely believe, it will be the most successful application, we yet have made. I enclose you an exact copy of a note,[8] for you to write to Larz Anderson—Galloway & C. Bullitt [9] of New Orleans—If you do as I wish—I am sure, you will find yourself better off, *this spring* than you have been for a long

for payment, will do eight months hence & charge no Interest. I will not do any further business with Stackpole for you. Bentley has his promise to pay. I'll write you this evening." (MS. owned by Herman Blum, Philadelphia, Pennsylvania.)

[6] Identified on p. 169.

[7] Samuel Galloway, prominent lawyer of Columbus, Ohio, was one of Lincoln's good friends and earliest supporters for the presidency.

[8] Not preserved.

[9] Cuthbert Bullitt, named by Lincoln in January 1865 as U.S. Marshal for the Eastern District of Louisiana, had in 1864 been appointed Acting Collector of the Port of New Orleans under the military government of Louisiana. John Hay commented at the time that Bullitt had Louisiana "in his trousers pocket."

time. I propose for you to address them letters—from Wash- *not written*, as if you were in *any* department or on *Treasury* letter paper—neither franked by French—and signed by another name than yours—say Charles Forsyth—I give you an earnest letter to copy, speak of yourself, as a warm friend of the family & mortified by result of Congress—and appeal to their kind feelings, in my behalf. *Each* of the parties, I request you to address, know me *very well*, warm friends of the family and will not refuse. Of course, if they do, any thing, they will send to me, but as a woman of honor, I will faithfully enclose any communication, I receive from them and the $50- on each thousand, shall be religiously yours—Bullitt —has the finest office in the Govt almost at New Orleans—the Andersons—Larz A is a grandson of [Nicholas] Longworth of Cin —and they count their money, by millions. We must try for the sake of humanity never breathe a word of this, to living mortal—We will soon see the result—When you write & start the letters, telegrap[h] me—perhaps—we can *outwit, old French* yet. The letter, I send you—you can take 3 copies—word for word—one to Hon Larz Anderson—Cin- one to Hon Samuel Galloway—Columbus O the 3rd to Hon Cuthbert Bullitt New Orleans La- in Bullitt's letter & Galloway's you of course will *omit*—the allusion to Mr Fogg [1]— also in Bullitt's letter (put *10 of March* house for sale—instead of *4 March*—to the Ohio gentleman) do not sign your own name—but please write, as I have directed *change* your hand a little, if you can.

yr friend

This action will benefit both of us—if you do as I wish. burn this letter.

To Alexander Williamson

Feb 20th [1866]

Mr Williamson

Please do not fail, to write the letters *word for word*—as I send you copy also, you might throw in a sentence in alluding to the

---

[1] Probably George G. Fogg, a New Hampshire lawyer who had served as minister to Switzerland from 1861–5.

Congressional action saying, "that no man had ever done so much for his country & from knowledge gained from those, who knew the circumstances, you were informed that the family were compelled to board in the plainest way and articles of clothing had to be sold to make boarding expenses (which in Chicago are very great easier—Also in settlement of debts—Mrs L. had disposed of greater part of her jewellry—many gifts from dear friends—" Pray do not fail to insert this sen[ten]ce & *urge* Anderson to show letter to Fogg & send to Clifton House, any means that can be spared—Write to Galloway also *all the three for 4th March*—Bullit [sic] for *10 of March*—do not fail to write the sentence about not having seen lady for months—On reflection—*write yourself* signed *Charles Forsyth*—the first line I receive *from any* of the parties I will send you—In the case of *these four men* remember—to every thousand, they send $50- for you—in your Wash applications $35- for *each* [$1,000]—Please see Blow Mem C—also McNeil [sic] & Myers [sic] Phil— [2] & get *him*—to add their names—never say you hear from me—telegraph me the hour—you send the letters—*Write them yourself*—communicate not to wife—daughter *no one*

You will find if you write each word, to *them* as I send—*fail*—is *not* the word—I understand the *tone* of the people you are writing to—

Change your hand, as much as possible Insert the sentence, I give you in this—& do not fail to write telegraph me

To Alexander Williamson

Chicago—Feb. 27th [1866]

My dear Sir:

Your letter is received. We might as well call S[tackpole] the "invisible *gentleman*," the *law can* reach *him*—to pay the money, due the estate & *it will*—I advise you not to go near Bentley in N.Y. he has *no energy*—means well enough & *above all*—listen to me—if

[2] Republican representatives Henry T. Blow of Missouri, Leonard Meyers and Charles O'Neill of Pennsylvania. (O'Neill, whom Mrs. Lincoln mistakenly referred to as "McNeil," was the brother of her close friend Mrs. James H. Orne.)

you should see him—do not tell him your business—Have Col Hardie—or some gentleman write a note certifying to their acquaintance with you, as an honorable gentleman but *do not* I beg you, let the one who writes such a note, know to what use, you are going to [page missing] the check to me—*Take note of each check* & in each you will find your reward—Stop in Phil—go to Union League there—Christian association—James Orne—Chesnut [sic] St Phil and be sharp & find out names—of rich merchants on Ches St get them—to give the check to my credit—as of course, your being a stranger, they would never do [to yours]—Go to New York —see Wm B. Astor—*Lord & Taylor Bull & Black* A. T. *Stewart—Tiffenay* [sic]—Cornelius Vanderbuilt [sic] *Moses Taylor Moses Grinnel* [sic] [Simeon] *Draper*[3]—*give Andrews* a regular blowing up—but for heavens sake—do not tell *him* your business in N.Y.- go to *Moses F. Odell*[4]—your sagacity when in *NY* can make you find out—all the rich men—besides—"let not your right hand know what the left doeth"—in other words, do not say to any party [page missing]

I write you in haste, write from Phil—New York be *very very* prudent—say you have not seen me for months, but you & others are anxious we should have a home—

very truly
M. L.

Tell *no one this business—I beg you.*

To David Davis

Chicago March 7 [1866]

My dear sir:

Presuming you will be leaving Washington, before long, I have concluded to request you, as soon as possible, if not troubling

---

[3] This listing included merchants with whom Mrs. Lincoln had at one time dealt heavily; in addition, Taylor and Grinnell, both wealthy New York politicians, had been members of the committee which raised $100,000 to pay off the mortgage on U. S. Grant's Washington home. Stewart, Taylor, Astor, Vanderbilt, and others of their ilk were contributing unprecedented amounts of money to the Republican party.
[4] A wealthy former congressman from Brooklyn.

you too much, to send the bill, which Stackpole, owes the estate—to him for collection. R[obert] thinks, it was about *$360*. You will know, the interest on it now, I should think would amount to near $500. *He, may* leave *W*, so it is best, to secure the debt in time. R. wrote you a few days since, with my receipted acknowledgments, of the money received from you. *He,* is quite solicitous to receive your reply & be advised by you, about what he has written.

This has been a most severe winter to me, bodily and mentally, if it were not, for the terrible anniversary, we are now approaching, my anguished heart, would almost welcome Spring. In the desolation that surrounds us, as a deeply bereaved family, the returning seasons, can bring little comfort *to us*. With kind regards, to Mrs Davis, I remain very truly & resp—

Mary Lincoln

To Alexander Williamson

March 12th [*1866*]

My dear Sir—

Your note also Mr [M. O.] Roberts', is just received. Mr R- is one of the best of men, yet, he mistakes—just now the country feeling the painful contrast, between the two Presidents and the terrible anniversary—almost upon us, will cause many a man, to put his hand, in his pocket—I advised you, that every move must be kept entirely private—each man you approach, must not know, you have been near another—Only, lest *not* knowing you they suspect you wrongly—have them in your presence make out a check—& see *they* send it—I wrote you on yesterday, full particulars—Let *Phil-* be the field of your operations—Use—the list I give you & many others—you will ascertain—let it be a *very private* matter— Stop—an hour or two in *Baltimore* to see [B & O] Pres Garret[t]— *casually,* show my note—I sent you—regarding you visiting C- & Taddie do not go on Saturday—leave *next* ~~Sunday~~ eve Monday morn—March 19th telegraph me if you conclude to go—so I can send you money

Not a line, from Ohio people or N[ew O[rleans]   This shows you—if action is not immediately taken—*time*, will not improve it —Let not your wife or *any one* know your business—Your reward is sure—if you succeed—Telegraph me your decision & abide by it —*Delay*, will be entire loss—Genl Spinner—sent me receipts—on the bills am yet owing almost $800- I am feeling very poor, as you may be sure—There is a very rich Mr Harrison in Phil- [5] *see him*— an elderly gentleman & living in great style—I have studied this subject well & know, if you try quietly & *assiduously*, you will succeed—Telegraph me, the hour you receive this—

Your friend M. L.

do not go farther than Phil- See May & Co- in Wash- Tell them, as others in W- did not ask interest, I *am sure*, *they* will not Tell them, I have paid out all I have (Between ourselves) *their* suggesting it —is *very contemptible* return answer of May & Co- Find out, many rich parties in *Phil*- without giving reasons to any one *when* in Phil

See John R. Gittings [sic] [6] in Bal- incidentally show note to Garrett & *himself*

To Alexander Williamson

March 13th [1866]

My dear Sir:

Even, with such a good man, as Mr Roberts—"there are wheels, within wheels," the explanation, of his timidity is this—In Feb. about six weeks, since *his* lawyer wrote me, urging me to sign my name, to an article he wrote—Mr Roberts *has been* & *still is* anxious—for the Custom House of N.Y. and *Mrs* R a great friend of mine & a very lovely [lady] wrote me, recently that a high govt Officer, had brought it up *against* Mr R. that *he*, R- had presented

---

[5] Joseph Harrison, Jr., who made his fortune in railroad-building in Russia, lived in splendor on Rittenhouse Square.
[6] John S. Gittings, a Baltimore financier and a director of the Baltimore & Ohio Railroad.

me $10,000- in fulfilment of a promise, made my husband & myself
—in return for the Govt using his vessels—during the war. This
vile story is like all the rest, too contemptible to notice. I think that
wicked Seward, invented it. I beg you not to mention this to any one

Strangely enough, he never asked a favor of my good husband
—yet is the only person almost—who feels, the neglect we have
received at the hands of a people, who owe my husband so much—
Those who are indebted to *Him*, for their all, are the most prominent
persons, opposed, to our having a home—As Mr R. *still desires*, the
place, I mention—he is necessarily timid, about his name, given as
another donation—To each person you apply, say it will never
escape your lips—their gift will be kept secret with you—I do not
trouble myself, about their villanous stories. I expect—Mr Galts bill
could disclose where all my spoons came from—At the W. H. we
had enough only, of small sized spoons, for about half a dozen persons, and had to borrow, when we had company—so I purchased
from Galt rather than ask old French & have paid for them myself
—Mark me now—I have a great mind to get Galt, to make out a
separate bill for spoons—a receipted bill—will be a shield from their
vile attacks which do not trouble me very much, having a good
conscience—You will find you will not lose much by going to Phil-
as I propose next week—

Stop in Baltimore to see the parties

To David Davis

Chicago—March 14th, [1866]

My dear Sir:

Your note is just received. Robert & myself have concluded,
that it will be unnecessary to *sue* Stackpole on the note, if you have
not written to him, you need not do so. If *you* have & if he is willing
to pay it well & good. *He*, will doubtless, not be very solicitous, on
the subject & most likely, it will go, as a bad debt Stackpole, had
been kind & thoughtful towards us, as a family, in our deep trouble,
at the W. H.—was the occasion of my exonerating him, from the

debt,—as no reliance probably, could be placed upon him, as to the payment, in *the absence* of the note—*rather* than *sue* him, of a necessity, we will have to abandon it without he should come forward & pay it, which is not *likely*—

M. L.

We are quite well & with kind regards to Mrs Davis, remain truly

To Sally Orne

Chicago   March 15 [1866]

Private

My dear Mrs Orne:

I neglected to request you to send the pamphlet, you spoke of, if you have a spare copy—My own intense misery, has been augmented by the *same thought*—that, *that* miserable inebriate Johnson, had cognizance of my husband's death—*Why*, was *that card* of Booth's, found in his box, [7] some acquaintance certainly existed— I have been deeply impressed, with the harrowing thought, that *he*, had an understanding with the conspirators & *they*, knew *their man*. Did not Booth, say, "There is one thing, he would not tell." There is said, to be honor, among thieves. No one ever heard, of Johnson, regretting my sainted husband's death, he never wrote me a line of condolence, and behaved in the most brutal way. Why, is not [Jefferson] *Davis*, brought to trial? As sure, as you & I live, Johnson, had some hand, in all this—if he does not receive his condemnation here (and I think, he is receiving it, if there is a place of reward & punishments—as there surely is—his fate, will be to suffer—he is *too* hardened to feel, in this world—I will trouble you no more to day or perhaps, for some time—I remain with assurances of regard,

Your friend
Mary Lincoln

[7] On the day of Lincoln's assassination, Booth had called at the Kirkwood House hotel, residence of the Vice-President (whom he had met once) and of his secretary William Browning. Booth had asked to see either Johnson or Browning, but since both were out, left in Browning's box a calling card bearing his name and

Another most important *item* in this *case*—why did Preston King, commit suicide [8]—I knew him well & naturally, a more cheerful man, never lived did this lady, cite his case a bosom friend of Johnson—having knowledge of this transaction, naturally good hearted—he could not live . . . Talk of insanity—*it was not so*

To Alexander Williamson

Chicago—March 25th [1866]

My dear Sir:

Your telegram was received to day. I regret to learn, of your indisposition and hope you will soon recover—Do not give a thought to the business, I proposed to you—your best efforts, would have doubtless been unavailing—and I must submit, to my fate—I have not received a line, from any of the parties you or I wrote to —& presume, it is, only an index—to *all the rest*—Please see Mr [Edward A.] Rollins—Com[missioner of Internal Revenue] relative to tax—on the *generous Con*[gressional] donation—and my smaller given sum—ask him, as *gifts* & placed in *seven thirties*—if they are *not* exempt—I write in great haste, remaining truly your friend

M- L

To Mary Ann Foote [9]

Chicago March 27 [1866]

My dear Mrs Foot [sic]

The painful announcement, of the severe illness, of your noble and distinguished husband, has so troubled me, that I cannot re-

the message, "Don't wish to disturb you. Are you at home?" Browning later decided the card was meant for Johnson, planted deliberately in order to embarrass him, which it did.

[8] In November 1865, while serving as collector of customs at New York, Johnson's close friend and supporter Preston King died by walking off the Hoboken ferry with a bag of shot tied around his waist. He had had a history of mental instability.

[9] Wife of the venerable Senator Solomon Foote of Vermont. Foote died shortly after this letter was written.

frain from writing you a few lines, expressive of my deep sympathy for you, in this your hour of deep trial, I pray that our Heavenly Father, may be merciful to you, and restore, the Senator to health & spare you, the cup of affliction, which I have been called upon so freely to receive. I have passed through *such* a baptism of sorrow, as but few have known, and my heart, can most readily enter into your anxious feelings, over the illness, of one so dear to you and to all the country. In my hours of deep affliction, I often think it would have been *some* solace to me and *perhaps* have lessened the grief, which is now breaking my heart—if my idolized had passed away, after an illness, and I had been permitted to watch over him and tend him to the last. No such assuaging thought, comes to my relief and only the knowledge, that no sign of recognition from my dearly beloved husband or a loving parting word or farewell, no such thoughts come to soothe *this* distracted brain.

The prayers, of a suffering woman are yours, that the life of your good husband, may be spared, yet if the Divine will, orders differently, I trust you may be prepared to bow in submission to so terrible a decree. With apologies, for troubling you, with so lengthy a note—when your time and thoughts are so sadly & anxiously occupied. I remain

truly & affectionately
Mary Lincoln

To Alexander Williamson

Chicago—March 29th [1866]

My dear Sir:

I regret to learn, that you have been very sick, I trust by this time, you have recovered. I enclose you a portion of your wife's letter, which startled me—*Stop*, all *such* proceedings—as it would bring a notoriety, from which, I beg to be excused—Did you see Mr Roberts or any one in N.Y.? Every plan has failed—so we will consider *this* business, entirely at an end—I pray you caution your wife, who appears to be conversant—with the matter, never to breathe a word, about what you have communicated to her—No

good, I see can come, of any further efforts—If you had succeeded—
I should have rewarded you, as promised—Pray stop—*this English
business*—and all other—*save Roberts*—if you can do any thing,
quietly there—I write in great haste—*no need either*, of consulting
Rollins—the Commissioner—I am poor enough, but if they see fit,
to unjustly tax & rob me—so be it. Say to Mrs W- when I am able to
get into my [boxes of] clothing, I will send herself & daughter some
remembrance—This is a miserable season of the year—to me—and
I have very little thought, to the cares—that have pressed so heavily
upon me—all is submerged, in my great & terrible loss—All are
well—

Truly your friend M L

To Charles Sumner [1]

Chicago April 2d 66

My dear Sir:

I am reminded, whilst reading this simple and natural poem,
"Snowbound," that its author, "Whittier," is a resident of your
State and doubtless, a personal friend of yours, and presuming that
amidst the cares and anxieties, of the past winter, this little volume
may have escaped your notice, therefore I take the liberty of sending
it, to you. I thank you kindly, for your speech you sent me, I have
already read it with much interest. How much misfortune, would
we be spared, as a Nation, if our faithless & unscrupulous President,
entertained the same views, as yourself and all other *true* patriots—
unfortunately, he is endeavouring to ignore all the good, that has
been accomplished and returning the slave, into his bondage. The
contemptible act, of refusing, the freedmen of Richmond, the
privilege of celebrating the anniversary of their freedom, is but
too sure an indication, of *his* feelings towards that oppressed race.
His, wicked efforts, will fail, and justice and liberty triumph.

How sad & melancholy, at this peculiar time, the death of our
noble friend, Senator Foot [sic]! Such good men, at any time can be

---

[1] This letter was found among the papers of John Greenleaf Whittier.

illy spared, but, when each & every voice, is needed, to silence the Traitors, that still infest our land, his loss, is very painful. His, "passing away," was so peaceful and triumphant, so much in unison, with his cheerful and well spent life, that it appears, almost sinful, to wish, him back. How many of the cherished friends, of my beloved husband, have within the past year, entered into their rest and been reunited, to *one*, they loved so well, whilst here. I am forgetting myself, in writing you so lengthy a note, when I had merely intended a few lines. With apologies, and assurances of friendship, I remain

always truly
Mary Lincoln.

With the arrival of the spring of 1866, the first year of Mary Lincoln's widowhood drew to a close. Sitting alone in her rooms at the Clifton House, a "genteel" Chicago residential hotel to which she had moved the previous August (after which Robert had taken an apartment of his own), she grimly contemplated another year, perhaps a lifetime, of boarding, of exposing her grief to strangers. She saw her son Tad, now a rambunctious thirteen-year-old, stifled by the atmosphere of a boardinghouse, and her heart went out to him.

If she were ever to have a home of her own, now would be the time to make her move. The $22,000 salary payment was not, by her lights, a fortune, but it was at least sufficient to buy a substantial house in a good neighborhood, at the inflated prices of the day. Moreover, she continued to anticipate the possibility that outside help would materialize at any moment, in which case her own money would be needed only for furnishings—or, hopefully, not at all.

In late March, after months of casting her lines into a sea of indifference, she was rewarded by a nibble from a rather big fish: Simon Cameron, that wily Pennsylvanian who had been Lincoln's first Secretary of War, later his minister to Russia. Even though

Cameron was in the throes of a Senate campaign, he seemed anxious to help the President's widow, with whom he had been on friendly terms during her years in Washington. Alexander Williamson had made the initial contact for her, but by April she had taken over, writing "General" Cameron long, confidential letters, marked by her usual blend of candor and calculation. She must have been relieved to deal directly with a prospective benefactor and not to have to rely on Williamson to get her message across.

Her correspondence with Cameron during April and May dealt almost exclusively with the purchase of a house, for which she claimed to need as much as $30,000. At first she had every reason to rejoice. A copy of a letter exists, unsigned, which is probably one "the General" circulated among his affluent friends. "Profoundly impressed with a belief that these orphans and this widowed Lady have claims upon every patriotic man in the land," it read in part, "I have conceived the idea of providing for their pressing necessities by raising twenty-thousand dollars soon, and placing that sum at the disposal of Mrs. Lincoln . . . To this end I give one thousand dollars. . . . I suggest that such a sum as I have named shall be subscribed." [2]

Results were slow in coming, and the waiting nearly drove Mrs. Lincoln to distraction. Her subsequent letters to Cameron form a heartbreaking chronicle of high hope diminishing into doubt which she hesitated to admit even to herself. As weeks went by, her letters came faster and faster, full of cringing deference, panic, and the grim tenacity that is born of desperation. On May 19, still awaiting word, she lost the first house she had liked, and wrote Cameron she had found another: a builder had offered her what then passed for terms on a $20,000 home: $12,000 to be paid down, with the remaining $8,000 due on the first of July. "How I am to accomplish this, it remains for you to say," she wrote pointedly. There was no reply.

In mid-June Cameron answered her at last, enclosing several letters from those he had approached, including a particularly churlish refusal from the banker Jay Cooke, to whose Washington establishment Mrs. Lincoln already was in debt. But by that time it was too late. The builder had come down in price to $17,000 and,

[2] MS. owned by Philip D. Sang, River Forest, Illinois.

with her usual impulsiveness, she had bought the house, a stately, stone-fronted dwelling, part of a row, at 375 West Washington Street. Cameron may have supplied enough for furnishings, but the large sums he had promised to raise never reached her. Her correspondence with David Davis leaves no doubt that the $17,000 paid for the house came out of her own funds: specifically, the salary payment made her by Congress. There is even reason to believe she had to borrow money and sell some possessions in order to equip and maintain the house.

To Simon Cameron

Chicago, April 6, [1866]

Confidential
My dear Sir:

Your very kind letter was received last evening and presuming you may require the *enclosed* one, I return it to you. There is no other person, in the world, I believe, to whom I would have written, as I did to you, I was too well aware, of your great kindness & nobleness of heart, not to know that you would sympathize with us, as a deeply bereaved family, in *every phase* of our afflictions. You will of course exercise your own good judgment, in your action of the case suggested—Only allow me, to be perfectly frank with you —as regards Judge Davis. So far as pecuniary matters are concerned, he is perfectly honorable, yet there is no warmth in his nature—and cares only for himself—Notwithstanding, *he* became known and distinguished, through my noble husband & received an office for *life* at his hands—in *Wash*, last winter I am informed by *reliable* persons—he said—the first year's salary was sufficient for us & *we should* return to Springfield to live—After the many years of happiness there, with my idolized husband—to place me in the home, deprived of *his* presence and the darling boy, we lost in Washington, it would not require a day, for me to lose my entire reason—I am distracted enough, as it is, with remembrances, but I will spare myself & my poor sons, this additional grief. After the death of my little Willie, my loving and indulgent husband told me, that he would never carry me back, to a place, which would remind us both, of so great a loss—Therefore, in settling in C- I am only carrying out the intentions of my lamented husband—Judge Davis —said to me, last fall, on leaving for Wash—*very coolly*—"If Congress only gives you $22,000—you will be unable ever to have a home." I replied, "it rests with *you*, to see that justice is done us—" "*Judd*, who blamed *me*, for having *no* place, in the cabinet [3]— went to Wash- and diligently joined with Trumbull & worked against, the 4 years salary—Gov *Oglesby* whose *ostentatious* plans, I thwarted, as regards the monument in Springfield, *he*, after I had decided to have my husband's remains, placed in the cemetery, in the suburbs—insisted the *monument, itself* should be placed *away* from it—in the center of S- as I *had* it *arranged* otherwise—*he* assisted Judge D- Judd & others—in depriving us, of a home, with only *sufficient* for me quietly & without the knowledge of our *warm hearted* friend Judge D to liquidate every debt, against the estate— Therefore, you may suppose, that with whatever is kindly bestowed upon us for a home—I trust no communication will be made to Judge D- He would like to force us back to S- but I would eat the *bread* of *poverty* first *here*—Property is very high—& with very little prospects of it lowering. There is a place here, to be disposed of this month—very much to my taste, it is [a] plain, yet elegant brick house, very much like the one *you* occupied in Wash- whose occupant goes to Europe, the first of May—it will cost—more than $20,000 yet that sum, will be gratefully received in part payment —As he closes his offer for sale, by the 20th of this month I am sure, you will advise me, when you receive any news—as to what pros- pects, there may be, that I can purchase it. Every cent, that is given, shall be *sacredly* applied for the purpose and my sons, ever after me—shall certify—that they will never part with it & retain it as a home—Any communication made, as soon as you are informed yourself, will be most gratefully received. Please erase the sentence about Judge D & believe me always truly & gratefully

Mary Lincoln

Let *all* I have written be most confidential & private—

---

[3] See letter to David Davis, January 1861.

To Simon Cameron

Chicago April 6th [1866]

My dear Sir:

In my letter of *this* morning, I neglected to request you, not to mention, about my speaking, as I did of Judge D- I can *substantiate*, all I say. Like his cousin "Winter Davis,[4] he loves to rule, cannot appreciate how others, unblessed by his "hundred thousands," *feel deprived* of *their all*—in every sense, of the word—My beloved husband, was my life & if it were not for my boys, I would rather *die* than live. For life, is a torture, a misery to me—without my husband—Living in a boarding house, is most revolting to my sons & myself—and certainly the thought that *his* family—would have had to come to this—would have been a most aggravating sorrow to *One* so devoted to his family, as my husband *was*—and *still is*, in his Heavenly home.

I am sure you will use every exertion to raise the sum you named $20,000— yet if I make a suggestion, will you kindly pardon it. I wish to live plainly—yet very genteely—Plain two story frame houses here, cost the sum you have named $20,000—and if, from an other quarter—you can *outside* of that have it increased to $25 or 30,000 I am sure you will—to be enabled to procure *the house* I wish, *this month*—as my opportunity will pass away after *that*. Confidentially, I will inform you of a circumstance that came within my knowledge 2 weeks ago—*so* recently—A gentleman friend from Wash- [Williamson] sent me a letter received by him from Mr M. O. Roberts, N.Y- saying, that he had been informed, that *we* were without a home, in Chicago—and *whenever means were* being raised, to secure us one, he would desire & expect to be called upon—If you of *your own* accord, without mentioning *my* name in it, if you write to him, *when* you receive this, say next week, you will doubtless be gratified by his *response*. The letter of *Mr R's* I returned to the

---

[4] Representative Henry Winter Davis of Maryland, one of the leading radicals in Congress and co-sponsor, with Senator Ben Wade of Ohio, of the Wade-Davis Manifesto of 1864, which had accused Lincoln of "studied outrage" against the popular will when he vetoed a bill embodying the radical position on Reconstruction.

gentleman in *Wash-* With many apologies for again troubling you, I remain most gratefully

M. L.

May I request, my dear Genl, as a great favor to me, to burn *these* & *my former letter*—and do not speak of them, to any one. I am almost humiliated, that I have written as I have done—but *you*, will *kindly* excuse me

To Lucy A. Little [5]

Chicago—April 9th 66

My dear girl:

Your kind and most touching little letter, has been received & believe me, in the midst of my terrible bereavement, your expressions of sympathy, for myself & my afflicted sons, are most welcome. Our Heavenly Father, has afflicted you, in the deprivation of your sight, yet you are surrounded by loving friends, whose lives are passed in contributing to your comfort. My dearly beloved husband, was the *light* of our eyes—we never felt, notwithstanding our *great* love for him, so *good* and great as he was, that we could love him sufficiently. As you [say], truly in midst of his happiness & rejoicing, *he* was called hence, to the "glorious home," prepared for all those, who truly love and serve *him*, *here*, on earth. Whilst we weep, *so* broken hearted, he is "rejoicing before the Throne of God & the Lamb for evermore"—*To me*, as you may well believe, life is *all darkness*, the sun is a mockery to me, in my great sorrow—My dear young friend, although unknown to me, I love you, for being able, so thoroughly to appreciate the noble character of my idolized husband—I pray, that your days, may be passed in happiness and peace, whilst I remain always, your deeply afflicted friend

Mary Lincoln

P.S. Remember [me] to your kind Grandmother.

M. L.

[5] A blind girl of West Milton, Wisconsin, who had written a letter of condolence to Mrs. Lincoln.

To Charles Sumner

Chicago, April 10, 1866

My dear Sir:

The letters of the Queen of England and Empress of France,[6] were received the last week of my sad sojourn in W- and if I had been capable of a thought beyond the great overwhelming affliction, which distracted me, I am sure, *you* would have been the first friend, to whom I would have handed them for perusal. I enclose them to you, knowing full well you can appreciate them, & as well as the two *very* opposite characters, who wrote them. The one a deeply bereaved wife and the other, a woman—a stranger to sorrow and to whom life was all [words indecipherable].

I have received innumerable letters and resolutions from distinguished persons in all portions of the habitable globe, that would greatly interest you to look over, and last week a large scrap book, comprising all the speeches & resolutions passed in England after the news of the heart rending tragedy, was received by the Nation. *Their* eyes, were only beginning to comprehend the nature and nobility, of the great, good man, who had accomplished, his work, and before *his Judge*, it was pronounced complete. The past year, as you well may believe, has been a long Eternity to me, *it is* slowly, solemnly drawing to a close and there are moments, now, of each day, when if it were not for my boys, who look to me, for guidance & comfort, I would pray God to be merciful and remove me from a world, so filled with darkness and blight. If like poor Mrs Foot [sic], even with trembling anxiety I had been permitted to watch over

[6] The letter of condolence written Mrs. Lincoln by Queen Victoria is reproduced on pp. 230–1. Eugénie's letter, dated "Paris 28 Avril, 1865. Tuileries," read as follows: "Madame: L'Empéreur fait parvenir à Washington les témoignages officials de l'indignation et de la douleur qu'inspire à la France le coup fatal qui vient de frapper le Président Lincoln.

"Mais a côté de cette calamité nationale il y a un malheur domestique qui éveille dans mon coeur une emotion profonde. Je veux, Madame, vous en offrir personnellement l'expression, ainsi que l'assurance de voeux que j'addresse au ciel pour qu'il vous donne la force de supporter cette cruelle épreuve. Croyez, Madame, à ma vive sympathie et à mes sentiments les plus sincères. Eugénie."

and minister to my idolized husband, through an illness and receiving his loving farewell word in return, I could have thanked him for his lifelong—almost; devotion to me & mine, and I could have asked forgiveness, for any inadvertant moment of pain, I may have caused him, perhaps *time*, could partially assuage my grief, and leave me to perform more calmly, the life duties, that remain to me. And then too, comes thoughts, of our beloved & *still*, greatly distracted country! How admirable is Whittier's description of the thraldom of Slavery and the emancipation, from the great evil that has been so long allowed, to curse the land. The decree, has gone forth, that all men are free and all the perfidious acts, of Johnson and his unprincipled partisans cannot eradicate, the seal, that has been placed on the "Emancipation Proclamation." [7] It is a rich & precious legacy, for my sons & one for which I am sure, and *believe* they will always bless God & their father. Yet, after all *your* life-long struggles in the cause of freedom, after battling for the right, so long and nobly when you felt, all your hopes were being crowned with success, how it must try, your soul to see a man, placed in *his* high office, to protect the Nation, from its wrongs, to take these rebellious traitors so kindly, by the hand, and willingly place them in places & positions, that should only be claimed, by those, who had "fought the good fight"—and rejoiced with us, in victory. I cannot express to you my dear Mr Sumner, my great indignation, when I hear of these men, who almost bowed the suppliant knee, to my husband affirm & insist that "*Johnson*—is carrying out President Lincoln's policy."

Retain the letters I send you as long as you please & show them to whom you are disposed. I have been thinking so little of any thing save my great great grief or I should long since have acted differently. As it is, some few here—have read them—the letters— I send you will excuse the tedious one I am now closing—so I will not apologise,

> Truly your friend
> Mary Lincoln

[7] A probable reference to the Senate vote, engineered by Sumner and the radicals, which on April 6, 1866, overrode Johnson's veto of the Civil Rights bill.

To A. R. Thompson [8]

Chicago April 15th [1866]

I regret, that I am unable to comply, with your request, regarding the Autograph, of my deeply lamented husband. We have given away, all we have and being unable to reach the private papers, at present, it will be impossible, to oblige you

I remain, very respectfully
Mary Lincoln

To Simon Cameron

Chicago April 17th [1866]

Private—
My dear Sir:

Knowing full well you will excuse, my writing so soon again— as I am anxious, to have some idea, of the result, of the work you have so kindly undertaken, in my behalf—We have to make a change by the 1st of May and I have to give an answer to a party, in a few days & very naturally I should like to have an idea, of what is to be done—I do not wish to trouble you, yet if you have any news, when you receive this, please apprise me—and oblige always truly

Mary Lincoln.

To Simon Cameron

Chicago April 21st [1866]

Private
My dear Sir:

As I am compelled to return an answer, on Thursday next— about the purchase of a house—may I trouble you—if you are pre-

[8] Unidentified.

pared to give me an answer—to telegraph me—when you receive this—either "yes or no"—addressed to Clifton House—so that I may form an idea—as to what I shall do—Before warm weather—I am anxious—to be removed—into a house of our own—even if it is small —even if you have *not*, been able to secure *all* the sum, you desired to raise, a portion or half of it—at this time—would be gratefully received—of course all of it would be very acceptable—as we are without a home—and we are most unpleasantly situated, at a boarding house—Little did my beloved husband—ever suppose that those so very very dear to him—would be left thus. I wish to trouble you, no farther than to request you to telegraph me, when you receive this— in a few words—so that I may know—what to do—With great respect, I remain always truly

Confidential—   Mary Lincoln

To Alexander Williamson

[*April 24, 1866*]

Mr Williamson—

I want you to write a letter to Mr Roberts of N.Y. *the hour* you receive this. Of course—*I am not a* party to it—You can say, you have just received *this* sad note from me and ask him—in your name, if means cannot *now*, be raised to get me a home, the present month. This letter, received from Halsted,[9] this morning, evidently means R- [has] the $5,000—assure Robert's—that waiting for Congress—to do any thing more—will be entirely unnecessary, *yet do not* allude to Halsted's letter—*He* will think it is a premeditated plan. In writing you can enclose *my letter* to Roberts—saying that it is so sad, *you cannot* refrain, from doing so—Of course, I am to have no knowledge, of any, thing—write & entreat him now to forward *his* & *other* assistance—In *every* instance—you will be remembered [by] *$200*—Write the hour you receive this & oblige—

[9] Two fragments of Halsted's letter have been preserved with Mrs. Lincoln's. The first scrap bears the date "Newark April 21st 66" and the salutation "Mrs Lincoln—My dear Madam"; the second reads ". . . until I could get them in better shape & partially redeem some heavy losses which had befallen me—I regretted as much as [I poss]ibly could, my inability . . ."

To Alexander Williamson

April 25th [1866]

My dear Sir:

Your letter of *21st* is just received. I think you are very wise in removing to the country for the summer—both as regards health & economy. I cannot tell you how sorry, I am, to be unable to comply with your request—to loan you "$70 or 80"—I am now owing, Robert, who is himself hardpressed—for my last month's—board—what I am going to do, for this month I cannot say. Between all my settlements & every thing—the interest on my small amount of money, only enables me to live in the plainest manner (in *this* most expensive place Of course you will not give up your place in the Treasury D?—who is *Mr Collins?* Of whom you write?—I know no such person, & he has not written to me. Not *one* of *the* parties you or I wrote to—have ever returned me a line—If through Mr Roberts—you can *now* get any thing towards a house, for me—I will send you from it $200—that is an offer for *you*—on which to exert yourself—Yr friend

Mrs—A. L.

To David Davis

Chicago, April 26th 66

My dear Sir:

On consultation, with Robert, who says, it will be all the same to you & the estate & will greatly accommodate me at this time, I write to request you, to allow me to have, (the $17,000—in Springfield—placed in seven thirties)—in exchange for $17,000- of mine, placed in same way—with *my* name written on them—I presume you will have *no* objection, *thus*—to oblige me—*if you have not*, will you favor me, by writing so soon as you receive this letter to S- for them—so that I may receive the bonds, by *next Wednesday*.[1] Any hour I am ready to remit, my $17,000—the awkwardness & inconvenience, of my name being upon those, of mine, occasions me thus, to trouble you—

It will also be desirable—to have a guardian appointed for our little Taddie early in June—Robert proposes—going to S[pringfield] at that time—yet, the only trouble is, that the guardian, if selected from S- will scarcely see Taddie, *yearly*—S & C are so distant.

Hoping you will oblige me, by immediately exchanging the bonds & with great respect—I remain Truly

Mary Lincoln

To David Davis

Chicago May 4th 66

My dear Sir:

Your note, has been received, and you will allow me to assure you, that I should not have written to you, asking to exchange the seven thirties, if Robert, had not mentioned, that there was *no name*, upon those in S[pringfield]. Your account changes, it entirely. It is not my intention, to ask any thing, which is not perfectly just & consistent—I regret, if you have interpreted any of my expressions otherwise. Gen Cameron, is proving himself a *true friend*, he is not unforgetful, as so many others, have been, of the kindness, of my beloved husband. He appears to wish to see us in a comfortable home—and we are the party, most naturally interested in it—I suppose any success he may have, he will soon apprise me of—I am sure

---

[1] Davis had opened an account at the First National Bank in Springfield, in his name as administrator, depositing therein several of Lincoln's uncashed salary warrants and other substantial amounts paid into the estate. With the money in this account, he had then purchased $17,000 worth of 7–30 bonds. Mrs. Lincoln's $17,000 had come out of the $22,000 salary payment made her by Congress, and was also invested in 7–30 bonds. She apparently did not wish to publicize her identity by turning over to the seller of the house she was purchasing bonds that bore her name. Davis considered her request an odd one and wrote her that the exchange she proposed would not be feasible. (Pratt, pp. 134–6.)

—you will enjoy—seeing us, more genteely & quietly housed, than we are—My sons are well—

I remain very truly
Mary Lincoln.

To Simon Cameron

Chicago, May 4th 66

Private—
My dear Sir:

I am in receipt of a letter from Judge Davis, who, in a most friendly manner informed me, that you had written him, mentioning your interest in our having a home && His expressions, would instantly put to flight, any impressions, that had been made upon my mind, by persons, in Wash- that *he* had considered *the small* appropriation sufficient for us. I am sure, as *we* are naturally, more interested, than he could possibly be, so soon, as you have any success, you will apprise me. I am so anxious to be settled before warm weather. Hoping to hear from you, when you receive this.

I remain very truly
Mary Lincoln

To Alexander Williamson

Chicago May 6th [*1866*]

My dear Sir:

I send you a line in great haste. When you wrote to Mr Roberts —*did you*, enclose *my* note also—and urge upon him & others—that you were perfectly assured—Congress—would do no more for us[?] On Wednesday morning when you receive this, telegraph me [2]—if

[2] On May 9 Williamson wired: "Received your letter. Wrote you with letter from Commissioner Rollins and one from Mr Roberts. Will see to your wishes. Alex. Williamson." MS. owned by Herman Blum, Philadelphia, Pa.

you have heard from Mr Roberts & others & they promise to assist say "all right"—if not, "no success," I will understand—Write when you receive this. Write to Paul S. Forbes [3] New York—on subject of house—A. T. Stewart—do not fail

Your friend

Mrs A. L

Can you not manage to *see* George Peabody,[4] of London, now in this country—*be sure*, of this—a rich reward, will be *yours*, if successful—

To Noah Brooks

Chicago, May 11th 66

My Dear Sir:

A few days since I received a very sad letter, from poor Mrs Henry—in which she vividly portrays her great desolation and dependence upon others, for every earthly comfort. I am induced to enclose you the *Nevada Claims* & also a *petroleum* claim,[5] hoping you may be able to secure a purchaser for them, in which case, I will most cheerfully, give Mrs Henry, some of the proceeds. I am aware that I am taxing your kindness very greatly, yet the remembrance of your great esteem, for my beloved husband & Dr Henry, would excuse the intrusion upon you. I wish you were not, so far removed from us—*true* friends, in *these* overwhelming days of affliction, I find to be very rare. I find myself clinging more tenderly, to the memory, of those who if *not* so remote, would be more friendly. I hope, you will be able to visit Mrs Henry, the coming

---

[3] A wealthy financier.

[4] An American banker and philanthropist who had been making his home in England.

[5] Enclosed in this letter were three certificates for wildcat stock that Brooks was never able to sell. A letter written on April 6, [1866] by Mrs. Lincoln to O. S. Halsted Jr. is in existence (location unknown). In it, Mrs. Lincoln reproved Halsted for not forwarding the "Nevada Claims," which were apparently in his hands at the time. Metropolitan Art Association, Lambert Sale, April 1, 1914, Third Session. Item 583.

summer. I sometimes, in my wildness & grief, am tempted to be-lieve, that it is some *terrible terrible* dream, and that my idolized husband—will return to me. Poor Dr Henry, he, who wept so truly & freely with us, in our great misfortune, how, soon he, was called to join the beloved one, who had so recently "gone before." In my great sorrow, how often I have prayed for death—to end, my great misery. My sons are well & a great comfort to me. I have another and *the right* Nevada Claim—with "Mary," instead of "Frances," upon it,[6] which I will send you, in the event—of your being able to dispose of it. Robert, & Taddie, remember you, very kindly. I hope you will write to us, more frequently. I am well aware of the deep sympathy, you feel for us—and the great affection & confidence, my husband, cherished for you, draws you, very near to us. With apologies, for troubling you, as I am now doing, I remain, always

Sincerely, your friend
Mary Lincoln

To Alexander Williamson

Chicago—May 11 [1866]

Private—
My dear Sir:

Your letter, with one from Mr R[oberts] is received. It is all perfect nonsense, to apply to any one or more Senators.—Some of them mean well enough, but they have resolved, there shall be *no precedent*, in our case, & so nothing will come of all that. As to Sumner—such things, are not, in *his line*, so do not, I pray you, appeal to him. As to attacks made upon me by *miserable* Congress-men & Wash- resident[s]—write to R.s and say, that *they* would attack, an angel of light, if it served their purposes. Write *him this* —*be sure*—The die is cast—boarding house life has become so offen-

---

[6] The enclosed certificates were purchased in the name of "Frances T. Lincoln." Francis Whiting Hatch in an article published in the *Journal of the Illinois State Historical Society* (Spring 1955) has suggested that Mrs. Lincoln had not wished company records to list her as a stockholder while her husband was President.

sive to me—I have engaged to buy a house, in a block for $18,000 —which must be paid, by first of June so, we will see, whether Roberts, will make his word good—and help me *now*, to pay this— The house, is considered a great bargain and if I am to be assisted surely they will do it now—to pay this—Write to Roberts & urge him to use his influence, for the *last* time, very positively & I shall never trouble them again—I write you a letter to send him—of course—*not* as if designedly—*this* of course you keep, yourself— Appeal to Roberts, in most earnest way, to see me, assisted through this payment—Say to him R.—in your letter—that appealing to Congress & Sen's—is absolutely, lost time—speak in yr letter of the disgrace, it is—that I am *so* situated—If *he* (R returns you a favorable answer—to telegraph me "yes" or contrary "no"—

Your reward in the former event, is sure Write—write I wrote to Genl Strong [7]—and no reply—Write to *Genl Cameron*

Yr friend
Mrs L.

Private for your own reading.
Write to *Genl Cameron*

To Alexander Williamson

Chicago—May 15th [1866]

My dear Sir:

You must certainly see, that *this* is my last chance—and if I am not assisted in paying, for *this* house, I do not know, what I shall do—Write a *most fervent*, *urgent* letter to Mr R[oberts] when you receive this—*plead* with him, to see his monied friends—I have given a written promise in consideration of the property being given to me, at a lower figure—I have to settle—the 1st of June—Write— write—if I was able to pay yr expenses—I should say go to N.Y. But you were *so unfortunate* the last time—and you saw *no one*—& I lost

---

[7] William K. Strong of New York, who before his military services to the Union was a New York merchant and Democratic politician.

$10 by it—I could not with my *present* means—advise you to [do] that—By all means—breathe to *no one*—my purchase of a house— you can enclose the note *not* marked private to Mr R *the hour* you receive this *Send this other* letter, I enclose to Mr R- with an urgent note, from yourself—*do not fail*—the *hour*, you receive it. *Not this* note send him

yr friend
Mrs L

To Alexander Williamson

[*May 16, 1866*] [8]

My dear Mr Williamson enclose—*the letter*, written on "mourning paper,"—with a most urgent *one* from yourself, *the hour*, you re- ceive this—It is my last chance & I am distracted to have *this* debt [on the house] settled—Speak of *me* most kindly to R[obert]s and urge him, to see that this money, is raised before 1st of June— write him—that I have given, my written promise on it—

Mr R. Appeals to *your judgment*, in his note—*when* the proper hour—shall be—by all means—*pray* & urge him—to consider *this hour*—of indebtedness the one—Write most fervently & enclose— the proper letter

M- L-

To Simon Cameron

Chicago, May 19 66

My dear Sir:

Your very kind note, was received two days since, and appre- ciating the interest you feel, that *as a family* we shall be more

[8] Date based on internal evidence.

pleasantly & *becomingly* situated, I have concluded to write you a frank letter, well knowing your great nobleness of nature & feeling assured, you will sympathise and I trust endorse, the course I have pursued. It is unnecessary to dwell upon my own and my son's great unhappiness of mind and our desolate condition, no wife, no children, ever had *such cause* for grief & despair—and notwithstanding the great services of my beloved husband to his country & his friends—we have been forced, by our embarassed circumstances, to remain without a home—and consigned to a boarding house. Such a fearful life, has injured my health, to such an extent, that at least 3 days, of each week, I am unable to sit up, with my severe headaches—My eldest son is pained & mortified continually & my little Taddie—the idol, of his darling father, is hourly thrown with persons & hears expressions—in the place, *where* we *now are* (considered the most genteel boarding place) in the city—bringing up this tender child *thus*, has only added, another pang, to my already broken heart. The remembrance of your kind promise to exert yourself to secure us, a plain unpretending home & the knowledge, that your great influence, can effect *so much*—has caused me, to effect an arrangement, which I am sure, you will see, that I am assisted through—Ten days since a gentleman, building some houses —came to me & made me an offer—which under *all* the circumstances we are laboring, I accepted—and now, my dear General, will you not with your kind affectionate heart, and indefatigable energy, see me assisted, through this difficulty? The house, is in a retired situation—& being one of a row (and consequently much cheaper) *he* the builder, offered it to me—at first cost, in consideration of my living in the row & he deducted—six thousand from the price, he charges the others. He has shown me his books, where it becomes very manifest—that he is truthful—He has the reputation of being a very honest man. Each of the houses, they are of stone, I am assured, cost him $18,000—& with the stables, to be added, will be $2,000—more)—making the sum, you are so generously trying to raise a home, for us—The builder, however, made a provision that $12,000 should be paid down, the 1st of June—and the remaining $8,000 the 1st of July—and how I am to accomplish this, it remains for you to say. In consideration of the painful circumstances, in which we are placed & fully understanding, that those, who so nobly subscribed their names, for our benefit—would not be particular to wait, until the whole $20,000 was raised—as of course, when their names were given—they meant it all—as they wrote— Could you not manage to gather the $5,000—you mention as *certain* & *the "promised $5,000,"* in Phil. & other sums; you may since, have added—to the list [9]—so that the payment to be positively made by 1st of June next—may not harass me, with my sorely troubled mind, quite so much. In continuing to raise the remaining sum—I can but trust, you would meet with no difficulty. The thanks of a bereaved widow and orphans, will be yours *forever* & *forever*—if you can grant this request of mine, made with a trembling and *most* anxious heart. Hoping that I may hear from you, when you receive this—*the day*, I remain always respectfully & gratefully,

M. L.

To Simon Cameron

Chicago- May 26- [1866]

My dear Sir:

The papers, announced that you have been in Wash- but as you have doubtless returned home, ere this, I take the liberty to direct our attention, to the letter, I wrote you a week since, to which, with your kind heart, I am sure, will immediately, respond. I should not have written you, except in *this extremely* urgent case—the *1st of June* is so near & I am so troubled about this pecuniary business. Pray relieve my anxiety, *when* you receive this & oblige

Yrs truly
Mary Lincoln

[9] A copy of the circular letter through which Cameron attempted to raise funds for Mrs. Lincoln has been preserved and is owned by Philip D. Sang of River Forest, Ill. It began with the observation that the family of the late President were "pennyless . . . in dread of poverty," and continued as quoted on p. 350.

[*To Caroline Roberts*] [1]

[EXCERPT]   [*June 1866?*]

I take the liberty of sending you, by Express, a snuff box, its only value consisting in its having belonged to Henry Clay, and having been presented to my dearly beloved husband. A cane, for Mr Roberts,[2] cut from Fort Sumpter; and one for the Rev Dr [J. P.] Thompson, your minister, also a memento of Mr Clay. Dr Thompson I am personally unacquainted with, yet both his preaching and practice, during the rebellion, in the cause of the Union and our suffering soldiers, has endeared him, to the hearts, of the whole nation, and—my good and noble husband, respected and appreciated him most highly, and I trust Dr Thompson, will excuse this very unceremonious presentation.

To Derby & Miller

Chicago- June 3rd [1866]

Private

Mess Derby & Miller—

Your note, also accompanying engraving of the "Emancipation Proclamation[3] has been received. I have always regarded the original painting, as very perfect, and the engraving, appears to me quite equal to it—With thanks, for your kind remembrance, I remain very respectfully

Mary Lincoln.

---

[1] Wife of Marshall O. Roberts. Her identity as recipient is based on internal evidence.

[2] See letter to O. S. Halsted, Jr. May 29, [1865].

[3] The painting by Francis B. Carpenter.

To Alexander Williamson

Chicago
June 9th 66

My dear Sir:

I enclose you the notes requested. *Mrs* Roberts wrote me a few days, since—requesting me to write to Col Frank E. Howe [4]—New York—and *not* mention her husband's name—so that *he*, might strait[en] the affair—I write to *Col Howe* to day—*Where are*—all *Mr R's promises, to assist*—I hope for nothing—any where—you can also write to Col Howe—if you choose—perhaps you *had better do so at once—stating the case* as *most urgent*——

Col Frank E. Howe—New York City

Does not Gen Cameron—reply to yr letters? I send a quilt to Mrs Dr Smith [unidentified]—for the fair [5]—will it be too late? Write when you receive this *to one & all*

Yr friend
Mrs A. L.

To Simon Cameron

Chicago June 16th [*1866*]

My dear Sir:

Your kind note, also accompanying letters, were received by me, this morning. It is painful for me to reflect from the *heartless* specimen, of Jay Cook's [sic] [6] letter, what an ordeal, *you* must have passed through—Let misfortune visit an individual in this blessed

[4] A wealthy New York politician, in whose Staten Island home Robert Lincoln had once been a guest.
[5] In July of 1866, a fair was held in Washington for the benefit of the widows and orphans of the Union soldiers.
[6] Jay Cooke, a Philadelphia banker who had made his fortune through financing the Union cause during the Civil War. Mrs. Lincoln, as has been seen, had borrowed from Cooke's Washington bank and had not yet repaid the loan.

land, even if it be an innocent yet unfortunate woman—and still more, the cherished wife of the man, to whom the nation, owes so deep a debt of gratitude, after *power*, has passed away, as *you* are aware,[7] all claims are ignored—and every act—denounced. I am personally unacquainted with Mr Cooke—and as my conscience acquits me of any flagrant transgression, save obeying the mandate of *such* sordid persons, as himself, in returning to *our shell*, of a house, in Springfield from whence—as we were leaving its doors, en route to W- my dear husband—told me, he would not carry me back there again—Robert, prefers a larger field than S. and as it is most natural—we should all be together—and moreover dear Genl *my feelings* must be allowed, to have something to do with my actions—occuping the same rooms, breathing the air, where so many happy years were passed—the contrast without my husband, would simply deprive me of my reason. It is such men as Cooke & a few others and indeed many, who owe everything to my husband—their wealth, station—& their all—these are the *especial* persons, who would most willingly, see Wife & sons—of their benefactor, eating the bread of poverty & *humiliation*—if they could—*We* have plenty of them in *this* State, as you are aware—and *they* have influenced— others, elsewhere—to their own base way of thinking. As to Mr Cooke—so unheard of, before the war—and who has made his millions by it—As *I* did not bow in reverence—to two of his Gods, *Chase & daughter*, and did not do violence to my feelings, by re- turning to a place—where my husband, positively assured me—he would not return—*his denunciation*, does not trouble me—I am endeavouring in every act—to carry out, what I believe, would have been, my idolized husband's wishes—Since I have been in C- I have led a most secluded life—scarcely seeing my best friends—It is very well—for such men as Cooke—to have *such a subterfuge*—as *preju- dice*—to resort to—Thank Heaven! I have some warm good friends, who, if not *so* wealthy as the renowned—Mr C. are better & greater men—Anticipating, some favorable result & having the offer of a most excellent new house, reduced to the sum of $17,000—I pur- chased it—time, being extended me to pay for it—by *1st* of July. Certainly, those who subscribed the $5,000—in good faith—will advance it—to assist in meeting the demand at that time—If I am

[7] A pointed reference to Cameron's recent political difficulties.

not assisted, I shall have to dispose of it—which I scarcely think some generous hearts—would like to see me do—I propose—to dispose of many personal effects—to purchase furniture—Judge D's —letter, is very just and truthful—How cruel, *those persons*, who misrepresent our straitened means!—Please write me on receipt of this, about the sum already subscribed, if it would not, be *now* allowed to assist in payment—Your friends, are anticipating yr return to the U.S. Senate—which I anticipate as truly & fervently as any one, possibly could do—My gratitude, will be unbounded, if you see me assisted, in the matter, I request.

I remain, very gratefully,
Mary Lincoln

Please send Judge Davis' letter to Col Frank E. Howe—New York—so soon as you receive this—Will explain hereafter—Please *do not* mention to him (Col Howe) about money subscribed (*condition of payment, being* when $20,000 is raised—*This* will be *unnecessary* with him & others there—If you can secure the $5,000 —*now* for me—in settlement—I would be pleased—Judge D- has all I have in the world—which is little—not a cent, *in any bank* I am sorry to say.

M. L.

To Alexander Williamson

Chicago—June 24th [1866]

My dear Sir:

A note from Mrs Smith and one from yourself announce the safe arrival—of the afghan &&—I hope, they will be disposed of, to good advantage. Col Howe, has written me a very beautiful & sympathising letter, assuring me, that he would, act immediately, on the case—Please mention to *no one*, this business or Col Howe's name—there are so many miserable minded people—that they would take steps to stop, any thing that might be done—*On this* account, I am sure you will be guarded. Mrs Roberts—is a very lovely Christian woman—and a very great friend of mine. Unlike so many other females—who are envious of any lady—who has enjoyed distinction. I presume, that those, to whom you refer, are of this numerous class—who prevented their husbands—exertions, in my behalf. If Mr R- *does not now*, keep his word, when another party, makes a move—he will prove himself a different man, from what I expect— Nous verrons—*A very short* time, will decide all this—I pray Heaven, Col Howe may succeed—or I do not know, what I shall do, with the unpaid property—now on my hands. It appears the necessity of my life, that I shall *now*, retain this home—Bad health & great unhappiness of mind—require a quiet shelter. Please write most urgent letters to *Howe* who is a most tender hearted, excellent gentleman—with great means *himself* also—Come out & see us on fourth of July—We will gladly welcome you—come *via New York* —be sure & see those gentlemen.

I enclose another request to Genl Hardee [sic]—Write *most* urgently to Howe—Roberts &&—When you receive this—also to me —If the fair does not terminate *before the 4th* of July—I can send, other articles to it. We who are so deeply bereaved—have indeed lost our All, can fully sympathise with the orphans of the war—for such we are ourselves—

Mr Wm Whiting, formerly solicitor of the War D- called to see me, a day or two since—He was always a warm personal friend

Truly
M L-

To Alexander Williamson

Chicago June 26 [1866]

My dear Sir:

The telegram of *Mrs R*[oberts]—is received. I cannot understand *why* Mr R- goes to Wash- Certainly if *he* applies for aid from that miserable Congress he will fail—Raymond—backed by *Seward*, *Weed* & *Stevens*—would destroy every chance for poor me—

Do telegraph me & write if *Howe* & Roberts, are *acting* together—There are *so* many *fiends* at work—there is positively no hope from Congress—assure them of *this*—

I write in haste anxiously looking for results—*Mrs R-* good woman as *she* is, appears to be mixing herself up considerably with matters—There will be nothing but failure—if application is made to Congress—*The* New *York people*, friends of *both*, those gentlemen *H & R*, can remedy the evil—Write— [8]

To Alexander Williamson

Chicago—Friday morning June 29th [1866]

My dear Sir:

I sent by yesterdays Express (free) *a cane of Genl Jackson's* —and one or two other articles, for the fair, addressed to **Mrs Dr Smith.** I have received only *one* letter from **Mr Howe**—almost despair of any success—if I do not hear from *him*, in a day or two— Do telegraph & write, if you hear any thing. In the zeal of these *false* Ill- men, to collect money, for the Monument, in every direction, I am informed, *they* have represented, we were in very good circumstances—by way of securing *more*, themselves—Every week or two, the Springfield paper—announces seven or eight hundred dollars—received—yet strange to say, and many people *here* & elsewhere shrug their shoulders—when it is mentioned—for the last 6 months, the whole sum, as they announce it—is $67,000. It is sometimes asked, *where* are the intermediate sums? *All this*, is entre nous. Because, we did not choose to live in their midst, *where* my husband, did *not*, intend residing—they have endeavoured to injure us, as much as they could. When I see you, I can tell you much about them—Answer me candidly if you believe *Howe & R-* will be successful as regards, my affairs—Will you, as a favor—to me, go & see Fahnstock—tell him I have been prevented, sending him, *the* money by *1st* of July—but by *10th* of the month—he will have it.

---

[8] On the back of the original letter is a notation, very likely in Williamson's hand: "Congress will not do anything, Stevens is in the way."

(Those, who have made *millions* by the War—would positively take the last cent from us, if they could) [9]—I am so very anxious to know the result of the N.Y. proceedings—

In haste truly M.L-

To Alexander Williamson

June 29th [*1866*]

My dear Sir:

Your note & the papers, containing notice of the gifts,[1] have been received—Would it not be *as well*—to send a copy *of each* of these papers to *Howe—Roberts &&* with *your* signature. I think it would have a good effect, *in expediting* matters—God knows—how much, I have the interests of all the widows & orphans, in the land, at heart—we have been so terribly bereaved ourselves—I can deeply feel, for all who suffer, not hearing from Howe again, makes me very anxious—I have suffered so much sorrow & disappointment, that I am fast learning, to expect very little—Please write to me & all parties—if I should prosper a little you & yours will not be forgotten—

Yr friend
Mrs A-L.

To Alexander Williamson

July 5th [*1866*]

Personal—
Mr W-

I have written you the note. I insist you shall not have it published—by [but] *quietly* show it to *all* proper persons—(*remember this—if you please*) A letter from Howe this week, saying he was doing *all* he could—regretted the *very persons*—necessary for the

[9] A reference to Jay Cooke.
[1] Sent by Mrs. Lincoln to the Washington fair.

work were absent from N.Y. *but* would use *his* greatest exertions
—*He* writes it has been so misrepresented—that *we have affluence!*
on *that ground* he has met with opposition—*H-* means well—and I
hope will not prove *faint hearted*—Write faithfully to R[oberts] &
himself it will soon be time for *these gentry* to be leaving N.Y. and
the heated term will find mine—a hopeless case. Write to them
urgently—

To Alexander Williamson

Chicago—July 5 [1866]

My dear Sir:

I have just sent off a letter to you to day but yr note of 3d just
received deserves a reply. You speak of the [monument] Committee
—from S[pringfield] being in N.Y. was this *before* Roberts, *was* in
W- do answer me *this*—The money *these* millionaires *have* given—
would be very well & good—if it would *ever* be appropriated *for the
purpose*—they solicit it for. It is *these* same miserable men from S-
who have stopped any thing being done for me—If *Mr R*[oberts]
and *H*[owe] are "sincere," towards *me*—they have *now,* an opportunity of proving it—I am beginning to despair—what think you?
Do write to H- & R's when you receive this—truly

M.L

Please answer me the question I ask in this note—Write to *them all
in N.Y*—

To Alexander Williamson

Chicago—July 21st [1866]

My dear Sir:

I have not received a line from you for the last week. I am
anxious, to have you return me the last two letters, of Andrews &
Howe. Please do so, when you receive this. I have not heard—

whether the few small articles, for the Fair, sent ten days since, have been received—among the collection, say to Mrs Smith—is a cloth—table cover presented me, by a friend & sent from Constantinople it is a curiosity & should bring—a very good price. I received a letter from Col Howe, this week, full of kindness & *promises for the future*—I have had *so* many of *these* latter that they have become rather painful. I wish you would write him a note, when you receive this—speak of *my* great interest in the Wash Fair & enclose *my* letter to you, on the subject of an *equal* distribution—You have never written me whether you showed *this*, to any persons—Col Howe—says his work for me, was interrupted *just*—as he was *beginning* to think of agitating it—by a call for the relief of the *Portland* [fire] sufferers. Just, as I expected there will always be something to *set* aside any thing—for my poor benefit—

I write in haste—hoping to hear soon from you. Did Fahnstock, reply to yr letter? I have a great curiosity, to find out what has become of the medal [2]—advertised to be sent me from France—Do make enquiries about it—if *Seward Hay* or *Nicolay* could stop its reaching me—they would do so—They are a great set of scamps—

Your friend
Mrs A.L

To Francis E. Spinner

Chicago
July 23, 1866

Private
Dear Sir:

You will kindly pardon my delay in refunding to you the $10 you loaned to Mr Williamson on my behalf. For your consideration, pray accept my thanks. At the same time may I trouble you to

[2] Issued by the "Committee of the French Democracy" to commemorate Lincoln's services to the cause of republican government and of liberal ideas. The committee represented forty thousand French citizens who paid for the medal by contributions limited to two sous per person. Mrs. Lincoln eventually received the medal; her letter of thanks was written on January 3, 1867.

have sent to Galt & Bros. the remaining sum due them, and in return receive their receipt? Also will you return the receipt to me? With high respect, I remain, very truly

Mary Lincoln.

To Alexander Williamson

Chicago Aug 5th [*1866*]

My dear Sir:

Another letter from Mr Huntingdon, of Jay Cooke & Co. Will you go to him & say, that I am just recovering from quite a severe indisposition (which is true) and so soon, as I am able to leave the house, I will send the money, he writes about. God, help these miserable people! Say to him, on the 10th of this month, Aug- at furthest, I will start it from *here*—do send him this message, say to him—by 15th of *this* month he will have it—My Heavens, what a fate, is mine! Can it be, after all the promises of Howe & Roberts —they will make no exertions, in my behalf? As gentlemen, it certainly cannot be so—Not a line, do I receive from Howe—do you hear from either of them? Can you not get a free pass, to go to New York & see them, when you receive this—have you, no friend's house, there, where you can stop—in N.Y. without any expense—to see them—*H. & R.* if I had the money—I would freely offer it to you—settling up every thing leaves me almost without a dollar. If *they* do not keep *their word*—in the future, I know not, what I shall do. I have not heard from you, the past week. Why, not study, over some friends house & go to N.Y.? Certainly, they do not consider *this*, child's play. Mr Bing [unidentified] writes me, proposing that *Robert* should write to France, about the medal. *This, would never do—He*—B. has many acquaintances in F. who could give him information. Seward, is capable of *any meanness*—and I should not wonder—if *the medal* is lodged in the *State D-* in W- Seward—has before, on his *shelves*—secreted a gift—to me from Europe—four years ago—which the donor—General C[ameron]——[3] wrote &

---

[3] Mrs. Lincoln wrote out this name, erased it poorly, and drew a heavy line through the erasure.

made them, give [to me]. *this*, is *entre nous*— but very correct. How *small* & *contemptible*, some of these people are, when we come to know them. *Can it be*—that men who call themselves gentlemen— like H & R. *are not* sincere—in what they profess—to undertake? Write me, all you know—I wish you had shown Sumner—the letter, I wrote you, about the *fair gifts*—before *he* left Wash- yr friend

Mrs A. L.

To Frank E. Howe

Chicago 12th Aug. [1866]

Personal and Private
My dear Sir:

Fearing that absence from the City, may have prevented the receipt of my last letter, after painful deliberation, I have concluded to write to you. I am just recovering from an illness of two weeks, and my recovery, as you may suppose has been greatly retarded, by my anxiety of mind, relative to my embarrassments. Relying upon your kind promises and generous sympathy for me in my most heart rending afflictions, may I, not soon, realize my anxious expectations & be relieved, of the load of pecuniary trouble, which renders daily life so annoying. Without the object being effected, which you are so nobly, endeavouring to promote, I shall be compelled to part with & dispose of every superfluous article in my possession, which will be a painful ordeal, for me to pass through. Living, with the most rigid economy, weekly, daily, I find, I am unable to meet the wants, that ill health & necessary requirements, call forth. I rely greatly on your great good heart & influence, to counteract, the severe trials I am now passing through. Bowed down, with my fearful bereavement, I feel assured, the noble people, in our great nation, would soon relieve me of these difficulties, if they were made known to them. Trusting, I am not trespassing too much, on your patience, and goodness—I remain

With great respect
Very truly
Mary Lincoln

In the month of August 1866, President Andrew Johnson was making preparations for a lengthy speaking tour through the North and West. Hounded by congressional radicals, he had designed this "swing around the circle" to salvage what was left of his prestige and to try to influence the mid-term elections. Johnson was scheduled to visit almost every major city in eight states, including Illinois, bearing in his wake such luminaries as Generals Ulysses S. Grant and George Custer, Admiral and Mrs. David Farragut, Secretary of the Navy and Mrs. Gideon Welles, his daughter Martha Patterson, and several members of his White House staff. The caravan would later include Secretary of State Seward and various local officials who joined it en route. On September 5, after a week of receptions which ranged from enthusiastic to indifferent to downright hostile, President Johnson arrived in Chicago. The following day he would place a wreath on the grave of Stephen A. Douglas and go on to Springfield to render a similar tribute to Abraham Lincoln.

Mrs. Lincoln regarded what she called "the royal progress" with even more jaundiced an eye than the radical press. Her personal antipathy to the President had been encouraged by Charles Sumner, whom she continued to worship, and who was one of Johnson's most vocal enemies in Congress. Wishing to slight the Chief Executive, and possibly anticipating a slight from him, she determined to be out of the city on the day of his visit. Although her good friend Mary Jane Welles would be in the presidential party, and would surely be anxious to see her, her resentment at the Welleses' continued fealty to the administration was so deep that she decided to risk the friendship rather than remain in Chicago. The only place she had an excuse to go to was Springfield, where she could visit her husband's tomb for a second time—an infinitely painful prospect but apparently more appealing than breathing the same air as Andrew Johnson.

Her trip was to have unexpected consequences, bearing no relation to the purpose for which it was undertaken. The seeds of future difficulty lay in a letter she wrote to William H. Herndon on August 28, the same day the President set out from Washington. Herndon had informed Robert earlier that he intended to do a bit of speaking or writing on the subject of his late, illustrious law partner, and would be grateful for any assistance Mrs. Lincoln could give him in the way of recollections. Considering her disdain for Herndon, and the fact that something he had just written had displeased her, the letter she sent him, agreeing to an interview during her stay in Springfield, was remarkably friendly. For once she allowed sentiment to carry the day. Lincoln, so generous even to his enemies, would have wanted her to be kind to Herndon, whom he had genuinely liked—and so she would be, for the sake of her husband's memory.

The meeting took place on the morning of September 5 at the St. Nicholas Hotel. Mrs. Lincoln, sitting across a table from her interrogator (and somewhat discomfited by the smell of liquor which emanated from his person), replied to questions about her husband's private life with exceptional candor and good nature. She innocently acknowledged that, although Lincoln had been a deeply religious man and "a true Christian gentleman," [4] he had never become formally affiliated with any church. She praised him lavishly, dwelling tenderly upon his devotion to her and the children. Afterward she no doubt congratulated herself on how well the interview had gone, feeling sure she had clarified a number of matters with Herndon.

She slipped out of Springfield the next night, before President Johnson arrived to—as she put it—"desecrate" Lincoln's grave with his presence. Herndon meanwhile began incorporating his sketchy notes into other material he had been assembling for months, all in behalf of a project designed to win him the fame and fortune that had hitherto eluded him. He was planning to write an intimate biography of his former partner, beginning with Lincoln's earliest life and ending with a brief summary of his presidency. The book, which would not be published until 1889, would combine known fact, personal observation, recollections of the President's friends,

---

[4] Mary Lincoln to James Smith [Marienbad, June 8, 1870].

family and associates, with a large amount of sheer speculation and extrapolation. Herndon's "research" had already led him to an intriguing new theory about Abraham Lincoln, which he planned to reveal to the public in a series of lectures. Part of the public was Mrs. Lincoln, who would have cause to regret her impulsive Springfield visit and her kindness to Herndon for the rest of her days.

To David Davis

Chicago, August 12 [1866]

My dear Sir:

Remembering your kindness of last year, in procuring us a pass to & from Springfield, I write, yet feel that I am taking a liberty, whilst doing so—to request you, if it is practicable, to procure for my sons & myself another pass. I propose in a few days accompanied by Taddie & perhaps Robert [5] to visit the cemetery at S- where rest the remains of the beloved husband and father. Robert has gone to Mackinaw—a change was very necessary for him. I expect his return every day. I have heard nothing further from you, regarding the guardianship of Taddie or it may be presumed, from the silence however that Mr Conkling, declines the charge. We will also be glad to receive the interest—which you so kindly said you would write to Wash- for so soon as it reaches you. To live in the most economical manner, requires more—than I can summon to my aid. With regard to the pass, if you, feel the least hesitation in requesting it, I hope you will not inconvenience yourself—yet—as I have made up my mind to take the trip—with my boys to S- the pass —will be very gratefully received—Would there be a possibility of getting it, within a very few days?—I remain, with great respect

Mary Lincoln

[5] Robert did not go to Springfield. (See Mary Lincoln to Charles Sumner, September 10, 1866.)

To Alexander Williamson

Chicago 19th Aug [1866]

My dear Sir:

Your last letter was received on yesty. I am obliged to you, for writing to Lyons,[6] about the Medal—You are right about *not* applying to the State Dept about the Medal, until you hear from France. As to the autograph letters [7]—*entre nous*—I shall decline to hand *even* copies of them over to Seward—*Say nothing* about it however. I must correct the erroneous impression, you have about Mr Sumner. When I sent the letters in the spring to him—I wrote him, to retain them, as long as he wished or until I sent for them. If I had *not* done so—he would have returned them in a week's time—He is a high toned gentlemen—and one of my best friends. For the past four years, he was a constant visitor at the W. H. both in office & drawing room—he appreciated my noble husband and I *learned* to converse with him, with more freedom & *confidence* than with any of my other friends—I received a long & beautiful letter from him, from Boston—on yesterday—and one last week—written as he was leaving Wash- He appreciates his *few* friends highly, yet in many respects —*is a peculiar* man When you receive *this*—write me, whether you showed to Wade [8]—& himself—the letter—I wrote you relative to the distribution—of fair gifts—you will understand me—*which one.* Do not fail to tell me—if you did so—I have some curiosity, on the subject & will explain to you, some other time—Please, do not mention that Sen Sumner wrote *me*, lest *Seward* will suspect, *he*, advised me *not* to allow the letters, to be published. I am learning fast to trust, but *very few*—I wrote to Howe—a few days since, faithfully portraying my necessities & requesting a reply. After all the *fair* promises—of those *gentlemen*—if they do not exert themselves in my cause—they are very false—When the "royal progress,"

[6] Probably Lord Lyons, British minister to Washington during the Civil War, at this time minister in Paris.

[7] From Eugénie and Victoria. (See Mary Lincoln to Sumner, April 10, 1866.)

[8] Benjamin F. Wade, Senator from Ohio, a leading congressional radical and co-author of the Wade-Davis Manifesto. (See p. 353.)

arrives in Chicago—I shall be absent—I propose on next Wednesday week—to go down to Springfield and visit the cemetery—where my idolized husband & darling Willie, rests—I wish you were here to accompany myself & sons—Are you never coming out to see us? Why not now? Leave, so soon as you receive this & take New York en route—You can procure a pass from War D- Those New York people, are indeed a mystery—*see them* en passant—could *Howe* after his letters, play false? Answer me about showing the letter to S[umner] & Wade—say nothing, of what I have written you—to any one.

Yr friend

M. L.

To David Davis

Chicago Aug 20th 66

My dear Sir:

Quite a severe indisposition, has prevented an earlier acknowledgment, of your kindness, in so soon acceding to my request & procuring through the favor of Mr Jones, a pass for my sons & myself, to Springfield. Also your letter of Aug 17th enclosing a check, for $1,000, was duly received, for which, I will send you, a more formal receipt. We propose going down, to S- about the time, the *"royal progress,"* is expected here. It will be quite as well to be absent, from the city on *that* occasion. I will endeavour whilst in S. to see Mr Conkling on the subject of the guardianship. I remain, with great respect, very truly

Mary Lincoln—

To William H. Herndon

375 *West Washington Street*
Chicago Ills. Aug 28th [1866]

Private—please burn
My dear Sir.

Owing to Robert's absence from Chicago your last letter to *him* was only shown me last evening. The recollection of my beloved husband's truly affectionate regard for *you* & the knowledge of your great love & reverence for the best man that ever lived, would of itself cause you to be cherished with the sincerest regard by my sons & myself. In my overwhelming bereavement, those who loved my idolized husband aside from disinterested motives [sic] are very precious to me & mine. My grief has been so uncontrollable —that in consequence I have been obliged to bury myself in solitude —knowing that many whom I would see, could not fully enter into the state of my feelings. I have been thinking for some time past that I would like to see you & have a long ~~talk~~ conversation. I wish to know if you will be in Springfield *next* Wednesday week—Sept 4th [9]—if so—at 10 o'clock in the morning, you will find me, at the St Nicolas Hotel—please mention this visit to S. to no one. It is a most sacred one—as you may suppose to visit the tomb which contains my All, in life—my husband. You will excuse me enclosing you this sentence of yours & asking its meaning. With the remembrance of years of *very, very* great domestic happiness—with my darling husband & children—my sons & myself fail to understand your meaning—will you be pleased to explain. If it will not be convenient—or if business at the time specified should require yr absence—should you visit Chicago any day this week I will be pleased to see you. I remain

Very truly,
Mary Lincoln

[9] September 4, 1866, fell on a Tuesday; Mrs. Lincoln clearly meant the 5th, and it can be assumed that that is when the interview took place.

To Alexander Williamson

Sept 2d 66

Dear Sir:

Your letter is received. I do hope that as you will be in N.Y. you will not leave—without seeing—& ascertaining the *exact truth* & prospects from H[owe] & R[oberts]. Their *utter* silence, after *all* their promises is very peculiar & unsatisfactory—We will be pleased to receive a visit from you, the address *here* is 375- West- Wash- St I have promised—Judge D to be at Bloomington—on Tuesday, day after tomorrow, to see him on business—as it will be half way to S. I may proceed thither—yet when you visit us, I can procure you a pass to S- I shall be home on Friday eveg—when we will be happy to see you—You know—it is an absolute necessity, for me to be absent *this* week—will reserve news, until I see you. Do pray, see *those* people in N.Y. and glean all the information, you can—

In haste truly
yr friend
M L

To Alexander Williamson

Friday noon
Sept 7th [*1866*]

My dear Sir:

When the postman rang the bell this morning, with yr note, from Phil- we expected, you had arrived—We greatly regret that you have concluded not to visit us at present. 2 hours since, I arrived from Springfield, missed seeing Mrs Welles & *the party*, of course, in consequence of absence—will write her in a few days also others. *Do see* Howe & R[oberts] when in N.Y. & report me—what does *their silence mean?* I wrote you a letter, directed to French's

Hotel N.Y. *do* get it—We hoped to see you in Chicago—Pray see *about that* N.Y. business I will write, to all parties about yours [1]— Write me often from N.Y. & believe me

yr friend

M. L

To Charles Sumner

Chicago, 10th Sept. 66

My dear Mr Sumner:

The "Presidential Progress," is soon in Illinois [Washington?] & I enclose you a brief yet correct account of the reception given them whilst performing their pilgrimmage through this State. The President encountered much that would humiliate any other than himself, possessing such inordinate vanity & presumption as he does.   Being absent from Chicago, I escaped seeing any of the party, yet Robert whilst making a private call on Edgar Welles, a former particular friend, encountered *them all*, and was made an *especiality* by Mr Seward who pressed him to breakfast with him on the morning of their departure, an invitation which he was *unable* to accept. Robert reports kind inquiries for me, from all, *save Johnson*, in which case I considered myself more honored "in the breach than in the observance" A note from Mrs Welles informed me that most of the party had proposed, making me a call, en masse. I remember Mrs Welles with sincere affection and gratitude, during my illness—fearful bereavement in Washington. She gave me all a sister's love & care under other circumstances, than her recent visit to Chicago, it would have afforded me the nicest pleasure, to have received a visit from her. *Her* heart is all right, yet the desire of some persons to be in office, will cause them to bend the knee— even to treason. The most painful thought to me, in my great sorrow is that the party *desecrated* my beloved husband's resting place, by their presence having just returned from the sacred spot myself with a renewed sadness upon me, it was felt all the more keenly by me,

---

[1] See Mary Lincoln to Orville H. Browning, September 24, [1866].

and added another pang to my Gethsemane of woes. All the scenes that are transpiring, at times appear to me like some hideous dream, our Country is in a fearful state & another civil war appears inevitable. May heaven avert it! My dear Mr Sumner, I was very forcibly, reminded of you & your remarks in the Senate, on yesterday by receiving a note from Miss *Vinnie Ream*,[2] on the subject of her proposed statue of the late President. "Washington lobbying," has evidently, *not* improved the young lady, very greatly, the tone of her letter, was self-satisfied & rather presuming. Nothing but a mortifying failure, can be anticipated, which will be a severe trial to the Nation & the World & the Country will never cease to regret that your wise admonitions were disregarded—

Speaking of art—at the Crosby Art Gallery in Chicago, very near "Bierdstadt's [sic] Rocky Mountains,[3] and a few other choice paintings, hangs a full length portrait of that exquisite poet, "Longfellow," executed by [George P. A.] Healy, quite an eminent American artist. It is considered very fine, and is it true that the expression of his eyes, have *such* depth & beauty, as that canvass depicts Yet when we remember, his poems && we can accord him every thing. You must have had a charming visit to the White Mountains, I sincerely hope, you found, the desired rest, and return with renewed health & spirits. As usual, I find myself sending you, quite a lengthy even *womanly* letter, which you will excuse!

I remain truly &&
Mary Lincoln

---

[2] A sculptress who, at the age of sixteen, won permission to model a bust of Lincoln as he sat at his desk working. Miss Ream visited the President's office frequently over the course of several months before the assassination, and Lincoln was said to have enjoyed the quiet sessions immensely. In securing her commission to extend the bust into a statue to stand in the U.S. Capitol, the sculptress did display what was then considered unladylike persistence and aggressiveness, but she had talent, and her work received high praise when in was unveiled in 1871. On July 27, 1866, in the Senate debate on the resolution to grant Miss Ream her commission, Sumner had warned against giving away $10,000 to an "unknown artist," declaring they "might as well place her on the staff of General Grant."

[3] Albert Bierstadt, founder of the "Rocky Mountain School" of American painting.

If the letters written by Mary Lincoln in the latter half of 1866 and in early 1867 had a single dominant theme it was her losing struggle to survive in the house she had purchased so impulsively and so hopefully. Once again she had bitten off more than she could chew. The vast sums Simon Cameron had promised to raise never arrived, but she dared not antagonize him with further supplication; instead she urged David Davis to write Cameron (who would in January 1867 win a bitter fight for the Republican nomination for U.S. Senator) in the hope that "the General" would recall "the promises made, when his future, was uncertain." [4] But Cameron apparently failed to respond. After February 1867 Mrs. Lincoln's letters contained no further mention of his name.

Meanwhile she renewed her efforts to pull a few last irons from the fire, by herself. Williamson had made no progress whatsoever, and at the turn of the year her stream of letters to him dried up abruptly. He would write her several times in 1867; her replies would be heavy with hints of dismissal. She wrote Davis of her difficulty in meeting the winter's fuel bills and the spring's taxes. For a brief period a new name was added to her roster of potential saviors: Leonard Swett, Lincoln's long-time friend, now practicing law in Chicago. She clung to a faint hope that Swett and Davis would work together in one last attempt to raise money; otherwise, she would be obliged to move out of the house, a wearisome and humiliating prospect that appeared more inevitable with each day that passed.

To Leonard Swett [5]

Chicago 13th Sept [1866]

My dear Sir:

You will pardon me for being solicitous about hearing from the result of your communications, with the friends to whom you pro-

---

[4] Mary Lincoln to David Davis, Chicago, January 14, [1867].
[5] A lawyer who had been born in Maine but who had pursued a successful career

posed writing. With the most rigid economy, which I am compelled to practise, I find it will be absolutely impossible to continue house-keeping on my present means two, mont[h]s longer. Seeking retirement as a necessity, with my great sorrow upon me—it would be to me the greatest conceivable pain, that I should have to rent this place, to assist me, in living—*With the sum*, with the amount of which you are apprised—I cannot attempt to struggle through the coming winter—with the requirements—which the winter necessarily brings —All I desire to know is, what prospect, there is of a *change*—or if you have been advised of any—please inform me—so that I may make my arrangements. I can assure you, it will add another pang, to my afflictions—if I have to give up—for want of means to keep it up—my present situation. If so—my pride would not allow me to remain in a land, under so many obligations to my noble husband. I would go, with my son, where I could live retired & at less expense— *far distant* from here. Without hesitation in case of nothing being done, I shall proceed in a few weeks, to dispose of all personal effects —which in the future—will not be required—Please write me, if you have heard any thing & believe me

Most respectfully
Mary Lincoln.

To Leonard Swett

Chicago 15th Sept. [1866]

My dear Sir:

In my note written two days since, I neglected to mention to you, the embarrassment, to which I am almost daily subjected—by the receipt of letters & calls, from indigent persons, who are impressed with the idea, that the family of the late beloved President, have had ample means, placed before them. When I have been compelled, to turn aside from their wants, without a dollar, I could *justly* give them, it has been with an aching heart oftentimes, the "bread which my idolized husband, so freely cast upon the waters,

---

in Illinois during the course of which he had become closely associated with Lincoln in legal and political ventures. He was now practicing law in Chicago.

to all sufferers who came near him, was not returned to his family by a country, he so faithfully served. I cannot *begin* to meet the wants of our little household, even in the simplest way, for the coming winter & shall place this house for rent, very soon. I have never been interested, in any of my surroundings, plain though they be, it was only, the pride & knowledge, what was due my husband & our former station ever made me attempt, with our stinted, meagre *unjust* means, even a passable appearance. This is all over, the rent of *this* house, *elsewhere*, may make, *this* portion of life easier. The families of soldiers & others, who come to me, for assistance, will *then* be assured, when I assert, that my own means are limited & I have not the wherewithal to give them. Of course, this is not, as it should be, I feel, in *all this*, my noble husband's name, is dishonored. If the country, had *truly* loved him, *such want* would not have been inflicted upon the household. I write hastily, but truly.

Very resp

Mary Lincoln

To Alexander Williamson

Sunday Sep 23rd 66

My dear Sir:

It is understood, that Johnson, has placed the *removals* into the hands of the *Departments*—therefore, I have concluded to address a note to Browning,[6] Gen Spinner & McCullough [sic] [7]—A note to *Mrs Welles*, will not avail much—I fear she is a little inclined to be offended with me, on account of my *absenting myself* when the party visited Chicago. At any rate we will try, *these three* persons first. I cannot believe, they would consider it necessary to remove you—yet it is best, to guard against it. I wish you to give me, when you receive this letter, *the details* of your interviews with Howe &

[6] On September 1, 1866, Orville H. Browning, former senator from Illinois, had been appointed by President Johnson to succeed James Harlan as Secretary of the Interior.

[7] Hugh McCulloch, Secretary of the Treasury, 1865–9.

Roberts—can it be possible after *three* months of *promises* they have secured nothing, and have ceased to be interested—Why does not Howe, write me—Do you think, in consenting to the *$5*- subscription I will escape *newspaper* notice—*my great aversion* Write to H & R. also myself

Yr friend
M L

To Orville H. Browning

Chicago Sept 24 [1866]

My dear Sir:

Only a circumstance of much interest to a devoted friend, of my beloved husband, as well as former tutor, to my idolized son Willie, would prompt me to intrude upon your kindness and occupations. Mr Williamson, after the sorrowful death, of our precious Willie, in return for his great interest, in our child, was placed by my husband, as clerk, in the Treasury Department. All, will bear testimony, to his faithful performance, of those duties, for he is considered by all persons, who are acquainted with him, an honest, upright man. He has a family, entirely dependent upon him—without any support than his small salary yields him. I am trespassing upon your valuable time, by writing you, to solicit from Mr Johnson & Sec McCullough, a promise, that he may be retained, in the Treasury Department. He Mr Williamson, fears, that amongst other removal[s], without kindly interference, *his* may be effected. He is a most loyal man & my great & noble husband, valued him most highly.

In the midst of my great sorrow—*under* the *circumstances*, may I request you, by your great influence with the parties named— to grant my special request.

I remain, always & truly
your friend
Mary Lincoln

To Charles Sumner

Chicago 1st Oct 66

My dear Mr Sumner

Your kind note has been received & I hasten to offer you my congratulations, on an event that will bring you so much happiness and consequently afford your numerous friends so much pleasure.[8] The confirmation of the rumor will doubtless be an agreable surprise to many, but its truth appeared to me very probable with my knowledge of your intimacy with the family and my recollection of the attractiveness of the lady. You have devoted your life so entirely to your country, that your friends will be greatly gratified by the assurance that your bachelor life has almost closed and that henceforth you will not stand *alone*, in your greatness. You may remember, that the lady in question, called one evening with you, to see me. The pleasant impression then made by Mrs H[ooper] cannot easily be erased. I had the pleasure of receiving a call from Senator Wilson, a few days since, his speeches, in the West, have been very effective. I will not weary you to day, with a lengthy letter you will please accept my thanks, for the distinguished mark of your good feeling towards me, in making known the pleasant prospects before you in life, which your past noble life, entitles you.

> With highest regards
> I remain always, truly &&
> Mary Lincoln

[8] Sumner had written to Mrs. Lincoln of his forthcoming marriage to Mrs. Alice Mason Hooper, the lovely widowed daughter-in-law of Representative Samuel Hooper of Massachusetts. The couple separated within a year and were divorced in 1873. In subsequent letters Mrs. Lincoln made several references to rumors concerning the Sumners' marital difficulties.

To Alexander Williamson

Chicago 17th Oct 66

My dear Sir:

I wrote you a letter on yesterday, which I presume you will receive, explanatory of my views and my reasons, that *Chicago*, should not be included in the list.[9] My son, who proposes making this place, his future home, would be subject to great annoyance & mortification, if action, were *otherwise* taken in the case. Col Howe, will understand all this. I would prefer myself, to endure penury, rather than ask a favor, at the hands—of such penurious, money loving people *as these*—It is rather a singular coincidence, that just as Col Howe, is proposing active measures, in my unfortunate behalf—the *Quebec* fire, like the *Portland one*, comes on the *tapis*. The cases however are *very* different, the English and Canadians were not such friends of our Country during our War, that the wants of the family, of the President, whose life was sacrificed in his country's cause—should be set aside—and ignored—to oblige its enemies. Certainly, thus far, with my daily wants pressing upon me—and the Country, understanding so well, the *needs* of those so very precious —to the great man, whom they have professed to love—It is certainly, a remarkable way, of showing their affection, slighting *those*, that were *more than* life, to *him*. To meet actual necessities, I have been compelled to resort to measures, that at first, made me tremble at the thought—such as disposing of my cast off clothing, to procure mourning garments, and even home comforts. This has been permitted so long, by the American people, that I can scarcely after this *long delay*, anticipate a change. With my great sorrow, pressing upon me, the future looks very dark & dreary.

I remain yr friend
Mrs A. L.

9 Of possible private donors of funds.

To Alexander Williamson

Chicago, 30th Oct 66

My dear Sir:

Your note is just received. "No news from Howe"—Do you not think it is *quite* time, to despair of *those gentlemen*—after *all* their promises. How true it is, "where there is a will, there is a way." With so much in their power—The long delay of H- & R- have proved to me the want of interest—*All this* is *entirely between our-selves*—*Howe* not writing *me*, looks strange *that* letter of mine, about *Quebec*, was very true—I am inclined to believe that *Howe's resort*, to the [Chicago] city *contributions*—was only a *blind*. He might be sure, we could not *live* here *even for the present* & have this thrown at us, all the time. All we can do, is to bide results, the hand-writing is already on the wall—*their procrastinations* have defeated any result, in my favor—save bad luck. Say *nothing* of this or my news—I pray you—So poor Fanny Seward [1] is dead—I am very sorry to hear it—She was an amiable, *inoffensive* girl—When you hear, from Howe—please advise me. I regret not being able to oblige you —I am without any autographs, of my beloved husband, save on some private letters—which I would not part with for the world.

yr friend—

M. L.

To Alexander Williamson

Chicago Nov 5—1866

Private

My dear Sir:

Your note, with enclosure is just received. It appears to me, to be an impossibility, *under the circumstances*—if my necessities *were*

---

[1] Frances Seward, young daughter of Secretary of State William H. Seward, had died after a lingering malaise presumably brought on by the attacks on her father and brother on the night of the assassination and the subsequent death of her mother.

made known, to the rich & generous men of N.Y. & Boston—that the demands, would not be met—A poor return, for my beloved husband's services, to his country! If *you* knew, how debts, were staring me in the face, which I cannot meet & depending, as I have been doing, on Col Howe's assistance to settle them, you would understand —how, being unable to meet them—as a matter of course—with my great need upon me—I cannot do—what under other circumstances —with a well filled purse—I should like to do—help you about your house. I borrowed money, at a high rate of interest, to purchase this house,[2] at a moderate cost & am unable to keep it—so shall relinquish it very soon—which I deeply regret being compelled to do— My income, is about equal to your salary—and there is no place more expensive than Chicago, any where—So the *"shoe,* pinches," with us all—For the last 3 months, to meet the most ordinary expenses, I have had to part with my clothing and I assure you, I am at the end of *that line*—all that is left are simple things [3] enough, but as gifts—of my precious husband, only absolute starvation would induce me to part with them—If I am not assisted ere long—I shall give up, every thing, to meet every indebtedness formed here —take my little Taddie in the spring & go—where I can live cheaper —I sometimes think of Germany, where Tad, can be educated at a moderate rate & certainly I can keep him & myself at a more moderate cost—than here—How little, did my good husband ever imagine—*his family* would be reduced to *this*, last extremity—I am *now* suffering so much mortification and with my great sorrow upon me—that in this country—situated as I am, unable to meet, what I am owing & the simplest daily necessities—I cannot endure it much longer—and my pride will compel me, to leave the land— a necessity most painful to me—and which I shrink from. You will understand, in a measure, my situation, but it would be impossible, for you fully to do so—If my purse, was equal to my good will, you would have what little assistance I could give—As it is

[2] Mrs. Lincoln actually paid for her house out of the first year's salary granted her by Congress; she stated as much in her letter to Elizabeth Keckley of November 9, 1867. Earlier letters to Williamson indicate that she used the borrowed funds to pay her debts in the East.

[3] A few of these "simple things" are listed in Mrs. Lincoln's letter to Elizabeth Keckley, November 9, 1867.

alas! with unpaid bills pressing upon me—I wish I could forget my-self.

I write in great haste & remain Truly

Yr friend

M L.

To Leonard Swett

My dear Sir:

As the season of *taxes* has come, and I am in daily apprehension of a notification to that effect, may I remind you of your promise so kindly made to speak a word for my benefit to Collector Wallace, or being absent from the city, if you will enclose a note to him, directed to myself. Only the most *painful* necessity compels me to make *this* request, a recapitulation of my straitened circumstances, I will not again trouble you with—time, with the most rigid economy, only renders them more embarrassing. In your visits to Boston, seeing Gen Cameron & others, who have hearts to feel for the distressed, I cannot bring myself to believe that you have been *entirely* unmind-ful of the promises you made me three months since, to advance my interests sufficiently, so that I may be enabled to keep my sons & my-self together. I only ask for sufficient to do this—no more—Can the Country be so forgetful, to my beloved husband's memory, as to deny me, this simple request. With yr feelings, all kindly interested, that we should be comfortably situated and not subjected to the hu-miliations I have been passing through, for want of adequate means, at times, to secure the common necessities, and remembering your influence, socially & politically I am relying on your success. I am struggling for a short time longer, but shall soon *be compelled* to give up this house, without you will send me some good news, which will happily continue us here. Hoping, you *will* write when you re-ceive this. I remain truly and respectfully

Mary Lincoln—

P.S. Please reply to this & relieve my anxiety.

M. L.

To Orville H. Browning

Chicago 3d Dec [1866]

My dear Sir:

The bearer of this note to you, Thomas Cross,[4] who was a faithful serving man, at the Executive Mansion, during our stay there, desires me to address you a line & request a favor—which is this. That you will assign him some employment, he has been out of service since July last, he is an honest, industrious man and was always highly esteemed by my beloved husband.

Knowing your great kindness of heart, I feel confident you will listen to his petition and afford him, the relief of employment. With great respect, I remain very truly

Your friend
Mary Lincoln

To Alexander Williamson

Dec 14 [1866]

Private
My dear Sir:

It is just as well to weigh every thing fairly. Since the meagre gift of Congress—I have felt there was no hope of other assistance— save through H[owe] & R[oberts]. For twelve months past, no hope of any other, has been offered me, and on my own small means, I feel assured, it is impossible to get along. Your wife, in her note, mentioned, the ridiculous story of C[uthbert?] manufactured out of whole cloth that I had received $25,000 from two parties, to whom

---

[4] During the Lincoln administration, there were two White House employees named Thomas Cross, one a furnaceman and one a doorkeeper. The latter had also served as companion-guard to Tad and had accompanied the family on their journey to Chicago.

you had written—I wish it were so, and most willingly, you should
have yr promised $50- on each thousand. Not a cent have I received
in 11 months from any quarter—My husband always enjoined upon
me to be quiet—Your wife is not different from womankind generally—and if in her visit to N.Y. she should see H, & mention to him,
my promise to you—of giving $50- on each thousand—my word for
it—not a dime from him or his collections, would ever be received by
me—and the only source from which I ever hope or expect—will be
baffled and I shall be unable to send you the promised remittance—
by not receiving any thing myself—I never fail in my word & faith
—if a dime from H- is ever re[ceiv]ed—you shall be duly repaid as
promised—Please write to Mrs W- to be cautious, as regards H-
and not mention the business to any one—I think it will annoy H- to
see any lady, in the case, I dread myself to write him—I want to be
able to serve you—and thr H- will be my only chance—so we must
be cautious. With yr excellent sense & kind heart, you will understand—It would best for Mrs W- not to call. H- has acted so mysteriously, that I am not very hopeful. We can only "watch & wait
—H- is the only one, who can or will assist us—Yr friend

To Alexander Williamson

Dec 16th [1866]

My dear Sir:-

    Your note is received. Within the last ten days, I have written
twice, to *H*[owe] as yet, no reply. Should I ever hear, I will notify—
you—and should any remittance ever be received my word and truth
is unchanging, that the promised sum on each thousand shall be
given you. H- is the only hope of a year past, and *if he fail*, as his
silence inclines me to fear, my limited means, will be almost unendurable. Mrs W[illiamson] chose a very cold season to visit her
friends in N.Y. I hope, she may return to W- in good health. In her
note, she did not mention H- or a call on him, I hope she did not do
so—& perhaps have been coldly received. My respect for you, causes
me to excuse her note which I regret having mentioned to you—I

am not accustomed to having my truth doubted, should she be called to pass through *half* the suffering I have, she will become calmer— May, you both, escape any unnecessary sorrow, in this life—Taddie is well Can now read, quite well—as he did not know his letters when he came, here, you will agree he learns rapidly. In the event of news from H. you will be informed. he is the only hope & expectation—

Yr friend
Mrs L

The untruthful statement made to Mrs W-[5] if it was only true, *by half*, would contribute greatly to our comfort—alas! it is only tantalizing to hear of it—H- is a mystery to me, I cannot understand such unfaithfulness to his word. I shall never write him again—as he has acted so strangely.—

To James Smith[6]

[INCOMPLETE] *Chicago 17th Dec "66"*

My dear Sir:

Your very welcome and interesting letter, was received a few days since, on the anniversary of my birthday, when my fearful bereavement and desolation, was *if possible*, more than ever apparent to me and with the exception of my dear Sons, I felt alone and uncared for in the world. Under these circumstances, your words of friendship, breathed from a far distant land, were most acceptable to my broken and weary heart, and my gratitude, in being so kindly remembered was very great. Only those who have suffered and have been called upon, to relinquish those, who were *far far* dearer than life, can understand the painful emotions, that the return of those days, that once brought joy and gladness; and without the presence of my dearly beloved husband, who was my all, in this life, you can

---

[5] See letter to Williamson, December 14, [1866].
[6] The elderly former minister of Springfield's First Presbyterian Church who had been appointed by Lincoln as American consul at Dundee, Scotland, in 1863, at the urging of Mrs. Lincoln.

well imagine how dreary every thing appears to me. *To me*, crushed and broken hearted, *"time*, brings no healing on its wing," and I would most gladly leave a world, so full of darkness. Under the blow, which has fallen upon my sons & myself, so heavily, I fear "calmness and resignation," can never visit this troubled spirit, so long as I am separated from one so necessary, to my life and happiness. How little in former years, did we anticipate, the darkness of the present hour! You can readily believe that no place is home to me *now* and I have sometimes thought, in the course of a year or two, I would carry out the intentions of my beloved husband, who proposed the last week, of his precious life, that at the expiration of his second term, we would visit Europe and he appeared to anticipate much pleasure, from a visit to Palestine—But a few days, after this conversation, the crown of immortality was his—he was rejoicing in the presence of his Saviour, and was in the midst of *the* Heavenly Jerusalem, where his troubles were ended, and his life, had been sacrificed, for his love to his Country—Only, the all sustaining hand of our Merciful Father, could have supported me, through my agonizing woe and distraction. There are hours of each day, that I cannot bring myself to believe, that it has not *all*, been some hideous dream, and in my bewildered state, I sometimes feel that my darling husband, *must* & *will* return to his sorrowing, loved ones.

The winter of *this* cold & ungenial climate, has commenced and as the residences of Mrs [Frances?] Wallace & myself, are quite distant, I fear I shall have the privilege of seeing her but seldom, until spring, which I very sincerely regret. I am so miserable, that I receive but few strangers & consequently the friends of other days, are dearer than ever to me.

To Alexander Williamson

Dec 17 [*1866*]

My Dear Sir—

As a matter of course, with such *false promising* men as H[owe] those who have trouble, and are not prosperous—are all "unpopular"—I am willing to risk my "popularity" against *his*—when put to the test—He has never made the least trial to do any thing—It has been *three* years since I have laid eyes on S. Draper & never saw him—but two or three times, in my life I never saw one of his family, in my life—I never received a line from him or a cent in my life—If I had been assisted, in the settlement, of my business I should not be pressed as I now am—I am sick of the name of *H*-—We have had enough of it—H- got up the false story that I had enough, as well as others to keep from doing any thing. This subject is banished for the future—This is a *patriotic* country! If H- is false in one story—he is in all *others*—In haste yr friend.

I am pleased that yr anxiety is relieved about Mrs W- a pleasant Christmas to you & yours (A sad one to us!

To David Davis

Chicago Dec [1866]

My dear Sir:

As Gen Cameron, is generally an habitué of Wash- during the session of Congress, may I not hope that ere this, you have been enabled to see him & others, and perhaps have written the few letters, you so kindly suggested. The daily experience of the last two months has convinced me that with my present reduced means, I can but a short time longer struggle, as I have been doing. This place, for the past few months has been a refuge to me in my great great sorrow, with the entirely inadequate income of $2,000 per year—it must be resigned into other more *fortunate* hands, who *can* afford a home. Living in the plainest manner, day by day, here or elsewhere, it will be impossible with the most rigid economy, to keep house on less than $2,000 a year, more than I now have, and if possible I should have $500 more yearly, to procure my mourning habiliments, the plainest of which is expensive. Being well aware, in consequence of the love you bear my beloved husband's memory & your very natural pride of country & mingled with the nobleness & generosity of your nature, to see us differently situated, not struggling for every meal that is placed upon the table—I am sure you will exert yourself in my behalf. You are scarcely conscious, *how far* your distinguished name and your word, which would become a law, could effect in this peculiar case. It would be to me, a great additional grief, if I am compelled to resign this quiet home, and with my breaking heart, be deprived of its solitude & retirement. Necessity will compel me, if I am not assisted as *before mentioned*, on the 1st of Feb. to rent it— as that is the month *here*, when houses are placed on the market— by that time, certainly the result of any efforts, can be known, & by continuing *here*, with little or nothing to live upon, I may lose a good tenant—Robert is careful of his means—but a young man's simplest clothing is expensive—and in consequence of his position & well established nobleness of character, many calls are made upon him —and his meager $2,000 a year is soon gone—after the 1st of Feb. I have resolutely determined never to call upon him again—*he*, has as little to spare as myself—Being well aware of your interested wishes —in our pecuniary behalf, and with the prospect so appalling of *change* to me, may I not hope soon, to hear favorable news from you. I remain dear Judge, with great respect

Truly Yours
Mary Lincoln

To David Davis

Chicago 25th Dec [1866]

My dear Sir:

Your kind letter has been received and I am aware that it is oc-cupying your valuable time too much, even to reply to it. I am deeply grateful for your great interest in our welfare, as a family, and it is oftentimes very painful to me to reflect, that you have been given so much trouble; annoyances, which we may be entirely unconscious of. I feel assured it will be as great a satisfaction to you, as to our-selves, if we can be permitted to remain, *just as we are*—but as I am now situated with regard to it—instead of keeping house, *a year* longer it will be impossible to do so—two months. In that time, *if there is a disposition*, to change our embarrassed state—sure *evidence*, will be given. I can struggle but a few weeks longer as I am now doing. Aside from selfish reasons, I hope Gen Cameron will be elected U.S. Senator. He is a kind tender hearted man. It appears that his daughter, Jennie, is to be married this week—She is a very pretty girl. I write to state to you, exactly the circumstances of the case. A word, a line, from you, dear Judge, in any accessible quarter, will be "all powerful," believe me—

Very respectfully-
Mary Lincoln

To Francis Bicknell Carpenter

Chicago 25th Dec 1866

Private
My dear Sir:

Your very kind letter was received a day or two since & I address you, whilst all the world is rejoicing over the return of an anniversary, so welcome to the glad world generally, my desolate broken heart, feels more than ever its great, great sorrow. I write you to day, to thank you, for the most perfect likeness of my beloved husband, that I have ever seen, the resemblance is so accurate, that it will require far more calmness, than I can now command, to have it continually placed before me. [7] Time only increases my great anguish of mind, over the fearful loss sustained in the death of my idolized husband.

As regards, the volume you so kindly sent my "little Taddie," I feel that many apologies, are due you. When it was received, I was suffering from chills and just as my health was being partially restored—your last kind favor was received. I had the pleasure of a call from Mr [Isaac] Arnold recently, whom you doubtless remember, he spoke of you, very pleasantly.

Knowing, how precious the memory of my sainted husband is

---

[7] Mrs. Lincoln had requested this portrait of Carpenter in a letter written on October 26, 1865.

to you, may I request the acceptance of a simple memento, which was *his*, and has been handled by *him*. It is a very plain cane, yet it has his name upon it, and will be treasured by you & yours. *This day*, is so sad to me, separated from my husband—that I can scarcely compose myself to write, even to you—so connected as you were for months, with the White house, and so many painful associations, that distract my brain.

With many happy returns of this day, to yourself and Mrs Carpenter, I remain

Very truly your friend
Mary Lincoln

"P.S."

The cane will be sent by Express to you, tomorrow, to your address.

M. L.

To The Committee of the French Democracy [8]

Chicago, Ill
January 3d 1867

Gentlemen:

The Medal which you were delegated to present, has been placed in my hands.

I cannot express to you the emotions, with which I receive this manifestation of the feelings of so many thousands of your fellow countrymen. So grand a testimonial to the memory of my husband, given in honor of his services in the cause of liberty, by those who labor in the same great cause in another land, is deeply affecting, and I beg you to accept for yourselves and for those whom you represent, my most grateful acknowledgments.

With profound respect I am, your obedient servant

Mary Lincoln

To Messieurs:

Etienne Arago, Ch. L. Chassin, L. Greppo, L. Lament-Pichat, Eug Despois, L. Kneip, A. Thomas, Albert J. Michelet, J. Barni,

[8] See letter to Alexander Williamson, July 21, [1866].

V. Chaffons, E. Littre, V. Schoelcher, T. Delord, P. Joigneaux, V. Maugin, Edgar Quinet, Louis Blanc, Eugene Pelletan, and Victor Hugo.

To David Davis

Chicago Jan 9th [1867]

My dear Sir:

I find myself again troubling you, by requesting you to send me—my half yearly interest—and notwithstanding the most rigid economy—with the high prices of every thing—this will carry me— a very short distance. *Your name*—will be very powerful—in your kind undertaking to secure means, that I may remain in this house —otherwise—I shall be compelled to relinquish it—the 1st of March —the thought to me is terrible!—Robert—sometimes speaks of accompanying—*Mr Fuller* [9]—to Wash. this winter. I fear *he* is in earnest & I think under present existing circumstances, it would be impracticable. Do you not? He may not be in earnest, *yet*, I fear he is. Will you not write to him, (not mentioning my name) speak of it as a rumor—and advise him not to do so. Mr Fuller—I believe— leaves next week—for Wash—& perhaps considers that R. may be useful to him. The thought of Robert, *so soon* repairing to W- is painful to me—I will rely on you, not mentioning my name to *him* in this—I think you will agree with me, about it. Very Resp

Mary Lincoln

To Leonard Swett

Jany 12th [1867]

My dear Sir:

Mr *Trumbull* has arrived in S[pringfield] & I fear with his smooth plausible stories—*will be* reelected. As a devoted friend, of

[9] Probably Samuel W. Fuller, partner in the firm of Scammon, McCagg and Fuller, where Robert Lincoln was serving his legal apprenticeship.

my husband's & knowing all his cold, selfish, treachery towards him, can you not write *to day*, to influential parties in S- and tell them, *the whole truth*. His past conduct to my darling husband, is always *fresh*, in my mind. I observe that *McGinnis'* [1] name is *not* among the confirmations. Important persons in W. have written & questioned me about this insignificant personage yet his antecedents—had been questioned. Should Gen Cameron, be confirmed by the Senate, as he unquestionably will, will you immediately write him? Also give me any news, when you receive letters from Judge Davis.

I remain with great respect

Truly

Mary Lincoln

P.S. I neglected to mention, in discussing the McGinness' [sic] on yesterday. that in parting Mrs *Mc.* insisted upon, some memento of Mr Lincoln—I asked her, what she would like—she replied "*a cane.*" You may imagine my reply & secret indignation. I declined of course, and in the coldest manner—Such profanation a *cane* of my Martyred husband, in the hands of a low Copperhead!!

To David Davis

Chicago Jany 14th [1867]

My dear Sir:

In consideration of Genl Cameron, having received the nomination for U.S. Sen from Penn- with the certainty of confirmation, may I request you to write to him without delay, whilst his triumph is still fresh in his mind—Gen Cameron is generous minded and *impulsive* and will most probably be only *too glad* to remember the promises made, when his future, was uncertain—and *now* he can effect much—Armed with *authority* from you, with your high name & character—both Cameron—Mr Dodge [2] & others, can accomplish all that is necessary—

[1] Probably John L. McGinnis, Jr., son-in-law of Illinois' former Democratic governor, Joel Matteson.

[2] William E. Dodge, the wealthy New York businessman who headed the Sanitary Commission during the war, was at this time serving as a congressman from New York.

I know that it will be a relief to you to know, and that within two or three weeks—that I can remain *here* quietly and without the "wolf at the door," as it is, at present. You will soon be able to ascertain every thing, as I *now* am, I cannot remain here one day, longer than 1st of March. It pains me thus to trouble you, but believe me, gratefully yours

Mary Lincoln

To Leonard Swett

Jany 18th [1867]

My dear Sir:

Another week of anxiety has passed and I am sure you will pardon me, if I write to you, relative to any news from Judge D. Mr W. E. Dodge, or it may be nearer home. Under the present circumstances without a prospect and assurance of change, I must make arrangements—that will bring fresh trouble to me, with health greatly impaired and feelings already so crushed. But to linger on, as I now am, is utterly impossible. I hope you will deal with me candidly and if you are *not* hopeful inform me—I remain very resp & truly

Mary Lincoln

Next week will bring us news from Genl Cameron, if he means to act, have you heard from him?

To David Davis

Chicago Jany 27 [1867]

My Dear Sir:

Only quite severe indisposition, has prevented an earlier reply to yr kind note, expressive of my most grateful thanks, for the interest you manifest in the subject, of so much importance to me, at present. I cannot realize, after all Gen Cameron's promises, his recent political success—and the consequent influence it will give him —united to the great ungercency of the case, how it is possible for him, not to use all his endeavours, during the month of Feby- to see that I am assisted—I hope ere this you have both heard from & seen Cameron & that he is now at work—With such men as himself & Mr Dodge, sactioned by your word, which will be of inestimable value —they cannot fail to succeed. Otherwise, it is utterly impossible, for me to remain here, four weeks longer, without becoming much embarrassed & in arrears—The check which was received, with the many requirements of the winter, such as fuel, taxes, I have just paid, & many little necessary expenses, will soon consume, my little allowance, with the greatest economy. Without the required assistance is received by 1st March, my fate is inevitable to give up this house—and if so my pride would not allow me to remain here, under such painful circumstances. I would prefer, if in need, to be among entire strangers—I *can but believe*, such an additional trial—will be spared me, with ill health & so much sorrow upon me—I hope you can give me some agreeable information, when you receive this—I remain most respectfully

Mary Lincoln—

To Leonard Swett

375 West Wash St.
[February 1867]

My dear Sir:

Owing to an intense headache, I was unable to read your kind note of yesterday until this morning, and I avail myself, of a moment's respite of sitting up, to reply to it. I can appreciate Judge Davis', desire that I should remain in this house, very especially as I am so much interested in doing so myself, *this place*, has for the last few months, been a refuge to me in my great sorrow & desolation, and it will be a very great additional grief, if *circumstances* remain *unchanged* & I find myself soon compelled to leave it. I am sufficiently brokenhearted *now*, in the event, that sufficient is not added to my meagre income, to live upon—by the 1st of March. What else is left me, but to leave the only place, where I can remain quiet? The prospect of no change, from my present circumscribed means & being cast forth, once more upon the world—causes many a head—as well as heartache—I am very deeply grateful to yourself & Judge D- for your great interest in this troublesome business. It is a painful gratification to me, that the two friends, whom my dearly beloved husband, most loved—should be the one's, to use their influence in endeavouring to extricate me from this painful & humiliating *dilemma*. The God of the widow & orphans, will bless you in all time to come, for your kindness! When you write to Judge D- please say to him, that I shall be only too glad to remain where I now am, in the event of a sufficient sum, being raised to allow me to live, even plainly here, *without it*, I cannot attempt it, after a *very few* weeks —& *no one*, could feel the change so much as my unhappy self— When you have leisure I should like to see you—if you would allow our boy, to call for you tomorrow at 1½ o'clock—he will return you to town—In the midst of your business cares, you are very kind to interest yourself, in my behalf. I fear you cannot decipher this scrawl—My eyes pain me so much, I can scarcely see.

Very truly & respectfully
Mary Lincoln

To Leonard Swett

375 *Wt Wash St*
[*February*, 1867]

My dear Sir:

If perfectly convenient, I would be pleased to see you this afternoon, I have some things to say, which I would like to mention to you. I do not wish to be troublesome yet I am daily convinced that I must make some *definite* arrangements for the future.

I remain respectfully & truly
Mary Lincoln

To David Davis

Chicago 24th Feb [1867]

My dear Sir:

    Mr Swett, appeared to suppose, that the Supreme Court, would adjourn for a few days about the first of March & consequently you would return to Ill- taking Chicago, en route. As the papers makes no mention of it, I presume there is some mistake. The severe winter & very high prices of every thing, with utter inability to meet expenses on so small an income & no apparent prospect of a remedy, has determined me, to end this folly of keeping house on a clerk's salary—and there is no other resource but giving up this house. On next Friday (first of March) I shall place every thing, in the hands of a house agent, either to sell or rent—If I can dispose of my furniture, for what I have paid for it, I must be satisfied. To be homeless & a wanderer in future, is to me, pressed down with care and sorrow —a very great additional grief. My income is barely sufficient, with the most rigid economy, to procure the plainest table fare & my coal bills & living this winter, has completely exhausted, the half year's sum—which is my portion until 1st of July—I can no longer struggle thus—and must remedy it, with the painful resort of giving all up—With apologies for troubling you with this recital—I remain very respectfully

Mary Lincoln

In the midst of the crisis over the house, Mary Lincoln was struck by a fresh blow, so startling and painful that her financial woes were temporarily forgotten. On November 16, 1866, William H. Herndon had presented in Springfield the fourth in a series of lectures on Abraham Lincoln, whom he claimed to have known better than any man alive. The lecture, improbably entitled "A. Lincoln—Miss Ann

Rutledge, New Salem—Pioneering, and THE poem called 'Immortality'—or 'Oh, Why Should the Spirit of Mortal Be Proud,'" had created a sensation. In it Herndon had delivered himself of an astonishing piece of intelligence: the great love of Lincoln's life had not been his wife of twenty-three years but a young girl named Ann Rutledge, an innkeeper's daughter he had befriended in New Salem when he was in his early twenties. "Abraham Lincoln loved Miss Ann Rutledge with all his soul, mind and strength," declared Herndon emphatically.[3]

Herndon had seized on the Rutledge affair, about which he had once heard only the vaguest of hints, as a vital, hitherto unexplored aspect of Abraham Lincoln's life and personality. Ann's untimely death from malaria had driven Lincoln to despondency and, eventually, into a marriage that was without love—or so Herndon sincerely believed. During the course of 1866, he had returned to New Salem's Menard County and had conducted there a series of interviews designed to corroborate his preconceived theories, his "intuition" about what lay behind the late President's recurring spells of melancholy. The men and women he had consulted had had to look back over thirty years in order to call forth some hazy recollection of Lincoln or Ann, but Herndon had used his lawyer's skill at suggestion to prod their memories.[4]

From threads of evidence that Abraham Lincoln had known Ann Rutledge well, had cheered her in the absence of her fiancé, John McNamar, and had been inordinately grieved by her death, Herndon wove a touching tale of love that lingered beyond the grave. "All New Salem encouraged [Lincoln's] suit,"[5] he asserted, in a statement subsequently denied by McNamar himself. There are other, nagging discrepancies between Herndon's theories and the evidence of later years. Lincoln's most conspicuous siege of melancholy came, not over Ann, but during the period of his estrangement from Mary Todd. Not even in his intimate correspondence with Joshua Speed is there so much as a veiled reference to Ann, and

[3] From a pamphlet bearing the text of Herndon's fourth lecture. Photostat in the Illinois State Historical Library, Springfield.
[4] The most thorough and convincing refutation of Herndon's statements is provided by Ruth Painter Randall in her book *Mary Lincoln: Biography of a Marriage*, pp. 36–51; 395–407; 425–9.
[5] Herndon lecture, *ibid.*

Speed claimed never to have heard of her. Finally, the mutual devotion of Mary and Abraham Lincoln must have been all the stronger to have survived their personality differences and the strains of public life—a point that would have been obvious to Herndon had he combined his skill at perception with an objective eye.

Through the efforts of her son Robert, who wished to spare her undue distress, word of Herndon's "revelations" was—somehow —kept from Mrs. Lincoln for four months. Immediately after the Rutledge lecture, Robert had written David Davis that Herndon was "making an ass of himself," [6] which was as much as he could say without knowing how much truth, if any, lay behind the allegations. Robert even went to Springfield and, with great restraint under the circumstances, attempted to deflect Herndon from his cruel course; he got nothing for his trouble but a torrent of abuse.

In March 1867, when the text of the lecture finally fell into Mrs. Lincoln's hands, rage followed on the heels of astonishment. A year earlier she had written Mrs. Welles, "It was always music in my ears, both before & after our marriage, when my husband, told me, that I was the only one, he had ever thought of, or cared for. It will solace me to the grave." [7] Now this boor was trying, for the sake of his own advancement, to snatch away her last comfort. He had to be stopped.

It is well to remember that these events occurred in an era when women were treated with extravagant chivalry, when they were protected, patronized, and idealized to a ridiculous extent. Although others of Herndon's disclosures would be roundly condemned for their assault on Lincoln's saintly reputation, little or no attention was given the fact that his comments on the Lincoln marriage subjected a lady, and a President's widow at that, to the worst sort of public embarrassment—perhaps because the lady in question had already had the bad taste to "make herself conspicuous." Not for nearly a century could any serious attempt to be made to investigate Herndon's sources or refute his contentions, but even at the time few people criticized his cruelty to Mrs. Lincoln. Most of the public swallowed whole his statements regarding the "unfortunate" rela-

[6] Robert Lincoln to David Davis, November 19, 1866. MS. in the Illinois State Historical Library, Springfield.
[7] Mary Lincoln to Mary Jane Welles, Chicago, December 6, 1865.

tionship between the Lincolns. With the Ann Rutledge story, Herndon planted a seed of speculation which in time blossomed into a legend, taking hold so completely that even now many Americans see it as one of the great love stories of all time. In a day when women wept delicious tears over novels of doomed love, and men understood quite well the tragedy of "a heart in the grave," Lincoln's public image acquired a new and romantic dimension, in perfect harmony with Victorian fantasy.

Shaken though she was, Mary Lincoln dismissed out of hand Herndon's fanciful theories about her marriage. Whatever the public was led to believe, she knew the union had been, on balance, an extremely happy one. Far more worrisome would be Herndon's subsequent allegations regarding Lincoln's religious beliefs, or lack of them. She would soon realize that she had made a grave error in admitting that her husband had never joined a church. Her statements in the September 1866 interview with Herndon, so clear and unequivocal to her mind, would be deliberately misconstrued, with malice aforethought. She herself had never doubted her husband's faith in God; who would know better than she that that faith had grown rather than diminished in the face of personal tragedy and awesome responsibility? But to a majority of the population in that day, lack of formal church affiliation meant that one was not a "technical Christian" and was, perhaps, (this, of Lincoln!) *not a Christian at all.* The notion that Abraham Lincoln might have been an "infidel" delighted its proponent, who was of the "non-believing-and-proud-of-it" school. Herndon had put forth his view of Lincoln as a freethinker privately a number of times, particularly in a letter to Dr. James Smith, the Lincolns' former pastor, now serving as an American consul in Scotland. In March of 1867, Dr. Smith sent Herndon's letter to the *Chicago Tribune*, together with his own scathing reply, in which he also took his correspondent to task on the subjects of Ann Rutledge and the Lincoln marriage. The exchange in the newspapers prompted a letter from Mrs. Lincoln to David Davis, whom she was obliged to regard as her protector in such matters. She stated, in the most inelegant language she had ever permitted herself, that Herndon was a "dirty dog," who, should he ever utter another word, would find his life "not worth living." [8]

[8] Mary Lincoln to David Davis, Chicago, March 6th [1867].

Herndon retaliated in time by branding her a "liar," who was subject to fits of madness. "From then on it was open warfare," wrote Herndon's biographer, David Donald. "Year after year went by and Herndon became more and more bitter. . . . Mrs. Lincoln, he thought, was a 'tigress;' a woman, 'imperious, proud, aristocratic, insolent witty and bitter,' 'a she-wolf,' 'soured . . . gross . . . material . . . avaricious.' Twenty years after Lincoln's death he concluded that Mary Todd Lincoln was 'the female wild cat of the age.' " [9] Thanks to Herndon's authoritative air and skill at persuasion, millions of his countrymen came to share this belief.

To David Davis

Chicago, March 4th 67

My dear Sir:

Permit me to point your attention to another sentence, in a lecture of the *distinguished* W[illiam] H[erndon] which is of great significance and indicates more clearly if possible, the malignity of *his* remarks, than any thing else. *He* pointedly says, "for the last *twenty three* years, Mr Lincoln has known no joy,"—it was evidently framed, for the *amiable* latitude he was breathing and was intended to convey a false impression. There is certainly "method in his madness." Will you please direct his *wandering* mind, to *that* particularly offensive & truthless sentence—he will find, if he has no sensibility, himself, *he will* be *taught it*—I will rely on you for *this*. This is the return for all my husband's kindness to this miserable man! Out of pity he took him into his office, when he was almost a hopeless inebriate and although he was only a drudge, in the place, he is very forgetful of his position and assumes, a confidential capacity towards—Mr Lincoln—

As you justly remark, each & every one has had, a little romance in their early days—but as my husband was *truth itself*, and as he always assured me, he had cared for no one but myself, the

---

[9] David Donald. "Herndon and Mrs. Lincoln." *Books at Brown*. Providence, R.I., Vol. XII, Nos. 2 and 3. April, 1950, pp. 4–5.

false W. H. (au contraire) I shall assuredly remain firm in my conviction—that *Ann Rutledge,* is a myth—for in all his confidential communications, such a romantic name, was never breathed, and concealment could have been no object, as Mr H's vivid imagination, supposed this pathetic tragedy to occur when Mr L was eighteen [1] & I did not know him, until he was thirty years old! Nor did his life or his joyous laugh, lead one to suppose his heart, was in any unfortunate woman's grave—but in the proper place with his loved wife & children—I assure you, it will not be *well with him*—if he makes the *least* disagreeable or false allusion in the future. *He* will be closely watched. You mentioned seeing Mr Dodge of N.Y. the evening before you left. Did *he* abandon all hope—please let me know. *It is* so painful to me *now* without sufficient to live upon, and in such a nervous afflicted state, to be compelled to give up a home—May I hope you will write me, after you see, that man Herndon.

Hoping your daughter's health is improving, and with kind regards to Mrs Davis, I remain, always truly & gratefully

Mary Lincoln

I would not believe an assertion of Herndon's if he would take a thousand oaths, upon the Bible—

To David Davis

Chicago March 6th [1867]

My dear Sir:

John Forsyth, the son in law, of Dr [James] Smith saw Robert, on yesterday & says Dr S- sent him the same article.[2] *As it* appears in *this morning's* Tribune, we conclude Dr S- sent the article to the paper. W[illiam] H[erndon] may consider himself a ruined man, in attempting to disgrace others, the vials of wrath, will be poured upon his own head. My love for my husband was so sacred and the

[1] Lincoln was in his early twenties when he knew Ann Rutledge.
[2] An open letter written by Reverend Smith and sent to the Chicago *Tribune,* denouncing Herndon's allegations concerning Lincoln's "romance" with Ann Rutledge.

knowledge it was fully returned so well assured, that if W. H- utters another word—and is not silent with his infamous falsehoods in the future, *his* life is not worth, living for—*I have* friends, if his *low* soul thought that my great affliction—had left me without them. In the future, he may well say, *his prayers*—"Revenge is sweet, especially to womankind but there are some of mankind left, who will wreak it upon him—He is a dirty dog & I [do not?] regret the article was sent to the papers—it shows him forth, in his proper colors—& I think he will *rue* the day, he did not take your advice

Truly
Mary Lincoln

To Alphonso Dunn

Chicago, March 18th [1867]

PRIVATE
Mr Dunn—

Mrs Welles writes to my son Robert [3] in regard to the suit of clothes [4] I gave you—and which have been in the possession of Mr [Matthew] Wilson the artist. She desires them for a Miss Vinnie Ream, un unknown person, who by much forwardness & unladylike persistence, obtained from Congress, permission to execute a statue of my husband, the late President. From her inexperience, I judge she will be unable to do this, in a faithful manner. For your devoted attentions to President Lincoln, I gave you those clothes, and, after the loan you *have* made of them—without you see proper, you need not let them go farther. Retain them always, in memory of the best and noblest man that ever lived.

You will understand me, when I say that it is *now* time for you to claim them, and you need feel under no obligations to allow them

[3] It is interesting to note that Mrs. Gideon Welles directed her request to Robert and not his mother, formerly one of her closest friends. The Welleses' participation in Johnson's "royal progress" in 1866, and Mrs. Lincoln's reaction to it, brought the friendship to an abrupt end.

[4] This suit, worn by Lincoln on the night of the assassination, is now on display at the Lincoln Museum in Ford's Theatre. It was purchased for the Museum from Alphonso Dunn's granddaughter in 1967.

to pass out of your possession at this time. Let me hear from you on this subject when you receive this letter—and show this letter to no one—only burn it. I feel as I gave them to you—I can dictate a little about them. Write on receipt of this. What you say will not be mentioned—as I remain your friend

Mrs Lincoln.

Use *your own* discretion about lending the clothes but as they are a gift from me you are under *no* obligations to yield them into other hands. All this you will understand. I do not wish my name mentioned in it. Write me all about it.

Burn this & mention contents to no one.

PRIVATE

To William H. Crook [5]

Mar 19 [*1867*]

W. H. Crook—

Taddie received your letter this morning & will reply in a few days—Please hand this letter to *Dunn* [6]—it may be, he is now doorkeeper at White House. Tell him, to reply to it, we are quite well.

Your friend
Mrs Lincoln

To Elizabeth Keckley

[INCOMPLETE] [7] [*March, 1867*]

. . . I have not the means, to meet the expenses of even a first-class boarding-house, and must sell out and secure cheap rooms at some

---

[5] A former police officer, appointed guard at the White House in January 1865. After Crook accompanied Mrs. Lincoln on her journey to Chicago, he returned to the Executive Mansion where he served until Chester Arthur's administration.

[6] See letter to Alphonso Dunn, March 18, [1867].

[7] The above excerpt appeared on pp. 267–8 of Elizabeth Keckley's ghost-written memoirs *Behind the Scenes*, published in the spring of 1868, and was dated by her. All the letters from Mrs. Lincoln to her former dressmaker are here reproduced exactly as they appeared in the book.

place in the country. It will not be startling news to you, my dear Lizzie, to learn that I must sell a portion of my wardrobe to add to my resources, so as to enable me to live decently, for you remember what I told you in Washington, as well as what you understood before you left me here in Chicago. I cannot live on $1,700 a year, and as I have many costly things which I shall never wear, I might as well turn them into money, and thus add to my income, and make my circumstances easier. It is humiliating to be placed in such a position, but, as I am in the position, I must extricate myself as best I can. Now, Lizzie, I want to ask a favor of you. It is imperative that I should do something for my relief, and I want you to meet me in New York, between the 30th of August and the 5th of September next,[8] to assist me in disposing of a portion of my wardrobe. . . .[9]

To Alphonso Dunn

April 2d 67

Mr A. Dunn—

I write you in haste, merely to say—that you can act as you please in the matter. This Miss Ream, is an entire stranger to me and mine—and I expect very inexperienced in her work, but I trust very sincerely, she may succeed.

I remain your friend

Mrs A. Lincoln

To David Davis

Chicago 6th April 1867

My dear Sir:

Feeling assured that you would feel interested in the result of the visit of the gentleman, who called to inspect the house, with a

[8] Later, plans were changed; Mrs. Lincoln did not meet Mrs. Keckley until the end of September.
[9] This adventure became known as "The Old Clothes Scandal." It is discussed on pp. 429–33.

view to renting, I have concluded I would write you to day. The party declined taking it on account of distance &&—I will not be able to get the worth of my new furniture in rent, and as it is utterly impossible with my small, contracted means to keep house—in order to meet even ordinary expenses—I shall have to dispose of my furniture which you may be assured will be a fresh trial to me. Mr Butters, who is considered the best auctioneer, of private sales called to see me on yesterday, and says that if I intend to sell to advantage, I must do so, by the 20*th* of this month, as all parties are requiring furnishing articles at that time—and to sell in *the house*, with furniture just as it stands, *he* can realize 50 per cent more than to send it to the auction. This disposal, will render it much easier for me to live and without I make this effort, on my little pittance of an income I cannot possibly live. Families who reside in the handsomest homes, here do so—but *the same pride*, that made me *endeavour*, for the sake of *our country* & position, to keep up a genteel appearance, that *same* feeling causes me to shrink, from a *flag* from our windows. Yet, *not* to be harrassed for fear of debt, and to rest & live easier, I must take up *this cross*, however unwillingly. *Gladly*, would I remain where I am, but I cannot undertake another year of servitude, being compelled to count *every cent* I must spend—Mr Butters, assures me, what I feel may prove true, that a year hence, prices will decrease and I cannot obtain a third of the value of the furniture—selling the furniture, and renting the house—will make it better for me. Tad—must be allowed enough to pay his board & expenses. Of course having an auction sale, at the house—will be as great a trial to Robert & as well as myself—But *I find* that *pride* does not give us bread & meat—With my taste for comforts, if when *stern necessity*, requires it, I am willing to fare plainly, the world, which (after all its professions) have been so willing that we should *do so*, need not complain. A poor return *all this is*, for the immortal services rendered by my beloved husband, to his Country! My poor health would make it most agreable to remain, where I now am, yet alas! I have no choice.

I remain very respectfully,
M. L.

Mary Lincoln, with Robert and Tad, occupied her house for a single, joyless year. As early as March 1867, she wrote Elizabeth Keckley of her reluctant decision to "sell out" and look for "cheap rooms"; a month later she was negotiating with an auctioneer for the sale of her furniture. The painful business of breaking up housekeeping (as well as a total absence of financial prospects) probably caused her to curtail her correspondence during the months of April, May and June; hardly any letters exist for that period. But by midsummer, having put up the house for rent or sale, she was forced to settle with David Davis a matter that she had been pushing aside too long in the face of other problems: the future welfare of her son Tad.

In the two years since his father's death Tad Lincoln had emerged from childhood into adolescence. At fourteen, he was still his mother's "troublesome *sunshine*," [1] but he was no longer the little imp whose charm and capers could reduce his elders to jelly. He had begun his formal education in September of 1865, at a public school in Chicago; the following year he was enrolled at the Brown School, a boys' academy within walking distance of his new home. The adjustment to discipline, routine, and casual, knockabout relationships with other children had not been an easy one and was never to be entirely accomplished. The inevitable isolation of a White House childhood, followed by the loss of an idolized father and the normal difficulties of dislocation, were only a few of his problems. If the Lincolns had doted on all their sons, they had spoiled Tad hopelessly, especially after Willie's death. They had encouraged his pranks with rueful laughter, given in to his whims, and neglected his training in the essentials of daily life. When he came to Chicago at twelve, he was, by his mother's own admission, unable to read or write any but the simplest words. A marked speech impediment, at first considered endearing, was probably responsible for his slow progress, but, whatever the reason, his mental processes were as

[1] Mary Lincoln to Elizabeth Emerson Atwater, June 30, [1867].

capricious as his conduct, his powers of concentration practically nil. Nor did his role as his mother's constant companion and mainstay help matters. Caught up in her own agonies, which could not have failed to affect an impressionable boy, forced to change residences four times in two years, Mary Lincoln could hardly surround her son with that atmosphere of continuity and stability which frees the young for self-development.

But Tad was a good boy, anxious to please his mother and live up to the example set by Robert, whom he adored. After two years of schooling he had learned to channel his energies into constructive projects and was beginning to be able to compete on equal terms with others of his age. He was growing increasingly malleable (perhaps too much so) but was still in need of discipline and direction, and this, his mother was conscientious enough to realize, would have to be supplied by someone other than herself. As long as Tad was underage he was required by law to have a guardian, preferably a male. At first Robert accepted the charge, but later wrote Judge Davis that he thought "some older person" with the authority to provide Tad with "advice and restraint" would be more suitable.[2] After several family friends in Springfield declined the responsibility, it fell ultimately to Davis himself.

Even while the guardianship question hung in abeyance, the problem of Tad's education arose, and again Mrs. Lincoln turned to Davis for advice. Immediate steps had to be taken to set Tad on the road to adult responsibility, to broaden his associations and experience, and to allow him a taste of independence. A room and an income of his own were only preliminaries; what he clearly needed was to go away to school, and on this subject his mother was, to say the least, ambivalent. She wanted the best for Tad but she was understandably loath to be separated from him.

In late June 1867, Tad and Robert were called to Washington to testify at the trial of John Surratt.[3] Mrs. Lincoln, who was also requested to appear, gave ill health as the reason she could not. Instead, she took advantage of her sons' absence to make a brief excursion to Racine, Wisconsin, site of an Episcopal secondary

---

[2] Robert Lincoln to David Davis [February 1866]. Quoted in Ruth Randall. *Lincoln's Sons*. Boston, 1955, p. 230.

[3] See Mary Lincoln to David Davis, June 30, [1867], *note*.

school that had been recommended for Tad. Her letters from Racine provide evidence that she was prejudiced against the school—against any boarding school—almost before she saw it. This one seemed a bit too "*high church*." The tuition was prohibitive. An "air of *restraint*" about the place put her off. In the end, the sight of "the little white cots of the boys, where they are wont, to repose, so far away, from the[ir] loving mothers" sealed her determination to keep Tad by her side.[4] After her sons returned and the house was rented, she took rooms at the Clifton House and enrolled Tad in the Chicago Academy for the school year 1867–8.

To Alexander Williamson

[INCOMPLETE] [5]   [*May 26, 1867*]

. . . I intend doing so—I have learned to view all these articles emanating from these unknown individuals—with perfect scorn—*The* world, understands the object of these persons, *to see* themselves in print—they soon sink to *their own level*—which is *low enough*.

I enclose you an article sent me a few days since—I wish you would oblige me—without *my name* appearing in it—to have it inserted in the daily [Washington] Chronicle—send me a copy—also enclose copies—to the New York Papers & Boston—My health continues very bad—*This climate* and my great grief are certainly shortening my life—Except for precious Tad—I would gladly welcome death—If you can quietly, use yr influence—have this appear —immediately—I will be pleased—I will not be here after this day week—and know not where I shall go—so please be expeditious & forward copies to me & elsewhere—send the whole Chronicle—I enclose you a letter sent me—Please write a little article, mentioning how much *my* gifts realized for the Fair—*without* publishing

[4] Mary Lincoln to Elizabeth Emerson Atwater, Racine, June 30, [1867].
[5] All that has been preserved of this letter are the final four pages, the first marked "5." by Mrs. Lincoln. The date "26th May/67'" has been superimposed on her handwriting on the last page.

the letter—*Bing*—would make a good notice of it—return me *the* letter I write in haste, *after* a week, I scarcely know where I *will* be —Tad sends his love

Yr friend
Mrs L

To David Davis

Chicago June 17th [1867]

My dear Sir:

In the probable event of Robert, *not* visiting Springfield, during your visit there, I have concluded to write you, in reference, to our dear little Taddie. As you are aware, our expenses are necessarily very heavy and it would be a great relief to us—to have a guardian appointed for him—at the present time—this month. I regret to learn that Mr J Williams [6] is unable to undertake it, but I trust, Mr Condell—[7] will not decline. Taddie, is very gentle in character and gives trouble to no one—If my means, were not so straitened, I would most willingly spare all I could, for his clothing, board & education—As it is, his unavoidable bills—thus far reach $400— certainly—eight or nine hundred, I hope will be allowed, at the present time, of high prices and little prospect of a change—for his support—Knowing your great kindness of heart, I feel assured, you will make this all right, without delay—I believe each of our interest, is due 1st of July—and if not inconvenient to you—I shall be pleased to get mine—All particulars, relative to ourselves—I shall give you—on yr next visit to Chicago. I remain always truly & sincerely—

Mary Lincoln

[6] John Williams, Springfield drygoods merchant. One can surmise that his and others' reluctance to assume the guardianship was due to the difficulty of dealing with Mrs. Lincoln on financial matters, especially at a distance.

[7] Thomas Condell, Jr., a Springfield merchant and banker. Condell was a close friend of A. T. Stewart; his son Moses was a nephew by marriage of Mrs. Lincoln's sister Elizabeth Edwards.

To David Davis

[INCOMPLETE]   *Racine Wis*
June 30th [1867]

My dear Sir:

I cannot express to you, my disappointment whilst seated in the cars last Tuesday afternoon in looking over the paper, to find your name among the arrivals—at the Tremont. I had wished so much to see, consult you and say so much—that I have no time to write—My health, after I saw you, broke down so completely, that I concluded Physician's visits daily, would break me up, if the *stupendous* Chicago prices *did not*—So I have closed my house and placed it in the hands of an agent for rent or sale—My very small income, is unequal to the task of keeping house at present prices— The time has now come, when Taddie must have some of his means at disposal to defray expenses—can this not be arranged this coming month—July? You are doubtless aware we were all summoned by Judge Pierrepoint [sic] & Mr Stanton, To Wash in the Surratt case—[8] of course, as I have been scarcely able to leave my lounge, I declined—Robert & Taddie, went on—and I am expecting their daily return—I came up to Racine, to see something about the school here—Mrs Senator Doolittle [9] (who resides here drove to the college on yesterday with me. I am very much pleased with its location & strange to say, their *present* term, does not end, until the *25th* of *Sept.* The College is situated in a grove of 90 acres—and scholars are compelled to board in the institution. A great many boys, of dear little Taddie's age were there & appeared quite happy. The board & tuition for the year was about $400- not including clothing & many *et ceteras*—Then the board of about 3 months— between the two vacations will make it absolutely necessary that $900—at the least should be allowed by the Court for Taddie. Your

[8] From June 10 to August 10, 1867, was held the trial of John Surratt, son of Mary Surratt, in whose Washington boardinghouse John Wilkes Booth and his fellow conspirators had met. Because Tad had encountered on board the *River Queen* a rough-looking man who might have been Surratt, he was called to Washington to testify at the trial, with Robert accompanying him. Judge Edwards Pierrepont presided.

[9] Wife of Senator James R. Doolittle, Republican of Wisconsin.

influence will I am sure obtain any necessary sum, from the Court —Robert, will be with you at any time you desire. *He* has in his possession, [records] which [show] *he* has paid many unavoidable bills against Taddie—I will be here, perhaps, several weeks at any time, you will be [page missing]

To Elizabeth Emerson Atwater [1]

Racine, June 30th [1867]

My dear Mrs Atwater.

Feeling assured you would be interested in my movements, I have concluded to write to you to day. A few hours after I saw you last Monday, a telegram was received from Robert, urging that Taddie should immediately proceed to Washington. Which he did on Tuesday afternoon at four o'clock—At the same hour, I left in a contrary direction, politely attended by my son's gentlemanly friend Norman Williams [2] and the *ever* faithful Thomas [Cross?] —to the depot. I am anxiously awaiting the return of my sons—you may be sure, I miss my little troublesome *sunshine* Taddie every hour—I find the house where I am stopping very neat, clean and every one anxious to please. I have a parlor & bedroom—fronting the lake & I find the air very refreshing. I may probably remain here some weeks—I am finding the rest very beneficial to me— Without I am compelled from the necessity of my house, *neither* being rented or sold, to return to it, I think I shall never undertake housekeeping again. That good husband of yours, will agree with me, that I am returning to my senses. After all, without my All in this life, my dearly beloved husband, why should I seek to find a house, the ever vacant chair is always there and I cannot have a settled feeling, where none exists in my heart. Alas! Alas! how every thing has changed. I find some friends residing here—Senator

[1] Wife of Samuel T. Atwater, a successful Chicago insurance agent. Mrs. Atwater was for many years active in the city's civic and charitable affairs.
[2] A young Chicago lawyer, born in Vermont. At this time Williams was thirty-two years old and building the lucrative practice that eventually made him one of the most prominent and philanthropic Chicagoans of his day.

Doolittle's family. *He* himself has stooped very low politically [3] but his wife is a very sweet & unpretending woman with great good sense & a very sympathetic heart—she has been twice to see me & last evening she called for me in her carriage to visit the College. I cannot express to you, how beautiful the last is situated on the banks of the lake, the grounds, 90 acres in all, a complete grove and the building situated in its midst. We were of course most graciously received, by the head professor, Dr Dekooven—attired very much like a *Jesuit* Priest, with an air of great suavity he conducted us throughout the building—My feelings were especially *moved*, by seeing the little white cots of the boys, where they are wont, to repose so far away, from the loving Mothers, who would at any moment, give almost their life to see them—Every thing is beautiful & comfortable, yet how could I, who have been deprived of so much and am left so little to love—how can I be separated from my precious child. It appears to be an exaction, that each child must board at College, Saturday they attend school & *Monday* is their holiday. As much as I am *now* feeling the necessity for Taddie, being especially cared for, and taught obedience by kind & gentle school treatment, yet there was an air of *restraint* which I did not exactly like. Yet it must be a most excellent school. It is still in session & remains so until 25*th* of *Sept*—Is it not a strange order of things?—and then begins again, early in Nov- Sen Doolittle, resides almost adjacent to the College. The walks here are shady & very pleasant. Each morning I have walked two miles—I scarcely know what I shall do about Taddie—I had *not* made up my mind to send him to school this summer & scarcely think I shall. We found the boys assembled in the chapel, practising their music—as you are aware it is an Episcoplain institute—yet scholars of all denominations attend. I should judge they were *high church*, their singing amounted to *almost* a *te deum*—how I wish I could see you. *Do* spare me a day or two down here. Hoping you will soon write, I remain yours

M. L.

---

[3] A reference to the fact that Senator Doolittle had allied himself with those Republicans who supported President Johnson in his troubles with the radicals in Congress.

To David Davis

My Dear Sir:

Your kind note has been received, and I fully concur with you, that with regard to Taddie, an arrangement should be made for him immediately. My sons were to reach Chicago, this morning & will be here tomorrow early. I came up here for rest & quiet, *temporarily*, even in the event of placing Taddie, at school here for the next two months, with the opportunity of seeing him *only once* a week, I should scarcely be here, but little of the time. On the other hand Robert is in Chicago, yet whilst I remain here, he will come out every Saturday evening & pass the Sabbath. I cannot afford to close up my house longer than the 1st of Sept if it remains *unrented* or unsold. It would be a most disagreeable necessity to have to return to it, owing to the unending expenses, the keeping of it, draws upon me, and my health & spirits are incapable of properly undertaking *such* a charge—I will rely upon the agent, doing the best he can for me by Autumn—I cannot certainly lose by the house—it will certainly *more* than cover the cost. Is it now your opinion, that a *more liberal* allowance would be given Taddie at Chicago than Springfield? In C it is better understood how much it takes to live —to board, clothe, & educate a boy, at schools *appropriate* for him —in S- their ideas are more contracted & would even deem a city school quite sufficient—My husband, always spoke of Mr. Matheney [sic] [4] as an excellent man. The sum of $900- that I mentioned in my former letter, would barely cover the entire cost of Taddie at a school, such *as this*, at Racine, clothing & boarding, between sessions. As he grows older, of course, his expenses increase & with my limited income—I would be unable to supply the deficiency. I will leave it all, to your good judgment, & kindness of heart. During the past year, I have been so harrassed to *avoid* debt & try to live comfortably, that come what may, I am determined to

[4] Probably James H. Matheny, lawyer and court clerk who had been one of Lincoln's oldest friends in Springfield.

thrust aside, all *such* care as much as possible in the future—The school at Racine remains in session, until Sept 25th yet in the uncertainty of *not* knowing what Taddie's allowance may be—I will not undertake to place him in school until it is decided—and I am very anxious to do so—as there is no time to be lost. I neglected to request in my letter, my *third* of the half yearly interest—my half yearly portion. May I trouble you to send it to me—as soon as you can. I remain very respectfully

Mary Lincoln

To Elizabeth Emerson Atwater

Racine July 13th 67

My dear Mrs Atwater:

Your kind note has been received, and only the knowledge, that every moment of your time is occupied and that a dull correspondent is never missed, has caused my silence. The pure air of this place still pleases me, yet think dear lady, that my boys are still in Washington and *life*, without my little Taddie, is indeed a miserable existence. The Secretary of War telegraphs me, that they will soon *be allowed* to return—the [John Surratt] trial appears to me only a *mockery* and only a repetition of the Jeff Davis one—What injustice and treason, is permitted in this land!⁵ Do you wonder, that I long to leave it! I suppose the "Brown will"—struck you as a little remarkable—What a large soul *W. H. B.*⁶ must have had, to allow his wife, who had toiled and *economised* for him always, such a noble pension, as $3,000 a year—Does Mr Atwater know, how much his estate is valued at? *This*, will be a lesson for ladies who have rich husbands—I hope she will be more successful, than *myself*, in her experiment, of keeping house on a *small pittance!* I shall never regret, having retired in disgust and given up the vain attempt—are your friends, the Andersons, still with you? If they have

⁵ John Surratt, like Davis, was freed on bail and never brought back for a second trial.
⁶ William H. Brown. Mrs. Brown is mentioned in the letter to Davis of September 12, [1865].

left, do run up here and make me a visit, even if it is, for a day or two—I wish to see you *so* much—*When*, will I have that pleasure? I have surrounded myself with books & propose a great deal of reading, whilst I remain here. Indeed this is the only resource that is left me. I occasionally, see persons who call, and have made a *few* desirable acquaintances, yet to be candid, I would prefer, that my present solitude, should be unbroken. *You* understand me— and yet being unacquainted with grief, *you* can scarcely do so. Do write, whilst I remain always,

> truly yours
> Mary Lincoln

May I hope to see you in Racine—So short a time, will bring you here—

> M. L.

No sooner had Mary Lincoln temporarily resettled in the Clifton House with Tad in August of 1867 than she began seriously planning an enterprise she had been considering for months. In a last, desperate attempt to raise money, she would go to New York, taking with her for sale trunks full of finery that she had accumulated in years past: gowns, furs, shawls, lengths of lace, pieces of jewelry, all of it costly and none of it of any use in her state of perpetual mourning. She intended at first to offer these things to a dealer at face value, keeping their ownership a secret—anything rather than expose herself to adverse publicity. But somewhere in the recesses of her mind must have lurked the knowledge of what these items might bring were it known they had once been worn by Mrs. President Lincoln.

Nearly every money-raising scheme that she had concocted alone had ended in disappointment; this one ended in debacle. What Billy Herndon could not do to her reputation, then and in the future, she did herself with what came to be known as "The Old Clothes Scandal." Ill-conceived and badly managed, it brought down on her head such a spate of criticism that she was ultimately forced to flee the country in humiliation.

Because she could not face the experience alone, she asked Elizabeth Keckley to come up from Washington and stay with her in New York until her business was completed. Mrs. Keckley would come not as a servant, but as a friend, ready to provide companionship, assistance, and moral support, as the occasion demanded. Much of what is known of the expedition is contained in a chapter of Mrs. Keckley's controversial memoir, *Behind the Scenes*, published the following spring. Her account, designed to exculpate her former employer, only succeeded in making public the unsavory details of an episode that had, by that time, received its full measure of unfortunate publicity. But the incidents she described, the conversations she recorded, the letters she published, all have about them a distressing air of authenticity. Moreover, key aspects of her narrative are corroborated in other sources. Here, in essence, was her story:

Despite grave misgivings, "Lizzie" agreed to meet Mary Lincoln—traveling under her old pseudonym "Mrs. Clarke"—in New York in mid-September. Somehow the pair missed connections. Mrs. Lincoln, arriving alone and failing to find her friend, grew frantic with apprehension, as evidenced by her letter of September 17. Mrs. Keckley's eventual arrival created new and unexpected problems. Because she was a Negro she found it difficult to engage regular quarters at the hotel; Mrs. Lincoln joined her in a cramped attic suite and, later, when Lizzie was refused service in the hotel dining room, offered to accompany her, unescorted, to a public restaurant. (The seamstress went hungry that night rather than allow the President's widow to indulge in such a breach of propriety.)

The following morning the two women settled on a bench in Union Square Park, heavily veiled against prying eyes, to discuss the matter at hand. Mrs. Lincoln announced that she had already selected, from a newspaper listing, a firm of commission brokers, W. H. Brady & Company, to handle the sale of her possessions and had, in fact, called at their establishment the day before. She had been treated rudely until her identity had been "accidentally" discovered. From that moment on, the brokers had been all smiles and blandishments.

Before long, Mrs. Keckley saw Brady and his partner S. C. Keyes for herself. Instead of a pair of conservative businessmen, drones in a musty Broadway office, Messrs. Brady and Keyes revealed themselves as promoters, tenth-rate Barnums. They assured Mrs. Lincoln that by placing matters entirely in their hands, she would have a hundred thousand dollars within a few weeks. But she must first forget any naive notions of anonymity: the key to success lay in capitalizing on her name. An initial step would be for her to write "certain letters" for the brokers to show to prominent politicians in the city, most of whom had at one time or another received favors from the Lincoln administration. Brady promised that these men would make "heavy advances" rather than let it be known that Mrs. Lincoln was in such want that she had to sell her wardrobe. The letters would hint at past consideration in the hope of embarrassing the politicians into present generosity.

Mary Lincoln dutifully sat down in her hotel room and composed a series of sorrowful letters, addressed to the brokers and pre-dated "Chicago," to make it appear as if the impulse were entirely her own. She was perhaps so caught up with enthusiasm that she failed to appreciate the import of Brady's corollary proposal: after showing the letters to the politicians, he would threaten to publish them in the newspapers if assistance were not forthcoming. The idea smacked more than slightly of blackmail, but Mrs. Lincoln was not unreceptive. In her sickness, her obsession about money, her mind had often run in the same channels.

Brady took around the letters, but the politicians, not surprisingly, refused to bite. After several days, during which the two women were forced to remove to the country to escape the curious stares of hotel guests, the brokers admitted that the scheme had been a failure. "Aside from a few dresses sold at small prices to second-hand dealers," wrote Mrs. Keckley in her book, "Mrs. Lincoln's wardrobe was still in her possession. . . . and she was goaded into more desperate measures. Money she must have, and to obtain it she proposed to play a bolder game. She gave Mr. Brady permission to place her wardrobe on exhibition for sale, and authorized him to publish the letters in the *World*." [7] On the day the

---

[7] Keckley, pp. 295–6.

letters were published, their author was on her way back to Chicago. She had an eventful journey, which she described "graphically" to Mrs. Keckley in a letter written on October 6.

Once Mrs. Lincoln was out of sight, her clothing was put on display, and though crowds came to stare and pick over it, no one came to buy. Not at all daunted, Brady and Keyes suggested still another tack: the issuance of a circular letter describing Mrs. Lincoln's plight, to be signed by numbers of well-known figures, the weight of whose names would presumably induce the general public to open its purses. This too fell flat when no one of any stature could be persuaded to sign his name to such a document. But the brokers had in mind one final project, even more dubious than the others: to send the wardrobe on touring exhibition around the country (and perhaps even in Europe), not for sale but as a curiosity, for which admission would be charged. The display would even include the bloodstained garments Mrs. Lincoln had worn on the night of the assassination. Desperate though she may have been, she was horrified to discover that this plan had been put into operation without her consent. She need not have worried. The "traveling show" scheme died a-borning when civic authorities in Providence, Rhode Island, refused to allow such an exhibition to take place in their city.

Once again matters had gotten out of hand, and the public repercussions were deafening. Their effect on Mrs. Lincoln can be discerned in her despairing communications to Elizabeth Keckley throughout the winter of 1867–8. With the publication of her letters to the brokers in the New York *World* (a Democratic paper never known for its charity to the Lincolns, man or wife), the whole undignified business was revealed, and Mary Lincoln was castigated and ridiculed from all sides.

Soon newspapers everywhere were reprinting the letters, often to the accompaniment of venomous editorials. Not since her Washington days had Mrs. Lincoln been subjected to such a barrage of imprecation, insinuation, and outright falsehood. The *World* culled the most damning passages from these editorials, publishing a new selection of excerpts every day for a week. Their general tone was reflected in an item from the Springfield (Mass.) *Republican*, which deplored the fact that "that dreadful woman . . . in the open market with her useless finery . . . persists in forcing her repugnant individuality before the world." The Cincinnati *Commercial* dismissed her as "an intensely vulgar woman," adding for good measure that "her relatives were all secessionists, and it was suspected that her sympathies were rather with the rebellion." [8] The radical faction of the Republican party, particularly, denounced and disowned her, although her heart had always been with them; her late husband's friends and those who opposed the radicals shook their heads sadly and accused the radicals of playing into the hands of the Democrats by dwelling on the foolishness of a miserable woman. The Democrats exulted: off-year elections were coming up. "If I had committed murder in every city of this *blessed Union*," lamented the victim of this scorn to Lizzie Keckley on October 9, "I could not be more traduced."

At Mrs. Lincoln's request, Mrs. Keckley stayed on in New York for most of the winter, keeping an eye on Brady and Keyes and on the property in their possession. As might have been expected, the adventure ended up costing more in expenses than it reaped in profits. Trunks full of unsold goods were returned, and on March 4, 1868, Mrs. Keckley handed Brady and Keyes Mary Lincoln's personal check for $824. With that, her account with the brokers, as well as the whole sorry affair, was closed.

To Elizabeth Keckley

St. Denis Hotel, Broadway, N.Y.
Wednesday, Sept 17th [1867]

My dear Lizzie:

I arrived *here* last evening in utter despair *at not* finding you. I am frightened to death, being here alone. Come, I pray you by *next* train. Inquire for

Mrs. Clarke
Room 94, 5th or 6th Story.

---

[8] Both passages quoted in the New York *World*, October 6, 1867.

House so crowded could not get another spot. I wrote you especially to meet me here last evening, it makes me wild to think of being here alone. Come by *next train*, without fail.

Your friend,
Mrs. Lincoln.

I am booked Mrs. Clarke; inquire for *no other person. Come, come, come.* I will pay your expenses when you arrive here. I shall not leave here or change my room until you come.

Your friend,
M. L.

Do not leave this house without seeing me. *Come!*

To W. H. Brady [9]

Chicago, [*September 1867*]

Dear Sir:

A notice that you sold articles of value on commission, prompts me to write you. The articles I am sending you to dispose of were gifts of dear friends, which only *urgent necessity* compels me to part with, and I am especially anxious that they shall not be sacrificed.

The circumstances are peculiar and painfully embarrassing; therefore I hope you will endeavor to realize as much as possible for them. Hoping to hear from you, I remain, very respectfully,

Mrs A. Lincoln

---

[9] This letter to Brady and those that immediately follow were published in the New York *World* with Mrs. Lincoln's consent. They are dated "Chicago" but were actually written in New York at Brady's instigation.

To W. H. Brady

Chicago, September 14 [1867]

My dear Sir:

Please call and see Hon. Abram Wakeman.[1] He was largely indebted to me for obtaining the lucrative office which he has held for several years, and from which he has amassed a very large fortune. He will assist me in my painful and humiliating situation, scarcely removed from want. He would scarcely hesitate to return, in a small manner, the many favors my husband and myself always showered upon him. Mr. Wakeman many times excited my sympathies in his urgent appeals for office, as well for himself as others. Therefore he will be only too happy to relieve me by purchasing one or more of the articles you will please place before him.[2]

Very truly,
Mrs. A. Lincoln.

To W. H. Brady

Chicago, Sept 18, 1867

Mr Brady

A notice in a New-York paper having attracted my attention, I have this day sent to you personal property, which I am compelled to part with, and which you will find of considerable value.

---

[1] For an account of Mrs. Lincoln's dealings with Wakeman see pp. 165–6, and letters to Wakeman, *passim.*

[2] This letter was published in the New York *World* on October 7, 1867, with a sarcastic editorial which read in part: "The English language affords few things more exquisite, in its way, than this letter. Its frankness and simplicity are touching. Its directness leaves open no avenue of escape. . . . Mr. Wakeman will not resist this appeal! He cannot! . . . Let Mr. Wakeman instantly take the whole lot, and send his check for the amount. The sum will be but a drop in the ocean of his reputed wealth."

The articles consist of four camels' hair shawls, lace dress and shawls, a parasol cover, a diamond ring, two dress patterns, some furs, &c.

Please have them appraised, and confer by letter with me.

Very respectfully,
Mrs Lincoln

To W. H. Brady

Chicago, September 22, 1867

W. H. Brady, Esq.

You write me that reporters are after you concerning my goods deposited with you—which, in consideration of my urgent wants, I assure you I am compelled to relinquish—and also that there is a fear that these newsmen will seize upon the painful circumstances of your having these articles placed in your hands to injure the Republican party politically. In the cause of this party, and for universal freedom, my beloved husband's precious life was sacrificed, Not for the world would I do anything to injure the cause. My heart is very anxious for its success, notwithstanding the very men for whom my noble husband did so much unhesitatingly deprived me of all means of support and left me in a pitiless condition. The necessities of life are upon me, urgent and imperative, and I am scarcely removed from want—so different from the lot my loving and devoted husband would have assigned me—and I find myself left to struggle for myself. I am compelled to pursue the only course left me—immediately within the next week to sell these goods, and if not wholly disposed of by Wednesday, October 30th, on that day please sell them at auction, after advertising *very largely* that they are my goods.

Very respectfully,
Mrs. A. Lincoln

To W. H. Brady

Private

W. H. Brady, Esq.

I have reflected upon your remarks, and have concluded to leave everything to your good judgment and excellent sense. My great, great sorrow and loss have made me painfully sensitive, but as my feelings and pecuniary comfort were never regarded or even recognized in the midst of my overwhelming bereavement—*now* that I am pressed in a most startling manner for means of common subsistence, I do not know why I should shrink from an opportunity of improving my trying position.

Being assured that all you do will be appropriately executed, and in a manner that will not startle me very greatly and excite as little comment as possible, again I shall leave all in your hands.

I am passing through a very painful ordeal, which the country, in remembrance of my noble and devoted husband, should have spared me. I remain, with great respect, very truly,

Mrs. Lincoln

P. S. As you mention that my goods have been valued at over $24,000, I will be willing to make a reduction of $8,000, and relinquish them for $16,000 in five-twenties—*nothing less*. If *this* is not accomplished, I will continue to advertise largely until every article is sold. I must have means to live, at least in a *medium* comfortable state.

Mrs. L.

To Elizabeth Keckley

My Dear Lizzie:

My ink is like myself and my spirits failing, so I write you to-day with a pencil. I had a solitary ride to this place, as you may imagine, varied by one or two amusing incidents. I found, after you left me, I could not continue in the car in which you left me, owing to every seat's berth being engaged; so, being simple *Mrs. Clarke*, I had to eat "humble pie" in a car less commodious. My thoughts were too much with my "dry goods and interests" at 609 Broadway, to care much for my surroundings, as uncomfortable as they were. In front of me sat a middle-aged, gray-haired, respectable-looking gentleman, who, for the whole morning, had the page of the *World* before him which contained my letters and business concerns. About four hours before arriving at Chicago, a consequential-looking man, of formidable size, seated himself by him, and it appears they were entirely unknown to each other. The well-fed looking individual opened the conversation with the man who had read the *World* so attentively, and the conversation soon grew warm and earnest. The war and its devastation engaged them. The bluffy individual, doubtless a Republican who had pocketed his many thousands, spoke of the widows of the land, made so by the war. My reading man remarked to him:

"Are you aware that Mrs. Lincoln is in indigent circumstances, and has to sell her clothing and jewelry to gain means to make life more endurable?"

The well-conditioned man replied: "I do not blame her for selling her clothing, if she wishes it. I suppose *when sold* she will convert the proceeds into five-twenties to enable her to have means to be buried."

The *World* man turned towards him with a searching glance, and replied, with the haughtiest manner: "That woman is not dead yet."

The discomfited individual looked down, never spoke another word, and in half an hour left his seat, and did not return.

I give you word for word as the conversation occurred. May it be found through the execution of my friends, Messrs Brady and Keyes, that "that woman is not yet dead," and being alive, she speaketh and gaineth valuable hearers. Such is life! Those who have been injured, how gladly the injurer would consign them to mother earth and forgetfulness! Hoping I should not be recognized at Fort Wayne, I thought I would get out at dinner for a cup of tea. . . .[3] I will show you what a creature of *fate* I am, as miserable

[3] Mrs. Keckley informed readers of her book that she had "suppress[ed] many

as it sometimes is. I went into the dining-room alone, and was ushered up to the table, where, at its head, sat a very elegant-looking gentleman—at his side a middle-aged lady. My black veil was doubled over my face. I had taken my seat next to him—he at the head of the table, I at his left hand. I immediately *felt* a pair of eyes was gazing at me. I looked him full in the face, and the glance was earnestly returned. I sipped my water, and said, "Mr. S[umner], is this indeed you?" His face was as pale as the table-cloth. We entered into conversation, when I asked him how long since he had left Chicago. He replied, "Two weeks since." He said, "How strange you should be on the train and I not know it!" [4]

As soon as I could escape from the table, I did so by saying, "I must secure a cup of tea for a lady friend with me who has a head-ache." I had scarcely returned to the car, when he entered it with a cup of tea borne by his own aristocratic hands. I was a good deal annoyed by seeing him, and he was so agitated that he spilled half of the cup over my *elegantly gloved* hands. *He* looked very sad, and I fancied 609 Broadway occupied his thoughts. I apologized for the absent lady who wished the cup, by saying that "in my absence she had slipped out for it." His heart was in his eyes, notwithstanding my veiled face. Pity for me, I fear, has something to do with all this. I never saw his manner *so* gentle and sad. This was nearly evening, and I did not see him again, as he returned to the lady, who was his sister-in-law from the East. . . . What evil spirit possessed me to go out and get that cup of tea? When he left me, *woman-like* I tossed the cup of tea out of the window, and tucked my head down and shed *bitter tears* . . . At the depot my darling little Taddie was waiting for me, and his voice never sounded so sweet. . . . My dear Lizzie, do visit Mr. Brady each morning at nine o'clock, and urge them all you can. I see by the papers [A. T.] Stewart has returned. To-morrow I will send the invoice of goods, which please to not give up. How much I miss you, tongue cannot tell. Forget my fright and nervousness of the evening before. Of course you were as innocent as a child in all you

---

passages of Mrs. Lincoln's letters, as they are of too confidential a nature to be given to the public."

[4] Sumner, whose marriage to Alice Hooper had by this time disintegrated, was on a month-long lecture tour in behalf of his new doctrine of "Continentalism," the cornerstone of which was the purchase of Alaska.

did. I consider you my best living friend, and I am struggling to be enabled some day to repay you. Write me often, as you promised.

Always truly yours,
M. L.

To Elizabeth Keckley

Chicago Sunday Morning
Oct 6 [1867]

My dear Lizzie:

I am writing this morning with a broken heart after a sleepless night of great mental suffering. R[obert] came up last evening like a maniac, and almost threatening his life, looking like death, because the letters of the *World* were published in yesterday's [Chicago] paper. I could not refrain from weeping when I saw him so miserable. But yet, my dear good Lizzie, was it not to protect myself and help others—and was not my motive and action of the purest kind? Pray for me that this cup of affliction may pass from me, or be sanctified to me. I weep whilst I am writing. . . . I pray for death this morning. Only my darling Taddie prevents my taking my life. I shall have to endure a round of newspaper abuse from the Republicans because I dared venture to relieve a few of my wants. Tell Mr Brady and Keyes not to have a line of mine once more in print I am nearly losing my reason

Your friend,
M. L.

To Elizabeth Keckley

Chicago, Oct. 8 [1867]

My dear Lizzie:

Bowed down with suffering and anguish, again I write you. As we might have expected, the Republicans are falsifying me, and doing *just* as they did when they prevented the Congressional appropriation. Mrs.——knows something about these same people. As her husband *is living* they dare not utter all they would desire to speak. You know yourself how innocently I have acted, and from the best and purest motives. They will *howl on* to prevent my disposing of my things. What a *vile, vile* set they are! The *Tribune* here, Mr. [Horace] White's paper, wrote a very beautiful editorial yesterday in my behalf; yet knowing that I have been deprived of my rights by the party, I suppose I would be *mobbed* if I ventured out. What a world of anguish this is—and how I have been made to suffer! . . . You would not recognize me now. The glass shows me a pale, wretched, haggard face, and my dresses are like bags on me. And all because I was doing what I felt to be my duty. Our minister, Mr. Swazey,[5] called on me yesterday and said I had done perfectly right. Mrs F[owler] [6] says every one speaks in the same way. The politicians, knowing they have deprived me of my just rights, would prefer to see me starve, rather than dispose of my things. They will prevent the sale of anything, so I have telegraphed for them. I hope you have received from B[rady] the letters I have consigned to his care. See to this. Show none of them. Write me every day.

M. L.

To Elizabeth Keckley

Chicago, Wednesday, October 9th [1867]

My dear Lizzie:

It appears as if the fiends had let loose, for the Republican papers are tearing me to pieces in this border ruffian West. If I had committed murder in every city in this *blessed Union*, I could not be more traduced. And you know how innocent I have been of the intention of doing wrong. A piece in the morning *Tribune*, signed

[5] The Reverend Arthur Swazey, pastor of the Third Presbyterian Church of Chicago from 1860 to 1870. He was also widely known as an editor and polemicist.
[6] A housekeeper at the Clifton House, where Mrs. Lincoln had been living just prior to her New York trip.

"B," pretending to be a lady, says there is no doubt Mrs L- *is* deranged—has been for years past, and will end her life in a lunatic asylum. They would doubtless like me to begin it *now*. Mr. S[wazey], a very kind, sympathizing minister, has been with me this morning, and has now gone to see Mr. [Joseph] Medill, of the *Tribune*, to know if *he* sanctioned his paper publishing such an article. . . . Pray for me, dear Lizzie, for I am very miserable and broken hearted. Since writing this, I have just received a letter from Mr. Keyes, begging and pleading with me to allow them to use my name for donations. I think I will consent . . .

Truly yours
M. L.

To Elizabeth Keckley

Chicago, Sunday, Oct 13 [1867]

My dear Lizzie:

I am greatly disappointed, having only received one letter from you since we parted, which was dated the day after. Day after day I sent to Mrs F[owler] for letters. After your promise of writing me every other day, I can scarcely understand it. I hope to-morrow will bring me a letter from you. How much I miss you cannot be expressed. I hope you have arrived safely in Washington, and will tell me everything. . . . Was there ever such cruel newspaper abuse lavished upon an unoffending woman as has been showered upon my devoted head? The people of this ungrateful country are like the "dogs in the manger;" will neither do anything themselves, nor allow me to improve my own condition. What a Government we have! All their abuse lavished upon me only lowers themselves in the estimation of all true-hearted people. The Springfield *Journal* had an editorial a few days since, with the important information that Mrs. Lincoln had been known to be *deranged* for years, and should be *pitied* for all her *strange acts*.[7] I should have been *all*

---

[7] The article to which Mrs. Lincoln referred appeared in the *Illinois State Journal* on October 10, 1867. It read: "A special dispatch from Chicago to the St. Louis *Democrat*, in referring to Mrs. Lincoln's recent mortifying statements in re-

right if I had allowed *them* to take possession of the White House. In the comfortable stealings by contracts from the Government, these low creatures are allowed to hurl their malicious wrath at me, with no one to defend me or protect me, if I should starve. These people injure themselves far more than they could do me, by their lies and villany. Their aim is to prevent my goods being sold, or anything being done for me. *In this*, I very much fear they have succeeded.

Write me, my dear friend, your candid opinion about everything. I wished to be made better off, quite as much to improve your condition as well as for myself. . . . Two weeks ago, dear Lizzie, we were in that *den* of discomfort and dirt. *Now* we are far asunder. Every other day, for the past week, I have had a chill, brought on by excitement and suffering of mind. In the midst of it I have moved into my winter quarters, and am now very comfortably situated. My parlor and bedroom are very sweetly furnished. I am lodged in a handsome house, a very kind, good, *quiet* family, and their meals are excellent. I consider myself fortunate in all this. I feel assured that the Republicans, who, to cover up their own perfidy and neglect, have used every villanous falsehood in their power to injure me—I fear they have *more* than succeeded, but if their day of reckoning does not come in this world, it *will surely* in the next. . . .

Saturday—I have determined to shed no more tears over all their cruel falsehoods, yet, just now, I feel almost forsaken by God and man—except by the *latter* to be vilified. Write me all that Keyes and Brady think of the result. For myself, after *such* abuse, I *expect* nothing. Oh! that I could see you. Write me, dear Lizzie, if only a line; I cannot understand your silence. Hereafter direct your letters to Mrs. A. Lincoln, 460 West Washington Street, Chicago, Illinois, care of D. Cole. Remember 460. I am always so anxious to hear

gard to her financial condition, says: 'Her conduct has greatly distressed her intimate friends and relatives in this city, and the most charitable construction that they can put on her strange course is that she is insane, which I fear is the case.' The same explanation of her conduct, we understand, has been suggested by those who are acquainted with her in this place. Indeed an impression generally pervades our community that she has not been entirely in her right mind for several years. In this view, she deserves pity and commiseration instead of harsh and uncharitable judgment for her singular behavior."

from you, I am feeling so *friendless* in the world. I remain always your affectionate friend

M. L.

To Rhoda White[8]

Chicago, Oct 18th 1867—

My dear Mrs White:

Your kind note so full of sympathy, was received a day or two since. Overwhelmed with my deep sorrow, I cannot express to you, how soothing to my wounded and tired spirit your amiable words of consolation are—Never was an act committed with a more innocent intention than mine was. Having no further use for the articles proposed to be sold—and really requiring the proceeds—I deposited them with an agent & I presumed no publicity would result from it—I was not more astonished than *you* must have been to see my letters, in print. It is impossible dear Mrs White, for me to write as I would converse with you, on this painful subject. By *the men*, who took every advantage of my beloved husband's position & good nature, I have been persecuted & their influence exerted to deprive me of what the country would otherwise have given me —and when I feel the necessity upon me, to do, as I best can—every act is seized upon & distorted. I am endeavouring to look Upward & be submissive to the will of our Heavenly Father, whom we are taught to believe, does not willingly afflict us. "Pray for me."

How grieved I was, my kind friend to learn that your dear and noble husband, had been taken from you. With my own heart bleeding over its desolation, I am fully prepared to enter into your feelings. What a change, the past two & half years has brought! Broken hearted as we both are, our only refuge in our distress, is in the Saviour, who suffered & died for us. Our sorrows must certainly draw us *very near* to the loved ones, who have *only* "gone

[8] Widow of Judge James W. White (see letter to Oliver S. Halsted, Jr., November 22, [1864], *note*). On June 12, 1867, Judge White had died at his home in Suffern, New York.

before." Hoping you will soon write me again, I send you my address. With kind regards to your family—

I remain very truly yours
Mary Lincoln.

To Elizabeth Keckley

[EXCERPT] [9]   [*October 24, 1867*]

. . . I cannot send this letter off without writing you two little incidents that have occurred within the past week. We may call it *justice* rendered for *evil words*, to say the least. There is a paper published in Chicago called the *Republican*, owned and published by Springfield men. Each morning since my return it has been thrown at my door, filled with abuse of myself. Four days ago a piece appeared in it, asking "What right had Mrs. L- to diamonds and laces?" Yesterday morning an article appeared in the same paper, announcing that the day previous, at the house of Mr. Bunn [1] (the owner of the paper), in Springfield, Illinois—the house had been entered at 11 in the morning, by burglars, and had been robbed of *five* diamond rings, and a quantity of fine laces. This morning's paper announces the recovery of these articles. Mr. Bunn who made his hundreds of thousands off our government, is running this paper, and denouncing the wife of the man from whom he obtained his means. I enclose you the article about the recovery of the goods. A few years ago he had a *small grocery* in S-. These facts can be authenticated. Another case in point; the evening I left my house to come here, the young daughter of one of my neighbors in the same block, was in a house not a square off, and in a childish

[9] Mrs. Keckley identified the above as a postscript to a letter written on October 24, 1867.
[1] Jacob Bunn, a successful merchant and banker in Springfield. Bunn would later perform valuable services for Mrs. Lincoln, for which she would be genuinely grateful, but for the moment he was part of the hated "Springfield clique" who she believed had risen to fame and fortune on the coattails of Abraham Lincoln and were now indifferent to her distress.

manner was regretting that I could not retain my house. The man in the house said: "Why waste your tears and regrets on Mrs. Lincoln?" An hour afterward the husband and wife went out to make a call, doubtless to gossip about me, on their return they found their young boy had almost blinded himself with gunpowder. Who will say that the cry of the "widow and fatherless" is disregarded in *His* sight! If man is not merciful, God will be in his own time.

M. L.

To Alexander Williamson

Chicago—Oct 29th 1867

My dear Sir:

Your kind note is received and I felt assured you would sympathize in my present overwhelming troubles—What I did—was undertaken with the idea that *no one* save the agent, Lizzie & myself would know of it—I am sure from what you knew of the circumstances you were not unprepared for my action—Articles which I required no longer—and which *necessity* compelled me to part with—Those who swindled *our Government*, in war times, are the ones who most deprecate my movements forgetting, that in the absence of my natural protector & unprovided with the means of support—I am left to do the best I can for myself. Call on Lizzie Keckley at *388—12th Street* Wash- and she will explain every thing to you—I can write no more—I will with pleasure the first opportunity that presents itself—send your daughter a souvenir— Taddie is well & going to school—

Your friend
Mrs L

Consider this note entirely private—

To Elizabeth Keckley

My dear Lizzie:

I received a very pleasant note from Mr. F. Douglass [2] on yesterday. I will reply to it this morning, and enclose it to you to hand or send him immediately. In this morning's [Chicago] *Tribune* there was a little article *evidently* designed to make capital *against* me just now—that *three* of my brothers were in the Southern army during the war. If they had been friendly with me they might have said they were *half* brothers of Mrs L-, whom she had not known since they were infants; and as she left Kentucky at an early age her sympathies were entirely Republican—that her feelings were entirely with the North during the war, and always. I never failed to urge my husband to be an *extreme* Republican, and now, in the day of my trouble, you see how *this* very party is trying to work against me. Tell Mr. Douglass, and every one, how deeply my feelings were enlisted in the cause of freedom. Why *harp* upon these *half* brothers, whom I never knew since they were infants, and scarcely then, for my early home was truly at a *boarding* school. Write to him, all this, and talk it to every one else. If we succeed I will soon send you enough for a very large supply of trimming material for the winter.

Truly,
M. L.

To Elizabeth Keckley

My dear Lizzie:

Your letter of last Wednesday is received, and I cannot refrain from expressing my surprise that before now K[eyes] and

[2] Frederick Douglass, a former slave who had become a widely respected speaker in behalf of Negro causes.

B[rady] did not go out in *search* of names, and have sent forth all those circulars.[3] Their conduct is becoming mysterious. We have heard enough of *their talk*—it is time now they should be *acting*. Their delay, I fear, has ruined the business. The circulars should all have been out before the *election*. I cannot understand their slowness. As Mr. Greeley's home is in New York, he could certainly have been found had he *been sought;* and there are plenty of other good men in New York, as well as himself. I venture to say, that *before* the election not a circular will be sent out. I begin to think they are making a political business of *my clothes*, and not for *my* benefit either. Their delay in acting is becoming very suspicious. Their slow, bad management is *ruining* every prospect of success. I fear you are only losing your time in New York, and that I shall be left *in debt* for what I am owing the firm [for expenses]. I have written to K. and B., and they do nothing that I request. I want neither Mr. Douglass nor Garnet to lecture in my behalf.[4] The conduct in New York is disgusting me with the whole business. I cannot understand what they have been about. Their delay has only given the enemies time to *gather* strength; what does it all mean? Of course give the lady at 609 [Broadway] permission to sell the dresses cheaper. . . . I am feeling wretchedly over the slowness and *do-nothing* style of B. & K. I believe in my heart I am being used as a tool for party purposes; and they do not design sending out a circular . . .

Your friend, M. L.

To Elizabeth Keckley

Chicago, Nov. 9, 1867

My dear Lizzie:

. . . Did you receive a letter a few days since, with one enclosed for F. Douglass? also a printed letter of mine, which I wished

---

[3] Designed to publicize Mrs. Lincoln's need and advertise her clothing for sale. (See p. 432.)

[4] Both Douglass and the Reverend Henry Highland Garnet of New York, a well-known Negro minister, offered to aid Mrs. Lincoln by lecturing in her behalf, but when she declined their services, the project was abandoned.

him to read? Do write me every other day at least, I am so *nervous and miserable*. And Lizzie, dear, I fear we have not the *least* chance of success. *Do* remain in New York a little longer, and occupy yourself with the sewing of your friends. *Then* I shall be able to learn *some*thing about my business. In *your heart* you know there will be no success. *Why* do you not candidly express yourself to me? Write me, if only a few lines, and that very frequently. R[obert] called up on yesterday, with Judge Davis . . . R. goes with Judge D. on Tuesday, [November 12], to settle the estate, which will give us each about $25,000,[5] with the income I told you of $1,700 a year for each of us. You made a mistake about my house costing $2700[0]—it was $1700[0].[6] The $22,000 Congress gave me I spent for house and furniture, which, owing to the smallness of my income, I was obliged to leave. I mention about the division of the estate to you, dear Lizzie, because when it is done the *papers* will harp upon it. You can explain everything in New York; please do so to every one. Please see H[enry] G[arnet], if it should come out in the papers. I had hoped, if something was gained, to have immediately placed *you* in more pleasant circumstances. Do urge F. D. to add his name to the circular; also get them to have [Henry Ward] Beecher's. There must not be an hour's delay in this. R[obert] is very spiteful at present, and I think hurries up the division to *cross* my purposes. He mentioned yesterday that he was going to the Rocky Mountains so soon as Edgar Welles joined him. He is very *deep*. . . . Write me, *do*, when you receive this. Your silence pains me.

Truly yours,

M. L.

[5] Mrs. Lincoln was perhaps unaware that the estate had appreciated from $85,000 to $110,794 in two years. In the final disposition, each of the survivors would receive $36,765.

[6] These figures, as published in *Behind the Scenes*, were obviously missing the final digit. See Mrs. Lincoln's letters to Simon Cameron, May 1866.

To Elizabeth Keckley

Chicago, Nov. 9 [1867]

My dear Lizzie:

I closed and sent off my letter before I had finished all I had to say. Do not hint to K[eyes] or B[rady], or any one else, my doubts of them, *only watch them.* As to S[umner], so many false-hoods are told in the papers that all the stuff about his wife and himself may be untrue. I hope it may prove so. I received a letter from Keyes this morning. I believe I wrote you that I had. How hard it is that I cannot see and talk with you in this time of great, *great* trouble. I feel as if I had not a friend in the world save your-self. . . . I sometimes wish myself out of this world of sorrow and care. I fear my fine articles at B.'s are getting pulled to pieces and soiled. I do not wish you to leave N.Y. without having the finest articles packed up and returned to me. The *single* white camel's hair shawl and the two Paisleys I wish returned to me, if none of them are sold. Do you think there is the least chance of *their* being sold? I will give you a list of the articles I wish returned to me from Mr Brady's before *you leave* New York for Washington.

> 1 camel's hair shawl, double black centre.
> 1 Camel's hair shawl, double white centre.
> 1 Single white camel's hair shawl.
> 2 Paisley shawls—white.
> 1 Pair bracelets and diamond ring.
> 1 Fine lace handkerchief.
> 3 Black lace shawls.
> 2 Black lama shawls.
> 1 Dress, silk unmade, white and black.
> 1 White boa.
> 1 Russian sable boa.
> 1 Russian sable cape.
> 1. A. sable cape, cuffs and muff.
> 1 Chinchilla set.

The lace dress, flounce, and shawl, is there no possibility of their being sold. Also all other fine articles return to me, save the dresses which, with prices lowered, *may be sold* . . .

M. L.

To David Davis

My Dear Sir:

I have regretted since your visit on yesterday, that especial mention had not been made, at that time about the supervision of Taddie himself. It was suggested by you last spring, that you would take charge, of the money belonging to him, only, whilst as a matter of course, as his mother I should have charge of himself. Taddie's nature is very amiable and I do not anticipate the least trouble in his management, and shall expect to have the guardianship of my child myself.[7] I am sure this arrangement will be more agreeable to us both, sparing you trouble & anxiety, whilst to me it will be the occupation of my life. His beloved father, had he lived would have insisted upon Taddie receiving the advantages of an education, and with the knowledge that my boy has of his backwardness in his studies, he will most readily embrace the opportunities, I shall urge upon him, to remain at school & college, until he is *twenty one*. *In this*, I shall not have the least difficulty. Wherever I shall place him at school, he will be well watched & cared for. I am aware, that with your great influence, you can secure a most ample support for him, even in these times of high prices. I believe, I omitted to say, that it is my intention, in the future, not to be separated from Taddie, for a day. Going & remaining with him, wherever he will be. Heretefore, he has never had a room, hereafter, this must be different, and he certainly cannot occupy one, under $12 a week. Thus far, his washing has not been charged to him, which will be another expense. Robert's expenses for the last few years of his college life were $1800- a year—they have not diminished since then. These

---

[7] Despite Mrs. Lincoln's offer to take on the guardianship herself, Davis assumed it at the same time the estate was settled.

details are very painful to me & if I had the wherewithal, after paying my own board, to make up any deficiency, that might occur, in the event of a very moderate sum, being allowed, for Taddie's yearly support, I should willingly give it & say nothing. Trusting to your kindness of feeling, in this business and with apologies for so lengthy a note, I remain very respectfully

Mary Lincoln—

To Alexander Williamson

Chicago, Nov 10 1867

My dear Sir:

Your note is received and you will allow me to say, that I have not the least intention of going to Europe. If I should ever do so, with my *present means*, it would be with the hope, that I might be more comfortable *there* on my small income than here. You, men have the advantage of us women, in being able to go out, in the world and earning a living. There need be no more correspondence on the subject of sending your daughter one of my dresses—When they are returned to me I shall do so—I am having chills, every other day, therefore I am unable to keep up a correspondence with any one—therefore my silence, with this explanation, and with your good sense & feeling, will not be attributed to any want of friendship. I am greatly indisposed & my physician orders quiet—as little writing & reading as possible. This climate is very trying to me in the winter season. When my dresses are returned to me, I will remember my promise, I cannot do so before. My health is too poor, for me to be disturbed by idle rumors. I would gladly keep up a correspondence with yourself & other friends, if I could do so without injury to myself. At the proper time, my promise, regarding your daughter will be kept—so there will be no more writing on the subject—I have given up housekeeping & am boarding in the plainest manner, so I can appreciate your expression, about high prices—I wish *we, all* could be unmindful of our daily necessities, by having sufficient to live upon. There is no more expensive place than Chicago. I am writing, with a fever on me, after a chill—and against a positive promise given my physician so, in the future, my silence by all friends, I hope, will be understood! I remain, truly your friend.

Mrs L—

To Elizabeth Keckley

Chicago, Nov 15th [1867]

My dear Keckley:

Your last letter has been received, and believe me, I duly appreciate your great interest in my affairs. I hope the day *may* arrive when I can return your kindness in *more* than words. As you are aware of my beloved husband's great indulgence to me in pecuniary matters, thereby allowing me to indulge in bestowing favors on those whom I considered worthy of it, it is in this respect I feel chiefly the humiliation of my small circumscribed income. If Congress, or the Nation, had given me the four years' salary, I should have been able to live as the widow of the great President Lincoln should, with sufficient means to give liberally to all benevolent objects, and at my death should have left at least half of it to the freedmen, for the liberty of whom his precious sacred life was sacrificed. The men who prevented *this* being done by their villanous unscrupulous falsehoods, are no friends of the colored race, and, as you well know, have led Johnson on in his wicked course.

"*God is just*," and the day of retribution will come to all such, if not in this world, in the great hereafter, to which those hoary-headed sinners are so rapidly hastening, with an innocent conscience. I did not feel it necessary to raise my weak woman's voice against the persecutions that have assailed me emanating from the tongues of such men as Weed & Co.[8] I have felt that their infamous false

---

[8] One of the harshest editorials criticizing Mrs. Lincoln had appeared in Thurlow Weed's New York *Commercial Advertiser* on October 4, 1867. It accused her of everything from taking bribes to padding the expenses for the state dinner for Prince Jerome Napoleon in 1861.

lives was a sufficient vindication of my character. They have never forgiven me for standing between my pure and noble husband and themselves, when, for their own vile purposes, they would have led him into error. *All this* the country knows, and why should I dwell longer on it? In the blissful home where my worshipped husband dwells God is ever merciful, and it is the consolation of my broken heart that my darling husband is ever retaining the devoted love which he always so abundantly manifested for his wife and children in this life. I feel assured his watchful, loving eyes are always watching over us, and he is fully aware of the wrong and injustice permitted his family by a country he lost his life in protecting. I write earnestly, because I feel very deeply. It appears to me a very remarkable coincidence, that most of the good feeling regarding my straitened circumstances proceeds from the colored people; in whose cause my noble husband was so largely interested. Whether we are successful or not, Mr F. Douglass and Mr Garnet will always have my most grateful thanks. They are very noble men. If any *favorable* results should crown their efforts, you may well believe at my death, whatever sum it may be, will be bequeathed to the colored people, who are very near my heart. In yesterdays paper it was announced that Gov. Andrew's [9] family were having $100,000 contributed to them. Gov. A. was a good man, but what did *he* do compared to President Lincoln? Right and left the latter gave, when he had but little to bestow, and in consequence his family are now feeling it; yet for my life I would not recall a dollar he ever gave. Yet his favorite expression, when I have playfully alluded to the "rainy day" that might be in store for *himself and his own* on several occasions, he has looked at me so earnestly and replied, "Cast your bread upon the waters." Although the petty sum of $22,000 was an insufficient return for Congress to make me, and allowanced to its meagreness by men who traduced and vilified the loved wife of the great man who *made them*, and from whom they amassed great fortunes—for *Weed, and Seward and R[aymond]* did this last. And yet, *all this* was permitted by an American people, who owed *their* remaining a nation to my husband! I have dwelt too long on this painful subject, but when I have been com-

[9] John A. Andrew, three-term governor of Massachusetts, died on October 30, 1867.

pelled from a pitiful income to make a boarding-house of [as] my home, as I now am doing, think you that it does not rankle in my heart?

Fortunately, with my husband's great, great love for me—the knowledge of this future for his petted and idolized wife was spared him, and yet I feel in my heart *he* knows it all. Mr. Sumner, the intimate friend of better days, called to see me two or three weeks since—he who had been an habitué of the White House—both the rooms of the President and my own reception-room, in either place he was always sure of a heartfelt welcome; my present situation must have struck a painful chord in his noble, sympathizing heart. And yet, when I endeavored to ameliorate my condition, the cry has been so fearful against me as to cause me to forget my own identity, and suppose I had plundered the nation, indeed, and committed murder. This, certainly, cannot be America, "the land of the *free*," the home of the *brave*." The evening before Mr. Sumner's last call I had received Mr. Douglass's letter; I mentioned the circumstance to Mr. Sumner, who replied, "Mr. Frederick Douglass is a very noble, talented man, and I know of no one who writes a more beautiful letter." I am sending you a long letter, Lizzie, but I rely a great deal on your indulgence. My fear is that you will not be able to decipher the scrawl written *so* hastily.

I remain, truly yours,
Mary Lincoln

To Elizabeth Keckley

Nov 17 [*1867*]

Private for yourself
Lizzie:

Show the note enclosed with this to B[rady] & K[eyes]; do not let them retain it an instant after reading, nor the printed articles. I knew these falsehoods would be circulated when the estate was divided. What *has* been the cause of the delay about the circulars? I fear, between ourselves, we have reason to distrust those men,——. Whatever is raised by the colored people, I solemnly give my word, at my death, it shall *all*, every cent, be returned to them. And out of the sum, if it is $50,000, *you* shall have $5,000 at my death; and I cannot live long, suffering as I am now doing. If $25,000 is raised by your people, you shall have the sum at my death; and in either event, the $25,000 raised, or $50,000, I will give you $300 a year, and the promised sum at my death. It will make your life easier. I have more faith in F[rederick] D[ouglass] and G[arnet]'s efforts, than in B. & K., I assure you. This division [of the estate] has been trumped up just now through spite . . . I have written to Judge Davis for an exact statement, which I will send to you when received. Write if anything is doing . . .

Truly,
M. L.

To Elizabeth Keckley

Chicago, Nov. 17 [1867]

My dear Lizzie:

By the time you receive this note, you will doubtless find the papers *raving* over the large income which we are *said* to have. Knowing exactly the amount we each will have, which I have already informed you, I was going to say, I have been shocked at the *fabulous* sum set down to each, but I have learned not to be surprised at anything. Of course it is gotten up to defeat success. *You* will *now* see the necessity for those circulars being issued weeks since. I enclose you a scrap from yesterday's *Times* of C[hicago] marked No. 1; also No. 2, in to-day's *Times*. The sum of $11,000 has been subtracted in twenty-four hours from the same paper. If it continues for a few days longer, it will soon be right. It is a secesh paper—says Congress gave me $25,000 as a *present*, besides $20,000 of remaining salary. The $25,000 *you* know to be utterly false. You can show this note to B[rady] & K[eyes], also the scraps sent. Let no one see them but themselves, and then burn them. It is all just as I had expected—that when the division took place, a "mountain would be made of a mole-hill." And I fear it will succeed in injuring the premeditated plans. If the *war rages*, the *Evening News* might simply say that the sum assigned each was false; that $75,000 was the sum the administrator, Judge Davis, filed his bonds for. But by all means *my authority* must not be given. And then the *Evening News* can descant on the $25,000 each, with income of $1,700 each, and Mrs. Lincoln's share she not being able to touch any of her son's portion. My *word* or *testimony* must not appear in the article; only the paper must speak decidedly. It must be managed very judiciously, and without a day's delay.

Yours truly
M. L.

To David Davis

Chicago Nov 17th [1867]

My dear Sir:

The papers are abounding with notices of the settlement of the Estate, and the amount left each of us. As I have not heard a word from Robert on the subject, I consider it necessary that *I* should be quite as well informed as the Press—regarding our own business.

Therefore, by way of possessing accurate information on a subject so important to our comfort—May I request you to send me a definite statement, of the *whole* business, as I am anxious to be apprised of it—please reply immediately—I enclose you a statement, made in the "Evening Journal," of Friday last [1]—As Robert on leaving for S[pringfield] mentioned that he had drawn from you $7,000- I cannot understand it—Not knowing exactly when R

---

[1] The clipping has been preserved. It reads, "The Hon David Davis, administrator of the late Abraham Lincoln, made a final settlement of the estate, at Springfield, yesterday. After paying all debts, there remained $110,294.62, which, divided among the widow and heirs, gives $36,765.30 to Mrs. Lincoln, and the same amount to each son. Robert T. Lincoln has received his share and also that of the minor heir, Thomas (Tad). The amount due Mrs. Lincoln, less about $4,000 heretofore drawn, is subject to her order."

would return to C- I have concluded to write you soliciting an entire statement of the business—to satisfy myself & others, which *I* am sure you will willingly give—as Tad & myself are quite as much interested as R-

> With great respect,
> I remain very truly
> Mary Lincoln

To David Davis

Chicago Nov 18th [*1867*]

My dear Sir:

Robert visited me last evening and made a full report of the business. Permit me to say, that in no hands save your own, could our interests have been so advantageously placed—please accept my grateful thanks for all your kindness to myself & family—

I remain truly & gratefully

Mary Lincoln

To Elizabeth Keckley

Chicago, November 21 [*1867*]

My dear Lizzie:

Your letter of Tuesday is just received. I have just written B[rady] a note of thanks for his kindness; also requesting the articles of which I gave you a list. Do see Keyes about it; K. will have it done. And will you *see* that they are forwarded to *me* before *you* leave New York? K. sent me a telegram on yesterday that eight names were on the circulars, and that they would be sent out *immediately*. What success do you think they will have? By all means assure K. & B. I have great confidence in them. These circulars must bring some money. Your letter made me quite sad. Talk to K. & B. of the *grateful feelings* I express towards them. Do pet up B., and see my things returned to me. Can you not, dear Lizzie, be employed in sewing for some of your lady friends in New York until December 1st? If I *ever* get any money you will be well remembered, be assured. R[obert] and a party of young men leave for the Rocky Mountains next Monday, to be absent three weeks. If the circulars are sent out, of course the *blasts* will be blown over again. So R. is out of the way *at the time*, and money comes in, I will not care. Write the hour you receive this. I hope they will send out 150,000 circulars. Urge K. & B. to do this.

Your friend,
M. L.

To Rhoda White

Chicago, Nov 21st
1867—

My dear Mrs White:

I cannot express to you, how heartfelt my grief was, on receiving the Obituary notice, of your beloved daughter's death. I know by experience how powerless, *words* are, to console us, in our fearful, irreparable bereavements. God alone can administer comfort in the trying hour of affliction and soothe the anguish of our broken hearts. I remember your lovely daughter so distincly, possessed of so much loveliness, talents, and so highly accomplished. "*Death*, truly loves a shining mark," and believe me, on learning the painful news, which brought so much sorrow to you, I sympathized with you, in my tears & prayers. How desolate *we both* have been made within the last few years! Overwhelmed with my great, great sorrow, I am prepared fully to share the afflictions, of all those who are called upon to sustain them. I have thought of late, whilst enduring the persecutions with which I have recently been assailed—that our Heavenly Father, had brought them upon me, to divert my mind, from the troubles, that have fallen so heavily upon me. It is the lot of humanity to suffer—otherwise we would cling too fondly to earth & its transitory enjoyments. Our noble friend Sen Sumner who was so closely associated with us in Washington, called to see me a few weeks ago, while in Chicago. *His* brow too was troubled, and his heart I presume more so— owing to the cruel rumors afloat, regarding his wife & himself—

It appeared to me particularly trying, that whilst he was journeying for his health & lecturing purposes, that he should be compelled to encounter such odious comments, as the press so *freely* & I believe falsely indulged in. We had become such friends, that immediately after his engagement was formed, he wrote me respecting it—and when he visited me after his marriage *for fear*, there might be some *truth* in the rumor, I could not allow myself the privilege of mentioning his wife's name. Mr Sumner, is a very sensitive man. I wish we could see *some such* men President, do not you? I will my dear Mrs White, direct my letter, according to the card you sent me, not knowing whether you have returned to town. Hoping to hear from you at your leisure, I remain truly yours.

Mary Lincoln.

To Elizabeth Keckley

Saturday Morning November 23rd [1867]

My dear Lizzie:

Although I am suffering with a fearful headache to day, yet, as your note of Wednesday is received, I must write. I am grieved to find that you are so wretchedly low-spirited. . . . On Wednesday, the 20th of November, K[eyes] sent me the telegram I send you. If he is not in earnest, what does it mean? What is the rate of expenses that B[rady] has gone to in my business, that he dares to withhold my immense amount of goods? Do you believe they *intend* sending out those circulars? Of course, you will be well rewarded if we have any success, but as to $500 "now," I have it not for myself, or any one else. Pray, what does B. propose to charge for *his expenses?* I pray God there will be some success, although, dear Lizzie, entirely between ourselves, I fear I am in villanous hands. As to money, I haven't it for myself just now, even if nothing comes in. When I get my things back, if ever, from——, I will send you some of those dresses to dispose of at Washington for your own benefit. If we get something, *you* will find that *promises* and performance for *this* life will be forthcoming. . . . It is *mysterious* why B. NEVER writes, and K. *once*, perhaps, in three weeks. All this is very strange . . .

M. L.

To Elizabeth Keckley

Chicago, Sunday, Nov. 24th

My dear Lizzie:

I wrote you on yesterday and am aware it was not a pleasant letter, although I wrote what I fear will turn out to be *truths*. It will be two weeks to-morrow since the legally attested consent from me was received by B[rady] and K[eyes], and yet *names* have not been obtained for it [the circular], when last heard from. . . . However, we will soon see for ourselves. If you and I are honest in our motives and intentions, it is no reason *all* the world is so. . . . If I should gain nothing pecuniarily by the loud cry that has been made over my affairs, it has been a losing game indeed . . . And the laugh of the world will be against me if it turns out as I *now* think; there is no doubt it will be *all* failure. If they had issued those circulars when they should have done, before the election, then it would have been all right. Alas! Alas! what a mistake it has all been! I have thought seriously over the whole business, and know what I am about. I am grateful for the sympathy of Mr F. Douglass and Mr. Garnet. I see that F. D. advertised to lecture in Chicago some time this winter. Tell him, for me, he must call and see me; give him my number. If I had been able to retain a house, I should have offered him apartments when he came to C.; as it is, I have to content *myself* with lodgings. An ungrateful country this! I very much fear the malignity of Seward, Weed, and R[aymond] will operate in Congress the coming winter, and that I will be denounced *there*, with their infamous and villanous falsehoods. The father of wickedness and lies will get those men when they "pass away;" and such fiends as they are, always linger in this mortal sphere. The agitation of mind has very much impaired my health . . . Why, why was not *I* taken when my darling husband was called from my side? I have been allowed no rest by those who, in my desolation, should have protected me. . . . How dearly I should love to see you *this very sad day*. Never, dear Lizzie, think of my great nervousness the night before we parted; I had been so harassed with my fears . . .

Always yours,
M. L.

To David Davis

Chicago Nov 27th [1867]

My dear Sir:

Robert is absent for a few days, travelling *towards* the Rocky Mountains, accompanied by Norman Williams & a few other young gentlemen. As Norman Williams, is to be married to Judge [John D.] Caton's daughter, Miss Carrie, on the 11th of Dec, I presume they will soon be returning. I wish to understand from you, especially in regard to Taddie & his expenditures. In the future wherever we are, he must have a room to himself, however small, & this, cannot be obtained for him under twelve or fourteen dollars a week. I considered it quite a privilege to get into the private family, where we are now stopping, although it was an accommodation on their part—Although, they are only a kind plain family, it is entirely unnecessary for them to have boarders, as from the rent of the stores, houses && he has built, his income is about $20,000, a year—we are occupying rooms, the family really need, therefore I fear, I cannot remain very long, in this quiet retreat. Consequently, whilst I remain in Chicago, I must either go to the Clifton House, or some Hotel—where *prices* are charged. It is always just as well to have a fair understanding, on such subjects. Wherever Taddie goes to school, he must remain & board where I do. It is impossible for me to separate myself from him & I prefer not to lodge in a private house, as a general thing & of course, in the best quarters. I wish to understand from you— how much will be allowed for his board per week. Will you please inform me so soon you receive this, and before you leave for Washington. *After this winter*, I shall withdraw him from public schools & place him, where his tuition must be paid for. *His* means are very ample and a liberal allowance, will not I am sure be withheld.

    Hoping to hear from you, by return mail I remain

Very respectfully
Mary Lincoln

To Henry C. Deming [2]

[EXCERPT]   *Chicago, December 16* [1867]

. . . Notwithstanding my letter of Saturday to you, I feel inclined to write you a few lines this morning. My doing so, is occasioned by seeing an article in last weeks "Independent" from the pen of the indefatigable F. B. Carpenter. I can scarcely express to you, my dear Mr Deming, how indignant I feel, when such men, mere adventurers, with whom my husband had scarcely the least acquaintance, write & publish such false statements about him. With regard to Mr Seward & Mr Lincoln, being & speaking together in Boston, in 1848, is devoid of all truth.[3] After Congress adjourned in Sept. of that year Mr L. accompanied by my two little boys & myself, visited B & remained there 3 weeks, detained by the illness of our youngest son, whom we lost a year afterwards. Neither Mr. L. or

[2] Colonel Deming, representative from Connecticut, had known Lincoln relatively well. A speech he delivered on June 8, 1865, reprinted in pamphlet form, is considered one of the most perceptive brief analyses of Lincoln's character ever written.

[3] Mrs. Lincoln's memory was faulty. The Boston *Atlas* of September 23, 1848, described a mass meeting at Tremont Temple in that city, at which both Lincoln and Seward spoke.

myself knew any young or old lady, by the name of Fanny Mc.[4]
. . . Perhaps Seward wrote the article & meant "McCracken." I
know you are a noble man; my beloved husband respected & admired you too much, not to be assured that you value the truth.
This man Carpenter, never had a dozen interviews with the late
President and the latter complained more than once to me, that C.
presumed upon the privilege he had given C. to have the use of the
State dining room, for a short time, whilst he was executing his
painting. This was only done, in consequence of the rumor we had
heard of his indigent circumstances. He is a second edition of Mr
L's crazy drinking law partner, Herndon, endeavouring to write
himself into notice, leaving truth, far, far, in the distance. C. in-
truded frequently into Mr L's office, when time was too precious to
be idled. Of this fact, I am well aware. To think of this stranger,
silly adventurer, daring to write a work, entitled, "The inner life of
Abraham Lincoln." [5] Each scribbling writer, almost strangers to Mr
L., subscribe themselves, his most intimate friend! With apologies,
I remain truly &&

Mrs A. Lincoln

To Sarah Bush Lincoln [6]

Chicago, Dec. 19th 67

Private
My dear Madam:

In memory of the dearly loved one, who always remembered
you with so much affection, will you not do me the favor of accept-

---

[4] Without a copy of the original letter it is impossible to know whether Mrs. Lincoln wrote out the last name of "Fanny Mc." A letter exists from Lincoln to Miss
Fanny McCullough of Bloomington, expressing condolences on the death of her
father and his friend, Colonel William McCullough, in 1862.

[5] The second edition of Carpenter's book *Six Months at the White House* was
given this title.

[6] Lincoln's stepmother, whom he never saw after 1861. Sarah Bush Johnston
had married Thomas Lincoln in 1819, less than a year after the death of Nancy
Hanks Lincoln, Abraham's mother. She had brought peace and order to the
household, and Abraham Lincoln had loved her dearly. This letter is the only
one that exists from Mrs. Lincoln to her mother-in-law, and shows the warmth
of her own feelings.

ing these few trifles? God has been very merciful to you, in pro-
longing your life and I trust your health has also been preserved—
In my great agony of mind I cannot trust myself to write about,
what so entirely fills my ~~mind~~ thoughts—my darling husband;
knowing how well you loved him also, is a grateful satisfaction to
me. Believe me, dear Madam, if I can ever be of service to you, in
any respect, I am entirely at your service. My husband a few weeks
before his death mentioned to me, that he intended *that* summer,
paying proper respect to *his* father's grave, by a head & foot stone,
with his name, age && and I propose very soon carrying out his intentions.[7] It was not from want of affection for his father, as you are
well aware, that it was not done, but *his* time was so greatly occupied always. I will be pleased to learn whether *this* package was
received by you—Perhaps you know that our youngest boy, is
named for your husband, Thomas Lincoln, this child, the idol of
his father—I am blessed in both of my sons, they are very good &
noble. The eldest is growing very much like his own dear father. I
am a deeply afflicted woman & hope you will pray for me—I am,
my dear Madam,

affectionately yours
Mary Lincoln.

This letter please consider entirely private—I shall be greatly
pleased to hear from you.

[*To Sarah Bush Lincoln*]

Dec 20th 1867

Enclosed is the Express receipt—also ten dollars which please
accept for the making of the dress && An answer is requested,
whether the box, money && has been received & oblige

Mrs Lincoln

Mrs A Lincoln's address is 460 West Washington St, Chicago, Ill.

---

[7] Thomas Lincoln had died in Coles County, Illinois, on January 17, 1851, and
is buried there in a cemetery in Shiloh Church. In 1880 Robert Todd Lincoln
would have a monument erected over the grave; it would be replaced in 1924 by
a new stone inscribed with the names of both Thomas and Sarah Lincoln.

To Elizabeth Keckley

December 26 [1867]

My dear Lizzie:

Your letters just received. I have just written to K[eyes] to withdraw the C[ircular]. Go to him yourself the moment you receive this. The idea of Congress doing anything is ridiculous. How much —— could effect *if he chose*, through others. Go to B. & K. the moment you receive this.

Yours,
M. L.

To Elizabeth Keckley

Chicago, December 27 [1867]

Dear Lizzie:

I wrote you a few lines on yesterday. I have twice written to Mr K[eyes] to have the C[ircular] stopped. Go and see him on the subject. I believe any more newspaper attacks would *lay me low* . . . As *influence* has passed away from me with my husband, my slightest act is misinterpreted. "*Time makes all things* right." I am positively suffering for a decent dress. I see Mr. A. [unidentified] and *some recent* visitors eyeing my clothing askance . . . Do send my black merino dress to me very soon; I must dress better in the future. I tremble at the bill that B & K may send me, I am so illy prepared to meet any expense. All my articles not sold must be sent to me. I leave *this* place *early* in the spring; had you better not go with me and share my fortunes, for a year or more? . . . *Write.*

Yours, etc.,
M. L.

To Alexander Williamson

Dec 30th 67

Mr A. Williamson:

   Your note is just received. Believe me my disappointment is far greater than your own can possibly be—that I have not been able this Christmas, to send the 2 dresses—I intended doing— When I can possibly see my articles from N.Y. my promise will assuredly be remembered. *So*, no more, *until then.*

Truly, your friend
Mrs L

To Alexander Williamson

Jany 9th [*1868*] [8]

My dear Sir:

   I am visited with quite a serious affliction—within the last few days—very sore & inflamed eyes—so much so—that I am unable to write or read & consequently am compelled to relinquish correspondence with all my friends. The physician insists upon my not using my eyes in any way for some time to come—I am disobeying his orders for a moment—to write you & say—that my son & myself —remember the [White House] gardeners so kindly—that we will both sign our names—to the document—you sent. No one loses any thing by my silence, for this is a very gloomy winter to me—I fear you will be unable to read this, as I am almost unable to see—

Yr friend
Mrs Lincoln

[8] Although Mrs Lincoln dated this letter "67," it has been placed in the following year for three reasons: (1) On January 9, 1867, she wrote to David Davis, on different stationery and in a clear, legible hand, a letter which, unlike the above, makes no mention and shows no evidence of disability; (2) There is a tone of finality in this letter that argues against there having been further correspondence between the two, yet Mrs Lincoln wrote Williamson several times in 1867; (3) Written as it was so soon after the first of the year, the letter could easily have been misdated, in a reflex common to many, including Mrs. Lincoln.

To Elizabeth Keckley

Clifton House
January 12 [*1868*]

My dear Lizzie:

Your last letter was received a day or two since. I have moved my quarters to *this house*, so please direct all your letters *here*. Why did *you* not urge them *not* to take my goods to Providence? For heaven's sake see K[eyes] & B[rady] when you receive this, and have them immediately returned to me, *with their bill*. I am so miserable I feel like taking my own life. My darling boy, my Taddie *alone*, I *fully* believe, prevents the deed. Your letter announcing that my clothes were to be paraded in Europe—those I gave you—has almost turned me wild. R[obert] would go *raving distracted* if such a thing was done. If you have the *least regard* for *our reason*, pray write to the bishop [9] that it *must* not be done. How little did I suppose you would do *such a thing;* you cannot imagine how much my overwhelming sorrows would be increased. May kind Heaven turn your heart, and have you write that *this* exhibition must not be attempted. R. would blast us all if you were to have this project carried out. Do remember *us* in our unmitigated anguish, and have those clothes, worn on those fearful occasions, recalled. . . . I am positively dying with a broken heart, and the probability is that I shall be living but a *very* short time. May we all meet in a better world, where *such grief* is unknown. Write me all about yourself. I should like you to have about four black widow's caps, just such as I had made in the fall in New York, sent to me. . . . Of course, you would not suppose if I had you come out here and work for me six weeks, I would not pay your expenses and pay you as you made *each* dress. The probability is that I shall need *few* more clothes; my rest, I am inclined to believe, is *near at hand*. Go to B. & K., and have my clothes sent me without further publicity. . . . I am feel-

[9] Bishop Payne of Wilberforce College, a Negro institution for the benefit of which Mrs. Keckley donated clothing presented her by Mrs. Lincoln. Among the garments were a bonnet and cloak stained with the President's blood. The European scheme was, of course, abandoned.

ing too weak to write more to-day. Why are you so silent? For the sake of *humanity*, if not *me* and my children, *do not* have those black clothes displayed in Europe. The thought has almost whitened every hair of my head. Write when you receive this.

Your friend,
M. L.

To Elizabeth Keckley

Clifton House, Jan 15, 1868

My dear Lizzie:

You will think I am sending you a deluge of letters. I am so very sad to day, that I feel that I must write you. I went out last evening with Tad, on a little business, in a street car, heavily veiled, very imprudently having *my month's living* in my pocket-book— and, on return, found it gone. The loss I deserve for being so careless, but it comes very hard on poor me. Troubles and misfortunes are fast overwhelming me; may *the end* soon come. I lost $82, and quite a new pocket-book. I am very, very anxious about that bill B[rady] & K[eyes] may bring in. Do go, dear Lizzie, and implore them to be moderate, for I am in a very narrow place. Tell them, I pray you, of this last loss. As they have not been successful (BE-TWEEN OURSELVES), and only given me great sorrow and trouble, I think their demand should be very small. (Do not mention this to them.) *Do*, dear Lizzie, go to 609, and talk to them on this subject. Let my things be sent to me immediately, and *do* see to it, that nothing is left behind. I can afford to lose nothing they have had placed in their hands. I am literally suffering for my black dress. Will you send it to me when you receive this? I am looking very shabby. I hope you have entirely recovered. *Write* when you receive this.

Very truly yours,
M. L.

To W. H. Brady

Chicago, Feb 7 [1868]

Mr Brady:

I hereby authorize Mrs. Keckley to request my bill from you; also my goods. An exact account must be given of everything, and all goods unsold returned to me. Pray hand Mrs. Keckley my bill, without fail, immediately.

Respectfully,
Mrs. Lincoln.

To Elizabeth Keckley

Saturday, Feb 29 [1868]

Dear Lizzie:

I am only able to sit up long enough to write you a line and enclose this check to Mr. K[eyes] Give it to him when he gives you up my goods, and require from him an exact inventory of them. I will write you tomorrow. The hour you receive this go to him, get my goods, and do not *give him the check until* you get the goods, and be sure you get a receipt for the check from him. . . . In his account given ten days since, he said we had borrowed $807; now he writes for $820. Ask him what this means, and get him to deduct the $13. I cannot understand it. A letter received from K. this morning says if the check is not received the first of the week, my goods *will be sold;* so do delay not an hour to see him . . . My diamond ring he writes has been sold; the goods sold have amounted to $824, and they appropriate all this for their expenses. A precious set, truly. My diamond ring itself cost more than that sum, and I charged them not to sell it under $700. Do get my things safely returned to me . . .

Truly,
M. L.

On October 13, 1867, shortly after her return from New York, Mary Lincoln ended a letter to Elizabeth Keckley with the plea, "Write me, dear Lizzie, if only a line; I cannot understand your silence." Aside from the fact that not even the most devoted correspondent could keep up with Mrs. Lincoln, the reasons for Lizzie's occasional silences were several: she was busy tying up loose ends with Brady and Keyes and enlisting the aid of such prominent Negro friends as Frederick Douglass and the Reverend Henry Highland Garnet, both of whom offered to lecture in Mrs. Lincoln's behalf—not only out of a residual regard for the Great Emancipator, but because they recognized in the President's widow a woman as free of racial prejudice and condescension as was possible in that day.

Cut off from her Washington clientele, Mrs. Keckley was attempting to support herself through the New York winter by taking in any small sewing job that came her way. (Like Alexander Williamson, she had been promised a commission on contributions she helped to raise; like Williamson, she raised nothing and received nothing.) But, most importantly, she was engaged in a time-consuming endeavor: she was writing her memoirs, recalling her girlhood as a slave, her career as modiste to several southern gentlewomen, her years of White House service, and her friendship with Mrs. Lincoln. The work would culminate in a participant's account of the Old Clothes Scandal, supplemented by a collection of relevant letters, twenty-four of them from Mary Lincoln. By late 1867, she had begun dictating her reminiscences to a professional writer,[1] in hopes that the book would be polished enough to have a wide sale. (She later claimed she had planned to turn over at least part of the proceeds to Mrs. Lincoln, and that she had never intended that the letters be included.)

---

[1] Various names have been suggested as ghost writer of *Behind the Scenes*, including that of Jane Grey Swisshelm; however, the most likely candidate is Hamilton Busbey, the journalist, whose autograph appears in a copy of the original edition of the book.

Behind the Scenes, published in the spring of 1868, was an early example of what has come to be a popular if questionable literary genre: a former employee's backstairs glimpse into the private lives of public figures. The book was candid in tone, remarkably accurate in observation, and generally sympathetic to the Lincolns. Historians approach it with a mixture of fascination and guilt, recognizing it as excellent source material but realizing that its publication constituted an appalling breach of friendship and good taste. Mrs. Keckley dealt freely with the weaknesses of a woman who was not only very much alive and in the public eye, but who had unconsciously relied on the protective instincts of those close to her. *Behind the Scenes* had an even more devastating effect on Mary Lincoln than Herndon's maunderings over the years. She had come to expect the worst from that quarter, as well as from other malicious and gossipy strangers. But she never knew what prompted her "best living friend" [2] to reveal overheard conversations between herself and the President, to discuss openly the emotional and financial difficulties she had always been at such pains to conceal from the world. And how could Lizzie have stooped so low as to permit the publication of letters meant for no one's eyes but her own?

As it turned out, the book had scant effect on public opinion. Although widely publicized and excerpted, and despite its sensational content, it sold few copies. Perhaps Robert Lincoln, already shattered by his mother's indiscretions, paid or pressured the publishers to withdraw it; it may simply have died from lack of interest. But the fact that it had been written at all ended forever an almost sisterly friendship between two women drawn to each other in defiance of contemporary attitudes toward race and station. As far as is known, Mrs. Lincoln never mentioned Elizabeth Keckley again in letters, except to dismiss her once, derisively, as "*the colored historian.*" [3]

The earlier newspaper abuse had been cruel enough; after this final betrayal Mary Lincoln felt she could no longer hold up her head among her countrymen. A long-festering desire to escape from the

[2] Mary Lincoln to Elizabeth Keckley, October 6, [1867].
[3] Mary Lincoln to Rhoda White, Chicago, May 2, [1868].

United States now became an imperative, and for once she had the means to accomplish it. In November 1867 Lincoln's estate had been settled, the widow and her two sons each receiving some $36,-000 in cash and securities. By 1868, too, the burden of debt had at last been lifted from her shoulders, precisely when and how being to this day a matter of conjecture. Certainly Robert had long since been told (or had discovered) the truth about his mother's situation, possibly even before the furor over her New York adventure, and had made sacrifices of his own in order to clear the family name. Mrs. Lincoln herself stated what was no doubt a painful truth when she wrote a friend from Europe, "I had every Wash- & every other indebtedness—sent to me & out of every dollar—I could command—I paid to the uttermost farthing [Except] in some cases, known by the administrators—but in a very few—it was all done by ourselves my son & myself out of my money." [4]

The cost of paying off the debts had been a terrible one. Robert's ultimate involvement in the effort, together with his near-violent reaction to the events of late 1867, resulted in a growing antagonism between mother and son. Perhaps it was just as well that he was to be married in September to the girl he had loved through three long years of separation: Mary Eunice Harlan, the pretty daughter of Senator and Mrs. James Harlan of Iowa. With Robert embarking on a family and law practice of his own, his mother felt free to turn her full attention to Tad, the one person who never criticized, never questioned, never wavered in his absolute loyalty to her.

At the time of the settlement of the estate, Justice Davis assumed legal guardianship of Tad, putting him on an allowance of $100 per month. The boy had matured considerably, and was now more comfortable in the role of student, but he still lacked discipline, a quality that European—especially German—educators excelled at instilling. And so Mrs. Lincoln began considering schools abroad, planning to leave for Europe in time for the opening of the fall term.

Another reason she thought it advisable to live in Europe was

[4] Mary Lincoln to James H. Orne, Marienbad, Bohemia, May 28, 1870. It is clear that Mrs. Lincoln felt she could, in good conscience, consider gifts made her as "her money."

her failing health. In a letter to Rhoda White in May of 1868, she alluded delicately to troubles of a "womanly nature" that had plagued her off and on since Tad's birth. The recurring migraines, chills, and general weakness of limb had been aggravated by the coming of the menopause and by extraordinary emotional stress. On the continent were numerous spas, where mineral waters and a strict physical regimen were believed to benefit almost any ailment known to man. In a day when "a change of scene" was recommended for everything from depression to dyspepsia, Mrs. Lincoln was told that new sights, new experiences, would do her good. Finally, she anticipated living far more cheaply abroad than at home. Yet to some extent these were all rationalizations; the fact remains that she was literally hounded from American shores.

In June she paid a brief, quiet visit to Springfield, for the "sad purpose" of taking one last look at the tomb and discussing with her cousin John Todd Stuart and others plans for the completion of the monument. Shortly thereafter she and Tad left Chicago to spend the rest of the summer in the Alleghenies, chiefly at a health resort in Cresson Springs, Pennsylvania. Located halfway between Altoona and Johnstown, Cresson Springs was a popular vacation area, boasting lovely mountain scenery and many natural springs high in mineral content; certainly it was the latter attraction that drew Mrs. Lincoln to the spot.

During her stay there she made the acquaintance of Mrs. Felician Slataper, wife of a well-to-do civil engineer from Pittsburgh, who was occupying a cottage at the resort with her husband and young son Daniel. Having "Danie" Slataper as companion was a great boon to Tad, and the mothers formed such an attachment to one another that, when Mrs. Slataper went home to Pittsburgh, an intimate correspondence sprang up between them. Mary Lincoln's letters to Eliza Slataper are a relatively recent find. They span three years, the first group written toward the end of her time in America and her early months in Europe, one written toward the close of her sojourn abroad, and a final three coming from Chicago in 1871. In the earlier letters—particularly those from abroad— Mary Lincoln for once lived up to her potential as an entertaining correspondent, evoking her surroundings, relating her experiences, and expressing her feelings without repeating herself unduly or falling into that aggrieved tone which characterized nearly every letter she wrote after 1865. The two women apparently never saw each other after Cresson Springs, but Mrs. Lincoln, hungry for friendship, quick to respond to warmth in others, wrote to Eliza Slataper as if she had known and loved her all her life.

It is through the Slataper letters, and several to Rhoda White, that one learns something of her reactions to Robert's marriage, which took place on September 24, 1868, at the Washington home of the bride's parents. It had been a hideous ordeal for her to visit even briefly the city where her husband had reigned and died, but the nature of the occasion and the fact that she "did not look around" [5] when she arrived, made things easier. Only after she returned to her quarters at Barnum's Hotel in Baltimore (the city from which she would embark for Europe) did an adverse reaction set in.

To Rhoda White

Chicago, May 2d [1868]

My Dear Mrs White:

It has been quite a time, since I have had the pleasure of hearing from you & in fact, I believe you are owing me a letter. This, however, will not deter me from writing you to day, as serious considerations prompt me to do so. I am *permitted* to sit up, whilst I write you a few lines as for the past three weeks, I have been seriously sick. ~~My disease is of a womanly nature, which you will understand has been~~ [6] greatly accelerated by the last three years of mental suffering. Since the birth of my youngest son, for about twelve years I have been more or less a sufferer. My physician, Dr [William E.?] Clarke, a brother of Mrs Lippincut [sic] (Grace Greenwood) [7] told me on yesterday, that he must prescribe an en-

---

[5] Mary Lincoln to Eliza Slataper, Barnum's Hotel, [Baltimore], September 27, [1868].

[6] This part of the sentence was violently crossed out in black ink on the original letter; it cannot be determined whose sense of discretion dictated the excision.

[7] Sarah Jane Clarke Lippincott, a popular authoress who wrote under the name of Grace Greenwood.

tire change of air, scene, for me. He thought going abroad—would alone benefit me—& advised me, as soon as I could bear the change, to go to Scotland for the summer. Our old Minister a very good and intellectual man, resides there & has been always writing that I should visit Scotland—and has promised to accompany me to some places of interest in that country. I have also a first Cousin in Edinburgh Mrs Judge Dickinson, [sic] [8] of Cincinnati—who is at present residing there. If I go, I shall be accompanied by my youngest son—a very promising, lovely boy of 15—In the autumn, I shall place him, in some desirable school—In the winter, if my health continues so delicate—I shall pass it in the South of Europe. I am thus minute, in my details—as I am anxious that we should understand each other. Your daughter, Mrs [Rhoda] Mack, wrote me, that she proposed going to Europe, early in the autumn, hoping that you had intended accompanying her—I write this almost unintelligible note. How dearly I would love to have you go over at the time I do, I fear from what my physician tells me, I cannot delay it longer than the 1st of July—Will you not consider the subject and join me at *that* time? We both, have many pleasant friends in E and a summer tour in S[cotland] & early in the Autumn in Switzerland, would be delightful. I am only anticipating, a visit to Europe which my dear husband, intended we should take at the end of his term, with myself. *Ill health* and much sorrow, forces me *now* to go & I earnestly hope you will favorably consider, what I have written—& give me an immediate reply. This proposition from me, does not argue *a debt of $70,000! !* as *the colored* historian asserts. It was Judge Davis (the administrator's) particular pride that only $11- (eleven dollars) was owing on my husband's estate—and that for a country newspaper,[9] which he knew nothing about. If such a debt or any debts—existed—what good fairy, would have canceled them? It is my comfort to know, that I do not owe a dollar in the world—but what little I have, I intend enjoying —and can make myself more comfortable in Europe, than I can for the same amount of means in Chicago, which if possible, surpasses, N.Y. in high prices. My health *now* demands the change & I do

[8] Mrs. Lincoln's cousin was Annie Parker Dickson, wife of Judge William M. Dickson.
[9] The *Illinois Gazette*.

hope, my dear Mrs W—we may cross the Ocean together && This communication, I am sure you will regard as entirely confidential. Through what fearful trials—I have been recently passing! My trust has been in our Heavenly Father & he has sustained me. Hoping to hear from you, I remain

Always truly yours
Mary Lincoln.

Under the circumstances, pray excuse the scrawl I send you.

To Jesse K. Dubois [1]

Chicago Thursday
June 19 [1868]

My Dear Sir:

Notwithstanding the warm weather & the remonstrances of my physician, I have concluded to make a visit of a day or two to Springfield—for the sad purpose—which your sympathizing heart can well imagine. It is necessary for me to remain as quiet as possible whilst in S- seeing as few persons who would agitate me and recall the fearful past. I am so heart broken, over the loss of my beloved husband—that I fear I shall never be calm again—

However I am very anxious to see yourself & Mrs Dubois and hope you will call to see me tomorrow afternoon about 3 or 4 o'clock—I desire to have an especial conversation with you on a subject in which you have taken a deep interest—the monument—future action && I write in great haste as Taddie & myself, will soon follow this letter—

Always yours truly
Mary Lincoln

[1] Identified on p. 55.

To John W. Forney [2]

Chicago, June 27 [1868]

My Dear Sir:

Allow me to thank you for your kind attention, in sending the telegram, a few days since. I have also received a letter from Hon Reverdy Johnson,[3] politely assenting, to the care of my little son & myself, whilst crossing the Atlantic. I have just written Mr Johnson, and have in accordance with his request, whilst securing state rooms for himself, asked him to have one reserved for ourselves. I should like to secure passage, for a waiting woman but if I have to pay full fare for her—I shall have to decline her services as invaluable as they will be to me, among strangers, & so frequently visited by severe sickness, as I now am. I feel that I am troubling you so much, but this is an anxious consideration with me, as well as with the person in question. If I may trouble you to ascertain, what her fare would be in full on the Steamship, I would be grateful & soon inform me. After having had so indulgent a husband—every want anticipated—you will understand how greatly I feel the change. But my great great sorrow, overshadows all such minor considerations, and it is only in such, as the present exigencies—the subject is pressed home, upon me. Only severe health & extreme nervousness, compels me to make the change & I must sacrifice my little property, to meet necessary demands. These are the reasons, why, I would trouble you, regarding, the third party accompanying me.

[2] Identified on p. 200.

[3] Democratic senator from Maryland, who left the Senate before the completion of his term to assume the post of minister to Great Britain. Despite the plans discussed in this letter, Johnson left for Europe before Mrs. Lincoln, probably because she decided to remain in the United States for Robert's marriage to Mary Harlan. She gave another reason in a letter written on September 5, 1868, to Jesse K. Dubois, the full text of which is unavailable. Dated "Altoona," it read in part: "Sudden illness prevented me from sailing Aug 1st under care of Hon Reverdy Johnson. Expecting soon to sail, I am desirous of obtaining some information from you before doing so, regarding the monumental designs. If a design has been accepted, please advise me of the plan & all particulars. (Of course no one is as interested as myself in regard to it.)" Excerpt published in *The Collector*, January & February 1954. Item e70.

Will you also ascertain and inform me, whether the Steamship Baltimore, sails from B- or New York. With many apologies for the trouble I am giving you, I remain, my dear Mr Forney, respectfully yours—

Mrs A. Lincoln

To Rhoda White

Cresson, Penn
July 18th '68

My dear Mrs White:

Your letter, as well as your recently written book, has been forwarded me, in this beautiful Alleghany Mountain retreat. The work has interested me very greatly and your great grief, on the occasion of the death of so lovely & Christian a daughter is very natural. My beloved husband's, devotion to me was so great, that it always inclined him to view with consideration all those whom I liked—towards your family, in conversing with him, I never failed to express a great regard and he therefore felt an interest in yourselves, as well as your daughter, from whom you were called upon to be separated in her far distant home. I only wish, she had visited Washington more frequently & that Mr Lincoln & myself could have become better acquainted with her—Alas! Alas! the ways of Providence are inscrutable.

We sail from *Baltimore* the 1st of August and in my very feeble health, I am endeavouring to catch every mountain breeze, in hopes that strength may be given me, for the sea voyage before me. In my hours of great bodily suffering which now occur quite frequently, I often fancy I shall not much longer be separated from my idolized husband, who has only "gone before," and I am certain is fondly watching & waiting for our reunion, never more to be separated. Can it be, that one, with whom every association since I was fifteen years old,[4] has been connected and who was only happy

---

[4] Mrs. Lincoln had been twenty when she met her husband. The possible reasons for her decision to lie about her age are given on pp. 532–3.

when I was in his presence, does not watch over my sorrows & yearns for the time, when they will be over? If we had sailed from New York, I should have hoped to have seen you—as it is,—I shall indulge in the anticipation of hearing from you occasionally, whilst abroad. My address until the 1st of Oct—will be Edinburgh, Scotland.[5] My dear Mrs White, I have brooded over my great great loss so much, that with others, I now feel assured, the change, that I am now about making, is the only thing left me to prolong my life. And I have two noble, devoted sons, who would be very desolate without me. Hoping to hear from you very soon, I remain always your affectionate friend.

Mary Lincoln

Will you be able to decipher this scrawl. I am suffering so much, I am scarcely able to sit up.

M. L.

To Martha Stafford [6]

Cresson, Pennsylvania
July 18 [*1868*]

Dear Martha:

I am sure you will be surprised to hear from me—We arrived most safely at this place—on the high Alleghany Mountains—it is more beautiful than I could possibly have imagined—Owing to Mrs Sullivan's lateness, I had much trouble the last hour. Mrs Fowler & herself undertook putting in my last things & I find they left out a small green box containing my hair braids. They had it in their hands & it was not put in the trunks. If it was left in the room, will you, with a package Mrs Sullivan has, send it to me by Express by return mail. I will settle the Express bill here. I must have the box. Please see Mrs S. *the hour* you receive this note & hand *her* note to

---

[5] In fact, Mrs. Lincoln went directly to Frankfurt, and did not go to Scotland until the following summer.

[6] Housekeeper at the Clifton House, Chicago; the others mentioned were also employees at the hotel.

her. If I have left anything else, please send it to me. Also say to Mr Barrell to please direct any letters that may arrive to me *here*. I write in great haste, always remaining truly your friend

Mrs Lincoln

Robert was with us, at the depot & was shocked at *so much* baggage. I feel very sad about having to leave him for such a time. I wish you every prosperity. I wish I could describe the loveliness of this place to you. Tad has met some fine boys here & looks very happy.

M. L.

To Rhoda White

Altoona Penn.
Aug. 19, '68

My dear Mrs White:

Your telegram has been received, & I greatly regret to hear of your indisposition. As you are aware I am peculiarly situated, being exceedingly anxious to witness the marriage of my son—with a young lady, who is so charming & whom I love so much, the terror of having to proceed to *Washington* to witness it, almost overpowers me. My little son is so anxious to remain, until that event takes place & perhaps the regret I may also feel in the future that I had not gratified them all, by remaining, has quite determined me. Of course it will be the 1st of Oct before I sail. I will then go immediately to Carlsbad & place myself under medical treatment & place my little son in school—somewhere in Germany. I write you hastily, for I am feeling this morning, much indisposed. The intervening time, I shall endeavour to take care of my health & will remain in this mountainous region. If I do not continue so well, may return to Bedford [Springs]. I have half promised Gov & Mrs Curtin [7] with whom we came up from Bedford a few days since to join them

---

[7] Andrew J. Curtin had been governor of Pennsylvania from 1861 to 1867.

at a charming retreat, on the Susquehanna. I hope to hear from you
& if you will direct your letters *here*, they will be forwarded me. I
can scarcely express to you, what a source of comfort they are to
me. With much love, I remain always truly yours

Mary Lincoln

To Rhoda White

Altoona Aug 27th [1868]

My dear Mrs White—

Your letter is just received & I cannot sufficiently express my
regret on account of your illness. In regard to the proposed marriage of my son, it is the only sunbeam in my sad future. I have
known & loved the young lady since her childhood, our families
have been very intimate and as she recently & sweetly expressed
herself to me—that she felt, she was only passing from one mother
to another." I think my absence will be less felt the first year or
two, than afterwards, by them. Therefore, you will conclude, I
consider this marriage, a great gain—A charming daughter will be
my portion & one whom my idolized husband loved & admired,
since she was very young. You will be persuaded, that no feeling
save the natural horror I would entertain about returning to Washington, even for a few hours, would have caused me to have written
to you as I did. I feel that I may rely upon yourself & daughter
guarding well the mention I made you of the proposed marriage. I
am anxious that it should soon be consummated as it is time my
son was in some good school, and I am not well here. Any information regarding German schools, will be gratefully received. I will
not weary you to day, with a lengthy note. Praying that you may
soon be restored to health & with much love—I remain very truly
& affectionately yours

Mary Lincoln—

To Eliza Slataper

Altoona Penn
Sept 21st '68

My dear Mrs Slatafer [sic]: [8]

We arrived here in safety, through the rain. I found a letter from the Baltimore steamer—mentioning that they sailed on the 1st of Oct—& would take Taddie & myself to Bremen for $135.00—in gold—very cheap indeed. Another letter addressed to Mr McClellan from N.Y.[9]—stating that the *Hermann* sailed Oct 1st & would take lady & Son for $130- gold—if the lad was under 12 years of age—(They did not know what party was applying & perhaps if they did, would not make a deduction). I want you to write me so soon as you receive this letter—giving your views. Taddie appears a little obstinate & *inclined* to be *argumentative* on the subject if I sail from Baltimore, it is such a round about way—to visit "*Browns mills*"![1] and again the continual desire of the boy, to be running backwards & forwards to Washington, will be *annoying*, to say the least. I leave here to morrow evening (Tuesday for Baltimore, please direct your letter to Barnums Hotel. Robert writes me that the marriage takes place on *Thursday*, evening, I am much pleased with the delay. On Friday *afternoon* from Barnum's, I will write you again—giving many particulars—the letter will reach you *this* day week—just as I hope, dear Mrs [Augustus] Gross & yourself will be starting to meet me—

Say to Mrs Gross, that I can never be sufficiently grateful to her, for her great kindness to my little boy. He became very much attached to the young ladies, who were so kind to him. He expresses himself, as having enjoyed himself, beyond bounds, which

---

[8] Mrs. Lincoln apparently never learned the correct spelling of her friend's name.
[9] "Mr McClellan" was perhaps a pseudonym used by Mrs. Lincoln in inquiring about fares, in order that she not be overcharged because of her identity. However, according to Stephen Birmingham in his book, *Our Crowd* (New York, 1967), Mrs. Lincoln's passage was paid by Joseph Seligman, New York banker, who wished to perform a service in memory of the late President, and it may have been he who inquired about costs under an assumed name.
[1] A town in Franklin County, Pennsylvania.

often happens to youths of his age, & thoughtlessness—not to say to larger persons sometimes. When he parted with me, I slipped some loose change in his hand, & by some manner of means, he dropped it. He says it mortified him to be without change—but I think it will teach him to be more careful, *next* time. Yet, as you may be sure, my Mother's heart, was tenderly touched, at his expression of mortification when he found he was away from me, having dropped his money. He was fortunate, in being situated just as he was, in such a dilemma. He sheds tears, whenever I allude to it. How much I miss you this morning. Mrs Murdock [2] is well & as bright as ever, enquired very particularly after you both. I regretted in the confusion not to be able to say adieu, to Mr Slatafer. When will we all meet again? Prepare yourselves to meet me early next week. The fan I send by Express today. Address to Baltimore —let me have a letter by Friday morning

With much love, I remain Always truly yours

M. L.

To Eliza Slataper

Barnum's Hotel [Baltimore]
Sept. 25th "68"

My Dear Mrs Slatafer:

I have just sent you a telegram—praying that you may immediately come down here. I have just returned from Washington. Tad—remained there—and I feel that I shall be lonely beyond expression, without you—*come to me*. The marriage—passed off finely—no more than 30—persons present—very elegant presents given. *Mr Scammon's* wife [3] was taken sick at Columbus O- did not arrive—but instead—two *very thin* gold bracelets—half an inch in width & very *thin*, arrived! All this is entirely *entre-nous—breathe it not!* The presents from every other person were very rich—if they had had a large wedding they would have had an immense as-

---

[2] Wife of a Pittsburgh physician, and a friend of Mrs. Slataper and Mrs. Gross.
[3] Mrs. Charles T. Scammon, wife of Robert Lincoln's law partner in Chicago.

sortment. I am tired & will write you no more—praying in the love
of mercy—you will come to me, without delay—it is best, I should
sail from here. We took an especial trail [train] from W. this morning with the bridal party & some friends, who accompanied them to
N.Y. *I landed here*—they insisted upon my accompanying them to
N.Y. but I thought it was best to remain here until you *come—do
come both*,[4] if you love me.

Always yours
M L

leave P[ittsburgh]. Sunday morning at 11- A. M. You will arrive
here in 13 hours—if you value my peace—*come*

M L

To Eliza Slataper

Barnums Hotel
Sept 27th [*1868*]
Sunday

My dear Mrs Slatafer:

You have not yet arrived—& I have been anxiously awaiting
you!

Did I tell you, that on my arrival at Baltimore, I found two
telegrams, urging me to proceed immediately to Senator Harlan's
in Washington. On our arrival at the depot there—I found Robert
Mary & Senator Harlan in their carriages. Quite a number of
friends called to see me & as I did not look around me in W- the
feeling of BEING THERE, did not oppress me as much, as I supposed
it would. Yet I felt the after effects, on my mind, when I returned
to Baltimore. On Friday, after writing you a letter and sending you
a telegram I went to dinner & after seating myself at a table near
the door, I found my head becoming dizzy & every thing appeared
black before me—I endured the feeling as long as I well could, and
whilst attempting to rise, found myself sinking to the floor—a very
distingué looking gentleman—gave me his arm—and led me to my

4 Mrs. Slataper and Mrs. Gross.

room door—was not *this a contretemps?* There was no help for it, but you may be sure—my meals are now served in my own room. Come—come to me—the hour you receive this—Do not mention the word dress—you are quite well enough & I may never see you again. I hope I shall see you, before you receive this.

With much love to *Mrs Gross & all*—I remain

Always yours
Mary Lincoln

To Eliza Slataper

*Barnum's Hotel
Tuesday Sep 29th*—[1868]

My dear Mrs Slatafer:

Can I begin to express my disappointment, at not seeing your dear face, before I leave this blessed land? Instead of yourself, your telegram came this morning. I am feeling very anxious, about your health and will continue to feel so, during my voyage. How anxiously I have been expecting you within the last week, *you will never know.* The hours are drawing near, for us to leave. Mrs Harlan has just telegraphed me, that she will come to Baltimore bringing Taddie. Poor child he doubtless feels like a victim. He will soon be happy in the change. I will write you, when I arrive in Bremen. On Thursday morning, I will write you a line, where to direct a letter in Bremen—and so soon as you receive the direction—write to me directed to Bremen—so that I may hear from you, so soon as I arrive there. I will be feeling, very anxious about you,—we sail on Thursday. No more happy hours, with you, for a long time, perhaps never again in this world. The change from this gloomy earth, to be forever reunited to my idolized husband & my darling Willie, would be happiness indeed! I write very hastily. Oh that I could see you, before I leave—With love to all—I remain, forever yours

Mary Lincoln.

Address your next letter to me—to the care of Brothers "Kulenkampff" Bremen—

IV

A Land of Strangers

October 1868

August 1871

The steamer *City of Baltimore* sailed from that port on October 1, 1868, with Mary and Tad Lincoln aboard. It docked at Bremen, Germany, two weeks later, and from there mother and son traveled directly to Frankfurt-am-Main. Mrs. Lincoln had planned on stopping in Frankfurt no longer than a week, but she found herself lingering. The city was not only rich in history; it was a center of educational, commercial, and medical activity. It lay only a short distance from several celebrated watering places and, perhaps for all these reasons, had a large English-speaking colony. It seemed a good place to settle for the time.

She enrolled Tad in a boarding school, the "Institute" of Dr. Hohagen on the Kettenhofstrasse, and arranged for him to have special instruction in both German and English. She herself took up residence nearby in the city's most fashionable hostelry, the Hôtel d'Angleterre (though she could afford only one room), and established connections with those two necessary evils, a physician and a banker. Her first months abroad must have been busy ones; not a single letter written from the time of her sailing to the beginning of December is known to exist.

Off in "a land of strangers," an ocean away from her detractors and from past associations, with Robert married and Tad well supervised, she experienced a brief sense of deliverance. There was little here to remind her of the United States except the silly ostentation of touring Americans. Like a Jamesian exile, she would seek refuge in Europe from the shameless striving and expensive vulgarity that marked the postwar years at home. (Her distaste, one can be certain, was rooted in envy rather than esthetics.) In Europe she could revel in the novelty of antiquity; here, too, this widow of one of the greatest democrats of all time could indulge her fascination with royalty and nobility, of every era and degree. She was entranced to walk upon floors trod by German emperors for a thousand years, pleased at the number of dukes and duchesses stopping at her hotel, and by the fact that the dressmaker she used also made clothes for Queen Victoria's daughters and had once even run something up for the Queen herself!

But fairy tale fantasies faded quickly amid the exigencies of daily life. The medicines prescribed by the German physicians were not as effective as anticipated, and mineral baths were no cure for depression. After an initial mild spell, the chill gloom of a northern winter set in, compounded by an "imperfect" understanding of heating techniques that were commonplace in America. Had means permitted, she would have followed her doctors' advice and gone immediately to Italy. Worst of all, she could not lose herself for long in the anonymity of a foreign city. Here as at home she was torn between conflicting desires, longing on the one hand for the recognition due a President's widow and on the other for the precious privacy of an ordinary citizen. Everyone seemed to know who she was, but her celebrity put her at a disadvantage. Meals in the hotel dining salon were ruined for her by stares and whispers from neighboring tables; soon she was having food sent up to her room, which served to increase both her expenses and her isolation. Local entrepreneurs—including the hotel management—believing her a woman of wealth, charged her top prices. Physicians' bills began eating into her tiny income.

The notion that she could live more comfortably and cheaply abroad was dispelled in short order; if anything, she was more painfully conscious of her limited means than ever before. She had hoped to have made her first trip to Europe with her husband, sharing with him the new sights and experiences. Her path would have been smoothed at every turn, the glances of passers-by envious and admiring rather than merely curious. Instead she was alone and sick, at the mercy of grasping strangers, forced to settle for second best in everything. Her letter to David Davis of December 15, 1868, withdrawing her promise of a loan to Robert, gives evidence of a fresh concern about money; so, too, do her letters to legislators, requesting their support of a pension bill for her.

After December of 1865, when Congress had voted her only one year's Presidential salary, she had abandoned all hope of further government assistance. For nearly three years she had undertaken the fruitless task of raising money from private sources, and the notoriety resulting from these efforts had driven her from America. But toward the end of 1868, some prominent person—presumably Charles Sumner—had informed her that there was talk in Washington about granting her a pension. Sumner himself had helped to draft a pension bill (with an as yet undetermined provision) which was scheduled to be introduced in the Senate in January of 1869. Long before that date, Mrs. Lincoln was back in harness, lobbying for herself. Emboldened by distance, spurred by a spark of hope, she composed a series of letters to individual congressmen and one directed to the Senate as a body, mining the old veins of her husband's sacrifice and of her straitened circumstances, now aggravated by ill health.

To George S. Boutwell [1]

Frankfort-on-the-Maine [2]
Germany Dec 4th '68—

My dear Sir:

In consequence of very ill health, caused by great mental suffering & by the advice of physicians in America, I came to Germany, in search of health. Physicians here insist upon my going immediately to Italy & suffering as I am, I would willingly do so —if my restricted means did not prevent such an undertaking. For with the high price of living there, and being compelled to take a

---

[1] A former governor of Massachusetts, Commissioner of Internal Revenue, and now representative from Massachusetts.
[2] Mrs. Lincoln did not adopt the German spelling of Frankfurt until almost a year after her arrival, perhaps because the city's Kentucky namesake, with which she had been familiar since childhood, was spelled with an "o." Her American reflexes also prompted her to add an "e" to the name of the city's river.

servant with me—without some change is made in my condition, I cannot go—I have to practice the most rigid economy by myself, and in this country, to judge from the heavy bills I am made to pay, they are under the impression I have been allowed a pension from Congress. Only the most rigid necessity compels me to address you these lines. Will you not, as the true friend of my beloved husband, exert your great influence & have Congress give me an appropriation *as soon* as possible of at least $3000 a year—whilst I am in such infirm health. I cannot tell you, how great my physician's bills are & have been & how much entirely they have swallowed up my little income. I feel that I am writing to a noble man—one whom my idolized husband respected & loved most truly, and one who can sympathize with [the] unparalleled sufferings of his bereaved widow. Praying that my petition will be granted, for thus troubling you— I remain, with great respect

> Always truly &&
> Mrs A. Lincoln

To Nathaniel P. Banks [3]

Suffering from ill health caused by great mental distress . . . I have come over to Germany to place my son in school here & to . . . have my condition a little improved. I am now ordered to the south of Europe, but with my limited income, cannot go without Congress will kindly grant me a small pension, say $3000 a year. Surely the remembrance of my martyred husband will cause them to remember his widow in her ill health and sorrow! . . . I almost doubt my own identity when I think over the present & the time when the smallest wish was anticipated by a most indulgent husband! Hoping you will exert your influence . . .

[3] Former Union general and governor of Massachusetts, now U.S. representative from Massachusetts. The letter is significant in its contrast to Mrs. Lincoln's vehement attacks on Banks in her letters to Charles Sumner and Oliver M. Halsted, Jr., in November 1864.

To the United States Senate [4]

[*Frankfurt, December,* 1868]

To the Honorable Vice-President and Members of the Senate:

I herewith most respectfully present to the honorable Senate of the United States an application for a pension. I am a widow of a President of the United States whose life was sacrificed to his country's service. That sad calamity has greatly impaired my health; and by the advice of my physician I have come over to Germany to try the mineral waters and during the winters to go to Italy. But my financial means do not permit me to take advantage of the advice given me, nor can I live in a style becoming to the widow of the Chief Magistrate of a great nation, although I live as economically as I can. In consideration of the great service my deeply lamented husband has rendered to the United States, and of the fearful loss I have sustained by his untimely death—his martyrdom, I may say—I respectfully submit to your honorable body this petition, hoping that a yearly pension may be granted me so that I may have less pecuniary care. I remain, most respectfully,

Mrs A. Lincoln.

To Eliza Slataper

Hotel *D'Angleterre*
Frankfort A'Maine
Dec 13*th.* '68

My dear Mrs Slatafer:

In this distant land, how can I sufficiently express the great pleasure, your kind letter, has afforded me! It is such a pleasure to be thus remembered, when we are separated from those we truly love!

[4] This letter was read in the Senate on January 26, 1869, at the order of Senator Benjamin Wade of Ohio.

I came to Frankfort, expecting to remain a week, and now Christmas, is almost upon us. When I was reading *"John Ross Bean's"* description of a winter & very especially a "Christmas" in Frankfort, I then scarcely expected to be here, to witness & pass through similar scenes. It was in the famous Alleghanies, last summer, that his account was read. Certainly I expect in no place on the habitable globe, do they make greater preparations for these holy days, than in F. There appears more to tempt one here than elsewhere—the shops are very beautiful and the [visit?]ing [page torn] Americans [are] said to have increased the prices. We are considered in Europe (& very justly) a most prodigal people—and this place has become a great resort for more quiet Americans. We have quite a little colony, at our hotel—which is considered the aristocratic one, in F. All the nobility stop here, counts, dukes & dutchesses abound in the house, and on my table, their cards are frequently laid. Yet in consideration of poor health & deep mourning, I have of course accepted no dinner invitations & have kept very quiet. Popp, the most charming of *all* dress makers, who receives many orders from America, and makes for the royal family of Prussia & all the nobility, has just made me up some heavy mourning silks, richly trimmed with crape. The *heaviest* blk English Crape here, is only in our money $1.50 cts per yard. think of it! when in *war* times—I once gave, *ten* dollars per yard, for the *heaviest!* He (Popp has made dresses for Queen Victoria's daughters so long, that a few years since, when [she passed] through [F. an]d stopped at this house—she sent for him & of course he obeyed the summons. He is a very modest man & never speaks of it himself. How different *some* of our boastful Americans, would be! I like Frankfort exceedingly, the true secret is, I suppose I am enjoying *peace*, which in my deepest, heart rending sorrow, I was not allowed, in my native land! I find it quite as expensive here as in America & as I am urged by my physicians to proceed to Italy very soon—at least I expect to start about the 22d of January & remain until 1st April. *That* fearful, sorrowful month, will be spent very quietly here on my return. I wish those dear eyes of yours, could become clairvoyant & visit sunny Italy—its churches, paintings & all objects of interest with me. What happiness it would be if you, were only with me! I am beginning to realise, why it is, that

Europe spoils so many men & especially women. There is [a]n
ind[ependen]ce here [and a *reverence*] which we do not dream of
in America. My rooms are on the same floor with Consul Murphy
& wife, Mrs Mason of N.Y. & Mrs General Robert Allen & daughter of U.S. Army.[5] Mrs M. is the wife of the Organ Mason, a very
superior woman, we are much together—yet the attraction is so
different—from what I feel towards you. Her children have been so
long going to school here, & she has been in Germany, so much herself, that she has imbibed many of their philosophical ideas, which
are often startling to me. She requires that softness of character,
without which no woman, can be lovely. Notwithstanding I like
her. I can perceive that she has been demoralised, as we called our
Army men often. On yesterday, two American gentlemen friends,
called to see me, they asked me, if I was homesick. I told them I
pined for a glass of American ice water—the latter here is impossible & really dangerous to drink. Wine, of course is universally
used & yet I have never seen a person the least intoxicated. [A fe]w
days since, I visited a building 1,000 one thousand years old, to see
the portraits of about fifty German Emperors, some of them older
than the building. The chairs on which these men sat, the stone
floors, on which they trod, every thing, of course, possesses a
charm for me—as I advance in my travels, the interest will certainly increase. I am sending you, my dear friend, a tedious account
of my movements, write me, I pray you & tell me what dear Mrs
Gross & yourself are doing. The weather is so mild here, at present,
that my fire has died out, so different from *your weather* I suspect.
I often here from Robert & Mary—the latter writes me often calling
me "Dear Mother—" and says she is so happy. Wonders whether I
am not almost ready to return to them. Dear child, it may be a
weary day, ere I recross the broad Atlantic, not that my thoughts
will not be daily, hourly with you all so dea[rly be]loved. I am convinced, the longer I live, that life & its blessings are not so entirely
unjustly distributed, are [as] when we are suffering greatly, we are
inclined to suppose. My home for so many years, was so rich in
love & happiness; now I am so lonely & isolated—whilst others live

[5] Those referred to by Mrs. Lincoln were: William Walton Murphy, American
consul at Frankfurt, 1861–9; Mrs. Henry Mason, wife of the co-founder of the
Mason and Hamlin Organ Company; and Brigadier General Robert Allen, formerly of Springfield.

on in a careless lukewarm state—not appearing to fill Longfellow's measure. "Into each life, some rain must fall." I have read his "Tragedies,[6] there is no doubt, but what he is a spiritualist—Himself & daughter are now in Paris. I hope we will all meet "somewhere." Taddie, has some little Christmas remembrances for your daughter & Mrs Gross'—which, I hope ere long, he will have an opportunity to send. He likes his school & is a most affectionate, amiable tempered child—he is *recovering* from his homesickness. Do write me soon as you receive this—so that I may hear from you, before I leave for Italy. With much love to all your family, Mrs Gross & husband I remain with much affection.

[Alw]ays yours—M Lincoln

Will you be able to decipher this scraw[l]?

M. L.

To David Davis
———

Hotel D'Angleterre
Frankfort-on-the Maine
Germany Dec 15th 68

My dear Sir

I wrote you quite a long letter, on my arrival in Germany, which I presume you have received. Taddie is settled in his school & I hope he will make up for lost time. When you see Robert, may I request you—to speak to him about forwarding the money to Dr Hohagen for Taddie's first quarter. Owing to a false impression which has gone abroad that I receive a liberal pension from our government, I am charged very high for my living && and of course I have no means of my own to advance, as it is, the school where Taddie is placed, is very moderate in terms.[7] On the subject

[6] The quotation is from the third stanza of "The Rainy Day." Longfellow's *New England Tragedies*, dealing with the witchcraft mania in Salem, was published in 1868.

[7] Tad attended Professor D. Hohagen's "Institute" from October 26, 1868, to April 26, 1870. According to the guardianship files at the Illinois State Historical Library, the quarterly tuition was 150 florins ($87.75 to $96, depending on fluctuating rates of exchange).

of Robert, I wish to write you. Please consider all I say, as perfectly private. About three weeks since I received a letter from
Robert, in which he requests the loan of my *1881* bonds,[8] to be converted into money—and to be used—in connection with John Forsythe of C[hicago] [9] in building 28 houses on the North Side—
thereby of course increasing his money & he offering me 10 percent
on the money, for four years. (R. has been a noble & devoted son
to me & I love his sweet little wife very dearly, & their advancement
is my first desire—With the thought of this before me—soon after
I received the letter, without much reflection, I wrote him that I
would consent. But the thought since of parting with *those* bonds—
which were *so* placed by my dear husband, has made me unhappy
—so, on yesterday after consultation with Consul Murphy & a
banker, who could be relied on—they, greatly disapproving of my
giving them up—I sent R. a telegram, saying that I could not part
with them. The telegram cost me 56 *florins*, & of *course*, I made it,
as short as possible. I was compelled to send the telegram, for fear
—poor fellow, he would receive my letter & make arrangements
which might involve him in a difficulty. With my great love for
my good son, the necessity for refusing his request, has made me
quite ill. My health continues very poor, & the physicians here
urges me to go immediately to Italy. The trip & living there will
involve such an amount of money, that thus far, I have had to remain in this damp climate—and I cannot explain to these strange
physicians, why I do not obey their commands. I cannot but believe
if Congress knew the circumstances of the case, they would allow
me a pension of say $3,000- a year—to help me out of my diffi-
culties. With my certain knowledge of your great goodness of
heart, dear Judge—I am sure if *it is*, brought up before Congress,
you will rather aid, than oppose it. Owing to my station, which of
course is greatly regarded in Europe, I am charged—the highest
prices & I am living in one room, in the most economical manner—
And to go to Italy, where I am daily urged, by my physicians to go
& where prices have become so exorbitant—I shall have *myself* to
dispose of a few bonds—which it appears a sacrilege to do—without

---

[8] Purchased by Lincoln in 1865, the 1881 bonds were by this time worth over
$55,000.
[9] Son-in-law of Dr. James Smith.

Con- will grant me the pension. *Thad Stevens is gone* & they speak of increasing [President-elect] Grant's salary to a $100,000- a year. My husband, was Commander in Chief & directed every move Grant ever made—Surely, surely with ill health upon me & physician bills, that often *appall* me—*I will be remembered. You can do much*, dear Judge, in influencing public opinion, will you not use, that great influence? I am sure you will. I wish you would write me your opinion, regarding the *1881* bonds. Did I do right? all you say, will be sacredly regarded, and never mentioned.

If Mrs Davis and your daughter are with you, please present, my kindest regards—

Hoping to hear from you, very soon, I remain, always, with great respect

Yours truly,
Mary Lincoln

I did not mention to you that I should be required to take a maid or companion with me to Italy as I could not travel alone. As it is with such prices as we have to pay in Italy—I could barely with great economy, go there alone—Will not Congress, while ill health is upon me, grant me a pension?

M. L.

To John Todd Stuart

Hotel D'Angleterre
January 18th 1869
Frankfort-on-the-Maine Germany

My Dear Cousin.

I have been intending writing to you for some time past, on a subject, very near to my heart. Of course it regards the resting place of my beloved husband—the monument—Very ill health, the past winter, has prevented my writing you, on this subject. Seeing the name of Mr Mead the sculptor [1] in the American papers, as being in Chicago, en route to Springfield, to perfect the arrange-

---

[1] Larkin G. Mead, who was to create the marble monument to Lincoln over the tomb at Oak Ridge.

ments, I thought I would write you. I have brought over to Europe, your last letters of assurance, which have been a great comfort to me. For in *your hands*, I feel all will be safe, and all the promises made me, will be most faithfully kept. I wish you would write me on the subject, in which I am so especially interested. Please address to "Care of Philip, Nicol, Schmidt, Bankers. Frankfort à Maine Germany"—Wherever I am, the letter will be forwarded me. I have just received a call from Mr McChesney,[2] you may remember him, as Mr [Tom?] Campbell's relative. He is said to have married a very accomplished lady, who is at present in Dresden. I am earnestly advised by two physicians—who have for the greater part of the winter, been attending on me—to go to Italy. I sometimes feel that I may never return alive to my own country, but if I should die abroad, my remains will be taken home & placed beside my husband. You will say, I am "nervous" truly, I am—With much love to all your family & all friends, not forgetting cousin "Lizzie"[3] I remain always, your affectionate Cousin

Mary Lincoln

On January 14, 1869, Oliver P. Morton of Indiana introduced in the Senate a joint resolution for the relief of Mrs. Abraham Lincoln. The resolution was based upon the consideration that her husband, Commander-in-Chief of the army and navy, had been killed in wartime by enemies of the republic, and that his widow was entitled to a pension "upon the same principles and for the like reasons with any other officer who fell in the war."[4] The amount was left blank. Charles Sumner, who had been largely responsible for formulating the resolution, suggested that the amount be fixed

[2] J. H. McChesney, former Assistant State Geologist for Illinois. He had been awarded a consulship in England in 1861.

[3] Mrs. Lincoln's widowed cousin, Elizabeth Todd Grimsley, who had married the Reverend John H. Brown of Springfield in 1867.

[4] The factual information in this section, and the quotations from the *Congressional Globe*, are taken from an article entitled "Mrs. Lincoln's Pension" by F. Lauriston Bullard. *Lincoln Herald*, June 1947, pp. 22–7.

at $5,000 a year, a figure roughly equivalent to interest on the $75,-
000 salary for the three years of Lincoln's unexpired term. The
resolution was referred to the Committee on Pensions, which took
ten days to issue a report recommending rejection, on the grounds
that the members were "unable to perceive that Mrs. Lincoln . . .
is entitled to a pension under the letter or spirit of any existing
law." The Senate debate on the resolution (during the course of
which the widow's letter of application was read) was long and
acrimonious. It covered not only matters of precedent and prudence, but also details of Mrs. Lincoln's financial affairs. Finally,
on March 3, at the last session of the Fortieth Congress, Sumner
brought about a vote: 23 for adoption, 27 against, 16 Senators absent and not voting.

For most of the period of the debate, Mary Lincoln was in the
South of France. Bitter cold had driven her from Frankfurt at the
beginning of February and, Italy being too far and too expensive,
she had settled in Nice. For the first time she experienced the rare
pleasures of a winter's sojourn under the southern sun, and the contrast in climates enraptured her. In Nice, too, she was mercifully
removed from "*hostile American* newspapers," [5] many of which
had taken the occasion of the debate to renew their attacks upon
her. She was still in Nice on March 5 when Sumner himself introduced a second pension bill specifying the $5,000 figure at a spe-
cial session of the new Forty-First Congress. He had hoped and
worked for immediate consideration of the measure, but George
Edmunds of Vermont, chairman of the Senate Pensions Committee, objected. The bill went back to committee, where it was destined to languish for over a year.

To Eliza Slataper

Nice, France, Feb 17th. '69

My Dear Mrs Slatafer:

I have been anxiously hoping to receive an answer to my last,
for a long time. As I have written to Frankfort for letters, I trust

[5] Mary Lincoln to Eliza Slataper, Nice, France, February 17, 1869.

in a day or two, I may be favored. After the first of January, cold weather set in and I became so greatly indisposed about six weeks since, that my physicians insisted upon my going South, so here I am and have been, for the last two or three weeks. I left it so cold, in Germany, on arriving here, I find the weather as sunny & balmy as June with us. Flowers growing in the gardens, oranges on the trees, my windows open all day, looking out upon the calm, blue Mediterranean. The contrast is inconceaveable. I live out in the open air & am gradually finding myself, grow stronger day by day, for I had been very sick in Frankfort. Another winter, will find me here, I think *much* earlier in the season. For more reasons than my health, am I congratulating myself that I am in the South of Europe, quite removed from *hostile American* newspapers. For as you are aware I have made a formal application to Congress, for a pension, which is my due—and for this *brave* act, *at this time*, I suppose according to custom, I am being most unmercifully assailed. The only papers, I have seen, since I have been here—have been the N.Y. Times, Tribune & Herald, and they all, with *one* accord, urge my rights. I am *not* in the least hopeful, that *justice*, will me done me & I am anticipating a refusal. Doubtless they are *tomahaw[k]ing* me *now*, to slay me afterwards! Nous verrons, yet I greatly fear my misgivings will prove correct. How dearly I would love to see you once again & talk over so many many things. If my health improves, my sight-seeing has only commenced. En route to Nice, I stopped for a day or two at Baden to see a lady from America, who resides most of the time in Europe. We visited a castle near Baden, where the veritable "White Lady,[6] is said, delights most to dwell, and where Napoleon signed his memorable treaty, in roaming over the immense building, I said to our two attendants "have you ever seen her"—to which of course, they both replied—"We often do." As you know the Germans are very superstitious, and from the King of Prussia, down to his humblest subject, believe in *her* frequent appearance. Speaking of royalty, reminds me that my dress swept past the Prussian Princess, on yesterday, in a Turkish store. She had alighted from her carriage and was selecting some gor-

---

[6] Many royal and noble families, including the Hohenzollerns, claimed a "White Lady," the apparition of an ancestress come back to haunt the castle where she died.

geous tablecovers—our eyes met & we looked earnestly at each other, yet until she left the store, I did not know, *who* she was. Of course she will always remain in ignorance, regarding *me*. Such is life! There are so many with Nobility attached to their names in this country, who live in apartments, and do not assume, *near as much* as *our nouveaux riches!* I had so much to harrass & excite me at home, in America, that I think it is the best thing, I could have done to "place the waters, between myself & unkindness," at present. Yet the distance *only* draws me nearer *to the few*, I loved so—truly. In consequence, should I ever regain my health & my strength of mind partially even returns to me, the restoration to those so dear to me, will be, *all the sweeter*. Oh if you were only with me here! Was there ever such a climate, such a sunshine, such air?—You cannot turn for flowers, beautiful bouquets, thrust into your very face. I never return from my walks without my hands being filled—and yet to me, they bring sad, deeply painful memories. I often wonder, how I could have touched them. Time brings to me, no healing on its wing and I shall be only too glad, when my mission which I know, to be my precious child Taddie, is completed, to be rejoined to my dearly loved ones, who have only "gone before." Such a dream as I had of my idolized Willie, last night. Some day, I will tell you *all*. I took the liberty of sending—your daughter & Mrs Gross', lately a simple set of amber each. I trust ere this, they have received them. I have also crosses of the same, for them—and it was yesterday, when I was selecting you both, *two fans*, that pleased me well & which I will send, when I return to Frankfort—that the Crown Princess & *myself* met face to face—

Present my kindest regards to Mrs Gross & the rest of your families. Also *please do—do*—write soon, directed to me at Frankfort—on the Maine, "Care of Phillip Nicol Schmidt bankers."

Ever yours most affectionately
Mary Lincoln

Will you be able to read such a scrawl?

To Rhoda White

Nice, France March 16th-'69

My Dear Mrs White:

Your letter recently received, has afforded me much pleasure & believe me, in this far distant land, you are frequently remembered, both in my thoughts & prayers. Past friendship, through the trying years of the war—and the fearful loss, we both have sustained—in our dearly beloved husbands, are ties, too strong for time or distance to sever.

Ill health, rendered it absolutely necessary that I should come South, & by degrees, I find myself regaining strength. *For sorrow*, such as ours, there is no balm, the grave and Heaven, with reunion with our loved ones, can alone heal, bleeding, broken hearts. *Wherever I am, feeling* so *sadly*, I lead a life of isolation & retirement, although I have been here several weeks, I am sure few or none are aware of it. I am not feeling sufficiently well in mind or body, to undertake Italy *this* winter. Next winter, I will try to come come down in Nov- The season is already so far advanced & nothing I could see now could interest me in the terrible month of April —I feel that in a few days, I must make the effort & return to my young son, who is now in Frankfort. When I visit Italy some months hence, it would be such a pleasure to have you as a companion. We could visit places of interest without being recognized. Of course, Americans abound everywhere—& in my morning walks in the sunshine, you can always recognize them, very often, by their loud voices, so *early* as ten or eleven in the morning, VELVET COSTUMES &&—*Full dress*, when one is sight seeing or in quest of *health* & *change*, must certainly be a trial. After we have suffered heavy afflictions, life is at best, a fearful endurance. To me—everything looks so desolate. I often wonder, why, I was spared, when my darling husband was taken, and to suffer so much too! I hope, my dear friend, you will write to me often—Please direct to, Phillip, Nicoll, Schmidt, bankers Frankfort a Maine—Germany. With apologies, for so hurried a letter & with remembrances to your amiable family, I remain always truly yours

Mary Lincoln

To Mary Harlan Lincoln

[INCOMPLETE]   *Frankfort March* 22 [1869] [7]

My very dear Mary:

After a most tedious journey from Nice of constant travel for three days, I arrived here this morning. Of course, I sent immediately for my Taddie and as he has just left me for an hour, I feel that I cannot refrain from writing you, for your most welcome letter of March 1st has just been read. It pains me beyond expression, to learn of your recent illness and I deeply deplore that I was not with you to wait upon you. My dear child, do take good care of your precious health—*even the thought* of you at this distance is a great alleviation to the sorrow I am enduring.

I may quietly return to you, as it is, nothing can please me in what is beyond doubt most necessary at the present time both to my health and to my peace of mind—this change of scene. My thoughts have been constantly with you for months past, and oh! how I have wished day by day, that you could be with me and enjoy the air and the sunshine of the lovely climate I have just left. It would have been utterly impossible for me with my present health and sad state of mind, to have taken the least interest in Italian cities this winter. I return to find my dear boy much grown in even so short a time and I am pained to see his face thinner, although he retains his usual bright complexion. He is doubtless greatly improving in his studies, yet I am very sure the food he gets at his school does not agree with him. This you may be sure is a most painful belief to me. When I am here, I can always give him his dinner as he has their permission to be absent. His presence has become so necessary even to my life. In two days' time he will have his Easter vacation for ten days and he is urging me to take him

[7] This letter, as published by Katherine Helm, bore no year. The greater portion clearly was written in early 1869: Mrs. Lincoln made only one trip to Nice, in the spring of that year. The reference in the final paragraph to young Mary having a "devoted husband and darling child" leads to the supposition that Miss Helm put together parts of two letters, and that the final paragraph, at least, was from a letter written in late 1869 or early 1870, after Robert and Mary had welcomed their first child, a daughter, born October 15, 1869.

somewhere at that time and if I were not so fatigued would gladly consent to do so, but I suppose it will end in my acquiescing with his wishes . . .

Do oblige me by considering me as a mother for you are very dear to me as a daughter. *Anything* and *everything* is yours—If you will consider them worth an acceptance. My mind was so distracted with my grief in that house, 375,[8] I cannot remember where anything was put. It will be such a relief to me to know that articles can be used and enjoyed by you. . . . Remember everything is yours and feeling so fully assured as you must be of my love, will you now, my dear girl, consider them as such? Oh! that I could be with you! for with the lonely life I impose upon myself, separation from those I love so much, at this trying, heart-rending time, is excruciating pain. If when we meet I find you restored to health, I will feel in a measure compensated for the dreary absence. I am glad you enjoyed your visit to Springfield. They are all so pleasantly situated—so hospitable and so fully prepared to receive you with the greatest affection. Do make the promised visit to Mrs. Edwards—in the summer and then go to the seaside and rest quietly for a month, no less time. Let me beseech you, dear Mary, to take care of your health.

My head aches now for the tears I have shed this morning in thinking of you and our loving boy. Taddie with his great good heart loves you so devotedly. I shall try to think of you as with your dear mother while it is so cold in Chicago at present. I know they will be careful of you. I never see anything particularly pretty —that I do not wish it was yours. My spirit is very willing but my purse not very extensive.

I am pained to hear of Bettie Stuart's death.[9] She was a most amiable woman, and her father is a very dearly loved cousin—a most affectionate relative. Did you see Mrs. Lizzie Brown in Springfield?—a very sweet woman. I shall, dear Mary, await most anxiously news from you. If I do not hear soon I shall imagine every trouble. If you will write to dear Taddie, you will gratify him very much.

[8] The house that Mrs. Lincoln still owned and now rented out at 375 West Washington Street, Chicago.
[9] "Bettie," daughter of John Todd Stuart and wife of Christopher C. Brown, died on March 2, 1869, in Springfield.

Referring to that speech Mrs. ——— made you last winter that housekeeping and babies were an uncomfortable state of existence for a young married lady I think her experience was different from most mothers who consider that in the outset in life—a nice home—loving husband and precious child are the happiest stages of life. I fear she has grown moody, but at the same time I hope you will have a good rest and enjoy yourself *free* for a year or more to come. The Doctor has just left me and says he wonders to find me sitting up.

You should go out *every day* and enjoy yourself—you are so *very young* and should be as gay as a lark. Trouble comes soon enough, my dear child, and you must enjoy life, whenever you can. We all love you so very much—and you are blessed with a devoted husband and darling child—*so do go out* and enjoy the sunshine. I do so hope your dear mother has recovered her health. When I can I will write to her. Do, I pray you, write frequently. I do wish you would take out the double India shawl, with a red center, which I never wore and make faithful use of it.

Mary Lincoln

To Charles Sumner

Frankfort à Maine
March 27, 1869

Private
My Dear Mr Sumner:

Permit me from this far distant land, to send you & other noble friends, an expression of my most grateful thanks, for your kind perseverance in my behalf, to secure me a pension, which the whole just, civilized world, acknowledges, I should receive.

If ill health and in fact the exigencies of the case did not require it, you may assuredly believe me, that I should not have made such an appeal, nor would I have done so, even under *these* circumstances, if I had not believed, the great heart of the American Nation, would *not* have responded immediately to my request—

Made under *such* trying circumstances—such a painful ordeal, as I am now passing through. My good husband, always surrounded me with such tender care, that in my great sorrow, desolation & illness you can imagine, I am feeling the contrast very greatly—I can but believe, that Gen Shurtz [sic] [1] will use his great influence, on the Committee, in my behalf, and with my impression of Senator Edmunds character—when he is *rightly* informed of the extent of my means, he will advocate the justice of the cause. Gen Grant too will not surely be unmindful of the past, & will urge upon the Committee & others my claim.

It is a satisfaction for me, whatever the result may be, to remember, that those who most urgently pressed the pension and its justice, even the whole souled men whom my husband, most highly regarded and loved as if they were brothers. I enclose Dear Mr Sumner, a card, which may I trouble you, to hand Gen Grant? [2] I am quite an invalid today, or would not send you, so hasty & illegible a letter

With many assurances of gratitude, I remain, always truly

Mary Lincoln

In July of 1869 Mary Lincoln embarked with Tad on a journey that was to provide one of the happiest interludes of her life. At the invitation of the Reverend James Smith, that loyal friend of twenty-five years, mother and son spent seven joyous weeks together in Scotland. They stopped in Paris and London en route and returned by way of Brussels, but Mrs. Lincoln's letters describing the

[1] Carl Schurz, the distinguished German-American, had served as minister to Spain from 1861 to 1862, then as a Union brigadier general, and was now senator from Missouri and a member of the Committee on Pensions.

[2] On the engraved visiting card enclosed with this letter, Mrs. Lincoln wrote: "In memory of my great and good husband will not President Grant exert his great influence with the Senate Committee & others, in order that an immediate pension may be granted me? Most respectfully Mrs. A. Lincoln March 27th 69." (Text published in Parke-Bernet Catalogue, Barrett Sale, February 19 and 20, 1952. Item 760.)

trip wasted not a word on those three great cities. Even the French capital, in all the fading grandeur of the Second Empire, paled beside "dear old Scotia." Her sojourn in that land of poets and warriors, of her own ancestors, touched a romantic chord in her nature; so full of wonder was she that for days at a time she forgot to feel sorry for herself. She and Tad traveled from one end of Scotland to the other, exploring Edinburgh and Glasgow, then wandering slowly north to the bleak country where in summer daylight breaks at three A. M. and lingers until eleven at night. They gazed on mountains and lochs, castles and abbeys, went down to Fingal's Cave and up into the Highlands near Balmoral. (She was certain that, had Queen Victoria been in residence there, she would have warmly welcomed a "sister in grief.") [3]

Returning to Frankfurt in mid-August, she experienced the inevitable letdown. Tad went back to school, and she was once again alone. Her earlier stay in the South of France had so depleted her resources that she had long since abandoned the Hôtel d'Angleterre for a second-class establishment. There was only one ray of light to brighten prospects of the cold, anxious winter ahead, the winter when the pension question would surely be decided for good or ill: on her arrival she found in her accumulated mail a note from Mrs. James H. Orne, a good friend of Washington days and a faithful correspondent since. Sally Orne, wife of a wealthy carpet manufacturer from Philadelphia, was making an extended tour of Europe, accompanied by two young daughters, a maid, and a valet. She had been in Hamburg, but by the time Mrs. Lincoln returned from Scotland had already left for Frankfurt on the chance that her friend would be there.

To her surprise, Mrs Orne found her friend also registered at the Hôtel de Holland. "I followed the waiter to the *fourth story* and the back part of it too—" she later wrote Charles Sumner. There, "in a small cheerless desolate looking room with but one window—two chairs and a wooden table with a solitary candle," she found Mary Lincoln.[4] It was an emotional reunion. For three days and nights, the two women spent every waking moment to-

[3] Mary Lincoln to Rhoda White, [K]ronberg, August 30, 1869.
[4] Sally B. Orne to Charles Sumner, Baden Baden, September 12, 1869. MS. in the Houghton Library, Harvard University, Cambridge, Massachusetts.

gether, reminiscing about the past and lamenting the present. Not since she had last seen Lizzie Keckley (and how could she bear to think about *that?*) had Mrs. Lincoln had the pleasant company and undivided attention of an old friend, someone who could appreciate her altered circumstances and who had nothing in the world to do but listen, commiserate, and try to cheer her up.

Nothing that was said appalled Mrs. Orne more than the conditions under which "*the wife the petted indulged wife* of my *noble* hearted just good *murdered* President Abraham Lincoln" was living. Her letter to Sumner was charged with passionate feeling. "My very blood boiled within my veins and I almost *cried out— shame on my countrymen—*Mrs. Lincoln was completely overwhelmed with grief—her sobs and tears wrung my own heart and I thought . . . if her *tormentors* and *slanderers* could see her— they surely *might be satisfied.*"[5] The time soon came for Mrs. Orne to resume her travels, but she never lost touch with Mary Lincoln or ceased efforts to communicate her plight to those in power in Washington. Her husband was an intimate of prominent political figures, even closer to President Grant than he had been to Lincoln; her brother, Charles O'Neill, was a Republican congressman from Philadelphia. Sally Orne used the family's formidable connections for all they were worth during those endless months when the pension bill lay ignored in committee.

"No action" in Washington put an intolerable strain on Mrs. Lincoln's nerves. Her intense interest in the pension grew into an obsession. The longer the delay, the more convinced she became that she would be forgotten, that other legislative business would be given priority over hers, and that enemies were attempting to prejudice her case in subtle and sinister ways. Her letters to Sally Orne during that time of waiting form a dreary catalogue of bodily ailments and nervous crises. In a frenzy of anxiety, she could have been writing from Frankfurt, Germany, Frankfort, Kentucky, or the bottom of a well, for all she conveyed of her surroundings. She had no heart for the cultural enticements of that cosmopolitan city, no eye for the cataclysmic changes taking place in neighboring Prussia, as Bismarck prepared to go to war with France within the year. She focused all her attention on America and on her own

[5] *Ibid.*

predicament. References to herself, Tad, her late husband, were drenched in sadness; references to others were caustic and occasionally cruel.

She reserved her harshest comments, her most scathing sarcasm, for any person who received public honors or gifts of money while she was reviled and her claims ignored. She had always disdained Ulysses Grant, that "butcher" of a general who would never have become President had Lincoln not "made" him. (The fact that Grant had, in a sense, "made" Lincoln probably never entered her mind.) The President would be forgiven his various meannesses only if he would "work" for her. With so many enemies lurking about, every friend must pitch in and work doubly hard to overcome opposition. Even such a loyal champion as Charles Sumner came in for gentle criticism when he appeared to be slackening his efforts to promote the pension.

The death of Edwin M. Stanton in December of 1869 overwhelmed her at first, until she learned that more than $100,000 had been privately raised for his survivors; similar assistance rendered the family of General John A. Rawlins, Grant's former Chief-of-Staff who had died destitute within a year of his appointment as Secretary of War, filled her with impotent rage. The news from America did, however, bring its occasional grim satisfactions. When it was rumored that Mrs. Grant had been indirectly involved in the gold scandals of September 1869, Mary Lincoln hoped the public would realize that a woman "more dreadful . . . than Mrs L- may *yet* occupy the *W. H.*" [6]

Through it all she was unstinting in praise of Sally Orne: her energy, her compassion, her "*executive ability.*" Although Mrs. Orne only managed to return to Frankfurt twice—when Mrs. Lincoln was out of town—she sent a continual flow of bulletins, newspaper clippings from America, and letters filled with encouragement and concern. For seven long months Mary Lincoln clung to those letters as to a lifeline.

[6] Mary Lincoln to Sally Orne, Frankfurt, February 11, 1870.

To Sally Orne [7]

Frankfort a M
August 17th '69

My dear Mrs Orne—

After six weeks absence from town, I returned last evening & amongst my package of letters, I found one from your dear, kind self. I can scarcely express the pleasure, I feel, to think that you are so near—but yet the sad thought will intrude itself, lest you may *not* be still at Homburg. I write this, hoping for the best. If you are still at H- please telegraph me "yes"—simply—I will understand—Address me, Hotel de Holland. room 72—My young son, has Thursday afternoon to himself, so if you have not left which I devoutly trust not, we will run out to see you, about 3- p.m. of that day. If I could leave earlier, I would do so—I am so impatient to see you—With much love & in great haste, I remain

Always affectionately yours,
Mary Lincoln

To Mary Harlan Lincoln

[EXCERPT]   *August 20* [1869]

Dear Mary:

. . . My very pleasant and affectionate friend arrived in town since I wrote the first part of this letter—Mrs. Orne. She came from Hamburg in search of me, and has rooms at the same hotel where I am now stopping. We are together all the time. She is a very lovely woman and will remain here some time, she says, to be with me. I feel quite made up . . .

---

[7] This letter apparently did not reach Mrs. Orne before she had left for Frankfurt. She later wrote Charles Sumner that she had come in search of Mrs. Lincoln and found her, by chance, in the hotel where she herself had reserved rooms.

To Eliza Slataper

My Dear Mrs Slatafer:

On my return from Scotland, three days since, I found your most acceptable letter quietly awaiting me written *now*, so many weeks since. Taddie & myself had been absent from this place seven weeks & have been so far *north* in Europe, as to see daylight closing in upon us at *eleven o'clock*—P.M. and morning light, at 3. A.M. Our old & dear friend, Dr Smith, 73—years of age [8] & very feeble, anticipating that he will not live much longer & desirous of seeing us before his departure, insisted so much upon our visit to him this summer, that we concluded to do so. We went to London via Paris, remaining at the latter place only 5 days, but sight seeing *every* moment of our time. In London—the kind good old man, came down by steamer & met us—there we also remained 5. days. Beautiful glorious Scotland, has spoilt me for every other Country! It appears to me, that we saw every place, yet I presume we might remain five months there, continually travelling round, without doing so. We visited—Abbotsford, Dryburgh abbey—passed six days in charming Edinburgh—seeing *oh so much!* Glascow, journey on the Clyde—all through the west of dear old Scotia, Burn's birthplace, saw *the nook in* the wall where he first saw *light*, went to Greenoch—heaved a sigh, over poor "Highland Mary's" grave—went out into the ocean—entered Fingal's cave Visited Glencoe—*Castles unnumerable*—Balmoral—Drummond the latter *perfectly fairy land* visited GLAMIS castle—saw the room & the bed on which poor king Duncan was murdered. Stepped *on the same* step—that Mary Queen of Scots jumped into the canoe from her prison home at *Lochleven*. I cannot begin to enumerate, all the places of interest we visited. I *am convinced*, that I shall never again be able to arouse myself to take *such another* interest in any other country, I may chance to visit. I hastened back as Taddie, had been delayed, ten days after the commencement of his school. We returned via—Ostend—Brussels went out to the battle field of

[8] Mrs. Lincoln overestimated Dr. Smith's age by five years. He died two years later, at the age of seventy.

Waterloo. I returned here—with rather a heavy heart, my usual accompaniment, of the last few years. But have had a very agreeable surprise in finding a very particular friend with her family—from Philadelphia a most charming lady, she had searched for me every where written me letters enquiring my whereabouts when I was in Sc- went out to Homburg, and strange to say—but it will not surprise either *you* or *I*—the day after my return—stopping myself, at an hotel here, where I never dreamed I should be she came here also—bag & baggage—as she said in quest of me. She is now here —and we sat up in my room last night & until 3. this morning— talking over former *happy* days. We were very intimate in Washington. They remain in E. three years & I suppose we will be much together. Her name is Mrs James Orne of Phil- they are immensely wealthy & she is as unaffected & overflowing with love for her friends, as if she were penniless. She is accompanied by two very sweet young daughters—her maid & valet. I forgot to mention a brother. She is very much shocked—that I should have no waiting woman & says a *better time*—is coming for me. Poor me! Heaven grant it. Her brother, Charles O'Neil [sic], is a member of Congress, from Phil. They are a very delightful family—and has written to me continually, since the fearful loss—of my darling husband. If you remember, her writing me when we were at Bedford, to come on to Phil & make her a visit—before sailing for E. I wish you knew, this sweet woman. She said it was an irresistible impulse, for her two or three [days] ago, to leave Homburg— for F- & on entering the hotel, remarked to her daughters—"I have a presentiment, that Mrs Lincoln, is in this house" and before she had taken off her bonnet—she was in my room & we sat up *that* whole night together too. A *gentleman* next door, knocked several times, during the night saying, "ladies, I should like to sleep some." We amused ourselves very much, over his discomfiture, last night—another sufferer—rang the bell—for the waiter & *quiet* at 2½ oclock THIS A.M.

Please burn this & oblige me, by telling no one save Mrs Gross of my recent journey to S. Will explain *hereafter*— [9]

[9] Mrs. Lincoln's plea for secrecy about her visit to Scotland probably stemmed from the fact that, while there, she had enlisted the aid of Dr. Smith (see letter which follows) in lobbying with senators for her pension. Perhaps she wished it to appear as if Smith's activities in her behalf were purely spontaneous. She might also have wished to avoid giving Washington the impression that she was able to afford the luxury of travel.

To James Smith

Frankfurt A Maine
August 26th '69—

My dear Sir:

Your kind note is just received & I am pleased to hear that you are enjoying the benefit of the waters, you mention. The weather is intensely warm here, and I leave tomorrow for the country. The friend from Phil- I mentioned to you, found me the day I wrote you, came direct to the hotel where I am stopping— and we have been together day & night ever since. Two or three entire nights, dear Mrs Orne & myself, sat up until daylight, talking over the happy past. She has been my most intimate friend—in Wash & elsewhere—for the last 8 or nine years—Her husband is a millionaire, and they are very noble people—Her brother is a member of Congress, & writes *her*, that I am to have my pension early next winter—Mr Orne, a very great Republican, wrote her, that 3 weeks since, he was sitting next Gen Grant at Long Branch, when the latter turned to him & said "Mr Orne, it shall be my first duty, when Congress reassembles, to see that Mrs Lincoln, has her pension. "Nous verrons"—this is entirely *entre nous*. They travel with a maid & valet—and think very justly, it is a disgrace that I am alone—I do trust, dear Dr—that you will recover your health —and I hope you will take great care of yourself & that your valuable life may be spared many years—Your constitution is naturally so strong, that I do not see why you cannot live 10 or 15 years still—I hope you will write a line to "Mr Phillip—N. Schmidt acknowledging the receipt of the cheque—Also in a letter to me— please return "my promise to pay & greatly oblige—Address my letters as usual to the care of the banker *here*—as they will be called for,

I remain very truly yours
Mary Lincoln

Private. If you receive *any* replies to your letters, written to the Senators—please forward them to me—I am glad, Miss Allen, is with you.

M. L-

To Rhoda White

Cronberg,[1] *August 30th* 69

My dear Mrs White:

On my return two weeks since, from the North of Scotland, I found your very welcome letter and if I had had, a moment of leisure since, you would have had an earlier reply. I considered myself very fortunate in having returned in time to see Mr Williams, who kindly handed me your note of introduction. I was very much pleased with him & found him a most gentlemanly young man and greatly regretted that owing to his hurried visit, to Europe, he could only allow himself so short a time in Frankfurt. Mrs James H. Orne & family, who remembers you with *so much* pleasure, were stopping in the same hotel, with myself, were disappointed not to make his acquaintance, very especially as he had seen you so recently. I feel assured, you remember seeing Mrs Orne of Philadelphia at Willard's five or six years since—she is a very sweet, affectionate woman, and both in joy & sorrow, has proved a very dear friend to me. Her husband, is an earnest Republican and having much means, and a noble generous heart, did much during the war for our brave soldiers. Mrs Orne & myself have been together for many days & *day* & NIGHT—we have been conversing incessantly. How much dear Mrs White, I wish you could have been with us—for I am sure a change of scene would benefit you greatly—We are both unfortunately too much alike with regard to thinking too much—over our fearful bereavement—yet broken hearted as we both are, how can it be otherwise? My first thought in the morning, when I awaken from my troubled slumbers & my last at night, is of my beloved husband, and my daily prayer is, that the time of my terrible probation HERE on earth may be short —ere we are reunited—*never more* to part! The ways of Providence, are indeed mysterious, if during my darling, husband's lifetime, I had been told, that a dark future was before me & notwithstanding the invaluable services, the one, dearer to me than life, was rendering his country, the idolized and indulged wife of that man,

---

[1] Kronberg, a mountain village near Frankfurt, was best known as the site of the castle used as a summer retreat by the Prussian royal family.

would have found it necessary to seek a foreign shore—to insure the *peace* & quiet, absolutely necessary, that she might retain her reason, surely, surely, I would have considered, the tale an idle & wild foreboding & would not have given it credence—and how would it have been with *that* husband & father, whose greatest weakness, was his excessive love for his wife & children? We were spoilt by his indulgence. Since he has passed away, the only soothing thought; that has visited my heart, has been, the consolatory one, that a merciful Father, would graciously permit him to watch over the dearly loved ones, from whom he was so cruelly torn. Life would be a torture to me, if I did not thus believe.

I feel that I am wrong, in writing to you in such a sad strain, but how true it is that "from the heart, we both write & speak. Mrs Orne & myself separated three days since—*temporarily*—she to go to Wiesbaden for a short time, when she will join me here, in this quiet region in the Taunus Mountains. But my surroundings here are beautiful *beyond description*. Three ruined castles are in sight, one, a very *near neighbour*—all of them dating back to the 12th & 13th centuries—when the robber knights inhabited them— and committed riotous depredations upon the country at large. As they had the good taste, always to build on high mountains you can imagine, dear friend, that my present habitation is very high up also—which is not at all disagreeable, in consideration of the warm weather we have had for the last few days. As regards my travels in Scotland of *seven* charming weeks, accompanied by my young son—during his summer vacation, I can scarcely permit myself to attempt a description. We were so far North—where daylight does not entirely cease until 11 P.M. and morning light breaks in upon us at 3 A.M. It does appear to me, that Scotland has spoilt me for seeing any other place in Europe. Edinburg is a beautiful city—no nook & corner of interest—did I leave unvisited, as I now think. We were at Abbotsford—all through the *Rob Roy* Country—visited all the lovely locks—Lock Lomond—Lock Catherine & *all—all*—saw the great mountains—castles visited Burn's birthplace & sighed over poor "Highland Mary's" grave. and greater than all—went down into the deep & entered "Fingal's cave," not equal to our Niagara, yet it is *wonderful*. The "old hundred sung in that vaulted region, by about two hundred people on *that* day—will ever sound in my ears. It is only in visiting such a spot, that we can fully realize the greatness & power of the Creator. At Oban—we visited the ruined castle where the *first* 28 kings of Scotland lived—a most interesting spot. You may have gone over all this ground. We travelled entirely INCOG- *Mrs Lincoln's* name, was never *breathed* —My health is so far from being restored, that absolute quiet is enjoined upon me, and I went to Scotland, quite reluctantly this summer and only to see a very dear old friend of my husband's & my own—whose days I fear are numbered. We also visited Balmoral—when the Queen was absent—I *have every* assurance, that as sisters in grief a warm welcome would be given me—*wherever* she is—yet I prefer quiet—I hope to hear from you *very very* soon. Please address—to the banker at Frankfurt a Ma[in], letters—will be forwarded me. Please regard this communication as private— With much love—I remain always affectionately yours

Mary Lincoln

We have indeed, *many*, many pure & true men & women in our land—*all* are not false. Gov Fenton, of New York [2] was the last person I saw three days since in Frankfurt—I had a most agreeable interview with him—what a charming gentleman he is, & what *a* proud & noble speciman *he is* of the great & good men, our beloved country has produced!

Do write

I expect to remain here, six weeks—until cold weather.

Will you be able to decipher this scrawl? I was deeply pained to learn of your recent affliction—in the loss of your little beloved granddaughter—My son & his wife write that they are *more* in love, with each other than ever—

M. L.

To Sally Orne

Cronberg
Sept. 10th '69

My dear Mrs Orne:

I have been thinking over our little conversation regarding [U.S. Consul] *Murphy* && am inclined to think it will be best not

[2] Reuben E. Fenton had been governor of New York from 1865–6, and was at this time beginning his first term in the U.S. Senate.

to mention his name to Col Forney or indeed any of our friends in Penn. For reasons I will give you, when I have the *great* happiness of seeing you again. Heaven grant *that* may be, in a day or two. Sunday, is very near, instead of a warm day in F- remember from my hill of tristesse, I look down upon you in sorrow if you refuse my prayer—Come·*direct* I pray you to me—I will show you that our rural land lady ("Lady Armüller") as she styles herself—can get us something to eat—though served as you may be sure, in a very plain way. Do come & break bread with *me*—for once. I received long & loving letters from Robert & Mary on yesterday—I have some funny things to tell you that M- relates me of *gala doings* at Long Branch && *all entre nous*. As I am "Micawber"-like hoping for "something" in the way of *gracious speech*—from that *small specimen* of humanity—G[rant]—I will not commit the on dit to paper. Mr & Mrs Glazier—the Vice Consul at F- drove out to see me on yesterday & we went to *Herveistein* as they had never been there—He tells me that it was telegraphed from the Tyrol on Wednesday to him that Mrs Murphy was very badly bitten by a dog, on that day, it jumped up to her face & bit near her eye & would probably have torn it out, if it had not been that in her fright she fell back on a pile of stones. Murphy was telegraphed for & was found in Berlin—where Glazier said Mr Gratz of Penn [3] had gone. I never said a word—but thought a good deal. In discussing *such great men*, one would suppose we were a *little* inclined to be politicians—If I had not formerly been so much interested in my beloved husband's career & allowed my thoughts to dwell so much upon that *sea of trouble* (politics) perhaps such *perfect solitude* unattended by even a *menial*, would not now be mine—All that I ever did was actuated by the purest motives, but where there are designing wicked men & I truly may say women—such acts are so often misinterpreted—A deep interest in my idolized husband & country alone caused me—ever to trouble myself, about other than womanly matters. We will only hope, that all, may yet be right. I have just finished *re*-reading [Trollope's] Phineas Finn—and think you will be exceedingly pleased with it.

All the *"nich fur sta"* ["insensitive"] inmates of my floor—

---

[3] Researchers at the Historical Society of Pennsylvania have been unable to determine which member of the illustrious Gratz family this may have been.

left for their homes this morning—Do you not envy me—*my deep* solitude. Believe me—"the cross"—is hard to be borne, if I could only leave to day "*God's* Will be done." Alas, no—I am so rebellious.

Tad was out yesterday. Such kindness as you have shown that dear boy—will be remembered all his precious life.—Much love to your dear family. If you care for me in the least come to me.

Always lovingly yours
Mary Lincoln

To Sally Orne

Frankfurt A Maine
Oct 18th '69

My very dear friend:

Two days since in the midst of one of my most tiresome headaches, your *more* than welcome letter of the *10th*—was handed me—My boy Taddie was absent last week on a little excursion with his Professor & I had not sent to the bank for letters, therefore the delay—*Words* are powerless to express the delight—I felt on hearing from you once more, I imagined you or your dear daughters might be ill—my fears were especially for Susie—for she looked very pale—when I last saw her. I regret very much to hear of your indisposition and hope ere this you may have recovered. In the midst of your illness, how kind it was in you to think of me in my loneliness & sad desolation. Although your silence was extremely painful to me & I sadly missed your agreeable and sympathising letters—yet believe me, my faith in your unwavering sincerity & great goodness of heart, *nothing can change*—but I hope henceforth, I will hear from you more frequently—and the prospect of seeing you once again & *that soon.*

Hoping to hear from you in a *very few* days believe me—with much affection

Always truly yours,
Mary Lincoln

Two or three weeks since I saw [in a newspaper] your names —registered at the Hotel de Louvre [in Paris] & wrote you a letter, directed *there* will you send your valet for it?

M. L.

To Sally Orne

Frankfurt
Oct 23rd 69

My dear Mrs Orne:

Notwithstanding the disadvantageous circumstances under which I am now labouring, I hasten to reply to your last, most acceptable letter, received so gladly on yesterday. The first finger of my right hand is painfully sore, enveloped in cloths—all arising from the smallest prick of a needle. *It (the finger)* has been to consult with a physician and the salve administered by him, I trust will prove efficaceous—It is very much inflamed & I scarcely closed my eyes during the night. Last week, sick most of the time & this week unable to use my hand and I am feeling so anxious *all* the time about that very precious little Mary in A- for her time of trouble has surely now come—and I do not know why, but I am fearing a suffering time for her—She is so innocent & lovely in character, my son is greatly blessed in so sweet a young wife—and she writes me that she never imagined *such* devotion, as she receives from him.

When I had gone out on yesterday, about my painful finger— the new Consul & his wife called. I found their cards—*She* is a sister of *Mrs* Ben Butler. Very soon—I expect to return it. From what Mrs Glazier tells me, I am prepared to like her. Pray, present ever so much love to your very sweet daughters—With kind regards to your brother & a world of love to your dear self—I remain always most affectionately.

M. L.

To Sally Orne

Frankfurt, Nov 7th 1869

My dear Mrs Orne:

Instead of writing you a dull, uninteresting letter this *unusually* bright morning, how much more agreeable to me, it would be, if we were only together, with hours before us, to indulge in a long pleasant conversation. I am *anxiously, most anxiously,* waiting that you should redeem your promise of "soon returning to Germany." But knowing your loving, *motherly* heart as I do, I have my fears, that you will remain, some little time longer in Paris. Although I am sure dear Sallie, would study *far* better if you were away. It is the same, I know as regards my boy, but I am so differently situated from you and have to accomodate myself, to the sad & unpropitious circumstances of the case. If that brighter day *should* come *ere* long I hope *that day* of "thanksgiving & praise" will be passed together. I am well aware—I have not a friend *in the world*, who would as gladly rejoice as yourself over my changed fortunes—I hope you will oblige me, in the event of your receiving ANY intimation, either favorably or *if unfortunately adverse*, to my interests whatever the opinion may be—INFORM ME. I know you to be good & true & that you would not for an instant, that I should be deceived by false expectations. You will, I am sure, unite your prayers with mine—that all may be well. If we succeed I shall be more indebted to *you* & *yours* that to any one else. Sumner *has been considered,* to be a man, who entertains but ONE IDEA, at a time— (entirely between ourselves) *I* know him to be, all that is excellent, yet *by this time*, my claims *may* have passed out of his mind & his thoughts may be absorbed in *Cuba* & something else. Your husband, your brother Charles & your other Phil- Members, will agitate & make it effectual—I know—ERE Congress are *immersed*— in other business. *On this subject*, my dear friend, I will not trouble you again—only—when you indite your "farewell addresses" to your own family & *perhaps Col* Forney on *the* subject—close your *portfolio* & come to Frankfurt. It appears—a weary, weary age, since I lost you—A week ago, I received the welcome news from my son that on the 15th of October our dear Mary—became the mother of a sweet little daughter—after great suffering of eight hours & she was doing *well*—Heaven be praised, for *that* mercy. *She*—is a dear child to me, indeed. He wrote—after a sleepless night & *four hours* after the birth of the child therefore *no names* were mentioned—but as *the other* GRANDMA PRESIDED with the Dr & nurse over the advent of the darling child perhaps *she* may consider *herself* entitled to the name—surely—myself, as *one Grandmother* (how very queer that sounds *to me*) being named Mary, the mother of the child *Mary*, the child being called *so* too, would be rather too much in the beginning. Mrs Harlan, has written me a few times & signed herself *A. E. H.* whether the *A.* stands for ANGELICA or ANASTASIA && I know not.[4] I abominate ugly names —if *they can* be avoided. I write you, my dear Mrs Orne—always confidentially. With a great deal of love to Susie, and hoping that she has now entirely recovered, I pray that it may be so. I have called on the Webster's & like them very much. My fingers are well. Write please *so soon* as you receive this—Very affectionately your friend

Mary Lincoln

To Sally Orne

Frankfurt, Nov [*13th* 1869]

My dear Mrs Orne:

In my portfolio I find only a scrap of paper—on which I will write you a line—tomorrow I shall do better. I am sitting up whilst my "*10 x 14*"—is being arranged, so that I shall return to my bed. I have been suffering for three days, with neuralgic headaches, pain in my limbs && The discomforts, by which I am surrounded and which I am unable to remedy, are doubtless, making inroads into my health you may well believe that my very affectionate young

---

[4] Mrs. Harlan's name was Ann, but the baby was, to Mrs. Lincoln's delight, named Mary after herself.

son, is almost continually by my bedside. In his loving & tender treatment of me at all times, & very especially when I am indisposed—he reminds me so strongly of his beloved father—for *he* was never himself—when I was not perfectly well—My condition pecuniarily, could not be much worse, but it is said, "the darkest hour is before day." We have too many noble, highsouled men in Congress—not to change this sad state of affairs—*so soon*, as it reassembles—Go where we will—we meet no such *grand* natures, as our own American people—Although my idolized husband, was not permitted by an inscrutable Providence to take leave of the wife & children whom he worshipped so fondly, or as *unlike* the case of Gen Rawlins [5]—was deprived of the power of pleading with his country—to keep his loved ones from want—yet, *even at this* hour, I cannot but believe—*justice* & mercy, will be remembered. The letters you have written me, this week, have been the greatest source of consolation to me—none but your own good, noble self, would be so unforgetful of SELF, in the midst of your *own* indisposition. I hope to receive a letter from you in a day or two—announcing your recovery. I will write you tomorrow, if able to sit up. The letter to Mrs G[rant] is admirable beyond expression—worthy of *yourself.*

Best love to your dear daughters—Taddie, always begs to be remembered. Your kindness to himself & Mother—is treasured in *his*—"*heart* of hearts" Tomorrow I hope to write you a long letter —Do write yourself, dear, dear friend. With much love

I remain

Always yours most aff

M. L-

Will you be able to decipher this scrawl? Sickness alone would excuse it.

M. L.

[5] General John A. Rawlins, Grant's valued wartime Chief of Staff, died of tuberculosis within a year of his appointment as Secretary of War in the Cabinet of his friend and former commander; his family was left in desperate financial straits.

To Sally Orne

Frankfurt
Sunday Nov 14 [1869]

My dear Mrs Orne:

I have been taking especial care of myself, since I wrote you, those few lines on yesterday, so that I might *inflict* you, with a longer letter to day. I am sitting up & *that is all*, for my limbs are as painful & unbending, as an old veteran of *seventy*, should be. I hope you have entirely recovered & that dear Susie, is in far better health, than when you last wrote, concerning her. The copy of the letter you sent me to *Mrs G*[rant] could not be surpassed for gentle womanly persuasion & nobleness of feeling—*if it is read* & *made use of* in *the same spirit* as in which it was written, my lot, pecuniarily will be miraculously changed. *To day*, my *wrists* even, pain with neuralgia—if possible, I will prevent *it*, creeping into my fingers, so that they may be able to use the pen to return *"thanks"* towards Christmas. I startle when I find myself *jesting*, on this subject. For when I gaze on my *uncarpeted* floor & my uncomfortable position generally, the bitter reflection, immediately follows—if my claims to a country's favour, in behalf of my beloved husband's memory, is not recognized—how much more sorrow & humiliation, is in store for me. If ever, in former happier years, with a loving & indulgent husband by my side, who never denied me a request, *the place*, where I have now *found* I TRUST only a transient abiding place—had been pictured to me—as where I would have to stay & BEWAIL with a broken heart, my existence—in the happiness—which is enjoyed by few, I should not have believed—such a fate could be realised—*Death* would be far more preferable to me, than my present life, believe me—the young life of my Taddie, is all that makes life endurable to me—I can well understand, my dear friend, how gay & delightful a life you could lead in Paris, if you were so disposed, for there must be at present a very pleasant society of Americans *there*—and I am sure, many of your friends —*If you will insist* upon remaining, you ought to go out more frequently—It will do you good & *I am very certain*, your presence

will afford much pleasure, to those you meet—You may well believe, that I would willingly exchange places with the LATTER—
such an *age* as it appears, since I last saw you. Between indisposition, sad, anxious *thoughts* & every thing else—I have grown very
nervous, & can now scarcely read & certainly cannot do any thing
useful. I hope the VERDICT will soon be RENDERED—the *earthquakes
we* have passed through here, are not worse than my *agitated* mind
—Is Sallie with you or at boarding school? Present my best love to
your daughters.—My thoughts are so much with you—if you
thought my life—desolate in *that summer* time—what would you
pronounce it *now*—in *this* "winter of my discontent?" Write, I pray
you; often—to your attached friend

Mary Lincoln

To Sally Orne

Frankfort a Maine
Nov 20th 1869

My dear Mrs Orne:

Words would fail me, were I to attempt to express the pleasure
your last letter afforded me, at *this particular time,* I feel that I am
a *very* "Martha"—indeed. I hope you will pray for me, that I may
personnate instead "the Mary" of *the Bible*—sitting at the feet of
Jesus—resigning myself to *his* will. But whilst we are of the
"earth, earthy," with a mind filled with ANXIETY & *fear,* how hard
it is to direct, our thoughts Heavenward. How kind & good it is in
you, in the midst of "gay, delightful Paris"—to be working in my
interests as you are doing, I often lie awake at night, & think over
it all—the word, *gratitude* would scarce suffice, as *sufficiently* expressive of *all* that I feel for such unselfishness. I have always loved
you, since the first time we met, my darling husband, had the
highest appreciation of your many excellencies. *I* am not EITHER a
spiritualist—but I sincerely believe—our loved ones, who have only,
"*gone before*" are permitted to watch over those who were dearer
to them than life—The work of love, you are now performing is

recorded on High. So cruelly severed from his idolized wife & children—believe me, my husband with his watchful tenderness, *still* exercised towards us, with the "holy, happy smile," you describe, regards you, in your acts of beneficence—It would, be impossible for him, in *his* Heavenly home, to feel reconciled—to the *present* situation, of those so very dear to him—I should have lost my reason long ere this—if I had entertained *other* views, than I do, on this subject—I am very glad, my dear friend, that you have seen Gov Fenton The world, I think does not contain a *nobler* man—We are proud to feel that he is an American—and can assure *"these foreigners"*—as poor Johnson said on *that memorable* [inauguration] *day*, our beloved land claims many grand characters. You & myself think, that *their great* worth—will soon be tested—Did you see Senator Fenton's daughter? I have understood that she was *very* —*very* beautiful—how much admired & how great a belle she will be this winter in Wash—I don't wish you to feel offended with Mr Sumner. It has certainly been very remiss in him, in not replying to your letter—it is not from want of great respect for you—but *it is his way*, so that his *deep* voice is raised *long & loud on the subject* SOON—you will surely excuse him. From the mention, Sen Fenton has made to you—of Mr Chandler [6]—I am more than ever confirmed in my previous conviction—that untruthful impressions —have been made upon *his* mind—regarding the necessity of Congressional action. I hope you *will* write to him—also to Gen Shurtz [sic] please have Sen Fenton talk to these gentlemen—also your brother Charles & your good husband—I have every confidence in your *executive ability*, be assured. Your Sallie, one day playfully said, "my Mother, is a great woman"—I feel that *justice* to you, requires the *superlative* degree—to be applied in the case—"the greatest woman"—my pen is *execrable* but if it only *makes a mark*, you will kindly excuse imperfections. I was so much obliged for the *Phil.* paper—any scraps—where *we* are interested—please send me in the future. Col Forney, has acted very *judiciously* in not making comments in his two papers—Until the *proper time*. If you see Sen Fenton again, which I am sure you will—please *quietly* ascertain, *if—Sen* Chandler—is averse to *our interests*. All you write, I con-

[6] Zachariah Chandler, senator from Michigan, another leader of the radicals in Congress.

sider confidential. I am very much annoyed *at myself*—for feeling SUCH anxiety, as I am now doing—over all this. The last *four* years —should have taught me more *discretion*—for "the iron, has indeed entered my soul." Can it be, that I am always to be surrounded with such darkness—It is very hard, to endure—such terrible changes as have come upon me. If *we fail*, I know not *where* I shall fly—

I am slowly recovering from my *neuralgic* woes—I hope *other* troubles *less* easily endured will not take its place—My best love to your daughters—Taddie was very grateful for the stamp. The beloved face of his father! You are so thoughtful & kind—write often to yours—*most* affectionately

M. L.

Please burn this—when read—

To Sally Orne

Frankfurt A Main
Nov 28th "69"

My dear Mrs Orne

You are an exceedingly naughty woman to neglect me so long, but with the rain beating against my windows & my heart filled with dreariness, I feel that I must inflict another letter upon you to day. My bright little comforter *Taddie*, is of course with me to day and we have been *speculating* upon your silence as lonely friends often will & we fear that some of you are sick—I trust such may not be the case—and that you may be rather enjoying yourself in the gay world of Paris—so filled this winter—with *so many* of our most agreeable Americans. Yet I am too well acquainted with your affectionate and benevolent heart not to be aware, that notwithstanding, whatever your surroundings may be—your thoughts as ever kindly turn towards me in my great desolation—and that you sympathise with me in the peculiar trials, that within the last few years—have been alloteded me—The darkness is very great—we can only pray—that the dawn is at hand. As you may imagine, this is a season of great anxiety for me. Any news you may receive—please transmit me—of whatever nature not forgetting *Philadelphia* newspapers—I want you, my dear friend—when you receive this, just to sit down & write me one of your letters—that my good boy hands me with such eagerness—& which are read with such indescribable emotions by me. The loneliness of *this Winter* words could not express nor pen *write* its terrors!!

You must have missed your cousins, very much when they left Paris for Italy—but you doubtless were worn out—with continual going out & required rest. I see that Washburne [7] is in high favour, with the Emperor. Have you yet seen his *little* wife? I have only seen her once—and I never heard from her, that she was not going out—with a young baby—I am sure she is a very good little woman, but scarcely fitted for a FRENCH Court—All of which manner of confidential expression on *my part*—YOU will never whisper—I am sure—Oh, if I could see you! When will it be—If we fail, I fear, I shall sink under the blow. I have grown so *nervous*.

Please present a world of love to your daughters, kind regards to your brother—whilst Taddie joins me in all—As ever, most affectionately your friend

Mary Lincoln—

To Sally Orne

Frankfurt A Maine
Dec 2d 1869

My dear Mrs Orne:

Your two letters arrived at the same time a day or two since & I cannot tell you, how glad I was, *once* more to hear from you. I greatly feared you were sick. I hope you are now much better—you must take good care of your cough. I was confined to my bed on yesterday, with a neuralgic headache—and am feeling very far

---

[7] Elihu B. Washburne, former congressman from Illinois and an intimate friend of President Grant, had been appointed Secretary of State in 1869, holding the post just long enough to acquire the prestige necessary for his next appointment, ambassador to France.

from well to day. Dear, charming Mr Sumner, did I not tell you *he was all right* If Congress, was *entirely* composed of *just* such men—there would be no more sleepless nights & trembling fearful days—such as I am now experiencing, regarding *our* business—I am grateful that Congress *so soon* meets—and I hope *some* decision may be made—*before Christmas*—I trust *not* an adverse *one*, or I shall have to emigrate to *Australia* or some such region. Those bright sunny letters of yours! how cheering they are—to my sorrow stricken heart—If success comes—it will all be through you—God, will bless you in this life for your noble efforts in behalf of the widow & oppressed—what think you, your reward in that *Hereafter* will be—for all your goodness! I have given you a day or two —to read over the letters of your other beaux—ere I return you, *Mr Sumner*. I have so many such treasures of his in America—the "yours faithfully" appears very familiar to me. In future, I will be deserted by him for *you*, but I will forgive you both—in my great regard, for *both* parties—In your future acquaintance with him, you will find him the most agreeable & delightful of men—How could his wife, have acted as she has done? It was a great mistake *he* made in marrying so late in life!!

You will not forget, my dear friend, *any* LITTLE NOTICES, pleasant or *otherwise*—the latter will *surely* come—please send me *any* such—so soon as read—My face begins in advance to *burn*— but may perhaps grow *ghastly* pale, when *the* DECISION reaches me —Tell me all about yourself, when you write—Susie—I hope is well and Sallie is not dimming her very sweet eyes—by *too* hard study—I am sure—if she is with you, you will often make her laugh & forget her book[s]—Oh that I could see you! I believe I never fail in this expression, in all my letters— "From my heart, it is spoken, I can tell you. Taddie is hurrying me greatly—to mail the letter —Do write just as soon as you receive it. Please present my best love, to your dear daughters—Taddie sends his best love. Believe me, always most truly & gratefully—

lovingly yours—
Mary Lincoln

To Sally Orne

[EXCERPTS]   *Sunday evening*
                                                    Dec 5th '69

My dear Mrs Orne:

Three evenings since, "Taddie, Lincoln, Lincoln," mailed a
letter to you, with Mr Sumner's enclosed within it. I *do so* hope,
you received the letter. Senator Fenton is, by this time, doubtless
on the stormy deep. Knowing what a power he will be in the Senate,
I wish very much, he had been present, the first day of the session
. . . Congress will only, most probably remain in session about
two weeks . . . So even if I had *hope*—that charming but deceitful
syren on my side—I could scarcely suppose any good, would be
effected in my cause by the time, when happier people are rejoicing
over their comforts—alas, what can I expect, but to be left out in
the cold . . . Oh that we could be together this *wintry* night. I
can readily imagine, that your good, kind husband is *even now* in
Wash and that his voice & influence will be exerted to the utmost.
I must acknowledge—a *great weakness* about wishing to see what
our friend Col Forney, will have to say, dinna forget me, should
you receive any of his papers. I am very glad—that the time has
come for Congress, to meet—that for weal or woe—I shall not be
long kept in ignorance, *perhaps it may be bliss* . . . Poor Gen
Sickles I suppose *he*, too, is watching & waiting.[8] It cannot be—
that he will *not* be confirmed . . . What changes—*time* brings to
us all—I sometimes feel as if I had lived a century. *My life* is not
dated by years. Taddie, as usual is hurrying me so I will close . . .
You are a wicked woman to be carrying on so *many* flirtations—
you must remember that you have a very handsome & agreeable
husband in America . . . In great haste, hoping very soon to hear
from you—I remain always

                              Your affectionate friend
                              Mary Lincoln

[8] President Grant appointed General Daniel Sickles minister to Spain in 1869,
but the American press and Sickles' political enemies created such an uproar over
his fitness for the job that Senate confirmation was delayed for a year after he
had assumed the duties of the post.

To James Smith

My dear Sir:

It is a very painful necessity for me, to find cause to have to write you *again* concerning *the box*—Taddie says *he* carried it down to your office and that your clerk—Mr Smail marked it—at least *he* requested him to do so—Now, I wish you to ascertain from *this* person, *the exact* address, he placed on the box—and I must also know the *name* & *address* of the London agent. I hope you will kindly gratify me in these most reasonable wishes—as, if you will not write to the agent in London, yourself, I must do so immediately —I do not desire to enter into a correspondence with your clerk— but if I do not hear from you in *eight* days—I will write him & he must be forced to look *this* box up—I do not know what possessed me to send it from your office, knowing that you were not there yourself & had a clerk in whom you placed no confidence—I must know, firstly the direction—& also the London agent. This matter must be looked into. In that box, there were some rare things— some I had procured in Paris—& souvenirs of Scotland, which I valued very highly. I believe it has never crossed the ocean, it has been repeatedly enquired for, by persons *really* interested in it— that it should be recovered—your man must see after it, just so soon as you receive this—tell the name he wrote on it &&—Other- wise I will employ a business man. I hope your health has improved. Hoping you will write *without delay*, on this subject, I remain, truly yours

Mary Lincoln

"Tomorrow is the anniversary of my birthday—" wrote Mary Lin- coln to Sally Orne on December 12, 1869, the day before she was fifty-one. "I will be 46. . . ." She went on to announce that her husband had been "14 years & 10 months" older than she, and to imply that she had married him at eighteen. (There had actually been less than ten years difference in their ages, and she had not met him until she was nearly twenty-one.) On an earlier occasion she had written Rhoda White—who, like Mrs. Orne, was a friend of comparatively recent standing, with no Springfield connections— that Mr. Lincoln had been a part of her "every association" since she was fifteen; later she would inform the same friend that she had been "not twenty" when Robert was born.[9]

It is at first amusing, and rather touching, to find Mary Lincoln cherishing this last little vanity in the midst of all her tribulations. At the same time there is something purposeful about the deception, which began about 1868, something not quite casual. It is strangely at variance with her relentless self-portrait of a woman whose life had all but ended at the moment of her husband's death, who was so sick and wretched that at times she seemed almost weary of herself. Curiously, also, she never volunteered her age in letters except to compare it to her husband's or to state it in the context of their mutual past. Only when these scattered references are considered in the light of another series of misstatements does the anomaly seem to resolve itself.

Early in December 1865, Mrs. Lincoln wrote three letters— to Josiah Holland, Mary Jane Welles and Francis Carpenter— describing the circumstances of her husband's near-duel with James Shields. In each, she declared that the incident had occurred "six months" before her marriage in November 1842—an obvious error, since the "Rebecca verses" which had provoked Shields in the first place had not appeared in the *Sangamo Journal* until September of 1842. And what of the fact that the couple was, from all evidence, still not reconciled six months before their marriage? Mary Lincoln skirted that in her letter to Mrs. Welles with a statement that was not quite a lie and not quite the truth: her close relations with Lincoln at the time of the duel, she said, "would have been the same eighteen months previous—We were engaged & greatly attached to each other—two years before we were married."[1]

---

[9] Mary Lincoln to Rhoda White, Chicago, July 18, 1868; [Frankfurt] December 20, 1869.
[1] Mary Lincoln to Mary Jane Welles, Chicago, December 6, 1865.

Perhaps, then, her campaign to convince everyone that she had, in fact, been Lincoln's "child-wife" had the same ulterior purpose as that deliberately ambiguous statement to Mrs. Welles: concealment of the broken engagement and the eighteen-month estrangement that followed. These events were not only painful to recall; they were personal, complicated, and, by that time, irrelevant. If revealed to the public they could so easily be misinterpreted and used to reflect on Lincoln's honor, his self-esteem and, most of all, on his love for her. She might well have concluded that the simple excision of five years from the past would forever absolve her of the need to explain (particularly in view of the Ann Rutledge story) just why her marriage had been delayed until she was practically twenty-four, an age at which most of her friends had given birth to their third child. If such were the case, the lies about her age were due not to petty vanity, but to a touch of the same pride that once had enabled her to hold her head high for eighteen months after Abraham Lincoln had broken off their engagement.

To Sally Orne

[INCOMPLETE]²   [*December 12, 1869*]

Private & burn

. . . I hope Mrs Grant has had the GRACE, to reply to your letter. I am possessed with the idea that our business will at least *come* up this week—*Sumner* is about receiving YOUR LAST *letter* and his mind is in an *exercised state*—*his heart* & voice will be heard this week—Fenton I hope will take his seat tomorrow and he with his good & genial nature—will soon make known—what you have told him—I do hope it will be settled one way or the other before Christmas—But *that* is so near at hand—and will be so long, ere we know the result. *This suspense is terrible*—Those few words in Sumner's letter—"I read with sorrow," is all far more expressive than many men's *pages*—would be. How little we all thought in that so much happier time—that true friends—would be so put to the test—When good Senator [Ira] Harris—would come in our drawing room so

² The first four pages of this letter are missing.

frequently in the W. H. & finding Mr S- would say in his cheerful way—"Ah Sumner we are sure of finding you here." and S- would often laugh & reply—"This is the first administration, in which I have ever felt disposed to visit *the house*—and I consider it a *privilege*" And *I* was pleased, knowing he visited no other lady— His time was so immersed in his business—and that cold & haughty looking man to the world—would insist upon my telling him all the news, & we would have such frequent & delightful conversations & often late in the evening—My darling husband would join us & they would laugh together, like *two* school boys. These are delicious memories, which even the terrible anguish of the present hour cannot efface—And yet the *memory* is *sad & bitter* When I think over the wrong & injustice that has been done me, I do not refer to pecuniary matters for "He, who steals my purse, *steals* trash! but those in the midst of my *unparalleled* bereavement, because I had not the sustaining hand of my husband to support me would dare falsify me. With your gentle & affectionate nature— you will sympathize with me in all these trials. You are indeed blessed, for you may *so well* love the brother who is so beloved in his own country and is regarded as one of its finest & most noble minded statesmen—gifted with fine intellect & unerring judgment. It is very hard, not to make *idols* of just such as these, when they are ours—My husband was so richly blessed with all these noble attributes that each day makes me worship his memory—*more & more*—Tomorrow is the anniversary of my birthday—I will be 46 —and I feel *86*—My husband always so playfully & tenderly reminded me of the day, if I *affected* to forget it. *He* was 14 years & 10 months older than myself, & was from my eighteenth year— Always—lover—husband—father & *all all to me*—Truly my all.

To Sally Orne

Frankfurt a Main
Dec 16th 69

My very dear friend:

Your kind letter was received last evening, with much pleasure, you may be sure. Yet it found me confined to my bed, with a neuralgic headache, which was not lessened, when my darling boy produced a *late London* paper published about *ten* days since, announcing that "Mrs Lincoln, the widow of President Lincoln, was soon to be married to the Baden Count"—with so unpronounceable a name, that I could not *attempt* to remember it [3]—The same evil spirit, that originated this rumor last spring, is evidently again at work, and in the most malignant form too—probably anticipating, that by *this* time, Congress might be turning their attention, to my *sad* & *unfortunate* case. The notice was in a budget of items of an Anglo-American paper—and is without doubt—*just now* being republished—with SUCH eagerness in *our* public journals—I tremble lest my name coupled with a person—whom I have never seen or never expect to do so—may not entirely ruin my prospects of any future comfort—for believe me—at present—I am in the most trying & humiliating position—which you well know. In my indignation—last evening, if means had allowed, I would have sent a telegram to our good friend, Col Forney, that "Mrs Lincoln was unacquainted with such a person." As it was, I passed a sleepless, miserable night & must remain very quiet to day—as I have fever upon me—with great & burning pain in my spine—with no one near me to hand me a glass of water—If I was dying—*The hour* you receive *this* note—will you write to Col Forney & your brother —so that mention may be made—that Mrs L sees no gentlemen & knows no such person as *this Count*—It is evidently a most *malignant invention.* When I am able to sit up—I will write you more fully regarding the contents of your last &&& I fancy, my dear friend, you yourself are a *little* wavering, regarding your *former hopes* & *anticipations. Withhold* nothing from me—my health has again become so poor—that I do not expect to rally—if defeat comes —Perhaps when the *end* comes, we can hope that it will be "well with me-"

Please have your letter go off—by *next* Saturday's *Dec 18th*

[3] The London paper had apparently taken seriously a cruel, heavy-handed satire reprinted from the Portland, Maine *Eastern Argus* by the New York *World* on November 13, 1869. The vivid imagination of the author had Mrs. Lincoln engaged to marry "Count Schneiderbutzen, Grand Chamberlain to the Duke of Baden." The Count, short of funds, was "said to be in ecstasies" at "securing an heiress for a wife." The court tailor, "Count Kotzenbratzen," was thriftily cutting down Abe Lincoln's clothes to fit the "tiny" bridegroom. "Poor little S!" lamented the article. "We don't begrudge him a stitch of the sacred wardrobe. He will have earned it all before he is done with Mary L."

steamer. I fear *this* new trouble may create mischief—I am in much pain—*do write* me—often—With much love—I remain always, most affectionately yours

Mary Lincoln.

To Rhoda White

Frankfurt, Germany
December 20, 1869

[EXCERPT] [4]

I cannot tell you, my dear friend, what a comfort this precious child has been to me, in a land of strangers. I am particularly blessed in my children & so are *you*, therefore with the terrible trial of separation from our beloved husbands, who have only gone before us & are watching & anxiously waiting, until we rejoin them, we must derive all the satisfaction we can from our children. I have written you about my lovely young daughter-in-law, who is just as dear to me, as if she were my own child—for she possesses such an amiable, charming character. She was only 22 years old—a month or since—and she has an infant—going on three months. I cannot realize, that I am a *grandmama*—it appears to me, *at times*, so short a time, since my darling husband, was bending over me, with such love and tenderness—when the young father of that babe— was born—My son Robert was just 26 the first of last August—So, is he not, a young Papa? It is all the better I think for young men to settle down early—but if I had a daughter—I think I would not give her up so easily—I was not twenty, by several months, when my first child was born, and you I suspect, was also married early— [5]

---

[4] An excerpt from a letter to Mrs. White was printed in *The Collector*, Whole No. 736, Item e71, which may have been the last page of the above: "You with your tender sensitive nature, understand, the life of retirement I have passed since my all, my husband, was so cruelly torn from me. And you can conceive how much my feelings have been wounded, when American papers, are placing my name, with some imaginary 'Baron or Count' whom I have never seen. . . . Write me just as soon as you receive this unintelligible scrawl—Will you not? Do you not dread these approaching anniversaries?"

[5] See pp. 532–3.

To Sally Orne

[EXCERPTS]   [*December 21, 1869*]

I have suffered so deeply that an adverse decree is only a very small sorrow in comparison with the great ones that have already made me a broken hearted, dispirited woman . . . I consider myself very fortunate in not having seen the "World" article—coming from that low sheet. No doubt it was a falsifying democratic mass of vituperation very worthy of that class of writers—and written for that occasion. The article I referred to—was simply an announcement of my proposed marriage with a Baden Count—with some outlandish name attached . . . Even this made me sick. There is no doubt that parties opposed to Congress doing anything for me created that "World" document. I am sufficiently aggitated already without reading such vile & wicked trash. So far I have not seen anything against myself—but of course it will come . . . I think myself that the most dignified course would be, by our friends, not to notice any article against me—which simply means —our Country's recognition—of my beloved husband's services— but if they are so inclined—speak well of me and my claims.

To Sally Orne

Frankfort a Maine
Dec 29th 1869.

My dear Mrs Orne:

I am *just again* recovering from a severe attack of neuralgic headache, or, I should have written to you, several days since. And I may add its after-effects—from an *unconscionable* dose of *blue mass*—which I took without consulting a physician. The day before Christmas, I found myself with *such* a headache & desiring to feel well on my dear boy's account, during *the holidays* I sent him to an

English apothecary's where he procured, what they told him was a *large dose*—which my sore bones—*can now* properly attest—On Sunday, Taddie brought the physician, *who*, of course is administering Mineral water—I am sitting up to day—feeling so much better—but of course must be very careful—He has directed me to wear flannel next my skin—and dear careful Taddie has just brought me in, some soft *woollen* ones—Taddie, is like some *old woman*, with regard to his care of me—and two or three days since —when I was *so very* sick—his dark loving eyes—watching over me, reminded me so much of his dearly beloved father's—so filled with *his* deep love. He also brought me a London Times, to day, to read—published about Christmas, announcing the death of that noble & patriotic man *E. B.* [sic] *Stanton.*⁶ Just too, as he had received the appointment & it *had been confirmed* by Congress—of *Supreme Judge!* What a misfortune his death!—How nobly, he served his country, in its darkest hours—history can well affirm! In my present weak state, the news, almost overwhelms me. My husband & himself, were very warmly attached to each other & we can well *believe*, that they are *now* together—*I do*—do you not? Whilst I am mourning over *my most* uncomfortable *situation* & the mortification & daily annoyance it gives me in this land of strangers— subjecting our country to *criticism* but living, as I must solemnly assure you—in the best manner my means will allow—I may not be left long—to endure all the pain—which I am now enduring. With your own noble and affectionate heart—I am sure *you* are hoping all things—my health would be much better than it *now* is—if I could view the future in the same light. *So much disappointment*— within the last *four years*—has driven *that* blessed comforter HOPE —from my heart—If *our affairs* are much longer delayed—if it is not taken up—*very* soon—after Congress *re*-assembles *you* may begin to despair—*Where is Grant all this* time—Where is his *memory* of my husband—who, made him, *just what he is? The papers are teeming*, with the rewards he is *continually* bestowing on those who have *enriched* HIM—*Private*—Did not my husband—*elevate him* from obscurity & you may say & most truly, place him on his *present* pinnacle of greatness? Your great intelligence, compre-

⁶ Edwin M. Stanton died on December 24, 1869, four days after having been confirmed as an Associate Justice of the Supreme Court.

hends the entire situation & to you ALONE—do I *thus* express my-self—With *you*—all I say *I know is sacred*—I could say much to you, that I cannot write—Will not, your husband, your brother, *our true good men* in Congress—*make him* G- manifest himself? *He*, G is not the only person in the world—In looking over the Sen-ate App[ropriations] Committee—I find the name of *Sen Wilson &* *Sprague*—I hope *these two*—will be friendly—I think Sumner—only needs a *hint* from our friends—to begin *his* part of the work—Where is Gov Fenton *all this time*—I hope his ardor, has not abated —The letters perhaps—that you will be *now* receiving—will throw *light* upon "*much* & *many*" Tell *me all* every thing—"*Life is short, at best*," and *yet—if an adverse decree is given*, I believe, the hand of fate, has written it—that I will sink, *from that hour*—Through the *malignity* of a Pennsylvanian [7] my comfortable support *was lost* —through the loving-kindness of that *very state*—it may be recov-ered—If we win—to *you*, my very dear friend & *yours*, will belong the victory. And yet, NO presentiment, comes to me, that we will win the day. The *dark* array—of the opposing ones—I ever see

    With so much love—I remain, always most affectionately yours

M. L.

To Sally Orne

Frankfurt
Jany 2d 1870

My Dear Mrs Orne:

    You will perhaps observe, that I am repaying you in full—for your kind letters of last week. You will never be able to know, how much comfort you administered to me, by writing to me *thus* fre-quently—Sick in body & worn out in mind, my present state, has be-come unendurable—To day, I am suffering so much with my back —at times I am racked with pain—my quarters have been cold & un-

---

[7] It is difficult to be certain to whom Mrs. Lincoln was referring, but it might have been the late Thaddeus Stevens, who fought against her being given any as-sistance by Congress.

comfortable this winter—I must either become an invalid or make a change—and I dislike to do so—for the next month—until we know *the best*—or the worst. *Germany* is the damptest climate, that can be conceived of, in the winter season! In the *midnight watches*, I often find myself, wondering, *where* will *all this* end. Most likely, for me, in the grave. I suppose, you had a day of enjoyment yesterday—many callers—and in my dreary monotonous existence—*ten* callers, ventured—the U.S. Consul & his son—two Doctors, 3 of *the women kind*—& three other *miscellaneous* individuals, whose names, I scarcely remember—(*The Count*, be assured, did not present himself.)—Perhaps this unwonted excitement, has occasioned such pain in all my limbs. I fear very much—*it is still*—that heavy *American* dose of calomel, from which I am suffering. Please burn that *copied note* from Genl Shurtz—I consider it *very far* from encouraging, do you not? *Any news*, good or bad, you receive, please advise me of immediately. What a friend, you are proving yourself, to be to me! I am powerless to express, all that I feel—Be assured, my heart is deeply filled with gratitude, your name will live in the memory of all good people—and as to myself, whatever may be the result—my last breath shall praise you for your efforts in my greatly afflicted self—I often find myself wondering what new villanous charges—were brought against me in that "World," article—and then again, I am grateful, that I *do not know*—I dread to have my name again before the people—and find myself in such a poor state of health—this winter—that my nerves could scarcely stand, many more attacks—Well may Mr Sumner speak flatteringly of your appeals, in my behalf—he is so kind & good himself, that he can thoroughly appreciate—nobleness of heart—in others—He will canonize —you as a saint almost—I hope the news is true that his wife & himself are together again—only I trust, she will give him some peace —I write dear friend, with much difficulty for I am in much pain.

Do write me, just *so soon* as you receive this—With a great deal of love to your dear daughters, I remain, always most affectionately, your friend.

Mary Lincoln

Do *pray*, that *that maid* will be forthcoming, very soon—I could employ her this moment in rubbing my poor back—with *camphor*—

To Sally Orne

My dear Mrs Orne:

I have been anxiously watching & waiting, for a reply to some of the *three* letters, written you within the last few days. The last letter, I have received from you, was dated Dec *27th* '69—hence you can realise, *in a* measure, my disappointment, at your silence. I cannot believe you have left Paris, or you would have written me, announcing your departure. I earnestly trust, that you are not ill or any one belonging to you. *You* can scarcely picture my *dismay* almost, as my dear son, returns each day, from the bank—without a line of remembrance from you. If you have bad news & are withholding it from me—I pray you, *do not do* so—*the bitterness* has become more familiar to me than the *sweet*, since I have been left *alone* and so desolate, in my misery. I will not write you, but a short note, my dear friend to day, lest in the event of your removal, into some other quarter—it may fall into other hands—My *three* recent letters, have been addressed (*your last* address)—just as I am doing this. Two days out of each week at *least*, I am confined to my bed & often unable to raise my head—with headache—therefore, you can imagine, I have nothing, especially pleasant to write about—added *to all this*, *great anxiety*, about our A[merican] affairs—does not improve *my condition*. If you are still in Paris—I imagine it will be impossible for you, to keep yourself aloof from its amusements—yet in the midst of all—I feel assured, your memory will often revert to your wretched & isolated friend—and am sure you will send me instead of that little artistic & beautiful note paper—one of those large old fashioned sheets—that I so delight to receive from you. Your silence is becoming, a painful wonder to me—I hope soon the mystery will be unravelled by a long letter from you.

With much love, I remain, always

Most affectionately yours,
Mary Lincoln.

To Sally Orne

Frankfort a Maine
Jany 13th 70

My Dear Mrs Orne:

Your very kind letter of yesterday is *just* received & I will write you a hurried note—whilst Taddie is near to mail it. How thankful, I am, that you have recovered, you must indeed have been very sick. Oh, that I could see you & *talk* over every thing! About *ten* days since when from the *earnest convictions* of my heart—regarding my belief of Grant & his wife's—*utter* indifference & heartlessness— after the letter was sent off, I quite reproached, *myself*, that I had so plainly expressed myself. *They* are intensely SMALL selfish peo- ple & it will be more than fully realised, ere *their* administration is over. I have seen no account of *their* Christmas festivities *at the house*, which I shudder to write the name—But, do you tell me, that already, THIS Congress *an* appropriation has been given Grant, for refurnishing the *W. H! !*— whilst the wife of the great Chieftain, whose life was sacrificed for his country & *made* the *present* occu- pant of the house, is living in an *uncarpeted* appartment—often ly- ing ill in bed, without a menial to hand her a cup of cold water! It appears strange, that God in his mysterious Providence permits such terrible *changes & contrasts*—My only prayer *now* is—that my life will soon be passed—my health has completely broken down— under all the privations, I have been called upon to pass through. Will you write & tell me, *exactly* if Grant, has not *yet* been called upon to exert himself—Where is *Gov Fenton*, all this time, dear Mrs Orne—I am beginning to perceive, that even your hoping, af- fectionate heart begins to fail you—Will our friends *not brand* Grant openly, if he does not aid in this matter.

A portrait of Gen Rawlins! During the war he was a *clerk* in the telegraph war office [8]—The evening after *his* funeral—Grant hur-

---

[8] This statement is not true. According to the *Dictionary of American Biography*, Volume VIII (New York, 1935, pp. 402–3), Rawlins entered the army in 1861 as a major, and was almost immediately appointed aide-de-camp to Grant; his fortunes continued to rise along with his commander's.

ried up to N.Y. and in a few days time—after *his royal decree* went forth—over 43 thousand was raised for Mrs R- besides 20- thousand from Cuba—yet for the wife of the man, *who* made him what he is he cannot faintly respond to the appeals of the great & good men, who voted for him—This is indeed a lovely specimen of humanity— Taddie is hurrying me fearfully—I will write in a day or two again.

Do write just *so soon* as you receive this—Is there *no* news from Col Forney—Please send me his paper—Tell me *candidly,* every thing. Always lovingly yours.

Mary Lincoln

Burn this—I pray you.

To Sally Orne

Frankfurt a Main
Jan 21st- 1870

My dear Mrs Orne:

Your letter of the 20*th* is just received—with Col Forney's & *the* newspaper—very many thanks for all your goodness to me, dear friend. I write to you immediately on the receipt of your letter— lest, you may have left Paris. I am very glad, that you are going to a *sunnier* & more agreeable climate than Paris—Italy, charming Italy! my fondest & best wishes, will accompany you, on your jour- ney—It will be the best place for you & your daughters to go to— Although it will appear to me, that *you are still* farther away—I am feeling so desolate & lonely, this winter. Whatever *fate*, befalls me —of one thing, I shall be assured—that both you and yours, will have done all that you could possibly *do* in my behalf. I am *so* plunged in gloom, that I can see *no* "sunny side," to the picture—yet if a failure should come to me, I scarcely know, what, will become of me. I presume you will still continue to receive *news*, in regard to *our* business—if so—*I feel assured* you will *candidly* transmit the news to me—as received.

A very pleasant little Penn lady from West Chester lives very near me—the wife of Dr Brown—the dentist—she is a very sweet

person & is acquainted with many of my friends—Jennie Cameron
& others—who lives at W. Chester. Dr B has been living in F- about
7 years—& she has just come on 3 months since—for the *first* time
—only a few doors separate [us]—*yet*—*no one* approaches to you in
my regards. *When, when* shall I see you? You will at least write
very *often*—will you not? *Do excuse* all my impatience—for I am so
nervous this winter. Even the Grant's *will be excused*—if *they will
work*

Hoping *very, very* soon to hear from you & with ever so much
love to all—your daughters—I remain *always* lovingly yours

Mary Lincoln

Dr Brown *fortunately* takes Col Forney's press & sends it to me—so
in that way—I will hear from that good friend

M L

To Rhoda White

*Frankfort a Maine
Jany 30th 1870*

My dear Mrs White,

In this land of strangers, words are powerless to express the
great pleasure I feel, when I receive letters from the friends, so
dearly loved, separated by the broad Atlantic. Notwithstanding *our*
acquaintance first commenced, in prosperity, with our beloved husbands, by our side, with not a cloud to mar our happiness, yet we
met as Strangers, surrounded by the cold, heartless throng, but *even
then*, we were drawn to each other—and sorrow & adversity finds us
true & undivided in our friendship for each other. My thoughts *so*
often wander to you & I sometimes feel as if I would give worlds, to
have daily communion with you, who have alike with myself, been
so *deeply, deeply*, bereaved. We can at least write to each other—
that satisfaction, is at least not denied us. I can fully understand &
appreciate your feelings—returning to Wash, in sorrow & gloom—
after having visited it, in former years, surrounded by all the delights, that make *life* so precious. I am so broken hearted myself,

that there is no suffering of mind, I cannot fully sympathize with—
In *Gods Own Time*, the veil will be removed, and the chastenings
that are *now* so grievous to be borne, will be made clear to us—in
that great *Hereafter*, our present sorrow, will be turned into joy—
"Life & immortality," will be brought to "light". "Over the river,"
our loved ones, are watching & waiting for us—But yet the time of
that reunion, appears so far distant. With sorrow, as a companion,
the time passes, *but* slowly. We have had a cold winter here, and as
in *this* country, the comforts of our home life, in America, are *most*
imperfectly understood, suffering greatly with neuralgia myself, the
winter has passed most unpleasantly. It is a great pleasure to me to
receive the kind remembrance of Mrs Admiral D[ahlgren]. I have
considered her one of our most amiable, accomplished & intellectual
women. She requires to be known, to be understood. And she has a
grand husband, do you not think so? If I had known you were going
to Washington, knowing how much you delight in benefitting others, I would have requested you to see Genl Butler & urge him to
favor my cause. Should any business for me be brought up before
the *House*, I believe you are well acquainted with him & I am
greatly disposed to ask you to write to him. *He* is one of our noblest
and most patriotic men [9] & would not desire to see the widow of the
great and good man who did so much to save his Country, in the
Rebellion, *so* very embarrassingly & painfully and I may say Hu-
miliatingly situated as I now am, surely *his* kind and powerful voice
will be raised in my behalf. Please dear Mrs White, write him so
soon as you receive this, on this subject. I would be so deeply grateful to you, & if it was ever in my power, would *so* love to oblige you
in any way.

I feel that by making this request, I am taking a great liberty
with you. Your great, good heart will, I am sure, kindly excuse. I
fear, you will be unable to decipher this scrawl—With kind regards
to your daughters, & *ever so much*, love to yourself, I remain, always aff yours

M. L.

Please write soon and BURN THIS.

---

[9] Mrs. Lincoln had apparently changed her mind about Benjamin Butler since
she discussed him in a letter to Charles Sumner in November 1864.

To Sally Orne

My *very* dear friend:

It is to me, an *inexpressible* relief, once more to receive letters from you. Since I last wrote you, I have been quite ill, confined to my bed, for ten wearisome days—and now I am *just able*, to creep about my room. A fearful cold, appeared to settle in my spine & I was unable to sit up, with the sharp, burning *agony*, in my back. I have now a plaster from my shoulders down the whole, extent of the spine & I am lying on my sofa most of the time—The Dr says, this present trouble, arises more from a distressed agitated mind, than a real local cause, but says of course there is a *great* tendency to spinal disease—You can imagine or rather you *cannot*—but I have lived through *this recent* time, with only a *grim* faced landlady, to look in upon me, once in a few hours. I, often think, I must be invisibly supported, loving ones, must be watching over me in silence & *it can be*, BUT grief, to see me so desolate & lonely & *at times* so *very helpless*—Tomorrow is the anniversary, of my precious, *husband's* birthday—and it may be, if my health continues to fail me, as it *now*, is so fast doing, another birthday may find me with him. I am very much pained to learn, that your dear daughter Susie, has been so much indisposed this winter—I wish very much, that from Paris, you had gone on to *Pau*, where it is said to be so delightful, *this* winter. Such a terribly cold winter, I have never before experienced, *it is now, intensely* cold, *trying* to snow. And as you are aware, in Europe, they do not understand, how to make themselves comfortable, as it is known in America. I suppose with means, even strangers, can do so, in a measure—but I am *alas! out in* THE COLD, & very much fear from the present appearance of things, gathered from an occasional paper, that the demon—*want*—will still pursue me. I, too, dearly loved Mr Stanton & greatly appreciated the services he rendered his country, our loved, bleeding land, during the trying rebellion. Yet he died peaceably on his bed—almost five years—

after the close of the war. My husband, great, good & glorious, *beyond* ALL WORDS of praise—was cruelly murdered, snatched from the side of the wife & family who adored him—without being able to sigh—a farewell. For Mr Stanton's family—125,000 dollars have already been raised, the first year's [Supreme Court] salary—have been given them—and they own, by far—the handsomest residence in Wash [1]—drive their carriage—whilst the family of the martyred President—are very poor *reviled & persecuted*—In the midst of my overwhelming grief, with a *most slender* purse—to save my life by avoiding further persecution, from the vampyre press—which sucks the life blood, out of the hearts—of even the bereaved widow & fatherless I had to flee to a land of strangers for refuge—all this—*you*, dear kind hearted friend—alas know to be—but—TOO TRUE—*News*, *has come*—dear, dear Mrs Orne. On the 24th of Jany—so says a N.Y. Tribune—of the next day, a resolution of *Sen* Wilson's, was referred—to the Committee granting Mrs Lincoln—a pension of $2,000—a year—of course in *greenbacks* from the date of her husbands death. You will observe that it was referred. I saw no particulars—so—IF IT IS granted—which is excessively doubtful, I will be enabled—to descend ONE flight of stairs—say, instead of lodging in the fourth story—of a DISCONSOLATE boarding house—I may take an uncarpeted room, such as I am *now compelled* to occupy, in the THIRD story, MINUS, however the maid—you well know how money is *wrested* from us every where—and I have found that *my name* only enhances the eagerness to grasp it. The wife of the Secretary, at the Consulate, often sends me, a daily N.Y. Tribune—On yesterday, she sent me one, of the 27 of Jany—with an editorial—from good, kind Mr Greely [sic]—no doubt—trying to shame our National Councils—*into* giving me a more decent maintenance. "Bark & Tray & all the small dogs, to judge, from his quite lengthy article —had not only in both houses—*already*—*three* days after the RESOLUTION—commenced their attack—as he appears to be fighting *some* of them off—The blood hounds—that would leave the widow & fatherless, of the *great man*, who FAR FAR above ALL OTHERS—was the terrible victim of the war to starve—had began *my* remarks.

[1] Actually, Stanton's family, at his death, were in financial difficulty. Several prominent Republicans, acting as the conscience of a nation which had worked Stanton to death, raised $111,466 for his survivors.

Greely says—the prevalent & unjust idea was that *Mrs L* would make *ill use*—of any money given her. Some fiends—had been doubtless advancing the idea. If living in garrets—nearly—not far removed—from bread & water as my daily food—is a proof of extravagance *then* I must be throwing away money. I have never yet been tried—with the money, of a *grateful nation*—so they should not judge. Have *you* ever heard of any *demonstrations* from the Grants, this winter, in my behalf, or have my predictions regarding *them*, been verified? Does he (G- sit by, smoking his *pipe*, whilst $2,000 per year—is offered me? Where is Sumner—all this time? I hope, dear Mrs ~~Lincoln~~ Orne *you* will consider ME SPEECHLESS whilst this *carnage*—of our hopes, is going on. Speak only for your dear good self. *One word*—from me, would cut me off from a florin— Your blood will boil—when you think of the world of wealth heaped upon the Stantons & RAWLINS—whilst I am living in poverty & *most* painful exile—You have of course seen the papers by this time—Fisk —of gold Sept memory,[2] testifies before the banking Committee that *Mrs Grant's* portion was to be $500,000!!!—& he swears—that he sent her a checque for $25,000- yesterday's Tribune says the Committee—were hesitating whether Mrs Grant & Mrs Corbin, G's sister,[3] should be summoned, before the Committee—As, in the midst of all my wickedness & transgressions, I never indulged in gold speculations, perhaps a more dreadful woman than *Mrs L-* may *yet* occupy the *W. H.-* Mrs Brown, a little Pen- lady, sent me last Sunday, a Forney Press—where he was rejoicing over the overflowing Stanton fund—she promises me the one—of the 29th perhaps—my poor, unrequited claims—the great debt, that has been *so long* & hopelessly hanging over the head of the American people—perhaps —F[orney] will kindly allude to it. *Even now*, whilst I am writing, that claim may be ignored—& all hope shut off from me—*If so*, if they have failed in Congress, my life may be required at their hands in the *great day of reckoning.*

[2] A reference to the panic created in September 1869, when "Robber Barons" Jim Fisk and Jay Gould attempted to corner the gold market. Only by flooding the market with U.S. gold could Grant thwart their scheme.

[3] Mrs. Abel Rathbone Corbin, née Virginia Grant, was the wife of a lobbyist and speculator who was involved in the activities of Gould and Fisk. Though President and Mrs. Grant were exonerated of wrongdoing by the congressional investigating committee, the odor of scandal still clung to them by virtue of their association with Fisk, Gould, and the Corbins.

I took the great liberty, dear Mrs Orne, in my nervous anxiety a week since—to write to your good husband, requesting his opinion & information. I am sure, you will excuse, the intrusion upon his time & my impatience. *Do write me* all the news—you have, *just so soon*—as you receive this—With a world of love to yr family—I remain always most aff- yours

M. L.

To Sally Orne

[INCOMPLETE]   [*February 18, 1870*] [4]

. . . We have so recently seen an exhibition of *the extent of the* [presidential] influence in the case of Mrs Rawlin's—in whose case almost a hundred thousand was raised—whilst I, the beloved wife, of the great & good man—whose life was sacrificed in his country's cause—have often to endure privations—which I would not venture to whisper to any one. I mention all this, by way of showing you what Gen Grant *can* do—if he *so* desires—Certainly our friends will call upon *him* & expect his support and if it is not undertaken in the beginning of the session & allowed to be delayed, no success, may expect to be obtained. With my knowledge of Mr Sumner's great & noble nature, rely upon it he will highly appreciate your communication to him—and depend upon it, he will be heard from—regarding it. One word from Gen G- *could* do every thing he cannot possibly withhold it—But there is one thing, my dear Mrs Orne—I earnestly request—it is this—that *whatever* views your friends write you, regarding the probable result of the action in Congress—do not withhold them from me—even if they are not flattering to the cause —I would prefer not to deceive myself with vain hopes—and yet when I think of failure—I tremble much, my situation mortifies me very much now—without a recognition either in shape of a pension or a generous allowance—I can only see—*still greater*—future discomfort. Regarding Mr Washburne—may I request you not to *say a word* to him *on the* subject—he is a self willed man—and if *he*

---

[4] Date taken from postmark on envelope.

wills that Grant should *not* use his influence in my behalf—*it will be withheld*. This is all ENTIRELY between ourselves. Not that W- is an enemy of *mine* yet *we*—he considers have passed away. The "rising sun"—in America, is very powerful. I can trust YOU with all this, regarding W-.

How very much I long to see you—Oh for some more of those long, pleasant chats. How they linger in my memory! Do write me dear friend, *just* so soon as you receive this, hastily written note—I have not yet recovered my strength—*last* week—was a desolate one indeed to me—Write me all the views that are given you—regarding Congressional action. I suffer very much in mind—but the *strength* does not come with it. Please present my kindest regards to your family. Tell Sallie—*compliments* from *her* I consider a very cold term. *Your* children—even on the slightest acquaintance, would have my love [page torn] Gen Grant—rolling in prosperity *cannot fail to be brought*—to use his unbounded influence in my behalf—I am sure the senators & members—*will not* allow him to *ignore* his duty in this respect. A request to one & all of them, made by him, *just* as soon as Congress meets—would [page torn] relieved from my present mortifying position. My all—my support in all respects was torn from my side—the eyes of the world—marks every thing. What do you think, dear friend of writing to Grant yourself, for your brother in Phil- to hand to him so soon as Congress meets— your good judgment—can best decide—

To Sally Orne

Frankfurt Feb 18th 1870

My very dear Friend:

Now that I am again *en rapport* with you, I fear you will weary of my frequent letters. Confined to my room, as I *now* am, you can imagine that with so much solitude & weary anxious thoughts, I am having a *very sorry* time of it.

Your description of your journey over the famous Cornice road was most interesting to me. Thank Heaven no accidents befel your

party, I am just in such a nervous state, that I can see *every* preci-
pice, you have passed over and appreciate all your fears, by the way
side. Now, I hope your dear roving ladyship, will take a good rest,
where you are and that *in the spring*, if such a season of balmy sunshine will *ever* come, after such an interminable winter, we may
again meet. What a pleasure, that will be, to me! Of course you
found a formidable budget of letters, from your loved ones at home.
I shall soon hope to hear from you & I am sure you will *candidly*
inform me, of what your friends consider to be, *my prospects* in
Wash. Your letter dear friend, *was a week* in reaching me, dated
Genoa, it has even a *London* postmark, upon it—*I am not jesting.*
You omitted "Germany" on your letter—which as I am anxious to
receive *all letters* that you write me, I hope you will in the future
avoid. If I continue, in this strain, this hastily written note, may
turn out a sermon. Of course you have read with interest of Prince
Arthur's visit to Wash &&.[5] I do not see Mrs Sprague's name,
among the gay notices of the winter. Is she in Wash—or South? I
hope her truelly kind hearted husband, will favor our interests. Our
best, most reliable papers, contradict the reckless assertion of Fisk,
that Grant or his wife, had anything to do, with the gold operation!
What freedom & insolence there is, in our American Press—I have
always, had a curiosity to know what villanous & malignant falsehoods, that "World" article contained. Something base of course.
Ignorance of their lying malice, is best for me. I see the name, of
a "Mrs Smith," *said* to be a cousin of Mrs Grant, flourishing largely
in the *Court* Circle this winter. *Is it our* Mrs Smith—who tried to
thrust herself, so much in former times, upon public notice? I hope
to receive some long letters now, from you. *Do not* disappoint me.

    With a great deal of love for your daughters & any quantity
for yourself, who both in prosperity & adversity have been so true
in your friendship. The "cup of cold water," to the parched lips &
the loving words to the suffering ones of earth are always recorded
in the *Great Book of Remembrance*.

Affectionately yours
Mary Lincoln

[5] Prince Arthur, Duke of Connaught, youngest son of Queen Victoria, had been
on an extended tour of Canada followed by a brief visit to the United States.

To Sally Orne

Frankfurt a Maine
March 31st [1870]

My very dear Friend:

It is so kind & good in you—to feel anxious about me, during my late very severe illness—I am sitting up in bed, whilst I am writing this—The banker has just sent me your letter to Tad—also a telegram which was returned to you, in reply to the one, you so kindly sent to day—I enclose a copy of the one that appears to have been sent you.[6] *The English is very striking*—if I could *smile* again —it would amuse me. I am enjoined by my physician who has just left to write a very few lines—my hands tremble so much—I cannot write—to return again to my troubled life—is so hard. I have been so near my husband—there were days of delirium—when I can *quite* recall—that my dearly loved ones—were hanging over me, would that I could have joined them. I am sorry indeed to hear that dear Susie is not well. I shall never forget your very great kindness to me always—in the days of my overwhelming sorrow & desolation —how unspeakably precious. Please write me *always where* to address you—as you are such a wandering JEWESS. Burn this shocking letter—for I am so very weak & nervous. Always your affectionate friend.

Mary Lincoln

To Sally Orne

Frankfurt A M
April 3d. 70

My dear Mrs Orne

My thoughts are so often directed to *you* & am feeling so grateful for your kind solicitude in my behalf that I find myself daily calculating, *when* I shall be able to write you again. I wrote

[6] Not preserved.

you some unintelligible lines, a few days since. I am sitting up for a little while, whilst I am writing this, but altogether as you may believe, I am having a *weary*—sad hearted time. My Physician urges me to go Marienbad, for the waters & baths—so soon as I am able to travel. It is near Dresden—There are many difficulties in the way, such as you can scarcely imagine—nor could *I* have *done so*, WHEN my beloved husband was near to anticipate every wish & the necessity of *each hour*. After serving *his* country so faithfully & unselfishly, as *he* did, well may *his brow be clouded*— whilst he is *still* permitted to watch over his dearly loved ones—My hourly prayer is—that I may soon be with him, far removed from such trying vicissitudes. My husband, was *above all*—in his country's service—*yet his family* are the only ones, left out—of benefits —we are considered unworthy of *grateful* recognition. $150,000 is said to have been given Mrs Stanton—their mansion in Wash- is certainly worth $75,000- more & only the other day—the first year's salary of Judgeship—was given her. Whilst *all this*, was going on —*where*—*where*—*were the friends*—who were interested, in my be- half *I* have to pass *sleepless* nights—grieving over the smallest ex- penses, medical & otherwise, I am unable to meet—*Instead* of WRIT- ING *that* man of *adamant* G[rant] why do they not *one & all* GO to him—I have heard—*not a word*, of my business has been mentioned in the House of R- this winter—Where is Col Forney Dear Mrs Orne—*believe* me—if there was earnestness of purpose I should not be left in the *sad state I am now in.*

All my sorrow—my uncomfortable surroundings—have brought me very near the brink of the grave, and there are mo- ments of each day, when I feel the greatest repugnance—to return to the *fearful battle of life*—which has broken my heart. I must accept my terrible fate—to undergo *daily crucifixion*—knowing that in *God's Own Time*"—the weary & heavy laden—will be loosed from the bonds of earth. With my darling ones, "watching & waiting," so anxiously for me—*Can it be*, that the time is far distant? I weary you & am feeling very weak myself.

Hoping you are all well—& with much love from dear Tad & myself. I remain always—

Your affectionate friend
Mary Lincoln

I am pleased to learn that Gen Sickles, has been confirmed. You need not visit *Spain*—without your husband but *do*—write the Gen'l a letter of congratulation—It will please him for he is certainly very kind hearted.

Forgive & burn this blotted—*tear* stained letter—Tad—had settled with the Banker, so I take the liberty of returning your change. I would be willing to pay daily, for news from you—dear dear friend.

M L

To Charles O'Neill

Frankfurt a Maine
April 26th 1870

My Dear Sir:

I feel that many apologies are due you, for *thus* trespassing upon your valuable time. The great friendship existing between your good & amiable sister & myself, and the assurances she has given me, that owing to past associations, between her & myself, as well as your great love for the memory, of my deeply lamented husband, and your just views, regarding the justice that is due those, his own dearly loved ones, from whom he was so cruelly torn, may excuse the liberty, I am taking, in writing to you, at the present time. "Hope deferred, regarding Congressional action in my case, has indeed made my heart sick. Added to all this, I am suffering with ill health, & am earnestly advised by my Physician to go into Bohemia—for the baths & mineral water. I write this note, hoping some definite information may immediately be given me, whether any expectations, can longer be indulged in—regarding the Bill—in my favor before Congress—I cannot believe that those who revere *even the* name, of their late beloved President, whose precious life was sacrificed for his Country, will longer delay action in the case. A gentlemen of great respectability in this city, a German, but an American citizen by adoption,[7] addressed

---

[7] Probably Henry Seligman, partner in the Frankfurt banking house of Seligman & Stettheimer. See pp. 556–7 for a discussion of his efforts to aid Mrs. Lincoln.

me a note a few days since, saying that his brother—a banker in
N.Y. had just received a note from Gen Horace Porter, the President's—private secretary, saying that Genl Grant had recently written a letter to the proper Congressional Committee on the subject
requesting—favorable consideration of the bill & without doubt,
you will be informed on the subject. I enclose the note mentioned
to Senator Harlan to day, which please have him show you. As you
are aware, owing to Mr Harlan's near relationship to our family
he is precluded from *actively* urging the business. We have too
many noblehearted *true* men, in our National Councils, longer to
neglect the bereaved widow & orphaned family, of the great & good
man, who *so* faithfully, served his bleeding country & saved it, from
its rebel foes. If I have acted injudiciously in writing & urging my
claims upon you & the friends of our country, pray pardon, the
error. Most respectfully

Mrs A. Lincoln

Just as Mary Lincoln was beginning to despair of her pension,
there was a burst of activity in Washington. On May 2, 1870, a
bill was introduced in the House, granting her $3,000 per year
(not the $5,000 Sumner had fought for in the Senate). It was
passed without debate by a margin of 80 to 65, with 77 members
absent and not voting. On the following day, when the House bill
was read in the Senate, Lyman Trumbull expressed his desire that
it pass "unanimously and graciously." It was a vain hope. George
Edmunds declared that his Pensions Committee still had before it
the original Senate bill, specifying the $5,000 amount, and was at
that moment drafting a report on it. Thwarted in his efforts to obtain consideration for the House bill, Sumner sat back to wait for
the committee's verdict. Mrs. Lincoln, in Frankfurt, waited too.[8]

In her anxiety about her "American affairs," she had begun
haunting the "English Reading Room" in Frankfurt. In its peaceful

[8] Bullard, "Mrs. Lincoln's Pension," *Lincoln Herald*, June 1947.

precincts she could, to her heart's content, pore over the British and American press for mention of her name. One morning late in May, her practiced eye picked out an ominous piece of intelligence in an English newspaper. A majority of the Senate Committee on Pensions had reported their decision to table her bill indefinitely, on the grounds of lack of precedent and insufficient need. The report cited the $25,000 salary payment made her in 1865 which, together with her share of Lincoln's estate, brought her personal wealth to $58,756.60.

It is not known whether the dispatch she read carried the rest of the committee's report: its insinuation that she had appropriated public property for her personal use, and that she was living beyond her means, even "royally." The closing statement was heavy with sinister implication, asserting that "other facts bearing on the subject which it is probably not needful to refer to, but which are generally known," were in the hands of the committee.[9]

So shattered was Mary Lincoln on reading of this latest setback that she collapsed on the spot. Her doctors, by now bored with her symptoms, at a loss to prescribe for her, solved their problem by removing her from their sight. She was bundled off to Bohemia, to take the waters at the Marienbad spa.

On the day of her departure she paid a visit to a close friend and counselor, Henry Seligman, formerly of New York, now returned to his native Frankfurt as a partner in the family banking firm of Seligman & Stettheimer. The Seligman family in both its American and European branches had played a vital role in financing the Union cause. As a gesture in memory of the President they had revered, Henry and Joseph Seligman determined to assist his widow. Joseph had presumably paid Mrs. Lincoln's passage to Europe; now, hours of weeping on Henry's sympathetic shoulder brought a further reward: a touching, indignant letter from the banker to an unidentified gentleman whom she had termed "her special friend." Awkward English only enhanced the poignancy and sincerity of Seligman's plea that "the Committee should hear the truth & not listen to lying reports perhaps from some one who doubtless got punished for disloyalty during the war & now wants

[9] Quoted from the *Congressional Globe*, Proceedings of the Fortieth and Forty-first Congress, in Evans, p. 207.

to get even. . . ." In a postscript, the banker identified himself as "one of 8 brothers who have been ardent friend to the late Mr Lincoln. . . ." [1]

Mary Lincoln remained in Marienbad throughout the month of June 1870, gaining strength from the baths and waters and a measure of peace from long, solitary strolls along the wooded mountain paths that wound about the resort. At nightfall she retired to her third-floor cubicle to marshall her forces in one last attempt to overrule the committee's verdict. She wrote to Mr. and Mrs. Orne in her usual plaintive vein, cautioned Reverend Smith to beware of antagonizing their mutual enemy Herndon at this critical juncture, and contacted individual members of Congress. Long-standing grudges were forgotten in the face of this fresh exigency. Now that she required their good offices, even such "scamps" as Judd and Trumbull were bathed in warm waves of flattery.

To Charles O'Neill

Frankfurt A. Maine
May 9th 1870

My dear Sir:

It is with feelings of the most profound gratitude that I acknowledge the receipt of your kind & considerate telegram. After your powerful efforts in my behalf, it must be a great relief to your mind to have had such a success [in the House]. We can only hope, that the Senate, which is composed of so many noble minded and patriotic men *also*, will respond with their affirmative votes. I shall always continue to be thankful & appreciate the great favor, that has been so generously extended toward me, and shall earnestly, in all time to come, pray for my beloved country's welfare.

I remain, with much respect, your greatly obliged friend,

Mrs Abraham Lincoln

[1] Henry Seligman to "My Dear Sir." Frankfurt, May 20, 1870. MS. formerly owned by Justin G. Turner. A letter from James H. Orne to President Grant has been preserved along with this one, indicating that Orne might have been the "special friend" to whom Seligman had addressed his letter.

To James H. Orne

Frankfurt a Maine
May 16th 1870

My Dear Sir:

Your very kind letter of April 30th has been received this morning & I hasten to return you, my most grateful acknowledgments for the great interest you have manifested in my behalf. It is the first time I have heard from you, the letter you mention having written in Feb. has never reached me. It may have been lost on the ocean. Words, my dear Mr Orne, are powerless to express my deep sense of gratitude, for the cheque which your letter contained —My continued illness of the last few months, has naturally, very greatly increased my expenses—Yet at the same time, this valuable memento, of our noble hearted Americans, shall remain untouched, until the final decision of the Senate, is made known—On the 3rd of May, I received a telegram, from Wash- signed by Mr Charles O'Neil, [sic] and Mr [Leonard] Myers [sic]—stating that the resolution, had passed the House, to give me a pension, of $3,000- per year. *All this* unmerited kindness has greatly affected me—to each of these gentlemen, I have written an expression of thanks,[2] no language can express my feelings, on the subject. I am anxiously awaiting, the decision of the Senate. My physician frequently urges an immediate departure for some medical baths in Bohemia —which he thinks will benefit my health—of course, I shall have to await the decision of the S and we can only hope, it will be favorable. The unparalleled kindness of yourself & Mrs Orne, as well as other influential persons from Penn- have very greatly advanced my interests—Under all circumstances my gratitude to you & all my friends, will be deeply fixed in my heart—and will continue there, while life lasts. With many apologies, for troubling you with so long a letter—Believe me, your greatly obliged friend—

Mary Lincoln

[2] See letter to Charles O'Neill, May 9, 1870.

To Mary Harlan Lincoln

Oberursel, Germany [3]
May 19th 1870

My Dear Mary:

I have come out here to pass a day or two with Taddie (his new school quarters) as I leave most probably tomorrow for Bohemia—a journey which will require fully twenty hours to accomplish. The first evening I will stop at the very old town of Nuremburg, so full of interest and perhaps remain there a day to see the old castles and churches. This morning in this old village five minutes by rail from [Bad] Hamburg, I entered an old church with dates of 1610 on it. The Christs that are suspended on the walks around the town—bear dates 1704—until we get accustomed to seeing these things they appear very strange to *fresh American* eyes. When I came out here two or three days since, I had just returned from a most charming trip in the Odenwald Mountains, where the scenery is very beautiful, also Tad went with me to Heidelburg, to Baden for a few hours and traveled in the *Black Forest*. At Heidelburg we ascended the mountain one morning about nine o'clock roamed through the ruins of the magnificent old castle and took our breakfast in the grounds where there is a very fine restaurant—at noon, we proceeded to Baden and ascended another mountain height, in the evening to visit the ruins of another grand old castle—centuries back. The next day we went out to "La Favorita" the abode of the "White Lady." Taddie & I were continually wishing that you and Bob and that precious baby were with us.

[3] Tad spent two months in a school at Oberursel, outside of Frankfurt, after finishing at Hohagen's Institute.

To Sally Orne

Marienbad, Bohemia
May 22nd, 1870

My very dear friend:

How strangely surprising, are the events that are hourly oc-
curring—in our lives! The morning after I wrote you from Oberursel—I went into F[rankfurt]—only 20 minutes by rail—to get Taddie some school books—see my physician about a new medicine—
he had given me & *see the papers*— With a lady friend, I went to
the Eng- reading room—and there met my *terrible fate*—dear Mrs
Orne need I say more—an Eng- paper said the Senate Com. had
decided against on the ground, that I had property to the amount
of $60,000!!! A fearful & wicked invention of the enemy—which in-
famous falsehood will consign me to a most painful state of existence all my days—Will our country, with its many noble hearted
men allow this? Neither you or I will believe it—I became very
sick—I was assisted into a cab—went to the house—of this good
friend—my physician was sent for & after seeing me, he declared—
another attack of sickness—such as I had in the winter—would
follow—if I was not hurried away—and he said *this* must be the
place—so in 12 hours time my carpet satchels were packed & two
or three of these friends drove me to the depot—introduced themselves *not me* to some nice looking couple a lady & gentleman—who
were en route to Carlsbad—via Eger—I arrived here worn out & am
just sitting up long enough—to write to yourself & dear Taddie—
This is a most lovely place—Although my disappointed hopes—
still & ever will—notwithstanding my villanously REPUTED fortune of $60,000!!! consign me to the *troisieme*—without a serving
woman—a mortification to myself—hourly praying that my life
—*at this dark* rate—will not much longer continue—God is merciful, if *man* is *not*— *Where, where* are my beloved husband's
works of love & mercy—that his family are thus requited, for those
services? I cannot tell you, dear friend, what a great privilege—it
is for me to write you again—if I had known for the last 2 months
—that your letters were still to be directed to your Paris bankers or

even that they *knew* your address—I should have written you very frequently—I wrote you a *very* long letter last week, have you received it—Please write just as soon as you receive this, but do not direct *here*—direct as usual to me at Frankfurt "Care of Phillip N. Schm *from there* letters will be forwarded me. I expect to remain here 6 weeks—will give you particulars in my next So, just *imagine* me an heiress!—I am feeling *very* miserable as you may be sure— *you* would enjoy this place—It is situated on a hill—with lovely mountain walks—through pine forests—the air is perfumed with the smell of cedar—In two or three days—I will write again—

With a world of love—I remain, yours—

Mary Lincoln

Do not direct to me here!!

To James H. Orne

Marienbad, Bohemia
May 28th 1870

My dear Sir:

The letter & paper of May 3d, which you so kindly sent me, was received *here*, a day or two since. Since *that* time alas, to judge from the report of the Senate Committee && there is to *my* mind, so troubled with anxiety & sorrow—but little chance of the noble work of the House, being responded to—by the Senate. Mr Edmunds, the Sen- (in the place of that good, noble & true gentleman, dear Senator Foote) appears vehemently determined—that cruel injustice shall be rendered to the bereaved family of the man, who was above *all others*, in the great work of the War. If I could possibly live, otherwise than to be a mortification to myself—I would not make the least request—at the hands of those—who could so ameliorate my sad condition. I am almost helpless—there are days when I cannot walk straight—I am unable to wait upon myself— from very frequent illnesses—as in the only *plainest* & *most obscure way*, I can keep myself—assuredly with my small means I cannot keep a servant. I wrote you, dear Mr Orne, a hurried but sincere statement of facts, a week since from Egèr, en route here— Then I told you, what my eldest son & myself, have always kept to ourselves—that so soon—as my senses could be regained—I had every Wash- & every other indebtedness—sent to me & out of every dollar—I could command—I paid to the uttermost farthing. [Except] In some cases, known by the Administrator—but in a very few—it was all done by *ourselves* my son & myself out of my money so that it should be said—that President Lincoln—was not in debt. This is one of the causes, why I am so straightened now—for living as we *were compelled to*, my husband not being a rich man & we had to pay enormous prices for everything—those war times— When I now hear, from cruel—wicked reckless assertions—*how rich I am*— often wanting *for a meal*—that I would daily offer a hungry wayfarer—If I could—my broken heart, cries aloud & I sigh more than ever to be at rest by my darling husband's side. Under any circumstances, I believe I should have hastened to settle any indebtedness against the estate, but being often told—that the remaining salary of the four years, would be given to the family— All I wished *then* was to die, if it had been Our Heavenly Fathers will—and the great sorrow & oftentimes cruelty—I have endured since, does not soften the aspect of life—or deprive it of its bitterness. Please write me on receipt of this a candid statement & your just views of the situation of affairs.

I wrote you in my letter from Egèr that on receipt of the refusal of the Sen- Com to confirm the bill—it was deemed best by my physician & two or three friends, that I should come on here— my mind is in such a disturbed state and truth to say—I am so unpleasantly situated—*so unable* to place myself in quarters—that one bearing my name, should occupy—that I am uncomfortable here. My health is very poor—so much so, since I have been here, now one week—I have had to send for the old physician of the place, two or three times—no menial near to assist me, if I was dying. Will not this condition of affairs, be rectified by a people—who are the *nobles* of the earth, could my devoted & indulgent husband, ever have anticipated—*such a return*—for the work of freedom & saving his country—from a rebellious foe! Whilst I am writing, I am in receipt of a letter from my young son, saying that Mrs Orne

& her family have arrived at Frankfurt & *he* has seen them! I feel like flying back—but will certainly very much shorten my stay here—to return to see them. There never was such goodness & nobleness of heart, I believe in any other woman in the world, as Mrs Orne possesses—Her loving sympathy—has been a great comfort to me—I will write her at once. If she had written me, she would have been coming earlier than July to Germany—I would have waited for her—as it is—two weeks hence—I return to Frankfurt.

Hoping you will excuse this letter—which in your great goodness—under the present trying circumstances—I am sure you will —and earnestly requesting—your views of affairs & prospects in A- I remain most respectfully your friend

Mary Lincoln

To Norman B. Judd [4]

Marienbad, Bohemia
June 2d 1870.

My dear Sir:

I am in receipt of information from my good son Robert, as well as others, mentioning the earnestness & zeal, with which you worked, to secure the passage of the bill, in my favour, in the House of Representatives. I cannot refrain from expressing to you, my deep sense of gratitude ~~to you~~, also to Judge Trumbull, for services rendered in my behalf. Remembering the warm affection my deeply lamented husband, always entertained for yourself, and the great regard, he had for Senator Trumbull,[5] I consider it therefore, an especial privilege, thus, to return you, my grateful thanks. I am aware that the Senate Committee, have reported adversely upon the bill, and by this time, *may* have voted accordingly—but

---

[4] Now a member of Congress from Illinois.
[5] It is interesting to contrast the sentiments expressed here toward Judd and Trumbull with those written to David Davis (January [?], 1861) and to Leonard Swett (January 12, [1867]).

with my knowledge of your great influence and indefatigability—
where you are interested to achieve an object, I can but hope, pray
& believe that ere the vote is given in the Sen. you will lend your
powerful influence, *to that body* & exert yourself, with *each Senator*, so successfully, that the bill may be carried. I have always been
deeply sensible, of your exertions to promote my beloved husband's
advancement & realise, very fully, the benefit, you afforded him.
Of those happy times, dear Mr Judd, I have not the strength of
mind, to speak. I am a broken hearted woman, my health has entirely failed & I assure you, that the means requested at the hands
of our Government, consisting of so many noble minded & patriotic
men, I am in fearful want, of the wherewithal to make me *even*
comfortable. Other explanations, after saying so much, I am sure
you will deem unnecessary. In my heart, I believe, you will do your
utmost for me & *succeed*. In all *coming time* my loving sons, will
remember your disinterested kindness & that of other friends, who
were so dear to my noble hearted husband. In the midst of my great
overwhelming sorrow, the memory of happier days, when life appeared all sunshine, with my beloved husband to love & protect me
—all these remembrances come back to me—amongst the friends
of that blessed time—there is none, who present themselves to my
mind, who was gentler, more amiable & accomplished, than your
own sweet wife. Be pleased to present her my kindest love—With
many apologies for writing you, believe me most respectfully yours

Mary Lincoln.

To James Smith

Marienbad, Bohemia
June 4th, 1870.

My dear Sir:

It was a great pleasure to me, in this far *out* of the *way* place
to receive your last letter. I, have been here, now, *just* two weeks,
faithfully drinking the waters—and taking the medicinal baths. I
am already beginning to feel, that I am improving, two more

weeks, will I think greatly strengthen me. For the last cold winter, had almost used me up. Nature has done a great deal for this place it is situated in the midst of pine mountains & forests—the walks through them very beautiful & finely kept up—seats every where & on pleasant days, I often take my books & pass hours in the fragrant forests. The Catholics reign supreme here, their clergy, I believe own the lands about & I see their priests at every corner. A few days since as I was quietly seated in my room at the Hotel, a knock came to my door—I said "Horine"—the German for enter— when who should step in—but a long robed *young* priest. Looking just as much in face and manner as we remember Richard Dodge [6] —20 years since. He spoke in German—asking alms, for the church. I replied—that I had but little money about—but would hand him—what I could spare—so I gave him *three* florins & you should have seen his look—almost of contempt—when it was enclosed—in his fat—well fed hands. The next morning I met him whilst I was walking & he scarcely bowed. He doubtless expected 50—or a 100 & perhaps had heard of the "IMAGINARY" $3,000- a year!! Referring to this *trying* theme, I must tell you—what you have perhaps heard that four or five members of the *Senate* committee—after *the House* had voted me $3,000—a year signed their names to a resolution—*adversely*—against my having it. It is said— that my friends—& they are the great & good men of the Senate— are determined to put it to the vote & get it for me—if they possibly can. The few men who signed their names—committee men—*I do not know*—Sen Wilson & *the most* distinguished Com. mem my very warm friends—would not sign it—There will be a hard battle over it yet—Was there ever such contemptible meanness—as our nation is showing—

Hoping you are tolerably well, I remain, truly your friend

Mary Lincoln

Please direct *always* to care "Phillip, Nicoll, Schmidt Frankfurt

[6] Pastor of Springfield's Third Presbyterian Church during the 1840's and '50's.

To James Smith

[INCOMPLETE] [7]   *[Marienbad, June 8, 1870]*

I scarcely know whether I did right, to send you those news-paper scraps, lest in your ill health, your mind might be again become excited over the vagaries, of this man, Herndon. I am sure, during your residence in Springfield, you never met him & as regards myself, during my deeply lamented husband's life time, I can well remember—that, socially, we never met or I never had the least conversation with him—You were so frequently at our house, making informal calls, meeting a few friends and very frequently large companies, yet you cannot recall the presence of this man, who through the mere circumstance of being a partner in the law office—has since my husband's death, so persistently thrust himself before the public—as the "life long friend of Lincoln" as he so familiarly styles himself. It is well known—that in early life—Mr Herndon's drank very much—and only through compassion—in the hope of reforming him—and bringing the man Herndon up from low associations & the wine cup—that Mr Lincoln placed him in his office. Never on an equality, you may be sure—Herndon, did the drudgery of the office—brought a message to my husband at his own home—when he was there—As you well know, notwithstanding Mr Lincoln's deep amiable nature, he was not a demonstrative man—and certainly, could not familiarly associate, with a person, so entirely uncongenial.[8] I can well understand, your indignation, regarding our family library which Herndon, has appropriated to himself, falsely saying that Mr L—gave him *our* books—Mr Lincoln was near when the family books were packed and he remarked, So Long as Herndon's name is on the *law books*, he may have those. Although such strange assertions for the last few years,

---

[7] The first six pages of this letter have been lost, but it can be assumed it was the one to which Mrs. Lincoln referred as a "fearful scrawl" in her letter to Dr. Smith of June 22, 1870.

[8] These statements are colored by Mrs. Lincoln's antipathy toward Herndon. Although Lincoln had many reservations about Herndon and did not see him socially, he had respect for his ability, gave him much responsibility, and found him "congenial" in many ways.

at least, have been continually emanating from his mouth & pen—
yet never was a greater untruth than this—My husband, would
sooner have parted with his right hand, than given away, his *private* library—books belonging—to each of us—which we had read
together & treasured from association.[9]

My husband also possessed among his other noble attributes,
great truthfulness and sincerity of character—and very naturally,
had mentioned all persons, with whom he had been particularly
acquainted or intimate in his life. You may well suppose—that understanding Mr Herndon's style of talking & remembering Mr
Lincoln's assurances always to me—that for no other lady, had he
ever cared, but myself—When Herndon came out with that pathetic
& sensational love story—which he had racked his brains to invent—to bring himself into notice—we who knew Mr Lincoln so
well—smiled at his falseness, knowing that time would make it
right. It has just been made to appear as it really was—in the
recent ~~note~~ published note from Mr McNair [McNamar] the
Scotch gentleman, to whom the young lady was engaged when she
died—and who says, that for *his* life, notwithstanding his own exact
story, to Herndon, he cannot tell, why Herndon's persists in thus
falsyfing. As my husband was known to be the most loving and
devoted husband & father we will allow these falsehoods a place
where they deserve. We all—the whole world have been greatly
shocked—at the fearful ideas—Herndon—has advanced regarding
Mr Lincoln's religious views. You, who knew him so well & held so
many conversations, with him, as far back as twenty years since,
know what they were. A man, who never took the name of his
Maker in vain, who always read his Bible diligently, who never
failed to rely on God's promises & looked up to him for protection,
surely such a man as this, could not have been a disbeliever, or
any other but what he was, a true Christian gentleman. No one, but
such a man as Herndon could venture—to suggest such an idea.
From the time of the death of our little Edward, I believe my hus-

---

[9] It is interesting to compare this statement with Herndon's description of Lincoln's library in his *Life of Lincoln* (p. 386): "He [Lincoln] had, aside from his
law books and the few gilded volumes that ornamented the centre-table in his
parlor . . . comparatively no library. He never seemed to care to own or collect
books. On the other hand," continued Herndon, "I had a very respectable collection. . . ."

band's heart, was directed towards religion & as time passed on—
when Mr Lincoln became elevated to Office—with the care of a
great Nation, upon his shoulders—when devastating war was upon
us—then indeed to my own knowledge—did his great heart go up
daily, hourly, in prayer to God—for his sustaining power. When
too—the overwhelming sorrow came upon us, our beautiful,
bright, angelic boy, Willie was called away from us, to his Heavenly Home, with God's chastising hand upon us—he turned his
heart to Christ—

Pardon this scrawl, for I am too tired to copy.

M. L.

To James Smith

Marienbad, Bohemia
June 22d 1870

My dear Sir:

I feel that I owe you, very many apologies for the fearful
scrawl, I sent you about two weeks since. The truth is, when my
mind referts to that wretched Herndon & all his falsehoods, and
villanies, I believe *I am* truly deprived of my reason, *almost.* Yet
for the last few days, I have been thinking over the matter quite
seriously & I think under the *present* trying circumstances, in
which I am placed it is certainly much more advisable & prudent,
for the PRESENT to *postpone* publishing *the article* you propose on
that renowned scamp & humbug. I am sure you will do so—of
course you can prepare your SCORING & I will earnestly watch the
American newspapers & *warn* YOU, when *he* brings himself into
notice *again*—advise you—of his boldness—THEN will be *the* time—
Is it not so? I received a letter from Robert this morning, dated
May 28—in which he says—if nothing is said by any of us—notwithstanding the SENATE Committee, have decided against my bill
—our strong & ardent friends in the Sen- INTEND that it SHALL be
forced through, before the session closes. Sen Harlan, wrote me the
same a few days since—I am as you may be sure, anxiously, await-

ing the result. Hence the *very* great necessity of being quiet at *present*. I should like very much to see your article on H—when it is written—of course long before you will publish it, I will carefully return it to you. I am sure, it will be so good, that it can afford to "*bide its time*." Please modify & improve many of my expressions —which I used concerning the villain—for instance when I referred to his falsehoods—you can express it—in a gentle yet sarcastic manner—also clothe the language more elegantly, only conveying the same strong meaning *always*—and especially as I am a woman —placed on so high an eminence that the free American low minded press would like to *get hold* of—quote my letter as a very private one, written entirely for your own perusal—yet under the circumstances, owing to our family friendship & the true statements I make you—you give my assertions as proof—with your own—But I earnestly hope some time will elapse before you publish it—When you write it & whilst it is lying idle in your drawer —will you let me see it? I write you *confidentially* about one other matter also—it concerns a *very very* first rate English school for Taddie. Where the English spoken is of the very purest—where are the best & most *earnest, vigilant* teachers & where there are not many scholars—where he will be *compelled* to study—yet treated especially well—I do not wish OUR name to be breathed. Does Mr Allen know of such a FIRST class school—Would y*ou* write him CONFIDENTIALLY—for I would like to hear all particulars in three weeks time at farthest.

I leave here in a few days, to join Taddie & my dear friend Mrs Orne of Phil- who is now awaiting me near Frankfurt—an hour since I received a telegram from Tad, asking permission to join me at the quaint old town of Nurenburg on Saturday next. I am writing him to do so. Hoping soon to hear from you, I remain truly yours

Mary Lincoln

Direct always to. "Care Phillip Nicoll Schmidt" Bankers Frankfurt A Maine

To Mrs. Paul R. Shipman [1]

Frankfurt am Main
June 29, 1870

My dear Mrs. Shipman:

Although weary months have passed since your very kind and welcome letter was received, yet notwithstanding it has so long remained unanswered, you have been very frequently in my thoughts and I have been mentally wishing you such a world of happiness in your new marriage relations. Your letter in the early spring found me quite an invalid and I have just returned from a long visit to the Marienbad baths and waters in Bohemia and I find my health greatly benefited. I can well imagine how greatly you have enjoyed your journeyings in Europe and I truly hope we may meet whilst we are both abroad. You with your life so filled with love and happiness, whilst I alas am but a weary exile. Without my beloved husband's presence, the world is filled with gloom and dreariness for me. I am going with my young son in a day or two into the country to remain for some weeks. If you will kindly write me and direct to care of Philip Nicoll Schmidt, Bankers, Frankfurt, Am Main, Germany, I will receive it. The name of the gentleman you have married is too prominent a one in America not to be familiar to me and associated with one so highly gifted as Mr. Prentice [2] was. The gems of poetry he has written will always fill our minds and hearts with remembrance of him. Dickens too has passed away. How much delight it would give me to meet you this summer. Do you ever hear from our amiable and lovely friend, Mrs. Speed? With compliments to Mr. Shipman and many affectionate congratulations to yourself.

I remain always truly yours,
Mary Lincoln

---

[1] Katherine Helm identified Mrs. Shipman as "the daughter of one of Mrs. Lincoln's intimate girlhood friends." She had called on Mrs. Lincoln in the '60's in Chicago with regards from Mr. and Mrs. Joshua Speed, and a warm friendship began. Paul Shipman was a former associate editor of the Louisville *Journal* (Helm, p. 270).

[2] George D. Prentice, editor of the Louisville *Journal*.

To Catherine Hurst [3]

Frankfurt a Maine
June 30th 1870

My Dear Mrs. Hurst:

I had hoped to have been able to make you a call, before I left for the country, but I find that I am unable to do so. I am leaving town tomorrow for some weeks, the noise and crowd of a city, are very distasteful to me in summer. I hope you will greatly enjoy your visit to England & Scotland, and return with improved health. You can scarcely imagine what a delight it was to receive a call from that great and noble man. Bishop Simpson! [4] Oh that he could have remained in town longer—I felt as if I had so much to say to him. On my return to Frankfurt I shall do myself the pleasure of calling to see you. With kind regards to Mr Hurst and great esteem for yourself, I remain dear Mrs Hurst, yours, very truly

Mary Lincoln.

By the beginning of July 1870, tensions on the continent had reached fever pitch. War between Prussia and France was expected at any hour, but for Mary Lincoln the events leading to the clash of two great armies could have been taking place on the moon, so absorbed was she in the fate of her pension bill in the Senate. The negative report of the Committee on Pensions was followed by two weeks of delaying tactics and debate. Charles Sumner, still trying to force a vote, found himself confronted with insinuations

---

[3] Wife of John Fletcher Hurst, Methodist Episcopal minister, then teaching at the Methodist Mission Institute in Frankfurt. As a bishop, Hurst founded the American University in Washington, D.C., and became its first chancellor.
[4] Matthew Simpson, Methodist Episcopal Bishop of Washington, D.C., had delivered the eulogy at Lincoln's Washington funeral service.

and accusations no less outrageous for their being familiar. Mrs. Lincoln's foes in the Senate could not have been more insulting or ungracious. The nadir of bad taste was achieved by Richard Yates of Illinois who, on July 9, stood on the floor of the Senate and sorrowfully intoned, "There are recollections and memories, sad and silent and deep, that I will not recall publicly, which induce me to vote against this bill. . . . A woman should be true to her husband. . . . I shall not go into details . . . God almighty bless the name and fame of Abraham Lincoln. . . . [but Mrs. Lincoln] and her family all through the war sympathized with the Rebellion." Even Mrs. Lincoln's supposed friends tended to be apologetic and condescending in their expressions of support. He who had been "noble" Senator Fenton of New York admitted that Mrs. Lincoln might at times have been "indiscreet," and thereby have forfeited "a measure" of respect, but she was still the widow of the Great Emancipator; Lyman Trumbull questioned the fitness of "bring[ing] Mrs. Lincoln's character here for discussion." Henry Wilson urged the Senate to get on with the Army Bill.

Twenty-four hours before the close of the session, the pension bill was finally scheduled to be voted upon. Still there was debate, still a senator to bring up Mrs. Lincoln's lack of need, still another to mention the Old Clothes Scandal. Then Simon Cameron of Pennsylvania asked to be recognized. Perhaps to make amends for having failed Mrs. Lincoln financially four years earlier, he delivered a moving plea in behalf of the bill and its beneficiary. In doing so he called forth a few "recollections and memories" of his own, memories of nine years past when "Mr. Lincoln and his family" came to Washington. "The ladies, and even the gentlemen, the gossips of the town, did all they could to make a bad reputation for Mrs. Lincoln, and tried to do so for the President. . . . They could not destroy him, but they did . . . destroy the social position of his wife. I do not want to talk, and I say, let us vote." And so they did. On July 14, 1870, a bill granting Mrs. Abraham Lincoln a lifetime annual pension of $3,000 was passed in the Senate by a vote of 28 to 20, 24 senators absent and not voting. It was signed by President Grant the same day.[5]

Mrs. Lincoln learned the good news through a telegram from

[5] Factual information and quotations from Bullard, "Mrs. Lincoln's Pension." *Lincoln Herald*, June 1947.

James Orne, to which she replied on July 16 from Innsbruck, Austria, where she was vacationing with Tad. In her letter of acknowledgment and thanks, she took note for the first time of the "agitation" on the continent. The outbreak of hostilities had obliged her to cash a check sent by Mr. Orne in order to *"secure"* her baggage in Frankfurt and to settle what she called "little business matters" there.[6] Deeply shaken by the turmoil (which had apparently taken her by surprise), she advanced long-held plans to take Tad at least as far as England, leaving with him at the beginning of September.

Even though the $3,000 was not the sum she had hoped for, and the payments were not retroactive from 1865, Mary Lincoln vowed to Sally Orne that she would utter "not a murmuring word" on the subject,[7] a resolve which lasted almost a year. At least she now had a bit of security, as well as the satisfaction of having exacted her due from the United States government in the face of determined opposition. (How pleased she would have been to know, too, that she had set a precedent for every presidential widow to come.) The transformation in her personality was immediately noticeable to her friends, and those who met her for the first time wondered that she was considered imperious and eccentric. She still interested herself in politics, but her comments on the subject held less and less rancor.

Now, for the first time, she could derive some pleasure from her existence. Among the few gratifications of the grim winter of 1869–70 had been the birth of a daughter to Robert and Mary in October 1869, and the fact that the child had been named after her. On leaving Germany, she felt the first stirrings of desire to return to America and see her tiny namesake and the young woman she thought of as a daughter. The relationship between the two Mrs. Lincolns, maintained through letters in the first years of the marriage, had begun and continued on a note of mutual warmth and generosity. In a great rush of love, Mary Lincoln had offered her daughter-in-law access to any of her possessions she could use and enjoy. "Remember everything is yours," she wrote.[8] Later, in the grip of violent anger, she would demand the return of her

6 Mary Lincoln to James H. Orne, Innsbruck Tyrol, July 16, 1870.
7 Mary Lincoln to Sally Orne, [Frankfurt, August 17, 1870].
8 Mary Lincoln to Mary Harlan Lincoln, Frankfurt, March 22, [1869].

belongings, but at the moment all she could feel for young Mary was love and a desire to give.

Her first known letter from England was a note of profuse thanks to Charles Sumner; it was dated "York." The second, to Robert's Mary, was written three days later in Leamington, site of a world-famous spa in the heart of the Shakespeare country. With the increase in her income, she was now able to attend to her health with some degree of ease; she could also engage a servant for herself, a private tutor for Tad, and enjoy her surroundings to the extent that she was able to enjoy anything. In mid-November after a short trip back to Frankfurt, she moved to London, taking rooms in Woburn Place, off Russell Square.

There she was plagued throughout the winter with coughs and colds and by Tad's growing homesickness. So acute was his longing to see Robert and the baby that his mother was almost persuaded to send him home for Christmas and have Robert arrange for his schooling in America. But she herself was not yet up to returning and, in the end, rather than trust Tad to the North Atlantic gales, she put him in a school at Brixton, outside of London, and shortly thereafter went south to Italy. She left early in February 1871, traveling by way of the Tyrol and visiting Milan, Lake Como, Genoa, Florence, and Venice. In March she returned to London via "dear old Frankfurt," and, at last, on April 29, sailed with Tad from Liverpool for New York aboard the *Russia*.

To James H. Orne

Innspruck, Tyrol
July 16th '70

My Dear Sir:

Your telegram has been this hour most gratefully received. I had run down here with my young son, to give him a little holiday, but shortly after our arrival was notified from Frankfurt that the *French* were on the Rhine [9] and if we wished to *secure* our baggage

---

[9] Mrs. Lincoln once again reacted hastily to rumor. France had declared war on Bismarck's Prussia only the day before this letter was written. Louis Napoleon's forces did not reach the Rhine until the first of August and never got much farther.

which had been deposited at the house of a friend, we must return & see after our effects—also, to entirely arrange our affairs in Germany, I was compelled four days since, in the absence of necessary funds, to send the cheque which you so kindly placed at my service to Frankfurt to be cashed—to settle little business matters —THERE. You can well believe that when my funds will be placed before me, and we have quiet times again (for the agitation in Europe, is very great, the obligation will be remembered—The kindness of yourself & your family, will always be deeply engraven on our hearts. In these tumultuous times, my great anxiety, is to see dear Mrs Orne again. With the most unbounded gratitude, I remain, always,

Most respectfully yours
Mary Lincoln.

To Sally Orne

[EXCERPT][1]   [*Frankfurt, August 17, 1870*]

. . . The sum, that was voted me, will greatly assist me and not a murmuring word, shall be heard from me, as to the amount—I feel assured that if a larger sum had been insisted upon, it would have fallen through, all together. So, your large soul, must be satisfied. . . . Taddie, on our arrival in London, will find your City address from the banker—You must excuse my paper as my usual mo[u]rning paper is somewhere in a trunk, which I am too lazy to unpack. . . . Gen Sheridan [2] is in town—Tad is just going to see him—So I may have a call from him in an hour or two.

---

[1] Another passage from this letter was published by Katherine Helm in her book (p. 285): "I must speak of my young boy. He has become so homesick and at the same time his English education has become so neglected that I have consented with many a heartache to permit him to go home [from England]."

[2] During the Franco-Prussian War, General Philip Sheridan went abroad to visit the German armies in the field. He met Bismarck, von Moltke, and the Emperor, and witnessed the battle of Sedan.

To Charles Sumner

York, England
September 7th 1870

My dear Sir:

Only the impression, that you were absent from Washington has occasioned my silence in the expressions of my feelings of deep heartfelt gratitude in return for your unparalleled efforts in my behalf. Dear Mr Sumner, you are noble and good & can fully understand how much my tired feelings would express on the subject. Words are inadequate to express my thanks, for all your goodness to me. I have been with some very dear friends in London, we have all been staying at the Langham, and although the sight of those so familiar to me in far happier days occasioned me many pangs of sadness from past associations, yet I find the reunion has benefitted me very much. My mind has dwelt so much upon its sorrows, that I feel morbidly sensitive at times, about meeting those, I love the best. Whilst I was in London, your great & distinguished, yet very badly treated friend, Mr Motley,[3] with his family, were absent, visiting at some country seat. A few hours after Mr Motley's return he called to see me, as I had unfortunately gone out, with a lady friend, we missed each other—when I return in a few days to London, I will not fail to see them. The Secretary of Legation, Mr [Benjamin] Moran, called several times to see me. You can well understand how greatly Mr Motley's removal has been lamented. He is so universally admired & esteemed, and is so eminently fitted, for the high position as Minister to England. It was one of Genl Grants fearful mistakes which lessens him very much, in public estimation, Mr Motley is only elevated, by such

---

[3] John Lothrop Motley, appointed minister to Great Britain chiefly in order to negotiate the Alabama Claims, had been, almost from the beginning of his mission, at odds with Grant and his State Department over the conduct of the negotiations. A close friend of Sumner, he tended to side with the radical element in Congress which demanded retribution for the damage the British-built *Alabama* had inflicted on Union shipping during the war. Several attempts were made to force Motley's resignation, and he learned of his dismissal through the newspapers. Motley's recall was considered a deliberate affront to Sumner, who had recommended him for the post.

injustice. My heart has been made sick the past summer, by being *almost* in the midst of the fearful war, which has convulsed the Continent. With many apologies for this hastily written scrawl, and with assurances that your untiring devotion to the cause of the "fatherless & widow" will always be prayerfully remembered by me.

I remain always
Most truly, your friend
Mary Lincoln

To Mary Harlan Lincoln

[INCOMPLETE]   *Leamington, England* [4]
                       Sept. 10, 1870

My dear Mary:

Your very welcome letter was received last evening. Taddie and his tutor began their studies together on yesterday, both appear deeply interested. He comes to us most highly recommended, and I shall see that not a moment will be idly passed. From eight until one o'clock each day Tad is seated at his table—with his tutor studying and from five to seven each evening with his tutor he is studying his lessons. On no occasion do I intend that he shall deviate from this rule. I have just been in to see him studying, and they are earnestly engaged—for dear life. The gentleman who is teaching him is very highly educated—very quiet and gentlemanly and patience itself. Tad now realizes the great necessity of an education, and I am sure will do well. I am coughing so badly that I can scarcely write. I left Liverpool last Saturday afternoon so completely sick that I determined to come on here to be well attended to. This is the first day I have sat up since then and a physician tells me that as soon as possible I should go to a dryer climate. It will be a great trial to separate myself from dear Mrs. Orne who has proved so loving a friend to me. But my health is

[4] Leamington Spa, in Warwickshire, 98 miles northwest of London, was renowned for its mineral baths.

again beginning to fail me as it did last winter. I can only hope
that I can secure some quiet Southern nook to rest—until the dis-
turbances in Italy have ceased.[5] When I see you I can tell you a
great deal about the War which I cannot now write—

To Mrs. Paul R. Shipman

Leamington, England
October 27, '70

My dear Mrs. Shipman:

Your very kind and welcome letter of September 27th has
just been received from Frankfurt. I cannot express to you how
deeply I regret not being in Frankfurt when you were there. I have
been absent most of the time from Germany since last June,[6] have
been occasionally in London but this I have considered my resting
place. I am exceedingly anxious to meet you, and if you could not
come here to the loveliest garden spot of Europe I would run up
any time to London. In three hours and a half we arrive there
passing through Oxford. Very possibly you may have been here—
surrounded by Kenilworth Castle, Warwick Castle, Stratford-on-
Avon, nine miles distant, and only a very pleasant drive. My son
of course is here with me. I have been fortunate enough to secure
a very fine English tutor for him who comes to us very highly
recommended, a very fine scholar and a gentlemanly, conscientious
man. He recites his lessons with his tutor seven hours of each day,
so you can imagine that I see very little of my dear, good son. If
he improves as he is doing I shall be satisfied. Many Americans
are always here. One especial family with whom I have been very

[5] Two months after this letter was written the troops of King Victor Emmanuel
entered the Holy City, and the last battle for the unification of Italy was over.
[6] Evidence that Mrs. Lincoln returned briefly to Frankfurt can be found in a
fragment of a letter published in *The Collector* (Whole No. 716, Item R284):
It was dated "Union Hotel, Frankfurt-am-Main, Oct. 17, 1870" and addressed to
Thomas Fowler, whom Mrs. Lincoln had known in Chicago: "I left Taddie in
England, with his tutor & some American friends & he desired to be especially
remembered should I see you—I have heard of you the past summer playing the
good Samaritan and have felt, that it was very much in keeping, with your kind
& noble heart."

intimate for years, has been with me all the time. Again, I repeat, I long to see you. My remembrance of you is of a very agreeable nature, and in this strange land those whom we have formerly loved become doubly dear. Hoping that I may soon hear from you, my dear friend, and with compliments for your husband and much love for yourself.

Your affectionate friend,
Mary Lincoln

To Eliza Slataper

Leamington England
Nov. 7th. 1870

My Dear Mrs Slatafer:

It has been more than *a year*, since I have received one of your very agreeable & most welcome letters. With my own heart, so filled with love for you, I cannot understand your painful silence. Can it be that I am forgetten, whilst memory of you, dear dear friend, is so fresh & unimpaired?

We have left Germany, some months since & we have been here, *most* of *the time*, for the last two months. We are three hours & half, by rail from London, where I have been, very frequently. *This* place, is the garden spot of England, Kenilworth Castle three miles distant, Warwick Castle—*still* nearer—and Stratford on Avon —nine miles distant. Only pleasant drives all of them—& spots, where I have lingered, with so much pleasure. Would that you had been with me! As much as I prized your charming society, in the Alleghanies—which appears to me, so *"long, long ago"* your presence, would be doubly dear to me, *now*. Taddie, became quite a proficient in the German language, & is now studying very diligently, under an English tutor—7 hours—each day. I have been reading, a little book—which made me think much of you. It is called, "Gates Ajar," by Mrs Phillips [7] do get it & read it—it is by an American lady, & has created quite a sensation in Europe, this

---

[7] *The Gates Ajar*, by Mrs. H. D. Ward, who wrote under the name of Elizabeth Phelps (not Phillips).

Autumn. I have wandered—over the greater portion of Europe—
and have become, weary of sight seeing. Oh that I could see you
this night, to converse with you, about *ever so many things*. Only
care for me, as I have for you & I will be satisfied.

Do write me *immediately*.

Whilst life lasts & *afterwards*—I shall always love you. Please
present my regards to dear Mrs Gross—your own family && Please
write me on receipt of this, directed to me, Care of Phillipp N.
Schmidt Banker, Frankfurt a Maine Germany. I remain, your
loving friend

Mary Lincoln.

To Mary Harlan Lincoln

[INCOMPLETE]   *London*
                                      No 9 Woburn Place
                                      Russell Square
                                      [November, 1870]

My dear Mary—

Your most acceptable letter was received to-day. Need I say
to you, how much delight it affords me to hear from you. That
blessed baby, how dearly I would love to look upon her sweet
young face. If my boy Taddie and myself are wanderers in a strange
land, our thoughts are continually with you and we speak of you
very frequently—I have just received a letter from Mrs. [Matthew]
Simpson who is en route to Italy. When she left here we came to
some understanding that I might join her about Christmas, in
Rome. As a matter of course, even if it suited pecuniarily, which
it does not, it would never do to have Taddie or his tutor accompany me. Taddie is closeted with his tutor seven and a half hours
each day, and from Saturday to Saturday. When I am with him
for three hours to listen to his examination of his studies of the
week I can see a great improvement in him. But of course if I go
to Italy the tutor must be relinquished and he placed in school or
I must trust him to the stormy waves and the merciful Providence
of our great Father in Heaven for safety and protection until he
lands in America! Driving down to the bank at noon to-day for
letters I proposed to Tad with a trembling voice and aching heart

you may be sure, that he would embark on the *Russia* which sails next Saturday week for the U.S. Dec. 10th and go home pass his Christmas with you and Bob and immediately afterward be placed in school. Study more than he does now he could not possibly do. If he only had the information of his tutor, who is most indefatigable, I told him to-day, I would be willing to live on a crust of bread a day—*almost*. To-night, we are engaged to meet Governor Evans [8] and family and I am going to ask Governor Evans' candid advice on the subject. He came over last week on the same vessel. To trust my beautiful, darling *good* boy to the elements, at this season of the year, makes my heart faint within me. Each breath I drew would be a prayer for his safety, which only those who have been as deeply bereaved as myself could fully understand. On the other hand, the English schools have vacation for a month after Christmas which if I did not send Tad home would delay my going to Italy until the 1st of Feb., keeping him with his tutor in the mean time at hard study.

I am troubled to hear of your dear mother's continued ill health. I do so trust that Bob will come over with you if it is only for a few months, it would do him such a world of good. He loves you so *very dearly* and misses you very greatly. I was such an excessively indulged wife—my darling husband was so gentle and easy. You know you will always be FIRST LOVE of daughters -in-law. I often tell Tad I can scarcely flatter myself he will ever marry to suit me quite as well as dear Bob has done. Please present my warmest love to your mother and father . . .

To Adam Badeau [9]

9 Woburn Place
December 21st 1870

My dear Sir:

Gov & Mrs Evans, with their family, including Miss Simpson (the Bishop's daughter) will make me a little visit tomorrow

---

[8] Probably John Evans, governor of the Colorado Territory, 1863–5. Evans had apparently come to England to place his son in school.
[9] Military secretary to General Grant from 1864–6, now U.S. Consul General at London. Badeau's reminiscences of Mrs. Lincoln's embarrassment at City Point in 1865 are on p. 207.

evening, (Thursday, if you will kindly join us, about eight o'clock, we will *all*, be very much pleased.

With kind regards, believe me,

Your true friend
Mrs A. Lincoln

To Mrs. Paul R. Shipman

9 Woburn Place
Russell Square, Jan 13, 1871

My dear Mrs. Shipman:

I have concluded in the weakness of my *Mother* heart to accompany my son out to his school and perhaps remain a day or two near him. As the movement is somewhat unexpected, I have in consequence not a moment to lose and it grieves me to say not even an opportunity of saying to you, for whom I entertain so true and firm a friendship, farewell. Even now I am being hurried, yet I could not leave your neighborhood without committing my regrets to paper. I shall hope soon to hear the good news that your health has improved. I go myself coughing most disagreeably and a bundle of wrappings. My servant woman has proved herself within the past week a good nurse. With kind regards to Mr. Shipman and ever so much love to your dear self, believe me always

Your truly affectionate friend
Mary Lincoln

To Mary Harlan Lincoln

[EXCERPT]   *London, January 26th, 1871*

My dear Mary

Count de Paris [1] came in about a week since, twelve miles from T[r]uckenham, to see me, having only heard the day before

[1] Louis Philippe d'Orléans, Bourbon pretender to the throne of France was, like former Emperor Louis Napoleon, living in exile in England. Mrs. Lincoln had

that I was in town. He then wished me to name a day when I would drive with them, and on my table this morning I find a most urgent note to come out to visit them. I will do so, on my return in the spring . . .

Be sure to write often to me for every thing connected with you or yours is of *deep, deep* interest to me. How pained I am, dear Mary, to hear of your beloved Mother's continued illness. Tad is often very anxious to hear of your brother for he, with his loving heart, is very much attached to him. Tad is almost wild to see Bob, you and the baby; he thinks the latter must be a rare young lady, I am also of his opinion. I scarcely imagined when I began this letter that my strength would hold out for more than three pages, but the themes which we discuss together in our epistles are decidedly exciting and exhaustless . . .

To Mary Harlan Lincoln

[INCOMPLETE]   *Florence, Italy*
                                Feb 12, [1871] [2]

My dear Mary:

My servant woman and I have arrived safely after much fatigue in this beautiful Florence. We came through the charming Tyrol, via Milan and Lake Como, had a day's sail on the latter the beauties of which are simply *indescribable.* Passed three days at Geneva [Genoa?] and found Mrs Simpson and Ida here wondering what had become of me. Yesterday we went together to the Pitti Palace where the King resides and saw the room where the beautiful Princess Marguerite sleeps. We can only wish *her* health and happiness *all her days.* knowing full well by experience that power & high position do not ensure a *bed of roses.* Mrs S. has been here already four weeks . . . Armed with my guide book, a desire to

---

met the Comte on several occasions when he had come to the United States to observe the Union forces during the Civil War.

[2] This letter was misdated "1870" either by Mrs. Lincoln or by Katherine Helm, who published it. Miss Helm probably also misread the Italian spelling of Genoa, "Genova," as "Geneva."

see all that is wonderful and strange and with my faithful domestic following in my wake, I must pursue my journey alone. At Venice, where Mrs Simpson has not yet been, in three weeks' time we will meet and wend our way up to dear old Frankfurt, thence to England. I received a letter this morning from dear Tad, I write you that until the middle of April next he is placed with young Evans in an English school. I am neglecting to tell you that we visited the studio on yesterday of [Larkin Mead] the man to whom the commission was given for the statue of my dearly beloved husband.

To those who saw him on his return from Europe, eighteen-year-old Tad Lincoln bore little resemblance to the bumptious boy of three years earlier. Tall and handsome, beautifully mannered, he behaved decorously and spoke clearly, with a slight trace of Teutonic accent. Aside from a few trips taken separately, he and his mother had never been more than a few hours' distance from one another throughout their European sojourn. In Frankfurt especially, Tad had spent much of his free time ministering to his mother's wants, running errands for her, nursing her through illnesses so solicitously that she once described him as being "like some *old woman*" [3]—a telling phrase, which, for all its rueful overtones, was intended as a compliment.

She was as concerned about Tad's delicate health as he was about hers; her sharp eyes noted instantly, after each parting, whether his face was thinner, his complexion more flushed, or his manner more listless than when she had seen him last. Arriving in New York on May 11 after a stormy voyage, she doubtless regretted having kept him in England over the preceding winter. The bone-chilling climate, from which she herself had fled in February, had aggravated a congenital weakness in his lungs; the slightest cold invariably went to his chest and lingered for weeks.

[3] Mary Lincoln to Sally Orne, Frankfurt a Maine, December 29, 1869.

Tad was ill with a cold when they docked in New York, but he and his mother remained in the city for five days, staying at the Everett House and visiting with old friends, among them Rhoda White. The two women idly discussed the possibility of Mrs. Lincoln's making her home in New York; perhaps they would buy neighboring cottages at the edge of Central Park. She knew it was not practical; Tad wanted to be near Robert, now established in Chicago, and she too felt the tug of family ties. But all the talk had aroused in her the old dread of poverty: despite her $3,000 pension, she still considered herself poor, unable to invest in a home. For the first time in over a year she began to fret about money, to complain of the meagerness of the government's provision.

Any notions that the Lincoln family stood at the brink of destitution would have been dispelled by a glimpse of Robert's "charming" new house on Wabash Avenue, purchased with the proceeds of his burgeoning law practice. The family reunion there was marred only by the sudden departure of Mary Harlan Lincoln for Washington, where her mother lay ill, and by the fact that Tad was confined to bed with the chest cold he had picked up at sea. Several days later he was well enough to move with his mother to the Clifton House, but from then on there was a steady deterioration in his health. On June 8, Mary Lincoln wrote Rhoda White that Tad had been "*very very* dangerously ill" with water on one lung, but that he was recovering. The improvement was short-lived, for the other lung was soon affected. His condition (diagnosed as "dropsy of the chest," an accumulation of fluid in the pleural sacs surrounding the lungs), made it difficult for him to lie flat; he even slept sitting up in a chair. For a time he seemed to be out of danger, but a brief period of convalescence was followed by a serious relapse. At about 7:30 on the morning of July 15, after a night spent fighting for breath, he slumped forward in his chair and, under the anguished eyes of his mother and brother, died of what physicians later termed "compression of the heart." [4] He was only three months past his eighteenth birthday.

Mrs. Lincoln somehow managed to attend a short service held

[4] Chicago *Tribune*, July 16, 1871.

at Robert's home and to receive callers there, but she was in a stupor compounded of grief and exhaustion. She was not aboard the train that carried Tad's body in its rosewood casket to Springfield for burial. Robert traveled with James Harlan, David Davis, and other friends in a private car, while his mother remained in Chicago under the care of her cousin, Elizabeth Grimsley Brown. The funeral was held at the First Presbyterian Church, and from there the coffin was carried to Oak Ridge Cemetery and placed in the vault beside those of Tad's father and two brothers.

In many ways Tad Lincoln was the most tragic member of a family marked for tragedy. As a child he had lost a brother who was his closest companion, and then a father he worshipped. His life with his widowed mother seems to have been a hellish existence which bit by bit snuffed out much of what was carefree and spontaneous in his personality. Robert had been well on his way to manhood at the time of his father's death and had already enjoyed a certain amount of independence which he was neither inclined nor expected to relinquish. No matter how deep his concern over his mother's problems, no matter how morbidly sensitive he became as a result of her indiscretions, these things had never been central to his existence. A career, friendships, marriage, and a family of his own provided him with legitimate avenues of escape. Tad never had a taste of true freedom or a chance to involve himself completely with his contemporaries. Circumstance had thrust him early into the role of companion to a sick and troubled woman; trapped first by dependency, then by duty, he had no life of his own. It is probable that Mary Lincoln, beset as she was, never considered that she might have placed her own needs above her son's or that there was anything in the least unnatural about their situation. She saw only Tad's sweetness and manliness, his pleasure in caring for her, and believed to the end that he needed only a bit more discipline to make him perfect, the *beau ideal* of sons.

To Rhoda White

Chicago. Ill.
May 21st [*1871*]

My dear Mrs White-

Only great fatigue & indisposition have prevented my writing you, on my immediate arrival here—I found my son—his wife & child well & rejoicing over our arrival—*In seeing you* & yours, I felt almost compensated for our Atlantic voyage—If the kind fates, had so arranged, that our dwelling places—were nearer together—the *pleasant* side of life—would be more frequently viewed by me. In our *prospective* cottages overlooking that beautiful *beyond* compare of parks (*the N.Y. Central*) we *could* pass very many delightful hours together. *As it is*, we can only remember that we are true & steadfast friends, that life's changes cannot separate us, and that we can console ourselves in the hope, of frequently meeting each other. Tomorrow, I feel that I must at least locate myself for a little while, *and so* I must go forth in search of *lodgings*—My face burns at the *mere* thought. In my own country, *such* a necessity is to me a great trial—if the *two* additional yearly thousand, had been added to the pension, as my good friends so anxiously desired—or the pension for *the* back 5½ years *been* paid me, then I could have secured a cottage home for myself—where I could live quietly & in peace and collect around me *the true* & *tried* friends—of *these* days of sorrow & adversity. We must accept our fate & *pray* for grace, to bear meekly the dispensations of Providence. Dear Mrs Mack, with her kind husband & very lovely family of children, with the remembrance of their kindness to me—will never be forgotten. Your lovely daughter & accomplished young son—will be a source of great consolation to you. Dear Mrs White, I write you very hastily, whilst my head is throbbing with pain. So I am sure, you will kindly excuse this scrawl. Do write me, & chat with me, as if we WERE in THOSE cottages vis-à-vis—*the* park. My address is care of R. T. Lincoln No- 1 Marine Bank.

Please present my warmest love to Mrs Mack to whom I will

write in a few days—Also remember me to your sweet daughter Lucy & your son. Ever your affectionate friend.

Mary Lincoln

Any attempt to introduce an increase of pension, would very likely cause the present *delicate sum* to be entirely withdrawn.

I will write Mrs Mack—in a few days.

M. L.

To Eliza Stuart Steele [5]

Wabash Avenue [*Chicago*]
May [23, 1871]

My dear Cousin:

My young son is confined to his bed with a severe cold and in consequence we will not remove to the Clifton House until Saturday. We are received with so much affection here and notwithstanding the confined limits of this charming little home my son Robert, who is all that is noble and good and his lovely little wife will not hear to our removal. Yet as she is compelled to go instantly to her mother, who is in a most critical state, I think we had best make the change. In reality when they return, of course we will be almost always together. I love my son's wife whom I have known since she was a child just as well as my own sons and her warm heart has always been mine. You are so amiable and good and will appreciate all such kindly relations. Dear Cousin Eliza, when you are coming in town with Lizzie [Grimsley Brown] drop in and see me. Broken-hearted as I am over my deep bereavement, yet the memory of earlier years and the memory of those who were so kind to me in my desolate childhood is ever remembered by me. My life was so enriched by the most loving and devoted of husbands which

---

[5] Mrs. Lincoln's cousin, sister of John Todd Stuart and widow of the Reverend Samuel Steele of Hillsboro, Ohio. Eliza was born in Lexington in 1805 and lived there until her marriage in 1843.

makes the present all the more sorrowful to bear. Do come. I trust you will remain in town some days longer.

With much love I remain.

Your affectionate cousin,
Mary Lincoln

To Rhoda White

[INCOMPLETE] [*May 23, 1871*]

. . . My youngest son, is confined to his bed to day, with a severe cold. I hope by great care, that he will soon recover. My young daughter has just received a fresh summons, to her mother's bed-side in Wash- Sen Harlan writes, that his wife continues very ill—

I have secured *lodgings*, which we will enter upon on Saturday. Words spoken with you regarding the "*cottage* home"—in very *sad* jest—appear in strange contradiction, when viewed from the windows of "apartments." My husband, so fondly indulgent, would have shrunk back, in horror, if he could have imagined *his* loved family, *thus* domiciled. My husband, *did* the great work of the war, *but* Grant, had all the *pecuniary* compensation. As I now stand, I can BOARD! plainly & *economically* with all I have, including the *delicate* pension—if I had the home outside, I would desire no more. But when the decree went forth, that $3,000- was assigned me, not giving me the 5½ *years back*, not that I was ungrateful, but the certain knowledge, that from henceforth, I was a desolate wanderer without a home, wrung from me bitter tears—in a foreign land—surrounded by cold, unsympathising strangers, who never dreamed of my anguish—*I do want* a quiet, home & *there* to remain & wander no more.

It mortifies me, in *this* land, for which my beloved husband's precious life was sacrificed, that I am unable, in my gloom, to shelter myself under my own roof—

To Rhoda White

June 8th [1871]
Clifton House, Chicago, Ill.

My dear Mrs White:

Feeling assured that you will hear of my beloved young son's illness and being well convinced of your anxiety regarding him, I take advantage of a quiet sleep, which he is enjoying, to write you regarding him. My dear boy, has been *very very* dangerously ill— attended by two excellent physicians,[6] who have just left me, with the assurance, that he is better. May we *ever* be sufficiently grateful, should his precious life be spared. Dr Davis,[7] a very eminent lung physician, says, that *thus far*, his lungs are *not at all* diseased although water has been formed on part of his left lung, which is gradually decreasing. His youth, and vigilant care, with the mercy of God, may ward off future trouble. With the *last* few years *so filled* with sorrow, *this* fresh anguish, bows me to the earth. I have been sitting up so constantly for the last ten nights, that I am unable to write you at length to day. I regret to hear of the illness of Mrs Walker's [8] child. Ere this, I trust it has entirely recovered. When you write, please direct to room 21, the Clifton House. Please *burn* the letters, I have RECENTLY written you. In this *hard*, matter of fact world, such vain delusions must not be cherished. With ever so much love, believe me, your affectionate friend

Mary Lincoln

In your next, please give me your number & St—I lost the one you gave me.

M L

---

[6] Drs. Charles Gilman Smith and H. A. Johnson.
[7] N. S. Davis, then a professor at Rush Medical College, was one of the founders of the American Medical Association and of the Chicago Medical College.
[8] Mrs. George Walker, another daughter of Mrs. White.

To Eliza Slataper

Thursday July 27th [1871] [9]

My very dear friend:

In my great great agony of mind, I write you. I pray you, by all that is merciful to come to this place—if but for a few days—I feel that I *must* see you. Can you not come next Monday—*each* day we could be together. My son's health required that he should [lea]ve town, for two weeks,[1] I promised him that I would remain in his house. A gentleman friend occupies his only spare room *at night* yet each day I am entirely alone, in my *fearful sorrow. Come, come to me* My daughter in law is absent with her sick Mother—

Lovingly your broken hearted friend

M L

It is very cool in C.

To Eliza Slataper

Monday morning July [*August?*] *13th* [1871] [2]

My dear Mrs Slatafer:

I wrote you a note a week since directed to Cresson S[prings] urging you, from the depths of an agonized bereaved heart to come to me if only for a day or two.

[9] This letter was written twelve days after Tad's death.

[1] After Tad's funeral Robert wrote a friend, "My own strength was then used up & I was compelled to leave my office for as long a period as possible. I only returned in time to commence regular fall work." Quoted in Randall: *Lincoln's Sons*, p. 275.

[2] In her deep distraction, Mrs. Lincoln must have misdated this letter. Tad had died on the fifteenth of July and the letter was obviously written after that, perhaps sometime in August. Yet even the date "13th" is in doubt. On August 15, Tad would have been dead one month, but Mrs. Slataper could not have received a letter written on the thirteenth by the fifteenth, much less have reached Chicago by then.

I have been prostrated by illness—& by *a grief*—that the grave alone can soften. Could you not pass the *15th*—with me. With a world of love—believe me your deeply attached friend

M. L.

I have just received a letter from my son, who left here by order of his physician, being so ill & worn out. He will not return before next Saturday—Come, come to me.

V

The Destroying Hand
of Time

October 1871

July 1882

Letters written by Mary Lincoln in the period between 1871 and 1876 are today the rarest of items. Many of them have been lost, others were perhaps deliberately destroyed, but relatively few existed to begin with. In the years following Tad's death, Mrs. Lincoln all but disappeared from sight. Her son's illness and the shock of his death had taxed her physically almost beyond endurance; mentally, she was in a state of deep despondency. She was interested in very little and scarcely stayed in one place long enough to maintain a correspondence with anyone.

Yet the few surviving documents from these years are of considerable interest, for most of them touch on matters that concerned her deeply. In November of 1871 she wrote David Davis about the division of Tad's estate, generously offering to transfer part of her share to Robert, who could presumably make better use of the money than she.

Then, in May of 1872, came a new blow. That month a biography of Lincoln appeared, nominally written by the President's old crony Ward Hill Lamon but actually the work of Chauncey F. Black, a man who had never been a noted admirer of his subject. Lamon supplemented his personal reminiscences with copies of documents acquired at some expense from William H. Herndon, who had yet to produce his own *magnum opus*. It was not surprising, therefore, that his book perpetuated many of Herndon's pet theories and prejudices. It discussed the Ann Rutledge romance, alluded to a forced, unhappy marriage, bore down heavily on Lincoln's lack of formal religion, and toyed with a new pair of notions:

the possible illegitimacy of Lincoln's mother and perhaps of Lincoln himself!

Mrs. Lincoln would not allow the book to be brought into her presence, but she knew enough of its content to suffer renewed grief and humiliation. From the health resort of Waukesha, Wisconsin, she wrote an indignant letter to Judge James Knowlton, who had befriended her in Chicago, referring to Lamon in the harsh terms she had hitherto reserved for Herndon. She had no way of knowing how lightly history would deal with their theories, nor how completely Lincoln's character and achievements would overshadow conjecture about his birth or religious beliefs. At the time it seemed to her that such men as these were, simply for the sake of sensation and personal gain, injuring beyond repair the memory of the finest man who ever lived.

To Eliza Slataper

653 Wabash Av
Oct. 4th. 1871

My dear Mrs Slatafer:

I have been so utterly prostrated—by my deep deep grief, that my health has completely given away. Latterly, I am suffering greatly with violent palpitation of the heart—which has become the cause of much [un]easiness to my friends. Consequently, I am ordered perfect quiet—as much as can be obtained by a person so broken-hearted as my poor self. As anxious as I am to see you, I feel that *it is best*, at present that we do not meet. Bleeding wounds, would only be opened afresh, in God's Own Time—I MAY grow calmer, yet I very much doubt it. As grievous as other bereavements have been, not one great sorrow, ever approached the agony of *this*. My idolized & devoted son, torn from me, when he had bloomed into such a noble, promising youth. I will write you soon again, in the *meantime*—DO write.

Your deeply afflicted friend
M L

To C. L. Farrington [1]

Chicago, Ill.
Nov. 9th 1871

My dear Sir:

Your note has been received, requesting an autograph of my husband. Believe me, that I deeply regret that we have none left in our possession, save on very private letters.

I remain, very truly
Mrs A. Lincoln

To David Davis

Nov 9th 1871

My dear Sir:

I feel that I would be carrying out the wishes, of my dearly beloved son Taddie, when I suggest that an equal division be made of the bonds in your possession.[2] Dividing them equally between Bob & myself—I understand that by the law, I am entitled to two thirds of them, but I should prefer only the half. In making the division however, some other matters will be settled between us, so that of the bonds you have, I will receive the 19- thousand 1881-bonds, and also the 37 hundred & 50- lot 5/20—if it has not been broken by the sale just made for Bob. Otherwise $4,000- of the twelve thousand lot—Bob has read over his letter to me & what he says in it, meets my approval.

Dear Judge, I well know, how deeply you sympathise with us, in our great great sorrow—My beloved boy, was the idol of my heart & had become my inseparable companion—My heart is entirely broken, for without his presence, the world is complete

---

[1] Unidentified.

[2] The bonds which Davis, as guardian, held in Tad's name at the time of his death amounted to $35,750; the estate also consisted of $1,315.16 in cash. (Figures taken from Pratt, p. 184.)

darkness—I am sure under the circumstances, you will kindly excuse this scrawl. I remain your deeply afflicted friend

Mary Lincoln.

To Mrs. George Eastman [3]

May 26th 1872
Chicago

My dear Madam:

Please accept the enclosed sum, of ten dollars, for the purchase of flowers for "Decoration day," to strew over the graves of our brave and honored soldiers.

I am so much of an invalid at present that I cannot participate in this sacred duty, otherwise than by advancing, this small mite.

Believe me,

Very respectfully yours
Mrs A. Lincoln

To James H. Knowlton [4]

Waukesha, Wis.[5]
Aug 3d 72

PRIVATE

My dear Sir:

Your kind note has been received & for which, please accept my most grateful thanks. In regard to the infamous publication,[6]

[3] Wife of the postmaster in Chicago.
[4] A county judge and legislator from Wisconsin, at this time practicing law in Chicago.
[5] A spa in southern Wisconsin which called itself "The Saratoga of the West." According to newspaper reports, Mrs. Lincoln arrived in Waukesha during the first week in July 1872 and left in mid-August.
[6] *The Life of Abraham Lincoln*, bearing the name of Ward Hill Lamon as author but actually written by Chauncey F. Black from Herndon's material. For further discussion of the volume and its effect on Mrs. Lincoln, see pp. 595–6.

to which you allude, the vile, unprincipled and *debased* character of the author, are sufficient guarantees, of the truthfulness of his wicked assertions. The life of my pure, noble minded, devoted husband, requires *no* vindication, and one would only *lower* themselves, and lose their own self respect, were the attempt made to reply to the vile slanders, sent out from *this* book. I have not seen it, nor should not allow it, to be brought into my presence. This man, Lamon, thrust himself, upon my *too* good natured husband, through his kindness, had a lucrative office, the proceeds of which he squandered in debauchery. Now, when this good man is gone, he would draw the life blood, from his loved & deeply afflicted widow, & the son, who was so dear to him, his first born, by writing sensational falsehoods & base calumnies, wherewith he may again enrich *his* coffers—Severe retribution will yet visit this wretch. When I return to town, I hope to see you, to consult about a little business, *very* foreign to the one of which, we have been writing about. In confidence

Very truly yours,
Mrs L

I fear you will not be able to decipher this scrawl, it is most hastily written, for I am quite an invalid at present.

M. L.

To Norman Williams [7]

Waukesha, Wis
Aug 8th 1872

My dear Sir:

I expect to leave *here* next Monday, the 12th and write to request you not to direct any more letters here to me, AFTER—Saturday, *10th*—Please retain any that may come for me, *after* that date until the 22d of Aug, if you will be kind enough on *that date* (not afterwards) to direct to me (care of P. M. Madison Wis—at that

---

[7] Identified on p. 425.

time I will be merely passing through M. I am going up to a *wild* part of the country, North—in Wis. I am trying as you will perceive to make the most of *this fearfully* wearisome summer—Gov Fenton & daughter, have just left Waukesha, and I have seen them almost every day. Scarcely a day passed, without he called, we met in Europe & were together some weeks. The remainder of my stay, I shall miss them, very much—They are charmingly agreeable. I live in such a retired manner in a private house, in the outskirts of the town where there are *no other* boarders & have all the advantage of the country Gov F. said on his arrival, that he understood that I saw no one—but he was determined to penetrate the solitude. I am so miserable over my great sorrows, that at times, I feel that it is impossible to see a strange face—

The last letter which you so kindly sent me from Bob—was written just as *he thought*, he had concluded to leave London for Paris [8]—I wish you had opened the letter & read it. Such a HIGH time, as they were passing through! Doubtless he has written you, on the subject. I believe it will be utterly impossible—for him after *this*—to settle in poor *burnt out* Chicago [9]—Yet there are many friends there, to whom he is greatly attached—*yourself foremost* in the list——

The weather is oppressively warm *here*, what must it be in *C-!* What a relief it must be for you each Saturday, to return to your loved ones! Neither Bob or myself, can ever be sufficiently grateful to you, for your kindness to us—This letter business, must be very troublesome to you.

Truly, your friend,
Mary Lincoln

[8] Robert and Mary Lincoln had left on May 28, 1872, on a vacation trip to Europe, Robert's first journey outside of the United States.

[9] The great Chicago fire had occurred on October 8, 1871. This is the only known reference to it in Mrs. Lincoln's letters, although she was probably in the city at the time.

In mid-1873 Mary Lincoln fled to Canada, perhaps in search of another "cure," perhaps in embarrassment after the publication of Lamon's book. Only because of a casual statement in a letter to her cousin John Todd Stuart is it known that she was there at all. No document has been uncovered to date which could tell us in which province she settled, why she went, or what she experienced there. She returned to Chicago late in the year, only to find that the controversy surrounding her husband's religious views had been fanned into a *cause célèbre* by William Herndon.

On December 12, 1873, Herndon delivered a lecture in Springfield on the subject of Lincoln's religion, insisting once again that the late President had not been a "technical Christian" and giving as evidence Mrs. Lincoln's own admission in 1866 that he had never joined a church. Herndon's extrapolation from that innocent remark made seven years earlier infuriated Mrs. Lincoln so that she issued a public statement denying having had "the conversation with Mr. Herndon, as stated by him." [1] Her phrasing was somewhat ambiguous—perhaps deliberately so—and it opened the door to further contention. Herndon read it to mean that she denied having spoken with him. He promptly issued to the newspapers a defensive broadside entitled "Mrs. Lincoln's Denial and What She Says."

Mary Lincoln's subsequent letters to Stuart, written in the heat of anger, only add to the confusion regarding her intentions. On December 16 she wrote her cousin that Herndon's quotations from her were "utterly false" and "entirely perverted." But a month later she was begging Stuart, "Please deny to *every* one . . . that *the* interview *never* took place." The use of the double negative, not uncommon to her, leaves her meaning in doubt. Whether or not she was tempted to disavow the entire interview, after "a night's reflection," she resignedly wrote Stuart that even bothering to deny anything was giving Herndon too much importance.

If Herndon's allegations concerning Lincoln's religion troubled her, it was as nothing compared to his statements that the President may have been an illegitimate child—a possibility that filled her with horror and sent Robert off on a frantic search for the truth. He discovered that after Lincoln's death his cousin Dennis Hanks had removed from the family Bible in Coles County, Illinois,

[1] *Illinois State Journal*, December 19, 1873.

the page which bore the marriage date of Thomas Lincoln and Nancy Hanks and had folded it so minutely that it had fallen apart with age. The portion bearing the entry for the marriage was lost, and Herndon, taking note of this, felt supported in his belief that no marriage had taken place. Fortunately the page had been copied out by another relative, and it was this full copy, bearing the wedding date, to which Mrs. Lincoln referred in her letter of December 16 to Stuart.

The world, it seemed, was not willing to leave her alone. In October 1874 the old controversy about the site of Lincoln's tomb was revived in such a way as to embarrass her further; again she felt obliged to issue a public statement in self-defense, but this time there is no record that it appeared in the newspapers.

It is difficult to assess how much responsibility Herndon and Lamon—especially Herndon—must bear for what next befell Mary Lincoln, but it seems likely that the blows they inflicted contributed to her unsettled state of mind in the months to come. To assert that William Herndon's conduct was crude and ungallant is to let him off easily; his callous disregard for the feelings of a woman who was unable, either emotionally or by virtue of her position, to deal with or dismiss his allegations, amounted, in the end, to a form of persecution.

To Isaac N. Arnold [2]

January 18th 1873
Metropolis Hotel

My dear Sir:

I am quite anxious to learn whether you have received the papers from Scotland.[3] Unfortunately the letter Mr Reid [sic] [4] wrote me sixteen months since, when my mind was so deeply agonized,

[2] Lincoln's old friend, a lawyer and former congressman who now lived in Chicago.
[3] Possibly letters or documents in the hands of the late Dr. James Smith, pertaining to Lincoln's religious beliefs.
[4] Probably the Reverend James A. Reed, who held Dr. James Smith's old pulpit at the First Presbyterian Church in Springfield.

that I was unable to cast a thought upon any thing save my terrible bereavement—that letter must have been carelessly tossed aside—with so many others.

Yet I cannot realise that Mr Reid *left to himself*—would act otherwise than in good faith—should he have received our letters. Can you not write me a line on the subject—or if you had a moments time on *Tuesday* next about twelve o'clock—to call. I know that your time is precious, and I can scarcely venture to suggest the latter.

Most truly,
your friend
Mary Lincoln

Pray pardon this hastily written note-

M. L.

To John Todd Stuart

Chicago, Dec 15th 1874 [1873]

My dear Cousin:

Owing to much indisposition during the past year & whilst in Canada for months, seldom seeing an American paper, the controversy which appears to have been going on regarding my great & good husband's religious views, have entirely escaped me. With very great sorrow & natural indignation have I read of Mr Herndon, placing words in my mouth—*never once* uttered. I remember the call *he* made on me for a few minutes at the [St. Nicholas] hotel [5] as he mentions, *your* welcome entrance a quarter of an hour afterward, naturally prevented a further interview with him. Mr Herndon, had always been an utter stranger to me, he was not considered an habitué, at our house. The office was more, in his line. Very soon after his entrance, I remember well, he branched off to Mr Lincoln's religious beliefs—I told him in positive words, that my husband's heart, was naturally religious—he had often described to me, his noble Mother, reading to him at a very early age,

[5] See letter to Herndon of August 28, 1866.

from her Bible, the prayers she offered up for him, that he should become a pious boy & man—and then I told Mr Herndon, what an acceptable book, *that* Great Book, was always to him. In our family bereavements, it was *there*, he first turned for comfort—Sabbath mornings he accompanied me to hear dear good old Dr Smith, preach & moreover, I reminded Mr Herndon, that his last words, to his dear friends on leaving for Washington, with an impending Rebellion before the country were words uttered in great a[n]xiety & sadness "Pray for me"—

These words revealed his *heart*. What more can I say in answer to this man, who when my heart was broken with anguish, issued falsehoods, against me & mine, which were enough to make the Heaven's blush—

Very truly yours
Mary Lincoln

Please show Rev Mr Read [sic] this note.[6]

To John Todd Stuart

Dec 16th 1864 [7] [1873]

To the Hon John T. Stuart

Every word, Mr Herndon has stated as coming from me in a conversation held some years ago, is utterly false & has been entirely perverted. I hope you will kindly in my name, to parties interested pronounce it so.

Truly, your Cousin,

Mary Lincoln

[6] Dr. Reed had taken up his predecessor's defense of Lincoln's religious beliefs in the face of Herndon's allegations. On October 29, 1881, Herndon wrote Benjamin Underwood: "The Revd. Jas. A. Reed and myself had a discussion . . . about 1873–4 touching Mr. Lincoln's Religion—: I holding that Mr. Lincoln was an infidel in the very best sense of that abused word; and Mr. Reed holding that Mr. Lincoln was a Christian &c. . . . Mr. Lincoln was an Infidel and so died." Excerpt published in *A History of America in Documents* Part Three, Item 323.
[7] Mrs. Lincoln, in her distracted state, clearly wrote the year "1864" at the top of the letter.

P. S. My very dear son, has just left me and in his quiet way says, Herndon need not break his heart, over the *missing page*— [8] which you know will *once more safe & sure* make us Lincoln's *once more*—

Cousin John, how can you all—the true friends of my dear good husband, allow such a wretched creature in your midst—A worse man I believe, has never lived. Pardon these lengthy notes, but let every one know, what false words he has attributed to poor unhappy me.

M. L.

The missing page is deposited in my son's vault. However we would not dim our eyes, over Herndon's fears on the subject. If you write, please address to my son's care only the contents of *this page* must quietly be made known.

To John Todd Stuart

Chicago
Jany 20th 1874

My dear Cousin:

Your kind note has been received, also the enclosure, which puts *shame to the blush*. When Herndon, presented his disagreeable self to me, at the time, he mentions, his appearance & the *air* he brought with him, were so revolting, that I could scarcely ask him to be seated—as it was, you came in about ten minutes afterwards—in *that time*, scarcely *notes* could be taken—every word the man *there*, in those two columns utters is a falsehood—so far as *my* conversation was concerned—The flowing bowl, must have been *entirely* exhausted—when he wrote that intellectual production.

As my good friend, Professor Swing,[9] recently said to me in one of his calls, when the name of Herndon was mentioned. "Cer-

---

[8] Of the Lincoln family Bible, bearing the marriage date of Thomas Lincoln and Nancy Hanks. The controversy is discussed on pp. 601–2.

[9] Dr. David Swing had been minister of Chicago's Westminster Presbyterian Church since 1866. Because of his liberal opinions, he would be forced to resign from the presbytery a few months after this letter was written.

tainly, my dear Mrs Lincoln, your thoughts rise above such "small barking dogs as this creature Herndon & Lamon"—His tone was so lofty, that I have since felt it was beneath me, to desecrate my lips —with such vile names. My dear Cousin, I often think how kind & patient you have been, with all your many afflicted relatives, ever since I can remember. My heart is so entirely broken over my terrible bereavements, that I have no tears *left*, for those, whom my beloved husband, did *so much* and have vilified *his* memory—and those of his sorrowing family. Believe me, I am affectionately

> your Cousin
> Mary L

P.S. In this scrap [1] [H] PERFECTS what you told him about my letter. Please deny to *every* one——that *the* interview *never* took place.

To John Todd Stuart

Jany 21st [1874]

My dear Cousin:

I have had a nights reflection over what I wrote you on yesterday concerning H[erndon] & think it is best—not to give the wretched, drunken madman so much importance, either to show my letter to any one or to say, I had *no such* interview—He cannot tell the truth—If he finds no one takes any notice of his articles—yet I need not say this, for he will write until he fills *a drunkard's grave*. And again too, in the letter, I used Professor Swing's name, one of our most [prominent] Pres- divines who at the same time told me that at a dinner of 15 gentlemen recently, he [Herndon] was denounced at the table by Swett & others as a drunkard, an out-

---

[1] A scrap of a news clipping has been preserved with this letter. It is from Herndon's article "Mrs. Lincoln's Denial and What She Says" and reads: "She, in the Stuart letter *expressly admits* a conversation and says that Mr. Stuart came *into the* room while *I was taking down* the *substance* of the *conversation*, but that it *was stopped*—suspended during his stay. This I understood from Mr. Stuart, if I remember correctly." The underlinings in ink were probably Mrs. Lincoln's.

rageous story-teller—to use a mild term and as he stole my husband's law books & our own private library, *we* may *safely* call him thief

your affectionate cousin
M L

To Isaac N. Arnold

Monday noon
[October 20, 1874] [2]

My dear Mr Arnold:

Most hastily, I have scrawled these few lines, hoping they will meet your approbation.

I believe I will ask you, without you *absolutely* consider it necessary, *not* to change *the least word*—I hope you will have it appear in the same words *as soon* as possible, in a prominent place in the Tribune and Evening Journal—& [Chicago] Inter Ocean—

Very truly, your obliged friend
Mrs A. Lincoln

It is a great pleasure to state, that there is not a word of truth relaive to the assertions made, by newspaper reporters that unpleasant feelings ever existed between Mrs A. Lincoln and Mrs [Thomas] Mather [3]—On the contrary, Mrs Mather, at least 28 years in advance of Mrs Lincoln in years age, has always been devotedly attached to the latter lady, whilst Mrs L- has always *ever* been an ardent admirer & continual visitor of Mrs Mather, even when she has herself been in her deepest affliction. It is cruel indeed that such interpretations should be placed upon Mrs Lincoln

[2] The date of receipt is on the last page of the letter, presumably in Arnold's handwriting. On October 9, 1874, Lincoln's coffin was removed from the temporary vault to the newly completed marble sarcophagus. On October 15 the monument was dedicated, and it was apparently in connection with these events that the cemetery dispute erupted again.
[3] The Mather family had owned the land in Springfield on which the Monument Association had planned to erect Lincoln's tomb and monument, a site which Mrs. Lincoln had rejected in favor of Oak Ridge.

selecting Oak Ridge, as the final resting place of her dearly beloved & lamented husband. Such selection was made, on account of her absolute knowledge—that the beauty & retirement of the spot, would have been her husband's choice—

All of the controversy coming so soon after Tad's death placed a vast strain on Mrs. Lincoln's inner resources. She withdrew farther and farther into her shell, avoiding family and friends, seeing faults in everyone, including the daughter-in-law she professed to love so dearly. She made Chicago her base but left town frequently to wander aimlessly over the landscape in search of medical treatment. So worrisome was her behavior that Robert felt it necessary to hire a nurse, Mrs. Richard Fitzgerald, to watch over her and tend to her needs. Mrs. Fitzgerald's son was the actor Eddie Foy. As a young boy Foy heard at first hand of the mental deterioration of his mother's celebrated charge. "After her son died," he wrote, "she suffered from periods of mild insanity. She had many strange delusions. At times she thought gas was the invention of the devil and would have nothing but candles in her room. At other times, she insisted on the shades being drawn and the room kept perfectly dark. . . . the position was a trying one and Mother gave it up twice, but each time the kinsmen induced her to come back." [4]

Mary Lincoln's increasingly erratic behavior must have been a painful thing to witness. Isaac N. Arnold was to write, "After 1871, Mrs. Lincoln, in the judgment of her most intimate friends, was never entirely responsible for her conduct. She was peculiar and eccentric and had various hallucinations." [5] Death had deprived her of everyone who was dear to her, with the exception of Robert. Now, under the spell of her illness she became obsessed with the idea that he, too, would be taken from her, and in her susceptible, disordered mind this fear took on the dimensions of reality. On

[4] Eddie Foy and A. E. Harlow. "Clowning through Life." *Collier's Weekly*, December 25, 1926. Quoted in Evans, p. 307.
[5] Arnold, p. 433.

March 12, 1875, while in Florida, she sent Robert's physician, Dr. Ralph N. Isham, a frantic telegram stating her belief that Robert was gravely ill and beseeching the doctor to go to him at once; she was returning to her son's side as quickly as she could. Doing as he was told, Dr. Isham found Robert, quite whole, at work in his office. Could Mrs. Lincoln have been thinking of her son's wife or one of his children? They, too, were in excellent health.[6]

On her arrival in Chicago Mrs. Lincoln was met at the depot by Robert, who urged her to stay in his home on Wabash Avenue. When she refused, he took two rooms at the Grand Pacific Hotel, one for her, the other for himself. Her behavior at the hotel was decidedly abnormal, filling Robert with shame and dread. A number of times during her stay she came to his door in her nightdress, awakened him with tales of being followed and harassed, and begged him to let her sleep in his room. Once, half-dressed, she entered an elevator, thinking it was a lavatory; when Robert, in an agony of embarrassment, enlisted the aid of a hotel employee to draw her gently back into her room, she threw their hands off and screeched that Robert was trying to murder her. At various times she told him all manner of fantastic stories; that a man in Jacksonville, Florida, had tried to poison her at breakfast; that Chicago was to be entirely consumed by fire at any moment (a not unreasonable anxiety, considering that it had happened four years earlier), and she was planning to send her valuables to a country place for safekeeping. Her head ached constantly; it felt, she said, as if "an Indian" were pulling wires out of her eyes, or as if needles of flame were moving through her brain.

But the most disturbing manifestation of all was her mania about money, a subject about which she had been unable to think rationally for years. She carried $57,000 in securities in a skirt pocket and made reckless purchases of articles she did not need and would never use: lace curtains for $600, three watches for $450; seventeen pairs of gloves and three dozen handkerchiefs, $700 worth of jewelry, $200 worth of toiletries. Before his marriage Robert had written to Mary Harlan: "I have no doubt that a great many good and amiable people wonder why I do not take charge of

---

[6] This, and the following information regarding Mrs. Lincoln's eccentric actions in 1875 are taken from testimony at her trial, as reported in the Chicago *Inter Ocean*, May 20, 1875.

her affairs and keep them straight, but it is very hard to deal with one who is sane on all subjects but one. You would hardly believe it possible, but my mother protests to me that she is in actual want, and nothing I can do or say will convince her to the contrary. So you see that I am likely to have a good deal of trouble in the future to do what I can to prevent it." [7]

The trouble had come at last, and Robert had to deal with it. He hired a Pinkerton detective to follow his mother about for three weeks, but even this measure proved inadequate. She clearly needed rest and care as well as protective surveillance on a prolonged basis. Above all, some way had to be found to keep her from squandering what money she had on multiple purchases of useless articles, or of being robbed or "taken" by someone who knew of her irresponsibility. Control of her money had to be removed from her hands, and the only way Robert could do this was by securing a legal judgment of incapacity—in balder terms, insanity. After considerable soul-searching and with the most competent advice available to him Robert took that grievous step. On May 18, 1875, Dr. Isham certified that he had examined "Mrs. Mary Lincoln—widow—and that I am of the opinion that she is insane and a fit subject for hospital treatment." The following day Robert's attorneys petitioned the Cook County Court that it would be to his mother's "benefit" that she be confined in an institution for the insane; [8] seventeen witnesses offered to testify at the necessary hearing. In addition, Robert requested that he be appointed conservator of her estate. It had been a painful decision, but Robert was convinced he had acted wisely. In a letter to his mother's friend Sally Orne, he wrote, "Six physicians informed me that by longer delay I was making myself morally responsible for some very probable tragedy . . ." [9]

The task of escorting Mary Lincoln to the hearing—in effect, arresting her—fell to Leonard Swett. She was of course taken by surprise, and at one point questioned Swett as to the names of those who had advised Robert in his course. Cousin John Todd Stuart was one, David Davis another. She never forgot. Once in court, she

[7] Robert Lincoln to Mary Harlan, October 16, 1867. Published in Helm, p. 267.

[8] Certificate from Dr. Isham and Robert Lincoln's petition to the Cook County Court reproduced in Sandburg & Angle, pp. 146–7.

[9] Robert Lincoln to Mrs. J. H. Orne, Chicago, June 1, 1875. Published in Helm, pp. 295–6.

listened to the evidence with seeming interest and composure. She heard Robert declare, "She has no home, and does not visit my house because of a misunderstanding with my wife. She has always been kind to me. She has been of unsound mind since the death of her husband." Tears filled Robert's eyes as he spoke. After the other witnesses were heard, the jury declared itself "satisfied that the said Mary Lincoln is insane and is a fit person to be sent to a State Hospital."

On page 596 of the "Lunatic Record" for Cook County, State of Illinois, the name "Mary Lincoln" was entered. The record stated, among other things, that she did not manifest any "homicidal or suicidal tendencies," which had been true until that day. For all her longing for death, expressed in the lugubrious rhetoric of her letters, she was willing to wait until her time arrived. Now, when the full implications of the hearing penetrated her consciousness, she lost all desire to live. This was the ultimate betrayal, coming not from a stranger with a personal grudge and babbling tongue, but from her only living son. The evening of the hearing, she attempted suicide for the first and only time in her life, escaping from her attendants at the hotel and going from one druggist to another in search of the deadly mixture of camphor and laudanum. One druggist, noting her distraught manner, pretended to fill her order but omitted the laudanum. When the drink failed to produce instant oblivion, she returned for more. The next day, very much alive and thoroughly wretched, she was taken by Robert to Bellevue Place, a private sanitarium for women in Batavia, Illinois, thirty-five miles west of Chicago. Dr. R. J. Patterson, one of the physicians who had advised Robert, was head of the institution.

Her situation there was in essence distasteful, but in actuality far from uncomfortable.[1] She lived in her own airy room, associated freely with members of the Patterson family, took drives, walks, and many of her meals with them. Outwardly, she was calm and compliant—though occasionally, and not unnaturally, depressed and given to small acts of defiance. She received her son cordially for the most part, inspiring him to write Mrs. Orne, "We are on the

[1] An excellent study of Mrs. Lincoln's sojourn at Bellevue Place can be found in an article by Rodney A. Ross entitled "Mary Todd Lincoln, Patient at Bellevue Place, Batavia." *Journal of the Illinois State Historical Society,* Spring 1970.

best of terms. Indeed my consolation in this sad affair is in thinking that she herself is happier in every way, than she has been in
ten years." [2] Robert, hoping for the best and meaning the best, failed
to divine the turmoil in his mother's mind. Behind her subdued
façade, her brain seethed with schemes to obtain her release. She
could not turn to Robert; he was the one who had had her incarcer-
ated in the first place, and not for her protection, she believed, but
in order to get his hands on her money. And so she enlisted the aid
of others, particularly Judge and Mrs. James Bradwell of Chicago. The Bradwells visited her many times, and letters were exchanged. Myra Bradwell, who was Illinois' first woman lawyer, let
it be widely known that Mary Lincoln, though "no more insane
than I am," was a virtual prisoner in Dr. Patterson's house.[3] None
of Mrs. Lincoln's letters to the Bradwells remains, and there is reason to believe Robert had theirs to her destroyed, so damning were
they to him.

Another surprising pair of allies in her fight to regain her liberty were her sister and brother-in-law, Mr. and Mrs. Ninian W.
Edwards. There had been a marked estrangement between Mary
and Elizabeth in the years following Lincoln's death, but now the
older sister forgot the past and concentrated on helping the younger
in her desperate need. When Mrs. Lincoln had been in Bellevue
Place less than four months, the Edwardses, supported by the
Bradwells, persuaded Dr. Patterson to allow her to live in their
Springfield home for a trial period. The weeks lengthened into
months, nine in all, after which a second sanity hearing was held.
Leonard Swett, acting as Mrs. Lincoln's attorney (and thereby re-
establishing himself in her esteem), petitioned the court for full
restoration of her rights and the removal of her conservator. Ninian
W. Edwards declared in a sworn statement that friends all thought
Mrs. Lincoln was "a proper person to take charge of her own affairs." [4]

On June 15, 1876, Mary Todd Lincoln was adjudged "restored to reason" and given her freedom and control over her af-

[2] Robert Lincoln to Mrs. J. H. Orne, Chicago, June 1, 1875. Published in Helm,
pp. 295–6.
[3] Quoted in Ross article, p. 14.
[4] Photostat of record of Cook County Court, June 15, 1876, Illinois State Historical Library, Springfield.

fairs.[5] Robert, removed as conservator, rendered a scrupulous accounting of her finances during the period he had managed them. He had tried to do what was best and felt certain that his motives would in time be understood by his mother and her friends. But resentment had been boiling within Mary Lincoln for a year; it was directed primarily at her son, secondarily at all those who had advised or assisted him in having her confined. Three days after her rights were restored, she sat down and wrote a letter which must have shocked Robert to his shoes. The salutation read simply "Robert T. Lincoln" and the signature, "Mrs A. Lincoln." In between was a withering blast of contempt and righteous indignation in which Mary Lincoln curtly demanded of Robert the return of all her possessions that his wife had "appropriated." "You have tried your game of robbery long enough," she declared.

At scattered intervals over the years, various observers had noted in Mary Lincoln instances of hallucination, outrageous utterance, eccentric behavior. Credible, sympathetic witnesses such as Noah Brooks, Orville H. Browning, William O. Stoddard, Elizabeth Keckley, Emilie Helm—even Abraham Lincoln himself—all sensed at one time or another that there was something abnormal in her makeup. At the sanity hearing, Robert, obviously heartbroken, repeated words and reported actions that could only have indicated serious disturbance in his mother, and much of what he said was corroborated or supplemented by others. Six physicians, including one who specialized in nervous and mental disorders, unanimously agreed that Mary Lincoln was (by all legal definitions) insane, incompetent to manage her own affairs.

A logical place to look for confirmation of their verdict would seem to be Mrs. Lincoln's own writings. Her letters tell us a great deal: that she was irrational on, and obsessed by, the subject of money, that she could not control her compulsion to buy, that she was abnormally acquisitive. We can see that she often felt depressed, fearful, and persecuted, that she could be hysterical, vindictive, self-pitying, and self-deluding. She was not above stretching or abandoning the truth to serve her own purposes, however obscure. Yet there is no letter that wanders off into total

[5] *Ibid.*

gibberish or wild fantasy: even her repeated, frantic communications attempted to deal with real problems. Most of her fears and animosities had roots in reality. For all her excessive grieving, there is nothing unduly morbid or macabre in her letters, nothing in her hand to prove that she thought of her dead as anything but dead. If the tragedies that befell her made her long for release, she never—until the night of her commitment—seriously threatened to take her own life. Although she nursed burning dislikes and predicted heavenly retribution for her enemies, she never even went so far as to wish them dead. She was not violent.

The most striking manifestations of her illness have come down to us almost exclusively through the statements of others; these persons may have exaggerated or misinterpreted her behavior, but they did not lie. Some of their most damning observations were recorded in private diaries as many as twelve years before the hearing, and were neither intended nor used as evidence against her. Perhaps it was too much to expect that doctors and lawyers in that era distinguish between areas and degrees of incompetence before branding a human being forever with the mark of lunatic—a fearsome stigma in 1875. It cannot be denied that Mary Lincoln was in some ways mentally disturbed even before her husband's death. Yet whatever else she has revealed of her mind and character in letters, she has, interestingly and ironically enough, refused to testify to her own madness.

To Ira Harris

Springfield, Ill.
Dec 1st, 1875

My dear friend Judge Harris

It is with the greatest sorrow, that I learn through the papers, of your very severe illness.[6] Dearly, did my noble husband & myself, love you & my deeply afflicted heart goes out to you in my prayers, for your speedy recovery.

[6] Senator Harris died at his home in Albany, New York, the day after this letter was written.

Please present my warmest love to your wife & family, and accept for yourself, dear & honored friend, my sincerest love.

Most affectionately yours,
Mary Lincoln

To Robert Todd Lincoln

Springfield, Illinois.
June 19th—1876

Robert T. Lincoln

Do not fail to send me without *the least* delay, *all* my paintings, Moses in the bullrushes included—also the fruit picture, which hung in your dining room—my silver set with large silver waiter presented me by New York friends, my silver tête-à-tête set also other articles your wife appropriated [7] & which are *well known* to you, must be sent, without a day's delay. Two lawyers and myself, have just been together and their list, coincides with my own & will be published in a few days. Trust not to the belief, that Mrs Edward's tongue, has not been *rancorous* against you all winter & she has maintained to the very last, that you dared not venture into her house & our presence. Send me my laces, my diamonds, my jewelry—My unmade silks, white lace dress—double lace shawl & flounce, lace scarf—2 blk lace shawls—one blk lace deep flounce, white lace sets ½ yd in width & eleven yards in length. I am now in constant receipt of letters, from my friends denouncing you in the bitterest terms, six letters from prominent, *respectable*, Chicago people such as you do not associate with. No John Forsythe's & such scamps, including Scamman [sic]. As to Mr Harlan—you are not worthy to wipe the dust, from his feet. Two prominent clergy men, have written me, since I saw you—and mention in their letters, that they think it advisable to offer up prayers for you in Church, on account of your wickedness against me and High Heaven. In reference to Chicago you have the enemies, & I chance to have the friends there. Send me all that I have written for, you

---

[7] See letter to Mary Harlan Lincoln, March 29, 1869.

have tried your game of robbery long enough. On yesterday, I received two telegrams from prominent Eastern lawyers. You have injured yourself, not me, by your wicked conduct.

Mrs A. Lincoln

My engravings too send me. M. L. Send me Whittier Pope, Agnes Strickland's Queens of England, other books, you have of mine—

During Mary Lincoln's year-long stay in her sister's home following her release from the sanitarium she gradually regained a measure of stability. Ninian and Elizabeth Edwards were in a sense reverting to roles they had played nearly forty years earlier, when they had first welcomed "Sister Mary" to the house on the hill: once again they were her friends, confidants, guardians. Their efforts to obtain her release and their kindness in succeeding months dissolved any traces of acrimony between the two sisters. In coming months, Mary Lincoln referred to Elizabeth in letters only in the most loving terms.

Once she had calmed down a bit, other needs began to assert themselves. She still had within her a vast reservoir of maternal affection, a desire to bestow the benefits of her experience on someone who was just starting out in life. And so, with three sons dead and one despised, she looked with new eyes on Elizabeth's seventeen-year-old grandson, Edward Lewis Baker, Jr. "Lewis" Baker was living in his grandparents' home while his mother and father were in Argentina on a diplomatic mission. (Their absence doubtless made the attachment easier, for Mary Lincoln disliked both Julia and Edward Baker intensely. Throughout her correspondence, beginning in the 1850's, there is scarcely a reference to either that is not bitter or belittling.) When Mrs. Lincoln first met Lewis he was going to school; later he went to work for the *Illinois State Journal*, the paper his father had edited. In his gentle, cheerful disposition, his intelligence and lack of artifice, Lewis reminded her of

Tad. Just by being himself he made his great-aunt feel both needed and protected.

But not even her new-found interest in Lewis could keep Mary Lincoln in Springfield with all its memories of happier times. Her incarceration at Bellevue Place still rankled, the wounds it had inflicted were too deep, and her embarrassment too acute to permit her to be entirely comfortable there. She refused to be pitied or patronized, nor would she put anyone out with her illnesses; she alone could salvage what remained of her dignity, her life. To the twin stigmas of (imagined) poverty and (genuine) notoriety was now added a third: insanity. "I cannot endure to meet my former friends, Lizzie," she told her sister. "They will never cease to regard me as a lunatic. I feel it in their soothing manner. If I should say the moon is made of green cheese they would heartily and smilingly agree with me. I love you, but I cannot stay. I would be much less unhappy in the midst of strangers." [8] She would go back to Europe.

Mrs. Lincoln left Springfield at the end of September 1876. Hardly able to tear herself away from Lewis, she invited him to escort her as far as New York, where she would embark for France; she wrote first to him on her arrival at Le Havre.

To Edward Lewis Baker, Jr.

Havre France
October 17th 76

My dear Lewis:

I find myself, sufficiently recovered from my sea voyage, to write you, concerning my safe arrival, on a foreign shore. Tomorrow, I sail on a new Steamer, the Columbia, for Bordeaux. Such kindness, deference & attention, as I met with on my arrival here, it is impossible for me to describe to you. Our elegant & kind hearted friend Louis de Berbieu, had written several letters to the agents here & they immediately took me in charge, without opening an article of baggage. They were equally as gentlemanly and distingué in appearance as Mr de Berbieu, the latter I am told, is of royal

---

[8] Quoted in Helm, p. 298.

descent, is a widower, certainly, a very cheerful looking one, with a beautiful young daughter, an only child. Every where, reverses of fortune are met with.[9] Perhaps it has not been *his* fate financially. Each day, since I have been here, about eleven in the morning, a carriage with coachman & footman in livery, has called for me to drive, accompanied always, by the owner. It is pleasant to be *thus* received, although of course, I am aware, it is entirely my own fault, as in *N.Y-* & *Phil*, in keeping myself aloof from dear friends, who love me well. I propose to act in a more *civilized* manner in the future, which conclusion will greatly please your *very dear* Grandma. I fear the small sum of $27- scarcely, returned you, my dear Louis [sic] to S[pringfield]. *Words*, are impossible to express *how* near you are to my heart. Such attention, such kindness, as you have shown me in the past year I can say no more, I am indeed a broken hearted, bereaved woman, but God in his "Own Time," will restore me to my beloved ones.

Please write at once & direct to Pau, France. Present my best love to all your precious home circle—Write me every thing. I have just received from Galignani's at Paris, Guizot's History of France in 5 large volumes, handsomely bound, the latest history, of this beautiful land.

Do not fail to write me & tell my dearly loved sister to do the same. Love to all friends

Most affectionately
Your Aunt
Mary Lincoln

Will you be able to decipher this scrawl?
I am stopping at a very delightful Hotel. M. L.

✦

From Le Havre Mrs. Lincoln traveled by steamer to Bordeaux, from there by rail to Pau, a popular health resort in the French Pyrenees. She had chosen to settle there because of the clear mountain air and

[9] A reference to the hard times resulting from the financial panic of 1873.

the mineral baths and medical facilities at hand: these were important considerations for one in her precarious state of health. As she
aged, the number and severity of her ailments increased. What was
probably a dropsical condition had resulted in the bloating of her
tissues. She was subject to boils and colds, as well as the usual chills
and neuralgic headaches. It has been theorized that she also had dia-
betes and high blood pressure.[1] But she was not yet an invalid, and
she would make several excursions about France and Italy during
the course of the coming four years—always, however, returning to
Pau.

Her mind seems to have been remarkably keen. The obsessive interest in money matters that usually caused her so much
trouble for once worked to her advantage, enabling her to keep
painstaking track of her finances from a distance. She had left her
affairs in the hands of Jacob Bunn, one of Springfield's most prominent merchants and bankers and an old friend of Lincoln. At one
time she had vilified Bunn as a member of the "Springfield
clique." [2] Time had softened this animosity, as it had so many others, and despite confusing and upsetting misunderstandings in the
beginning, she was able eventually to place her entire trust in
Bunn, so much so that when he suffered serious financial reverses
early in 1878 she assured him, in a beautiful and touching letter,[3]
of her continued confidence in his management—a rare bit of generosity for one as self-protective as she.

Ninety-two of her letters to Bunn have been preserved. They
are business letters, some of them merely receipts. She scrupu-
lously acknowledged every mortgage, pension, and interest check
he forwarded her. She signed her quarterly pension certificates,
had them witnessed, and returned them with dispatch. When expected papers or checks failed to arrive, she wrote Bunn demanding to know the reason for the delay and always took care to inform
him of her whereabouts, lest any important documents go astray.
She advised him on her investments, figured accurately, and ac-
counted for every penny she drew.

Which is not to say that her attitude was wholly restrained:

---

[1] Evans, pp. 337–45.
[2] See letter to Elizabeth Keckley, [October 24, 1867].
[3] February 26, 1878.

some of her instructions were repeated a dozen times, and at one point her agitation over the absence of a pension paper bordered on panic. She was still convinced that the poorhouse lay but a step away, and her penny-pinching tendencies continued to be painfully apparent. In his personality study of Mrs. Lincoln, Dr. W. A. Evans found nothing pathological in this. "The three-cornered fight in her mental makeup," he wrote, "between the desire to get, the desire to spend, and the desire to hoard had lasted for nearly forty years. Sometimes one combatant was on top, sometimes another. In the final stretch, miserliness held the field of battle. . . . This complex mania for money, extravagance and miserliness—paradoxical as it appears to laymen—is well known to psychiatrists. It is present in many people who are accepted as normal. In Mrs. Lincoln . . . it was developed to the point where it did not prove actual insanity . . . at most, it made of her not more than a border-line case."[4]

Even for a "border-line case," Mary Lincoln, in her letters to Bunn, displayed an astonishing degree of perspicacity and control —the more so when it is realized that she was dealing exclusively with money, the one area in which she had been demonstrably irrational. When one considers further that it was chiefly because of her inability to handle her finances that she was sent to a mental institution, the Bunn correspondence becomes an even greater source of wonder. Or perhaps one should wonder at the confinement.

To Jacob Bunn

Pau, France
Oct 23d 1876

My dear Sir:

I arrived here, two days since & feel some disappointment, on account of not receiving a letter of remittance from you, of $125-[5]

---

[4] Evans, pp. 312–13.

[5] This amount, which Mrs. Lincoln continually and erroneously referred to as "rent" on her Chicago house at 375 West Washington Street, was actually a mortgage payment. Title records show that the house was finally sold on April 8, 1874. That Mrs. Lincoln held a small mortgage on it is evident from her letter to Bunn of January 31, 1877.

which was due the 1st of Oct- for the *preceeding month* of Sept. I will take the liberty of remitting you an envelope, with my address—

Please present my kindest regards to your family, whilst I remain, most respectfully your friend.

Mrs A. Lincoln

To Jacob Bunn

Pau, France
Oct 24th 76

My dear Sir:

Through some mistake, your note of the 2d of Oct, was not handed me on my arrival here. This morning, the P[ost] M[aster] gave it to me, & I hasten to thank you, for your kind attention, in the remittance of 580. France [sic] for the month of Sept.

Most truly yours.
Mrs Abraham Lincoln

To Jacob Bunn

Pau France
November 28th 1876
Grand Hotel de la Pa[ix]

My dear Sir:

Your note, with checque for 580. Fr has been received. Before this acknowledgement reaches you, my Pension [payment],[6] for Dec 4th will have become due; I feel assured, that the necessary papers, with instructions, will be sent me, from S[pringfield]. I have seen Mr [Musgrave] Clay, the Banker here & he has promised

---

[6] The pension of $3,000 per annum was paid Mrs. Lincoln in quarterly installments of $750 each. Each quarter, the Chicago pension office sent a form to Bunn, who forwarded it to Mrs. Lincoln; it had to be signed and returned before payment could be made, a cumbersome procedure which caused much difficulty.

to assist me, when the papers arrive. I have received a call from the Mayor of Pau, accompanied by his two adjutants, it was a mere visit of ceremony & etiquette. I mention the circumstance as Mr N. W. Edwards, my brother-in-law, appeared to think that perhaps, it would be necessary, to see him, in his official capacity, on the subject. The call was unexpected & of course no allusion, was made to the business. Mr Clay, is a man of intelligence & doubtless, understands, the whole routine. Regarding the interest that accrues, on the 1st of Jan 1877, on my $60,000. [federal] Bonds, the arrangement, we made in Sept. last, thoroughly settles that business—you *withdrew* from the $1800, in gold which you advanced me, the interest in gold, which would be due—January 1st 1877, *on the loan.* In other words—when the interest of $1800. (in gold) on my Bonds becomes due, in January next, my note, which you retained, assigns, that sum to you. I have expressed, myself, in a womanly like way yet I feel assured, that you will comprehend me —And, believe me, with so long & expensive a journey, before me, I was very grateful, for the arrangement—

My note of Sep last [7] has made it all satisfactory.

I remain,
Very respectfully
Mrs A. Lincoln

To Jacob Bunn

Pau, France
Dec. 12th 1876

My dear Sir:

The Pension paper, accompanied by your note, with instructions, have been received. I return the paper to you, signed by the proper authorities, Mr Musgrave Clay, is the Consul, connected with the American Consulate. Le Baron de Bennecker, is one of the high authorities here & one of the Government officers. I observe, by my Daily Galignani of Paris, which receives constant

[7] Not preserved.

news, from America, that gold on the 8th of Dec- was 107¼—quite a decline, making it however, so much better, if it continues, for the number of my francs. Living abroad, has greatly changed, *since* the war, between France & Germany & *this*, is a very expensive place—Doubtless the ag[it]ations caused by the difficulty of deciding, *who*, is to be our next President, overshadows everything, in our beloved country.[8] We can only pray, that no civil war, will occur, to blight our prosperous land.

My sister, Mrs Edwards, wrote me on the 20th of Nov, regarding the critical condition of Mr [Jesse K.] Dubois, therefore I was *not* unprepared, to receive the sad & painful intelligence of his death. With many kind remembrances to your family, believe me,

Most respectfully &&

Mrs Abraham Lincoln

To Jacob Bunn

Pau, France
Jan 31st. 1877

My dear Sir:

Several days have elapsed since the receipt of your letter containing 3550 Francs, the proceeds of my quarterly Pension $750. The delay in acknowledging the remittance, has been caused by my desire, *not* to *trouble* you with two letters, so near the same time. I have *not yet* received the rent [sic] *due* from Chicago, the 1st of Jany. 1877—for *December*.[9] I feel that it is due you, in return for your kindness, in undertaking to transmit me, monthly & at other times, my lawful allowance, to make a few statements, that in the event of your not having carefully perused the paper, may be considered necessary. The monthly rent of C[hicago] house, is not paid

---

[8] A reference to the disputed election of Rutherford B. Hayes, Republican candidate for President in 1876. Samuel J. Tilden, the Democrat, had a clear plurality, but returns from three southern states and Oregon were thrown out on a technicality, giving Hayes the presidency. At the time this letter was written, the electoral commission had not yet met to make its controversial decision.

[9] See letter to Bunn, October 23, 1876, *note*.

in advance—so that on the expiration of the period, May 1st 1881 when *all* rent ceases, the rent of the previous month (April will be paid on 1st of May 1881—Perhaps, it may also be as well to mention, that notwithstanding the first few sentences of the paper to which I have referred, that contains the assertion that "in consideration of the payment of $10,000 &&& which without doubt you may have noted in your mind, not *one* dollar [of interest] was ever required by me, of the party to whom the bequest was made, & very certainly also, nothing has been given me. The *paper* was drawn up, by the present owner & I, soon afterwards, showed it to Judge James Bradwell of Chicago (Legal News Office) [1] who was not pleased with it. I believe this latter gentleman to be a just, good man & a lover of *truth*. Should you chance to meet Judge B- he will explain every thing. With many apologies, for so long a letter (which I had not proposed at first) believe me, most gratefully &&

Mrs Abraham Lincoln.

To Jacob Bunn

Pau, France
February 5th, 1877

My dear Sir:

A few days since, I sent you an acknowledgement, of the receipt of 3550 Francs, the proceeds of my Pension money of Dec 4th 1876. I have not yet received the rent money of $125. due the 1st of Jany 1877. from Chicago, *from* the preceding month of December. The letter containing the cheque, may have been lost through the mails; in that event, I feel assured you will remit me another, so soon as you receive, *this* announcement. Also, will you have the kindness, to send me the Pension paper, for signature, as early in March, as possible. I remain, most respectfully.

Mrs Abraham Lincoln.

---

[1] For a discussion of Mrs. Lincoln's relationship with Judge and Mrs. Bradwell, see pp. 612.

To Jacob Bunn

Pau, France
Feb 13th, 1877

My dear Sir:

On the 5th of Feb, I sent you an acknowledgement of the cheque you sent me, for Pension payment of Dec 4th 1876—The *last letter* I have received of yours, enclosing rent from Chicago, was dated Dec 2d 1876—it reached me the 24th of the same month —it was due for the month of Nov. Without doubt, the letter you have written on Jan 2d '77 with checque for *Dec.* rent, has been lost through the mails, will you kindly send me another, I shall immediately inform you of its receipt—Also of the one, which I will have the latter part of this month, I am sure, without fail from you. With many apologies, for troubling you, I remain, most respectfully.[2]

Mrs Abraham Lincoln

To Jacob Bunn

Pau, France
Feb 20th 1876[7]

My dear Sir:

Your note, with enclosure, was received on yesterday. The Jany one, has undoubtedly been lost, through the mails. Enquiries have been made at the Post Office, at this place, for letters, and at the Hotel, they are always punctual.

It is too late now, I presume to expect to receive it; the month of January, was said to be very stormy at sea.

If you will have the kindness, to send me another cheque, for

---

[2] At the bottom of this letter is a notation in Bunn's handwriting which reads: "Duplicate #129—Pension papers remitted March 2, 1877."

the proceeds of \$125- for December rent, due Jany 1st I shall be much obliged. With great respect, I remain very truly &&

Mrs Abraham Linco[ln]

To Jacob Bunn

Pau, France
Feb 27, 1877

My dear Sir:

Your note, with cheque, of the 4th of Jany—has been received to day. Should a duplicate cheque be received from you, I will immediately return it, to you.

Most respectfully &&
Mrs Abraham Lincoln

To Elizabeth Todd Edwards

Pau, France
March 19th 1877

My dear Sister:

I wrote you a letter a few days since, on receipt of the [Illinois State] Journal, containing the afflicting intelligence of the death, of dear, sweet, affectionate little Florence,[3] whom I loved so well. The information saddened me greatly & rendered me quite ill. I have drank so deeply of the cup of sorrow, in my desolate bereavements, that I am always prepared to sympathise, with all those who suffer, but when it comes *so close* to us, & when I remember that precocious, happy child, with its loving parents—what can I say? In grief, words are a poor consolation—silence & agonizing tears, are all, that is left the sufferer. Immediately, on the receipt of your most

[3] Florence Edwards, daughter of Elizabeth's son Charles, died on February 21, 1877, at the age of four.

welcome, tender letter, with the enclosures of dear dear Florence's beautiful photograph, some weeks since, I wrote you a long letter & sent a loving kiss, to the sweet child—Do write me, when you can, every thing. What a fearful winter, my dear Sister—you have had—I have never received a line from Lewis Baker—and I often feel, that letters are sent, when I do not receive them—Yet, at this Hotel, they are very attentive. There is a carelessness, I fear, at the P. O. here. The French are a superficial people, yet, I live, very much alone, & do not identify myself with them—have a few friends & prefer to remain secluded. My *"Gethsemane"*, is ever with me & God, can *alone*, lighten the burden, until I am reunited to my dearly beloved husband, and children. Write as soon as possible.

Most lovingly,
Your Sister
Mary Lincoln

To Jacob Bunn

Pau, France
March 19, 1877

My dear Sir:

Your note of March 2d containing the duplicate checque No. 129 has been received to day. Until the 20th of February, I had not received the corresponding one, sent Jany 4th for Dec rent. Immediately on its receipt, I wrote you an acknowledgment,[4] therefore I enclose you in this note, the checque No. 129 just received, as I had the other already cashed. I trust it will reach you in safety.

About the 15th of Dec, I received the Pension papers, from you, for signature due from Dec 4th to March 4th. They were at once returned to you & near the same date in January, your checque for the amount, reached me—of this, I advised you.

In looking over the paper contained in note of March 2d I find that it is a duplicate Pension paper from Dec 4th to March 4th. On opening it, I had hoped it would have been the one from March

[4] See letter to Bunn, February 20, 1877.

4th to June 4th. Doubtless in a day or two, I will receive the latter, which shall be immediately forwarded to you. I shall never fail to make an acknowledgment of a paper without the least delay when, received.

The sad accounts of illness & death amongst children in Springfield this winter, are startling. I hope your family remain in good health. Believe me, most respectfully &&

Mrs Abraham Lincoln

To Jacob Bunn

Pau, France
March 19 [20], *1877*

My dear Sir:

On yesterday, I received your letter of the 2d of March, with enclosures of duplicate checque, No. 129 also a Pension paper, for signature from Dec 4th to March 4th. As I had already received at the proper time in Dec- the pension paper & in return had your acknowledgment of the return of it—also had your checque for the amount I had no use for it. I had hoped instead to have found enclosed a Pension paper for March 4th to June 4th. So soon, as I receive the *latter*, I will sign it & return it to you. I must confess myself a little disappointed. I shewed it to the Consul this morning & like myself he agrees, that in a day or two, I will receive the one for the 4th of March. This morning, before receiving your note of *3d* of March, containing the checque No 146 I had mailed a letter to you returning duplicate checque No 129—which I hope will reach you safely. The one for Jany, arrived in Feb- having been detained, somewhere in France. *When*, I receive the 4th of March Pension Paper, I will immediately sign it & return it to you—Many thanks for your attention, to my business. Most respectfully &&

Mrs Abraham Lincoln.

Many apologies for troubling you so frequently.

M L

To Jacob Bunn

———

Pau, France
March 21st, 1877

My dear Sir:

On the 21st [19th] (two days since) I wrote you, acknowledging the receipt of duplicate checque for rent dated January 3d which I returned to you, on same date—Also your letter enclosed Duplicate Pension papers, from Dec 4th to March 4th. The latter had been received by me on 12th of Dec- signed, returned, & very soon afterwards—I received the checque, from you.

I have not yet received the Pension papers of March 4th to June 4th which I feel assured you will forward me, at once. It requires so much, to live, in the plainest way, in a foreign land & as at different times, I have been here sufficiently, not to allow them, to take advantage of me, as is so frequently done, with *strangers* who do not understand their language. Happily, I am not in the latter category.

Most respectfully &&
Mrs Abraham Lincoln.

To Jacob Bunn

———

Pau, France
Basses Pyrénees
March 31st 1877

My dear Sir:

The month comes to a close to day & I have not yet received, the Pension Papers of March 4th to June 4th for signature. I cannot understand it, and I am anxious to have them, as I am in need of the money. The weather is also becoming warm & it will *soon* be necessary for me to leave town—I suggest this, by way of safety, the French are especially a *covetous* people and I would be so pleased to receive my Pension papers, for signature, *just as soon*, after *the 4th* of the months—when they become due in the U.S.A. *as possible*—On the 4th of June, for instance, *when* it will be exceedingly warm here—I should like to have the paper for signature —*as soon after*, the *latter* date as possible—Also may I request you, to send me *two separate* duplicates, the French, are a peculiar people & you will excuse me for saying to you, that I am very apprehensive that your printed name on the left hand corner, may have excited some suspicions, that money may have been enclosed within. Be assured always, that *when* your letters are received, I will immediately, as a conscientious woman, acknowledge them. Please write on a plain envelope & direct to Pau- France Basses- Pyrenees —"Poste Restante." in *two different* envelopes by *same* mail, in the event that one, *may* be lost—both for monthly rent—and also for Pension papers, for signature—send me if you please—two of the latter & also, when you send a checque for either rent or Pension papers—may I urge you to send me *two* checques for *each*—As a matter of course, as an honest person, on receipt of two checques— for each sum due me, be fully assured—the other will be *at once* returned to you. I am much disappointed, not to have received 4th of March Pension papers, for signature.

Most respectfully
Mrs Abraham Lincoln

P.S. The Hotel, where I have been stopping, closed a few days since—

M. L.

Mary Lincoln's businesslike letters to Jacob Bunn stood in sharp contrast to those she was writing young Lewis Baker. She was unfailingly gracious to the banker, but rarely touched on the personal or extraneous with him, confining herself, mostly as a courtesy one suspects, to an occasional comment on the death of a mutual friend (both were at that stage of life where contemporaries were departing in alarming succession), or to brief mention of public events in the United States.

Only in moments of great stress did she draw Lewis into her complicated financial affairs. He was the one to whom she confided her thoughts, her plans, details of her health, impressions of her surroundings. She wrote him more regularly than any other family member—and, at that, none too frequently—looked eagerly for his letters, and was concerned when too long a time elapsed between them. She shared his pleasures, disappointments, and griefs, worried over his health, and gave him motherly advice on his career, which must on no account be journalism. That would lead to a love of politics, she wrote, "anything, *but* desirable in a young man." [5] She had obviously ceased to think of her husband as the supremely gifted politician he was, or to recall her own addiction to that "unladylike profession." Politics was no more than a *"sea of trouble"* and politicians an unsavory crew who had taken advantage of her and then tossed her to the wolves.

She was anxious that Lewis broaden his horizons, urging him to visit places she herself had loved: the White Mountains, Lake George, Niagara. She even offered to finance a European trip for him—a delectable prospect, only slightly dampened by the stipulation that she must "first return to America, straiten out my bonds, and settle down." [6]

Lewis was her substitute son. She never contacted Robert, although she did send his daughter "Mamie" small gifts now and then. A letter written to Lewis in April 1877 revealed that time had, if anything, deepened her loathing for "that wretched young man, but *old* in sin." Before the insanity hearing, she would have willingly throttled anyone who dared criticize one of her children; afterward, her resentment colored the past, transforming Robert from the "good son" she had always said he was into a villain of a boy, "so different from our other sons." She even quoted Lincoln as wondering "from whence, such a mean nature came." [7] But she was human after all. In June 1879 her eye would fall on a news-

[5] Mary Lincoln to Edward Lewis Baker, Jr., Pau, France, April 11, 1877.
[6] Mary Lincoln to Edward Lewis Baker, Jr., Pau, France, June 12, 1880.
[7] Mary Lincoln to Edward Lewis Baker, Jr., Pau, France, April 11, 1877.

paper story in which Robert Todd Lincoln was mentioned as a future possibility for the presidency. Robert himself was not responsible for such speculation: he was abnormally reticent and had no particular love for politics. But he was a public-spirited citizen and a faithful Republican with a magic name. Despite Mary Lincoln's strong feelings, her maternal pride returned unbidden. Visions of a Lincoln dynasty provided moments of delicious reverie. She pictured *"Little Mamie"* skipping through White House corridors and even began speculating on Robert's Cabinet choices—the sort of thing which, she sweetly assured Lewis, "never once occurred to me to do in my good husband's time." [8]

To Edward Lewis Baker, Jr.

Pau, France
Basses Pyrénées
April 11, 1877

My dear Lewis:

About ten days since, I received your very welcome letter and I am now sending you an immediate reply. Truly, the past winter, has brought much sorrow with it, and you can well understand how fully, I have sympathized with you all, in your griefs, over the loss of those two sweet little girls. [9] We are never prepared for these things & I sometimes wonder, if *it is well*, for us *not* to anticipate them, in a measure. God, gives us our beloved ones, we make them our idols, they are removed from us, & we have patiently to await the time, when, *He*, reunites us to them. And the *waiting*, is so long! My bereavements, have been *so* intense, the most loving and devoted of husbands, torn from my side, my hand within his own, at the time—and God has recalled from this earth, sons, the most *idolising*, the noblest, purest, most talented—that were ever given to parents—Their presence grand & beautiful—too good for this

[8] Mary Lincoln to Edward Lewis Baker, Jr., Pau, France, June 22, 1879.
[9] On January 17, 1877, Annie Edwards, daughter of Mr. and Mrs. Albert Edwards, died at the age of four. Her death was followed a month later by that of Florence Edwards. Both girls were cousins of Lewis Baker and granddaughters of Mrs. Edwards. (See letter to Elizabeth Edwards, March 19, 1877.)

world, so full of sorrow—Yet the time will come, when the sever-
ance, will be over, together husband, wife & children—never more to
be separated—I grieve for those who have been called upon to give
up their precious ones, and until the sunlight of a happier clime
dawns upon us, we will never know *until then*, why, we have been
visited, by *such* sorrow. God wills it and we must bow to his irrevo-
cable decrees. Prayers, tears, are unavailing, and we are left to our
great desolation!! I am living through, a very sad time myself, this
season of the year, with its reminiscences, renders me anything, but
cheerful, I am leading a life of retirement and daily, send up my
supplications to Him, the ruler over us all, to reconcile and soften
the pathway, I have been called upon to tread within the last few
years.

I regret that I did not receive your letter, written last Nov. for
your letters, dear Lewis, could not fail to be interesting. You will
pardon me for expressing also a regret, that you, with your talents,
are not attending college. Perhaps, before the close of the *present*
year, such will be the case. Journalism, will naturally lead to a love
for politics, & I think, *that* is anything, *but* desirable in a young
man.[1] You always, find me expressing myself, very sincerely to you
on all subjects. With regard to your letter of Nov. last, without
doubt, it was properly directed—but those unpleasant failures to
receive letters, sometimes occur. I must confess that I was surprised to find, that Hayes, has placed in his Cabinet Key,[2] a man,
who served, in the Confederate Army, during the War; we have
many other men in our Country, with talents & patriotism to the
true cause, not to reward a Secessionist—Certainly, Hayes has committed a great *mistake*. How frequently, I wish I could see & converse with you all, once more, the kindnesses showered upon me in
the days, when I was so cruelly persecuted, by a bad son, on whom
I had bestowed, the greater part of my all, rankles, *still*, deeply in
my heart. It is impossible to forget, the love shown us in our days
of sorrow! That wretched young man, but *old* in sin, has a fearful

---

[1] When one considers Mrs. Lincoln's intense dislike of Lewis' father, who edi-
torialized against her in the *Illinois State Journal* during her early widowhood,
this "advice" takes on new meaning.
[2] Senator David M. Key of Tennessee had recently been appointed Postmaster
General by President Hayes. The appointment, designed to reflect Hayes' new
conciliatory policy toward the South, met with considerable opposition.

account, *yet* to render to his Maker! And God, does not allow, sin, to go unpunished. In our household, he was always trying to obtain the mastery, on all occasions—never daring of course to be insolent, to my amiable devoted children or myself, when my beloved husband, was near, it was a great relief to us all, when he was sent East to school, *then* we had a most loving peace [3]—So different from our other sons—he was always persecuting them and my husband so tender & loving—always said he never knew, from whence, such a mean nature came. Talents, are not every thing. My darling sons, were perfect in that respect & so worshipping to us both. *Distance* or time does not weaken *remembrance.*

My best love to all—Present my kindest regards to Mr Phillips [4] & Hatch when you see them. I think of you all a great deal—Write very soon, I pray you. Most affectionately your Aunt,

Mary Lincoln

Please hand this enclosed note, to your Grandfather.

M. L.

To Jacob Bunn

Pau, France
Basses Pyrénées
April 23, 1877

My dear Sir:

Your letter, enclosing 600. Fr- has been received. I regret to announce to you, that the March 4th pension paper, for Signature, has not yet reached me. I received the one in Dec- eight days after the fourth, of the *latter* month and daily enquiries are made here— at the Post Office for letters. The "Grand Hotel de la Paix," has closed and may I request you to direct to care of "Poste Restante." Also, will you please start *from* Springfield, by the 20th of May, the 4th of June, pension paper, for signature. I am very much in

---

[3] This statement should be contrasted with those in Mrs. Lincoln's letters to Hannah Shearer of August 28, [1859], and to Adeline Judd of June 13, [1860].
[4] David L. Phillips served the *Illinois State Journal* variously as editor, publisher, and co-owner from 1862 to 1878.

need of the money, from the 4th of March Pension. As I have not yet received (as I have informed you) the latter date of papers, for signature, I am sure, you will consider it best that you should be made aware of it—and if you should send the *last* mentioned paper, please send a checque for the amount with it. When you send the 4th of June papers for signature, may I request that you send a duplicate one, in the event, that one may go astray—and if you deem it proper, when you send a checque, for the 4th of March Pension please send in separate envelope, by same mail a duplicate checque, for the amount. Believe me, most respectfully.

Mrs Abraham Lincoln.

To Jacob Bunn

Pau, France
April 25, 1877

My dear Sir:

Your favor of the 5th of April was received on yesterday. As I wrote you on receipt of the Pension paper March 19th that I went at once to the Consul, who told me that neither of us, could sign it, as it was for Dec 4th instead of March 4th The former date had already been received by me. The delay of receiving the proper one, has caused some inconvenience, but if on receipt of this note you will send me one for March 4th I will be very grateful. As a matter of course, until my signature is given, no money, can be received upon the paper—Please send me duplicate papers, in separate envelopes for June 4th Pension paper.

Most respectfully
Mrs Abraham Lincoln

To Delia Dubois [5]

Pau, France
April 28, 1877

My dear Delia:

Your letter of the 4th of April, was received two days since. I have searched in vain, for lace suitable for your dress, there are only two lace stores here in the winter, and at the close of the season, they return to Paris. After careful enquiry, I have ascertained that one store was closed on the 12th of this month & the other on the 20th—

You can scarcely imagine my disappointment, it would have been such a pleasure [for] me, to have been able to procure the lace, *especially* for the occasion of which you wrote. You have been such an indefatigable student & I feel well assured, will have such a triumphant success at your examination.

Your mother has been owing me a letter for a long time, and I hope ere long, will write me. Please present her my best love— also remember me most kindly to Mr Hatch—

Believe me, very truly your friend,

Mary Lincoln.

To Jacob Bunn

Pau, France
May 18, 1877

My dear Sir:

Your letter enclosing checque for rent as well as the Pension Certificate for signature of *March 4th* has just been received. I enclose it to you signed, and presume by *this date* in June, I shall receive from you the amount. It is becoming exceedingly warm

---

[5] Daughter of Mr. and Mrs. Jesse K. Dubois.

here and when I receive money from the 4th March Pension, 4th of June and the gold interest on my [$]60,000 bonds, which will be $1800 in gold—will feel disposed to wander away, *for a time* from this place. Yet, I shall remain here six weeks longer until I receive the remittances from these three named resources—& my rent. Please send *as soon* as possible the 4th of June Pension paper for signature—also—the 1st of July, send the interest on my bonds— Please direct in all cases—*to this* place Pau—I assure you, that I have received *no* 4th of March Pension paper for signature, only the duplicate one of Dec 4 which you sent me on the 2nd of March. For fear of delay, or papers going astray, I think you will find my plan a good one when you send a Pension Certificate, to enclose another one in a separate envelope & send—I trust the 4th of June Pen paper will arrive just as soon after the *latter* date—as possible —This country has become fearfully expensive. Please address your letters to *Pau*. I regret to learn of the death of Mr [James H.] Matheny—With kind regards to your family, I remain very respectfully,

Mrs A. Lincoln.

To Edward Lewis Baker, Jr.

Pau, France
May 20, 1877

My dear Lewis:

Three days since I received *at last*—a Pension paper, for *March 4th* for signature from Mr Bunn—and it is the *only one* I have received for THAT DATE. *The one of date* Dec 4th which he sent me, March 2d I enclosed to your Grandfather. Within *this* letter I place, Mr Bunn's last—*he persists* in believing, notwithstanding my frequent assurances that I *have not* received other Pension papers from him, this is certainly very incorrect, as I have been & *am still*, very badly in want of the money, from the Quarterly Pension of March 4th. However the one he sent me *May 2nd* (*think of it!* has arrived and I write to you, dear Lewis, to request you *so soon* as you receive this letter—to see Mr Bunn and tell him that 3 days since the Pension paper he sent me, May 2nd has been signed by the Consul, witness & myself and I mailed it *myself*. —*Private*—If he had sent me a Pension paper, for March 4th I would have received it and I *do* trust I shall have a checque from him without the *least* delay. The Pension paper, just received by me from Mr B- had *not* a mark or *star where names* should be placed and it annoyed the Consul so much, that at first he said, he could not have any thing to do—with a paper, so sent, without any instructions. I managed to persuade him that *he* must sign it, which he did—so I trust this difficulty is ended—perhaps he, Mr B., will say, he has not received it—regarding the Pension business—Mr Bunn is acting very strangely. Get your grandfather, to read the last part of the enclosed note of Mr Bunn and I very much fear, that *he* (Mr B) is going to give me the same trouble for *June 4th*. Will you please say to Mr Bunn, that I received but *one* Pension paper for *March 4th* and that was *three* days since—therefore I have no Pension papers from him, on which I can place my name, for June 4th so he must at *once* send me a Pension paper of the *latter* date for signature—This delay & annoyance is insupportable —my hair is fast becoming grey, with *this* conduct, about the 4th of March Pension paper. Also, please say to him, *when* he sends a Pension paper for signature, if he will be so kind, as to mark, *where* names shall be placed. Just read the last two or three sentences of his note, which I here enclose you, & if you can make out any *sense* in it, it is more than I can do—As to *mislaying* any paper, he would send me, that would be very [un]likely, I am only too much in need of the money—to do so. Please request your Grandfather to see him also—And in the event any pension paper which he sends me, should go astray—he could *so easily* send two, for signature, in different envelopes—of course only *one* would be used. If *he had* sent me, any other, save the *one*—I sent your grandfather to see, in a *March 2nd* letter from Mr B- I should have received it—Just to think Lewis, that two months & half, since the March 4th Pensions, have been given, I have *not yet* received mine—There can be no excuse, however, now, for the paper for March 4th—which I received 3 days since, has been *signed* & *resent him*—About the little rent coming to me each month, Mr B- has been so kind in forwarding it to me—But if I *had* had the strength to work, I could have earned the money, *long since*, from *this* 4th of March Pension—Yet, even now, I *have not*, received the proceeds from it!

I wrote you a long letter, four weeks since—Not a line have I received from your Grandmother since April 1st. You must all write me.

Your very affectionate Aunt—
Mary Lincoln

To Jacob Bunn

May 22 1877.

My dear Sir

The Pension paper is received to day, for March 4th until June 4th 1877. We have signed it & I am going to mail it myself *within the hour—*

Very respectfully &&
Mrs Abraham Lincoln

To Jacob Bunn

Pau, France
June 5th 1877

My dear Sir:

Your favor of the 17th of May, is just received. In the letter, you enclose a [duplicate?] Pension paper to be signed for [March 4th to] June 4th. I will go at once to the Consul, for his signature & send it to you, by this evening's mail—

I have received your two letters of 3 & 4—of May, enclosing Pension papers from *Dec 4th to March 4th. Both* of these papers were immediately signed by the Consul, witness & myself and I

mailed them myself—without the *least* doubt, you have received
both of these signed papers by this time, as it has almost been
three weeks—since they were *resent* to you, with signatures—And I
do trust that *by the time* you receive *this letter*, I shall have a
checque for *the 4th of March* Pension *now* due me, three months.
I am greatly in need of it—also—please send me the proceeds of the
4th of June Pension—when this Pension paper is received by you,
which will certainly *be* in a little over two weeks. *Two Pensions* are
now due me—that of March 4th & June 4th I trust such a delay,
will not occur again. I shall anxiously await my *two* Pension remittances. I go at once to the Consul & shall mail this paper myself. I
presume you consider the paper to be signed to day for June 4th
as I have mentioned, two other papers were signed near 3 weeks
since & sent you for March *4th*—

Very resp—

Mrs A. Lincoln

To Jacob Bunn

Pau, France
June 6th, 1877

My dear Sir:

On yesterday, I received your letter of May 17th with Pension
paper for Signature dated from March 4th to June 4th I went at
once to the Consul, who signed it & I mailed it myself—This is the
3d Pension paper, within the last 3 weeks, we have signed & sent
you. I am now daily hoping that the 4th of June [to 4th of Septem-
ber] Pension paper for signature will be received by me. They are
very punctual here at the Office, when any letter arrives for me and
I feel assured that the 4th of June Pension is now on the way. It is
unpleasant for me to repeat, that I am now needing very greatly the
proceeds of March 4th Pension & June 4th Pension.

Believe me, very respectfully,

Mrs Abraham Lincoln

To Jacob Bunn

[*Pau, France*]
[*June 6, 1877*] [6]

The Consul, understands that this paper is for Pension paper from March 4—to June 4th. This is the 3d paper for March 4th to June 4th Pension—that has *now* been signed & sent you for *that date*— I hope a checque for the amount, has already been sent, as it has been now, almost three weeks, since the signed papers were sent you. *Now, two* Quarterly pensions are due me—I hope the Pension papers, for June 4th to Sept 4th will be received in a day or two. I assure you, I need my Pension remittances greatly. I write this, at the Office of the Consul & mail it at once. Please send me without any delay, my remittances, for the *two* quarterly pensions.

Very respectfully,
Mrs A. Lincoln

To Jacob Bunn

Pau, France
June 13, 1877

My dear Sir:

I have just returned from the Post Office & feel much disappointment that I have not yet received the 4th of June, Pension paper, for signature. There are now two pensions [payments] due me, that of March 4th & June 4th. The proceeds I am needing *very greatly*, and as I have sent you 3 Pension papers signed within the last four weeks, wanting *two* days, I can but hope that but a *very few days* will elapse, *ere* I receive my money from the Pensions, *one* of them *now* due me, so long. I observe that gold is again on

---

[6] The date appears on the face of the original letter in brackets. This covering note was hastily written on two sheets of paper obtained in the consul's office.

the decline, as the last quotation from New York marks it 105⅛ that of June 9th received here—Also the last papers mention, that the Illinois Legislature, did not adjourn until the 24th of May. Ours, has become a great State in the Union, once so far West, now so Central. I am pleased that Fannie Wallace, was so fortunate as to obtain the situation of Post Mistress, the past winter. I am waiting, most anxiously for checques, from my two Pensions, due me, and between the need of the *latter*, and the excessive heat, it is a *most serious endurance*, believe me.

I shall be compelled to draw the 1st day of July, *the day* for the drawing, my interest on my [$]60,000 bonds, amounting in gold to $1800—which with 20 pounds, on each hundred in gold, will make 500 Francs on each hundred in gold—this is invariable —and I shall have to draw it on the 1st of July. Therefore I write you in advance, so that you will have *more than time*, before the last mentioned date to receive this letter. On yesterday, I received a letter 16 days from Springfield and this letter, gives you 17 days & half, as I go immediately to mail it myself. Of course after this announcement my interest of $1800 will rest, until I draw on the 1st of July. It is absolutely necessary, that I have without delay my Pension money, when it becomes due.

I remain, very respectfully,
Mrs A Lincoln

Please direct to Pau—On the 1st of July, I will draw from *this* place Pau the $1800- in gold—which will be 500- francs, on each hundred of gold dollars—In the meantime beyond question, I shall receive checques, in return for Pension papers, returned—signed— within the last four weeks, to you.

Very resp-
Mrs L.

To Jacob Bunn

Pau, France
June 20, 1877

My dear Sir:

Your letter of the 2d of June, containing a checque for rent, has been received today. Two days hence will be *five* weeks since I returned you, *signed*, a Pension paper for 4th of March pension. Also two days after sending you the paper, you enclosed me May 2d I returned you another Pension paper signed for March 4th. Consequently, I am daily & hourly, in expectation, of receiving a checque, for my Pension, of March 4th of which I am in such great need. On the 5th of June, I received from you the Pension paper of June 4th for signature, which as you mention in your letter of June 2d you sent on May 17th. On the same day of the receipt of the June 4th Pension paper (June 5th) I went immediately, to the office of the Consul—to have signatures—and on the *same* day, mailed it to you, myself, and I feel assured that by *this* time you have also received the *latter*, as it was two weeks on yesterday, since it was sent. Two Pensions of $750. each, *are now* due me, and I am in constant expectation of receiving checques from *them*. I wrote you a week since, that on the 1st of July I would draw on you, for my $1800 in gold, being the interest, semi-yearly, on my [$]60,000 bonds. There being 20 pounds on each hundred dollars in gold, there will come to me 500 francs, on each hundred dollars in gold. I will draw on you, July 2 from *this* place, Pau. I trust there will be no *further* disappointment, in receiving checques for my 2 Quarterly Pensions *now* due me of March 4th & June 4th. I am pleased to see by the daily, American quotations, that gold, is having such a downward tendency.

I remain very respectfully,
Mrs. A. Lincoln

To Jacob Bunn

Pau, France
June [2]6th, 1877 [7]

Your letter of the 6th of June, with enclosure of checque for 3550 Francs, is just received. The payment is for the 4th of March Pension. The checque for 4th of June Pension, now due me, I hope to receive in a day or two—as the Pension papers for 4th of June were sent you signed, by the Consul, a young man in his office & myself, June 5th. There will certainly be no trouble in consequence about the Pension paper of June 4th with three witnesses—of course the Consul included as one of them. As I wish to leave town at once—I hope to have immediately a checque, for this 4th of June Pension.

I will draw on the 2*d* of July, Monday, from the Consul, who is also a Banker, the $1800 in gold, the interest on my $60,000-Bonds, semi annually—which will be on each hundred in gold,—500 Francs. I notified you, now nearly 2 weeks since, that I would draw on the 1st from *this* place—Pau—the amount. I am anxious to get into the country amongst the mountains—but on the *17th* of *each month* will return to town (Pau) for my mail—as my rent money arrives as always about that time, so please send as usual directed to Pau, France as I shall not fail to return to Pau, each 17th of month—for my letters.

I remain very respectfully,

Mrs A. Lincoln

To Jacob Bunn

Pau, France
June 27, 1877

My dear Sir:

Two days since I wrote you, acknowledging the receipt of a checque for Pension due, March 4th. After mailing the letter I

[7] Misdated by Mrs. Lincoln.

went to the Consul, who told me that the Pension paper sent you
June 5th for June 4th Pension, was as well signed, as any that had
been issued from his Office—I shall hope in a few days to receive
a checque from you, for the 4th of June Pension. May I request you
to place, "Poste Restante," on your envelope. The Consul informs
me, of what I already knew, that in regard to the $1800. in gold
which is my semi annual interest on Bonds—there are 20 Pounds—
on each hundred dollars also 500. Francs on each hundred dollars
—but he says, I shall have to pay you some Francs in *the exchange*,
as I wish to pay no interest, at any time whatever, please deduct,
any exchange from the 1st of August rent, when you send it to me.
It can be but very little. Each day henceforward, for the next week,
I shall expect my checque on the 4th of June Pension. It has been
two weeks to day, since I wrote you, that I would draw from this
place (Pau), the 1st of July—interest—twice since, I have mentioned it to you. I shall return to town on *the* 18th of July & 18th
August, to remain until the 22d of each month,—shall remain four
days in town—to get my letters—then return to my quiet sojourn
in the mountains—but before I leave—which will be in a week—
shall expect to receive checque for 4th of June Pension—I write under difficulties, as my right hand is bound up. I am very anxious to
get to the country. I remain, most respectfully.

Mrs A. Lincoln

From the 18th to the end of each month will be in town. Please
direct to Pau, France. "Poste Restante."

To Jacob Bunn

Pau, France
July 2d, 1877

My dear Sir:

    I drew from the Bank of Mr Clay, of this place, *to day* the sum
of nine thousand Francs £360- Pounds, being exactly the sum of
$1800 in gold the amount of my semi-annual interest on my $60,-
000 Bonds—due July 1st. There will of course be some Francs, in

exchange, which please deduct from my 1st of August rent, as I wish to have no interest to pay, at any time—Two days hence, will be three weeks since I notified you, that it would be necessary for me to draw this interest on the 2d of July, which letter and a subsequent one, you doubtless have received. *Four* weeks tomorrow since I sent you 4th of June, Pension paper signed, and I am daily in expectation of receiving the checque, from the 4th of June pension. On receipt of it, I shall go into the country but will *always* return to town (Pau) on the 18th of each month, to remain three or four days, for my letters. Please direct to Pau, as usual. I hope I shall not have to wait longer, than a day or two, for the checque for June 4th Pension. I am suffering so much from a disabled hand, that I fear you will scarcely be able to decipher this letter.

I remain, most respectfully,

Mrs Abraham Lincoln

To Jacob Bunn

Pau, France
July 9, 1877

My dear Sir:

Your letter of the 21st of June, is just received, containing Pension paper and enclosure of 4000 Francs—I regret that you have sent the latter, however it can very easily be arranged. *When* you receive the Pension paper, which I shall return you to *day* more properly signed, with witnesses && before the Consul— please retain the money, which the 4th of June Pension gives which I suppose will be the same amount 3550. Fr & deduct *from* 1st of August rent, the *remainder* of the amount, which will be 450. Francs—This will make the payment for the 4000 Fr received *to day* from you. As I wrote you several weeks since, that I would draw from this place (Pau) July 1st the $1800 in gold making 9000 Francs. On the 2d of July, I drew the amount from Mr Clay, & of course the notice was immediately forwarded you—Also please deduct any exchange that *may* arise from the transaction, from the 1st of August rent. Several times, I wrote you, that I would draw, the 1st of July, therefore I feel assured you will not remit the 1st of July interest on my bonds *now*, as I have drawn it. Retain, as I have mentioned, the 3550. Francs, of 4th of June Pension payment & deduct 450 Fr from 1st of Aug. rent—It appears to me the easiest way, to settle for the 4000 Francs, you have so kindly forwarded me the 21st of June—You will certainly not send me any money on July bond interest, as I have already drawn it—I can scarcely write with a suffering hand—Please direct to Pau.

Most respectfully.

Mrs Lincoln

To Jacob Bunn

Pau. July 9th [10] [1877]

Hon Jacob Bunn:

On yesterday, I returned you the Pension paper, for June 4th signed & witnessed by two persons, beside the Consul & myself. This time, I am sure you will find the paper correct. Please retain the amount 3550 Fr. from the 4th of June pension, in payment for the 4000 Francs, you sent me June 21st also take 450 Francs, from the August rent—to make the amount of 4000. Francs. complete, which you so kindly advanced me—

Very respectfully.
Mrs Abraham Lincoln.

Please pardon this hastily written note.

To Jacob Bunn

Pau, France
July 20th 1877

My dear Sir:

Your letter of July 3d has been received this morning, containing checque for rent. I am very grateful to you, for your management of my little business & as a matter of course, whatever expenses may arise, from the necessity of your going to Chicago or otherwise, I am most willing to pay them. I regret very much that you should have been annoyed, about the Pension papers not having been properly signed but in the future, I feel assured, it will be very different—Please indicate *every place where* signatures should be written, I am sure that all difficulties, regarding the papers are at an end. Neither the English Consul here, or myself were acquainted with the business. The little delay regarding the arrival of the money has passed & I trust you will excuse our stupidity. Only mark *each place*, if you please. I wrote you regarding the necessity of having to draw the $1800 in gold from this place July 2d. Soon after you wrote your letter of July 3d you must have received the notification I sent you, I received your checque for 4000. Francs which you sent July 21st to be deducted from 1st July interest—I did not receive the letter, until several days after I drew the 9000. Francs. Please retain the 4th of June Pension money, and deduct 450. Francs from August rent—also the $20- in gold from the last mentioned month, for your payment—as well as any other exchange that is necessary, as your payment for the 4000 Fr && It appears to me that this arrangement, will settle the business. Believe me always very grateful, for your kind attention to my affairs. Please present my kindest regards to your family. The death of our amiable friend, Mrs T Campbell, is very sad.[8] I remain, most respectfully,

Mrs A. Lincoln

To Jacob Bunn

Pau, France
August 6th, 1877

My dear Sir:

Doubtless, about the 20th of July, you received the Pension paper of June 4th resent to you properly signed by the Consul, two

---

[8] Mrs. Tom Campbell was the former Ann Todd of Columbia, Missouri, the cousin referred to so frequently in the first letter in this volume.

witnesses & myself. Please retain the 4th of June Pension money (3550 Francs add to it 450. Francs, deducted from 1st Aug rent— also deduct expenses to Chicago && from rent as payment for the 4000. Francs, you kindly advanced me June 21st. I feel assured that this plan of returning you the 4000. Fr with other expenses *just* mentioned, will meet with your approbation. I see no other way of settling it.

On the 5th of June I received the Pension paper of June 4th [to September 4th] for signature. Please send me the 4th of September [to 4th of December] Pension paper, so that I may receive it also by the 5th of Sept. Particular care will be taken to have it accurately signed. May I request you to indicate by a star, *each* place where signatures should be written, *otherwise* mistakes might again occur. Experience will teach us to avoid them, if the places are indicated by a star—when the paper is sent. I trust the railroad troubles, in our Country, have ceased.[9] They must have created quite an agitation.

Believe me, most respectfully,

Mrs Abraham Lincoln.

Please direct to this place, Pau, France.

M. L.

To Jacob Bunn

Pau, France

August 22 1877

My dear Sir

On my return from the mountains on yesterday, I received your letter, enclosing Pension paper for Sept 4th also checque for rent, for August. We have now settled for the July interest, it is a pleasure to have every thing made straight. This morning, I had the

[9] A reference to a milestone in the American labor movement, the "Great Railroad Strike of '77." The walkout was the response of the unorganized railroad employees to a wage cut by four lines and resulted in ferocious battles between militia and mobs. Federal troops were eventually called in to quell the unrest.

checque of 4000. Francs cashed at a Bank, in this place. The one you sent me, June 21st. All that business is settled. I regret that the Pension paper just received for September, has not the places marked where names should be signed. I can but hope that when you receive this, you will send me another paper with *each* place indicated. I am very grateful to you for your patience—

I have not only my own dullness to contend with, but that of the English Consul. You mention in your letter that the Pensions are paid now in Chicago. This appears to me strange as I should suppose that the Pensioner's list in Springfield & county was quite sufficient to justify a Pension Office. This change must have been very recently made, I have been away so much in the country, that I see so few papers. When I look over one, there is immediately the death of some pleasant acquaintance. This morning, in a New York paper of Aug 8th I read the announcement of Mr Wm B. Ogden's,[1] death. In former times, a very prominent citizen of Illinois. With apologies for so long a letter, I, remain, most respectfully,

Mrs Abraham Lincoln—

To Jacob Bunn

September 5, 1877
Pau, France

My dear Sir:

I enclose you the Pension certificate for Sept 4th signed. This time, I am sure you will find it correct. Please direct to Pau. On close examination, I found the places for signature marked. I remain

most respectfully,
Mrs Abraham Lincoln

---

[1] Ogden, the first mayor of Chicago, subsequently a financier and railroad baron, died on August 3, 1877.

To Jacob Bunn

Pau, France
September 20, 1877

My dear Sir:

Your letter containing checque, was received this morning. The Pension papers for Sept 4th were sent you September 5th. I feel assured that you will find them *this* time, very correctly signed. We are becoming a little more experienced in the business. With many thanks for your kind attention to my little *business*, believe me, most respectfully,

Mrs Abraham Lincoln

Please direct to Pau—as usual.

M. L.

To Jacob Bunn

[INCOMPLETE]   *October 1st 1877*
                               Pau, France

My dear Sir:

Your letter of 10th Sept containing Pension paper for Sept 4th was received this morning. On closer examination as I wrote you, I found the places indicated on the first one you sent me, therefore the Consul witnesses & myself signed it & enclosed it to you September 5th. I feel assured, that you will find it properly signed.

To Jacob Bunn

Pau, France
October 16, 1877

My dear Sir:

Your letter of September 25th, enclosing Pension checque, has been received. I wrote you two weeks since that the Consul declined signing the second Pension certificate you sent me, assigning as a reason, that the paper sent you on the 5th of September, was signed & properly witnessed. However as you have collected the money & sent it to me on the 4th of Sept. Pension, perhaps it will be unnecessary, to sign the last paper you have just sent me. I should have to go to Bordeaux, to the Consul there. It is a little unfortunate that we have no American Consul here. Mr Musgrave Clay, is a brusque Englishman, unpopular with every nationality here, but I am impressed with the belief that he has very little Sympathy, with *our* Government. A few years since, the American Consul died here, since which time Mr Clay, has been officiating in that capacity. But as this place, is more the resort of the English, than the Americans, his work in behalf of our countrymen, is very light. I suppose there will be no more necessity to approach him regarding the 4th of Sept. Pension paper, as you have already sent me a checque for it.

Believe me, most respectfully,

Mrs Abraham Lincoln

To Jacob Bunn

Pau, France
Oct. 24, 1877

My dear Sir:

Your letter with enclosure of checque, was received to day. Please send me the Pension paper, for 4th of December, for signature, by the 5th of December as on the 6th of the *latter* month, I will be leaving here, to go further South. I will always notify you, three weeks in advance, where a letter will find me.

Believe me,

very respectfully,
Mrs Abraham Lincoln

While abroad, Mrs. Lincoln lived in terror of being caught short of funds. She was loath to pay Illinois expenses out of money already forwarded her and continually urged Bunn to deduct such expenses from her income checks *before* they were forwarded. By going to elaborate lengths to avoid relinquishing a cent of what she had in hand, she sometimes succeeded in making things difficult for herself. She was adept at creating complications where none existed.

The episode of the trunk was a case in point. In the autumn of 1877 Mrs. Lincoln purchased several hundred dollars' worth of woolen garments for her sister Frances Wallace, who had suffered financial difficulties in later life. Fearful that she might be cheated, or that clerical incompetence would cause the trunk to go astray, she determined to "superintend" its shipment herself and traveled all the way to Paris for the purpose. She paid for its passage as far as New York, unwilling to lay out the full amount required to get it to Springfield: this could be paid out of home funds. But when "Fannie" had not received the trunk by mid-December, she began to fear that it was lost—her "superintendance" had not included insuring it.

Late in January 1878 she received word that the trunk had arrived and was being detained in the New York Customs House, awaiting payment of duty. In characteristically roundabout fashion, she contacted Rufus F. Andrews, that old friend of White House days, asking him to pay the duty and submit a bill to Bunn for reimbursement—anything but pay it herself. Andrews, knowing her habits too well to take chances, confined himself to securing an appraisal of the amount of duty required—$55.45—and promptly "disappeared." Mrs. Lincoln was furious at the "unpleasant light" in which his actions had placed her, but she should have known better than to rely on Andrews, playing on memories of those "*halcyon*" days when he had needed her friendship; he had washed his hands of her long ago. Eventually the duty was paid, and in March, four months after the woolens had been dispatched, they arrived in Springfield along with warm weather.

To Jacob Bunn

Paris, France
Nov 7th 1877

My dear Sir:

I find myself very unexpectedly here, in consequence of having a trunk of woolen articles to be sent to my sister, Mrs Wallace, and find that I must superintend myself regarding it, so that she may soon receive it—The trunk is paid for as far as New York— Any expenses that may *afterwards* arise upon it—please settle out of November rent due, 1st December. The remainder please forward to Pau, France—I am leaving for the latter place tomorrow. I had contemplated going further South, early in December, I have now concluded to remain at Pau, until the 22nd of January next.

I remain, most respectfully
Mrs Abraham Lincoln

To Jacob Bunn

Pau, France
Nov 16, 1877

My dear Sir:

Your letter containing checque for October rent, due Nov 1st was received this morning. I have received as yet no Pension paper, for signature for Dec 4th. I have carefully looked over the two Pension papers, I have for signature—one of the date of the 4th of last *June*—to *Sept* and the other is from 4th of Sept *to* 4th of Dec—of course I cannot NOW use *either* of these. Please send me one for signature for *4th of Dec*. I wish to leave this mountainous region, about the 20th of January. The cold is already beginning to be quite penetrating, so different from last winter—

Please accept my assurances of gratitude for your kind attention to my affairs.

Believe me Most respectfully,

Mrs Abraham Lincoln

To Jacob Bunn

Pau, France
December 8, 1877

My dear Sir:

I have been expecting for the last few days, to receive my Pension paper, for 4th of Dec. for signature. It is now the 8th of Dec. & I have not yet received it, much to my disappointment. I wrote you now, more than three weeks since, that I had an unsigned Pension paper for June 4th and one for Sept 4th 1877 *both* with *dates* plainly written upon them. Therefore, I could not venture to approach the Consul, with these, requesting his signature. I do trust, that I shall *soon* receive the proper one, for December 4th 1877— for signature—I feel assured that you will *at once* send it to me. Also, the Dec. rent due the 1st of January, please send me *here* to Pau—as well as the interest on my [$]60,000-Bonds which is 9000-(nine thousand) in francs. As a matter of course, if it is necessary, for you to go to Chicago, on account of collecting the interest therefrom, please deduct your expenses. I hope, I will receive this sum by the 20*th* of *January* as a lady friend & myself expect to leave here at that time together—and she remains here until that date—the 20th—on my account.

By the time this letter is received, perhaps another year, may have almost come to a close. Please present my regards & the best wishes of the season to your family, who are so pleasantly remembered by me.

Most respectfully,
Mrs Abraham Lincoln

To Jacob Bunn

Pau, France
December 10, 1877

My dear Sir:

Two days since I wrote & mailed you a letter, regarding the Pension paper. This morning, I received your letter of the 21st of November, enclosing the Pension paper, for December 4th for signature. I have just returned from the Office of the Consul, with the paper, signed in every place. It arrives in very good time, for Signature, as it will doubtless reach you & the checque be received by me, about the 18th or 20th of January. *As at that time*, I contemplate leaving here for three or four months. I am always grateful to you for your kind attention to my little business.

Most respectfully,
Mrs Abraham Lincoln

To Jacob Bunn

Pau, France
Dec 19, 1877

My dear Sir:

Your letter containing checque for rent, of date of Dec 3d has been received to day. On the 10th of this month, I sent you the Pension paper, which I received on the latter date, signed, for Dec 4th. Your letter which enclosed the Pension paper for signature was dated Nov 21st. Ere this reaches you, you will doubtless have received it. You speak in your letter received to day, of a Pension paper you were again enclosing for me, which I did not find in the letter. However, as a paper is already, en route to you, signed for Dec 4th it does not matter. You are so very kind, that I often feel that I am giving you a great deal of trouble. I am very grateful to you. To day's mail, brings me a letter from Fannie Wallace, who mentions that they are *not* in receipt of the trunk, which I placed in the hands of an agent in Paris Nov 7th to be immediately forwarded. The[y] have giving [sic] me *three* receipts for it, as far as New York—for which I paid them. One I retain, one I enclosed in a letter to Hon Rufus F. Andrews, N.Y. another I placed in a letter to Mr Phillips of the Journal Office. I can but hope, the trunk will not be lost. Will you speak to Mr Phillips regarding it—The contents were inexpensive, yet very choice & comfortable for the winter. I will destroy the Pension papers of June 4th and Sept 4th.

Very respectfully,
Mrs Abraham Lincoln

P. S. I will not write to the house in Paris, regarding the trunk, until I hear again from Springfield, this letter I fear you will find, incoherent, as some persons are conversing around me.

M. L.

Unfortunately I did not insure the trunk—

To Jacob Bunn

Pau, France
January 15, 1878

My dear Sir:

Your letter with enclosure of a checque for December Pension, was received today. Also there was enclosed a Pension Paper for signature for March 4, 1878—I shall place the latter away very carefully, until the necessary time for signature. As to the others you mention, they are already destroyed. It is a bitter cold winter here & in a few days, I am leaving with a lady friend for Naples. The rent of the 1st of February, please direct to me at Naples care of W. J. Turner & Cie.

Bança Napolitana
Naples, Italy.

It is a banking establishment; named on the letter of Credit, you so kindly furnished me with. It is unnecessary for me again to assure you of my continued gratitude.

Very respectfully
Mrs Abraham Lincoln

To Jacob Bunn

Pau, France
January 24, 1878

My dear Sir:

Your letter of the 7th of January was received this morning. Most truly, do I sympathise with you & your amiable, kind hearted family, in this unexpected trouble.[2] Afflictions are very terrible, whatever form they may assume & of late years mine have been so overwhelming, that they have left me a very broken hearted woman—I received from New York, a checque for the January interest, a cheque for December 4th Pension, also a checque for rent of Dec. due Jan 1st 1878—Allow me to thank you for your kindness in going up to Chicago, to collect money on interest. Your kind attention to my business, as well as your great promptitude, is most gratefully remembered by me. Please present, my affectionate regards to your family—

I wrote you to send the rent due 1st of February, to Naples. I have concluded to remain here a few weeks longer. The winter

---

[2] On January 1, 1878, Bunn's bank became a casualty of the long depression that followed the panic of 1873. The bank failed with liabilities of $800,000, nearly all of which was eventually paid off by Bunn's heirs.

has been extremely cold & disagreeable and even extends to Italy
—I will write to the Banker at Naples—to return the letter to Pau.
On the 5th of March—I will send you the Pension paper—signed,
obeying the instructions you have given me. In the meantime,
early in February, I will write you from Pau, as to *where* I will
be, the middle of March—to receive from you the rent due 1st
March. Please make these collections *just* mentioned for me.

   Believe me, most respectfully,

Mrs Abraham Lincoln

To Jacob Bunn

Pau, France
Jan. 26, 1878

My dear Sir:

   Two days since I wrote you, in reply to your letter of the 7th
of January. In the letter I requested you to continue sending me
the rent money each month, also I mentioned that when the time
arrived March 5th for signing the Pension paper of the latter
date, I would send it to you for collection. The letter you will
receive doubtless, a little in advance of this communication. I
write to day in reference to the trunk which has been *so long*
detained. The agent from Paris sent me on yesterday a *copy* of a
letter he had just *received* from New York regarding it. Through
an inadvertence I presume, the copy he sent me had no signature
—but in reading it, you will readily perceive it comes from the
New York Custom House—where it has been detained. I have
written Mr R. F. Andrews myself *three* times, concerning it and
have never received a reply. In the *halcyon* days, amongst the first
appointments my noble & good husband made—was that of Mr
Andrews to one of the most lucrative places in New York. In each
of my letters to Mr Andrews, I have *enjoined* upon him that the
Customs duties, should be forwarded to you, certainly expecting
there would be such upon the trunk. Instead of paying them &

sending the bill to you, for reimbursement, *he* has placed me in a very unpleasant light—I am the last person, who would wish to defraud our Government, which has certainly treated me very kindly in allowing me a Pension. I love my country & its institutions dearly and could not ever rest in France as I am now doing temporarily, *without* it was a Republic—

As a matter of course, Mr Andrews must *have* ~~not~~ known, that the payment he made on the charges of the C. H. would be *at once* refunded. In the days of sorrow & adversity, the changes of time & circumstance are painful lessons, we are taught. If you have a friend in New York on whom you can rely, who will *go* to Mr Andrews & see him—*without writing* to him but of course the trunk is in the Custom House. Will you please deduct the expenses from the next month's rent—and have Mrs Wallace in possession of her trunk—I shall be very grateful to you, I assure you. I now send you a copy of the New York letter.

> *New York*
> *12th January, 1878*

> When the trunk "F. J. W." arrived, we notified Mr Andrews who called on us, in relation to it. He being a gentleman of some influence, procured an appraisement of the articles, without the formalities of the owners affidavits and supposed that they would be passed duty free, but instead of this, they were declared dutiable, duty being $55.45 cts. in gold. In view of the above facts you can readily understand we did not feel disposed to pay this duty, without consulting Mr Andrews and therefore notified him of the actions taken by C. H. Officials and asked for his instructions. Up to present writing, he has not replied to our letters, although we have written to him, *three* times. This is the way the matter stands at present——"

— — — — —

As I have written there was no signature. Please let no one *write* Mr Andrews—only have someone see him—On reflection, I think this copied letter may have come from their house on Broadway, New York, No. 72. Baldwin, Bros & Co—If they can be seen or written to—Please address me Pau, France.

> Very Respectfully,
> Mrs Abraham Lincoln

To Jacob Bunn

Pau, France
February 12, 1878

My dear Sir:

I took the liberty two weeks since to enclose you a copy of a letter received from the agents at Paris, Messieurs Sherbette Thane & Co- *from* their correspondents in New York—Baldwin Bros & Co—72 Broadway—which was sent me unsigned. As a matter of course, it was relative to the missing trunk. I wrote to the agents at Paris, to send me a copy of the letter *signed*—I now send you their reply, also the original letter from 72- Broadway N.Y. The appraisement of the simple & inexpensive articles contained in the trunk is simply wonderful. I certainly never expended more than four hundred dollars of our money—in purchase of the articles. I am quite willing to pay the $55.45 cts in gold, (fifty five dollars and 40 cts) to get the trunk out of the Custom House. I cannot understand Mr Phillips action in the case as I wrote him—sending receipts and told him, that you would meet the charges. It is very painful to be misunderstood. Please, when you send me rent, due March 1st direct to Pau, France and if you will place "Poste Restante," upon the envelope, I will *more surely* receive letters. Today is the anniversary of my beloved husband's birthday!!

I remain, very respectfully,
Mrs. Abraham Lincoln

P. S. Please send the *two* enclosed letters, one from Paris agent & the other from Baldwin Bros & Co- to Lewis Baker—at "Journal Office," to show his Grandmother.

M. L.

To Jacob Bunn

February 26, 1878

Mr Bunn:

Most earnestly I request you to retain my Bonds, papers &&
in your possession, knowing well, that in your honorable hands,
they are entirely safe. Also, oblige me, by attending to my business as usual.[3]

> Most respectfully,
> Mrs Abraham Lincoln

To Jacob Bunn

Pau, France
February 26, 1878

My dear Sir:

Your letter of the 4th of Feb is just received. A few days
after you wrote me the *latter* letter, I feel sure you must have
received the two letters I wrote you, in reply to yours of the 7th
of January requesting you to continue your attention to my business for it is *very* painful for me to receive my remittances from
any other party. The letter from Morton Bliss & Co. containing
checque for rent, due Feb 1st has not yet been received, but will
doubtless be here, very soon. I *entreat you*, in the future, to send
my remittances *yourself*, take charge of my business & I will
endeavour to give you as little trouble as possible. Retain my
Bonds & my papers, for in your honourable hands, I feel well assured, they are perfectly safe. Will you please respect my wishes
in regard to this dear Mr Bunn—for I wish to feel *at rest*, regard-

---

[3] According to the letter which follows, Mrs. Lincoln wrote out this statement at
Bunn's request, as a formal expression of her continued confidence in him, despite
his recent difficulties.

ing these matters. On the 5th of March, I will sign the Pension papers you so kindly forwarded me & send it to you. In your hands alone, I wish the Pension business *also*. As the friend of my beloved husband, who respected you so highly continue your attention to my affairs. If when I first heard of your business trouble I may have expressed fright respecting my Bonds, lest creditors might have *the power* to seize on any funds in your possession—it arose you may well believe—from no want of *implicit* faith, in *you* but simply from ignorance—if I had *four* times, as much as I now have, most willingly would I place it in your hands for safe keeping. I can but believe, that you will adhere to the offer, you made me in your letter of the 7th of January—to continue my business. Allow no one but yourself to send me Pension papers, remittances for rent & retain my Bonds yourself. I feel that I can say no more to day. Believe me most grateful to you for the past. With many kind remembrances to your family, I remain most respectfully,

Mrs Abraham Lincoln

Please direct to Pau.

To Jacob Bunn

Pau, France
February 27, 1878

My Dear Sir:

Your kind letter of the 10th of Feb, with enclosure of a checque for rent, due Feb 1st was received this morning. In the midst of your own business cares, it is exceedingly thoughtful in you, thus, to remember me and as you may well believe I am very grateful. I wrote you a letter two days since urging you to continue my business, and desiring you to retain possession of my Bonds & papers. Only the thought, that you would feel some anxiety, regarding the arrival of the checque, causes me to trouble you so soon again. Invariably I acknowledge the receipt, the *same* day, of any paper from you, & shall continue to do so, in the future—

With my business or papers in any other hands *save* your own, I should feel greatly troubled. Therefore, as the friend of my own dear, good husband, I entreat you to retain possession of my Bonds, send me remittances *thereupon*, when due, send me my monthly rent & my Pension papers—I feel that I am asking a great deal at your hands, but I cannot but *believe* that you will still continue to oblige me *in* so *doing. Otherwise*, I would not know what to do, *no one*, must have my papers, save yourself. My husband esteemed you so highly & I should have *no confidence*, in any one else. As I wrote you two days since, on the 5th of March, I will send you Pension papers signed. It was *very un-necessary* in the parties, to apply to the Secretary of the Treasury. Please pay Custom House duties & safe *arrival* of trunk. I cannot excuse myself, for troubling you so much regarding it. You have acted very nobly towards me.

I remain, most respectfully,

Mrs Abraham Lincoln

To Jacob Bunn

Pau, France
March 5, 1878

My dear Sir:

I enclose you the Pension Certificate signed *to day*, for March 5th, 1878. When you enclose me a checque for the amount, please direct the letter to Naples, Italy, care of W. J. Turner & Co—Bankers. Also, please forward checque for rent, due April 1st to Naples, Italy. My lady friend, with whom I will make the little journey is detained in Toulouse, France by illness, but we expect to meet at Marseilles, in a few days. I have found the cold here very unendurable *this* winter—and as late as the season is, will not complain of the warm sunshine of Italy—I have just acknowledged to Mess. Morton, Bliss & Co- the receipt of £25-5- as a matter of course, I will not use it as I have received a duplicate checque of the same amount from you, for February 1st. I trust & believe, all remittances in the future will be sent by yourself. It has pained me more than I can express. Please present my kindest regards to your family.

> Very respectfully,
> Mrs Abraham Lincoln

To Jacob Bunn

Pau, France
March 22, 1878

My dear Sir:

Your kind letter of March 2nd has been received, informing me of the arrival of the trunk. Please accept my grateful thanks for your assistance in regard to it, for without your aid, I believe it would never have been received—I regret that you went to the trouble of sending any statement—I have received the remittance from New York and cannot for the moment find the letter which contained the checque.—Consequently, cannot acknowledge it, not remembering exactly the address. May I take the liberty of requesting you to write them a line regarding it—I truly hope that in the future no one but yourself, will forward me remittances.

Owing to quite severe indisposition I have been detained here so long. The weather is still cold. Please direct to Naples, Italy care of W. J. Turner & Co. Bankers. On the 5th of March I sent Pension Certificate for 4th of March, signed—I leave here this afternoon, & will be in Naples in ten days time, where I join my lady friend. Very respectfully

> Mrs Abraham Lincoln

To Jacob Bunn

Naples, Italy
April 10, 1878

My dear Sir:

When you receive the rent money due May 1st please send it to Rome, Italy addressed *to me*—care of Macbien & Co. Bankers.

As I wrote you, I sent you on the 5th of March, the Pension paper, properly signed & requested you to direct to this place (Naples— care of W. J. Turner & Co. I remain here, *only* a few days longer and *thence* to Rome—Any letter received from you, shall be within *the hour* answered.

I remain,

Most respectfully,

Mrs Abraham Lincoln

P. S. Any letters that may arrive for me, addressed to care of W. J. Turner & Co will be at once forwarded to me to the care of the address I have just given you of Macbien & Co Rome.

To Jacob Bunn

Naples, Italy
Hotel de Russie
April 29, 1878

My dear Sir:

On my return on Saturday, from Sorrento, where I have been passing the last two weeks, I found two letters from you, one of the date of March 25th and the other dated April 8th—The former contained a Pension Certificate for June 4th for Signature, also a checque for 4th of March Pension. The letter of April 8th contained checque for rent, due April 1st.

Please accept my sincerest thanks, for your kind attention, to my business. I find the climate of Italy very soft & pleasant; having visited here once before, in former years, prevents the feeling of novelty, yet as sorrowful as I *then* was, my grief has been greatly *intensified since*, consequently, I take no interest whatever in fresh scenes & objects. I have found the Messieurs Turner & Co, very polite and courteous, and they expressed themselves pleased at any moment to cash the checques. I expect to be passing through Marseilles about the 5th of June and will present the Pension Certificate to the U.S. Consul at the latter place—for his signature & from that place will forward it to you. Please enclose letter containing checque for rent due June 1st to me, care of the

United States Consul, Marseilles, France—he will forward it to me, as I will leave him, my address—

May I request you, to present my kindest regards to your family, whilst I remain most respectfully & gratefully

Mrs Abraham Lincoln

P. S. I do not know the name of the U.S. Consul at Marseilles. May I trouble you, to apply to Lewis Baker. Perhaps he can give it.

To Jacob Bunn

Rome, Italy
Hotel d'Italie
May 22, 1878

My dear Sir:

Your checque for rent, due May 1st was received this morning. It was cashed at the same time, also the day before leaving Naples, the Pension checque was cashed, as well as the one for April, by Mess. Turner & Co. All of which, doubtless you have been duly notified of, by the parties. On arriving at Marseilles, early in June, I will get the U.S. Consul, to sign the Pension Certificate—I wrote you requesting you send 1st of June rent to the care of the *latter* at Marseilles. The rent for 1st of July as well as interest on bonds, please direct to me at Pau, France, where I shall be by the 1st of July.

I remain, most respectfully,
Mrs Abraham Lincoln

To Jacob Bunn

Marseilles, France
June 5th, 1878

My dear Sir:

I enclose the Pension Certificate, signed by our U.S. Consul here. I will be in Pau, by the 1st of July, *where* if you please direct your letters, for the next three months. Also, the letter containing checque for Pension of June 4th direct with rent money of July 1st to Pau, France. I requested you in a recent letter to send checque for rent due June 1st to the care of the Consul here—I have directed him to forward any letters received within this month, (June) to Vichy—I leave here tomorrow for the latter place, where I scarcely expect to remain more than two weeks. I shall not object once more, to settle down in the Pyrénées—wherever I am, I make it a quiet retreat. With continued thanks for all your kindness I remain

Most respectfully
Mrs Abraham Lincoln.

To Jacob Bunn

Vichy, France
June 24, 1878

My dear Sir:

Your letter of June 3d, enclosing checque for rent due June 1st, was received this morning. On the 5th of June, I forwarded you from Marseilles, the Pension Certificate, duly signed, by the Consul witnesses & myself. If it is necessary for you to go to Chicago, to draw the interest on my Bonds, 1st of July, please repay yourself, for the expenses of the journey, by withdrawing the necessary amount. I will be leaving here in a few days for Pau—where I shall remain some little time.

I remain, very respectfully & gratefully,
Mrs Abraham Lincoln

To Jacob Bunn

Pau, France
July 13, 1878

My dear Sir:

Your kind letter of the 25th of June containing a Pension certificate for September 4th was received on yesterday. Also, this morning, a letter arrived from you, of the same date, enclosing a checque for Pension of June 4th. Please accept my best thanks, for your prompt attention to my business affairs. With kindest regards to your family, believe me very gratefully, and respectfully,

Mrs Abraham Lincoln.

To Jacob Bunn

Pau, France
July 20, 1878

My dear Sir:

Your letter of the 2d of July, containing a checque of nine thousand five hundred & thirty five francs (9535), was received this morning. I wrote you a week since acknowledging the receipt of Pension Certificate for September 4th also the checque for rent, due June 1st. I thank you very sincerely for your kind and prompt attention, to my business. Believe me, very respectfully & gratefully,

Mrs Abraham Lincoln.

To Jacob Bunn

My dear Sir:

I received this morning, your checque of 625. francs, for rent due Aug 1st. Please accept my thanks for the journey you made on my account July 11 to Chicago. All, was very satisfactory, & I never fail to be grateful, for your kindness—Please direct to Pau.

I remain,
Very respectfully,
Mrs Abraham Lincoln.

To Jacob Bunn

My dear Sir:

I enclose the Pension Certificate, for September 4th signed by the Consul, witnesses & myself.

Trusting you will receive it in due time, and with many thanks for your many kindnesses, I remain most respectfully,

Mrs Abraham Lincoln.

To Jacob Bunn

My dear Sir:

Your letter of the 6th of September, enclosing checque of 625. francs, was received this morning.

Please accept my thanks for your kind attention, whilst I remain very respectfully

Mrs A. Lincoln

Please direct as usual to Pau—

To Jacob Bunn

Pau, France
October 14, 1878

My dear Sir:

Your letter of the 25th of September, with the checque for the pension of the latter month, was received this morning. Will you please when you write again, send me the Pension paper for signature, for December next. I am remaining at Pau, for the present.

With kindest regards to your family, I am, very respectfully & gratefully,

Mrs Abraham Lincoln.

To Jacob Bunn

Pau, France
October 23, 1878

My dear Sir:

On the 14th of Oct- I wrote you acknowledging the receipt of checque, for pension of September 4th.

Two days afterwards, I received a letter from you, enclosing Pension Certificate for signature for next December, for which favor please accept my thanks.

This morning, I have received your letter of the 4th of October, with checque for rent, due October 1st. For all your kind attentions to my little business, I feel myself always, under renewed obligations. I remain, very respectfully,

Mrs Abraham Lincoln

To Jacob Bunn

Pau, France
October 25th, 1878

My dear Sir:

Your letter with enclosure of checque for 625 francs, for rent, due Nov 1st was received this morning.

On the 5th of December, I will forward you Pension Certificate duly signed. I remain, always, gratefully and very respectfully,

Mrs Abraham Lincoln

Please direct to Pau—

To Jacob Bunn

Pau, France
December 5th 1878

My dear Sir:

I enclose you the Pension certificate signed this morning, by Mr Clay, witnesses & myself, for December 4th.

Please present my kindest regards to your family, whilst, I remain, most respectfully,

Mrs Abraham Lincoln.

To Jacob Bunn

Pau, France
December 23, 1878

My dear Sir:

Your letter of Dec 3d with enclosure, of checque, was received this morning. Also, on the 5th of December, I forwarded you, the Pension Certificate, duly signed. With the kindest regards of the season, for yourself, and family.

> I remain very respectfully,
> Mrs Abraham Lincoln.

To Jacob Bunn

Pau, France
Jan. 13, 1879

My dear Sir:

Your letter, with enclosure of Pension certificate for March 5th also checque for Pension of December last, have just been received.

Please accept my most grateful thanks, for your great attention, to my interests.

> Very respectfully,
> Mrs Abraham Lincoln.

To Jacob Bunn

Pau, France
January 23, 1879

My Dear Sir:

Your letter, enclosing Pension papers for proper signature, was received last evening. This morning I went to the Consul & he looked it over very carefully & we both hope it is now signed, in all the necessary places—When he signed the one for Dec. 4th the imperfect one—he was conversing with two or three gentlemen, which may account for any mistakes—When he signed his name, as one of the witnesses, I remarked to him that it would be better for another person to sign it, but he appeared to think not —Afterwards I regretted that I had not been more firm. Another time, I feel assured, that all papers will be very exact. He promises to be more strict, regarding the signatures. Be kind enough to explain to Miss Sweet,[4] if you please. I feel that I am troubling you, very greatly.

I remain very gratefully & respectfully

Mrs. Abraham Lincoln.

To Jacob Bunn
———

Pau, France
January. 27, 1879

My dear Sir:

Your letter of the 4th of Jany, with enclosures of checque of interest & rent money due the 1st of the year, was received this morning. A few days since, I forwarded you the *last* Pension certificate signed & I trust properly arranged—As I wrote you, I feared that the Consul writing his own name as one of the witnesses, was altogether wrong, & I shall be careful, that it shall not occur again. The Consul means to act right, but he is uncommonly nervous, for an Englishman. I am always so grateful to you, for your kind attention to my business. It is raining continually here, this winter, while in our own Country, I believe the weather is severely cold. Please present my kindest regards to your family.

I remain very respectfully,
Mrs Abraham Lincoln.

To Jacob Bunn
———

Pau, France
February 11th 1879

My dear Sir:

May I request the favor, that you retain the rent money of $125- due 1st of March, in order that you may advance whatever

---

[4] A pension officer in Chicago.

money may be necessary in payment of two trunks which will arrive in New York, *early in March*. Their destination will be Springfield, Ill directed to my sister Mrs Edwards. As Mr Edwards is an invalid this winter, I trust you will kindly excuse the great liberty, I am taking. I am under so many obligations to you, that I shrink from troubling you so much. *One* trunk leaves this evening for Havre—The other, a few days hence. The trunk just leaving, has been paid for, so far as New York. The address of the office in New York is,

> "The Morris European & American Express, outward
> department, No 50. Broadway, New York."

With very many apologies, for giving you so much trouble, believe me, most gratefully & respectfully,

Mrs Abraham Lincoln

To Jacob Bunn

Pau, France
February 26, 1879

My dear Sir:

Your letter of the 5th of February, has been received, also the checque of 625 francs, due 1st of this month—

I had anticipated that some of my bonds might be called in, yet at the same time *hoped*, that such might *not* be the case. However, we have to make the best of it—I went to the Consul this morning, to request a power of attorney, for the sale of the four bonds, mentioned in your letter & he assures me that it is not in *his* power to give it, that it must be sent me from the United States & he mentioned that it was issued, in printed form—Of this, of course you know best—I can do nothing more, until I receive the paper, from you. Please before *any sale* is made of these bonds, consult with Mr N.W. Edwards & Judge *Treat*,[5] also, two of my husband's best friends, I wish their advice, as to their transmission into other bonds, of the safest & best paying interest.

[5] Samuel H. Treat had known Lincoln since the time when both rode the circuit, Treat as judge, Lincoln as lawyer. He was at this time on the federal bench.

When the whole is adjusted, please show the new bonds, to these gentlemen, give them the numbers, as well as send me the same. You have been so kind to me that I trust, I am not troubling you too much. Ten days since a blk trunk was shipped to New York, & I wrote you at the same time to please retain March rent for payment of *this* trunk and a box, which leaves here in a day or two, arriving I hope early in March. I fear this writing will not be easily read, as I am suffering much with neuralgia, in my right arm. I remain.

Very respectfully
Mrs Abraham Lincoln

The Pension Certificate has perhaps reached you some time since, I trust this time, it is correct. Yet when I turned away, for an instant, I found the Consul had placed a stamp on the power of Att- for collecting it—which may be wrong.

Mrs L

To Jacob Bunn

Pau, France
February 27th 1879

My dear Sir:

I feel assured that I am troubling you very much, yet as the box, under the care of the agent here, left *to day* for New York— I think it is best, to advise you of the fact. As I wrote you ten days since, that the trunk was paid for as far as New York, also I paid this morning, the same sum, 59. francs for the box—as a matter of course, the agent gave me a receipt for each of these articles, which it is best, for me to retain or send to you, in case any difficulty should arise, which I presume will not be the case—for the agent here, has the reputation of being *just* in his dealings. He certainly has a very honest look. I requested a second receipted bill, for each to send to you, but he said it was contrary to law. However, the two receipted bills—so far as N.Y. for these two articles, the trunk & box—are on my table before me at present—to be carefully retained. I am under so many obligations to you, for all your great kindness—

I feel assured that you will carry out my wishes, as I wrote you on yesterday. Please send me a power of attorney, with each place for signature *well* marked. I cannot express to you, how *inefficient* I find this English Consul about our affairs—Why we have not an American one here, is a mystery to me. These bonds are sacred deposits, as invested by my husband's hard earnings and I wish them safely *reinvested*—and with the joint advice of Mr N.W. Edwards & Judge Treat—and your own accurate knowledge of such things—I feel that they will be well converted into others—perhaps better than they have been. I remain, most gratefully and respectfully

Mrs Abraham Lincoln

Please present my kindest regards to your family. M. L.

To Jacob Bunn

Pau, France
March 5, 1879

My dear Sir:

I enclose you the Pension Certificate signed this morning. It has been so carefully studied over that it appears *impossible* that any defect, can be found in it. I feel assured that it will satisfy Miss Sweet. I was mistaken regarding there being *no* necessity for the Consul, placing his seal upon the paper, giving you the Power of Attorney, for collecting the Pension. He was correct in doing so, I am informed—Again, this morning, he mentioned that he could *not* make out a paper for me, for the sale of the four bonds. Therefore, I find myself depending upon your kindness for one.

I remain, very respectfully,
Mrs Abraham Lincoln.

To Jacob Bunn

Pau, France
April 1st 1879

My dear Sir:

Your letter of the 14th with enclosure of Power of Attorney, has been received to day. It has been signed by the Consul, Witnesses & myself & will be *resent* to you, in this letter. You mentioned that the blank line where a name should be written, could be executed on the return of the paper to Springfield. It would please me very much, if your own name, was placed there. You have been so kind to me about my business, that I feel especially grateful. The Consul, objected to my placing on the paper, the "Mrs" before my name, I hope his ideas were correct—I greatly regret that the trunk with its simple contents, is giving so much trouble. I fear the box will meet with the same fate. Please present my kindest regards to your family—I neglected to mention that the rent due March 1st was received ten days since.

I remain, very respectfully
Mrs Abraham Lincoln.

To Jacob Bunn

Pau, France
[April 10, 1879] [6]

My dear Sir:

Your letter of March 26th has been received this morning. I have been to see the Consul & he has again signed the Pension papers, which I trust may be found correct. I greatly regret always, when they are found defective. The paper for the *ensuing* June please make as plain as possible. My sister Mrs Edwards, writes me of the *safe* arrival of the trunk—She also mentioned something about a loan on real estate at 8 per cent might possibly

[6] The estimated date is in Bunn's handwriting.

be made with the four bonds—May I trouble you to say to Mr Edwards that I prefer the four bonds reinvested in the safest and most remunerative BONDS—I wish *nothing* to do with *property* && or *mortgages*—Many apologies for troubling you so much. I would so much like your counsel, united with Judge Treat's & Mr Edward's regarding the bond business.

Very gratefully & respectfully

Mrs Abraham Lincoln.

P. S. Please see Mr Edwards at once. One of the witnesses gave his occupation, without my knowledge, which I trust will not be found to be wrong. There is no reason why the bonds should not be *reinvested* in other bonds—paying the same interest—$60 dollars on each thousand per annum—mention *this* please to Mr Edwards—

To Jacob Bunn

Pau, France
April 23, 1879

My Dear Sir:

Your letter with enclosure of checque for rent, until the 1st of May, was received this morning. Please accept my most grateful thanks, for your kind attention, regarding the trunk. A box was shipped on board the "Labrador," the 15th of March, for New York, for Mrs N. W. Edwards, which I suppose has arrived ere this. The agent at Havre, notified this agent here, to that effect a few weeks since. For payment upon it, please deduct the necessary amount from May rent. Both the power of attorney & Pension paper for March 4th were returned to you two weeks since. The Consul, directed one to a friend of his, to affix his name as witness and as it will appear upon the paper, he gave his occupation. I returned to the Consul's office at once & on showing him the paper he remarked that it did not make the least difference, it was always the custom in England & very frequently he sent important papers to America—with the witness' occupation attached to his name. Will you be so kind, when you send Pension papers for June, on the power of Attorney, write the month & date as well as all other papers in the future. The Consul says, he cannot understand why it should not be dated the *same* month, it is signed. As regards the bonds, I wrote to my sister, Mrs Edwards, on the first notification, that I wished the four converted into other bonds, bearing the best interest—Very certainly, I wish no loans on real estate or mortgages—only the safest bonds—I wrote you concerning this, when I returned the power of Attorney—I hope the paper did not arrive too late. With the frequent return of Pension papers, (which I have so much deplored), as well as my business, you have had so much to exercise your patience. Deeply grateful I am, for your continual kindness. Please present my best regards, to your family.

> Very respectfully
> Mrs Abraham Lincoln

To Jacob Bunn

Pau, France
May 20th, 1879

My dear Sir:

Your letter of the 28th of April has been received, with enclosures of a Pension certificate for June 4th, as well as a checque of 3750 fr for March Pension.

This morning I received your letter of the 3rd of May, with the remaining sum of rent, due May 1st—after deducting expenses of the box. I regret that all the four per cent bonds, had been sold at Washington, when my four arrived, yet I feel well assured, that you will find other *Gov* bonds, equally as safe, & yielding as high a rate of interest. I, also, am satisfied, that you, three gentlemen [7] will carry out my wishes & invest, ONLY in *government* BONDS—With many apologies for troubling you so much.

Believe me, very gratefully & respectfully.

> Mrs Abraham Lincoln.

[7] Bunn, Edwards, and Treat.

To Jacob Bunn

———

Pau, France
June 5th 1879

My dear Sir:

I, enclose the Pension certificate, signed to day, for June 5th which without doubt, will be found to be perfectly correct.

I remain, very respectfully
Mrs Abraham Lincoln

P. S. Please continue to direct to Pau

M. L.

To Jacob Bunn

———

Pau, France
June 21, 1879

My dear Sir:

Your letter of the 3rd of June, with enclosures of checque due May 1st for rent—has been received—Also, you gave me information, regarding the transmission of the four Bonds, into others—Please, when you write again, give me the name of the new Bonds —as well as the amount of interest, to be received on *each* thousand per annum. At the same time, if I am not troubling you too much, please make out a new list of the $60,000 now in your possession & enclose it to me—On receipt of which, I will burn the two lists I now have. Please receive my most grateful thanks, for your kind attention in this matter. It is now more than two weeks since I sent you, the Pension Certificate duly signed, for June 4th.

I remain, very respectfully,
Mrs Abraham Lincoln.

To Edward Lewis Baker, Jr.

My dear Lewis:

It is impossible for me to express to you, the great pleasure your beautiful letter of the 1st of June, afforded me. I wrote to your Grandma, how much I was delighted with your photograph, which you so kindly sent me. Please say to that dear Grandma, who is *so dearly* beloved by us all, that I have not forgotten her promise, to send me *her own*. I loved you all very much whilst I was with you, but in this strange land, so *far* removed from you, my heart and my thoughts revert continually to your little circle, and very frequently, I wish myself in your midst—*Very* reluctantly, I left you all, and it was only for *self protection*, that I did so. Of this, dear Lewis, you are *fully* aware. The great God, removed from me my idols & when my last worshipped one, who so completely filled my heart & thoughts, & who idolized me as much in return, was taken THEN my heart broke—Your Grandma is indeed blessed to have *you* remain with her—and you may well believe, that Mr Phillips, loves you as well as if you were his own son. "Love crowned you at your birth," it would be almost sacrilege, if you left Springfield, with your many friends there. I remember, whilst in Washington in the Summer of *1861*—I sent your Mother a bottle of *Jordan* water, which had been sent me from Palestine, as she had mentioned that she was going to have her children christened. I believe that face of yours, loved by so many persons, *so* abounding in intelligence, good looks, & sweet sympathy, was watered by this same Jordan water—Yet, it required, my dear Lewis, nothing of the kind, to beautify that nature of yours, that gladdens so many hearts. I have been called upon to surrender—two, of the loveliest sons, that God ever gave to a Mother, possessing exactly your attributes, and for whom I shall never cease to grieve, with an almost unparallelled sorrow, until God reunites us—I am feeling too sad to write to day, but I am sure, you will excuse me. *This* is a fete day, among the Catholics, & the grandest procession, quite a mile in length, passed this street, half an hour since. Two or three bands of music, were interspersed in the line. Can I say to you, how much I wished your Grandma and yourself, had witnessed it. From *little* girls of 3 years of age, to those of 30—all dressed in pure white— then came a long line of nuns, priests, and an indescribable array of gilt glitter—*Music* such as would have rejoiced your brother Willis greatly. Has the latter, yet left you? What a comfort you must have found in him, the past winter! I trust the *benign* influence of J. T. Stuart [8] had nothing to do with the difficulty, concerning your property & that of your good Grandfather. In J. T. Stuart—I have not the *least* faith. It is a great pleasure to me to hear that your Grandpa is in a measure recovering the use of his right arm & hand —the latter in damp weather, I fear he will often find painful— please remember me to him, with much love. Fannie Wallace, *now* writes about *twice* a year—Remember me to Mr Phillips—whom I believe is a very warm hearted man, very true to his friends and possessing an infinite amount of talents—I shall never cease, dear Lewis, to be mortified when I recall the fact that Rufus F. Andrews who was once so *obsequious* for *office* sake, should have ventured *not* to reply to Mr Phillips letters, as well as that of *others*—a *very* wicked INFLUENCE was the cause—

There is a paper published at Pau, called the "American Register," which is issued once a week, & which I sometimes see. Recently, I had the privilege of seeing a short article in it, mentioning that Robert T. Lincoln and Stephen A. Douglas, [Jr.] were practising law in Chicago both prominent in their respective political parties, with *quite* the *certainty* of being at no distant day, candidates for the Presidency. You can imagine how elated I felt, in my quiet way, over such a prospect—the triumph of the "*just*" *slightly different* from the great & good father, however who was kind even to *his stepmother*—I began to study over in my own mind, with such a CERTAINTY in view, what never once occured to me to do in my good husband's time notwithstanding articles that often appeared in the papers, that "Mrs Lincoln was the power behind the throne" I found myself revolving in my own *feeble* mind, of what superior persons the *Cabinet* would consist—Swett of *Maine*—&

[8] John Todd Stuart had been relegated to the roster of Mrs. Lincoln's enemies by concurring in the decision to have her committed to the sanitarium.

Little Mamie with her charming manners & presence, in the event of *success*, will grace the place. By the way, dear Lewis, should I again enclose any thing for this dear child again, I will not trouble your good Grandmother—only if you will write R. T. Lincoln—a formal note—remitting what is sent. *The* young man, who makes *no* concessions to the *Mother*, whom he has so cruelly & unmercifully wronged—So that he will be a *temperate* man, is the boon, for which I *daily* kneel. How terrible is the death of young Lewis [sic] Napoleon! [9] The Ex-Empress is alone & desolate, like my own very sorrowful self! Cut to pieces, after receiving the fatal shot, in so unnecessary a cause. Write to me very frequently, my dear Lewis. I write so rapidly, that I fear my letters are not easily read. Please present my best love to all friends. Always, your very affectionate Aunt,

Mary Lincoln

Please burn this letter, so hurriedly written that I dare not read it over. Write *very frequently*, dear Lewis—

Aff
M. L.

To Jacob Bunn

Pau, France
July 10, 1879

My dear Sir:

Your letter of the 25th of June, enclosing Pension Certificate for September 4th also enclosing a checque for June 4th has been received to day. Please accept my continued thanks for your prompt attention to my business. With kindest remembrance to your family, believe me very respectfully & gratefully,

Mrs Abraham Lincoln.

---

[9] Louis Napoleon, the eldest son of Napoleon III and Eugénie of France had joined the British expedition to Zululand and was killed in an ambush by native warriors.

To Jacob Bunn

Pau, France
July 21, 1879

My dear Sir:

Your letter of the 3rd of July, has been received this morning. Also the enclosure of the checque for June 4th Pension, as well as rent money due July 1st—

I cannot express to you how grateful I am, for your unremitting attention to my business, not to mention your journey to Chicago, on my account. Believe me, very respectfully &&

Mrs Abraham Lincoln.

During her four years abroad Mary Lincoln was able to take brief trips to Paris, Vichy, Avignon, and Marseilles, to such seaside resorts as Biarritz and St. Jean de Luz, and once into Italy as far as Rome and Naples. But her health was too uncertain to permit her to go much farther afield or to sightsee extensively. In her younger days she had been an energetic and responsive tourist, relishing the novelty of travel and absorbing in full measure the beauty and history of her surroundings. From girlhood she had longed to visit Europe; the week her husband was killed the two had talked of plans for trips after his term in office ended. It was her sad fate that by the time she got her wish she was too sick and depressed to derive much pleasure from "fresh scenes & objects," [1] and that her times abroad were very much in the nature of exiles.

She loved France, knew its history and language, but could muster little warmth for its citizens. Sometimes they were "*peculiar*," at other times "*covetous*," finally they appeared "*the most unprincipled, heartless, avaricious people* on the face of the earth." [2]

[1] Mary Lincoln to Jacob Bunn, Naples, Italy, April 29, 1878.
[2] Mary Lincoln to Edward Lewis Baker, Jr., Pau, France, June 12, 1880.

The hallowed French cuisine held no charms for a woman reared on wholesome southern cooking: any country without *"waffles, batter cakes*, egg corn bread . . . biscuits, light rolls . . . *buckwheat cakes"* was a gastronomic desert.[3] She did feel a curious sense of kinship with the former French Empress Eugénie, as she did with royal unfortunates everywhere. She and Eugénie had been on top of the world at much the same moment in history. The comedown for both had been abrupt. After his country's defeat in 1870 at the hands of Bismarck, Louis Napoleon had been taken as a prisoner to Germany; after his release, he had gone into exile in England, where he died in 1873. When his son was killed in the Zululand in 1879, Mrs. Lincoln, ever the grieving mother, was moved to sympathize with the former Empress, "alone & desolate, like my own very sorrowful self." She thought perhaps she might go to Biarritz and tour Eugénie's old château. "It is only open on Mondays."[4]

If she was indifferent to European affairs, she was hardly more involved in those of her native land. An occasional newspaper story would evoke a spark of interest, but it quickly died. Still, she had opinions and loyalties that would not die. She was "surprised" when President Hayes appointed a southerner to his Cabinet, when so many others, supporters of the *"true cause,"* were available.[5] There was no room for charity when Mrs. John Tyler began applying for a government pension. It was, to Mary Lincoln, "an impudent request" coming "from so fearful a secessionist."[6] But times were changing; the world was moving on without her.

To Edward Lewis Baker, Jr.

Pau, France
August 3rd, 1879

My dear Lewis:

I have been absent for ten days at the seaside, returning on yesterday. This morning I called at the Post Office & found your

[3] Mary Lincoln to Edward Lewis Baker, Jr., Pau, France, October 4, 1879.
[4] Mary Lincoln to Edward Lewis Baker, Jr., Pau, France, August 3, 1879.
[5] Mary Lincoln to Edward Lewis Baker, Jr., Pau, France, April 11, 1877.
[6] Mary Lincoln to Edward Lewis Baker, Jr., Avignon, France, January 16, 1880.

very welcome letter, dated Dubuque, Iowa, July 10. I am so pleased
to think, dear Lewis, that you are having a summer vacation, &
visiting the beautiful upper Mississippi. It is always pleasant for
the young & happy to have something to anticipate in *advance*.
Therefore, permit me to suggest that *next* summer, you visit the
White Mountains, returning home by way of Lake George, so un-
rivalled in scenery, I wish you to pass *your fourth* of July, at the
Tip Top House on the White Mountains—(Do I give it the right
name?) [7] I am sure you will not think it amiss, if I offer for your acceptance, at the time stated, sufficient means for four weeks enjoyment, the month of July. Starting the 26th of June, you will easily
reach the White Mountains by our patriotic fourth—If you write
me on receipt of this letter, accepting my proposition for this *especial* journey, it will all be made right. Mr Phillips, will be well
pleased to acquiesce. The rent of June 1st will be handed you on
starting & Mr Bunn will forward my July rent to Boston to you,
which is paid the first of *each* month. This is writing in a business
like manner, but in this world of reality the *practical* is always the
best. Of course it is for the present, entirely entre nous, your Grandfather and Grandmother included—

I wrote you a very long letter on the 22nd of June. Have you
received it? It was enclosed, with one to your grandmother in a
very *frail* envelope, for *this* reason, I make special mention of it—I
passed a week on the seashore at St Jean de Luz, on the border of
Spain, the *Spanish* mountains, overhanging the old town—it is four
miles from Biarritz, & a much more quiet place, notwithstanding
all along the seashore, crowds have now congregated. I stopped at
Biarritz for three days, where the Ex Empress Eugenie has a fine
Château—which she will never again see, it is supposed. To the
deeply bereaved, grand mansions & broad lands, enter but little into
the thoughts—and yet whilst we have life, there is a positive necessity for the means of subsistence. I think I will visit Biarritz early
in October & then I will go through the Château. It is only open on
Mondays. Some time or other, I will send your grandmother, views
of the Château, here at Pau, the different sides—Tomorrow I am
going into the Mountains for this month of August, from one point
to another—yet in some places, we have to return to Pau, to take the

[7] The name was correct. Mrs. Lincoln had stayed there herself on a summer journey in 1863.

railroad. How dearly, dear Lewis, I would love to be with *you all to day*. I am writing you on Sunday, but yet, I do not travel, on *this sacred* day. Do write me often—It is a great pleasure to hear from you. With much love to all, believe me your very devoted Aunt,

Mary Lincoln

Write me, if you have ever visited the White Mountains.

The Hotel where I stopped at St. Jean de Luz was so near the sea, my window opening out upon it that oftentimes I felt myself quite sea sick. A *further distance* would have been more agreeable.

To Jacob Bunn

Pau, France
August 18, 1879

My dear Sir:

On my return from the country this morning, I received your letter of the 2nd of Aug with enclosures of monthly checque. For which favor, please receive my thanks. In consideration of the four bonds, having their numbers changed, when you have leisure, I would like to have the [$]60. Bonds again made out, to the date of your doing so, & the numbers sent me. I dislike to trouble you, so much. I remain, very respectfully,

Mrs Abraham Lincoln

To Jacob Bunn

Pau, France
September 5, 1879

My dear Sir:

I returned last evening, from St Sauvern, in the Pyrenees, in order to sign the Pension Certificate, for *this* date, which I now enclose you. When I wrote you acknowledging the receipt of rent, due

August 1st I had not received the *other letter*, containing the new account of Bonds which you so kindly made out for me, however the days afterwards, the letter was handed me. This explanation will enable you to understand why I requested the numbers a second time. I am aware as you stated in your letter that three Bonds of $1000 each are matured Dec 31st 1880—and the rest July 31st 1881—

You are aware that *after* the payment of rent May 1st 1881—my income suffers a decrease of $1500- per annum, and I cannot afford to lose a dollar, on the interest of the remaining $56,000- It is a positive & absolute necessity, that I receive $60. interest on each Bond a *year—as* at present, when they are exchanged for others—I only hope they will not be called in, by the Secretary of the Treasury, before the time indicated—

Please direct as usual to Pau, France.

With great respect, I remain very truly,
Mrs Abraham Lincoln

To E. H. Shannon [8]

Pau, France
October 4, 1879

E. H. Shannon

Your letter requesting an autograph of my husband, President Lincoln, has been received.

I regret to inform you, that all his letters to me, were enclosed in a small trunk & left in America—Hence I am unable to gratify your request.

Very Respectfully,
Mrs Abraham Lincoln

[8] Unidentified.

To Edward Lewis Baker, Jr.

Pau, France.
October 4th, 1879

My dear Lewis:

I am sitting up, for the *first* half hour, within the past week. I have been really ill, with a very severe cold taken in the mountains, where I suppose I lingered too long. I am enveloped in flannels from head to foot—my throat is almost closed at times, continual pain & soreness in the chest—& am coughing most of the time. I am well repaid for my love of mountain scenery, & detestation of town in summer—Rather a poor prospect for me, for the coming winter. I enclose a card of my *exact* weight *nearly* a month ago—since then, as a matter of course many pounds of flesh have departed. *Here*, in France, they are compelled to be *rigidly* exact in their weights—I am now, just the weight I was, when we went to Wash in 1861— Therefore I may conclude, my great bloat has left me & I have returned to my natural size—It was such a great pleasure dear Lewis to receive your interesting letter of the 8th of September—I am so pleased also that you will visit the White Mountains next summer, lake George & pass a day or two at Niagara falls—I have visited all these places & have always returned to Niagara with renewed interest—I think 24—hours, *however* will suffice you, on the Tip Top house. *One* 1st of August, we ascended the Mountain from the Glen house where it was *intensely* warm & found it snowing on top. There is so much pleasure, in anticipation for those who have never visited these places.

Without doubt, I must have been considered *quite* ill—as numerous cards are daily handed me & notes of enquiry, flowers, &&— I lead a life of such great quiet here that the *pleasant* thought occurs to me *sometimes* that I am not supposed to be in *this* latitude —How much I long to see you all—to have a taste of your dear Grandma's good food—*waffles, batter cakes,* egg corn bread—are *all* unknown here—as to biscuits, light rolls && they have never been dreamed of—*not* to speak of *buckwheat* cakes—It needs no assurance of mine, to convince you, that a long period of absence from

America, is not agreeable—but to an oppressed, heart broken woman it is simply an *exile*. You are spared a very long letter to day, my dear Lewis, for I cannot sit up a moment longer. Since the commencement of this letter, the enclosed card has been sent up to me—These *dignitaries* abound here & are so courteous—When you receive this letter, I hope you will *at once* write me—I see *no* American papers—send me slips of news—all the time, when you write—I hope our country—will never nominate for the Presidency, so BAD a man as Roscoe Conkling.[9] Adieu, for the present—With much love to all & a great deal for your dear self

I remain your devoted Aunt—
Mary Lincoln

To Jacob Bunn

Pau, France
October 21st 1879

My dear Sir:

Your letter enclosing checque for 4th of September, Pension—as well as blank certificate for signature for next Dec- has been received. Owing to illness, I failed to write you, acknowledging the receipt of checque for rent of September 1st—

This morning, I have received your letter, enclosing a checque of 825- francs—for rent of 1st October & interest on four Bonds, to the 1st of latter month.

I remain, very respectfully

Mrs Abraham Lincoln.

---

[9] Senator from New York and at this time acknowledged leader of the Republican party in his state. Conkling, an opponent of President Hayes, had been a serious contender for the Republican presidential nomination two years earlier. Mrs. Lincoln's reference to his "badness" probably stemmed from rumors linking him with Kate Chase Sprague and more particularly from the scandalous episode of August 1879 when ex-Senator Sprague attacked Conkling with a gun for supposed attentions to his wife. The Spragues were ultimately divorced, and Mrs. Sprague died in poverty.

To Jacob Bunn

———

Pau, France
December 5th 1879

My dear Sir:

I enclose you the Pension Certificate for Dec 5th signed to day.

Also, November 21st I received a checque, for the rent due the 1st of the *latter* month.

Please present my kindest regards, to your family, with the Compliments of the Season. Please direct as usual to Pau. France. I remain, very respectfully,

Mrs Abraham Lincoln

To Jacob Bunn

———

Pau, France
December 22, 1879

My dear Sir:

Your letter of the 2d of Dec enclosing checque for rent, due the 1st of this month has been received. Also, on the 5th of December I enclosed you the Pension Certificate signed. Please accept my thanks for your kind attention to my business, whilst I remain

most respectfully
Mrs Abraham Lincoln

Lewis Baker's great-aunt never failed to keep him posted on the state of her health. She wrote him of her pains, her colds, the fluctuations in her weight; it was good to know someone who would not object to such a tedious and depressing recital. In December of

1879 she had an accident. While hanging a picture over a mantel, she fell from a stepladder and severely injured her spine.[1] It had to be set in plasters, but even this treatment could not alleviate the intense pain in her left side, pain that made the slightest gesture an agony. This misfortune set the seal on her decision to end her exile, but she was slow to move. The following June, accompanied by a *bonne*, she made her painful way to the Hôtel de la Paix, where she had been staying in Pau before it was closed down. She was checking on her possessions, going to see which of her trunks needed repair or replacement. Coming down what must have been steep stairs her weakened left side gave way and she apparently stumbled. She had to be lifted into her carriage and her physician sent for. After describing her injury to Lewis she requested that he ask Ninian W. Edwards for "letters" that would expedite her passage through customs and secure free transport for her baggage. She would sail for home on October 16, aboard the steamship *L'Amerique*.

To Jacob Bunn

Pau, France
Jan 14, 1880

My dear Sir:

Your letter of the 27th of Dec, has been received to day, with enclosure of checque for Pension, as well as Pension Certificate for signature for March 5th.

The weather is exceedingly cold here this winter & in consequence of a very severe cough & neuralgia I think I will leave here in a few days for Italy. Therefore, if you will kindly direct your letter of the 2d or 3d of February, to Naples Italy, care of W. J. Turner & Cie Bankers, I shall be much obliged to you. I leave reluctantly & only ill health would occasion me to do so—With many thanks for all your kindness, I remain

Most respectfully,
Mrs Abraham Lincoln

[1] Helm, pp. 298–9.

To Edward Lewis Baker, Jr.

Avignon, France
January 16, 1880

My dear Lewis.

Five days since I arrived here, owing to excessive fatigue & illness however, the three first were passed in bed and now I am sitting up just long enough to write you—so much, for my poor broken back, with its *three* plasters & my left side always in pain— When I have sufficiently recovered (which I trust will be soon as it is *still* cold here, I will proceed to Marseilles & take the Steamer to Naples.

Two years since I was here for a few days, when I was not *so* bowed down with bodily pain, drove around, saw all the churches, viewed the quaint old town, so filled with historical associations, the house of the noble *John Stuart* Mills [sic], where he now rests from life's cares & ingratitude—I only wish, that you, dear Lewis, were here in my place, with your young, bright, intelligence, & I a broken hearted sorrowing woman in *your* place, with your dear Grandma, my own good, sweet sister—Tell her to take a good rest, retire early & sleep well—How much we will have to talk over, when we are once more together. Write me very often & direct to Naples—I am so isolated from the world, I know so little that is going on, *yet* I observed a little paragraph recently in the papers that Mrs John Tyler, was applying very vigorously for a Pension, from OUR Government. A woman, who was so bitter against our cause during the War, with much Northern property & money—as well as the South—but so *fearful* a Secessionist—Our Republican leaders will, I am sure, remember ALL THIS—& the Country will not have fallen upon such "evil times," as to grant her impudent request.

Please write me *without* fail all particulars. Tell your dear Grandma, I have now run down to 100- pounds, EXACTLY. With best love to all—I remain your devoted Aunt,

Mary Lincoln

To Edward Lewis Baker, Jr.

[INCOMPLETE]   *Pau, France*
                                          January 19, 1880

My dear Lewis:

I cannot send off to the mail a letter I have just written to your dear Grandma, without writing you a few lines. It was quite a coincidence that your letter was dated on the 13th of December the anniversary of my birthday & your Grandma's letter was received on the 1st of Jan, *when* I was groaning with an *almost* broken back—which is aching very badly at present—My letter to her will explain all—You will be relieved to day from a long letter—but in return, dear Lewis, write me, as soon as this note is received. Enjoy your Operas this winter—Youth does not always last—and you are so fond of music. I must close—I entreat you to write me frequently—I, cannot express to you, how much I enjoy your letters. Your letter of assurance regarding meeting me down the harbor on my arrival in N.Y. is a consolation to me. Also, the exemption from Custom House duties. The extremely cold weather & an unusual amount of pain forces me in a week or two, to leave for Naples. Please direct to W. J. Turner & Co, Bankers, Naples, Italy. How much I dread to make the change my maker, only knows. Very greatly, do I long to be with you all once more . . .

To Jacob Bunn

Pau, France
January 26, 1880

My dear Sir:

Your letter of January 5th with enclosure of checque for 9135. fr. has been received. Please accept my thanks for your kind attention to my business. As I wrote you recently, please direct to Naples, Italy care of W. J. Turner & Co. Bankers.

Very respectfully,
Mrs Abraham Lincoln

To Jacob Bunn

Marseilles, France
March 5, 1880

My dear Sir:

After a detention of three weeks at Avignon, France, with quite severe illness, two days since I arrived here with great pain & difficulty, to sign my Pension Certificate before the U.S. Consul. The Consul, was absent at Florence, but the Vice Consul I found to be well acquainted with all necessary proceedings & being empowered, in the absence of the Consul, with his business, arranged the paper for me. Mr Potter who signed the P. Certificate two years since for me, has been replaced by the present one—I enclose it to you to day, & when you send a reply, as well as enclosure of rent money for April 1st please direct my address care of Mr J. B. Gould. U.S. Consul, Marseilles, France—Wherever I am, he will forward to me. The Banker at Naples Mr W. J. Turner—sent your letters of February 5th to the Consul *here*—One, containing checque for rent, due Feb 1st. Please do not direct to Avignon, *only* to Marseilles—May, 2 or 3—direct to Pau, France, if you please. I return to Avignon, tomorrow where I seek, *absolute rest*. I am too ill, to travel & have not the least wish, to do so. Kindly pardon these details—as it is necessary to explain to you, that I have abandoned *all* idea of proceeding to Naples—With kindest regards to your family, I remain, very respectfully,

Mrs Abraham Lincoln

P.S. There is no American Consul at Avignon.

To J. B. Gould [2]

Avignon, France
April 22d, 1880

My dear Sir:

The letters you enclosed me, ten days since, have been received. On the 24th by the 10 o'clock morning Express, please send me, any others that may have accumulated. Also, *after* the 24th, may I request you to retain any others *until* the *first* of May, & send them to me here, at Avignon, with "Poste Restante" upon them. You are doubtless aware that the *French*, are a *peculiar* people. *After* the 1st of May, please send my letters to Pau, France. In all this, I feel well assured, that I am giving you a great deal of trouble, and I am very grateful to you I hope some day, to have the pleasure of thanking you personally. Mrs Rathbon[e],[3] of whom you wrote, was a dear friend of former days, *mentally*, a very superior woman & her dear, good father, Judge Harris, was an intimate friend, of my beloved husband, in Washington & was *always* a welcome guest at the Executive Mansion.

Believe me, very respectfully
Mrs A. Lincoln

To Jacob Bunn

Avignon, France
April 26, 1880

My dear Sir:

Your letter of March 3d, with enclosure of checque for rent due at that time has been received, as well as letter of April 8th

---

[2] The envelope for this letter was addressed to "Hon Mr Gould, United States Consul—Marseilles, France."

[3] Clara Harris Rathbone and her future husband had been guests in the presidential box on the night of Lincoln's assassination. Never mentally right after that experience, Major Rathbone, in 1894, would go berserk, shooting and killing his wife. He ended his life in an insane asylum in Hanover, Germany.

with enclosure of checque for rent, also checque for Pension & quarterly interest on 3 Bonds, all *have* arrived safely.

Please accept my thanks for your kind attention to my business—I have neglected to mention the receipt of Pension Certificate for Signature June 5th. I expect to leave here about the 10th of May for Pau—where if you please henceforth direct my letters.

I remain, very respectfully,
Mrs Abraham Lincoln

To Jacob Bunn

Pau, France
June 5th, 1880

My dear Sir:

Your letter of the 3d of May, with enclosure of checque for rent to *that* date, has been received. Also, on the 26th of April, I wrote you from Avignon, acknowledging the receipt of rent, until April 1st as well as checque for pension due March 5th. Ere this, I hope you have received my letter. I enclose to day Pension Certificate for June 4th signed—Please direct to Pau, France, all letters this summer, as I am remaining *here*, for the next four months. Believe me, very respectfully & gratefully

Mrs Abraham Lincoln.

To Edward Lewis Baker, Jr.

Pau, France
June 12, 1880

My dear Lewis,

Your very agreeable & welcome letter of May 6th, was received a few days since, having been detained a week at the Consul's office at Marseilles. I have not heard from your Grandmother, for at least two months, though from your letter, I am encouraged to believe that she has regained her health, which is so precious to us all, who love her so dearly. I shrink from writing almost to day, dear Lewis, having so poor a report to make of myself. On my return here, the day afterwards being utterly exhausted with the sufferings of my back & left side, & the journey, I was compelled to send for the physician, who insisted upon perfect rest, outward applications, & resting on the lounge, the greater part of the time for two months—Allowing me a drive of an hour *once* a week. In my desire to regain my former strength, I think I *faintly* promised him to do so—But in my great wish to leave this place, arrange my effects here, in a *fourth* story, with *almost* a broken back, four days since, I sent for a bonne, who had sometimes been of service to me —took her arm and *painfully* wended my way to the "Hotel de la Paix" closed & deserted—I wished to take a survey of broken trunks & to see how many had to be replaced. Alas, for my weakness, on attempting to *descend*, my left side gave way, she had to call the Concierge to lift me down, place me in a carriage, although my present Hotel Henry Quatre is as near to the Hotel, where I went, as Mrs James Lamb's is to you. The bonne, went for the physician, who ordered a warm bath, the bonne placed me in bed, & gave me a cup of warm soup, the physician returned towards evening, with fresh plasters & I am now sitting propped up, on my lounge. This is a weary recital to you dear Lewis, but with your great, good heart perhaps it will not be amiss, to write you the exact truth. But I feel assured, that I shall be completely cured, by following the directions of my physician. But it is a curiosity to see *how* angry, these French people can become. The *most unprincipled, heartless, avaricious* people, on the face of the earth. With the exception of a *very few*, I detest them all. I regret to hear of Mr Phillip's illness. *To this hour*, I do not know who is nominated for the Presidency,[4] you must write and enclose me, *all* news—I have been thinking over a good deal, dear Lewis, the last two or three days, in my darkened, solitary room and I think IF I DO NOT regain my health, a little more rapidly than I am now doing, *instead* of the trip to the White Mountains as I proposed to you several months since, a trip to Havre and a run down to Paris, the latter a journey of four hours to meet me, with a visit of ten days or two weeks to Paris—would be

---

[4] The Republican candidate, and next President, was James H. Garfield.

more pleasant to you *in the late autumn. Of this*, more hereafter. I shall never feel satisfied until you see the beautiful Pyrénées & have a four or five months, journey, on *this* side of the water—and, dear Lewis, it will not be my fault, be assured, if it is not accomplished. But I must first return to America, straiten out my bonds and settle down, THEN, I shall be only too pleased if you will undertake the journey by yourself. It is now too late in the season to begin any thing of the kind, you should leave the U.S. in May, returning in the autumn—I write you very sincerely, since last autumn, owing to illness and thieving generally by the *French physicians* && I shall be *better* enabled to carry out my wishes, after *my* RETURN. You wrote me that your kind, good Grandfather had letters that would pass me through the Custom House, I entreat you with *his* invaluable influence, to secure me *free* transport, for my baggage, which *has always* been accorded me in Europe without a *question* or a trunk being opened—My great & good Husband's service to his country, *should* grant me *this* favor, at least. I will write in a few days to your dear Grandmother further particulars. I *so* long to be with you all. In ill health & sadness quietude & loved faces, are far best. Have *perfect* confidence, in what I write you & *future movements best* love *to all*. Your Grandmother will understand every thing.

Most affectionately,
Your Aunt,
Mary Lincoln

Please direct to Pau, France Poste Restante—for the next four months.

To Jacob Bunn

Pau, France
July 21, 1880

My dear Sir:

Your letter of the 29th of June has been received. Enclosed was a Pension Certificate for September 4th also checque for June

4th Pension. To day, I have received your letter of the 3d of July, enclosing all remittances due to the latter date. Please accept my thanks, for your kind attention to my business. I may have neglected to acknowledge the receipt of checque for rent due June 1st. As there was two competent witnesses who signed the 4th of June, Pension Certificate, I can scarcely understand the difficulty. However, as they so kindly overlooked, what was considered a slight error, I can only return my thanks.

I remain, very respectfully,

Mrs Abraham Lincoln.

To Edward Lewis Baker, Jr.

[INCOMPLETE]   *Pau, France*
August 29th-1880

My dear Lewis:

Your very welcome & agreeable letter of the 8th of Aug—has just been received. It pains me greatly to learn that your health is not good and I feel assured that you will listen to my *entreaties*, and take better care of yourself—Retire early, each evening, take *much more* rest than you have *ever* done before, and as cool weather advances, wrap your chest & throat up, more warmly. You have always led too active a life, for one so young, I felt it, when I was with you dear Lewis. I have been so weakened by the intense suffering of my left side & back, that I will be unable to complete my preparations for my departure from Pau, before the 1st of October. Owing to the exertions of the past week, I am suffering *even* more than usual with my back to day, but *such* is my anxiety about you, that I cannot refrain from writing. Yesterday was a day of sadness in the hotel, as the good landlady was buried. I wrote your Grandmother recently, that my friend the Baronne de Brandenecker, had left for Austria. Two weeks since, she returned to look after her business & yesterday afternoon, she came & passed three hours with me, as she said she knew I would be nervous. But she leaves again soon even perhaps before I will, the 1st of October. I *so* long to be with you all, once more dear Lewis, I am *now* very unfit, to be separated from loving sympathising friends—I would love dearly to have you meet me at Havre or Paris but with the assi[s]tance of the agents, I hope I will not meet with much difficulty. BY ALL means, meet me in New York. Now, that you are not very well, I fear that crossing the Ocean, twice in succession with a few days of interval on land, *on this* side, would fatigue you. Do not disappoint me, dear Lewis, in accepting my proposition, for a six months journey to Europe, as soon after my return as possible—I am sure your Grandfather & Grandmother, would certainly not object—when your health, demands a rest & afterwards, you will feel so much better, for the journey. You can draw the 1st of each month, on Mr Bunn for $300- (1500 francs) when in Europe—& it will be such a pleasure to me—& it will be entirely between—your loving Grandmother, yourself & me—When you meet me in New York I wish to see you looking in such good health. Mr Bunn will hand you $125- the 2d of November for your trip to New York—I will write *him*, in time. Please say nothing about my return to *any one*—I earnestly pray, that my immense array of baggage, through the kind interference of your Grandfather, will not be subject to duty. *Never*, on any occasion, on this side, has an article been opened for inspection, nor in America—My good husband, certainly did sufficiently, for his country, that I should be exempted, from this painful ordeal; doubly so now in my delicate health . . .

To Jacob Bunn

Pau France
September 6th 1880

My dear Sir:

Enclosed you will find Pension Certificate, signed this morning. When you write, on receipt of this letter please direct to the address I now give you—NOT to Pau. Also please send checque for rent due October 1st to the *same* Paris address. The checque due August 1st was received about the 21st of same month.

Believe me, very respectfully
Mrs Abraham Lincoln

To Edward Lewis Baker, Jr.

Bordeaux, France
October. 7th—1880

My dear Lewis:

I have concluded to return by the Amerique, which sails for New York, from Havre. October 16th. I cannot trust myself, *any longer* away from you all—I am too ill & feeble in health. Tomorrow I leave for Paris—my baggage has now gone on to Havre. I entreat you, by all that is merciful, dear Lewis, to meet me on the steamer. The French vessels are swift—& doubtless we will make the passage in 9 days—*Do not* leave Springfield LATER than the 22d, (twenty second)—of October and please call at the French [Line] Office & accompany the small boat—"Down the bay"—Bring on your dear Grandmother with you—The small steamers *always* go out to meet the large French steamers. Give yourself a day or two of repose in New York, before the arrival of the Steamer—I shall have to ask quite a favour of your Grandfather—*It is this*, that he will hand you $125- to pay your way & I enclose a few lines to Mr Bunn, that he will hand your Grandfather $125- the second day of November—Please have your Grandfather speak to him by the 1st of Nov—I shall have no American money with me. Stop in New York—at the 5th Avenue [Hotel]—& when I arrive—we can go to some other—Too many associations of happier days with my beloved children at some of these places.

Rely, upon my passage, upon the Amerique October 16th—SIX days *later—without fail* start for me.

M. L.

To Jacob Bunn

Bordeaux, France
October 7th 1880

Mr Bunn, will have the kindness, to hand to Mr N. W. Edwards, the 2d of November 1880—The rent money, $125 & greatly oblige,

Mrs Abraham Lincoln

One day during the course of her return voyage, Mary Lincoln was preparing to descend a stairway when a sudden swell caused the ship to lurch violently. She would have hurtled headfirst down the steps had not a woman standing behind her seized her skirt. Her rescuer was none other than Sarah Bernhardt, who gave a melodramatic account of the incident in her book, *Memories of My Life*. The little woman, "dressed in black, with a sad, resigned face" was "very much hurt . . . and a trifle confused; she thanked me in such a gentle, dreamy voice that my heart began to beat with emotion. 'You might have been killed, madame,' I said, 'down that horrible staircase!' 'Yes,' she answered, with a sigh of regret, 'but it was not God's will.' " When Madame Bernhardt revealed her name, the reaction was not of the sort she had come to expect: the little woman recoiled. "I am the widow of President Lincoln," she hissed significantly. She had clearly lost her love for actors, no matter how celebrated. The tragedienne reflected then that she had "just done this unhappy woman the only service that I ought not to have done her—I had saved her from death." [5]

"When the AMERIQUE reached New York," wrote a reporter for the New York *Sun*, "a throng was assembled on the dock and a greater throng was in the street outside the gates. . . . Among the passengers was an aged lady; she was dressed plainly; her face was furrowed and her hair was streaked with white—this was the widow of Abraham Lincoln. She was almost unnoticed. . . . When the gangplank was swung aboard, Madame Bernhardt and her companions . . . were the first to descend. . . . The gates were besieged, and there was some difficulty in bringing the carriage, which was to convey the actress to the hotel. . . . Mrs. Lincoln, leaning upon the arm of her nephew, walked toward the gate. A policeman touched the aged lady on the shoulder and bade her stand back. She retreated with her nephew into the line of spectators, while Manager Abbey's carriage was brought in. Madame Bernhardt was handed in and the carriage made its way out. . . .

[5] Sarah Bernhardt. *Memories of My Life*. New York, 1907, p. 370.

After it went out the others . . . Mrs. Lincoln with the rest." [6] Lewis later wrote his family that his great-aunt had not been in the least upset to have been pushed aside; she had long since come to terms with anonymity.

After a short stay in New York, Lewis Baker took Mrs. Lincoln back to Springfield, where she withdrew into the familiar sanctuary of the Edwards home. Since no letters of hers survive for the year she was there, one must turn elsewhere for word of her. The available evidence is flattering neither to Mary Lincoln nor to Elizabeth Edwards. From the moment of her return, the same woman who had written lucidly to Jacob Bunn, lovingly to Lewis Baker, apparently lapsed into reclusion and eccentricity, putting great strain on the entire household. Mrs. Edwards was hard put to conceal her exasperation; the two sisters quarreled constantly. In the spring of 1881 Elizabeth wrote testily to Emilie Helm that Mary was "somewhat an invalid," but was exaggerating her condition so as to demand "every moment" of her time. "Her enjoyment of a darkened room, does not accord with my ideas of enjoying life—" declared Elizabeth. "I have suffered from indulging her with my company until I can scarcely see to guide my pen." [7]

Elizabeth's sixteen-year-old granddaughter, Mary Edwards, was in and out of the house at the time, helping out occasionally with "Aunt Mary," whom she recalled seventy-five years later as a pathetic, almost ridiculous figure. "Aunt Mary" wore a money belt at all times, even under her nightdress. Once, when Mrs. Lincoln accused her sister of stealing from her, Elizabeth and her daughter-in-law "Josie" Edwards lifted her bodily from her bed and, while one held her on top of a commode, the other reached under the mattress and brought out a huge roll of bills that Mrs. Lincoln had hidden there. In another room, the floorboards sagged under the weight of sixty-four trunks and crates, crammed with a lifetime's hoard of possessions. "Aunt Mary," recalled her great-niece, "had a lot of clothes in her trunks made of elegant foreign material she bought abroad and she had basted together to look like dresses—to escape the customs duty. . . . Every day she got up and went through those trunks for hours. Grandmother said it was funny, if

---

[6] The New York *Sun*, October 28, 1880.
[7] Elizabeth Todd Edwards to Emilie Todd Helm, Springfield, March 3, [1881]. MS. formerly owned by Justin G. Turner.

Aunt Mary was so sick, that she was able to be up all day bending over her trunks." [8]

In May of 1881 Mrs. Lincoln had a surprise visitor: Robert came, bringing along eleven-year-old Mamie, to make his peace with his mother. Hatred can be exhausting, and Mary Lincoln was weary; nonetheless she might have held out against Robert had it not been for the presence of her first grandchild and namesake. And too, the fact that Robert had just been appointed Secretary of War in President Garfield's Cabinet certainly did him no harm with his mother. Some bitterness may have remained, but at least the two were once again on speaking terms. Robert had come to Springfield deeply concerned about his mother's health, but left feeling reassured. He, like Mrs. Edwards, thought her condition exaggerated— by herself, and by the newspapers. "She is undoubtedly far from well," he wrote the ever-solicitous Sally Orne, "& has not been out of her room for more than six months and she thinks she is very ill. My own judgment is that some part of her trouble is imaginary." [9]

There was nothing "imaginary" about Mrs. Lincoln's back difficulties, however, or about her faltering vision. In the autumn of 1881, lame and ailing, partially blind from years of abusing her eyes, she traveled to New York to be treated by Dr. Lewis Sayre, one of the nation's leading orthopedic surgeons. Dr. Sayre visited her often in her room at Miller's Hotel on West Twenty-Sixth Street, an establishment which boasted "Turkish, Electric and Roman Baths." She could hardly walk and had to be carried everywhere; in her helplessness, her mania about poverty returned in full force, despite the fact that she was now a reasonably wealthy woman.

She was destined to be even wealthier. After all these years, Congress was considering a $2,000 increase in her pension, with an additional gift of $15,000, one thousand dollars for each year since her husband's death. The assassination of President Garfield in September 1881, which left a widow with five children to be provided for, had aroused the conscience of the nation. Mrs. Garfield was to get $5,000 a year; it was only right that Mrs. Lincoln's pension be increased commensurately. The bill was to pass with

[8] Mary Edwards Brown, quoted in the article "An Old Lady's Lincoln Memories," by Dorothy Meserve Kunhardt. *Life*, February 9, 1959, pp. 57–8.
[9] Robert Todd Lincoln to Mrs. J. H. Orne, Washington, June 3, 1881. MS. in the Illinois State Historical Library, Springfield.

minimal difficulty, but Mary Lincoln anticipated trouble; there was nothing in her experience to cause her to think differently.

And so she mustered her feeble resources for one last battle. Once again she was in need of loyal allies who would champion her cause as if it were their own. Into the picture stepped two persons: Rhoda Mack, daughter of her long-time friend Rhoda White, and the Reverend Noyes W. Miner, brother of another old friend, Hannah Shearer. Rhoda Mack, who lived in New York, came almost daily to Miller's Hotel, assisted Mrs. Lincoln in getting about, and wrote numerous letters in her behalf. Miner, who had come to the city to attend a pastors' conference, called on Mrs. Lincoln soon after the pension had become an issue in Congress. He was appalled at her wasted appearance, her weakened condition, and her apparent lack of friends, and, after leaving her, delivered a moving speech in her defense before the assembled clergymen.

He then put himself entirely at her disposal, asking if there were anything he could do to help her. There was indeed: he could go to Washington and plead her case before the senators and representatives in whose hands lay the fate of her bill. Once Miner had agreed to the mission, she filled page after page of hotel stationery with instructions for him, her once exquisite handwriting by now as huge and unformed as that of a child. When she could not see to write, Rhoda Mack wrote for her. "One or two points Mrs Lincoln forgot to mention when she saw you," wrote Mrs. Mack to Miner on December 16, 1881, "Dr Sayre with the best intentions in the world, but with *very* little tact, wrote to Sen Logan [sponsor of the bill] that 'matters had been so arranged for Mrs Lincoln that her living cost her next to nothing.' This is quite at variance with the facts. . . . The board here is high and every bath costs $2.50. Mrs Lincoln's only chance of recovery to even a comfortable state of health—is, in pursuing the treatment now prescribed for her, the remainder of her life. . . ."[1]

On January 3, 1882, as Miner prepared for a second pilgrimage to Washington, he received a frantic missive from Mary Lincoln with numerous postscripts and lists of names scrawled over the back, top, and sides. It was a letter filled with accusations and suspicion,

[1] Rhoda Mack to N. W. Miner, New York. December 16, 1881. MS. formerly owned by Justin G. Turner.

painfully reminiscent of those with which poor Alexander Williamson had been battered fifteen years before. A second communication
that day warned Miner not to approach "Robert T. Lincoln." His
mother was at least considerate enough to appreciate the embarrassment her lobbying might cause him.

Eighteen days later Congress voted Mrs. Abraham Lincoln a
$2,000 pension increase and an additional gift of $15,000. But suspicion had become a habit of mind by now, and even after she
learned of the vote, she refused to believe her good fortune. People
were withholding information from her; President Arthur would
somehow be prevented from signing the bill. She was quite irrational now, accusing everyone from David Davis (now a senator)
to the proprietors of Miller's Hotel and the faithful Rhoda Mack of
being unfriendly and deceitful.

Even when she was satisfied that the bill had been signed by
the President, her fears were not allayed. She wrote Miner, first,
that she doubted everything, then that the $2,000 was "paltry," and
that she would not believe the $15,000 until she "saw" it. She
needed an operation on her eyes, and Congress had not been generous enough to enable her to afford it. But once she was convinced
that the money was indeed hers, she had nothing left to fight for.
Nothing seemed to interest her any longer and, in March of 1882,
she wrote one last letter to Lewis Baker, telling him she was coming
home.

To Josephine Remann Edwards [2]

[*Miller's Hotel, New York*] [3]
October 23, 1881

My dear Joe:

I am too ill to day, only to write you a few lines. You will observe that I am situated here to receive daily Electric baths, al-

[2] Wife of Albert Edwards, son of Mr. & Mrs. Ninian Edwards.
[3] This letter and the ones that immediately follow were written on stationery
headed "Miller's Hotel, Nos. 37, 39 & 41 West Twenty-Sixth Street, New York
City, Between Broadway and Sixth Avenue, near Madison Park. Turkish, Electric
and Roman Baths Connected with the Hotel. Dr. E. P. Miller, Proprietor."

though it is a very choice Hotel, for those who *do not*. When I landed at the depot in N.Y. I was so thoroughly exhausted that the hackman lifted me in his arms into the carriage—also lifted me into the Clarendon Hotel—Dr Miller insists that his man shall lift me up stairs from the baths—indeed, it could *not* be otherwise.

Some former Washington friends are stopping here, Mr & Mrs [Silas] Robbins & Judge & Mrs [Joseph G.] Bowman. I have received several calls from them. Mrs Dr Sayre comes often to see me—I decline many callers, with painful sores & an aching back—it is necessary to do so.

I am frightened with the great expenses I am passing through —Baths a nurse physician's bill hotel &&—The 5 dollars a month, for the two rooms where my baggage is stored. Of course I have nothing whatever to do with the room, which I occupied as a chamber at Mr Edwards. I pay for no place I left open that as, you know was the agreement—I left 4 nails for the windows—to secure any party, who might occupy the room & to avoid the entrance from the roof. The agreement was to pay $3- a month for rooms when baggage was stored. Wherever I AM I have *more asked* than I should pay for—I pay for NO room, I do not occupy & leave open.[4] It is painful to know you are poor—when you are ill.

Dear Joe—I can write no more—The weather is as sunny & beautiful as September—I am too ill to ride out—Write—Love to Allie [and the] children—Frances Wallace & Mary Baker—

Always, truly—

M L

---

[4] From these references it may be concluded that Ninian W. Edwards was actually charging Mrs. Lincoln, his sister-in-law, for the use of the room in which her possessions were stored. Possibly she was even charged rent while she was in residence, which might have been a cause (or effect) of the renewed difficulties between the sisters.

Letter of Introduction

Dec. 5th, 1881

Permit me to introduce the Rev Dr Miner to you, our clergyman for fifteen years,[5] our opposite neighbor, and a friend very much beloved by my husband.

Very respectfully,
Mary Lincoln

To Noyes W. Miner

[*Miller's Hotel, New York*]
Jan 3d, 1882

My dear Mr Miner:

Only my great anxiety about your leaving for Washington tomorrow (Wednesday) causes me to write to day. Congress meets on Thursday morning—Dr Miller, Mrs Mack & myself MOST EARNESTLY urge you to be there at the opening of Congress Thursday *We all* consider it an ABSOLUTE necessity—with your VERY vigorous work Believe me, it is a positive necessity that you are there—and we feel assured that you will talk MOST earnestly with EVERY Senator & member, without the LEAST DELAY—Please do not listen to Springer [6] *when* he tells you there is *no* necessity for the most STRENUOUS exertion—NONE OF US here trust the Springfield clique—Please say nothing to Springer about my intention NOT to live in Springer [Springfield] Also be kind enough NOT to say a word about bonds—ONLY urge the $10,000- a year & the 5 years & four months back pension *with interest*. Will you also tell Springer & Logan [7] about the appointment of that old renegade

[5] The Lincolns had worshipped at the First Presbyterian Church in Springfield. Miner, a Baptist, had never been their minister.
[6] William M. Springer, Democratic representative from Springfield and sponsor of the pension bill in the House.
[7] Senator John A. Logan, Republican of Illinois, sponsor of the pension bill in the Senate.

Davis [8]—He, will prove himself an ungrateful villain in the matter. Please see [John S.] Ingalls—of the Senate—Do not read a
written statement your noble lip eloquence is VERY FAR BEST—

Four physicians came on Sunday to see me. Mrs Mack goes
to day at one o'clock to see about the report. I am very feeble with
my spine & limbs—*now*, quite unable to walk but a very few steps
& my vision VERY greatly obscured. As Dr S[ayre] says to be
lame & almost without the least eyesight—what an affliction—
Dear, Mr Miner, please oblige us all by starting tomorrow morning & leave no one *untalked to*. Please see & talk to Abram Hewitt,
Cox, Anthony, Cameron [9]—indeed *one & all*—Try, if you please,
to get before the Committees of the Senate & House—Do not *walk*
if you please—Overpower them all, by your good words. Please
go at once—

> Very truly &&
> Mrs A. Lincoln

Best love to your family
Again please *do not walk*
Do not forget *Gen Singleton* [1] by all means—

To Noyes W. Miner

[*Miller's Hotel, New York*]
Tuesday [*January 3, 1882*]
5 P.M.

Dear Mr Miner:

I write to inform you that Dr Sayre has just left me—He
informs me that the Physicians statements are *now* in the hands

[8] David Davis had resigned his Supreme Court seat in 1876 to reenter political
life. He was elected to the U.S. Senate in January 1877 as a Democrat and late
in 1881 was awarded the office of President pro tempore of the Senate. Mrs. Lincoln's animosity toward him stemmed from his concurrence in her commitment to
the sanitarium.
[9] The men listed by Mrs. Lincoln were as follows: Representatives Abram Hewitt
and Samuel S. Cox, Democrats of New York, Senator Henry B. Anthony, Republican of Rhode Island, and F. Donald Cameron, Republican of Pennsylvania, who
now sat in the Senate seat formerly held by his father, Simon Cameron.
[1] John W. Singleton, Democratic representative from Illinois.

of Mr Springer Please let every Senator & member know that I have never received a dollar of the 3 years pay of my husband I am informed that Judge DAVIS has started that rumor—

Do not approach Robert T. Lincoln you will understand how he is situated—I know that you will *plead* with *every member of Congress* & Senator—I cannot live on my income. *Never* will I forget your kindness—

Mrs Mack and myself think that I must have been given the $10,000 (ten thousand) a year some twelve months since, to judge of this *new invention* of the enemies

Mrs Mack will direct her letters to the Washington, D.C. P.O. until you inform her *where* you are stopping. Do not let your Baptist friends, seize on you—It would be as well also to enquire at the St James Hotel for letters

Excuse paper & everything. Please leave tomorrow for Wash

Very resp
Mrs L

J. H. Smith	Geo. W. Lader
Sen Logan	and the National *Party* [Committee]
Sen [Philetus] Sawyer	

To Noyes W. Miner

[Miller's Hotel, New York]
Feb 5th, 1882

My dear Mr Miner:

I write to you ON TWO subjects of the VERY greatest importance to me. I am growing VERY ill with ANXIETY—parties coming in tell me that no one knows accurately whether the Bill for $15,000 passed the house with the $2,000. a year pension bill. Without I see the handwriting of Mr Springer announcing that the $15,000 was passed with the *grand* Pension Bill, may I not implore you, the *hour* you receive this letter tomorrow morning—to write to Mr Springer and have *him* write to you at once—the truth about it all. Of course (between ourselves) if it passed with the other bill it would be kept from me, and if the $15,000 passed the House of Representatives, they would try to prevent [President] Arthur from *signing* it. I plead with you to write to Mr Springer about *it all* & please enclose me *his* reply without the least delay. The great anxiety about this business is rendering me very ill. Only a few lines from *Springer* will satisfy me. Many persons are now doubting it greatly. As you were not in Washington at the time of the voting Springer, will know best about it. Mrs Dr Miller returned from Wash. a few days since accompanied by Susan B. Anthony & other suffrage women who stopped at this house. Through *gossiping* Miller, I understand she had a conference with old Villain Davis. I feel assured Mrs M[iller] worked against my Pension. Avoid any conversation with Dr Miller save the *mere civilities* of life. He tells everything. No woman in the drawing room or at table *but* know everything that is whispered to him. Not a word from 575 Broadway [2]—moving may be a partial excuse. *Again* I implore you, Mr Miner, to write him again *the hour* you receive this letter. *This is* the only straw left us. Please write him at once and ask him what contributions he has received & tell him to send them to me. *This is our last week*. If you do not write to him *when* you receive this letter, there will be no success. Your $20. (twenty dollars) on any thousand henceforth received may help you in your little illness and through 575 & his friends it will come very easily by a few lines from you.

"Nothing venture, nothing have" and it appears *very, very* remiss and almost sinful to allow *this* opportunity to pass. I cannot bring myself to believe that you will neglect it any longer. The small checque received two weeks since has proved too much for her, Mrs Macks, delicate nerves. As to herself she has not called. Of course she requires no money. *Please, please Do Not* reply to *one* of her letters. On Thursday afternoon Dr Sayre called

---

[2] During the 1860's, 575 Broadway was the address of Edwin Brooks, a dealer in shoes and boots with whom Mrs. Lincoln did business. By the 1880's Brooks' establishment had long since been moved uptown. The most assiduous research has failed to uncover the identities of the several entrepreneurs located at this address in 1882; a further impediment to identification is the fact that the person to whom Mrs. Lincoln referred so cryptically was moving (either in or out) at the time.

& said "Did you receive the letter I sent you." I replied, "No, Sir."
Then he fumbled in his coat pockets and drew out a four page
letter, a fresh one from Mrs Mack. Evidently he wished to read
it to me. I said *please* spare me.[3] We began speaking about 575
& as quickly as possible I changed the subject.

Send me please Springer's letter.

Write Monday morning to 575 requesting to know what. . . .

Mrs Mack has acted very ugly. I do entreat you to write
Monday morning to Springer.

With best love to your family, I am

Very truly
Mrs A. L.

To Noyes W. Miner

[*Grand Central Hotel, New York*]
Feb 21, 1882

My dear Mr Miner:

A week ago, to day, I moved here. It was a great relief to get
away from Miller's, I considered it necessary to stop for a few
weeks from the Electric baths, the food was miserable & the
thought he could practise the slight swindle of $60- a week on me.
The whole house was disgusted with Miller. Since taking up my
quarters here, within the past week I have had two very severe
chills & I find myself in a very feeble state—I hope you have recovered your health. It is a fearful thing to be ill, *all the time*. May
I trouble you dear Mr Miner to write to Mr Springer for me,
notify him that I have left Millers, am here resting for a few
weeks from the baths, that I am in a very enfeebled state—It is
necessary also to enquire of him about the *$15,000* which *between*
ourselves, is beginning to be *somewhat* of a *myth*—It might as
well be sent me at once—Also—the *New* Pension Paper. Tomorrow morning—the *hour* you receive this letter—*will* you please

---

[3] Study of this letter in the published version from which it was taken indicates
that this statement was inadvertently placed at the end of the letter when it logi-
cally belongs here. The error was no doubt due to the fact that Mrs. Lincoln in
these letters finished her sentences wherever she found a space to write.

write Mr Springer to have the New Pension paper made out & the *New* Certificate sent me from Miss Sweet of Chicago—the Pension Agent. On the 6*th* of March it is necessary that I see a Notary Public *here* & sign the paper. I will rely with confidence in your obliging me without *any* delay in *this*. The time is *now* so short—*Please* write also to Mr S about the $15,000 I am ill with chills—& am resting from the Baths

Please write to him without any delay about these things—I have *great* reason to doubt every thing—I suppose it will be for Mr Springer to manage without any *further* delay, these affairs. I can only hope there will be *no deception* practised—as the paltry sum of $2000—alone was added to my Pension. Until I see the $15,000—I will not believe it. I never see Mrs Mack—without she lisps 575—My reply always is—a look into her face. Her naturally good sense always deserts her about that checque—Miller's was a very false place, I sent the letter you left for 575—by the servant girl & I believe it never left the office. *That man* 575 —meant assistance & if you will *still* follow it up, benefit on both sides—will arise—With the small additional Pension given—my eyes can never be operated upon—I will give you the $20- on each thousand henceforth—but I [page missing]

Please DO NOT reply to a letter of *Mrs* Mack & *do* NOT call to see her *when* you come to New York.

To Noyes W. Miner

[*Grand Central Hotel, New York*]
Feb 24th 1882

My dear Mr Miner:

I wrote you several days since—requesting you to write *at once* to Mr Springer regarding my new Pension paper & the $15,000—which both houses of Congress unanimously voted me —*Where* is the money—Please let me hear from you without any further delay. With best love to your family, believe me very truly—

Mary Lincoln

To Edward Lewis Baker, Jr.

[*Grand Central Hotel, New York*]
March 21st, [188]2

My dear Lewis:

May I request you to have a supervision over a box containing an invalid's chair & a smaller box—also a very small package
of medicine—I leave here tomorrow Wednesday evening at 5½
o'clock—for Springfield—I find that I must rest from the Electric
Baths, for a few weeks—I go west by way of Hudson River railroad—to Buffalo, Cleaveland Detroit & Toledo arriving at Decatur
before daylight Friday morning and Springfield at 7 o'clock—in
the morning—I dread the journey greatly, with my limbs still in
so paralzed a state—

Very truly yours,
Mary Lincoln

And so Mary Lincoln came back to Springfield, to her family, to
the house on the hill, and her lonely room. There she remained,
keeping the shades drawn even on the sunniest days; the only
light her eyes could bear was the faint glow of a candle. The world
went by beneath her windows, children laughed and ran along the
sidewalks she had trod so often; they whispered that a "crazy
woman" lurked behind the drawn blinds. She lay in her bed,
scarcely able to lift her head, lying to one side so as not to disturb
"the President's place" beside her. In July she suffered a severe
recurrence of boils, aggravated by the paralysis that was slowly
creeping over her limbs. Her strength gradually ebbed away, until, at 8:15 on the night of July 15, 1882, at the age of sixty-four,
she was freed of life at last. Dr. T. W. Dresser's death certificate

attributed the cause of death simply to "paralysis"; in his medical history of Mrs. Lincoln, Dr. W. A. Evans suggests that this was brought about by apoplexy; the symptoms also suggest diabetic coma.[4] She died believing she was poor; her estate would amount to nearly $90,000.

Her coffin was placed in the parlor, the same room where Lincoln had fidgeted when he had come to call on her and almost in the exact spot where they had stood to be married forty years before. The whale-oil lamps that had lit that ceremony flickered over her open casket, illuminating the faint smile on her lips and the dull gleam of the ring, so worn now that the words "Love Is Eternal," could barely be read. Funeral services were held at the First Presbyterian Church, the Reverend James A. Reed officiating. In his eulogy Dr. Reed likened Mary and Abraham Lincoln to two pine trees he had once seen growing toward the sky, so close to one another that their branches and roots intertwined. When one tree was struck down by lightning, the other seemed at first unharmed. But, said Reverend Reed, in a most sensitive analogy, "they had virtually both been killed at the same time. With the one that lingered it was slow death from the same cause. So it seems to me today, that we are only looking at death placing his seal upon the lingering victim of a past calamity." [5] From the church the body of Mary Todd Lincoln was borne in solemn procession to Oak Ridge Cemetery. The floral tributes were impressive; the pallbearers included the Governor of Illinois and some of Springfield's most distinguished citizens.

The recipient of these late-come honors would have wished her friends to be happy rather than grieved over her passing. Had she not told them often enough how badly she wished to rejoin her loved ones? In 1865, writing of her great grief, she had said, "*Time* does not soften it, nor can I ever be reconciled to my loss, until the grave closes over the remembrance, and I am again reunited with *him*." [6] The grave had closed at last.

[4] Evans, p. 344.
[5] Published in Sandburg & Angle (The Documents), p. 326.
[6] Mary Lincoln to Elizabeth Blair Lee, Chicago, August 25, 1865.

SOURCES AND LOCATIONS
OF THE LETTERS

BIBLIOGRAPHY

INDEX

Sources and Locations of the Letters

Each letter reproduced in this volume is listed below chronologically, together with the location of the original document (when known) and/or the source from which our text was taken. Unless otherwise indicated, a letter was copied directly from the manuscript or from a photostat of it.

The texts of those letters which were formerly owned by Justin G. Turner were of course taken from the original manuscripts while they were in his collection. (The collection was sold in 1967.) Other items listed here as owned by private individuals may have changed hands during the five years this book has been in preparation. Because it is not feasible to attempt to trace the peregrinations of a manuscript once it has been placed with a dealer or privately sold or bequeathed, we have listed as the owner of a letter that person whose property it was known or assumed to be in 1967, when most of the material for this book was brought together. The owner's place of residence, as it was at that time, has been given the first time his or her name appears in the listing.

NOTE: The abbreviation "MS." is used to denote the original manuscript. A/p stands for "as published."

1840

July 23. To Mercy Ann Levering. MS. owned by Philip D. Sang, River Forest, Ill. A/p in his article "Mary Todd Lincoln: A Tragic Portrait." *Jour. Rutgers Univ. Lib.*, April 1961.

December [15?]. To Mercy Ann Levering. MS. owned by Philip D. Sang. A/p in his article "Mary Todd Lincoln: A Tragic Portrait." *Jour. Rutgers Univ. Lib.*, April 1961.

1841

June [?]. To Mercy Ann Levering. MS. owned by Philip D. Sang. A/p in his article "Mary Todd Lincoln: A Tragic Portrait." *Jour. Rutgers Univ. Lib.*, April 1961.

1848

May [?].   To Abraham Lincoln. MS., Ill. State Hist. Lib., Springfield, Ill.

1853

September 17.   To Elizabeth Dale Black. MS. owned by Malcolm A. Black, LeMay, Mo. A/p in the article " 'Took Tea at Mrs. Lincoln's.' " *Jour. Ill. State Hist. Soc.*, Spring 1955.

1856

November 23.   To Emilie Todd Helm. MS. formerly owned by Justin G. Turner,* Beverly Hills, Calif.

1857

February 16.   To Emilie Todd Helm. MS. formerly owned by Justin G. Turner.

September 20.   To Emilie Todd Helm. MS. formerly owned by Justin G. Turner.

[No date, *c*1857].   To Mary Brayman. Photostat, Ill. State Hist. Lib. (Abraham Lincoln Association files), Springfield, Ill.

1859

[February 28].   To Ozias M. Hatch. MS. owned by Cornelia Hatch, Springfield, Ill. A/p in Sandburg & Angle: *Mary Lincoln: Wife and Widow* (The Documents),† p. 201.

[April 24].   To Hannah Shearer. MS. destroyed. A/p in " 'Your Truly Attached Friend, Mary Lincoln,' " by Charles V. Darrin. *Jour. Ill. State Hist. Soc.*, Spring 1951.

June [26].   To Hannah Shearer. MS. destroyed. A/p in " 'Your Truly Attached Friend, Mary Lincoln,' " by Charles V. Darrin. *Jour. Ill. State Hist. Soc.*, Spring 1951.

August 28.   To Hannah Shearer. MS. destroyed. A/p in " 'Your Truly Attached Friend, Mary Lincoln,' " by Charles V. Darrin. *Jour. Ill. State Hist. Soc.*, Spring 1951.

October 2.   To Hannah Shearer. MS. destroyed. A/p in " 'Your Truly Attached Friend, Mary Lincoln,' " by Charles V. Darrin. *Jour. Ill. State Hist. Soc.*, Spring 1951.

October 3.   To Ozias M. Hatch. MS. owned by Cornelia Hatch. A/p in Sandburg & Angle, p. 202.

---

* See introductory note to this section.
† See Bibliography.

1860

January 1.   To Hannah Shearer. MS. destroyed. A/p in " 'Your Truly Attached Friend, Mary Lincoln,' " by Charles V. Darrin. *Jour. Ill. State Hist. Soc.*, Spring 1951.

May 25.   To Mark Delahay. MS., Univ. of Chicago Lib., Chicago, Ill.

June 13.   To Adeline Judd. MS. owned by Philip D. Sang. A/p in his article "Mary Todd Lincoln: A Tragic Portrait." *Jour. Rutgers Univ. Lib.*, April 1961.

August 25.   To John Meredith Read. MS., Lib. of Cong. Washington, D.C.

October 20.   To Hannah Shearer. MS., Lib. of Cong., Washington, D.C.

October 29.   To Dyer Burgess. MS., Ill. State Hist. Lib., Springfield, Ill.

December 31.   To Samuel B. Halliday. MS., Ill. State Hist. Lib., Springfield, Ill.

1861

January 17.   To David Davis. MS., Ill. State Hist. Lib., Springfield, Ill.

March 22.   To William H. Seward. MS., Rush Rhees Lib., Univ. of Rochester, Rochester, N.Y.

March [28].   To Hannah Shearer. MS. destroyed. A/p in " 'Your Truly Attached Friend, Mary Lincoln,' " by Charles V. Darrin. *Jour. Ill. State Hist. Soc.*, Spring 1951.

March 29.   To Simon Cameron. MS., Lib. of Cong., Washington, D.C.

April [11].   To Ward Hill Lamon. MS., Henry E. Huntington Lib., San Marino, Calif.

April 27.   To Mrs. Samuel H. Melvin. MS. privately owned. Photostat, Ill. State Hist. Lib. (ALA files), Springfield, Ill.

May 12.   To Ward Hill Lamon. MS. privately owned. Typescript, Ill. State Hist. Lib. (ALA files), Springfield, Ill.

[May 31].   To Caleb B. Smith. MS., Lib. of Cong., Washington, D.C.

June 17.   To Mary Brayman. MS. privately owned. Photostat, Ill. State Hist. Lib. (ALA files), Springfield, Ill.

June 20.   To John Fry. A/p in Sandburg & Angle, pp. 204–5.

July 11.   To Hannah Shearer. MS. destroyed. A/p in " 'Your Truly Attached Friend, Mary Lincoln,' " by Charles V. Darrin. *Jour. Ill. State Hist. Soc.*, Spring 1951.

July [18?].   To Cambridge Telegraph Office. MS., Ill. State Hist. Lib., Springfield, Ill.

August 1.   To Hannah Shearer. MS. destroyed. A/p in " 'Your Truly Attached Friend, Mary Lincoln,' " by Charles V. Darrin. *Jour. Ill. State Hist. Soc.*, Spring 1951.

September 8.   To Caleb B. Smith. MS., Blumhaven Lib., Philadelphia, Pa.

[September 9].   [To Oliver S. Halsted, Jr.?]. MS. owned by Philip D. Sang. A/p in his article "Mary Todd Lincoln: A Tragic Portrait." *Jour. Rutgers Univ. Lib.*, April 1961.

September 12.   To Simon Cameron. MS., Lib. of Cong., Washington, D.C.

September 13.   To John F. Potter. MS., Lib. of Cong., Washington, D.C.

September 29.   To Elizabeth Todd Grimsley. MS. owned by Philip D. Sang. A/p in his article "Mary Todd Lincoln: A Tragic Portrait." *Jour. Rutgers Univ. Lib.*, April 1961.

October 3.   To Thomas A. Scott. MS., Blumhaven Lib., Philadelphia, Pa.

October 4.   To Montgomery Meigs. MS., Ill. State Hist. Lib., Springfield, Ill.

October 6.   To Hannah Shearer. MS. owned by Katrina van Asmus Kindel, Grand Rapids, Mich.

October 15.   To Carlos E. Farnham. Handwritten copy, Ill. State Hist. Lib. (ALA files), Springfield, Ill.

[c October].   To W. Hindhaugh & Co. MS., Blumhaven Lib., Philadelphia, Pa.

October 25.   To James Gordon Bennett. MS., Univ. of Chicago Lib., Chicago, Ill.

[October 26].   To Caleb B. Smith. MS., Lib. of Cong., Washington, D.C.

November 21.   To Ruth Harris. MS., Huntington Lib., San Marino, Calif.

[November 22].   To Ruth Harris. MS. privately owned. Photostat, Ill. State Hist. Lib. (ALA files), Springfield, Ill.

[November]   To "Mr Anthony." MS., Chicago Hist. Soc., Chicago, Ill.

November 27.   To William A. Newell. Handwritten copy, Ill. State Hist. Lib. (ALA files), Springfield, Ill.

December 15.   To Thomas W. Sweney. MS. privately owned. A/p in Parke-Bernet Catalogue, Forest G. Sweet Sale, Oct. 22 & 23, 1957. Item #192.

December 15.   To George Sykes. MS. owned by Catherine Newell, residence unknown.

1862

January 7.   To Robert T. Lincoln. MS. formerly owned by Justin G. Turner.

January 15.   To Joanna Newell. MS. privately owned. Photostat, Ill. State Hist. Lib. (ALA files), Springfield, Ill.

[February 1.]   [To Benjamin B. French?]. MS., Ill. State Hist. Lib., Springfield, Ill.

February [?].   To Clement Heerdt & Co. MS., Ill. State Hist. Lib., Springfield, Ill.

April 13.   To Francis L. Vinton. MS., Brown Univ. Lib., Providence, R.I.

[May 17].   To Ruth Harris. MS., Houghton Lib., Harvard Univ., Cambridge, Mass.

May 19.   To Mrs. Phineas D. Gurley. MS., Newberry Lib., Chicago, Ill.

[May].   To Ruth Harris. MS., Hist. Soc. of Pennsylvania, Philadelphia, Pa.

May 29.   To Julia Ann Sprigg. Photograph of MS. in Goltz. *Incidents in the Life of Mary Todd Lincoln.* *

July 3.   To John E. Wool. MS. owned by Edward Lustgarten, Encino, Calif.

* See Bibliography.

July 26.   To Benjamin B. French. MS., Ill. State Hist. Lib., Springfield, Ill.

July 26.   To Mrs. Charles Eames. MS., Lib. of Cong., Washington, D.C.

[August 21].   To Jeremiah T. Boyle. MS. owned by King V. Hostick, Springfield, Ill.

[September 28].   Ozias M. Hatch. MS., The White House, Washington, D.C.

[September 29].   Ozias M. Hatch. MS. privately owned. Photostat, Ill. State Hist. Lib., Springfield, Ill.

September 30.   To John E. Wool. MS. privately owned. Photostat, Ill. State Hist. Lib., Springfield, Ill.

September 31.   Daniel E. Sickles. MS., Lib. of Cong., Washington, D.C.

October 4.   To James Gordon Bennett. MS., Brown Univ. Lib., Providence, R.I.

[*c* October].   To "Mrs Lester." MS. privately owned. Photostat in possession of Justin G. Turner.

November 2.   To Abraham Lincoln. MS., Lib. of Cong., Washington, D.C.

[November 3].   To Abraham Lincoln. MS., Lib. of Cong., Washington, D.C.

November 13.   To Edwin D. Morgan. MS., New York State Lib., Albany, N.Y.

November 26.   To Gustav E. Gumpert. A/p in "Tad Lincoln and Gus Gumpert" by Gustav Gumpert. *Jour. Ill. State Hist. Soc.*, Spring 1955.

December 6.   To "Mrs Goddard." MS., Lilly Lib., Indiana Univ., Bloomington, Ind.

December 16.   To William A. Newell. Typescript, Ill. State Hist. Lib., Springfield, Ill.

December 30.   To Charles Sumner. MS., Brown Univ. Lib., Providence, R.I.

1863

February 11.   To Edwin M. Stanton. MS., Lib. of Cong., Washington, D.C.

[*c* February].   To Montgomery Meigs. MS., Yale Univ. Lib., New Haven, Conn.

February 21.   To Mary Jane Welles. MS., Lib. of Cong., Washington, D.C.

March 4.   To Mrs. Charles Heard. MS. owned by Katrina van Asmus Kindel.

March 10.   To Peter H. Watson. A/p in Sandburg & Angle, p. 216.

[March 20].   To George Harrington. MS., Ill. State Hist. Lib., Springfield, Ill.

[*c* April].   To Thomas W. Sweney. MS., Albany Inst. of History and Art, Albany, N.Y.

April 22.   To George Harrington. MS., Univ. of Chicago Lib., Chicago, Ill.

[*c* April].   To Gustav E. Gumpert. MS. privately owned. Photostat, Ill. State Hist. Lib.

May 17.   To Mary Jane Welles. MS., Lib. of Cong., Washington, D.C.

June 1.   To Thomas Stackpole. MS., Ill. State Hist. Lib., Springfield, Ill.

June 5.   To George B. Butler. MS., Ill. State Hist. Lib., Springfield, Ill.

June 16.   To John Meredith Read. MS., Lincoln National Life Foundation, Fort Wayne, Ind.

July 1.   To Antonio Bagioli. MS., Ill. State Hist. Lib., Springfield, Ill.

July 28.   To Edward McManus. MS., Brown Univ. Lib., Providence, R.I.

September 21.   To Edward McManus. A/p in Helm. *The True Story of Mary, Wife of Lincoln*, pp. 214–15.*

September 22.   To Abraham Lincoln. A/p in Helm, p. 215.

November 18.   To Abraham Lincoln. MS., Wills House Mus., Gettysburg, Pa.

November 20.   [To Mary Elizabeth Blair]. MS., New-York Hist. Soc., New York, N.Y.

December 1.   To John W. Garrett. MS., Ill. State Hist. Lib., Springfield, Ill.

December 4.   To Abraham Lincoln. A/p in Helm, p. 234.

December 6.   To Abraham Lincoln. A/p in Helm, p. 234.

December 6.   To Edward McManus. A/p in Helm, p. 235.

December 7.   To Abraham Lincoln. A/p in Helm, p. 235.

1864
———

January 4.   To Catherine Sumwalt. MS., Ill. State Hist. Lib., Springfield, Ill.

January 11.   To Julian Dartois. MS., Ill. State Hist. Lib., Springfield, Ill.

January 15.   To Benjamin F. Butler. MS., Univ. of Chicago Lib., Chicago, Ill.

February 6.   To Daniel E. Sickles. MS., Ill. State Hist. Lib., Springfield, Ill.

February 18.   To E. N. Drury. MS., Brown Univ. Lib., Providence, R.I.

February 20.   To Daniel E. Sickles. MS., Brown Univ. Lib., Providence, R.I.

February 21.   To Larz Anderson. MS., Ill. State Hist. Lib., Springfield, Ill.

February 25.   To Clement Heerdt & Co. Typescript, Ill. State Hist. Lib., Springfield, Ill.

February 26.   To Clement Heerdt & Co. Typescript, Ill. State Hist. Lib., Springfield, Ill.

March 4.   To "Mr Sanford." MS., Univ. of Chicago Lib., Chicago, Ill.

[March 6].   To Mary Ann Cuthbert. MS., Ill. State Hist. Lib., Springfield, Ill.

March 7.   To Mary Ann Cuthbert. MS., Ill. State Hist. Lib., Springfield, Ill.

[March 9].   To Mary Ann Cuthbert. MS., Ill. State Hist. Lib., Springfield, Ill.

[March 10].   To Mary Ann Cuthbert. MS., Ill. State Hist. Lib., Springfield, Ill.

* See Bibliography.

March 11.   Request for a Pass. MS., Lincoln National Life Foundation. Fort Wayne, Ind.

March 28.   To Charles Sumner. MS., Houghton Lib., Harvard Univ., Cambridge, Mass.

April 1.   To Emmanuel Uhlfelder. MS., Ill. State Hist. Lib., Springfield, Ill.

[April 1].   To Edwin A. Brooks. MS., Ill. State Hist. Lib., Springfield, Ill.

April 5.   To Charles Sumner. MS., Houghton Lib., Harvard Univ., Cambridge, Mass.

April 16.   [To A. T. Stewart?]. MS. owned by King V. Hostick, Springfield, Ill.

[April 27].   To Warren Leland. MS., Ill. State Hist. Lib., Springfield, Ill.

April 28.   To Abraham Lincoln. A/p in Helm, p. 239.

May 3.   To Abram Wakeman. Photostat, Ill. State Hist. Lib. (ALA files), Springfield, Ill.

May 27.   To Mary Jane Welles. MS., Houghton Lib., Harvard Univ., Cambridge, Mass.

July 15.   To Phineas D. Gurley. MS., Houghton Lib., Harvard Univ., Cambridge, Mass.

July 20.   To George D. Ramsay. Photostat, Chicago Hist. Soc., Chicago, Ill.

July 29.   To Robert T. Lincoln. MS., Ill. State Hist. Lib., Springfield, Ill.

July 29.   To Mercy Levering Conkling. MS., Hist. Soc. of Pennsylvania, Philadelphia, Pa.

August 1.   To George A. Hearn. MS., Ill. State Hist. Lib., Springfield, Ill.

August 10.   To "Mrs Agen." Handwritten copy, Ill. State Hist. Lib. (ALA files), Springfield, Ill.

September 23.   To Abram Wakeman. Typescript supplied by Elizabeth M. Benner, Neshanic Station, N.J., former owner of MS.

October 23.   To Abram Wakeman. Typescript supplied by Elizabeth M. Benner.

[November 2].   To Elizabeth Keckley. MS. owned by Katrina van Asmus Kindel.

November 2.   To Gideon B. Welles. MS. owned by King V. Hostick.

November 9.   To Edwin M. Stanton. MS. privately owned. Photostat, Ill. State Hist. Lib. (ALA files), Springfield, Ill.

November 19.   To Mercy Levering Conkling. MS., Ill. State Hist. Lib., Springfield, Ill.

November 20.   To Hannah Shearer. MS. destroyed. A/p in " 'Your Truly Attached Friend, Mary Lincoln,' " by Charles V. Darrin. *Jour. Ill. State Hist. Soc.*, Spring 1951.

November 22.   To Oliver S. Halsted, Jr. MS., Ill. State Hist. Lib., Springfield, Ill.

[c November].   To Edward Grosjean. MS., Ill. State Hist. Lib., Springfield, Ill.

[November 20].   To Charles Sumner. MS., Houghton Lib., Harvard Univ., Cambridge, Mass.

November 24.   To Oliver S. Halsted, Jr. MS. privately owned. Photostat, Ill. State Hist. Lib. (ALA files), Springfield, Ill.

November 24.   To Charles Sumner. MS., Houghton Lib., Harvard Univ., Cambridge, Mass.

December 8.   To Edwin M. Stanton. MS. owned by King V. Hostick.

December 11.   To Ruth Harris. MS., Ill. State Hist. Lib., Springfield, Ill.

[December 15].   To Ruth Harris. MS., Ill. State Hist. Lib., Springfield, Ill.

December 16.   To James A. Hardie. Typescript, Ill. State Hist. Lib., Springfield, Ill.

December 20.   [To George Harrington?]. Photostat, Ill. State Hist. Lib., Springfield, Ill.

December 28.   To Ruth Harris. MS., Ill. State Hist. Lib., Springfield, Ill.

1865

[January 5].   To John A. Dillon. MS., Ill. State Hist. Lib., Springfield, Ill.

[January 9].   To James K. Kerr. MS., Ill. State Hist. Lib., Springfield, Ill.

[January 10].   To John K. Kerr. MS., Ill. State Hist. Lib., Springfield, Ill.

January 26.   To Simeon Draper. A/p in *Blumhaven Digest*, August 1957.

January 30.   To Abram Wakeman. Typescript supplied by Elizabeth M. Benner.

February 12.   To Winfield Scott Hancock. MS., Hist. Soc. of Pennsylvania, Philadelphia, Pa.

[February 18].   To Abram Wakeman. Typescript supplied by Elizabeth M. Benner.

February 20.   To Abram Wakeman. Typescript supplied by Elizabeth M. Benner.

February 21.   To Ruth Harris. MS., Ill. State Hist. Lib., Springfield, Ill.

February 24.   To Ruth Harris. MS. formerly owned by Justin G. Turner.

February 28.   To Robert T. Lincoln. Typescript, Ill. State Hist. Lib. (ALA files), Springfield, Ill.

[March 12].   To Abram Wakeman. Typescript supplied by Elizabeth M. Benner.

March 19.   To Charles Sumner. MS., Houghton Lib., Harvard Univ., Cambridge, Mass.

March 20.   To Abram Wakeman. MS., Lib. of Cong., Washington, D.C.

March 23.   To Charles Sumner. MS., Houghton Lib., Harvard Univ., Cambridge, Mass.

March 24.   To Mary Ann Cuthbert. MS., Ill. State Hist. Lib., Springfield, Ill.

March 25.   To Alphonso Dunn. MS., Lincoln Mus., Ford's Theatre, Washington, D.C. Typescript supplied.

April 2.   To Abraham Lincoln. MS., Ill. State Hist. Lib., Springfield, Ill.

April 3.   Certification. MS., Ill. State Hist. Lib., Springfield, Ill.

April 3.   Certification. MS. owned by Katrina van Asmus Kindel.

April 3.   To Charles Sumner. MS., Houghton Lib., Harvard Univ., Cambridge, Mass.

April 4.   To Abram Wakeman. Typescript supplied by Elizabeth M. Benner.

April 4.   To Abraham Lincoln. MS., Ill. State Hist. Lib., Springfield, Ill.

April 6.   To Abraham Lincoln. MS., National Archives, Washington, D.C.

April 6.   To Edwin M. Stanton. MS., Ill. State Hist. Lib., Springfield, Ill.

April 6.   To Abraham Lincoln. MS., National Archives, Washington, D.C.

[April 6].   To Charles Sumner. MS., Houghton Lib., Harvard Univ., Cambridge, Mass.

[April 10].   To Charles Sumner. MS., Houghton Lib., Harvard Univ., Cambridge, Mass.

April 11.   To Charles Sumner. MS., Houghton Lib., Harvard Univ., Cambridge, Mass.

[April 13].   To James Gordon Bennett. Excerpt/p in Parke-Bernet Catalogue, Bennett Sale, November 23, 1926. Item #80.

April 13.   To Charles Sumner. MS., Houghton Lib., Harvard Univ., Cambridge, Mass.

[April 13].   To Ulysses S. Grant. MS., Berkshire Mus., Pittsfield, Mass.

April 13.   To Abram Wakeman. Typescript supplied by Elizabeth M. Benner.

April 13.   To Schuyler Colfax. Excerpt/p in *The History of America in Documents*, Part Three, Item #246.*

[April 13].   To Schuyler Colfax. Excerpt/p in *The History of America in Documents*, Part Three, Item #247.

April 29.   To Andrew Johnson. MS., Lib. of Cong., Washington, D.C.

May 3.   To Andrew Johnson. MS., National Archives, Washington, D.C.

May 9.   To Charles Sumner. MS., Houghton Lib., Harvard Univ., Cambridge, Mass.

May 11.   To Charles Sumner. MS., Houghton Lib., Harvard Univ., Cambridge, Mass.

May 14.   To Charles Sumner. MS., Houghton Lib., Harvard Univ., Cambridge, Mass.

[c May].   To Andrew Johnson. A/p in *Lincoln Lore*, No. 641, July 21, 1941.

May 16.   To "Mrs Off & Mrs Baker." MS., Headquarters, National Society, Daughters of the American Revolution, Washington, D.C.

May 20.   To Alphonso Dunn. MS., Lincoln Mus., Ford's Theater. Washington, D.C. Typescript supplied.

May 21.   To H.M. Queen Victoria. MS., The White House, Washington, D.C.

May 29.   To Oliver S. Halsted, Jr. MS., Ill. State Hist. Lib., Springfield, Ill.

June 5.   To Richard J. Oglesby. MS. privately owned. Photostat, Ill. State Hist. Lib. (ALA files), Springfield, Ill.

June 8.   To Harriet Wilson. MS., Pierpont Morgan Lib., New York, N.Y.

[c. June].   Request for Agreement. MS., Ill. State Hist. Lib., Springfield, Ill.

June 10.   To Richard J. Oglesby. Photostat, Ill. State Hist. Lib. (ALA files), Springfield, Ill.

* See Bibliography.

June 11.   To Richard J. Oglesby. MS., Ill. State Hist. Lib., Springfield, Ill.

June 15.   To Alexander Williamson. MS., Chicago Hist. Soc., Chicago, Ill.

June 26.   To Alexander Williamson. MS., Huntington Lib., San Marino, Calif.

June 27.   To David Davis. MS., Ill. State Hist. Lib., Springfield, Ill.

July 4.   To Charles Sumner. MS., Houghton Library, Harvard Univ., Cambridge, Mass.

July 11.   To Mary Jane Welles. MS., Lib. of Cong., Washington, D.C.

July 11.   To Elizabeth Blair Lee. MS. on deposit at Princeton Univ. Lib., Princeton, N.J.

July 17.   To Anson G. Henry. MS. formerly owned by Justin G. Turner.

July 26.   To James K. Kerr. MS., Hist. Soc. of Pennsylvania, Philadelphia, Pa.

July 26.   To Anson G. Henry. Photostat, Chicago Hist. Soc., Chicago, Ill.

August 17.   To Alexander Williamson. A/p in Sandburg & Angle, pp. 237–8.

August 25.   To Elizabeth Blair Lee. MS. on deposit at Princeton Univ. Lib., Princeton, N.J.

August 30.   To Alexander Williamson. MS., Huntington Lib., San Marino, Calif.

August 31.   To Sally Orne. MS., Ill. State Hist. Lib., Springfield, Ill.

August 31.   To Eliza Henry. MS. owned by Mrs. Frank A. Hollowbush, Savannah, Ga.

September 9.   To Alexander Williamson. MS., Lincoln Mus., Ford's Theatre, Washington, D.C.

September 12.   To David Davis. MS., Ill. State Hist. Lib., Springfield, Ill.

October 12.   To James K. Kerr. MS., Hist. Soc. of Pennsylvania, Philadelphia, Pa.

October 14.   To Mary Jane Welles. MS., Lib. of Cong., Washington, D.C.

October 20.   To Alexander Williamson. Excerpt/p Parke-Bernet Catalogue, Barrett Sale, Feb. 19 & 20, 1952. Item #737.

October 26.   To Francis B. Carpenter. MS. formerly owned by Justin G. Turner.

November 11.   To Oliver S. Halsted, Jr. MS., Ill. State Hist. Lib., Springfield, Ill.

November 11.   To Alexander Williamson. MS., Huntington Lib., San Marino, Calif.

November 11.   To Leeds & Miner. A/p in Sandburg & Angle, p. 239.

November 15.   To Francis B. Carpenter. MS., Lilly Lib., Indiana Univ., Bloomington, Ind.

November 19.   To Alexander Williamson. MS., Huntington Lib., San Marino, Calif.

November 26.   To Alexander Williamson. MS., Huntington Lib., San Marino, Calif.

November 28.   To Alexander Williamson. MS., Huntington Lib., San Marino, Calif.

November 29.   To Elihu B. Washburne. MS., Lib. of Cong., Washington, D.C.

November 29. To Derby & Miller. MS., New-York Hist. Soc., New York, N.Y.

December 1. To Alexander Williamson. MS., Huntington Lib., San Marino, Calif.

December 4. To Josiah G. Holland. MS., Chicago Hist. Soc., Chicago, Ill.

December 6. To Mary Jane Welles. MS., Lib. of Cong., Washington, D.C.

December 7. To Alexander Williamson. MS., Huntington Lib., San Marino, Calif.

December 8. To Francis B. Carpenter. MS., Lilly Lib., Indiana Univ., Bloomington, Ind.

December 9. To Elihu B. Washburne. MS., Lib. of Cong., Washington, D.C.

December 11. To Elizabeth Blair Lee. MS. on deposit at Princeton Univ. Lib., Princeton, N.J.

December 13. To David Davis. MS., Ill. State Hist. Lib., Springfield, Ill.

December 13. To Alexander Williamson. MS., Huntington Lib., San Marino, Calif.

December 15. To Alexander Williamson. MS., Huntington Lib., San Marino, Calif.

December 15. To Elihu B. Washburne. MS., Lib. of Cong., Washington, D.C.

December 16. To Alexander Williamson. MS., Huntington Lib., San Marino, Calif.

December 16. To James A. Hardie. MS., The White House, Washington, D.C.

December 18. To Noah Brooks. MS. owned by Francis Whiting Hatch, Boston, Mass. A/p in his article "Mary Lincoln Writes to Noah Brooks." *Jour. Ill. State Hist. Soc.*, Spring 1955.

December 24. To Sally Orne. MS., Univ. of Chicago Lib., Chicago, Ill.

December 26. To Benjamin B. Sherman. A/p in Sandburg & Angle, pp. 250–1.

December 26. To Alexander Williamson. MS., Huntington Lib., San Marino, Calif.

December 29. To Mary Jane Welles. MS., Lib. of Cong., Washington, D.C.

December 29. To Alexander Williamson. MS., Huntington Lib., San Marino, Calif.

December 30. To Francis E. Spinner. A/p in *The New York Times*, undated clipping in possession of Justin G. Turner.

December 30. To Sally Orne. MS., Huntington Lib., San Marino, Calif.

December 31. To Alexander Williamson. MS., Huntington Lib., San Marino, Calif.

1866

January 1. To Francis E. Spinner. A/p in *The New York Times*, undated clipping in possession of Justin G. Turner.

January 3.   To Alexander Williamson. MS., Huntington Lib., San Marino, Calif.

January 4.   To Sally Orne. MS. privately owned. A/p in Sandburg & Angle, pp. 251–2.

January 5.   To David Davis. MS., Ill. State Hist. Lib., Springfield, Ill.

January 10.   To Sally Orne. MS., Huntington Lib., San Marino, Calif.

January 11.   To David Davis. MS., Ill. State Hist. Lib., Springfield, Ill.

January 11.   To Francis E. Spinner. A/p in *The New York Times*, undated clipping in possession of Justin G. Turner.

January 13.   To Sally Orne. MS., Brown Univ. Lib., Providence, R.I.

January 17.   To Alexander Williamson. MS., Huntington Lib., San Marino, Calif.

January 17.   To Oliver S. Halsted, Jr. MS., Ill. State Hist. Lib., Springfield, Ill.

January 19.   To Alexander Williamson. MS., Huntington Lib., San Marino, Calif.

January 21.   To Oliver S. Halsted, Jr. MS., Ill. State Hist. Lib., Springfield, Ill.

January 26.   To Alexander Williamson. MS., Huntington Lib., San Marino, Calif.

January 27.   To Alexander Williamson. MS., Huntington Lib., San Marino, Calif.

February 2.   To Alexander Williamson. MS., Huntington Lib., San Marino, Calif.

February 5.   To Alexander Williamson. MS., Huntington Lib., San Marino, Calif.

February 9.   To Alexander Williamson. MS., Huntington Lib., San Marino, Calif.

February 17.   To Alexander Williamson. MS., Huntington Lib., San Marino, Calif.

February 20.   To Alexander Williamson. MS., Huntington Lib., San Marino, Calif.

February 20.   To Alexander Williamson. MS., Huntington Lib., San Marino, Calif.

February 27.   To Alexander Williamson. MS., Huntington Lib., San Marino, Calif.

March 7.   To David Davis. MS., Ill. State Hist. Lib., Springfield, Ill.

March 12.   To Alexander Williamson. MS., Huntington Lib., San Marino, Calif.

March 13.   To Alexander Williamson. MS., Huntington Lib., San Marino, Calif.

March 14.   To David Davis. MS., Ill. State Hist. Lib., Springfield, Ill.

March 15.   To Sally Orne. MS. owned by David Kirschenbaum, Carnegie Book Shop, New York, N.Y.

March 25.   To Alexander Williamson. MS., Huntington Lib., San Marino, Calif.

March 27.   To Mary Ann Foote. MS., New Jersey Hist. Soc., Newark, N.J.

March 29.   To Alexander Williamson. MS., Huntington Lib., San Marino, Calif.

April 2.   To Charles Sumner. MS., Brown Univ. Lib., Providence, R.I.

April 6.   To Simon Cameron. MS. owned by Philip D. Sang. A/p in his article "Mary Todd Lincoln: A Tragic Portrait." *Jour. Rutgers Univ. Lib.*, April 1961.

April 6.   To Simon Cameron. MS. owned by Philip D. Sang. A/p in his article "Mary Todd Lincoln: A Tragic Portrait." *Jour. Rutgers Univ. Lib.*, April 1961.

April 9.   To Lucy A. Little. MS., Univ. of Chicago Lib., Chicago, Ill.

April 10.   To Charles Sumner. MS., Houghton Lib., Harvard Univ., Cambridge, Mass.

April 15.   To A. R. Thompson. MS., Lib. of Cong., Washington, D.C.

April 17.   To Simon Cameron. MS. owned by Philip D. Sang. A/p in his article "Mary Todd Lincoln: A Tragic Portrait." *Jour. Rutgers Univ. Lib.*, April 1961.

April 21.   To Simon Cameron. MS. owned by Philip D. Sang. A/p in his article "Mary Todd Lincoln: A Tragic Portrait." *Jour. Rutgers Univ. Lib.*, April 1961.

[April 24].   To Alexander Williamson. MS., Huntington Lib., San Marino, Calif.

April 25.   To Alexander Williamson. MS., Huntington Lib., San Marino, Calif.

April 26.   To David Davis. MS., Ill. State Hist. Lib., Springfield, Ill.

May 4.   To David Davis. MS., Ill. State Hist. Lib., Springfield, Ill.

May 4.   To Simon Cameron. MS. owned by Philip D. Sang. A/p in his article "Mary Todd Lincoln: A Tragic Portrait." *Jour. Rutgers Univ. Lib.*, April 1961.

May 6.   To Alexander Williamson. MS., Huntington Lib., San Marino, Calif.

May 11.   To Noah Brooks. MS. owned by Francis Whiting Hatch. A/p in his article "Mary Lincoln Writes to Noah Brooks." *Jour. Ill. State Hist. Soc.*, Spring 1955.

May 11.   To Alexander Williamson. MS., Huntington Lib., San Marino, Calif.

May 15.   To Alexander Williamson. MS., Huntington Lib., San Marino, Calif.

[May 16].   To Alexander Williamson. MS., Huntington Lib., San Marino, Calif.

May 19.   To Simon Cameron. MS. owned by Philip D. Sang. A/p in his article "Mary Todd Lincoln: A Tragic Portrait." *Jour. Rutgers Univ. Lib.*, April 1961.

May 26.   To Simon Cameron. MS. owned by Philip D. Sang. A/p in his article "Mary Todd Lincoln: A Tragic Portrait." *Jour. Rutgers Univ. Lib.*, April 1961.

[c June].   [To Caroline Roberts]. Handwritten copy, Yale Univ. Lib., New Haven, Conn.

June 3. To Derby & Miller. MS., Pierpont Morgan Lib., New York, N.Y.

June 9. To Alexander Williamson. MS., Huntington Lib., San Marino, Calif.

June 16. To Simon Cameron. MS. owned by Philip D. Sang. A/p in his article "Mary Todd Lincoln: A Tragic Portrait." *Jour. Rutgers Univ. Lib.*, April 1961.

June 24. To Alexander Williamson. MS., Huntington Lib., San Marino, Calif.

June 26. To Alexander Williamson. MS., Huntington Lib., San Marino, Calif.

June 29. To Alexander Williamson. MS., Huntington Lib., San Marino, Calif.

June 29. To Alexander Williamson. MS., St. John's Seminary Lib., Camarillo, Calif.

July 5. To Alexander Williamson. MS., Huntington Lib., San Marino, Calif.

July 5. To Alexander Williamson. MS., Huntington Lib., San Marino, Calif.

July 21. To Alexander Williamson. MS., Huntington Lib., San Marino, Calif.

July 23. To Francis E. Spinner. MS., A/p in *The New York Times*, October 18, 1948.

August 5. To Alexander Williamson. MS., Huntington Lib., San Marino, Calif.

August 12. To Frank E. Howe. MS., Chicago Hist. Soc., Chicago, Ill.

August 12. To David Davis. MS., Ill. State Hist. Lib., Springfield, Ill.

August 19. To Alexander Williamson. MS., Huntington Lib., San Marino, Calif.

August 20. To David Davis. Photostat, Ill. State Hist. Lib. (ALA files), Springfield, Ill.

August 28. To William H. Herndon. MS., Lib. of Cong., Washington, D.C.

September 2. To Alexander Williamson. MS., Huntington Lib., San Marino, Calif.

September 7. To Alexander Williamson. MS., Huntington Lib., San Marino, Calif.

September 10. To Charles Sumner. MS., Houghton Lib., Harvard Univ., Cambridge, Mass.

September 13. To Leonard Swett. MS. privately owned. Photostat, Ill. State Hist. Lib. (ALA files), Springfield, Ill.

September 15. To Leonard Swett. MS., Ill. State Hist. Lib., Springfield, Ill.

September 23. To Alexander Williamson. MS., Huntington Lib., San Marino, Calif.

September 24. To Orville H. Browning. MS., Ill. State Hist. Lib., Springfield, Ill.

October 1. To Charles Sumner. MS., Houghton Lib., Harvard Univ., Cambridge, Mass.

October 17.   To Alexander Williamson. MS., Chicago Hist. Soc., Chicago, Ill.

October 30.   To Alexander Williamson. MS., Huntington Lib., San Marino, Calif.

November 5.   To Alexander Williamson. MS., Chicago Hist. Soc., Chicago, Ill.

November 27.   To Leonard Swett. Photostat, Ill. State Hist. Lib. (ALA files), Springfield, Ill.

December 3.   To Orville H. Browning. MS., Chicago Hist. Soc., Chicago, Ill.

December 14.   To Alexander Williamson. MS., Huntington Lib., San Marino, Calif.

December 16.   To Alexander Williamson. MS., Huntington Lib., San Marino, Calif.

December 17.   To James Smith. MS. owned by Mrs. Stanley H. Graves, Hadley, Mass. On deposit, Huntington Lib., San Marino, Calif.

December 17.   To Alexander Williamson. MS., Huntington Lib., San Marino, Calif.

December [?].   To David Davis. MS., Ill. State Hist. Lib., Springfield, Ill.

December 25.   To David Davis. MS., Ill. State Hist. Lib., Springfield, Ill.

December 25.   To Francis B. Carpenter. MS., Lilly Lib., Indiana Univ., Bloomington, Ind.

1867

January 3.   To The Committee of the French Democracy. Photograph of MS. in MacChesney. *Abraham Lincoln: The Tribute of a Century*, pp. 286–7.*

January 9.   To David Davis. MS., Ill. State Hist. Lib., Springfield, Ill.

January 12.   To Leonard Swett. Photostat, Ill. State Hist. Lib. (ALA files), Springfield, Ill.

January 14.   To David Davis. MS., Ill. State Hist. Lib., Springfield, Ill.

January 18.   To Leonard Swett. Photostat, Ill. State Hist. Lib. (ALA files), Springfield, Ill.

January 27.   To David Davis. MS., Ill. State Hist. Lib., Springfield, Ill.

[c February].   To Leonard Swett. Photostat, Ill. State Hist. Lib. (ALA files), Springfield, Ill.

[c February].   To Leonard Swett. Photostat, Ill. State Hist. Lib. (ALA files), Springfield, Ill.

February 24.   To David Davis. MS., Ill. State Hist. Lib., Springfield, Ill.

March 4.   To David Davis. MS., Ill. State Hist. Lib., Springfield, Ill.

March 6.   To David Davis. MS., Ill. State Hist. Lib., Springfield, Ill.

March 18.   To Alphonso Dunn. MS., Lincoln Mus., Ford's Theatre, Washington, D.C. Typewritten copy supplied.

March 19.   To William H. Crook. Photostat, Ill. State Hist. Lib. (ALA files), Springfield, Ill.

* See Bibliography.

[March ?].   To Elizabeth Keckley. A/p in Keckley. *Behind the Scenes*, pp.
    267–8.*

April 2.   To Alphonso Dunn. MS., Lincoln Mus., Ford's Theatre, Washing-
    ton, D.C. Typewritten copy supplied.

April 6.   To David Davis. MS., Ill. State Hist. Lib., Springfield, Ill.

[May 26].   To Alexander Williamson. MS., Huntington Lib., San Marino,
    Calif.

June 17.   To David Davis. MS., Ill. State Hist. Lib., Springfield, Ill.

June 30.   To David Davis. MS., Ill. State Hist. Lib., Springfield, Ill.

June 30.   To Elizabeth Atwater. MS. privately owned. Photostat, Ill. State
    Hist. Lib. (ALA files), Springfield, Ill.

July 8.   To David Davis. MS., Ill. State Hist. Lib., Springfield, Ill.

July 13.   To Elizabeth Atwater. MS., Ill. State Hist. Lib., Springfield, Ill.

September 17.   To Elizabeth Keckley. A/p in Keckley, pp. 277–8.

[*c* September].   To W. H. Brady. A/p in Keckley, pp. 291–2.

September 14.   To W. H. Brady. A/p in the New York *World*, October 3,
    1867.

September 18.   To W. H. Brady. A/p in the New York *World*, October
    3, 1867.

September 22.   To W. H. Brady. A/p in the New York *World*, October 3,
    1867.

September 25.   To W. H. Brady. A/p in the New York *World*, October 3,
    1867.

October 6.   To Elizabeth Keckley. A/p in Keckley, pp. 296–301.

October 6.   To Elizabeth Keckley. A/p in Keckley, pp. 332–3.

October 8.   To Elizabeth Keckley. A/p in Keckley, pp. 333–5.

October 9.   To Elizabeth Keckley. A/p in Keckley, pp. 335–6.

October 13.   To Elizabeth Keckley. A/p in Keckley, pp. 336–9.

October 18.   To Rhoda White. MS., Ill. State Hist. Lib., Springfield, Ill.

[October 24].   To Elizabeth Keckley. A/p in Keckley, pp. 339–41.

October 29.   To Alexander Williamson. MS., Huntington Lib., San
    Marino, Calif.

October 29.   To Elizabeth Keckley. A/p in Keckley, pp. 341–2.

November 2.   To Elizabeth Keckley. A/p in Keckley, pp. 343–4.

November 9.   To Elizabeth Keckley. A/p in Keckley, pp. 345–6.

November 9.   To Elizabeth Keckley. A/p in Keckley, pp. 346–8.

November 9.   To David Davis, Ill. State Hist. Lib., Springfield, Ill.

November 10.   To Alexander Williamson. MS., Brown Univ. Lib., Provi-
    dence, R.I.

November 15.   To Elizabeth Keckley. A/p in Keckley, pp. 348–54.

November 17.   To Elizabeth Keckley. A/p in Keckley, pp. 354–6.

November 17.   To Elizabeth Keckley. A/p in Keckley, pp. 356–7.

November 17.   To David Davis. MS., Ill. State Hist. Lib., Springfield, Ill.

November 18.   To David Davis. MS., Ill. State Hist. Lib., Springfield, Ill.

November 21.   To Elizabeth Keckley. A/p in Keckley, pp. 357–8.

November 21.   To Rhoda White. MS., Univ. of Chicago Lib., Chicago, Ill.

*   See Bibliography.

November 23.   To Elizabeth Keckley. A/p in Keckley, pp. 359–60.

November 24.   To Elizabeth Keckley. A/p in Keckley, pp. 360–2.

November 27.   To David Davis. MS., Ill. State Hist. Lib., Springfield, Ill.

December 16.   To Henry C. Deming. MS. privately owned. Excerpt/p in Swann & Co. Catalogue, Jan. 19, 1950. Item #250.

December 19.   To Sarah Bush Lincoln. MS., Lincoln Natl. Life Foundation, Fort Wayne, Ind.

December 20.   [To Sarah Bush Lincoln]. A/p in Sandburg & Angle, p. 280.

December 26.   To Elizabeth Keckley. A/p in Keckley, pp. 362–3.

December 27.   To Elizabeth Keckley. A/p in Keckley, pp. 363–4.

December 30.   To Alexander Williamson. MS., Lincoln Natl. Life Foundation, Fort Wayne, Ind.

1868

January 9.   To Alexander Williamson. MS., Lincoln Memorial Univ. Lib., Harrogate, Tenn.

January 12.   To Elizabeth Keckley. A/p in Keckley, pp. 364–6.

January 15.   To Elizabeth Keckley. A/p in Keckley, pp. 368–9.

February 7.   To W. H. Brady. A/p in Keckley, pp. 369–70.

February 29.   To Elizabeth Keckley. A/p in Keckley, pp. 370–1.

May 2.   To Rhoda White. MS., Univ. of Chicago Lib., Chicago, Ill.

June 19.   To Jesse K. Dubois. Photostat, Ill. State Hist. Lib. (ALA files), Springfield, Ill.

June 27.   To John W. Forney. MS., Hist. Soc. of Pennsylvania, Philadelphia, Pa.

July 18.   To Rhoda White. MS., Ill. State Hist. Lib., Springfield, Ill.

July 18.   To Martha Stafford. MS. owned by Katrina van Asmus Kindel.

August 19.   To Rhoda White. MS., Univ. of Chicago Lib., Chicago, Ill.

August 27.   To Rhoda White. MS. formerly owned by Justin G. Turner.

September 21.   To Eliza Slataper. MS. formerly owned by Justin G. Turner. A/p in his article "The Mary Lincoln Letters to Mrs. Felician Slataper." *Jour. Ill. State Hist. Soc.*, Spring 1956.

September 25.   To Eliza Slataper. MS. formerly owned by Justin G. Turner. A/p in his article "The Mary Lincoln Letters to Mrs. Felician Slataper." *Jour. Ill. State Hist. Soc.*, Spring 1956.

September 27.   To Eliza Slataper. MS. formerly owned by Justin G. Turner. A/p in his article "The Mary Lincoln Letters to Mrs. Felician Slataper." *Jour. Ill. State Hist. Soc.*, Spring 1956.

September 29.   To Eliza Slataper. MS. formerly owned by Justin G. Turner. A/p in his article "The Mary Lincoln Letters to Mrs. Felician Slataper." *Jour. Ill. State Hist. Soc.*, Spring 1956.

December 4.   To George Boutwell. MS., privately owned. Photostat, Ill. State Hist. Lib. (ALA files), Springfield, Ill.

December 4.   To Nathaniel P. Banks. Excerpt /p in Parke-Bernet Catalogue, Smith Family & Philip Ward, Jr. Sale, May 5, 1964, Item #131.

[*c* December]. To The United States Senate. A/p in the Chicago *Times*, January 26, 1869.

December 13. To Eliza Slataper. MS. formerly owned by Justin G. Turner. A/p in his article "The Mary Lincoln Letters to Mrs. Felician Slataper." *Jour. Ill. State Hist. Soc.*, Spring 1956.

December 15. To David Davis. MS., Ill. State Hist. Lib., Springfield, Ill.

1869

January 18. To John Todd Stuart. MS., Ill. State Hist. Lib., Springfield, Ill.

February 17. To Eliza Slataper. MS. formerly owned by Justin G. Turner. A/p in his article, "The Mary Lincoln Letters to Mrs. Felician Slataper." *Jour. Ill. State Hist. Soc.*, Spring 1956.

March 16. To Rhoda White. MS. owned by Philip D. Sang. A/p in his article "Mary Todd Lincoln: A Tragic Portrait." *Jour. Rutgers Univ. Lib.*, April 1961.

March 22. To Mary Harlan Lincoln. A/p in Helm, pp. 280–300.

March 27. To Charles Sumner. MS., Houghton Lib., Harvard Univ., Cambridge, Mass.

August 17. To Sally Orne. Photostat, Ill. State Hist. Lib. (ALA files), Springfield, Ill.

August 20. To Mary Harlan Lincoln. Excerpt /p in Helm, p. 286.

August 21. To Eliza Slataper. MS. formerly owned by Justin G. Turner. A/p in his article "The Mary Lincoln Letters to Mrs. Felician Slataper." *Jour. Ill. State Hist. Soc.*, Spring 1956.

August 26. To James Smith. MS. owned by Mrs. Stanley H. Graves. On deposit at Huntington Lib., San Marino, Calif.

August 30. To Rhoda White. MS., privately owned. Photostat, Lib. of Cong., Washington, D.C.

September 10. To Sally Orne. MS., Lincoln Memorial Univ. Lib., Harrogate, Tenn.

October 18. To Sally Orne. MS., Huntington Lib., San Marino, Calif.

October 23. To Sally Orne. MS. owned by Mrs. Richard Maass, White Plains, N.Y.

November 7. To Sally Orne. Photostat, Ill. State Hist. Lib. (ALA files), Springfield, Ill.

November [13]. To Sally Orne. MS., Huntington Lib., San Marino, Calif.

November 14. To Sally Orne. MS., Ill. State Hist. Lib., Springfield, Ill.

November 20. To Sally Orne. MS., Franklin and Marshall College Lib., Lancaster, Pa.

November 28. To Sally Orne. MS. owned by Mrs. Richard Maass.

December 2. To Sally Orne. MS., Univ. of Chicago Lib., Chicago, Ill.

December 5. To Sally Orne. MS. owned by Harry J. Sonneborn, Winnetka, Ill. Handwritten excerpts in possession of Justin G. Turner.

December 11. To James Smith. MS. owned by Mrs. Stanley H. Graves. On deposit, Huntington Lib., San Marino, Calif.

[December 12]. To Sally Orne. MS. owned by Mrs. Richard Maass.

December 16.   To Sally Orne. MS., Ill. State Hist. Lib., Springfield, Ill.
December 20.   To Rhoda White. Excerpt/p in *The History of America in Documents*, Part Three, Item #295.
[December 21].   To Sally Orne. MS. privately owned. Excerpt/p in Coins & Currency Catalogue, Spring 1969. Item #75.
December 29.   To Sally Orne. MS., Huntington Lib., San Marino, Calif.

1870

January 2.   To Sally Orne. MS., Ill. State Hist. Lib., Springfield, Ill.
January 8.   To Sally Orne. MS., Huntington Lib., San Marino, Calif.
January 13.   To Sally Orne. MS., Ill. State Hist. Lib., Springfield, Ill.
January 21.   To Sally Orne. MS., privately owned. Photostat, Ill. State Hist. Lib., Springfield, Ill.
January 30.   To Rhoda White. MS., Ill. State Hist. Lib., Springfield, Ill.
February 11.   To Sally Orne. MS., Ill. State Hist. Lib., Springfield, Ill.
[February 18].   To Sally Orne. MS., Brown Univ. Lib., Providence, R.I.
February 18.   To Sally Orne. A/p in Sandburg & Angle, pp. 294–6.
March 31.   To Sally Orne. MS., Ill. State Hist. Lib., Springfield, Ill.
April 3.   To Sally Orne. MS., Yale Univ. Lib., New Haven, Conn.
April 26.   To Charles O'Neill. MS., Ill. State Hist. Lib., Springfield, Ill.
May 9.   To Charles O'Neill. MS., John H. Scheide Lib., Titusville, Pa.
May 16.   To James H. Orne. MS., Ill. State Hist. Lib., Springfield, Ill.
May 19.   To Mary Harlan Lincoln. A/p in Helm, pp. 283–4.
May 22.   To Sally Orne. MS., Huntington Lib., San Marino, Calif.
May 28.   To James H. Orne. MS., Blumhaven Lib., Philadelphia, Pa.
June 2.   To Norman B. Judd. MS., Brown Univ. Lib., Providence, R.I.
June 4.   To James Smith. MS. owned by Mrs. Stanley H. Graves. On deposit, Huntington Lib., San Marino, Calif.
[June 8].   To James Smith. MS. owned by Mrs. Stanley H. Graves. On deposit, Huntington Lib., San Marino, Calif.
June 22.   To James Smith. MS. owned by Mrs. Stanley H. Graves. On deposit, Huntington Lib., San Marino, Calif.
June 29.   To Mrs. Paul R. Shipman. A/p in Helm, pp. 284–5.
June 30.   To Catherine Hurst. MS. owned by Philip D. Sang. A/p in his article "Mary Todd Lincoln: A Tragic Portrait." *Jour. Rutgers Univ. Lib.*, April 1961.
July 16.   To James H. Orne. MS., Ill. State Hist. Lib., Springfield, Ill.
[August 17].   To Sally Orne. MS., privately owned. Excerpt/p Coins & Currency Catalogue, Spring 1969. Item #76.
September 7.   To Charles Sumner. MS., Houghton Lib., Harvard Univ., Cambridge, Mass.
September 10.   To Mary Harlan Lincoln. A/p in Helm, pp. 286–7.
October 27.   To Mrs. Paul R. Shipman. A/p in Helm, pp. 287–8.
November 7.   To Eliza Slataper. MS. formerly owned by Justin G. Turner. A/p in his article "The Mary Lincoln Letters to Mrs. Felician Slataper." *Jour. Ill. State Hist. Soc.*, Spring 1956.
[c November].   To Mary Harlan Lincoln. A/p in Helm, pp. 277–8.

December 21.   To Adam Badeau. MS., in Lincoln College Lib., Lincoln, Ill.

1871

January 13.   To Mrs. Paul R. Shipman. A/p in Helm, pp. 288–9.

January 26.   To Mary Harlan Lincoln. A/p in Helm, pp. 289–90.

February 12.   To Mary Harlan Lincoln. A/p in Helm, pp. 279–80.

May 21.   To Rhoda White. MS., Univ. of Chicago Lib., Chicago, Ill.

May [23].   To Eliza Stuart Steele. A/p in Helm, pp. 290–1.

[May 23].   To Rhoda White. MS., Headq. of the Natl. Soc., Daughters of the American Revolution, Washington, D.C.

June 8.   To Rhoda White. MS., Univ. of Chicago Lib., Chicago, Ill.

July 27.   To Eliza Slataper. MS. formerly owned by Justin G. Turner. A/p in his article "The Mary Lincoln Letters to Mrs. Felician Slataper." *Jour. Ill. State Hist. Soc.*, Spring 1956.

[August] 13.   To Eliza Slataper. MS. formerly owned by Justin G. Turner. A/p in his article "The Mary Lincoln Letters to Mrs. Felician Slataper." *Jour. Ill. State Hist Soc.*, Spring 1956.

October 4.   To Eliza Slataper. MS. formerly owned by Justin G. Turner. A/p in his article "The Mary Lincoln Letters to Mrs. Felician Slataper."

November 9.   To C. L. Farrington. Photostat, Ill. State Hist. Lib. (ALA files), Springfield, Ill.

November 9.   To David Davis. MS., Ill. State Hist. Lib. (ALA files), Springfield, Ill.

1872

May 26.   To Mrs. George Eastman. MS., privately owned. Photostat in possession of Justin G. Turner.

August 3.   To James H. Knowlton. MS., privately owned. Photostat, Ill. State Hist. Lib. (ALA files), Springfield, Ill.

August 7.   To Norman Williams. Photostat, Ill. State Hist. Lib. (ALA files), Springfield, Ill.

1873

January 18.   To Isaac N. Arnold. MS., Chicago Hist. Soc., Chicago, Ill.

December 15.   To John Todd Stuart. M.S., Ill. State Hist. Lib., Springfield, Ill.

December 16.   To John Todd Stuart. MS., Ill. State Hist. Lib., Springfield, Ill.

1874

January 20.   To John Todd Stuart. MS., Ill. State Hist. Lib., Springfield, Ill.

January 21.   To John Todd Stuart. MS., Ill. State Hist. Lib., Springfield,
Ill.
[October 20].   To Isaac N. Arnold. MS., Chicago Hist. Soc., Chicago, Ill.

1875

December 1.   To Ira Harris. MS., privately owned. Photostat, Ill. State
Hist. Lib. (ALA files), Springfield, Ill.

1876

June 19.   To Robert T. Lincoln. MS. owned by Philip D. Sang. A/p in his
article "Mary Todd Lincoln: A Tragic Portrait." *Jour. Rutgers Univ.
Lib.*, April 1961.
October 17.   To Edward Lewis Baker, Jr. MS., Ill. State Hist. Lib.,
Springfield, Ill.
October 23.   To Jacob Bunn. MS., Ill. State Hist. Lib., Springfield, Ill.
October 24.   To Jacob Bunn. MS., Ill. State Hist. Lib., Springfield, Ill.
November 28.   To Jacob Bunn. MS., Ill. State Hist. Lib., Springfield, Ill.
December 12.   To Jacob Bunn. MS., Ill. State Hist. Lib., Springfield, Ill.

1877

January 31.   To Jacob Bunn. MS., Ill. State Hist. Lib., Springfield, Ill.
February 5.   To Jacob Bunn. MS., Ill. State Hist. Lib., Springfield, Ill.
February 13.   To Jacob Bunn. MS., Ill. State Hist. Lib., Springfield, Ill.
February 20.   To Jacob Bunn. MS., Ill. State Hist. Lib., Springfield, Ill.
February 27.   To Jacob Bunn. MS., Ill. State Hist. Lib., Springfield, Ill.
March 19.   To Jacob Bunn. MS., Ill. State Hist. Lib., Springfield, Ill.
March 19.   To Elizabeth Todd Edwards. MS., Lincoln Natl. Life Foun-
dation, Fort Wayne, Ind.
March 19.   To Jacob Bunn. MS., Ill. State Hist. Lib., Springfield, Ill.
March 21.   To Jacob Bunn. MS., Ill. State Hist. Lib., Springfield, Ill.
March 31.   To Jacob Bunn. MS., Ill. State Hist. Lib., Springfield, Ill.
April 11.   To Edward Lewis Baker, Jr. MS., Ill. State Hist. Lib., Spring-
field, Ill.
April 23.   To Jacob Bunn. MS., Ill. State Hist. Lib., Springfield, Ill.
April 25.   To Jacob Bunn. MS., Ill. State Hist. Lib., Springfield, Ill.
April 28.   To Delia Dubois. MS., Ill. State Hist. Lib., Springfield, Ill.
May 18.   To Jacob Bunn. MS., Ill. State Hist. Lib., Springfield, Ill.
May 20.   To Edward Lewis Baker, Jr. MS., Ill. State Hist. Lib., Spring-
field, Ill.
May 22.   To Jacob Bunn. MS., Ill. State Hist. Lib., Springfield, Ill.
June 5.   To Jacob Bunn. MS., Ill. State Hist. Lib., Springfield, Ill.
June 6.   To Jacob Bunn. MS., Ill. State Hist. Lib., Springfield, Ill.
[June 6].   To Jacob Bunn. MS., Ill. State Hist. Lib., Springfield, Ill.

June 13.   To Jacob Bunn. MS., Ill. State Hist. Lib., Springfield, Ill.
June 20.   To Jacob Bunn. MS., Ill. State Hist. Lib., Springfield, Ill.
June 2[6].   To Jacob Bunn. MS., Ill. State Hist. Lib., Springfield, Ill.
June 27.   To Jacob Bunn. MS., Ill. State Hist. Lib., Springfield, Ill.
July 2.   To Jacob Bunn. MS., Ill. State Hist. Lib., Springfield, Ill.
July 9.   To Jacob Bunn. MS., Ill. State Hist. Lib., Springfield, Ill.
July [10].   To Jacob Bunn. MS., Ill. State Hist. Lib., Springfield, Ill.
July 20.   To Jacob Bunn. MS., Ill. State Hist. Lib., Springfield, Ill.
August 6.   To Jacob Bunn. MS., Ill. State Hist. Lib., Springfield, Ill.
August 22.   To Jacob Bunn. MS., Ill. State Hist. Lib., Springfield, Ill.
September 5.   To Jacob Bunn. MS., Ill. State Hist. Lib., Springfield, Ill.
September 20.   To Jacob Bunn. MS., Ill. State Hist. Lib., Springfield, Ill.
October 1.   To Jacob Bunn. MS., Ill. State Hist. Lib., Springfield, Ill.
October 16.   To Jacob Bunn. MS., Ill. State Hist. Lib., Springfield, Ill.
October 24.   To Jacob Bunn. MS., Ill. State Hist. Lib., Springfield, Ill.
November 7.   To Jacob Bunn. MS., Ill. State Hist. Lib., Springfield, Ill.
November 16.   To Jacob Bunn. MS., Ill. State Hist. Lib., Springfield, Ill.
December 8.   To Jacob Bunn. MS., Ill. State Hist. Lib., Springfield, Ill.
December 10.   To Jacob Bunn. MS., Ill. State Hist. Lib., Springfield, Ill.
December 19.   To Jacob Bunn. MS., Ill. State Hist. Lib., Springfield, Ill.

1878

January 15.   To Jacob Bunn. MS., Ill. State Hist. Lib., Springfield, Ill.
January 24.   To Jacob Bunn. MS., Ill. State Hist. Lib., Springfield, Ill.
January 26.   To Jacob Bunn. MS., Ill. State Hist. Lib., Springfield, Ill.
February 12.   To Jacob Bunn. MS., Ill. State Hist. Lib., Springfield, Ill.
February 26.   To Jacob Bunn. MS., Ill. State Hist. Lib., Springfield, Ill.
February 26.   To Jacob Bunn. MS., Ill. State Hist. Lib., Springfield, Ill.
February 27.   To Jacob Bunn. MS., Ill. State Hist. Lib., Springfield, Ill.
March 5.   To Jacob Bunn. MS., Ill. State Hist. Lib., Springfield, Ill.
March 22.   To Jacob Bunn. MS., Ill. State Hist. Lib., Springfield, Ill.
April 10.   To Jacob Bunn. MS., Ill. State Hist. Lib., Springfield, Ill.
April 29.   To Jacob Bunn. MS., Ill. State Hist. Lib., Springfield, Ill.
May 22.   To Jacob Bunn. MS., Ill. State Hist. Lib., Springfield, Ill.
June 5.   To Jacob Bunn. MS., Ill. State Hist. Lib., Springfield, Ill.
June 24.   To Jacob Bunn. MS., Ill. State Hist. Lib., Springfield, Ill.
July 13.   To Jacob Bunn. MS., Ill. State Hist. Lib., Springfield, Ill.
July 20.   To Jacob Bunn. MS., Ill. State Hist. Lib., Springfield, Ill.
August 19.   To Jacob Bunn. MS., Ill. State Hist. Lib., Springfield, Ill.
September 5.   To Jacob Bunn. MS., Ill. State Hist. Lib., Springfield, Ill.
September 26.   To Jacob Bunn. MS., Ill. State Hist. Lib., Springfield, Ill.
October 14.   To Jacob Bunn. MS., Ill. State Hist. Lib., Springfield, Ill.
October 23.   To Jacob Bunn. MS., Ill. State Hist. Lib., Springfield, Ill.
October 25.   To Jacob Bunn. MS., Ill. State Hist. Lib., Springfield, Ill.
December 5.   To Jacob Bunn. MS., Ill. State Hist. Lib., Springfield, Ill.
December 23.   To Jacob Bunn. MS., Ill. State Hist. Lib., Springfield, Ill.

1879

January 13.   To Jacob Bunn. MS., Ill. State Hist. Lib., Springfield, Ill.
January 23.   To Jacob Bunn. MS., Ill. State Hist. Lib., Springfield, Ill.
January 27.   To Jacob Bunn. MS., Ill. State Hist. Lib., Springfield, Ill.
February 11.   To Jacob Bunn. MS., Ill. State Hist. Lib., Springfield, Ill.
February 26.   To Jacob Bunn. MS., Ill. State Hist. Lib., Springfield, Ill.
February 27.   To Jacob Bunn. MS., Ill. State Hist. Lib., Springfield, Ill.
March 5.   To Jacob Bunn. MS., Ill. State Hist. Lib., Springfield, Ill.
April 1.   To Jacob Bunn. MS., Ill. State Hist. Lib., Springfield, Ill.
[April 10].   To Jacob Bunn. MS., Ill. State Hist. Lib., Springfield, Ill.
April 23.   To Jacob Bunn. MS., Ill. State Hist. Lib., Springfield, Ill.
May 20.   To Jacob Bunn. MS., Ill. State Hist. Lib., Springfield, Ill.
June 5.   To Jacob Bunn. MS., Ill. State Hist. Lib., Springfield, Ill.
June 21.   To Jacob Bunn. MS., Ill. State Hist. Lib., Springfield, Ill.
June 22.   To Edward Lewis Baker, Jr. MS., Ill. State Hist. Lib., Springfield, Ill.
July 10.   To Jacob Bunn. MS., Ill. State Hist. Lib., Springfield, Ill.
July 21.   To Jacob Bunn. MS., Ill. State Hist. Lib., Springfield, Ill.
August 3.   To Edward Lewis Baker, Jr. MS., Ill. State Hist. Lib., Springfield, Ill.
August 18.   To Jacob Bunn. MS., Ill. State Hist. Lib., Springfield, Ill.
September 5.   To Jacob Bunn. MS., Ill. State Hist. Lib., Springfield, Ill.
October 4.   To E. H. Shannon. MS., Ill. State Hist. Lib., Springfield, Ill.
October 4.   To Edward Lewis Baker, Jr. MS., Ill. State Hist. Lib., Springfield, Ill.
October 21.   To Jacob Bunn. MS., Ill. State Hist. Lib., Springfield, Ill.
December 5.   To Jacob Bunn. MS., Ill. State Hist. Lib., Springfield, Ill.
December 22.   To Jacob Bunn. MS., Ill. State Hist. Lib., Springfield, Ill.

1880

January 14.   To Jacob Bunn. MS., Ill. State Hist. Lib., Springfield, Ill.
January 16.   To Edward Lewis Baker, Jr. MS., Ill. State Hist. Lib., Springfield, Ill.
January 19.   To Edward Lewis Baker, Jr. MS., Ill. State Hist. Lib., Springfield, Ill.
January 26.   To Jacob Bunn. MS., Ill. State Hist. Lib., Springfield, Ill.
March 5.   To Jacob Bunn. MS., Ill. State Hist. Lib., Springfield, Ill.
April 22.   To J. B. Gould. MS., Ill. State Hist. Lib., Springfield, Ill.
April 26.   To Jacob Bunn. MS., Ill. State Hist. Lib., Springfield, Ill.
June 5.   To Jacob Bunn. MS., Ill. State Hist. Lib., Springfield, Ill.
June 12.   To Edward Lewis Baker, Jr. MS., Ill. State Hist. Lib., Springfield, Ill.
July 21.   To Jacob Bunn. MS., Ill. State Hist. Lib., Springfield, Ill.
August 29.   To Edward Lewis Baker, Jr. MS., Ill. State Hist. Lib., Springfield, Ill.

September 6.   To Jacob Bunn. MS., Ill. State Hist. Lib., Springfield, Ill.
October 7.   To Edward Lewis Baker, Jr. MS., Ill. State Hist. Lib., Springfield, Ill.
October 7.   To Jacob Bunn. MS., Ill. State Hist. Lib., Springfield, Ill.

1881

October 23.   To Josephine Remann Edwards. MS., Ill. State Hist. Lib., Springfield, Ill.
December 5.   Letter of Introduction. A/p in *Lincoln Lore*, No. 1367, June 20, 1955.

1882

January 3.   To Noyes W. Miner. MS., Huntington Lib., San Marino, Calif.
[January 3].   To Noyes W. Miner. MS., Huntington Lib., San Marino, Calif.
February 5.   To Noyes W. Miner. A/p in Sandburg & Angle, pp. 122–4.
February 21.   To Noyes W. Miner. MS., Huntington Lib., San Marino, Calif.
February 24.   To Noyes W. Miner. MS., Ill. State Hist. Lib., Springfield, Ill.
March 21.   To Edward Lewis Baker, Jr. MS., Ill. State Hist. Lib., Springfield, Ill.

Bibliography

The following sources proved useful to the editors in annotating Mary Lincoln's letters and in writing the accompanying commentary.

Manuscript Collections

Many archives and private collections that contain Mrs. Lincoln's letters (see Sources and Locations) also have letters to and about her as well as other documents and records relevant to her life. The National Archives, Library of Congress, Illinois State Historical Library, and the Houghton and Huntington Libraries are among the most prominent repositories of such material. Mention is made in footnotes whenever records or original manuscripts, in public or private collections, have been quoted.

Newspapers

Consulted to varying extents for editorials and general reportage concerning Mrs. Lincoln and for confirmation of references in her letters were: *The New York Times;* New York *Herald;* New York *Tribune; The World* (New York); Chicago *Journal;* Chicago *Tribune; Inter Ocean* (Chicago); Sangamo *Journal,* later the *Illinois Daily State Journal* (Springfield); *Daily Morning Chronicle* (Washington, D.C.); *National Intelligencer* (Washington, D.C.). Scattered references to articles in other newspapers are cited in the footnotes.

Books

Abraham Lincoln: The Tribute of a Century 1809–1909. Edited by Nathan William MacChesney. Chicago, 1910.

Arnold, Isaac N. *The Life of Abraham Lincoln.* Chicago, 1885. Few but interesting recollections of Mary Lincoln by her husband's good friend and associate.

Badeau, Adam. *Grant in Peace.* Hartford, 1887.

Barton, William E. *The Women Lincoln Loved.* Indianapolis, 1927.

Bayne, Julia Taft. *Tad Lincoln's Father.* Boston, 1931. Intimate glimpses of the Lincoln family in the White House by a former playmate of Willie and Tad.

Bernard, Kenneth A. *Lincoln and the Music of the Civil War.* Caldwell, Idaho, 1966. In effect, a social history of the Lincoln administration, well documented.

Bernhardt, Sarah. *Memories of My Life.* New York, 1907.

Birmingham, Stephen. *Our Crowd: The Great Jewish Families of New York.* New York, 1967.

Boatner, Mark Mayo III. *The Civil War Dictionary.* New York, 1959. Straightforward, bare-bones entries, useful in identifying military officers written to or mentioned by Mrs. Lincoln and for general facts about the Civil War.

Bradford, Gamaliel. *Wives.* New York, 1925. Contains a perceptive analysis of Mary Lincoln's life and character.

Brooks, Noah. *Washington in Lincoln's Time.* Edited with an Introduction by Herbert Mitgang. New York, 1958.

Bruce, Robert V. *Lincoln and the Tools of War.* Indianapolis and New York, 1956.

Bullard, F. Lauriston. *Lincoln in Marble and Bronze.* New Brunswick, 1952.

Carpenter, F. B. *Six Months at the White House with Abraham Lincoln: The Story of a Picture.* New York, 1866.

Clemmer, Mary (Ames). *Ten Years in Washington: Or, Inside Life and Scenes in Our Nation's Capital as a Woman Sees Them.* Hartford, 1882. In a chapter on Presidents' wives, Mary Lincoln viewed in anger.

The Collected Works of Abraham Lincoln, Volumes I–VIII. Roy P. Basler, Editor; Marion Dolores Pratt and Lloyd A. Dunlap, Assistant Editors. New Brunswick, 1953. From this definitive compilation sponsored by the Abraham Lincoln Association, the editors have taken excerpts from Lincoln's speeches and from letters and telegrams to his wife and to others.

Concerning Mr. Lincoln: In Which Abraham Lincoln is Pictured as he Appeared to Letter Writers of his Time. Compiled by Harry E. Pratt. Springfield, Ill., 1944.

The Diary of a Public Man: An Intimate View of the National Administration December 28, 1860 to March 15, 1861. Prefatory notes by F. Lauriston Bullard. Foreword by Carl Sandburg. Chicago, 1945. This anonymous classic contains several caustic references to Mrs. Lincoln.

Dictionary of American Biography, Volumes I–XI. New York, 1937–58.

Donald, David. *Lincoln's Herndon.* New York, 1948. The definitive work on Lincoln's law partner and biographer, the man more responsible than any other for posterity's jaundiced view of Mary Lincoln.

————. *Charles Sumner and the Rights of Man.* New York, 1971.

Evans, W. A., M.D. *Mrs. Abraham Lincoln: A Study of Her Personality and Her Influence on Lincoln.* New York, 1932. A psychiatrist's analysis of Mary Lincoln's mental and physical characteristics as related to her life and to her family's history.

Forney, John W. *Anecdotes of Public Men.* New York, 1877.

Harper, Robert S. *Lincoln and the Press.* New York, 1951.

Helm, Katherine. *The True Story of Mary, Wife of Lincoln.* New York, 1928. Written by Mrs. Lincoln's niece and containing letters, family gossip, and excerpts from the diaries of Emilie Todd Helm, Mrs. Lincoln's half-sister, during whose lifetime the book was published.

Herndon, William H., and Weik, Jesse W. *Herndon's Life of Lincoln.* Introduction and Notes by Paul M. Angle. Cleveland, 1949. A "collector's edition" of the book originally published in 1889.

Holland, J. G. *The Life of Abraham Lincoln.* Springfield, Mass., 1866. The massive biography read by Mary Lincoln and commented upon in several of her letters.

Keckley, Elizabeth. *Behind the Scenes, or Thirty Years a Slave and Four Years in the White House.* New York, 1868. The ghostwritten account of Mrs. Lincoln's Negro dressmaker, interesting and surprisingly accurate. Contains 24 letters from Mrs. Lincoln unavailable elsewhere.

King, Willard L. *Lincoln's Manager, David Davis.* Cambridge, 1960. Of particular interest is Chapter XIX, " 'Dear Judge' 1865–1882," discussing Mary Lincoln's relationship with Davis as administrator of her husband's estate.

Leech, Margaret. *Reveille in Washington, 1860–1865.* New York, 1941.

Lewis, Lloyd. *Myths After Lincoln.* New York, 1929.

Lewis, Montgomery. *Legends that Libel Lincoln.* New York, 1946.

Lincoln and the Baltimore Plot, 1861. Edited by Norma B. Cuthbert. San Marino, 1949.

Lincoln and the Civil War in the Diaries and Letters of John Hay. Edited by Tyler Dennett. New York, 1939. Occasional references to Mrs. Lincoln are pungent and intriguing.

Lincoln Day by Day: A Chronology 1809–1865. Volumes I–III. Earl Schenck Miers, Editor-in-Chief; William E. Baringer and C. Percy Powell, Compilers. Washington, 1960. A meticulous record which includes much information about Mrs. Lincoln's comings and goings during her husband's lifetime.

Nicolay, Helen. *Lincoln's Secretary: A Biography of John G. Nicolay.* New York, 1949.

Pratt, Harry E. *The Personal Finances of Abraham Lincoln.* Springfield, Ill., 1943. Detailed discussion of a matter in which Mary Lincoln was intensely interested, both before and after her husband's death.

Randall, Ruth Painter. *Mary Lincoln: Biography of a Marriage.* Boston, 1953. The pre-eminent biography of Mary Lincoln to date, carefully documented and warmly sympathetic.

———— *Lincoln's Sons.* Boston, 1955.

———— *The Courtship of Mr. Lincoln.* Boston, 1957.

Sandburg, Carl. *Lincoln Collector: The Story of the Oliver R. Barrett Lincoln Collection.* New York, 1960.

Sandburg, Carl, and Angle, Paul M. *Mary Lincoln: Wife and Widow.* New York, 1932. Part I is a romantic Sandburg biography; Part II, entitled "The Documents," contains a broad sampling of Mrs. Lincoln's letters and of articles and documents relevant to her life, edited by Mr. Angle.

Stoddard, William O. *Inside the White House in War Times.* New York, 1890. Sympathetic comments on Mary Lincoln by the man who acted as her personal secretary.

Swanberg, W. A. *Sickles the Incredible.* New York, 1956.

Through Five Administrations: Reminiscences of Colonel William H. Crook: Body-Guard to President Lincoln. Compiled and edited by Margarita Spalding Gerry. New York, 1910.

Townsend, William H. *Lincoln and His Wife's Home Town.* Indianapolis, 1929. A history written by the late distinguished citizen of Lexington and Lincoln collector.

————. *Lincoln and the Bluegrass: Slavery and the Civil War in Kentucky.* Lexington, 1955. An expanded view of Lincoln, the Kentucky Todds, and the issues that drove them apart.

Villard, Henry. *Lincoln on the Eve of '61: A Journalist's Story.* Edited by Harold G. and Oswald Garrison Villard. New York, 1941.

Wilson, Rufus Rockwell. *Lincoln in Portraiture.* New York, 1935.

Articles and Pamphlets

Angle, Paul M. "The Building of the Lincoln Monument." A paper delivered on February 12, 1926, at Springfield and published in *Lincoln Centennial Association Papers*, Springfield, 1926. Gives details of Mrs. Lincoln's involvement in the long controversy over her husband's burial site.

Basler, Roy P. "The Authorship of the 'Rebecca Letters.'" *Abraham Lincoln Quarterly*, June 1942, pp. 80–90.

Bernard, Kenneth A. "Glimpses of Lincoln in the White House." *Abraham Lincoln Quarterly*, December 1952, pp. 161–87.

Bullard F. Lauriston. "Mrs. Lincoln's Pension." *Lincoln Herald*, January 1947, pp. 22–7. An accurate, dispassionate account of a complex matter.

Darrin, Charles V. " 'Your Truly Attached Friend, Mary Lincoln.' " *Journal of the Illinois State Historical Society*, Spring 1951, pp. 7–25. Contains 15 letters, annotated.

Donald, David. "Herndon and Mrs. Lincoln." *Books at Brown*, issue of April 1950.

Goltz, Carlos W. "Incidents in the Life of Mary Todd Lincoln Containing an Unpublished Letter." Bound pamphlet. Sioux City, 1928.

Grimsley, Elizabeth Todd. "Six Months in the White House." *Journal of the Illinois State Historical Society*, October 1926–January 1927, pp. 43–73. Written by Mrs. Lincoln's cousin and published posthumously.

Gumpert, Gustav. "Tad Lincoln and Gus Gumpert." *Journal of the Illinois State Historical Society*, Spring 1955, pp. 41–4.

Hatch, Francis Whiting. "Mary Lincoln Writes to Noah Brooks." *Journal of the Illinois State Historical Society*, Spring 1955, pp. 45–51.

Hunt, Eugenia Jones. "My Personal Recollections of Abraham and Mary

Todd Lincoln." *Abraham Lincoln Quarterly*, March 1945, pp. 235–52.

James, Jeanne H., and Temple, Wayne C. "Mrs. Lincoln's Clothing." *Lincoln Herald*, Summer 1960, pp. 54–65.

Klement, Frank. "Jane Grey Swisshelm and Lincoln: A Feminist Fusses and Frets." *Abraham Lincoln Quarterly*, December 1950, pp. 227–38.

Krueger, Lillian. "Mary Todd Lincoln Summers in Wisconsin." *Journal of the Illinois State Historical Society*, June 1941, pp. 249–53.

"The Lincolns Go Shopping." Edited by Harry E. Pratt. *Journal of the Illinois State Historical Society*, Spring 1955, pp. 65–81. Includes records of the Lincolns' purchases at several Springfield stores.

"Lincoln's Neighbors: A Dramatic Find." Picture essay accompanied by "An Old Lady's Lincoln Memories," an interview with Mary Edwards Brown by Dorothy Meserve Kunhardt. *Life*, February 9, 1959, pp. 48–60.

Monaghan, Jay. "Was Abraham Lincoln Really a Spiritualist?" *Journal of the Illinois State Historical Society*, June 1941, pp. 209–32. A scholarly discussion of the Lincolns' interest in a popular phenomenon of Victorian days.

"Mrs. Frances Jane (Todd) Wallace Describes Lincoln's Wedding." Edited by Wayne C. Temple. Pamphlet published by Lincoln Memorial University Press, Harrogate, Tenn., 1960. A rather garbled account from Mrs. Lincoln's sister, amended and annotated.

"Mrs. Lincoln's Visit to Springfield in 1866." Edited by Wayne C. Temple. *Lincoln Herald*, Winter 1960, pp. 170–2.

" 'My Tired & Weary Husband': Mary Lincoln on Life in the Executive Mansion." *Abraham Lincoln Quarterly*, September 1946, pp. 137–9.

Ostendorf, Lloyd. "The Photographs of Mary Todd Lincoln." *Journal of the Illinois State Historical Society*, Spring 1969, pp. 269–332. Reproductions and discussion by a noted authority of every known photograph of Mrs. Lincoln.

Peckham, Howard H. "James Tanner's Account of Lincoln's Death." *Abraham Lincoln Quarterly*, December 1942, pp. 176–83.

Pineton, Charles A. (Marquis de Chambrun). "Personal Recollections of Mr. Lincoln." *Scribner's Magazine*, January 1893, pp. 26–38.

Pratt, Harry E., and East, Ernest E. "Mrs. Lincoln Refurbishes the White House." *Lincoln Herald*, February 1945, pp. 13–22. Includes some records pertaining to purchases and alterations.

Randall, Ruth Painter. "Mary Lincoln: Judgment Appealed." *Abraham Lincoln Quarterly*, September 1949, pp. 379–404.

Roberts, Octavia. " 'We All Knew Abr'ham.' " *Abraham Lincoln Quarterly*, March 1946, pp. 17–29.

Ross, Rodney A. "Mary Todd Lincoln, Patient at Bellevue Place, Batavia." *Journal of the Illinois State Historical Society*, Spring 1970, pp. 5–34. Includes day-by-day physicians' records of Mrs. Lincoln's behavior during her stay in the sanitarium.

Sang, Philip D. "Mary Todd Lincoln: A Tragic Portrait." *Journal of the Rutgers University Library*, April 1961. Reprinted in pamphlet form. A sympathetic analysis and texts of 17 important letters from the collection of Mr. and Mrs. Sang.

Squires, J. Duane. "Lincoln's Todd In-Laws." *Lincoln Herald*, Fall 1967, pp. 121–8.

Temple, Wayne C. "Mary Todd Lincoln's Travels." *Journal of the Illinois State Historical Society*, Spring 1959, pp. 180–94. Reprinted in pamphlet form. A detailed account, based mostly on newspaper records.

———. "Mary Todd Lincoln as a Sailor." *Lincoln Herald*, Fall 1959, pp. 101–10.

———. "Alexander Williamson—Tutor to the Lincoln Boys." Address before the annual meeting of the Lincoln Fellowship of Wisconsin, 1970. Published in pamphlet form by the State Historical Society of Wisconsin as Historical Bulletin No. 26. Little-known facts about a close friend of Mrs. Lincoln.

" 'Took Tea at Mrs. Lincoln's': The Diary of Mrs. William M. Black." (Editor not given.) *Journal of the Illinois State Historical Society*, Spring 1955, pp. 59–64. Includes an early letter of Mrs. Lincoln.

Turner, Justin G. "The Mary Lincoln Letters to Mrs. Felician Slataper." *Journal of the Illinois State Historical Society*, Spring 1956, pp. 7–33. Includes 11 letters, annotated.

Two other publications are worthy of note as sources of interesting sidelights on President and Mrs. Lincoln and their era: *The Blumhaven Journal*, edited and published by Herman Blum, founder and director of the Blumhaven Library in Philadelphia; and *Lincoln Lore*, which has been published since 1929 by the Lincoln National Life Foundation of Fort Wayne, Indiana, and is edited by R. Gerald McMurtry. Information taken from articles in these two publications is cited in the footnotes.

Dealers' Publications

The editors have made extensive use of autograph dealers' listings of documents for sale, not only for the texts (or partial texts) of Mrs. Lincoln's letters when the originals were unavailable, but also for the texts of letters to or about her and for descriptions of articles of her clothing, jewelry, and furniture that came into the possession of private collectors and were eventually offered for sale. Beginning with the listings for the sale at auction of the Lambert collection by the Metropolitan Art Association in 1914, catalogues of the following dealers have been helpful to us:

Walter P. Benjamin, Autographs (*The Collector*)

Carnegie Book Shop

Charles Hamilton Galleries, Inc.

Parke-Bernet Sotheby's

The Rosenbach Company (*A History of America in Documents*, Philadelphia and New York, 1949)

Paul C. Richards, Autographs

Swann and Company

Coins & Currency, Inc.

Howard S. Mott, Autographs

Index

M

A Note on the Editors

For over forty years, Justin G. Turner has been a well-known collector of manuscripts and documents relating to American history and, in particular, to Abraham Lincoln and the Civil War. His recently sold collection of Lincolniana—considered by many to be one of the finest and most exhaustive private collections in the world—contained a great number of Mrs. Lincoln's letters; it was this that inspired him to undertake this volume. Mr. Turner has published numerous monographs on aspects of his collection in scholarly journals, including the *Journal of the Illinois State Historical Society*, *Lincoln Herald*, the *American Jewish Historical Quarterly*, *Manuscripts*, the *American Collector*, and the *Antiquarian Bookman*. He has served as president of the Southern California Historical Society, the Manuscript Society, and the Civil War Round Table of Southern California, and as an honorary member of the National Civil War Centennial Commission. Mr. Turner is currently a consultant to the Manuscript Department of the Library at the University of California at Los Angeles. He makes his home in Beverly Hills.

A former book editor, Linda Levitt Turner has been a student of history since her days at Bryn Mawr, where as an undergraduate she twice won the Elizabeth Duane Gillespie Prize for excellence in American history. A native of Baltimore, Maryland, she is married to Justin G. Turner's son, Paul. Having become imbued with the family passion for Lincolniana, she is presently at work on a biographical study of Mary Lincoln. Mrs. Turner lives in New York City with her husband and their daughter, Rebecca.

A Note on the Type

This book was set in Monticello, a Linotype revival of the original Roman No. 1 cut by Archibald Binny and cast in 1796 by the Philadelphia type foundry Binny & Ronaldson. The face was named Monticello in honor of its use in the monumental fifty-volume *Papers of Thomas Jefferson*, published by Princeton University Press. Monticello is a transitional type design, embodying certain features of Bulmer and Baskerville, but it is a distinguished face in its own right.

The book was composed, printed, and bound by Kingsport Press, Inc., Kingsport, Tennessee. Typography and binding design by Betty Anderson.

she reports as well as usual— Uncle J— was to to have them yesterday for Ky— Our little Eddy, has recovered from little spell of sickness — Dear boy, I must tell you a story about him— Roby in his wanderings to day, came in a yard, a little kitten, your hobby, he says he asked for it, he brought it triumphantly to the house, so soon as he espied it—

his tenderness, broke forth, he made them bring it water, it with bread himself, with his own dear hands, he to delighted little creature over it, in the midst of his happ— Ma came in, she you must know dislikes the whole cat I thought in a very unfeeling manner, she ordered a servant near, to throw it out, which of course, was done Ed— screaming & protesting loudly against the process she never appeared to mind his screams, which were lo loud I assure you— Tis unusual for her now a days, to do thing quite so striking, she is very obliging & accomm —ting, but if she thought any of us, were on her hands, a I believe she would be worse than ever— In it next she appeared in a good humor, I know she did not to offend me— By the way, she has just sent me up glass of ice cream, for which this warm evening, I am grateful— The country is so delightful I am going to s two or three weeks out there, it will doubtless benefit the chil Grandma has received a letter from Uncle James Parker of